S·O·U·R·C·E·S

NOTABLE
SELECTIONS IN

Crime,
Criminology,
and
Criminal Justice

About the Editors

DAVID V. BAKER received his bachelor's degree in political science from California State University, Northridge, a master's degree and a doctorate in sociology from the University of California, Riverside, and he is completing a juris doctorate from California Southern Law School. He is an associate professor of sociology and chair of the Department of Behavioral Sciences at Riverside Community College in Riverside, California, and he has held visiting lectureships at the University of California, Riverside, and Chapman University. His research and teaching interests are in race and ethnic relations with an emphasis on exploring the structure and dynamics of racism in the U.S. criminal justice system. Professor Baker has contributed works to several professional journals, including *Ethnic Studies, Social Justice, The Justice Professional, Social Science Journal, Women and Criminal Justice,* and *Criminal Justice Abstracts.* He is coauthor of *Race, Racism and the Death Penalty in the United States* (Vande Vere), *Sources: Notable Selections in Race and Ethnicity,* 2d ed. (Dushkin/McGraw-Hill), *Perspectives on Race and Ethnicity in American Criminal Justice* (West), *Structured Inequality in American Society: Critical Discussions on the Continuing Significance of Race, Ethnicity, Gender, and Class* (Prentice Hall), and a forthcoming work on the multicultural dimensions of domestic violence in U.S. society. Professor Baker has also received two National Endowments for the Humanities fellowships, and he is an associate editor for *The Justice Professional.*

RICHARD P. DAVIN received his bachelor's degree in sociology from the University of Wyoming at Laramie, a master's degree in communication from the University of Northern Colorado, and a master's degree and a doctorate in sociology and criminology from the University of California, Riverside. He is an assistant professor of sociology and criminal justice and director of the Center for Justice Studies at Riverside Community College in Riverside, California. His research interests focus on inequality in the American criminal justice system, and his teaching interests are in criminology and research methods. His work has appeared in *The Justice Professional,* and he has contributed to several other published works. Professor Davin is a credentialed California crime analyst and serves as research consultant to local police agencies.

S·O·U·R·C·E·S

NOTABLE SELECTIONS IN

Crime, Criminology, and Criminal Justice

EDITED BY

DAVID V. BAKER
Riverside Community College

RICHARD P. DAVIN
Riverside Community College

McGraw-Hill/Dushkin

A Division of The McGraw-Hill Companies

This book is dedicated to my wife, Tina Marie, and our three
young daughters—Jennifer Marie, Tiffany Ann, and
Stephanie Diane (D. B.)

To Gloria (R. D.)

© 2001 by McGraw-Hill/Dushkin, A Division of The McGraw-Hill Companies,
Guilford, Connecticut 06437

Manufactured in the United States of America

First Edition

10 9 8 7 6 5 4 3 2 1

Library of Congress Cataloging-in-Publication Data
  Main entry under title:
    Sources: notable selections in crime, criminology, and criminal justice/edited by
    David V. Baker and Richard P. Davin.—1st ed.
    Includes bibliographical references and index.
    1. Crime and criminals. 2. Criminology. 3. Criminal justice, administration of.
    I. Baker, David V., *ed.* II. Davin, Richard P., *ed.* III. Series.

                                                                                364
  0-07-238880-3   ISSN: 1530-0781

Preface

*A*merican abolitionist Frederick Douglass noted generations ago that "justice is often painted with bandaged eyes. She is described in forensic eloquence as utterly blind to wealth and poverty, high or low, black or white, but a mask of iron, however thick, could never blind American justice when a black man happens to be on trial." Generations later social scientists have shown irrefutably that historically based patterns of institutional discrimination remain deeply embedded in American criminal justice. Nevertheless, Americans continue to embrace the judicial maxim that justice is blind despite insurmountable social scientific evidence that the maxim remains as mythical today as it did during the life of Douglass. U.S. Supreme Court justice Thurgood Marshall admonished the naivete about inequality in the American criminal justice system when he noted that it is "wishful thinking that racial discrimination is largely a phenomenon of the past." Steven Bright, director of the Southern Center for Human Rights, echoed Marhsall's claim when he stated, "Citizens, judges, the bar, and the press would like to believe we have a system which equally and fairly dispenses justice. But neither legal presumptions nor legal fiction will make it so." The notion that inequality is an artifact of the nation's criminal justice past has been encouraged, to a large extent, by the illusion that the criminal justice reforms arising out of the civil rights campaigns of the 1960s alleviated the arbitrary, capricious, and discriminatory treatment of nonwhite minorities and women in the justice system. As a result, Americans continue to reject the notion that *racism*, *sexism*, and *classism* are systemic and fully institutionalized in the processes and procedures of criminal justice administration. Attorney and law professor Gerald F. Uelmen may have put it best when he said,

> Our criminal justice system is no different from our other human institutions. The problem of racism in our system of criminal justice is a systematic problem that keeps rearing its head. And we consistently ignore it and walk away.... It is time for a lot more candor and a lot less denial in assessing the role that race plays in our criminal justice system.

Moreover, we allow the adulteration of such work as William Wilbanks's *The Myth of a Racist Criminal Justice System* (Brooks/Cole, 1987) to rationalize the continued disregard for structured race, ethnic, and gender inequality in the American justice system. Citizens must recognize that the criminal justice

ii

*Notable
Selections in
Crime,
Criminology,
and Criminal
Justice*

system is one of society's most oppressive institutions. Inequality remains pervasive in the U.S. criminal justice system because the discriminatory conduct of justice professionals is built into the system's structure and legitimated by American cultural beliefs and legal codes. In short, social inequality in the U.S. criminal justice system has become fully institutionalized. One can no longer deny the consequences of structural inequality as aberrant, obscure, tangential, and unimportant in the administration of justice. Structural inequality is not fragmented and isolated in the system of justice; rather, it is endemic, integral, and central to its processes and procedures. It is indisputable that race, ethnic, gender, and class inequality are clearly associated with racial profiling and selective law enforcement; the vicious brutality waged against nonwhite minorities by state and federal police agents; the violent sexual exploitation of female inmates by male prison guards; the torture and murder of custodial populations by prison guards; the impunity with which adult men sexually exploit growing numbers of young girls; the politicalization of crime as a nonwhite problem; the warehousing of blacks and Latinos in the nation's jails and prisons; the prosecutorial impotence in gaining convictions for hate crime; the violence-related morbidity and mortality in Latino communities; the capriciousness with which society imposes death as punishment; and the continued pacification of critical race theory and feminist thought concerning American criminal justice. One can no longer continue to summarily reject as inconsequential the constitutional mandate that *all* Americans are to be afforded the fundamental rights of due process of law and equal protection of the law. One purpose of this book is to provide students with straightforward and candid observations about the existence of racial, ethnic, gender, and class oppression in the U.S. criminal justice system. The authors of the selections brought together in this book recognize the enduring struggle for evenhandedness and impartiality in the administration of justice in the United States. Through their writings, these contributors recognize that the fundamental notions of *decency, fairness,* and *equitable treatment* remain mythical in the American system of justice. They categorically understand that justice is *not* blind.

ORGANIZATION OF THE BOOK.   The selections in this book are organized topically around major areas of study within crime, criminology, and criminal justice. Part 1 includes selections on the Social Requirement for Control; Part 2, Law and Criminality; and Part 3, the Criminal Justice Process. Each selection is preceded by a short introductory headnote that places the selection in the context of its relevance to the literature in the field of criminology and that provides biographical information on the author.

ON THE INTERNET.   Each part of this book is preceded by an *On the Internet* page. This page provides a list of Internet site addresses that are relevant to the part as well as a description of each site.

A WORD TO THE INSTRUCTOR. An *Instructor's Manual With Test Questions* (multiple-choice and essay) is available through the publisher for instructors using *Sources: Notable Selections in Crime, Criminology, and Criminal Justice* in the classroom.

David V. Baker
Riverside Community College

Richard P. Davin
Riverside Community College

Contents

CHAPTER 4   Law and Criminality   145

vii

*Notable
Selections in
Crime,
Criminology,
and Criminal
Justice*

ix

*Notable
Selections in
Crime,
Criminology,
and Criminal
Justice*

The Social Requirement for Control

On the Internet . . .

Sites appropriate to Part One

This site features an extensive list of criminal justice links compiled by Dr. Matthew Robinson of Appalachian State University. Categories include crime data, criminal law, criminological theory, and law enforcement.

```
http://www.acs.appstate.edu/dept/ps-cj/
   cj-sour.html
```

This is an excellent starting point for a study of all aspects of criminology and criminal justice, with links to general and international criminal justice sites, juvenile justice, courts, police, governments, and so on.

```
http://www.bsos.umd.edu/asc/four.html
```

This Web site of the National Archive of Criminal Justice Data (NACJD) offers access to the most up-to-date information available on criminal justice. Browser and search possibilities plus additional Web resources are also available here.

```
http://www.icpsr.umich.edu/NACJD/
   archive.html
```

Here you will find links to basic criminology sources as well as resources developed within a critical sociology framework.

```
http://sun.soci.niu.edu/~critcrim/
```

CHAPTER 1

Law and Social Order

1.1 HERBERT L. PACKER

Two Models of the Criminal Process

In the following selection from *The Limits of the Criminal Sanction* (Stanford University Press, 1968), legal scholar Herbert L. Packer describes American criminal justice as the outcome of two separate value systems, the *crime control model* and the *due process model*, which compete for priority in the operation of the criminal justice process. He views them as the polar extremes of a continuum. At one end of the spectrum is the crime control model. This model of criminal justice in the United States reflects "traditional politically *conservative* values." The crime control model "is based on the proposition that the repression of criminal conduct (crime control) is by far the most important function to be performed by the criminal justice process." At the other end of spectrum is the due process model. This model represents "traditional politically *liberal* values," and its principal goal is to ensure that crime control is accomplished within the constitutionally prescribed protections afforded criminal defendants. Packer compares the crime control model with the due process model on their differing views of justice processing, their principal assumptions concerning the rights of the accused, their differing goals of justice, the type of justice processing emphasized by the models, their differing methods of achieving justice, and the differences in their requirements for punishment. Moreover, the nation's political climate dictates which "value system" dominates American criminal justice policy. For example, the U.S. Supreme Court extended substantive due process rights set forth in the Fourth, Fifth, Sixth, and Eighth Amendments to state criminal defendants through the Fourteenth Amendment, beginning in the 1950s. Since the mid-1970s, however, criminal justice policy has taken on "traditional politically conservative values" and chipped away at issues of substantive due process (the exclusionary rule, the right to remain silent, the right to counsel, the right to bail, the right to a jury trial, the right to confront accusers and witnesses, and double jeopardy) in an attempt to extend state police powers to control crime.

Key Concept: due process and crime control models and the American criminal justice policy

INTRODUCTION

People who commit crimes appear to share the prevalent impression that punishment is an unpleasantness that is best avoided. They ordinarily take care to avoid being caught. If arrested, they ordinarily deny their guilt and otherwise try not to cooperate with the police. If brought to trial, they do whatever their resources permit to resist being convicted. And even after they have been convicted and sent to prison, their efforts to secure their freedom do not cease. It is a struggle from start to finish. This struggle is often referred to as the criminal process, a compendious term that stands for all the complexes of activity that operate to bring the substantive law of crime to bear (or to keep it from coming to bear) on persons who are suspected of having committed crimes. It can be described, but only partially and inadequately, by referring to the rules of law that govern the apprehension, screening, and trial of persons suspected of crime. It consists at least as importantly of patterns of official activity that correspond only in the roughest kind of way to the prescriptions of procedural rules. As a result of recent emphasis on empirical research into the administration of criminal justice, we are just beginning to be aware how very rough the correspondence is.

At the same time, and perhaps in part as a result of this new accretion of knowledge, some of our lawmaking institutions—particularly the Supreme Court of the United States—have begun to add measurably to the prescriptions of law that are meant to govern the operation of the criminal process. This accretion has become, in the last few years, exponential in extent and velocity. We are faced with an interesting paradox: the more we learn about the Is of the criminal process, the more we are instructed about its Ought and the greater the gulf between Is and Ought appears to become. We learn that very few people get adequate legal representation in the criminal process; we are simultaneously told that the Constitution requires people to be afforded adequate legal representation in the criminal process. We learn that coercion is often used to extract confessions from suspected criminals; we are then told that convictions based on coerced confessions may not be permitted to stand. We discover that the police often use methods in gathering evidence that violate the norms of privacy protected by the Fourth Amendment; we are told that evidence obtained in this way must be excluded from the criminal trial. But these prescriptions about how the process ought to operate do not automatically become part of the patterns of official behavior in the criminal process. Is and Ought share an increasingly uneasy coexistence. Doubts are stirred about the kind of criminal process we want to have.

The kind of criminal process we have is an important determinant of the kind of behavior content that the criminal law ought rationally to comprise. Logically, the substantive question may appear to be prior: decide what kinds of conduct one wants to reach through the criminal process, and then decide what kind of process is best calculated to deal with those kinds of conduct. It has not worked that way. On the whole, the process has been at least as much a given as the content of the criminal law. But it is far from being a given in any rigid sense.

The shape of the criminal process affects the substance of the criminal law in two general ways. First, one would want to know, before adding a new category of behavior to the list of crimes and therefore placing an additional burden on the process, whether it is easy or hard to employ the criminal process. The more expeditious the process, the greater the number of people with whom it can deal and, therefore, the greater the variety of anti-social conduct that can be confided in whole or in part to the criminal law for inhibition. On the other hand, the harder the process is to use, the smaller the number of people who can be handled by it at any given level of resources for staffing and operating it. The harder it is to put a suspected criminal in jail, the fewer the number of cases that can be handled in a year by a given number of policemen, prosecutors, defense lawyers, judges and jurymen, probation officers, etc., etc. A second and subtler relationship exists between the characteristic functioning of the process and the kinds of conduct with which it can efficiently deal. Perhaps the clearest example, but by no means the only one, is in the area of what have been referred to as victimless crimes, i.e., offenses that do not result in anyone's feeling that he has been injured so as to impel him to bring the offense to the attention of the authorities. The offense of fornication is an example. In a jurisdiction where it is illegal for two persons not married to each other to have sexual intercourse, there is a substantial enforcement problem (or would be, if the law were taken seriously) because people who voluntarily have sexual intercourse with each other often do not feel that they have been victimized and therefore often do not complain to the police. Consensual transactions in gambling and narcotics present the same problem, somewhat exacerbated by the fact that we take these forms of conduct rather more seriously than fornication. To the difficulties of apprehending a criminal when it is known that he has committed a crime are added the difficulties of knowing that a crime has been committed. In this sense, the victimless crime always presents a greater problem to the criminal process than does the crime with an ascertainable victim. But this problem may be minimized if the criminal process has at its disposal measures designed to increase the probability that the commission of such offenses will become known. If suspects may be entrapped into committing offenses, if the police may arrest and search a suspect without evidence that he has committed an offense, if wiretaps and other forms of electronic surveillance are permitted, it becomes easier to detect the commission of offenses of this sort. But if these measures are prohibited and if the prohibitions are observed in practice, it becomes more difficult, and eventually there may come a point at which the capacity of the criminal process to deal with victimless offenses becomes so attenuated that a failure of enforcement occurs.

Thus, a pragmatic approach to the central question of what the criminal law is good for would require both a general assessment of whether the criminal process is a high-speed or a low-speed instrument of social control, and a series of specific assessments of its fitness for handling particular kinds of antisocial behavior. Such assessments are necessary if we are to have a basis for elaborating the criteria that ought to affect legislative invocation of the criminal sanction. How can we provide ourselves with an understanding of the criminal process that pays due regard to its static and dynamic elements? There are, to be sure, aspects of the criminal process that vary only inconsequentially from place to place and from time to time. But its dynamism is clear—clearer today, perhaps, than ever before. We need to have an idea of the potentialities for change in the system and the probable direction that change is taking and may be expected to take in the future. We need to detach ourselves from the welter of more or less connected details that describe the myriad ways in which the criminal process does operate or may be likely to operate in mid-twentieth-century America, so that we can begin to see how the system as a whole might be able to deal with the variety of missions we confide to it.

One way to do this kind of job is to abstract from reality, to build a model. In a sense, a model is just what an examination of the constitutional and statutory provisions that govern the operation of the criminal process would produce. This in effect is the way analysis of the legal system has traditionally proceeded. It has considerable utility as an index of current value choices; but it produces a model that will not tell us very much about some important problems that the system encounters and that will only fortuitously tell us anything useful about how the system actually operates. On the other hand, the kind of model that might emerge from an attempt to cut loose from the law on the books and to describe, as accurately as possible, what actually goes on in the real-life world of the criminal process would so subordinate the inquiry to the tyranny of the actual that the existence of competing value choices would be obscured. The kind of criminal process we have depends importantly on certain value choices that are reflected, explicitly or implicitly, in its habitual functioning. The kind of model we need is one that permits us to recognize explicitly the value choices that underlie the details of the criminal process. In a word, what we need is a *normative* model or models. It will take more than one model, but it will not take more than two.

Two models of the criminal process will let us perceive the normative antinomy at the heart of the criminal law. These models are not labeled Is and Ought, nor are they to be taken in that sense. Rather, they represent an attempt to abstract two separate value systems that compete for priority in the operation of the criminal process. Neither is presented as either corresponding to reality or representing the ideal to the exclusion of the other. The two models merely afford a convenient way to talk about the operation of a process whose day-to-day functioning involves a constant series of minute adjustments between the competing demands of two value systems and whose normative future likewise involves a series of resolutions of the tensions between competing claims.

I call these two models the Due Process Model and the Crime Control Model. In the rest of this [selection] I shall sketch their animating presuppositions.... As we examine the way the models operate in each successive stage [of the criminal process], we will raise two further inquiries: first, where on a spectrum between the extremes represented by the two models do our present practices seem approximately to fall; second, what appears to be the direction and thrust of current and foreseeable trends along each such spectrum?

There is a risk in an enterprise of this sort that is latent in any attempt to polarize. It is, simply, that values are too various to be pinned down to yes-or-no answers. The models are distortions of reality. And, since they are normative in character, there is a danger of seeing one or the other as Good or Bad. The reader will have his preferences, as I do, but we should not be so rigid as to demand consistently polarized answers to the range of questions posed in the criminal process. The weighty questions of public policy that inhere in any attempt to discern where on the spectrum of normative choice the "right" answer lies are beyond the scope of the present inquiry. The attempt here is primarily to clarify the terms of discussion by isolating the assumptions that underlie competing policy claims and examining the conclusions that those claims, if fully accepted, would lead to.

VALUES UNDERLYING THE MODELS

Each of the two models we are about to examine is an attempt to give operational content to a complex of values underlying the criminal law. As I have suggested earlier, it is possible to identify two competing systems of values, the tension between which accounts for the intense activity now observable in the development of the criminal process. The actors in this development—lawmakers, judges, police, prosecutors, defense lawyers—do not often pause to articulate the values that underlie the positions that they take on any given issue. Indeed, it would be a gross over-simplification to ascribe a coherent and consistent set of values to any of these actors. Each of the two competing schemes of values we will be developing in this section contains components that are demonstrably present some of the time in some of the actors' preferences regarding the criminal process. No one person has ever identified himself as holding all of the values that underlie these two models. The models are polarities, and so are the schemes of value that underlie them. A person who subscribed to all of the values underlying one model to the exclusion of all of the values underlying the other would be rightly viewed as a fanatic. The values are presented here as an aid to analysis, not as a program for action.

Some common ground.   However, the polarity of the two models is not absolute. Although it would be possible to construct models that exist in an institutional vacuum, it would not serve our purposes to do so. We are postulating, not a criminal process that operates in any kind of society at all, but rather one that operates within the framework of contemporary American society. This leaves plenty of room for polarization, but it does require the observance of some limits. A model of the criminal process that left out of account relatively stable and enduring features of the American legal system would not have much relevance to our central inquiry. For convenience, these elements of stability and continuity can be roughly equated with minimal agreed limits expressed in the Constitution of the United States and, more importantly, with unarticulated assumptions that can be perceived to underlie those limits. Of course, it is true that the Constitution is constantly appealed to by proponents and opponents of many measures that affect the criminal process. And only the naive would deny that there are few conclusive positions that can be reached by appeal to the Constitution. Yet there are assumptions about the criminal process that are widely shared and that may be viewed as common ground for the operation of any model of the criminal process. Our first task is to clarify these assumptions.

First, there is the assumption, implicit in the ex post facto clause of the Constitution, that the function of defining conduct that may be treated as criminal is separate from and prior to the process of identifying and dealing with persons as criminals. How wide or narrow the definition of criminal conduct must be is an important question of policy that yields highly variable results depending on the values held by those making the relevant decisions. But that there must be a means of definition that is in some sense separate from and prior to the operation of the process is clear. If this were not so, our efforts to deal with the phenomenon of organized crime would appear ludicrous indeed (which is not to say that we have by any means exhausted the possibilities for dealing with that problem within the limits of this basic assumption).

A related assumption that limits the area of controversy is that the criminal process ordinarily ought to be invoked by those charged with the responsibility for doing so when it appears that a crime has been committed and that there is a reasonable prospect of apprehending and convicting its perpetrator. Although police and prosecutors are allowed broad discretion for deciding not to invoke the criminal process, it is commonly agreed that these officials have no general dispensing power. If the legislature has decided that certain conduct is to be treated as criminal, the decision-makers at every level of the criminal process are expected to accept that basic decision as a premise for action. The controversial nature of the occasional case in which the relevant decision-makers appear not to have played their appointed role only serves to highlight the strength with which the premise holds. This assumption may be viewed as the other side of the ex post facto coin. Just as conduct that is not proscribed as criminal may not be dealt with in the criminal process, so conduct that has been denominated as criminal must be treated as such by the participants in the criminal process acting within their respective competences.

Next, there is the assumption that there are limits to the powers of government to investigate and apprehend persons suspected of committing crimes. I do not refer to the controversy (settled recently, at least in broad outline) as to whether the Fourth Amendment's prohibition against unreasonable searches and seizures applies to the states with the same force with which it applies to the federal government.[1] Rather, I am talking about the general assumption that a degree of scrutiny and control must be exercised with respect to the activities of law enforcement officers, that the security and privacy of the individual may not be invaded at will. It is possible to imagine a society in which even lip service is not paid to this assumption. Nazi Germany approached but never quite reached this position. But no one in our society would maintain that any individual may be taken into custody at any time and held without any limitation of time during the process of investigating his possible commission of crimes, or would argue that there should be no form of redress for violation of at least some standards for official investigative conduct. Although this assumption may not appear to have much in the way of positive content, its absence would render moot some of our most hotly controverted problems. If there were not general agreement that there must be some limits on police power to detain and investigate, the highly controversial provisions of the Uniform Arrest Act, permitting the police to detain a person for questioning for a short period even though they do not have grounds for making an arrest, would be a magnanimous concession by the all-powerful state rather than, as it is now perceived, a substantial expansion of police power.

Finally, there is a complex of assumptions embraced by terms such as "the adversary system," "procedural due process," "notice and an opportunity to be heard," and "day in court." Common to them all is the notion that the alleged criminal is not merely an object to be acted upon but an independent entity in the process who may, if he so desires, force the operators of the process to demonstrate to an independent authority (judge and jury) that he is guilty of the charges against him. It is a minimal assumption. It speaks in terms of "may" rather than "must." It permits but does not require the accused, acting by himself or through his own agent, to play an active role in the process. By virtue of that fact the process becomes or has the capacity to become a contest between, if not equals, at least independent actors. As we shall see, much of the space between the two models is occupied by stronger or weaker notions of how this contest is to be arranged, in what cases it is to be played, and by what rules. The Crime Control Model tends to de-emphasize this adversary aspect of the process; the Due Process Model tends to make it central. The common ground, and it is important, is the agreement that the process has, for everyone subjected to it, at least the potentiality of becoming to some extent an adversary struggle.

So much for common ground. There is a good deal of it, even in the narrowest view. Its existence should not be overlooked, because it is, by definition, what permits partial resolutions of the tension between the two models to take place. The rhetoric of the criminal process consists largely of claims that disputed territory is "really" common ground: that, for example, the premise of an adversary system "necessarily" embraces the appointment of counsel for everyone accused of crime, or conversely, that the obligation to pursue persons suspected of committing crimes "necessarily" embraces interrogation of suspects without the intervention of counsel. We may smile indulgently at such claims; they are rhetoric, and no more. But the form in which they are made suggests an important truth: that there *is* a common ground of value assumption about the criminal process that makes continued discourse about its problems possible.

Crime control values.   The value system that underlies the Crime Control Model is based on the proposition that the repression of criminal conduct is by far the most important function to be performed by the criminal process. The failure of law enforcement to bring criminal conduct under tight control is viewed as leading to the breakdown of public order and thence to the disappearance of an important condition of human freedom. If the laws go unenforced——which is to say, if it is perceived that there is a high percentage of failure to apprehend and convict in the criminal process—a general disregard for legal controls tends to develop. The law-abiding citizen then becomes the victim of all sorts of unjustifiable invasions of his interests. His security of person and property is sharply diminished, and, therefore, so is his liberty to function as a member of society. The claim ultimately is that the criminal process is a positive guarantor of social freedom. In order to achieve this high purpose, the Crime Control Model requires that primary attention be paid to the efficiency with which the criminal process operates to screen suspects, determine guilt, and secure appropriate dispositions of persons convicted of crime.

Efficiency of operation is not, of course, a criterion that can be applied in a vacuum. By "efficiency" we mean the system's capacity to apprehend, try, convict, and dispose of a high proportion of criminal offenders whose offenses become known. In a society in which only the grossest forms of antisocial behavior were made criminal and in which the crime rate was exceedingly low, the criminal process might require the devotion of many more man-hours of police, prosecutorial, and judicial time per case than ours does, and still operate with tolerable efficiency. A society that was prepared to increase even further the resources devoted to the suppression of crime might cope with a rising crime rate without sacrifice of efficiency while continuing to maintain an elaborate and time-consuming set of criminal processes. However, neither of these possible characteristics corresponds with social reality in this country. We use the criminal sanction to cover an increasingly wide spectrum of behavior thought to be antisocial, and the amount of crime is very high indeed, although both level and trend are hard to assess.[2] At the same time, although precise measures are not available, it does not appear that we are disposed in the public sector of the economy to increase very drastically the quantity, much less the quality, of the resources devoted to the suppression of criminal activity through the operation of the criminal process. These factors have an important bearing on the criteria of efficiency, and therefore on the nature of the Crime Control Model.

The model, in order to operate successfully, must produce a high rate of apprehension and conviction, and must do so in a context where the magnitudes being dealt with are very large and the resources for dealing with them are very limited. There must then be a premium on speed and finality. Speed, in turn, depends on informality and on uniformity; finality depends on minimizing the occasions for challenge. The process must not be cluttered up with ceremonious rituals that do not advance the progress of a case. Facts can be established more quickly through interrogation in a police station than through the formal process of examination and cross-examination in a court. It follows that extra-judicial processes should be preferred to judicial processes, informal operations to formal ones. But informality is not enough; there must also be uniformity. Routine, stereotyped procedures are essential if large numbers are being handled. The model that will operate successfully on these presuppositions must be an administrative, almost a managerial, model. The image that comes to mind is an assembly-line conveyor belt down which moves an endless stream of cases, never stopping, carrying the cases to workers who stand at fixed stations and who perform on each case as it comes by the same small but essential operation that brings it one step closer to being a finished product, or, to exchange the metaphor for the reality, a closed file. The criminal process, in this model, is seen as a screening process in which each successive stage—prearrest investigation, arrest, post-arrest investigation, preparation for trial, trial or entry of plea, conviction, disposition—involves a series of routinized operations whose success is gauged primarily by their tendency to pass the case along to a successful conclusion.

What is a successful conclusion? One that throws off at an early stage those cases in which it appears unlikely that the person apprehended is an offender and then secures, as expeditiously as possible, the conviction of the rest, with a minimum of occasions for challenge, let alone post-audit. By the application of administrative expertness, primarily that of the police and prosecutors, an early determination of probable innocence or guilt emerges. Those who are probably innocent are screened out. Those who are probably guilty are passed quickly through the remaining stages of the process. The key to the operation of the model regarding those who are not screened out is what I shall call a presumption of guilt. The concept requires some explanation, since it may appear startling to assert that what appears to be the precise converse of our generally accepted ideology of a presumption of innocence can be an essential element of a model that does correspond in some respects to the actual operation of the criminal process.

The presumption of guilt is what makes it possible for the system to deal efficiently with large numbers, as the Crime Control Model demands. The supposition is that the screening processes operated by police and prosecutors are reliable indicators of probable guilt. Once a man has been arrested and investigated without being found to be probably innocent, or, to put it differently, once a determination has been made that there is enough evidence of guilt to permit holding him for further action, then all subsequent activity directed toward him is based on the view that he is probably guilty. The precise point at which this occurs will vary from case to case; in many cases it will occur as soon as the suspect is arrested, or even before, if the evidence of probable guilt that has come to the attention of the authorities is sufficiently strong. But in any case the presumption of guilt will begin to operate well before the "suspect" becomes a "defendant."

The presumption of guilt is not, of course, a thing. Nor is it even a rule of law in the usual sense. It simply is the consequence of a complex of attitudes, a mood. If there is confidence in the reliability of informal administrative fact-finding activities that take place in the early stages of the criminal process, the remaining stages of the process can be relatively perfunctory without any loss in operating efficiency. The presumption of guilt, as it operates in the Crime Control Model, is the operational expression of that confidence.

It would be a mistake to think of the presumption of guilt as the opposite of the presumption of innocence that we are so used to thinking of as the polestar of the criminal process and that, as we shall see, occupies an important position in the Due Process Model. The presumption of innocence is not its opposite; it is irrelevant to the presumption of guilt; the two concepts are different rather than opposite ideas. The difference can perhaps be epitomized by an example. A murderer, for reasons best known to himself, chooses to shoot his victim in plain view of a large number of people. When the police arrive, he hands them his gun and says, "I did it and I'm glad." His account of what happened is corroborated by several eyewitnesses. He is placed under arrest and led off to jail. Under these circumstances, which may seem extreme but which in fact characterize with rough accuracy the evidentiary situation in a large proportion of criminal cases, it would be plainly absurd to maintain that more probably than not the suspect did not commit the killing. But that is not what the presumption of innocence means. It means that until there has been an adjudication of guilt by an authority legally competent to make such an adjudication, the suspect is to be treated, for reasons that have nothing whatever to do with the probable outcome of the case, as if his guilt is an open question.

The presumption of innocence is a direction to officials about how they are to proceed, not a prediction of outcome. The presumption of guilt, however, is purely and simply a prediction of outcome. The presumption of innocence is, then, a direction to the authorities to ignore the presumption of guilt in their treatment of the suspect. It tells them, in effect, to close their eyes to what will frequently seem to be factual probabilities. The reasons why it tells them this are among the animating presuppositions of the Due Process Model, and we will come to them shortly. It is enough to note at this point that the presumption of guilt is descriptive and factual; the presumption of innocence is normative and legal. The pure Crime Control Model has no truck with the presumption of innocence, although its real-life emanations are, as we shall see, brought into uneasy compromise with the dictates of this dominant ideological position. In the presumption of guilt this model finds a factual predicate for the position that the dominant goal of repressing crime can be achieved through highly summary processes without any great loss of efficiency (as previously defined), because of the probability that, in the run of cases, the preliminary screening processes operated by the police and the prosecuting officials contain adequate guarantees of reliable fact-finding. Indeed, the model takes an even stronger position. It is that subsequent processes, particularly those of a formal adjudicatory nature, are unlikely to produce as reliable fact-finding as the expert administrative process that precedes them is capable of. The criminal process thus must put special weight on the quality of administrative fact-finding. It becomes important, then, to place as few restrictions as possible on the character of the administrative fact-finding processes and to limit restrictions to such as enhance reliability, excluding those designed for other purposes. As we shall see, this view of restrictions on administrative fact-finding is a consistent theme in the development of the Crime Control Model.

In this model, as I have suggested, the center of gravity for the process lies in the early, administrative fact-finding stages. The complementary proposition is that the subsequent stages are relatively unimportant and should be truncated as much as possible. This, too, produces tensions with presently dominant ideology. The pure Crime Control Model has very little use for many conspicuous features of the adjudicative process, and in real life works out a number of ingenious compromises with them. Even in the pure model, however, there have to be devices for dealing with the suspect after the preliminary screening process has resulted in a determination of probable guilt. The focal device, as we shall see, is the plea of guilty; through its use, adjudicative fact-finding is reduced to a minimum. It might be said of the Crime Control Model that, when reduced to its barest essentials and operating at its most successful pitch, it offers two possibilities: an administrative fact-finding process leading (1) to exoneration of the suspect or (2) to the entry of a plea of guilty.

Due process values. If the Crime Control Model resembles an assembly line, the Due Process Model looks very much like an obstacle course. Each of its successive stages is designed to present formidable impediments to carrying the accused any further along in the process. Its ideology is not the converse of that underlying the Crime Control Model. It does not rest on the idea that it is not socially desirable to repress crime, although critics of its application have been known to claim so. Its ideology is composed of a complex of ideas, some of them based on judgments about the efficacy of crime control devices, others having to do with quite different considerations. The ideology of due process is far more deeply impressed on the formal structure of the law than is the ideology of crime control; yet an accurate tracing of the strands that make it up is strangely difficult. What follows is only an attempt at an approximation.

The Due Process Model encounters its rival on the Crime Control Model's own ground in respect to the reliability of fact-finding processes. The Crime Control Model, as we have suggested, places heavy reliance on the ability of investigative and prosecutorial officers, acting in an informal setting in which their distinctive skills are given full sway, to elicit and reconstruct a tolerably accurate account of what actually took place in an alleged criminal event. The Due Process Model rejects this premise and substitutes for it a view of informal, nonadjudicative fact-finding that stresses the possibility of error. People are notoriously poor observers of disturbing events—the more emotion-arousing the context, the greater the possibility that recollection will be incorrect; confessions and admissions by persons in police custody may be induced by physical or psychological coercion so that the police end up hearing what the suspect thinks they want to hear rather than the truth; witnesses may be animated by a bias or interest that no one would trouble to discover except one specially charged with protecting the interests of the accused (as the police are not). Considerations of this kind all lead to a rejection of informal fact-finding processes as definitive of factual guilt and to an insistence on formal, adjudicative, adversary fact-finding processes in which the factual case against the accused is publicly heard by an impartial tribunal and is evaluated only after the accused has had a full opportunity to discredit the case against him. Even then, the distrust of fact-finding processes that animates the Due Process Model is not dissipated. The possibilities of human error being what they are, further scrutiny is necessary, or at least must be available, in case facts have been overlooked or suppressed in the heat of battle. How far this subsequent scrutiny must be available is a hotly controverted issue today. In the pure Due Process Model the answer would be: at least as long as there is an allegation of factual error that has not received an adjudicative hearing in a fact-finding context. The demand for finality is thus very low in the Due Process Model.

This strand of due process ideology is not enough to sustain the model. If all that were at issue between the two models was a series of questions about the reliability of fact-finding processes, we would have but one model of the criminal process, the nature of whose constituent elements would pose questions of fact not of value. Even if the discussion is confined, for the moment, to the question of reliability, it is apparent that more is at stake than simply an evaluation of what kinds of fact-finding processes, alone or in combination, are likely to produce the most nearly reliable results. The stumbling block is this: how much reliability is compatible with efficiency? Granted that informal fact-finding will make some mistakes that can be remedied if backed up by adjudicative fact-finding, the desirability of providing this backup is not affirmed or negated by factual demonstrations or predictions that the increase in reliability will be x per cent or x plus n per cent. It still remains to ask how much weight is to be given to the competing demands of reliability (a high degree of probability in each case that factual guilt has been accurately determined) and efficiency (expeditious handling of the large numbers of cases that the process ingests). The Crime Control Model is more optimistic about the improbability of error in a significant number of cases; but it is also, though only in part therefore, more tolerant about the amount of error that it will put up with. The Due Process Model insists on the prevention and elimination of mistakes to the extent possible; the Crime Control Model accepts the probability of mistakes up to the level at which they interfere with the goal of repressing crime, either because too many guilty people are escaping or, more subtly, because general awareness of the unreliability of the process leads to a decrease in the deterrent efficacy of the criminal law. In this view, reliability and efficiency are not polar opposites but rather complementary characteristics. The system is reliable *because* efficient; reliability becomes a matter of independent concern only when it becomes so attenuated as to impair efficiency. All of this the Due Process Model rejects. If efficiency demands shortcuts around reliability, then absolute efficiency must be rejected. The aim of the process is at least as much to protect the factually innocent as it is to convict the factually guilty. It is a little like quality control in industrial technology: tolerable deviation from standard varies with the importance of conformity to standard in the destined uses of the product. The Due Process Model resembles a factory that has to devote a substantial part of its input to quality control. This necessarily cuts down on quantitative output.

All of this is only the beginning of the ideological difference between the two models. The Due Process Model could disclaim any attempt to provide enhanced reliability for the fact-finding process and still produce a set of institutions and processes that would differ sharply from those demanded by the Crime Control Model. Indeed, it may not be too great an oversimplification to assert that in point of historical development the doctrinal pressures emanating from the demands of the Due Process Model have tended to evolve from an original matrix of concern for the maximization of reliability into values quite different and more far-reaching. These values can be expressed in, although not adequately described by, the concept of the primacy of the individual and the complementary concept of limitation on official power.

The combination of stigma and loss of liberty that is embodied in the end result of the criminal process is viewed as being the heaviest deprivation that government can inflict on the individual. Furthermore, the processes that culminate in these highly afflictive sanctions are seen as in themselves coercive, restricting, and demeaning. Power is always subject to abuse—sometimes subtle, other times, as in the criminal process, open and ugly. Precisely because of its potency in subjecting the individual to the coercive power of the state, the criminal process must, in this model, be subjected to controls that prevent it from operating with maximal efficiency. According to this ideology, maximal efficiency means maximal tyranny. And, although no one would assert that minimal efficiency means minimal tyranny, the proponents of the Due Process Model would accept with considerable equanimity a substantial diminution in the efficiency with which the criminal process operates in the interest of preventing official oppression of the individual.

The most modest-seeming but potentially far-reaching mechanism by which the Due Process Model implements these anti-authoritarian values is the doctrine of legal guilt. According to this doctrine, a person is not to be held guilty of crime merely on a showing that in all probability, based upon reliable evidence, he did factually what he is said to have done. Instead, he is to be held guilty if and only if these factual determinations are made in procedurally regular fashion and by authorities acting within competences duly allocated to them. Furthermore, he is not to be held guilty, even though the factual determination is or might be adverse to him, if various rules designed to protect him and to safeguard the integrity of the process are not given effect: the tribunal that convicts him must have the power to deal with his kind of case ("jurisdiction") and must be geographically appropriate ("venue"); too long a time must not have elapsed since the offense was committed ("statute of limitations"); he must not have been previously convicted or acquitted of the same or a substantially similar offense ("double jeopardy"); he must not fall within a category of persons, such as children or the insane, who are legally immune to conviction ("criminal responsibility"); and so on. None of these requirements has anything to do with the factual question of whether the person did or did not engage in the conduct that is charged as the offense against him; yet favorable answers to any of them will mean that he is legally innocent. Wherever the competence to make adequate factual determinations lies, it is apparent that only a tribunal that is aware of these guilt-defeating doctrines and is willing to apply them can be viewed as competent to make determinations of legal guilt. The police and the prosecutors are ruled out by lack of competence, in the first instance, and by lack of assurance of willingness, in the second. Only an impartial tribunal can be trusted to make determinations of legal as opposed to factual guilt.

In this concept of legal guilt lies the explanation for the apparently quixotic presumption of innocence of which we spoke earlier. A man who, after police investigation, is charged with having committed a crime can hardly be said to be presumptively innocent, if what we mean is factual innocence. But if what we mean is that it has yet to be determined if any of the myriad legal doctrines that serve in one way or another the end of limiting official power through the observance of certain substantive and procedural regularities may be appropriately invoked to exculpate the accused man, it is apparent that as a matter of prediction it cannot be said with confidence that more probably than not he will be found guilty.

Beyond the question of predictability this model posits a functional reason for observing the presumption of innocence: by forcing the state to prove its case against the accused in an adjudicative context, the presumption of innocence serves to force into play all the qualifying and disabling doctrines that limit the use of the criminal sanction against the individual, thereby enhancing his opportunity to secure a favorable outcome. In this sense, the presumption of innocence may be seen to operate as a kind of self-fulfilling prophecy. By opening up a procedural situation that permits the successful assertion of defenses having nothing to do with factual guilt, it vindicates the proposition that the factually guilty may nonetheless be legally innocent and should therefore be given a chance to qualify for that kind of treatment.

The possibility of legal innocence is expanded enormously when the criminal process is viewed as the appropriate forum for correcting its own abuses. This notion may well account for a greater amount of the distance between the two models than any other. In theory the Crime Control Model can tolerate rules that forbid illegal arrests, unreasonable searches, coercive interrogations, and the like. What it cannot tolerate is the vindication of those rules in the criminal process itself through the exclusion of evidence illegally obtained or through the reversal of convictions in cases where the criminal process has breached the rules laid down for its observance. And the Due Process Model, although it may in the first instance be addressed to the maintenance of reliable fact-finding techniques, comes eventually to incorporate prophylactic and deterrent rules that result in the release of the factually guilty even in cases in which blotting out the illegality would still leave an adjudicative fact-finder convinced of the accused person's guilt. Only by penalizing errant police and prosecutors within the criminal process itself can adequate pressure be maintained, so the argument runs, to induce conformity with the Due Process Model.

Another strand in the complex of attitudes underlying the Due Process Model is the idea—itself a shorthand statement for a complex of attitudes—of equality. This notion has only recently emerged as an explicit basis for pressing the demands of the Due Process Model, but it appears to represent, at least in its potential, a most powerful norm for influencing official conduct. Stated most starkly, the ideal of equality holds that "there can be no equal justice where the kind of trial a man gets depends on the amount of money he has."[3] The factual predicate underlying this assertion is that there are gross inequalities in the financial means of criminal defendants as a class, that in an adversary system of criminal justice an effective defense is largely a function of the resources that can be mustered on behalf of the accused, and that the very large proportion of criminal defendants who are, operationally speaking, "indigent" will thus be denied an effective defense. This factual premise has been strongly reinforced by recent studies that in turn have been both a cause and an effect of an increasing emphasis upon norms for the criminal process based on the premise.

The norms derived from the premise do not take the form of an insistence upon governmental responsibility to provide literally equal opportunities for all criminal defendants to challenge the process. Rather, they take as their point of departure the notion that the criminal process, initiated as it is by government and containing as it does the likelihood of severe deprivations at the hands of government, imposes some kind of public obligation to ensure that financial inability does not destroy the capacity of an accused to assert what may be meritorious challenges to the processes being invoked against him. At its most gross, the norm of equality would act to prevent situations in which financial inability forms an absolute barrier to the assertion of a right that is in theory generally available, as where there is a right to appeal that is, however, effectively conditional upon the filing of a trial transcript obtained at the defendant's expense. Beyond this, it may provide the basis for a claim whenever the system theoretically makes some kind of challenge available to an accused who has the means to press it. If, for example, a defendant who is adequately represented has the opportunity to prevent the case against him from coming to the trial stage by forcing the state to its proof in a preliminary hearing, the norm of equality may be invoked to assert that the same kind of opportunity must be available to others as well. In a sense the system as it functions for the small minority whose resources permit them to exploit all its defensive possibilities provides a benchmark by which its functioning in all other cases is to be tested: not, perhaps, to guarantee literal identity but rather to provide a measure of whether the process as a whole is recognizably of the same general order. The demands made by a norm of this kind are likely by their very nature to be quite sweeping. Although the norm's imperatives may be initially limited to determining whether in a particular case the accused was injured or prejudiced by his relative inability to make an appropriate challenge, the norm of equality very quickly moves to another level on which the demand is that the process in general be adapted to minimize discriminations rather than that a mere series of post hoc determinations of discrimination be made or makeable.

It should be observed that the impact of the equality norm will vary greatly depending upon the point in time at which it is introduced into a model of the criminal process. If one were starting from scratch to decide how the process ought to work, the norm of equality would have nothing very important to say on such questions as, for example, whether an accused should have the effective assistance of counsel in deciding whether to enter a plea of guilty. One could decide, on quite independent considerations, that it is or is not a good thing to afford that facility to the generality of persons accused of crime. But the impact of the equality norm becomes far greater when it is brought to bear on a process whose contours have already been shaped. If our model of the criminal process affords defendants who are in a financial position to do so the right to consult a lawyer before entering a plea, then the equality norm exerts powerful pressure to provide such an opportunity to all defendants and to regard the failure to do so as a malfunctioning of the process of whose consequences the accused is entitled to be relieved. In a sense, this has been the role of the equality norm in affecting the real-world criminal process. It has made its appearance on the scene comparatively late, and has therefore encountered a system in which the relative financial inability of most persons accused of crime results in treatment very different from that accorded the small minority of the financially capable. For this reason, its impact has already been substantial and may be expected to be even more so in the future.

There is a final strand of thought in the Due Process Model that is often ignored but that needs to be candidly faced if thought on the subject is not to be obscured. This is a mood of skepticism about the morality and utility of the criminal sanction, taken either as a whole or in some of its applications. The subject is a large and complicated one, comprehending as it does much of the intellectual history of our times. It is properly the subject of another essay altogether. To put the matter briefly, one cannot improve upon the statement by Professor Paul Bator:

> In summary we are told that the criminal law's notion of just condemnation and punishment is a cruel hypocrisy visited by a smug society on the psychologically and economically crippled; that its premise of a morally autonomous will with at least some measure of choice whether to comply with the values expressed in a penal code is unscientific and outmoded; that is reliance on punishment as an educational and deterrent agent is misplaced, particularly in the case of the very members of society most likely to engage in criminal conduct; and that its failure to provide for individualized and humane rehabilitation of offenders is inhuman and wasteful.[4]

This skepticism, which may be fairly said to be widespread among the most influential and articulate contemporary leaders of informed opinion, leads to an attitude toward the processes of the criminal law that, to quote Mr. Bator again, engenders "a peculiar receptivity toward claims of injustice which arise within the traditional structure of the system itself; fundamental disagreement and unease about the very bases of the criminal law has, inevitably, created acute pressure at least to expand and liberalize those of its processes and doctrines which serve to make more tentative its judgments or limit its power." In short, doubts about the ends for which power is being exercised create pressure to limit the discretion with which that power is exercised.

The point need not be pressed to the extreme of doubts about or rejection of the premises upon which the criminal sanction in general rests. Unease may be stirred simply by reflection on the variety of uses to which the criminal sanction is put and by a judgment that an increasingly large proportion of those uses may represent an unwise invocation of so extreme a sanction. It would be an interesting irony if doubts about the propriety of certain uses of the criminal sanction prove to contribute to a restrictive trend in the criminal process that in the end requires a choice among uses and finally an abandonment of some of the very uses that stirred the original doubts, but for a reason quite unrelated to those doubts.

There are two kinds of problems that need to be dealt with in any model of the criminal process. One is what the rules shall be. The other is how the rules shall be implemented. The second is at least as important as the first. . . . [T]he distinctive difference between the two models is not only in the rules of conduct that they lay down but also in the sanctions that are to be invoked when a claim is presented that the rules have been breached and, no less importantly, in the timing that is permitted or required for the invocation of those sanctions.

Herbert L.
Packer

As I have already suggested, the Due Process Model locates at least some of the sanctions for breach of the operative rules in the criminal process itself. The relation between these two aspects of the process—the rules and the sanctions for their breach—is a purely formal one unless there is some mechanism for bringing them into play with each other. The hinge between them in the Due Process Model is the availability of legal counsel. This has a double aspect. Many of the rules that the model requires are couched in terms of the availability of counsel to do various things at various stages of the process—this is the conventionally recognized aspect; beyond it, there is a pervasive assumption that counsel is necessary in order to invoke sanctions for breach of any of the rules. The more freely available these sanctions are, the more important is the role of counsel in seeing to it that the sanctions are appropriately invoked. If the process is seen as a series of occasions for checking its own operation, the role of counsel is a much more nearly central one than is the case in a process that is seen as primarily concerned with expeditious determination of factual guilt. And if equality of operation is a governing norm, the availability of counsel to some is seen as requiring it for all. Of all the controverted aspects of the criminal process, the right to counsel, including the role of government in its provision, is the most dependent on what one's model of the process looks like, and the least susceptible of resolution unless one has confronted the antinomies of the two models.

I do not mean to suggest that questions about the right to counsel disappear if one adopts a model of the process that conforms more or less closely to the Crime Control Model, but only that such questions become absolutely central if one's model moves very far down the spectrum of possibilities toward the pure Due Process Model. The reason for this centrality is to be found in the assumption underlying both models that the process is an adversary one in which the initiative in invoking relevant rules rests primarily on the parties concerned, the state, and the accused. One could construct models that placed central responsibility on adjudicative agents such as committing magistrates and trial judges. And there are, as we shall see, marginal but nonetheless important adjustments in the role of the adjudicative agents that enter into the models with which we are concerned. For present purposes it is enough to say that these adjustments are marginal, that the animating presuppositions that underlie both models in the context of the American criminal system relegate the adjudicative agents to a relatively passive role, and therefore place central importance on the role of counsel.

. . . What assumptions do we make about the sources of authority to shape the real-world operations of the criminal process? Recognizing that our models are only models, what agencies of government have the power to pick and choose between their competing demands? Once again, the limiting features of the American context come into play. Ours is not a system of legislative supremacy. The distinctively American institution of judicial review exercises a limiting and ultimately a shaping influence on the criminal process. Because the Crime Control Model is basically an affirmative model, emphasizing at every turn the existence and exercise of official power, its validating authority is ultimately legislative (although proximately administrative). Because the Due Process Model is basically a negative model, asserting limits on the nature of official power and on the modes of its exercise, its validating authority is judicial and requires an appeal to supra-legislative law, to the law of the Constitution. To the extent that tensions between the two models are resolved by deference to the Due Process Model, the authoritative force at work is the judicial power, working in the distinctively judicial mode of invoking the sanction of nullity. That is at once the strength and the weakness of the Due Process Model: its strength because in our system the appeal to the Constitution provides the last and the overriding word; its weakness because saying no in specific cases is an exercise in futility unless there is a general willingness on the part of the officials who operate the process to apply negative prescriptions across the board. It is no accident that statements reinforcing the Due Process Model come from the courts, while at the same time facts denying it are established by the police and prosecutors.

NOTES

1. Mapp v. Ohio, 367 U.S. 643 (1961); Ker v. California, 374 U.S. 23 (1963).
2. See President's Commission on Law Enforcement and Administration of Justice, *The Challenge of Crime in a Free Society* (Washington, D.C., 1967), chap. 2.
3. Griffin v. Illinois, 351 U.S. 12, 19 (1956).
4. *Finality in Criminal Law and Federal Habeas Corpus for State Prisoners*, 76 HARV. L. REV. 441, 442 (1963).

1.2 DAVID E. BARLOW, MELISSA HICKMAN BARLOW, AND THEODORE G. CHIRICOS

Long Economic Cycles and the Criminal Justice System in the U.S.

Social historians have traced changes in the U.S. criminal justice policy to political and economic developments. As such, the United States adopts criminal justice policies that it needs to support its political and economic institutions. For example, statutory developments during the time of slavery suggest that capital punishment served to protect and control the institution of Southern slavery. Scholars have analyzed the political and economic functions of the convict lease system that developed after the Civil War as essentially "*de facto* enslavement of African Americans." Related studies suggest a relationship between capitalist production, labor needs, and extralegal mechanisms of social control in the postbellum South. One study examined the relationship between economic conditions and the lynching of blacks in the Deep South from 1882 to 1930 and found that black lynchings dramatically increased during periods of decline in cotton prices.

In the following selection from "Long Economic Cycles and the Criminal Justice System in the U.S.," *Crime, Law and Social Change* (1993), University of Wisconsin–Milwaukee professor David E. Barlow, University of Wisconsin–Green Bay professor Melissa Hickman Barlow, and Florida State University professor Theodore G. Chiricos analyze U.S. criminal justice history within the context of the social structure of capitalist development. They propose that the intensity of criminal justice policy to promote social control change is related to developments in economic conditions. As such, in times of economic expansion and capitalist accumulation, criminal justice policy on social control, social order, and social reform weakens. During these periods the criminal justice system adopts a more complacent posture, which in turn is reflected in a certain passivity of the criminal justice system to expand or reform its mechanisms of social control. Conversely, criminal justice policy accentuates mechanisms of social control during periods of economic crisis and capitalist contraction. In these periods capitalist accumulation is jeopardized, and general disenchantment flows from social institutions and is manifested in social unrest, public disorder, and crime.

In response to the crisis, the criminal justice system becomes procedurally more innovative, stiffens its control mechanisms, and gets tough on crime.

Key Concept: criminal justice history and the U.S. correctional policy

Abstract. *Long cycles in capitalist development have been utilized as an analytical tool for political economic theory and to explain major shifts in the social structure within capitalist political economies. However, the potential impact that these massive changes in the political economy have on the historical development of criminal justice institutions and policies is an area not addressed within the literature. This article explores the relationship between long cycles of capitalist development and the historical formation of criminal justice policy in the United States.*

POLITICAL ECONOMY AND CRIMINAL JUSTICE

That there is a relationship between economic conditions and criminal justice policy is well established in the literature. Georg Rusche observed in the 1930s that the political economy contributed significantly to the development of penal systems in various countries. According to Rusche, the political economic structure shapes the formation of criminal justice institutions and their operation. Specifically, he suggests that the conditions of the labor market and the standard of living greatly influence contemporary forms of corrections. Rusche broke from traditional criminal justice theory by suggesting that the societal response to criminal behavior is not a simple consequence of crime.

In relation to the United States criminal justice system, Rusche largely focused on the emergence and decline of hard labor as the primary mode of punishment. The historical investigations of Miller, Petchesky, Adamson, and Gardner support Rusche's ideas that confinement with hard labor was a very profitable enterprise in early 19th century America. Prison administrators and business people who utilized prison labor made a great deal of profit from confinement with hard labor. These investigations also suggest that convict labor was quite productive and played a major role in the growth of a new nation. The demise of confinement with hard labor in the latter part of the 19th century is primarily attributed to declines in both its profitability and its effectiveness in preserving social order.

Several empirical studies have found a significant correlation between unemployment and incarceration. The relationship between unemployment and incarceration is witnessed in studies which control for the crime rate, changes in the population, and the growth of non-criminal justice institutions, such as welfare caseloads and mental hospitalizations. In addition, Melossi's research shows a significant relationship between the yearly change in per capita income and incarceration. Myers and Sabol also provide support for the thesis that unemployment and incarceration are closely related; however, they report their findings to be sensitive to race and region. Although Galster and Scaturo's work found no relationship between unemployment and incarceration, they did find a significant inverse relationship between unemployment and unconditional releases. Hall et al. and Ratner and McMullan each connect criminal justice with economic conditions, within arguments that economic crises have lead to hegemonic crises, the response to which has been the emergence of an "exceptional state" within capitalist political economies.

Numerous authors, then, identify that a relationship exists between economic conditions and criminal justice. It is our contention that we will broaden our perspective on this relationship by investigating the history of criminal justice in the United States within the context of long cycles in capitalist development. Exploring criminal justice policy in relation to long cycles contributes both to the literature on criminal justice history and to political economic literature as well.

LONG CYCLES OF CAPITALIST DEVELOPMENT

The historical development of world capitalism is characterized by political economists in a variety of ways. The view of capitalist development as a series of long international cycles of accelerating and decelerating economic growth holds that these long cycles are quantitatively and qualitatively different from the shorter and less traumatic business or industrial fluctuations, typically referred to as business cycles. Kondratieff explains that these are massive cycles, lasting a total of approximately fifty years each, and affecting all capitalist countries, industries, and intermediate cycles.

According to Gordon, the long cycles of capitalism begin with an extended period of economic expansion, which is characterized by high profits, low unemployment, increasing investment, production, and consumption, and a generally positive business climate. These periods of expansion, though, are eventually followed by a prolonged phase of economic contraction and stagnation, characterized by low profits, high unemployment, decreasing investment, production and consumption, and a generally negative business climate. Political, economic, and social institutions are all greatly affected by these shifts in economic activity.

Profits are the driving force in capitalism and, because of this, capitalists will invest only if they have a high expectation of realization of profit. Without an environment favorable to the accumulation of capital, the cycle of production will not even begin. In the absence of a favorable environment, business confidence falls and investments decrease. When investments fall off, production, hiring, and consumption decline as well.

When the above described scenario occurs, the major determinants of whether capitalist relations will once again become productive are found in what Gordon, Edwards and Reich refer to as the social structure of accumulation. The social structure of accumulation consists of all of the societal institutions and processes which affect, either directly or indirectly, the accumulation of capital. The social structure of accumulation is made up of many different components which provide the necessary conditions for stimulation of the economy. However, historically, the social structure of accumulation has also been characterized by contradictions, which eventually bring the economy into a period of prolonged stagnation. Some of the major elements within the social structure of accumulation are technological development, the intensity of the class struggle, the organization of work, the structure of the labor market, and the form of the state. The social structure of accumulation is the entire configuration of institutions that play a role in the accumulation of capital.

Explaining the impetus for the cyclical nature of capitalist development, Gordon points out that economic crisis may itself produce the necessary environment for revitalization of the economy and the reproduction of capitalist relations. However, Gordon also notes that there is no guarantee that the period of decline will be followed by a period of growth. Economic crisis typically cheapens the cost of labor through high unemployment, the expansion of surplus populations, and the gradual introduction of labor-saving technologies. Crisis also weeds out unprofitable companies and industries, and enlarges the total amount of idle capital. Each of these is necessary but not sufficient to trigger another period of growth in the economy. In order for capitalism to once again become productive a substantial restructuring of old institutions into a new social structure of accumulation must occur.

The restructuring of the social structure of accumulation, the creation of a more favorable climate for accumulation, the restoration of business confidence, the increase in the rate of profit, and the acceleration of investment may produce a once more expansive economy, but it cannot last forever. According to Mandel, these resolutions to economic crisis contain specific contradictions that eventually return the economy to a state of crisis. Indeed, the concept of "contradiction" refers to the notion that resolutions to crisis contain within them precisely those elements that bring about another crisis. The particular resolutions to a crisis differ, as the impediments to capitalist accumulation differ. Usually, economic crisis is caused by the interaction of several contradictions, such as overproduction, underconsumption, the rising organic composition of capital, and class conflict, one of which is typically dominant. The contradictions and their consequences are historically specific and, thus, can only be identified through historical investigation. The criminal justice system is a vital component of the social structure of accumulation in capitalist societies. As the capitalist state's most openly coercive form of social control, criminal justice plays a critical role in maintaining social order and, thereby, establishing a favorable business climate.

In the following section, we summarize both developments in the political economy and developments in U.S. criminal justice, in order to begin to explore criminal justice history in terms of the wider social structure of accumulation. This overview of U.S. economic history and criminal justice history provides a basis for understanding the role of criminal justice in the long cycles of capitalist development.

THE HISTORICAL DEVELOPMENT OF LONG CYCLES AND CRIMINAL JUSTICE POLICY IN THE U.S.

First Expansion (1789/93–1820/26)

Mandel locates the first long cycle of capitalist development between 1789/93 and 1847/48, the period of the Industrial Revolution. This period is characterized by bourgeois revolutions, the Napoleonic wars, the constitution of the world market for industrial goods, and the gradual spread of the steam engine. The first long period of expansion is located between 1789/93 and 1825/26, in which there was accelerated growth and a high rate of profit. Particular features of this period of expanding competitive capitalism include artisan-produced machines and the slow expansion of the industrial proletariat.

Although the United States experienced tremendous urbanization, immigration, industrialization and change during this time period, general social conditions were relatively positive and peaceful. The new nation was filled with opportunity. As Walker points out, few efforts were made in the area of social control reform. Traditional methods of social discipline remained intact.

First Contraction (1820/26–1845/48)

Wright identifies the first period of expansion as the state of primitive accumulation and the contraction phase which followed as the period of transformation to manufacturing. He further explains that two of the central constraints which led to economic decline were the low level of technology and the shortage of labor. Mandel locates this depressed phase of the cycle between 1825/26 and 1847/48, and points out that it is characterized by decelerated growth and a low rate of profit. According to Mandel, this phase was brought on by increased competition, the rising cost of constant capital and a decrease in world market expansion.

Gordon et al. also locate the first long cycle between the 1790s and the mid-1840s. According to these authors, the downswing between 1820 and the mid-1840s signaled the failure of the organization of work and the structure of labor markets to produce sufficient accumulation. Capitalists had a shortage of labor due to the lack of proletarianization, i.e., the process of forcing people to work as wage-earners in order to survive. Capitalists need a large supply of laborers from which to draw, in order to lower their labor and production costs and increase the rate of profit. Ultimately, proletarianization was facilitated by the criminalization of begging and various forms of vagrancy during this period of contraction. As Rothman notes, anyone who did not work for a wage, could be forced into an almshouse or prison and then put to work.

In addition to the creation of vagrancy laws, many other significant innovations in the area of social control took place during this time period, largely in response to deteriorating social conditions and growing unrest. This period of American history is riddled with signs of decline, unrest and fear. Long-standing social institutions became fragmented as they confronted the new institutions of industry. Although riots occurred in colonial times,

> [i]n the 1830s an unprecedented and frightening wave of riots swept over urban areas. Philadelphia and Baltimore competed for the dubious title of "mob city", ... New York experienced three major strikes in 1834 alone. Nor was the problem confined to the east; Cincinnati, St. Louis, and Chicago had their own riots. To many Americans, the survival of the new nation seemed at stake.

In 1837, 20,000 unemployed people in Philadelphia assembled in protest. In New York City, thousands organized in City Hall Park to protest monopolies, and the high cost of food and rent. The Broad Street Riot in New York City began as a clash between volunteer fire-fighters and an Irish funeral procession which led to a riot involving one-sixth of the city's population and the eventual intervention of a cavalry regiment of 800 horse soldiers. According to Richardson, rapid population growth, high levels of immigration, increasing class distinctions, high mobility, and impersonal human work relationships all contributed to a sense of social disorder. But it was not until these elements were combined with severe economic depression in the world economy that official and organized government action was mobilized.

In response to these conditions within the political economy, major innovations in social control emerged. Possibly the most significant innovation during this period was the emergence of incarceration as the primary instrument for punishing criminals. In the mid-1820s, separate institutions were constructed for juveniles. In the 1830s, the general prison style that began to dominate was based on confinement with hard labor. Also, in the 1830s and 1840s, there was a substantial growth in asylums for child-care, from orphanages to reformatories.

Another important development in the area of social control took place in law enforcement. Lipson discovered that private police agencies emerged during this time and Platt et al, note that private police played a major role in the social control of immigrants, workers and the poor. In addition to private police, the first bureaucratically organized, partially trained, public salaried, uniformed police began to appear in the latter part of this period. Walker states that:

> [t]he police, the prison, and the first juvenile justice agencies had appeared since the 1820s. The apparatus of social control was now far larger and more extensive than it had ever been; it was able to intervene in the lives of American citizens as never before.

These innovations were not simple extensions of previous forms of social control, but, rather, they were radical departures from anything the world had witnessed prior to 1820. Many leaders of philanthropic organizations and members of the political elite struggled with other members of their own class, to convince them of the need for these new social institutions.

Second Expansion (1845/48–1873)

Mandel periodizes the second long wave from 1848 to 1893 and calls it the period of "free competition" in industrial capitalism. Mandel suggests that the second long cycle is particularized by the generalization of the steam engine and the transition to machine-made machines. He also observes that, during this period, there were increases in world market expansion, industrialization, gold production, and railroad construction. According to Mandel, this stage contains the first technological revolution, which led to cheaper fixed capital, and a rise in relative surplus capital, as productivity increased. Mandel observes that the steam machine was replaced by the steam engine and that handicrafts were replaced by industrial production, which increased the rate of growth in the productivity of labor.

Gordon, Edwards and Reich characterize the period between the mid-1840s to 1873 as the "consolidation" phase of "initial proletarianization". American labor was transformed into a workforce of wage earners. Working for a wage, as opposed to being a self-employed artisan, for example, became the common form of labor. This reorganization of the workforce was vital to the economic and industrial expansion which took place during this period. Proletarianization helped to solve the critical shortage of labor which existed in the previous long cycle.

As in the earlier period of economic expansion, social conditions during the second expansion were positive and productive. Industrial violence and riots in the streets were rare, especially in comparison to the number of industrial battles and hunger riots of the previous period of stagnation. According to Walker, there was no citizen outcry for public order during this period. Although criminal justice institutions did not remain dormant, there were very few innovations in this area. New police departments continued to be formed after 1845, but the initial excitement of the movement had passed and the pattern was established. Correctional institutions failed to produce the anticipated rehabilitation of offenders and, thus, the fervor concerning this form of control diminished. Some movements to reform and humanize the prison emerged during the 1860s, but no major policy changes occurred. According to Rothman, the term which best describes the 1850s and 1860s was "complacency". In comparison to the period of stagnation, enthusiasm for the creation of innovations in social control was notably absent during the period of the second expansion, and there was little concern expressed about the so-called "dangerous classes".

Second Contraction (1873–1893)

Wright identifies the intensification of class struggle as a major contributor to the onset of the second period of economic stagnation. He suggests that the growth in working class strength during this cycle was due to increased organization within the working class. Gordon et al. assert that class struggle also played a major role in the eventual failure of the process of proletarianization. They contend that growing intercapitalist competition and workers' struggles produced a squeeze on profits, which ultimately led to financial panic and the withholding of investment.

Wright and Mandel emphasize the "rising organic composition of capital" as a decisive contradiction in capitalism during this period. Due to the rising cost of raw materials, along with old technology, an increasingly higher proportion of capital was put into machines and raw materials. Only living labor can produce surplus value. Therefore, as a greater proportion of capital is invested into dead labor (machines and raw materials), all other things remaining equal, the rate of profit tends to decline. In addition, the intensification of class struggle kept the costs of labor relatively high, which also contributed to fall in the rate of profit.

Beginning with the devastating depression of 1873, social unrest and discontent spread throughout the cities of the United States. According to Dubofsky, from 1865 to 1897 some of the most violent industrial conflicts in American history took place. The Great Railroad Strike of 1877 and the Great Upheaval of the 1880s put fear in the hearts of industrial capitalists. With the introduction of new, labor-saving technologies, unemployment for the first time became structural. Millions were unemployed. In addition, "public relief was usually nonexistent, and private charity either insufficient or offered only on the most demeaning terms". Piven and Cloward note that unemployed people became involved in large demonstrations and riots. Dubofsky distinguishes 1877 as the most violent year in the late 19th century. Much of this violence was directed at the destruction of factories, which had brought about increases in labor discipline and labor-saving technology. As a result, even more unemployment and job insecurity were produced. Class struggle grew in scope and intensity, during this period, largely because workers had become powerful enough to pose a real threat to capitalist class interests.

For example, from 1881 to 1890 there were 9668 strikes and lockouts. Thirty-nine percent of the strikes in the 1880s were not initiated by unions, but rather, they were spontaneous. The Great Strike of 1877 virtually shut down Pittsburgh, Buffalo, St. Louis and Chicago as riots spread throughout the major rail cities in the country, and resulted in the deaths of dozens of people and $5 million in property damage. Other grand scale strikes also occurred, such as Chicago's McCormick Strike of 1886, the 1884 Longshoremen strike in Buffalo, and the street car strikes in Chicago, Columbus, Detroit and Indianapolis.

Within this period of decline, as in the previous depression, there appears to have been a merging of a moral crusade, anti-immigrant legislation, and concern about the poor. The moral crusade which occurred during the second contraction generated acute concern over victimless crime, as efforts were launched to counter what was perceived to be a wave of immorality and permissiveness in the 1870s. Walker observes that the "enforcement of vagrancy laws was a common response to the major depressions of the 1870s and 1890s." Through criminalization of the recreational activities of the working class, a direct attack was launched against the "dangerous classes", who were said to be causing the violent disorders of the period. According to Friedman, the law "exploded" after 1870, "creating new victimless crimes and revitalizing old ones." Even the federal government for the first time got involved in such legislation, with the Comstock Act of 1873. The Comstock Act prohibited the sale or use of contraceptive devices. The federal government followed this legislation with the Internal Revenue Act of 1890, which prohibited the smoking of opium, a practice almost exclusively restricted to Chinese immigrants. The recreational activities of the working class were subject more and more to regulation by the government.

This regulation was complimented by a revolutionary reorganization of major city police departments, and their transformation into the primary instruments for the repression of working class immigrants. According to Harring, this is the most significant development in the history of the urban police in the United States. The urban police experienced a revolutionary transformation in structure, design and technique. Remarkable changes were implemented in technology, discipline, and in the size of police departments. The early departments were small and did not play the dominant position in crowd, strike, and riot control that they did by the end of the nineteenth century. This revolutionary change in social control was an important aspect of the increasing socialization of the costs of production-reproduction and the general expansion of municipal services. The expanded role of municipal police in social control may also be attributed to the apparent legitimacy of the newly professionalized public police departments, which appeared in direct contrast to the corrupt, brutal and ineffective private police system.

The punishment realm of criminal justice also experienced significant innovations during the second period of contraction. Many of the programs that have traditionally been attributed to the Progressive Era (1900 to 1920) actually first emerged in the latter decades of the nineteenth century. As Walker notes, the reformatory first emerged in the 1870s, and with it came the models for indeterminate sentencing, probation, and conditional release. Between 1860 and 1880, there was a wave of legislation throughout the United States establishing good-time credit policies. Between 1880 and 1900, twenty-one states passed parole laws. The 1880s brought the advent of community corrections with the construction of the first settlement houses. Also, with the assistance of the previously mentioned moral crusade, separate institutions were established for women prisoners and women matrons were first introduced in the field of corrections. Juvenile institutions, specifically the Elmira Reformatory in 1877, spearheaded many of the reformatory-type guidelines. It is important to note, however, as Walker and Miller maintain, that these innovations should not be seen as institutional substitutes or humanitarian efforts to decarcerate individuals. These developments, like other reforms in criminal justice during this time period, are more realistically viewed as efforts to develop more effective forms of social control.

Third Expansion (1873–1913/15)

Mandel identifies imperialism as one of the solutions to the stagnation of the second contraction, pointing out that "large scale capital investment in raw materials helped to counteract the rising organic composition of capital by lowering the cost of circulating capital." This investment made raw material production more efficient through better technology and lowered the costs of raw materials. Such investment also brought about an expansion in world markets, with capital exports to colonies and semi-colonies, a practice which cheapens the cost of raw materials. Mandel locates this expansion between 1893/4 and 1913.

Wolfe also characterizes this period in terms of a wave of expansionism, as the "ruling classes turned to foreign expansion as a solution to domestic problems". Due to the problem of labor militancy, immigration became a major policy concern of the state. People were encouraged to migrate into areas without enough workers to lower the value of labor and they were discouraged from remaining in areas that had too many dislocated rural peasants. America's major urban and industrial areas were flooded with a massive wave of immigrants, who were used by capitalists to break strikes and lower labor costs.

Gordon et al., who locate this expansion period between the late 1890s and the First World War, also write about the demand placed on capitalists to quell labor militancy. They describe the consolidation of a process which they refer to as homogenization, which reduced the jobs of most American factory laborers to common, semi-skilled employment. The homogenization of labor made it easier to replace workers, opening the door for immigrants to take the jobs of disgruntled or striking workers. Employment insecurity grew rapidly and lowered the value of the industrial worker and his or her skill, thus weakening the bargaining power of labor.

The process of deskilling workers can only be accomplished through the introduction of proper technology. Mandel categorizes this period as the second technological revolution. From the 1890s to 1940, the machine production and application of electric and combustion engines began to take place in the capitalist world. The focus was on keeping markets and the economy expansive, while raising the level of labor exploitation to new heights.

The period from 1893 to 1913/15 was not characterized by the magnitude of concern about crime, nor the number of criminal justice innovations, noted in the previous period of decline. The period was not completely without social control concerns, for many of the reforms begun in the previous period of stagnation continued to expand during this period. However, no panic over or great demand for social control is evident in this period.

Third Contraction (1913/15–1940)

According to Wolfe, expansionism and immigration contained certain innate problems that prevented them from being permanent solutions to economic decline. The primary problem is that the world is a finite place and eventually market expansion reached a dead end. The immigration/migration phenomenon also reached similar limits. Instead of solving problems, immigration only shifted problems to new locations. The flood of immigrants into small urban areas produced social problems that the state was not equipped to handle. Reich refers to the period between 1870 and 1920 as the "era of mobilization", and points out that, during this period, the social structure was inappropriate for dealing with the enormous problems of mass unemployment, low education, poverty, disease, and the other social consequences of industrialization and urbanization. America's mobile, erratic, free-wheeling capital and labor markets served to stimulate the boom of the 1890s, but they lacked the planning, management and social responsibility necessary to offset the consequences of the boom.

Gordon et al. suggest that the successes of homogenization began to decay during the period of decline between the two world wars. Wright illustrates that the weakening of the working class lowered the cost of labor to a level that stifled economic growth. In other words, attempts to crush the power of labor, in order to raise the accumulation of surplus value, eventually lowered the accumulation of surplus value, as a crisis of underconsumption materialized. Mandel submits that the extremely high rate of exploitation led to a high level of speculation and investment. Gordon et al. state that the process of homogenization, and the other methods of crushing labor unrest, were too successful in extracting surplus value. The decline in real wages intensified the problem of underconsumption and antagonized the working class into becoming better organized.

Wright explains that, as capitalists continue to increase the absolute and relative level of surplus value, prices are pushed up and wages are pushed down, limited markets are expanded and production increased. It becomes increasingly difficult for demand and/or buying power to stay high enough to absorb the products at a level that will realize the expected surplus value. In other words, as more capital is accumulated privately, there is less capital available among other groups of consumers to buy products.

Disorder, riots, social unrest and fear characterized the period from 1913/15 to 1940. In 1918 and 1919, for example, a series of race riots in New Orleans, Charleston, Tulsa, Omaha, Washington, D.C., Knoxville, Chicago, and East St. Louis heightened public fears of breakdown of law and order. According to Piven and Cloward, much of the social disorder of this period was due to the collapse in the economy. The economic system was obviously not working and people lost faith in it. Demonstrations, protests, and riots became commonplace, as workers and the unemployed sought both to stimulate social change and simply to survive. In Chicago, five thousand men marched on the headquarters of the lodging houses in order to stop evictions. In 1931, evictions were temporarily suspended after three police officers were injured in a "rent riot".

There was a serious rise in looting in the early 1930s and organized unemployed people became a very real threat to the social order. People banded together to demand food; thirty to forty people would regularly organize and descend upon markets. In New York City, 1,100 men waiting on a Salvation Army breadline mobbed two trucks delivering bread to a nearby hotel. In Henrietta, Oklahoma 300 marched on storekeepers and demanded food. The chain stores and the media were scared to report these events for fear of starting a contagion effect. Unemployed people marched in New York, Detroit, Cleveland, Philadelphia, Los Angeles, Chicago, Seattle, Boston and Milwaukee under such banners as "fight—don't starve". "[I]n December 1931, participants in the first of two Communist-led national hunger marches on Washington were met on the ramps leading to the capitol by police armed with rifles and riot guns (backed up by machine gun nests concealed in the stonework above)."

Union membership increased dramatically. Labor militancy increased as well. "Between 1915 and 1916 the number of reported strikes more than doubled, and the latter year recorded more industrial disputes than any previous time in the United States." In 1917, for the first time in U.S. history, one million workers annually walked off their jobs. In 1919, over four million workers struck and the General Seattle Strike paralyzed the city for five days. In 1933, fifteen strikers were killed by police, and in 1934, forty strikers were killed. In 18 months, troops were called out in 16 states. Preston identifies "an eruption of mass strikes on a scale never before seen in American society." And, as riots and demonstrations by both the employed and unemployed threatened established institutions, the state responded both with relief and with violence.

The third phase of economic decline, like previous periods of decline, was characterized by innovations in the urban police and the correctional system; but the most substantial and radical changes occurred within the federal government. Fear of crime and social disorder increased during the depression and the government responded in full force. The federal government expanded into areas in which it had never before been involved. Federal authorities made an obvious effort to become more involved in the control of street crime.

The implementation and development of probation, parole, indeterminate sentencing and other reforms in corrections intensified between 1916 and 1940. A major shift in reforms occurred in the early 1920s, as crime control ideology shifted from an emphasis on societal reform to an emphasis on psychological and individual reform. Several important innovations occurred in the area of corrections during this period. For example, in 1913 Wisconsin established the first work release program. In the 1930s neighborhood and area projects began to multiply as the repressive apparatus moved securely into the community. The federal government also moved into the area of corrections, in 1925, with the first federal probationary law. This was followed by the establishment of the Federal Bureau of Prisons in 1930, and the 1935 enactment of the Ashhurst-Summis Act to modify prisons.

Concerns about inefficiency and corruption among police "sparked a movement for police 'reform' that was expressed in several ways during the period from 1910 to the early 1930s". Many of the progressives in business, government and the universities became critical of the police and this triggered a new wave of police professionalization. Police professionalization was connected to a move to increase police training and to technological developments, such as the radio patrol car. "By the late 1920s and 1930s, the crime-fighter model of policing moved to the forefront" of police departments throughout the country and improvements in technology reflected the desire to make the police more efficient.

As previously mentioned, the most significant development in the area of social control during this period was an increase in federal intervention into street crime. Walker refers to the 1920s and 1930s as the "crime control decades", as attitudes hardened toward crime and criminals. National crime commissions flourished and moral crusades against alcohol, vice and drugs led to Prohibition, the Harrison Act of 1914, and the Marijuana Tax Act of 1937. The number of federal agencies responsible for enforcing laws increased dramatically with the creation of the Federal Bureau of Narcotics, the Bureau of Prohibition, and the Federal Bureau of Investigations.

During this time period, J. Edgar Hoover took command of the Federal Bureau of Investigations (FBI) and made it the most important law enforcement agency in the country. The FBI played a major role in domestic spying and the suppression of socialists, labor unions and radicals. This process was facilitated by a series of sensational crimes and the creation of many new federal crimes, such as kidnapping, bank robbery, interstate theft, and anti-American activities. Clearly, the federal government began to play an unprecedented role in criminal justice during this period of economic stagnation.

Fourth Expansion (1940–1966/70)

The transformation of the social structure of accumulation that ushered in the fourth major expansion in capitalist development was characterized by efforts to raise demand, so that the crisis of underconsumption could be remedied. Wright explains that the Keynesian form of state intervention into the economy was designed to expand aggregate demand for products, especially through military spending. It was a conscious effort by state managers to increase the money and credit supply in order to artificially create demand. Wright also suggests that World War II helped the U.S. economy, "both through military spending and through the destruction of great quantities of capital". This destruction of capital was primarily in Europe and Asia, which facilitated the United States' domination of the world, economically, militarily and ideologically. This period of U.S. domination is sometimes referred to as *Pax Americana*. The United States dollar standardized international currency transactions with the Bretton Woods Agreement.

Reich observes that the United States moved full-force into high-volume machinery and production with large-scale organization. Mandel identifies the period between 1940/48 and 1966/67 as the third technological revolution and he associates this period with the generalization of machine production of electronic and nuclear apparatuses. Bluestone and Harrison note that this massive technological change was facilitated by a postwar social contract between capital and labor. Capitalists needed labor peace in order to increase accumulation; thus, they agreed to link unionized employees' salaries with their level of productivity. Harrison and Bluestone point out that, with the virtual destruction of foreign competition, U.S. corporations could simply raise prices to compensate for increases in production costs or labor concessions.

Gordon, Edwards and Reich identify "segmentation" as another strategy for securing labor peace in the post-World War II period. Job structures and labor markets became more separated and divergent. The segmentation process divided workers and decreased their sense of unity by separating their interests and using them against each other. As large corporations formed into definite core industries, peripheral and non-unionized workers developed antagonistic attitudes toward the better paid unionized employees of these core industries. According to Gordon, Edwards and Reich, the managerial revolution also led to more segregation as the numerous tiers of supervision divided and antagonized employees. The segmentation process helped to weaken labor organization and strength; thus, allowing industrialists to maintain their dominance in the class power relationship.

During the expansion period of the 1940s and 1950s, there was generally less concern about crime and far fewer criminal justice innovations than in the previous period of decline. The period was not without significant events in the area of social control, especially considering that this was the time of the McCarthy Era. But "in general the police received little scholarly attention during the 1940s and 1950s." There was no great concern over the criminal justice system and, thus, criminal justice essentially drifted without much direction until the 1960s.

Fourth Contraction (1966/70–Present)

The contradictions inherent in government efforts to stimulate demand, to preserve domestic order and to protect American business interests overseas, manifested themselves in the late 1960s. One of the major problems that developed was the creation of permanent inflation. Gamble and Walton suggest that spending by both the public and private sectors out-paced production and resulted in rising prices. The segmentation of labor became less effective in reducing labor militancy as worker dissatisfaction intensified. Wright suggests that Keynesian social reforms, such as unemployment insurance, reduced the effectiveness of unemployment in keeping inflation down.

In addition, as technology in the United States began to deteriorate and newer technology was generalized to other countries which could produce the high-volume products at lower costs, foreign intercapitalist competition intensified. As noted above, with the rising costs of social reforms, labor, and raw materials in the 1960s, the rate of profit was preserved by rising prices. However, with the onslaught of foreign competition, United States capitalists found themselves unable to raise prices and still remain competitive. U.S. dominance of the world economy began to deteriorate with the collapse of *Pax Americana*, the Bretton Woods Accords and the labor peace accords. U.S. corporations began to shift capital within and out of the United States in an effort to reduce labor costs. Capitalists found it increasingly difficult to realize their expected rate of profit; thus, investment declined, production slowed, and people were put out of work.

Social conditions since 1966 reflect this deterioration of U.S. economic, military and ideological dominance internationally and domestically. The turbulent sixties are a well documented period in United States history. Images of violent racial conflicts, civil rights marches and demonstrations, and massive student protests against the war in Vietnam are etched in the public's memory. The social rebellions which occurred during this period produced real fear within the general public. The militancy, the violence and the extensive property damage of the 1960s shook the nation.

Beginning in the 1960s, the powerful civil rights movement exposed inequality and challenged the forms of social control focused on Blacks. The student movement challenged the "establishment" and its traditional forms of social restraint. Student protests increased and ultimately centered on an anti-Vietnam war campaign. These challenges by young United States citizens often came into conflict with the legal system and the government did not appear to be able to control the situation. Race riots, violent demonstrations and prisoner rebellions escalated as the police often responded to protest with violence. "The rising tide of public disrespect and fear of crime in the streets" and growing disrespect for law and established institutions characterize this period.

As for the 1970s, although many of the movements calmed during this decade, economic deterioration continued and was accompanied by mass unemployment. Unemployment grew in the mid-1970s and again between 1980 and 1982 when it reached its highest level since the 1930s.

Although unemployment levels have dropped since 1982, high levels of underemployment, declines in real income for the majority of U.S. families, and increasing income inequality clearly suggest that economic and social conditions continue to deteriorate. From 1977 to 1989, the "real income of families in the middle fifth of the population actually fell 5.3 percent... and the incomes of poorer Americans fell even further during this period—10.4 percent." It should also be noted that as the economy worsens many unemployed people are not counted in official statistics. Much of the improvement in official economic statistics during the 1980s can be attributed to a "credit card" economy which has been supported by skyrocketing Federal Government deficits.

Economic and social conditions in the United States steadily declined under both the Reagan and Bush Administrations. Concern about the need for social control and discipline intensified, as official crime rates continued to increase. Traditional social institutions such as the government, the family and the church appeared to be losing their grip on society.

As the public began to lose faith in government, state managers started to search for new mechanisms with which to control social disorder. The criminal justice system was at the forefront of efforts to stop race riots and curb the militant activities of students. The correctional system underwent many adjustments and policy changes. Law enforcement agencies were criticized for their failures during the turmoil of the sixties, and money and innovations quickly appeared within this branch of criminal justice. With the establishment of the Law Enforcement Assistance Administration, the federal government grew larger and more repressive; its tentacles moved deeper into juvenile delinquency, drugs, the police, corrections, and domestic spying.

The first major policy change in U.S. corrections during this period was in the late 1960s with the re-introduction of decarceration, through various forms of community-based corrections, probation and parole. Between 1967 and 1974 the number of people on probation and parole increased dramatically. Connected to this development was the adoption of new methods of social control, such as behavior modification, psychosurgery and drug therapy, within the treatment-rehabilitation model in corrections. According to Hylton, these decarceration programs did little to reduce the use of incarceration. Numerous studies have shown that decarceration or diversion programs often involve individuals who would otherwise not be handled in an official manner. Thus, such programs "widen the net" of the state's social control function.

Beginning in the mid-1970s, a major shift from treatment to punishment took place in corrections. The popularity of the "justice model" grew rapidly as people were attracted to the idea of criminals receiving their just deserts. Alongside the justice model with its emphasis on retribution, a "crime control" model developed and provided further ideological support to "tough on crime" initiatives, such as stiffer flat-time sentences, preventive detention, the death penalty, and the abolition of plea bargaining and parole. Heightened concern about crime, and demands for retributive justice and deterrence through tough criminal justice, have continued through the onset of the 1990s.

Local police departments also went through radical changes during the 1960s and 1970s. As Platt et al. note, "in the late 1960s, the new forms of policing were strongly influenced by the unprecedented growth of the federal government." The police were heavily criticized in the 1960s for their inappropriate and often violent reactions and the federal government sought new, more effective methods of crime control by flooding the field with money for research, training, education and new technology. The local police in the United States implemented policy changes to enhance professionalization, management and supervision, police-community relations, and intelligence. The introduction of the computer radically increased the ability of law enforcement agencies to gather intelligence. Law enforcement experienced a tremendous boost beginning in the late 1960s, and still receives a tremendous amount of financial and political support.

A review of developments in law enforcement during this time illustrates that the intervention of the federal government into criminal justice during this period is extraordinary. Many of the major innovations in social control occurred at the federal level, beginning with President Johnson's "War on Crime" and the Safe Streets and Crime Control Act of 1967. However, the most significant piece of legislation in the war on crime, or possibly in the history of the police, was the Omnibus Crime Control and Safe Streets Act of 1968. This piece of legislation was "the most sweeping invasion-of-privacy legislation ever to be placed on the books." In the 1970s, the Nixon Administration continued the trend set by this Act with a variety of government programs, enactments and agencies. Nixon greatly expanded the role of the federal government in crime control, with efforts such as the "air marshals program" and massive domestic spying. In the mid-1970s, the federal government's policies reflected the crime control model. For example, Schroeder observed a shift in emphasis in federal drug legislation from a focus on research and treatment to enforcement and punishment.

Many of the get-tough, crime control policies were implemented within the Reagan Administration. This trend is reflected in the move from the rehabilitative treatment of drug addicts to the zero-tolerance for drugs ideology of the 1980s. Along these same lines, a National Drug Czar is created to wage a "war on drugs". In addition, the Reagan Administration rebuilt the FBI and CIA and greatly enhanced their intelligence gathering and enforcement capabilities. The U.S. Congress authorized fixed sentencing without parole, preventive detention, and wider authority for prosecutors to seize and sell the property of convicted drug dealers and users. The substantial growth in both the rate of incarceration and the number of people incarcerated in the 1970s and 1980s reflect the punishment orientation that has developed during this latter period of investigation. The rate of incarceration among state and federal institutions increased from 96 in 1970 to 139 in 1980, and to 244 in 1988, which reflects a 154% increase between 1970 and 1988. The total number of persons incarcerated in state and federal facilities increased from 196,429 in 1970 to 315,974 in 1980, and to 603,732 in 1988, 207% increase between 1970 and 1988. There can be little doubt that crime and its control have been major issues since the 1960s and appear to be gaining momentum.

Summary

We have identified patterns in the development of capitalism in the United States. Since the 1780s, the U.S. economy and the world economy have experienced long periods of economic expansion followed by sustained periods of economic stagnation. During the periods of economic deterioration, unemployment and economic inequality increase substantially and social unrest and crime become critical problems. Old forms of social control are typically replaced with newer methods of control. New techniques implemented during periods of economic decline have included the introduction of incarceration, the urban police force, community corrections, and federal enforcement agencies. It is not our contention that there is no repression of subordinate classes during periods of economic prosperity. However, the evidence presented here suggests that criminal justice innovations and radical shifts in policy appear to be concentrated in periods of poor economic conditions.

DISCUSSION AND CONCLUSION

If criminal justice innovations and radical shifts in policy are, as we suggest, concentrated within periods of economic stagnation, how is this to be explained? Although the events and conditions described here are structural, an explanation of these events must incorporate social structure and human agency. All social institutions and policy are human constructions. Therefore, the motivations and interests of criminal justice practitioners and state managers who develop policy must be incorporated into the analysis. While further research is needed to document the role of human agents in the processes described here, it is possible to infer some of the motivations and intentions of capitalists, state managers, and workers from examination of these processes. The following explanation of the relationship between long cycles of capitalist development and the history of criminal justice in the U.S. is based both on the structural conditions described above and on the motivations and intentions of actors which we believe are reasonably inferred from the historically specific material conditions.

First, certain structural conditions exist which influence the individual actions of capitalists, workers and state managers during periods of economic stagnation. The logic of capitalism suggests that as the rate of profit begins to fall, capitalists tend to restrict the investment of their capital. A decline in general business confidence is produced as capitalists fail to realize the expected return on their allocated capital. As investment slows, production also declines. New jobs are not created, old jobs are lost and opportunities become more limited. The slow-down in production is accompanied by increases in unemployment, underemployment and job insecurity. As state revenues decline, state managers often find it necessary to cut back social programs designed to assist marginalized workers, such as economic supports, education, training, and job placement assistance. It is not surprising that labor militancy, protests and social tensions spread in response to these conditions. Indeed, as we have seen, prolonged periods of economic contraction have historically been characterized by increases in levels of social unrest.

The economic conditions of labor continue to grow worse as capitalists seek to regenerate economic growth. An important part of the recovery process includes the lowering of production costs in order to bolster the rate of profit. Because a major element of production costs is the cost of labor, a key to increasing rates of profit is to cut expenditures for labor. Strategies to lower labor costs have included union-busting, slashing wages, cutting benefits, laying off workers, the introduction of labor-saving technology and the dismantling of the social security net for the poor and unemployed. Historically, these strategies have also included the use of convict labor, the use of police officers as strike breakers, and the suppression of labor militancy. These policies further aggravate feelings of anxiety, frustration and crisis among workers. As material benefits dwindle, workers lose faith in the economic system, the political administration, and/or certain social policies, depending on where the workers place the blame for their plight. The intensification of social unrest further exacerbates problems within the economy because of the negative effect on general business confidence. The individual capitalist is not likely to invest when property is being destroyed by riots and when laborers are resisting their work. The social environment is less predictable and, thus, a high rate of profit is not certain. Efforts to stimulate the economy must include restoring social order.

It is in the realm of securing and maintaining social order that the state plays one of its most vital roles in facilitating the accumulation of capital. Through its apparatuses of social control, including the criminal justice system, state managers attempt to preserve the peace both materially and ideologically. State managers understandably support economic growth, in order to increase revenues for the state, to lower unemployment, to minimize the effects of inflation, to relieve social unrest and to reduce class tensions. More fundamentally, state managers want a strong economy because, without it, the populous will likely vote in new leadership.

State managers also seek to secure social order for many of the same reasons that they support economic growth. Not only do they wish to preserve the current political structure, they receive pressure from both the rich and the poor to "do something" about the "crime problem". The important role that the preservation of order plays in the accumulation of capital may simply be an unintended consequence of the intentional efforts of government officials to reduce crime and disorder.

According to Box and Hale, the critical intervening variables between recessions and increases in state coercion are the following three beliefs among decision-makers. The first is that the social order is threatened by periods of economic decline. For example, Cook and Zarkin suggest that it is commonly believed that recessions cause crime. According to Box and Hale, the second common sense notion is that the most economically depressed groups (i.e. unemployed, homeless, young, male minorities) are the most likely to commit crimes and disrupt the social order. Finally, conventional wisdom maintains that increases in state coercion and punishment will deter these people from being socially disruptive.

Although increasing punishment serves to shore up class domination in times when power relations are potentially threatened, Box and Hale do not posit a conspiracy between state managers and capitalists to protect power relations. They introduce human agents into the analysis of the relations between the economy and criminal justice, but no all-knowing agents acting as instruments of the capitalist class. Rather, the preservation of class domination is viewed by Box and Hale as an unintended consequence produced by an aggregate of persons making common sense decisions in the face of economic and political upheaval.

Stephen Box maintains that the "logic of the situation" is that poor economic conditions, combined with high levels of unemployment make crime more attractive and, thus, increase the rate of crime. In addition, criminal justice administrators, judges, legislators, parole board members, and police and probation officers believe that unemployment causes crime. Therefore, when unemployment increases, state managers enter into a posture of readiness, preparing for the worst. Based on their beliefs about unemployment and crime, public officials seek out new strategies of social control. When one adds to this "logic" the popular, common sense notion that increasing the likelihood and severity of punishment will deter potential law violators, it follows that deteriorating economic conditions and increases in the unemployment rate will quite naturally lead to increased attention to the criminal justice system. What follows are increases in criminal justice innovations, policy changes and new institutions during the periods of economic stagnation. The increased focus on criminal justice in turn intensifies the apprehension about crime among the public.

As in other aspects of the social structure of accumulation, mechanisms for social control come to be seen as outdated and ineffective and state managers seek new mechanisms of control. They seek strategies which are more effective in stopping crime and social unrest, and which will, at the same time, legitimize the political economic system. In contrast to Hall et al.'s argument that such efforts reflect the development of an "exceptional state" during troubled economic and political times, we argue that there is nothing "exceptional" about this period in relation to the role of the state or the criminal justice system. As Wolfe points out, the capitalist state has always played a major role in the accumulation of capital. It is not necessary for the state to move into an exceptional mode in order to perform this function. State managers have only to continue their regular routines. It is in fact "business as usual", except for the fact that current methods of control have become ineffective and new methods must be developed in the face of declining economic conditions.

In conclusion, the findings of this project provide support for the assertion that the economy is a significant factor in the development of criminal justice policy and in the emergence of criminal justice innovations. The findings also support the notion that the long cycles of capitalism are important to the history of criminal justice in the United States.

1.3 RICHARD DELGADO

Words That Wound

With its beginnings in the mid-1970s with the work of Derrick Bell and Alan Freeman, *critical race theory* is a growing movement advocating racial reform in American law. Many of its proponents are minority scholars calling attention to the pervasiveness of racism as permanently structured in the American legal system. A major thesis of critical race theory is that "racism is normal, not aberrant, in American society." To many scholars, racism is so deeply rooted in the U.S. legal system that it systematically limits the possibility of justice to minority persons.

The following selection is from "Words That Wound: A Tort Action for Racial Insults, Epithets, and Name-Calling," *Harvard Civil Rights–Civil Liberties Law Review* (vol. 17, 1982), by Richard Delgado, a professor of law at the University of Colorado at Boulder whose work on critical race theory and the effects of racist speech has led to a new way of thinking about civil rights. In it, he suggests that one way to satisfy the social need for legal redress for victims of racial insults, epithets, and name-calling is to seek a tort remedy in civil court. Undoubtedly, many legal scholars would suggest that Delgado's proposal of seeking civil remedy for victims of racial insults is unrealistic given the limitations of American tort law and the federal Constitution's protection of free speech. In a related development, however, the California Supreme Court recently decided that "a remedial injunction prohibiting the continued use of epithets in the workplace does not violate the right to freedom of speech." The case involved a lawsuit by Latino employees of Avis Rent-a-Car who claimed that one of the company's managers at the San Francisco International Airport outlet repeatedly used "derogatory names and continually demeaned them on the basis of their race, national origin and lack of English language skills," which in turn "created a hostile or abusive work environment."

Key Concept: tort action for racial insults, epithets, and name-calling

PSYCHOLOGICAL, SOCIOLOGICAL, AND POLITICAL EFFECTS OF RACIAL INSULTS

American society remains deeply afflicted by racism. Long before slavery became the mainstay of the plantation society of the antebellum South, Anglo-Saxon attitudes of racial superiority left their stamp on the developing culture of colonial America. Today, over a century after the abolition of slavery, many

41

citizens suffer from discriminatory attitudes and practices, infecting our economic system, our cultural and political institutions, and the daily interactions of individuals. The idea that color is a badge of inferiority and a justification for the denial of opportunity and equal treatment is deeply ingrained.

The racial insult remains one of the most pervasive channels through which discriminatory attitudes are imparted. Such language injures the dignity and self-regard of the person to whom it is addressed, communicating the message that distinctions of race are distinctions of merit, dignity, status, and personhood. Not only does the listener learn and internalize the messages contained in racial insults, these messages color our society's institutions and are transmitted to succeeding generations.

THE HARMS OF RACISM

The psychological harms caused by racial stigmatization are often much more severe than those created by other stereotyping actions. Unlike many characteristics upon which stigmatization may be based, membership in a racial minority can be considered neither self-induced, like alcoholism or prostitution, nor alterable. Race-based stigmatization is, therefore, "one of the most fruitful causes of human misery. Poverty can be eliminated—but skin color cannot." The plight of members of racial minorities may be compared with that of persons with physical disfigurements; the point has been made that

> [a] rebuff due to one's color puts [the victim] in very much the situation of the very ugly person or one suffering from a loathsome disease. The suffering... may be aggravated by a consciousness of incurability and even blameworthiness, a self-reproaching which tends to leave the individual still more aware of his loneliness and unwantedness.

The psychological impact of this type of verbal abuse has been described in various ways. Kenneth Clark has observed, "Human beings... whose daily experience tells them that almost nowhere in society are they respected and granted the ordinary dignity and courtesy accorded to others will, as a matter of course, begin to doubt their own worth." Minorities may come to believe the frequent accusations that they are lazy, ignorant, dirty, and superstitious. "The accumulation of negative images... present[s] them with one massive and destructive choice: either to hate one's self, as culture so systematically demand[s], or to have no self at all, to be nothing."

The psychological responses to such stigmatization consist of feelings of humiliation, isolation, and self-hatred. Consequently, it is neither unusual nor abnormal for stigmatized individuals to feel ambivalent about their self-worth and identity. This ambivalence arises from the stigmatized individual's awareness that others perceive him or her as falling short of societal standards, standards which the individual has adopted. Stigmatized individuals thus often are hypersensitive and anticipate pain at the prospect of contact with "normals."

It is no surprise, then, that racial stigmatization injures its victims' relationships with others. Racial tags deny minority individuals the possibility of neutral behavior in cross-racial contacts, thereby impairing the victims' capacity to form close interracial relationships. Moreover, the psychological responses of self-hatred and self-doubt unquestionably affect even the victims' relationships with members of their own group.

The psychological effects of racism may also result in mental illness and psychosomatic disease. The affected person may react by seeking escape through alcohol, drugs, or other kinds of anti-social behavior. The rates of narcotic use and admission to public psychiatric hospitals are much higher in minority communities than in society as a whole.

The achievement of high socioeconomic status does not diminish the psychological harms caused by prejudice. The effort to achieve success in business and managerial careers exacts a psychological toll even among exceptionally ambitious and upwardly mobile members of minority groups. Furthermore, those who succeed "do not enjoy the full benefits of their professional status within their organizations, because of inconsistent treatment by others resulting in continual psychological stress, strain, and frustration." As a result, the incidence of severe psychological impairment caused by the environmental stress of prejudice and discrimination is not lower among minority group members of high socioeconomic status.

One of the most troubling effects of racial stigmatization is that it may affect parenting practices among minority group members, thereby perpetuating a tradition of failure. A recent study of minority mothers found that many denied the real significance of color in their lives, yet were morbidly sensitive to matters of race. Some, as a defense against aggression, identified excessively with whites, accepting whiteness as superior. Most had negative expectations concerning life's chances. Such self-conscious, hypersensitive parents, preoccupied with the ambiguity of their own social position, are unlikely to raise confident, achievement-oriented, and emotionally stable children.

In addition to these long-term psychological harms of racial labeling, the stresses of racial abuse may have physical consequences. There is evidence that high blood pressure is associated with inhibited, constrained, or restricted anger, and not with genetic factors, and that insults produce elevation in blood pressure. American blacks have higher blood pressure levels and higher morbidity and mortality rates from hypertension, hypertensive disease, and stroke than do white counterparts. Further, there exists a strong correlation between degree of darkness of skin for blacks and level of stress felt, a correlation that may be caused by the greater discrimination experienced by dark-skinned blacks.

In addition to such emotional and physical consequences, racial stigmatization may damage a victim's pecuniary interests. The psychological injuries severely handicap the victim's pursuit of a career. The person who is timid, withdrawn, bitter, hypertense, or psychotic will almost certainly fare poorly in employment settings. An experiment in which blacks and whites of similar aptitudes and capacities were put into a competitive situation found that the blacks exhibited defeatism, half-hearted competitiveness, and "high expectancies of failure." For many minority group members, the equalization of such quantifiable variables as salary and entry level would be an insufficient antidote to defeatist attitudes because the psychological price of attempting to compete is unaffordable; they are "programmed for failure." Additionally, career options for the victims of racism are closed off by institutional racism—the subtle and unconscious racism in schools, hiring decisions, and the other practices which determine the distribution of social benefits and responsibilities.

Unlike most of the actions for which tort law provides redress to the victim, racial labeling and racial insults directly harm the perpetrator. Bigotry harms the individuals who harbor it by reinforcing rigid thinking, thereby dulling their moral and social senses and possibly leading to a "mildly . . . paranoid" mentality. There is little evidence that racial slurs serve as a "safety valve" for anxiety which would otherwise be expressed in violence.

Racism and racial stigmatization harm not only the victim and the perpetrator of individual racist acts but also society as a whole. Racism is a breach of the ideal of egalitarianism, that "all men are created equal" and each person is an equal moral agent, an ideal that is a cornerstone of the American moral and legal system. A society in which some members regularly are subjected to degradation because of their race hardly exemplifies this ideal. The failure of the legal system to redress the harms of racism, and of racial insults, conveys to all the lesson that egalitarianism is not a fundamental principle; the law, through inaction, implicitly teaches that respect for individuals is of little importance. Moreover, unredressed breaches of the egalitarian ideal may demoralize all those who prefer to live in a truly equal society, making them unwilling participants in the perpetuation of racism and racial inequality.

To the extent that racism contributes to a class system, society has a paramount interest in controlling or suppressing it. Racism injures the career prospects, social mobility, and interracial contacts of minority group members. This, in turn, impedes assimilation into the economic, social, and political mainstream of society and ensures that the victims of racism are seen and see themselves as outsiders. Indeed, racism can be seen as a force used by the majority to preserve an economically advantageous position for themselves. But when individuals cannot or choose not to contribute their talents to a social system because they are demoralized or angry, or when they are actively prevented by racist institutions from fully contributing their talents, society as a whole loses.

Finally, and perhaps most disturbingly, racism and racial labeling have an even greater impact on children than on adults. The effects of racial labeling are discernible early in life; at a young age, minority children exhibit self-hatred because of their color, and majority children learn to associate dark skin with undesirability and ugliness. A few examples readily reveal the psychological damage of racial stigmatization on children. When presented with otherwise identical dolls, a black child preferred the light-skinned one as a friend; she said that the dark-skinned one looked dirty or "not nice." Another child hated her skin color so intensely that she "vigorously lathered her arms and face with soap in an effort to wash away the dirt." She told the experimenter, "This morning I scrubbed and scrubbed and it came almost white." When asked about making a little girl out of clay, a black child said that the group should use the white clay rather than the brown "because it will make a better girl." When asked to describe dolls which had the physical characteristics of black people, young children chose adjectives such as "rough, funny, stupid, silly, smelly, stinky, dirty." Three-fourths of a group of four-year-old black children favored white play companions; over half felt themselves inferior to whites. Some engaged in denial or falsification.

THE HARMS OF RACIAL INSULTS

Immediate mental or emotional distress is the most obvious direct harm caused by a racial insult. Without question, mere words, whether racial or otherwise, can cause mental, emotional, or even physical harm to their target, especially if delivered in front of others or by a person in a position of authority. Racial insults, relying as they do on the unalterable fact of the victim's race and on the history of slavery and race discrimination in this country, have an even greater potential for harm than other insults.

Although the emotional damage caused is variable and depends on many factors, only one of which is the outrageousness of the insult, a racial insult is always a dignitary affront, a direct violation of the victim's right to be treated respectfully. Our moral and legal systems recognize the principle that individuals are entitled to treatment that does not denigrate their humanity through disrespect for their privacy or moral worth. This ideal has a high place in our traditions, finding expression in such principles as universal suffrage, the prohibition against cruel and unusual punishment, the protection of the fourth amendment against unreasonable searches, and the abolition of slavery. A racial insult is a serious transgression of this principle because it derogates by race, a characteristic central to one's self-image.

The wrong of this dignitary affront consists of the expression of a judgment that the victim of the racial slur is entitled to less than that to which all other citizens are entitled. Verbal tags provide a convenient means of categorization so that individuals may be treated as members of a class and assumed to share all the negative attitudes imputed to the class. Racial insults also serve to keep the victim compliant. Such dignitary affronts are certainly no less harmful than others recognized by the law. Clearly, a society whose public law recognizes harm in the stigma of separate but equal schooling and the potential offensiveness of the required display of a state motto on automobile license plates, and whose private law sees actionable conduct in an unwanted kiss or the forcible removal of a person's hat, should also recognize the dignitary harm inflicted by a racial insult.

The need for legal redress for victims also is underscored by the fact that racial insults are intentional acts. The intentionality of racial insults is obvious: what other purpose could the insult serve? There can be little doubt that the dignitary affront of racial insults, except perhaps those that are overheard, is intentional and therefore most reprehensible. Most people today know that certain words are offensive and only calculated to wound. No other use remains for such words as "nigger," "wop," "spick," or "kike."

In addition to the harms of immediate emotional distress and infringement of dignity, racial insults inflict psychological harm upon the victim. Racial slurs may cause long-term emotional pain because they draw upon and intensify the effects of the stigmatization, labeling, and disrespectful treatment that the victim has previously undergone. Social scientists who have studied the effects of racism have found that speech that communicates low regard for an individual because of race "tends to create in the victim those very traits of 'inferiority' that it ascribes to him." Moreover, "even in the absence of more objective forms of discrimination—poor schools, menial jobs, and substandard housing—traditional stereotypes about the low ability and apathy of Negroes and other minorities can operate as 'self-fulfilling prophecies.'" These stereotypes, portraying members of a minority group as stupid, lazy, dirty, or untrustworthy, are often communicated either explicitly or implicitly through racial insults.

Because they constantly hear racist messages, minority children, not surprisingly, come to question their competence, intelligence, and worth. Much of the blame for the formation of these attitudes lies squarely on value-laden words, epithets, and racial names. These are the materials out of which each child "grows his own set of thoughts and feelings about race." If the majority "defines them and their parents as no good, inadequate, dirty, incompetent, and stupid," the child will find it difficult not to accept those judgments.

Victims of racial invective have few means of coping with the harms caused by the insults. Physical attacks are of course forbidden. "More speech" frequently is useless because it may provoke only further abuse or because the insulter is in a position of authority over the victim. Complaints to civil rights organizations also are meaningless unless they are followed by action to punish the offender. Adoption of a "they're well meaning but ignorant" attitude is another impotent response in light of the insidious psychological harms of racial slurs. When victimized by racist language, victims must be able to threaten and institute legal action, thereby relieving the sense of helplessness that leads to psychological harm and communicating to the perpetrator and to society that such abuse will not be tolerated, either by its victims or by the courts.

Minority children possess even fewer means for coping with racial insults than do adults. "A child who finds himself rejected and attacked ... is not likely to develop dignity and poise. ... On the contrary he develops defenses. Like a dwarf in a world of menacing giants, he cannot fight on equal terms." The child who is the victim of belittlement can react with only two unsuccessful strategies, hostility or passivity. Aggressive reactions can lead to consequences that reinforce the harm caused by the insults; children who behave aggressively in school are marked by their teachers as troublemakers, adding to the children's alienation and sense of rejection. Seemingly passive reactions have no better results; children who are passive toward their insulters turn the aggressive response on themselves; robbed of confidence and motivation, these children withdraw into moroseness, fantasy, and fear.

It is, of course, impossible to predict the degree of deterrence a cause of action in tort would create. However, as Professor van den Berghe has written, "for most people living in racist societies racial prejudice is merely a special kind of convenient rationalization for rewarding behavior." In other words, in racist societies "most members of the dominant group will exhibit both prejudice and discrimination," but only in conforming to social norms. Thus, "[W]hen social pressures and rewards for racism are absent, racial bigotry is more likely to be restricted to people for whom prejudice fulfills a psychological 'need.' In such a tolerant milieu prejudiced persons may even refrain from discriminating behavior to escape social disapproval." Increasing the cost of racial insults thus would certainly decrease their frequency. Laws will never prevent violations altogether, but they will deter "whoever is deterrable."

Because most citizens comply with legal rules, and this compliance in turn "reinforce[s] their own sentiments toward conformity," a tort action for racial insults would discourage such harmful activity through the teaching function of the law. The establishment of a legal norm "creates a public conscience and a standard for expected behavior that check overt signs of prejudice." Legislation aims first at controlling only the acts that express undesired attitudes. But "when expression changes, thoughts too in the long run are likely to fall into line." "Laws . . . restrain the middle range of mortals who need them as a mentor in molding their habits." Thus, "If we create institutional arrangements in which exploitative behaviors are no longer reinforced, we will then succeed in changing attitudes [that underlie these behaviors]." Because racial attitudes of white Americans "typically follow rather than precede actual institutional [or legal] alteration," a tort for racial slurs is a promising vehicle for the eradication of racism.

PART TWO

Law and Criminality

On the Internet . . .

Sites appropriate to Part Two

This excellent outline of the causes of crime, including major theories, was prepared by Darryl Wood at the University of Alaska, Anchorage.

```
http://www.uaa.alaska.edu/just/just110/
    crime2.html
```

The Criminal Justice page of the American Civil Liberties Union (ACLU) Web site highlights recent events, lists important resources, and contains a search mechanism.

```
http://aclu.org/issues/criminal/hmcj.html
```

Data about all aspects of criminal justice in the United States are available at this site, which includes more than 600 tables from over 100 sources. This site also has a search mechanism.

```
http://www.albany.edu/sourcebook/
```

The Partnerships Against Violence Network (PAVNET) is a virtual library of information about violence and youths at risk, representing data from seven different federal agencies.

```
http://www.pavnet.org
```

CHAPTER 2 The Historical-Contextual Nature of Crime

2.1 DONALD E. GREEN

The Contextual Nature of American Indian Criminality

Much of social science research has tended to overlook, ignore, or be unaware of the extent of diversity within racial and ethnic groups in the United States, particularly those classified as "minority." While much has been done to examine intergroup cultural diversity, substantively less has been done to examine or adequately account for intragroup diversity. Equally, much has been done to examine dominant-minority group patterns, but again, much less has been done to examine patterns across minority groups. The implication is that cultural minorities are homogeneous groups and may be classified as a single unit of sociological analysis. Hence, a single finding as to the social nature of a subordinate group can be generalized to that entire population, while it is unthinkable to apply

51

such a standard to the dominant group. This undoubtedly poses an inherent contradiction in sociological and criminological thinking. On the one hand, sociology rejects the mechanisms of stereotyping, the negative effects of ethnocentrism, and other misguided or unsupported generalizations, while solidly promoting the virtues of cultural awareness, understanding, and diversity. In fact, comparative studies in sociology are dedicated to that end. On the other hand, with respect to subordinate groups, much of the sociological and criminological literature has examined such diversity primarily within an intergroup context, while providing volumes of analysis and insight into the intragroup heterogeneity of the dominant group.

Donald E. Green is an assistant professor of sociology at the University of Wisconsin, Milwaukee. In the following selection from "The Contextual Nature of American Indian Criminality," *American Indian Culture and Research Journal* (vol. 17, no. 2, 1993), he offers insights and remedial strategies for criminological research to more accurately examine the intragroup dynamics of American Indians. After a comprehensive review of the research literature on American Indian criminality and criminal justice, the author concludes that the sociohistorical context in which such criminality and subsequent criminal justice outcomes occurred is substantively lacking. In addition, the propensity for researchers to employ aggregate and often national-level data to examine American Indian criminality assumes a monolithic conception of the Indian culture and subsequently fails to account for the vast diversity among Indian nations, tribes, and individuals. Green strongly suggests that failing to account for such diversity within and among American Indian groups and also failing to account for the varied historical and sociological context of culture conflict between American Indians and Anglos further compromises the validity of such research. The author concludes by offering a framework for future research.

Key Concept: intracultural and intercultural research methods

INTRODUCTION

Several reviews of the contemporary literature on American Indian criminality and criminal justice outcomes during the last decade have lamented the lack of volume, theoretical clarity, and methodological rigor of research in this area of criminology.[1] The present analysis of that literature suggests a somewhat more optimistic view. When these works are placed within the sociological framework of the Native American experience in the United States, several important contextual factors emerge that advance our understanding of crime patterns in this uniquely American racial group. This paper will review selected studies and present additional crime data from the Uniform Crime Reports (UCR) that establish the significance of these contexts and discuss their implications for future research.[2]

THE CONTEXTUAL NATURE OF CRIMINOLOGICAL RESEARCH ON AMERICAN INDIANS

Perhaps the most overlooked factors in the study of American Indian criminality are the sociological contexts of the studies themselves. Consider one of the earliest studies to appear in the contemporary literature, authored by Norman S. Hayner and published in a prominent sociological journal in 1942. Although this research was conducted during a period in which significant numbers of American Indians still lived on reservation lands that were relatively isolated from large, white, urban populations, extensive efforts by the federal government to dismantle traditional Indian culture and assimilate Indians into mainstream American society had taken their toll on many Indian nations. Not surprisingly, then, in this primarily descriptive work, Hayner stressed the importance of tribal social disorganization as an explanation for crime among American Indians. He utilized initial arrest statistics generated by the Federal Bureau of Investigation (FBI) to support his argument that crime among American Indians in the Pacific Northwest, who were the focus of his study, varied according to levels of social isolation from white populations and periods of economic prosperity resulting from monetary payments for natural resources. That is, less isolated populations and those that experienced greater monetary payments had higher rates of crime. Hayner concluded that these factors adversely affected tribal organization in these groups and provided the best explanation for their crime patterns.

Although social disorganization explanations for American Indian criminality have continued to appear in the literature, more recent studies have found support for refined conceptualizations of this approach. And while these reconceptualizations are internally consistent with the data presented in these studies, the literature has failed to address the exogenous relationships between the sociological contexts of these studies and the shifting theoretical relationships among social disorganization variables and American Indian crime patterns. For example, in their 1970s case study of violent behavior among the Eastern Cherokee, French and Hornbuckle also found support for social isolation explanations for crime among American Indians but placed their findings within a "cultural frustration/subcultural control" perspective.

In addition, the direction of the social isolation and crime relationship that French and Hornbuckle found is contrary to Hayner's earlier study. They argue that, rather than protecting traditional culture, years of living in a restrictive reservation environment created by paternalistic federal Indian policies resulted in a breakdown of traditional mechanisms of social control among the Eastern Cherokee. The authors stress that the breakdown was particularly evident among "marginal Indians," whom they defined as the majority of Native Americans living on and off reservations, torn between Indian and white worlds and not being fully accepted by either group. French and Hornbuckle contend that, as the influence of the traditional cultural norms and values of the Eastern Cherokee has continued to decline, nontraditional norms and values more supportive of interpersonal violence have emerged in response to the frustrating and tension-filled reservation experience. They conclude that the pattern of criminal behavior observed among this group is similar to that identified in urban Black ghetto communities by Wolfgang and Ferracuti.

Others have questioned whether these findings can be generalized, because the studies by French and Hornbuckle, Hayner, and others have lacked the possibility of statistical control for alternative explanations for criminal behaviors. Acknowledging this problem, Larry Williams and his colleagues assessed the relative impact of three different approaches to American Indian criminality: social background characteristics, personality, and cultural factors. Utilizing survey data from a randomly selected sample of Native Americans living in the Seattle area during 1972, their step-wise multivariate regression analysis indicated little support for cultural conflict explanations, while support was found for several indicators of social disorganization, although these were more contemporary conceptualizations not necessarily specific to American Indians. Williams and his colleagues found that indicators of familial disorganization, such as problems with marital adjustment and relative marital happiness, were significant predictors of self-reported arrests among these Seattle respondents, even after controlling for a number of personal and cultural variables such as self-esteem, degree of alienation, and support for assimilation into white culture.

Again, however, the sociological context of this study emerges as a neglected explanatory variable that is central to the theoretical implications of its findings. This research was conducted following a two-decade effort by the federal government to relocate large numbers of American Indians to urban areas in the United States. Therefore, these findings should be considered in light of the fact that many urban American Indians in the sample may have experienced some of the previously documented adjustment problems that occurred during these federal relocation programs. And while these experiences may have been no less difficult to endure than the conditions experienced by those who remained in rural/reservation areas, the lack of support for alternative explanations for the respondents' self-reported arrests may be due to unaccounted-for differences between urban and nonurban Indian populations.

The contextual nature of research on American Indian criminality is further demonstrated by two studies on the social reaction to American Indian offenders. Hall and Symkus compared sentencing decisions for both whites and Indians in a western state during the late 1960s and early 1970s. They controlled for the effects of a number of legal and extralegal variables that past research has found to be important predictors of criminal court sentencing patterns, such as prior adult offenses and juvenile dispositions, education levels, employment status, and other socioeconomic background variables. Hall's and Symkus's findings indicated that even when comparisons were statistically controlled for both sets of variables, Native Americans, more than non-Indians, were both more likely to receive sentences that included incarceration and less likely to receive deferred sentences.

A second study by Bynum also focused on criminal justice outcomes among American Indians during the 1970s. His research examined the effect of prior record and major disciplinary infractions while in prison—as well as selected sociodemographic characteristics of the offenders—on a parole board's release decisions in an upper Plains state. Bynum's findings indicated that not only did American Indians receive incarceration for offenses that non-Indians did not; they also served significantly greater portions of their original sentences than did non-Indians. Although the authors of these two studies did not explicitly acknowledge the social context in which their data collection occurred, it is significant to note that the time frame utilized in both coincides with that of increased Native American political activity. Given the widely held view among criminologists and criminal justice practitioners that race per se has no direct effect on criminal justice outcomes, one could possibly interpret these findings to mean that the differential criminal justice outcomes reported in these studies were evidenced only within the context of a highly visible political movement among various American Indian groups in these states and other regions of the country.

Another frequently ignored contextual factor in research literature on American Indian criminality is the lack of comprehensive data. This limitation forces researchers to omit a number of variables previously identified as significant predictors of crime patterns among other population groups. As a result, studies of American Indian criminality often propose theoretical arguments that extend well beyond the data presented. A good example of this problem can be found in aggregate-level analyses of national arrest data. Notwithstanding the numerous studies that have stressed the importance of alcohol abuse in explaining frequency of involvement in illegal behaviors, aggregate-level research on American Indian arrest rates has consistently documented the disproportionate number of American Indians involved in alcohol-related crime. A study by Peak and Spencer is representative of this series of studies conducted over the last three decades focusing solely on univariate arrest statistics. Although it is important to acknowledge Peak and Spencer for their efforts to examine Indian arrest rates both on and off reservations, they also devote considerable attention to "the Indian propensity for arrests involving alcohol-related offenses." With the inability of univariate analyses such as these to assess alternative theoretical explanations adequately, it is not surprising that conclusions drawn from these studies too often focus primarily on the role that alcohol plays in the etiology of crime among American Indians, rather than on variables that may be antecedent to both its abuse and relationship to illegal behavior.

In fact, despite these frequently cited physiological and/or psychological explanations, there are still other studies suggesting that at least within particular social contexts, structural and/or economic explanations often used to account for crime patterns among non-Indian populations might best account for American Indian criminality. For instance, sociodemographic population characteristics such as age and sex have consistently been linked to criminality in non-Indian populations. Similarly, in the previously mentioned study by Williams and his colleagues, the variables of age and sex were the most important predictors of self-reported arrests among their sample of urban American Indians. And in an earlier study of the Shoshone-Bannock tribe on the Fort Hall

Reservation, Minnis assessed the relationship between various indicators of the social structure of that Indian community and official tribal records of adult and juvenile law violations. Using households as the unit of analysis, she argued that overcrowded conditions, high percentages of individuals on public assistance, and low education levels were linked to high levels of crime.[3]

In the following sections, perhaps the most recent sociological context of the American Indian experience in the United States to influence research on American Indian criminality—changing conceptions of American Indian identity—is presented and discussed.

AMERICAN INDIAN IDENTITY AND UNITED STATES CENSUS DATA

Over the past few decades, demographic research on the American Indian has frequently discussed the consequences of a series of historical factors that have affected this population.[4] While debate continues concerning the exact number of American Indians prior to European contact, those who have focused their research efforts in this area generally agree that disease, war, and federal government policies directed toward these indigenous groups since their initial contacts with European societies have had devastating effects on American Indian populations. Nagel and Snipp, for example, have noted that even conservative estimates of the Native American population indicate a decline from approximately two million people at the time of Columbus's arrival in 1492 to as few as 237,000 people in 1900.

Since this population nadir, census figures from 1900 to the present suggest that the Native American population in the United States has increased over the past century at a rate that is perhaps as dramatic as the population declines prior to the 1900s. Nagel and Snipp, for instance, report that American Indian census data between 1890 and 1980 indicate an increase of 555 percent during this period. Moreover, these researchers note that the largest increase occurred between the years 1950 and 1980, when the American Indian population increased from 343,000 to 1,357,000. Even the most recent census data reveal a continuation of this trend, reporting the 1990 American Indian population at 1,959,234, although the degree of increase is less than that which occurred over the last three decades.[5]

Some demographers, however, have questioned whether this more recent American Indian population trend has been a natural one (i.e., the result of high birth and low death rates), arguing instead that the increase can be attributed primarily to changes in the way the Census Bureau counts American Indians.[6] Since 1950, the bureau has increasingly relied on respondents' self-identification of race in the enumeration process. Subsequently, some have suggested that more recent census data include a significant number of individuals, previously identified with other races, who now identify themselves as American Indian, at least for census-recording purposes.[7] Although explanations for this dramatic increase have been of significant interest to those concerned with the study of American Indian demography, criminological research on official rates of American Indian criminality—which employ census data to derive rates of involvement in crime—has completely ignored this issue. In the following review and extension of the literature on American Indian arrest rates, some preliminary indications will be presented of the degree to which this demographic phenomenon affects criminological research involving American Indian populations.[8]

CHANGING AMERICAN INDIAN IDENTITY AND AGGREGATE-LEVEL ANALYSES OF CRIME

As previously mentioned, some of the more widely cited research on American Indian criminality has been based on national-level arrest data. Collectively, this research can provide us with a rough chronological account of the rate of Native American involvement in crime since the FBI has been recording arrest data systematically by race. Native American arrest rates have consistently increased from a low of 1,699 per 100,000 in 1935 to a high of 15,123 in 1960. Following this peak, American Indian arrest rates show a more gradual decrease, with the most recently published studies (based on 1985 data) indicating an American Indian arrest rate of between 7,859.2 and 8171.5, depending on whether the census figures utilized to calculate the rate per 100,000 population included Alaska Natives.

These reported increases in arrests between 1935 and 1960 are consistent with similar trends in census data reported by demographic research on the Native American population, at least between the years of 1935 and 1960. Given these historical patterns, however, it is somewhat surprising that more recently published studies of American Indian arrest rates indicate a decrease in crime among this racial group while census figures indicate that the American Indian population continues to increase, especially during the last three decades. Perhaps more importantly for our efforts to understand American Indian criminality, these indicators of involvement in crime suggest that the total Native American crime rate has decreased during a time when the overall amount of crime in the United States in general, and among other racial groups in particular, has experienced dramatic increases.

This differential pattern of racial involvement in illegal behavior has continued into the 1980s. Table 1 presents the actual number of arrests for American Indians, Blacks, and whites for the years 1970, 1980, and 1990 for all crimes and index crimes only. Between 1970 and 1980, the total number of arrests for index crimes increased for all groups. On the other hand, while the total number of arrests for all crimes increased for Blacks and whites during the years 1970 through 1980, American Indian arrests for all crimes decreased during this period. An examination of the percent change in number of arrests provides a cogent illustration of these differences. As the bottom panel of table 1 indicates, the total number of Native American arrests for index crimes increased by 54.6 percent between 1970 and 1980, an increase that exceeds comparable totals for both Blacks (39.4 percent) and whites (48.6 percent). During the same

TABLE 1

Arrests for 1970, 1980, and 1990 for Index and Total Crimes by Race*

Arrests	Native Americans	Blacks	Whites
1970			
Index crimes	9,167	436,581	739,306
Total crimes	130,981	1,739,306	4,373,157
1980			
Index crimes	20,194	720,739	1,438,098
Total crimes	109,480	2,375,204	7,145,763
1990			
Index crimes	22,198	794,725	1,469,241
Total crimes	122,586	3,224,060	7,712,339
Actual Change in Number of Arrests:			
1970–1980			
Index crimes	+11,027	+284,158	+698,792
Total crimes	-21,501	+686,815	+2,772,606
1980–1990			
Index crimes	+2,004	+73,986	+31,143
Total crimes	+13,106	+848,856	+566,576
1970–1990			
Index crimes	+13,031	+358,144	+729,935
Total crimes	-8,395	-1,484,754	+3,339,182
Percent Change in Number of Arrests:			
1970–1980			
Index crimes	+54.6	+39.4	-48.6
Total crimes	-16.4	+28.9	+38.8
1980–1990			
Index crimes	-9.0	+9.3	+2.1
Total crimes	+10.7	+26.3	+7.4
1970–1990			
Index crimes	+58.7	+45.1	+49.7
Total crimes	-6.4	+46.1	+43.3

*The FBI classifies the following offenses as index crimes (or Part I offenses): murder, rape, robbery, aggravated assault, burglary, larceny theft, motor vehicle theft, and arson. Index crimes are basically felonies that are considered of most concern to the general public. The arson category is omitted from the table because it has been included as an index crime only since 1979. The total crime category includes both part I and part II offenses (which include simple assault, forgery and counterfeiting, fraud, embezzlement, buying, receiving, or possessing stolen property, vandalism, carrying or possessing deadly weapons, prostitution and commercialized vice, sex offenses, drug-abuse violations, gambling, offenses against the family or children, liquor laws, drunkenness, disorderly conduct, vagrancy, and all other offenses that are violations of state or local laws, except the above offenses and traffic violations).

Source: U.S. Department of Justice, Uniform Crime Reports, 1970, p. 131; 1980, p. 204; 1990, p. 192.

decade, however, American Indian arrests for all crimes decreased by 16.4 percent, while arrests for all crimes for both Blacks and whites increased by 28.9 and 38.8 percent, respectively. These figures indicate that, unlike the patterns observed for Blacks and whites, Native American arrests have both increased and decreased between the years 1970 and 1980, depending which category of crimes is examined.

In contrast to the 1970–80 data, table 1 indicates that the arrest patterns among these racial groups are considerably more consistent for the years 1980 through 1990. Arrests for the index and total crimes categories increased for all groups during this decade. The percent change figures indicate that arrests for index crimes were up 9.0 percent for American Indians and 9.3 percent for Blacks, while index crime arrests were up only 2.1 percent for whites. A similar pattern emerges for all crimes, with Blacks having the largest increase in arrests (26.3 percent), while American Indian and white increases were considerably smaller (10.7 and 7.4 percent, respectively).

Finally, a comparison of 1970–90 arrest data for these groups reveals a pattern more similar to the years 1970–80 than 1980–90. As was the case in 1970, the number of arrests for index crimes only has increased for all groups between 1970 and 1990, while the number of arrests for total crimes has decreased for American Indians only. The percentage change figures in table 1 indicate that, in the two decades since 1970, American Indians have experienced the largest increase in arrests for index crimes among all racial groups examined (+58.7 percent), while Blacks and whites have experienced increases of 45.1 and 49.7 percent, respectively. However, the percent change figures in the bottom row of the table indicate that, while arrests for all crimes have continued to increase between the years 1970 and 1990 for both Blacks and whites (46.1 and 43.3 percent, respectively), total arrests among American Indians during this same period have actually decreased 6.4 percent.

The differential patterns of arrest revealed by these data, particularly for the years 1970–90, clearly indicate the need for more scholarly inquiries to determine what factors have contributed to the varied picture of racial involvement in crime presented here. Sociological theories of law suggest that these rates are merely a reflection of an underlying practice of differential enforcement of criminal laws against Native Americans, as well as other racial groups. For example, conflict theories of criminal law posit that the formation and implementation of the criminal law is directly influenced by those groups in society that control its power and resources. Through this influence, these more powerful groups have the ability to avoid sanctions against those behaviors that are in their best interest, while ensuring that behaviors detrimental to their interest but frequently engaged in by those groups not in power or control over resources are more frequently and severely sanctioned. The so-called labeling perspective in criminology also suggests that social reactions against certain forms of behavior are racially linked. Proponents of this view of the criminal law argue that, although all members of society engage in behaviors that could be considered illegal, in reality only those individuals with selected social characteristics—for example, being in a racial minority—are the object of society's reactions to crime.

Still another possible factor to consider is the sociological context of changing patterns of American Indian identity and the potential measurement error

American Indian census data may create for research on aggregate arrest rates among American Indians. Table 2 presents two methods of calculating American Indian arrest rates and compares them with rates of arrests for both Blacks and whites for the years 1970, 1980, and 1990, in order to assess the degree to which these changing patterns of American Indian identity may alter arrest rates for this group. That is, two Native American arrest rates are presented: one based on actual census data and a second based on estimates derived from natural increases (the difference between births and deaths). These estimates have been determined previously by demographers who have examined the extent to which increases in the American Indian population, as indicated by census figures, are the result of changes in self-identification rather than a natural increase in the Native American population.[9] These latter figures then represent what would be considered the natural increase in the American Indian population in the United States over the last two decades.[10]

As table 2 indicates, based on actual census figures, American Indian arrest rates (per 100,000) for index crimes only were 1,156 in 1970, 1,419 in 1980, and 1,133 in 1990. The corresponding percent change figures reported in the bottom panel of the table indicate that American Indian arrests for index crimes increased by 18.5 percent between 1970 and 1980 and decreased by 20.2 percent between 1980 and 1990. The table also reveals a decrease of 2.0 percent in arrests for index crimes among American Indians over the past three decades.

Utilizing demographic estimates of the natural increase in the Native American population to calculate their arrest rates reveals a somewhat different picture of American Indian criminality over this period of time. This alternative population base produces a change in the American Indian arrest rate for index crimes between 1970 and 1980 of almost twice that based on actual census data (18.5 percent versus 32.5 percent), although the latter rate more closely approximates the rate of change in index arrests during the same period for Blacks (+39.5) and whites (+48.7). Differences among these two indicators of arrests for index crimes involving American Indians are not as pronounced for the 1980–90 period (−20.2 versus −25.6). In general, they follow a similar decline in arrests for index crimes among Blacks (−17.0) and whites (−9.0). Interestingly, the two percent change figures between 1970 and 1990 present completely opposite patterns of American Indian arrests for index crimes over these three decades. The actual census-based rate reveals a decrease of 2.0 percent in arrests for index crimes among American Indians, while the rates based on estimated natural increases indicates an increase of 9.3 percent. Again, however, the natural increase-based rates more closely follow the three-decade pattern of increased index arrests among both Blacks (+27.1) and whites (+43.6).

The percent change figures for American Indian arrests for all crimes consistently reveal a decrease in rates regardless of the population base employed, although there are considerable differences in the degree of change indicated for each. For example, when the natural increase base is utilized, the percent change figures for the periods 1970–80 (−53.4 versus −43.8) and 1970–90 (−62.1 versus −57.4) are reduced, while those for 1980–90 (−19.9 versus −24.3) are increased. Perhaps the more compelling finding in regard to these figures is the fact that, with the exception of the 3.9 percent decrease for whites between 1980

TABLE 2

*Arrest Rates (per 100,000) by Race for 1970, 1980, and 1990
Total and Index Crimes*

Arrest Rates	American Indian*	Black	White
1970			
Index crimes	1,156 (1,286)	1,932	415
Total crimes	16,517 (18,370)	7,471	2,457
1980			
Index crimes	1,419 (1,905)	3,192	809
Total crimes	7,694 (10,329)	10,519	4,020
1990			
Index crimes	1,133 (1,417)	2,650	736
Total crimes	6,258 (7,823)	10,752	3,862
Percent change in rates of arrests:			
1970–1980			
Index crimes	+18.5 (+32.5)	+39.5	+48.7
Total crimes	-53.4 (-43.8)	+29.0	+38.9
1980–1990			
Index crimes	-20.2 (-25.6)	-17.0	-9.0
Total crimes	-19.9 (-24.3)	+2.2	-3.9
1970–1990			
Index crimes	-2.0 (+9.3)	+27.1	+43.6
Total crimes	-62.1 (-57.4)	+30.5	+36.4

*Numbers in parentheses represent Native American crime rates based on demographic estimates of natural increases, defined by demographers as the difference between the number of births and deaths per year.

Source: U.S. Bureau of the Census, 1970, 1980, 1990; U.S. Department of Justice, Uniform Crime Reports, 1970, p. 131; 1980, p. 204; 1990, p. 192.

and 1990, overall rates of arrest for all crimes have increased for both Blacks and whites during these three decades, while rates of arrest for all crimes among American Indians have decreased dramatically.

While this analysis reveals significant differences in aggregate measures of American Indian arrests when alternate indicators of the American Indian population are utilized, the implications of these differences for future research are less clear. In general, the "natural increase" population estimates produce higher rates of arrests across all crime categories and time periods. Although the differences between the two indicators of criminality show some convergence between the 1970s and 1980s, comparisons between the 1980 and 1990 figures reveal that these differences may have started to increase again. This finding suggests that longitudinal research should further assess the extent to which this lack of congruence continues between American Indian census data and population estimates derived from alternative sources on American Indian populations.

Nevertheless, with the exception of the arrest rates for the 1970–90 period, these differences seem to raise more questions concerning the magnitude rather than the overall direction of these indicators. Assuming that these population differences are constant across all American Indian populations, this measurement issue may uniformly affect aggregate analyses of national arrest data only through the strength of various relationships among variables in this area of criminological research, rather than their direction. On the other hand, if the differential population figures reflect that changing patterns of American Indian identity are not invariant across Indian populations at state, county, and other units of analysis, future research that fails to account for this contextual factor would seem to be of limited value.

In this regard, it is instructive to note that several recent studies of American Indian demography have utilized a comparative strategy to assess the extent to which this measurement issue affects demographic research involving American Indian census data. For example, noting that the "overcount" previously identified by demographers is less problematic for nineteen "Indian states" (i.e., states that historically have had large numbers of American Indians and in which Indian identity has remained relatively consistent over the years 1960–80), Sandefur and his colleagues have assessed differences between these states and all others on a number of sociodemographic and social indicators of the population.[11] Based on 1980 census data, their findings suggest that Indians residing in traditionally Indian areas of the country do differ from Indians who live in the so-called non-Indian states. American Indians living in Indian states had higher rates of poverty and family social disorganization, as well as lower per capita household incomes, both of which represent factors that have been found by previous criminological research to be highly correlated with aggregate crime rates. Given these findings, it seems crucial that future aggregate-level analyses of American Indian arrests also assess the extent to which crime rates in "Indian states" differ from those in non-Indian states.[12] For example, should findings indicate that arrest patterns differ significantly on these grounds, states might prove to be the preferred unit of analysis for future aggregate-level research [on] American Indian arrest rates. Currently I am analyzing arrest data for all fifty states to determine the extent to which this measurement issue affects American Indian arrest rates.[13]

A FRAMEWORK FOR FUTURE RESEARCH ON AMERICAN INDIAN CRIMINALITY

As the previous discussion indicated, the contextual nature of research findings on American Indian criminality has been virtually ignored in the literature. However, a review of some of the more widely cited studies in this area of criminology suggests that the sociological context of the Native American experience in the United States is a crucial concept for our understanding of crime and criminal justice outcomes among this racial group. Indicators of the concept not only emerge as important exogenous variables capable of bridging the theoretical gap between often divergent findings of past criminological research on American Indians, but they also raise significant methodological issues for future quantitative research on American Indian arrest rates.

Several other contextual factors should also be considered in future research on American Indian criminality. As recently suggested by Biolosi, a problem with many studies that focus on the American Indian experience is the tendency to assume a monolithic conception of Indian culture. Although the history of the American Indian reveals that, in general, Indians have shared similar experiences as the victims of cultural, social, and economic deprivations, the degree of deprivation clearly differs by tribal group, as well as by individual. Regardless of the level of analysis, research on Native American criminality should assess more thoroughly those factors that can account for differential rates of criminal behavior within Indian populations.

The assumption of a monolithic Indian culture also raises questions concerning those studies that continue to suggest that culture conflict is a primary explanation for American Indian criminality. There is little argument that traditional Indian cultures have conflicted directly with Anglo-American culture, but the importance of this variable for our contemporary understanding of American Indian crime patterns may be considerably reduced. American Indians today comprise a diverse, young, and increasingly urban population that participates to varying degrees in both the remnants of the traditional tribal culture and that of the dominant society. To the extent that research on American Indian criminality fails to take into account the diversity of the Indian experience in the United States, our knowledge about Indian crime patterns will continue to be limited to overgeneralizations based on an unrealistic view of what it means to be an American Indian in contemporary society. In addition, many American Indians today have little knowledge of their traditional cultures precisely because of the continuous subjugation and exploitation of Indian people; therefore, the use of culture conflict variables to explain racial differences in patterns of crime could lead to a misspecified model of American Indian criminality.

In fact, it is plausible to argue that a decline in the degree of culture conflict among American Indians has paralleled the previously noted changing forms of Indian identity. Rather than culture conflict, American Indian identity may now be a more important variable to consider in future efforts to develop an etiology of crime among American Indians. As previously noted, scholars of the Native American experience in the United States have noted recently the emergence of new dimensions of American Indian identity. Consequently, it seems crucial that future studies of American Indian crime patterns incorporate a method of conceptually defining and measuring this dimension of "Indianness" to account for variation in the degree of American Indian identity among those individuals who engage in illegal behavior.

Research on this dimension of American Indian criminality may find that Indian identity and criminality are inversely related. For example, individuals of Indian descent who have lost ties to their tribal cultures may be more likely to engage in crime than those who have not. As an explanation for crime and delinquency, social control theories in criminology emphasize the importance of an individual's social bond to society through attachments to significant others and involvement in conventional activities. If this perspective is applied to American Indian criminality, involvement in illegal behavior among this racial group may well be explained by the lack of a social bond to contemporary Indian society. For example, findings from a recent study on American Indian delinquency suggest that illegal behavior among Indian youth is the result of a lack of attachment to and involvement in both Indian and non-Indian societies. Future research on self-reported American Indian criminality should test the applicability of social control theories as explanations of American Indian criminality by including indicators of individual involvement in contemporary Indian society, such as participation in powwows, membership in tribal, pan-tribal, or pan-Indian organizations, and perhaps other, more traditional ceremonies.[14]

It is also instructive to consider the findings of Williams's and his colleagues' study based on a random sample of American Indians in Seattle. They report that degree of Indianness, measured as a composite of their respondents' ancestry, religion, attendance at powwows, and perceptions of their ethnicity, was positively related to self-reported arrests. Based on this finding, they argue that active participation in Indian community affairs may raise the visibility of individual Indians to agents of social control. These findings, linked with the studies reporting differential treatment of American Indians in the criminal justice system during periods of increased political activity, support the argument that the Native American resurgence in the form of highly visible political activities may not bode well for the future experiences of politically active American Indians with the formal social control system in the United States.

The diversity of the American Indian experience in the United States requires that those who conduct research on American Indian crime patterns not view it as a generic phenomenon. In order to assess between racial group differences in general patterns of crime, future criminological research must include more comprehensive data on American Indians in current macro- and micro-level research efforts on the etiology of and social reaction to crime. Studies must also attempt to identify situational and contextual factors that can account for differences within the American Indian population by utilizing comparative samples of Indian offenders across tribal groups. The agenda outlined here may seem to involve as long and difficult a task as the struggle of American Indians themselves to achieve racial and social equity; nevertheless, it is deserving of just such an effort.

NOTES

1. Philip A. May, "Contemporary Crime and the American Indian: A Survey and Analysis of the Literature," *Plains Anthropologist* 27:97 (August 1982): 225–38; Donald E. Green, "American Indian Criminality: What Do We Really Know?" in *American Indians: Social Justice and Public Policy, Ethnicity and Public Policy Series,* vol. 9, ed. Donald

E. Green and Thomas V. Tonnesen (Milwaukee, WI: University of Wisconsin System, Institute on Race and Ethnicity, 1991), 223–70.

2. Although a number of studies have examined crime among indigenous groups in North America, the focus of this discussion will be on United States studies that have examined crime and criminal justice outcomes among American Indians living in the contiguous forty-eight states, because they are more directly comparable to the contemporary criminological literature. For example, research on Canadian indigenous populations is hampered by a lack of race-based data to facilitate comparative studies with United States crime figures. Moreover, race-based statistics on criminality and criminal justice outcomes continue to be a source of controversy in Canada. "Taboo on Race-based Figures Debated," *Milwaukee Journal*, 2 August 1992.

3. Again, however, methodological problems associated with these studies in many ways compromise their generalizability of these findings, particularly in comparison to the standards being applied to current criminological research on both individual and structural determinants of crime with non-Indian populations. See Green, "American Indian Criminality." For example, even though their refusal rate was a mere 7 percent, Williams's and his colleagues' best efforts to obtain a representative group of Seattle Indians generated only 28 percent of their original sample of respondents. On the other hand, Mhyra S. Minnis's research ["The Relationship of the Social Structure of an Indian Community to Adult and Juvenile Delinquency," *Social Forces* 41 (1963): 395–403] is based on inferences drawn primarily from univariate statistics on selected structural indicators of the community and adult and juvenile law violations, with only one bivariate cross-tabulation presented between the variables of degree of crowding and percentage of households with any reported arrests (adults or juveniles).

4. Joane Nagel and C. Matthew Snipp, "American Indian Tribal Identification and Federal Indian Policy: The Reflection of History in the 1980 Census" (Paper presented at the American Sociological Association annual meetings, August 1987); C. Matthew Snipp, *American Indians: The First of This Land* (New York: Russell Sage Foundation, 1989).

5. For example, according to data presented by Nagel and Snipp, and the Bureau of the Census, between 1960 and 1970, the American Indian population increased by 51.1 percent; between 1970 and 1980, it increased by 72.2 percent; and between 1980 and 1990, it increased by 37.9 percent. Also U.S. Department of Commerce News, Economic and Statistics Administration, Bureau of the Census, "Census Bureau Completes Distribution of 1990 Redistricting Tabulations to States," table 1 (Washington, DC: 11 March 1991).

6. Jeffrey S. Passel, "Provisional Evaluation of the 1970 Census Count of American Indians," *Demography* 13 (1976):397–409; Snipp, "American Indians," 26–61.

7. Jeffrey S. Passel and Patricia A. Berman, "The Quality of 1980 Census Data for American Indians," *Social Biology* 33 (1986):163–82; Snipp, "American Indians," and Nagel and Snipp, "American Indian Tribal Identification."

8. While previous studies of American Indian crime patterns have focused on a number of different indicators of criminality, the present discussion will focus, for a number of reasons, on aggregate-level studies that have utilized Uniform Crime Reports (UCR) of arrest figures and U.S. census data to assess Native American involvement in illegal behavior. These two forms of information are perhaps the most consistently reported, widely available, and frequently cited sources of data on United States criminal and general populations. Employed together, they have provided criminologists with the ability to assess the influence of a host of theoretically derived sociodemographic characteristics and social indicators of the population on rates of arrests at

national, state, country, and local levels of analysis. In addition to their amenability to studies on the etiology of crime, they also represent society's official reaction to crime in the form of the number of official arrests for crimes known to reporting police agencies throughout the United States, and allow researchers to assess the frequently hypothesized relationship between race and criminal justice processes.

9. Passel, "Provisional Evaluation of the 1970 Census Count"; Passel and Berman, "The Quality of 1980 Census Data"; and Snipp, "American Indians." These three sources provided the estimated natural increase figures for the American Indian population used to compute the arrests rates presented in table 2. According to these estimates, the 1970 census data indicated an "overcount" of American Indians of approximately 8 percent, while the 1980 census reported an "overcount" of American Indians of approximately 26 percent.

10. Actual estimates of the natural increase currently are not available for the 1990 figures. However, utilizing trend data on the natural increase in the American Indian population presented by Passel, Passel and Berman, and Snipp, a conservative estimate of the 1990 "overcount" for American Indians (approximately 20 percent) was employed to derive the 1990 arrest rates based on the natural increase in the American Indian population. Passel, "Provisional Evaluation of the 1970 Census Count"; Passel and Berman, "The Quality of 1980 Census Data"; and Snipp, "American Indians," 70.

11. The nineteen so-called Indian states identified by Gary D. Sandefur and his colleagues are Alaska, Arizona, Idaho, Michigan, Minnesota, Montana, Nebraska, Nevada, New Mexico, New York, North Carolina, North Dakota, Oklahoma, Oregon, South Dakota, Utah, Washington, Wisconsin, and Wyoming.

12. This resolution does not address two additional problems that have the potential to introduce measurement error in analyses of American Indian criminality. First, . . . UCR data does not include Bureau of Indian Affairs (BIA) crime reports from federal reservation lands. Second, we have no evidence to date that assesses the degree to which self-identification problems plague police reports of American Indian criminality. That is, we do not know the extent to which police arrest/crime figures include those individuals who may not be perceived as American Indian but who self-identify with the racial group on census reports, or visa versa.

13. Based on the data presented here, the extent to which this population measurement issue affects rates of American Indian arrests may be decreasing over time. According to census data, the American Indian population increase appears to have peaked in 1980, with a 72 percent increase over the previous decade. The most recent census figures for 1990 indicate that the Indian population increased by only 37.9 percent over the previous 1980 figures. However, even if this problem is ultimately limited to a three- or four-decade period when changing patterns of self-identification among Americans with American Indian ancestry were most pronounced, the problem remains an issue for those who examine arrests rates among this racial group during these years, and correction factors still may be warranted to assess rates during periods in which this "overcount" was particularly problematic.

14. In regard to the concept of Indian identity, a recent study of academic success among Indian students at a state university in the Midwest included measures of attachment to American Indian culture such as attendance at powwows and belonging to Indian organizations. The study found that these involvements were significantly inversely related to academic achievement. Wilbur J. Scott, "Attachment to Indian Culture," *Youth and Society* 17 (June 1986): 392–94.

2.2 ROBERT STAPLES

White Racism, Black Crime, and American Justice

In an attempt to understand the dilemma inequality poses for a society that espouses equal rights for all, sociologists have developed a set of conceptual approaches for the study of inequality—in particular racial and ethnic inequality. The race and ethnic relations theory that has been most prominent within the social sciences for several decades is the *assimilation theory*. This theory has been used to examine the experiences of immigrant groups that have become part of the United States, both voluntarily and involuntarily. Studies focusing on the assimilation of European immigrants have generally lauded these people's success, while studies on non-European racial and ethnic populations have frequently found these groups to be biologically, culturally, and structurally deficient. The perceived deficiencies of racial and ethnic populations have produced a characterization of these populations that is demeaning and that reinforces negative stereotypes of racial and ethnic populations. In an attempt to redress the limitations of assimilation theory in the study of racial and ethnic populations, some scholars have turned to an *internal colonial* framework.

In the following selection from "White Racism, Black Crime, and American Justice: An Application of the Colonial Model to Explain Crime and Race," *Phylon* (1972), Robert Staples, a professor at the University of California, San Francisco, applies the internal colonial model to explain the relationship between race and crime in U.S. society. To Staples, crimes committed by blacks are the products of their colonial relationship to the greater society, which, in turn, "is based on racial inequality and perpetuated by the political state." Staples maintains that blacks are not protected by American law, that police brutality is a fact of daily experience in black America, and that the cultural values of white supremacy place little significance on the lives of blacks in U.S. society.

Key Concept: white racism, black crime, and colonialism

*I*n the past hundred years criminologists have shown great interest in the relationship between race and crime. Various theories have been put forth to explain the association between racial membership and criminal activity.

These theories have ranged from Lombroso's[1] discredited assertion that certain groups possess inherent criminal tendencies to the more widely accepted theory that certain racial groups are more commonly exposed to conditions of poverty which lead them to commit crimes more often.[2] The purpose of this paper is to examine the relationship of race and crime in a new theoretical framework which will permit a systematic analysis of racial crime within the political-economic context of American society. One function of this model will be to delineate the nature of the solution required to reduce the magnitude of crime among certain racial groups.

The approach here used to explain race and crime is the colonial model. This framework has been formulated and used in the writings of Fanon, Blauner, Carmichael and Hamilton, Memmi, and others.[3] It is particularly attributed to Fanon, whose analysis of colonial relationships in Africa has been transferred to the American pattern of racial dominance and subjugation. While there are many criminologists who will summarily dismiss this model as lacking any relevance for understanding the relationship between race and crime, it merits a hearing since many blacks, especially those presently incarcerated, give it considerable credence. In fact, it is their self-definition as political prisoners that has motivated the many prison protests that have occurred in recent years.

Basically, the colonial analogy views the black community as an underdeveloped colony whose economics and politics are controlled by leaders of the racially dominant group. Using this framework, it is useful to view race as a political and cultural identity rather than to apply any genetic definitions. Race is a political identity because it defines the way in which an individual is to be treated by the political state and the conditions of one's oppression. It is cultural in the sense that white cultural values always have ascendancy over black cultural values, thus what is "good" or "bad," "criminal" or "legitimate" behavior is always defined in terms favorable to the ruling class. The result is that crime by blacks in America is structured by their relationship to the colonial structure, which is based on racial inequality and perpetuated by the political state.

Obviously, there are some imperfections in the colonial analogy as a unitary heuristic model to explain race and crime. More theoretical and empirical research is necessary before the structural forms characteristic of classical colonialism may be mechanically applied to the complexities of crime in America. Yet, the essential features of colonialism are manifest in American society. Blacks have been, and remain, a group subjected to economic exploitation and political control; and they lack the ability to express their cultural values without incurring serious consequences. While other colonial factors such as the geographical relationship of the colonial masters to the colonized, the population ratio, and the duration of colonization may be missing, they do not profoundly affect the form or substance of black and white relations in America: white superordination and black subordination.

In using this model I am not dissuaded by the complications of class often interjected into the issue of crime and race. Domestic colonialism is as much cultural as economic. While members of the white working class are more victimized by their class location than other whites, they are not subjected to the dehumanized status of blacks of all social classes. The racist fabric of white

America denies blacks a basic humanity and thus permits the violation of their right to equal justice under the law. In America the right to justice is an inalienable right; but for blacks it is still a privilege to be granted at the caprice and goodwill of whites, who control the machinery of the legal system and the agents of social control.

LAW AND ORDER

One of the key elements in securing the citizenry's obedience to a nation's laws is the belief of the citizens that the laws are fair. A prevalent view of the law among blacks is summed up in Lester's statement that "the American Black man has never known law and order except as an instrument of oppression. The law has been written by white men, for the protection of white men and their property, to be enforced by white men against Blacks in particular and poor folks in general."[4] Historically, a good case can be made for the argument that the function of law was to establish and regulate the colonial relationship of blacks and whites in the United States. Initially, the colonial system was established by laws which legitimated the subordination of the black population.

The legalization of the colonial order is best represented in the Constitution itself. While the Constitution is regarded as the bulwark of human equality and freedom, it denied the right to vote to Afro-Americans and made the political franchise an exclusive right of white property owners. In fact, blacks were defined as a source of organic property for white slave holders in the notorious 3/5 clause. This clause allowed the slaveowner to claim 3/5 constituency for each slave that he possessed. Since non-citizens are beyond the pale of legal equality, the Dred Scott decision affirmed that slaves were not citizens and could not bring suit in the courts. As the ultimate blow to the aspirations of blacks, in 1896 the Supreme Court upheld racial segregation in its "separate but equal" decision in the Plessy *v.* Ferguson case.[5]

In a contemporary sense, blacks are not protected by American law because they have no power to enforce those laws. They have no law of their own and no defense against the laws of the colonizers. Thus, the power to define what constitutes a crime is in the hands of the dominant caste and is another mechanism of racial subordination. How crime is defined reflects the relationship of the colonized to the colonizers. The ruling caste defines those acts as crimes which fit its needs and purposes and characterizes as criminals individuals who commit certain kinds of illegal acts, while other such acts are exempted from prosecution and escape public disapprobation because they are not perceived as criminal or a threat to society.

As a result of the colonial administration's power to define the nature of criminality, the white collar crimes[6] which involve millions of dollars go unpunished or lightly punished, while the crimes of the colonized involving nickels and dimes result in long jail sentences. The main executor of the colonial regime can wage a war that takes thousands of lives in direct violation of the Constitution, while the colonized are sent to the gas chambers for non-fatal crimes such as rape. It is no coincidence that the two criminal acts for which politicians wanted to preserve the death penalty were kidnapping and airline hijacking, the former a crime committed mainly against the wealthy while the latter is a political act against the state.

INTERNAL MILITARY AGENTS

In any colonial situation, there must be agents to enforce the status quo. A classical colonial world is dichotomized into two parts of society, and the policeman acts as the go-between. Fanon describes it in Colonial Africa:

> In the colonies it is the policeman and the soldier who are the official instituted go-betweens, the spokesman of the settler and his rule of oppression... By their immediate presence and their frequent and direct action, they maintain contact with the native and advise him by means of rifle-butts and napalm not to budge. It is obvious here that the agents of government speak the language of pure force. The intermediary does not lighten the oppression, nor seek to hide the domination; he shows them up and puts them into practice with the clear conscience of an upholder of the peace, yet he is the bringer of violence into the home and into the mind of the native.[7]

One could hardly find a more perfect analogy on the role of the policeman than in the findings of the United States Commission on Civil Rights in the 1960's. Police brutality was discovered to be a fact of daily existence for Afro-Americans and a primary source of abuse by whites against any challenge by blacks to the status quo. In essence:

> Police misconduct often serves as the ultimate weapon for keeping the Negro in his place, for it is quite clear that when all else fails, policemen in some communities can be trusted to prevent the Negro from entering a "desegregated" school or housing project, a voting booth, or even a court of law. They may do it merely by turning their backs on private lawlessness, or by more direct involvement. Trumped up charges, dragnet roundups, illegal arrests, the "third degree" and brutal beatings are all part of the pattern of "white supremacy."[8]

In order to enforce this type of colonial rule, policemen must have certain traits. First and foremost, they must be members of the dominant racial group. Almost every major urban area has a police force that is predominantly white, although the cities themselves may contain mostly blacks. The highest ratio of black policemen to the black population is found in Philadelphia, where 29 percent of the city's population is black and 20 percent of the police force is black. The lowest is probably New Orleans, with the black population composing 41 percent of the total population and 4 percent of the police force.[9]

It is not only that the police force is composed mostly of members of the colonizers' group, but they also represent the more authoritarian and racist members of that sector. One survey disclosed that the majority of white police officers hold antiblack attitudes. In predominantly black precincts, over 75 percent of the white police expressed highly prejudiced feelings towards blacks, and only 1 percent showed sympathy toward the plight of blacks.[10] A series of public hearings on police brutality in Chicago revealed that candidates for the police department who do poorly on the psychological tests or who demonstrate personality problems while undergoing training in the police academy are assigned to "stress areas" in Chicago's black and brown ghettos.[11] The predominantly black city of Oakland, California was recruiting its police officers among men recently returned from military service in Vietnam.

Considering the characteristics of policemen assigned to the black colony, it is no surprise to find that for the years 1920–1932, of 479 blacks killed by white persons in the South, 54 percent were slain by white police officers.[12] In more recent periods cities outside the South provide interesting statistics. Seventy-five percent of the civilians killed by Chicago police in 1971 were black.[13] The state of California reports that blacks, who make up 7 percent of its population, were 48 percent of the persons killed by policemen in 1971.[14]

Even less surprising are the studies which show blacks believe that policemen are disrespectful, that police brutality exists in their areas, and that blacks are treated worse than whites by the police.[15] Besides the abuse suffered at the hands of white police officers, two basic types of complaint are the basis for these beliefs. One is that the police in black communities are more tolerant of illegal activities such as drug addiction, prostitution, and street violence than they would be in white communities. The other is that the police see as much less urgent the calls for help and complaints from black areas than from white areas.[16]

Such complaints about the police force are due to ignorance of their functional role in colonial society. The police are not placed in black communities to protect the indigenous inhabitants, but to protect the property of the colonizers who live outside those communities and to restrain any black person from breaking out of the colonial wards in the event of violence. No amount of "proper" behavior on the part of the police, therefore, nullifies the fundamental colonial machinery which imposes law and order according to the definitions of the colonizers. The law itself constitutes the basis for colonial rule; and the ideology of white supremacy shapes the police force, the courts, and the prisons as instruments of continued colonial subjugation.

CRIME BY BLACKS

The colonial character of American society tends to structure the racial pattern of crime. In the urban areas, where most blacks live, the majority of serious property crimes such as burglary, larceny (over $50), and auto thefts are committed by whites. More blacks than whites are arrested for serious crimes of violence such as murder, rape, and aggravated assaults. These crimes of violence by blacks are most often committed against other blacks.[17] The homicide rate for blacks is about ten times the rate for whites. Indeed, homicide is the second leading cause of death among black males aged 15–25, the third leading cause between 25–44.[18] In interracial crimes of violence, whites attack and assault blacks more often than blacks attack and assault whites.[19]

The above statistics follow the typical pattern in the colonial world. The violence with which the supremacy of the values of whites is affirmed and the aggressiveness which has infused the victory of these values into the ways of life and thought of the colonized mean that their challenge to the colonial world will be to claim that same violence as a means of breaking into the colonizers' forbidden quarters. According to Fanon, colonized men will initially express against their own people this aggressiveness which they have internalized. This is the period when the colonized terrorize and beat each other, while the colonizers or policemen have the right to assault the natives with impunity. This is a pattern of avoidance that allows the colonized to negate their powerlessness, to pretend that colonialism does not exist. Ultimately, this behavior leads to armed resistance against colonialism.[20]

The cultural values of white supremacy place little premium on the lives of blacks in the United States. A native's death is of little importance to the continuation of colonial rule, except that it may deprive a particular colonizer of the labor of a skilled worker. Hence, while blacks are generally given longer prison terms than whites for the same crime, they get shorter sentences for murder.[21] According to Bullock,

> These judicial responses possibly represent indulgent and non-indulgent patterns that characterize local attitudes concerning property and intra-racial morals. Since the victims of most of the Negroes committed for ... [murder] were also Negroes, local norms tolerate a less rigorous enforcement of the law; the disorder is mainly located within the Negro society. Local norms are less tolerant (in Black crimes against white property), for the motivation to protect white property and to protect "white" society against disorder is stronger than the motivation to protect "Negro" society.[22]

THE COLONIAL MACHINERY

Colonial practices are not confined to the police. Rather, the political state, which is also dominated by whites, controls the dispensation of justice from police apprehension to prison; and these all serve the interests of the colonizers. In the courts, most judges in the state, federal, circuit, superior and supreme courts are appointed by the political state, and not elected. No black person in the United States has the power to appoint a judge to the bench. Consequently, there are almost no black judges in the South, and few in the North and West.[23] Moreover, any blacks appointed to the bench are likely to possess the values of the colonizers.

A trial by jury guarantees no more equal justice to the accused black offenders. Blacks are still systematically excluded from juries in some parts of the South, and are often underrepresented on juries in which they are allowed to serve. Sometimes they are excluded by more subtle and indirect means such as preemptory challenges by the prosecution, requirements of voter registration, property ownership, or literacy tests.[24] Despite the American creed of equal justice before the law, few black offenders before the courts will receive a neutral hearing before a jury of normal white Americans. As Fanon states, in a racist society the normal person is racist.[25]

Blacks are further victimized by the lack of adequate legal representation. Since colonial administrations allow few natives to attain professional skills and become members of the native bourgeoisie, there is a scarcity of black lawyers to represent black alleged offenders before the courts. Another feature of colonialism is the creation of dependency in the natives upon the members of the ruling group to achieve ordinary rights of citizenship. Thus, black defendants often choose white lawyers over black ones because they feel they can neutralize the impact of racism in decisions rendered by a white judge and jury. Many black defendants, of course, cannot afford an attorney and must accept a court-appointed lawyer. In federal larceny cases, 52 percent of the blacks did not have their own lawyers, as compared to 25 percent of the whites.[26]

Another disadvantage faced by black defendants is the illegitimacy of their cultural values. There are several examples of words and phrases used by blacks which have a totally different meaning in the white community. These cultural differences are particularly crucial in certain types of crimes such as assault and battery and public obscenity. But the colonial order insists that the natives' society is lacking in values, and that differences in cultural symbols, *i.e.,* language, are not recognized in a court of law. There are other linguistic barriers in the courtroom that affect black defendants. Often, they may not comprehend the legal jargon of the attorneys and give answers based on their mistaken interpretation of the language used in the courtroom.[27]

Given all these factors, black defendants are often shortchanged in the decisions of the courts and the length of their prison sentences. Most of the available data reveal that blacks usually receive longer prison terms than whites for the same criminal offenses. They are particularly discriminated against when one considers their chances of receiving probation or a suspended sentence. In larceny cases, for example, 74 percent of guilty blacks were imprisoned in state larceny cases compared to only 49 percent of guilty whites. The racial gap in larceny cases is greater than in assault convictions because larcenies by blacks are more often committed against whites, while assaults occur more frequently against other blacks. Hence, racial disparities in prison sentencing are not only related to the skin color of the alleged offender, but to that of his victim, too.[28]

It is in the area of capital punishment that the racial, and thus colonial, factors stand out. The statistics on capital punishment in the United States reveal most glaringly the double standard of justice that exists there: One for the wealthy and another for blacks and poor people. Even the former Warden of the Sing Sing prison once remarked, "Only the poor, the friendless, and the foreign born are sentenced to death and executed."[29] But it is particularly the colonial wards of America, *i.e.,* blacks, who have received the heaviest brunt of this dual standard of American justice.

For blacks in America, capital punishment is only a transfer of the functions of lynch mobs to the state authority. Under the auspices of the political state, blacks have been executed for less serious crimes and crimes less often receiving the death penalty, particularly rape, than whites. They were of a younger age than whites at the time of execution and were more often executed without appeals, regardless of their offense or age at execution. Of the

3,827 men and 32 women executed since 1930, 53 percent were black. The proportion of blacks on death row in 1972 was 52 percent. It is in the South that discrimination in capital punishment is most evident. Practically all executions for rape took place in the South. In that region, 90 percent of those executed for rape were black.[30]

Again, the colonial pattern emerges. The two things the colonizers fear most are the stealing of their possessions and the rape of their women, and they punish with special fury the crime of sexual violation of upper caste women. About 85 percent of the black rape offenders executed had white victims,[31] although the overwhelming majority of the black males' rape victims are black women.

POLITICAL PRISONERS

The combination of the colonial administration of justice and the oppression of blacks has resulted in the internment of a disproportionate number of blacks in the nation's prisons. The number of blacks in prison is three times their representation in the society at large.[32] There are actually more blacks in prison than in college. Yet, as Angela Davis has observed:

> Along with the army and the police, prisons are the most essential instruments of state power. The prospect of long prison terms is meant to preserve order; it is supposed to serve as a threat to anyone who dares disturb existing social relations, whether by failing to observe the sacred rules of property, or by consciously challenging the right of an unjust system of racism and domination to function smoothly.[33]

In recent years the number of prison protests by black prisoners have risen. Part of the reason is the prisoners' self-definition as political prisoners. Two basic types of political prisoners may be defined. One kind is the person arrested under the guise of criminal charges, but only because of the state's wish to remove the political activist as a threat to the prevailing racial conditions. Examples of this type are Angela Davis, Bobby Seale, and H. Rap Brown. The second type is more numerous and consists of those blacks who are arbitrarily arrested and then "railroaded" through the courts, where they face white politically appointed judges, all-white juries, without a lawyer, or with an appointed lawyer who suggests a guilty plea in exchange for a reduced sentence.

Since most crimes by blacks have black victims, not all black prisoners are *ipso facto* political prisoners. The incarceration of these blacks stems from the subjugated condition of black people in the United States. As Chrisman asserts, "a Black prisoner's crime may or may not have been a political action against the state, but the state's action against him is always political."[34] The basis for this judgment is that black criminals are not tried and judged by the black community itself, but that their crimes are defined and they are convicted and sentenced by the machinery of the ruling colonial order, whose interests are served by the systematic subjugation of all black people. As long as crime by blacks occurs within the context of racial subjugation and exploitation, blacks will continue to believe that their criminal acts will not be objectively and fairly treated, but rather that the treatment will be affected by the racial inequality which constitutes the essence of American colonialism.

In this paper the colonial model has been applied to explain the relationship between crime and race. While the fit between theory and empirical data is not perfect, it does point the way to reducing some of the racial inequities in American criminal justice. Among the remedies suggested by this model is community control of the police. Community control would respond to the charge that the police in black neighborhoods constitute an occupation army in their midst. Policemen would be chosen by the people in the community and required to live in their precinct. In this way, blacks would have greater assurance that the police are there to protect their interests rather than the property of whites who live outside the community.[35]

Another remedy to be considered is a trial by jury of one's peers. This means a jury whose experiences, needs, and interests are similar to those of the defendant. When this is not feasible, proportional representation of blacks on juries, in the legal staff, and on the bench might be considered. While these suggestions will not radically affect the socioeconomic conditions that generate crime, they will at least reduce the impact of domestic racism on the administration of justice to the black population.

NOTES

1. Gina Lombroso, "Ferrero," in *Criminal Man According to the Classifications of Cesare Lombroso* (New York, 1911).

2. C. F. Marvin Wolfgang and Bernard Cohen, *Crime and Race: Conceptions and Misconceptions* (New York, 1970).

3. Frantz Fanon, *The Wretched of the Earth* (New York, 1966); Robert Blauner, "Internal Colonialism and Ghetto Revolt," *Social Problems* XVI (Spring, 1969), 393–408; Stokely Carmichael and Charles Hamilton, *Black Power* (New York, 1967); Albert Memmi, *The Colonizer and the Colonized* (Boston, 1967).

4. Julius Lester, *Look Out, Whitey: Black Power's Gon' Get Your Mama* (New York, 1968), p. 23.

5. Cf. Mary Berry, *Black Resistance—White Law: A History of Constitutional Racism in America* (New York, 1971).

6. Edwin H. Sutherland, *White Collar Crime* (New York, 1949).

7. Fanon, *op. cit.*, p. 31.

8. Wallace Mendelson, *Discrimination* (Englewood Cliffs, 1962), pp. 143–44.

9. *Report of the National Advisory Commission on Civil Disorders* (New York, 1968), p. 321.

10. Albert J. Reiss, Jr., "Police Brutality—Answers to Key Questions," *Transaction,* V (July–August, 1968), 10–19.

11. Testimony of Dr. Evrum Mendelsohn of the Elmhurst Psychological Center before Congressman Ralph Metcalfe's Public Hearing on Police Brutality in Chicago, September 1, 1972.

12. Gunnar Myrdal, *An American Dilemma* (New York, 1944).

13. Testimony of a team of law students from Northwestern University at the Metcalfe hearing, August 30, 1972.

14. Report by Evelle Younger, Attorney General of the State of California, cited in *The Los Angeles Sentinel*, August 10, 1972, p. A2.

15. Report of the National Advisory Commission on Civil Disorders, *op. cit.*, p. 302.

16. *Ibid.*, p. 268.

17. United States Department of Justice, Federal Bureau of Investigation, "Crime in the United States," *Uniform Crime Reports*, 1969.

18. Lee N. Robins, "Negro Homicide Victims—Who Will They Be?" *Transaction*, V (June, 1968), p. 16.

19. Marvin Wolfgang, *Patterns in Criminal Homicide* (Philadelphia, 1958).

20. Fanon, *op. cit.*, p. 43.

21. Wolfgang, *Crime and Race, op. cit.*, p. 82.

22. Henry A. Bullock, "Significance of the Racial Factor in the Length of Prison Sentences," *The Journal of Criminal Law, Criminology and Police Science*, VII (November, 1961), 411–17.

23. United States Commission on Civil Rights Report, 1963, p. 124.

24. United States Commission on Civil Rights Report, *Justice* (Washington, D.C., 1961), p. 92.

25. Frantz Fanon, "Racism and Culture," in *Toward the African Revolution* (New York, 1967).

26. Stuart Nagel, *The Legal Process From a Behavioral Perspective* (Homewood, Illinois, 1969).

27. Daniel H. Swett, *Cross Cultural Communications in the Courtroom: Applied Linguistics in a Murder Trial*, a paper presented at the Conference on Racism and the Law (San Francisco, December, 1967), pp. 2–5.

28. Nagel, *op. cit.*

29. Cited in Hugo Bedau, *The Death Penalty in America* (New York, 1967), p. 411.

30. William J. Bowers, *Racial Discrimination in Capital Punishment: Characteristics of the Condemned* (Lexington, Massachusetts, 1972).

31. *Ibid.*

32. National Prisoner Statistics, 1971.

33. Angela Davis, "The Soledad Brothers," *The Black Scholar*, II (April–May 1971), 2–3.

34. Robert Chrisman, "Black Prisoners, White Law," *The Black Scholar*, II (April–May 1971), 45–46.

35. Cf. Arthur Waskow, "Community Control of the Police," *Transaction*, VI (December 1969), 4–5.

2.3 VICTOR E. KAPPELER, MARK BLUMBERG, AND GARY W. POTTER

Crime Waves and Crime Fears

Victor E. Kappeler and Gary W. Potter are professors in the Department of Criminal Justice and Police Studies at Eastern Kentucky University in Richmond, Kentucky. Mark Blumberg is on the faculty of the Department of Criminal Justice at Central Missouri State University in Warrensburg, Missouri. In the following selection from their book *The Mythology of Crime and Criminal Justice,* 2d ed. (Waveland Press, 1996), Kappeler, Blumberg, and Potter examine the social construction of the crime problem in America, and identify those public and private entities that create, perpetuate, and exploit its scope and intensity. They advance the idea that America's crime wave is a myth. The authors review evidence to support the notion that the popular conceptions of crime, its victims, and its contexts are grossly inaccurate and that such inaccuracies are a conscious and concerted effort to advance an economic and political agenda. Kappeler, Blumberg, and Potter refute the extent of crime, particularly as reported by so-called official governmental sources, including the FBI's Uniform Crime Reports (UCR) and the National Crime Victimization Survey (NCVS). These scholars dispel the incidence and prevalence of violent crime and the nature of crime victimization as reported through the popular media. They show that the typical portrayal of crime as the violent, interpersonal encounter between interracial and urban strangers is the exception rather than the rule. In fact, they maintain, the typical crime involves an intragroup altercation of simple assault or petty property crime most often perpetrated by a family member or other acquaintance with little or no noticeable injury or loss. The authors suggest that the incongruence between the facts about crime and the public's perception of crime stems from sensational media reporting, the politicalization of crime, and an alarmist's behavior entrenched within the criminal justice system. They conclude that the media is motivated by profits realized through advertising sales during prime time television or the sale of news media, the criminal justice system is motivated by enhanced public funding for institutional growth, and political actors are motivated by the probabilities of increased power and privilege. As a result, Americans' popular conception of crime is based upon erroneous and often fabricated information.

Key Concept: crime waves and the politicalization of America's crime problem

The people of this country are fed up with crime. The media report it. Statistics reflect it. Polls prove it.

—FBI Director Louis J. Freeh

When Federal Bureau of Investigation Director Freeh made the remark above to the National Press Club, in 1994 he was echoing the popular mood in America. That same year, a national news magazine published the following quotation and analysis:

> What are we going to do about these kids (monsters) who kill with guns??? Line them up against the wall and get a firing squad and pull, pull, pull. I am volunteering to pull, pull, pull.
>
> That's not a rap lyric. It's from an anonymous letter to a judge in Dade County Florida—part of the shared unconscious talking. And suddenly we're all ears. In one of the most startling spikes in the history of polling, large numbers of Americans are abruptly calling crime their greatest concern. Confronted by clear evidence of a big issue, politicians everywhere, including the one in the White House, are reaching for their loudest guns: prisons, boot camps, mandatory sentences. Months before the start of baseball season, the air is full of shouts of "Three strikes and you're out" (Lacayo, 1994:51).

A *Time* public opinion poll reported that 19 percent of all Americans regard crime as the country's most serious problem, up from only 4 percent one year earlier (Lacayo, 1994). The poll showed that twice as many Americans were more worried about crime than the economy or unemployment and four times as many were more concerned with crime than with the budget deficit. And, on the face of it, it's no wonder that they are so worried about crime in America. As Director Freeh (1994:5) went on to say in his speech: "In the past 30 years, homicides have nearly tripled, robberies and forcible rapes each are up over 500 percent, and aggravated assaults have increased more than 600 percent. According to the most recent National Crime Victimization Survey, nearly 37 million people have been injured by criminals in this country in the past 20 years. It is estimated that crime has cost America $19 billion since 1991."

Director Freeh's ominous report included seemingly irrefutable data from the National Crime Victimization Survey (NCVS). Another passage from that survey revealed:

> Persons age 12 or older, living in the United States, experienced 34.7 million crimes in 1991 according to the National Crime Victimization Survey (NCVS). Approximately 6.4 million of these victimizations consisted of violent crimes such as rape, robbery, and aggravated and simple assaults. Another 12.5 million victimizations were crimes of theft—larcenies both with and without contact between the victim and offender. Finally there were 15.8 million household crimes in 1991 (Bastian, 1992:1).

These are truly horrifying numbers that clearly suggest Americans are being attacked, killed, and maimed by criminals in such numbers and at such an alarming rate that drastic measures must be taken to deal with this national crisis. If these reports are correct, we are somewhere between three and six times more likely to be attacked by a violent criminal than in the past, and about one in four Americans are in dire danger of criminal victimization each and every year.

Not only are the crime trends as presented by Department of Justice officials very menacing, but our perception of the individual who will inflict this harm is equally menacing. Jeffrey Reiman (1990:42) details our view of the typical criminal as: "He is, first of all a he. Second, he is a youth—most likely under the age of twenty. Third, he is predominantly urban—although increasingly suburban. Fourth, he is disproportionately black—blacks are arrested for Index crimes at a rate three times that of their percentage in the national population. Finally he is poor." Reiman (1995:52–53) goes on to comment:

> This, then, is the Typical Criminal, the one whose portrait President Reagan described as "that of a stark, staring face, a face that belongs to a frightening reality of our time—the face of a human predator, the face of the habitual criminal. Nothing in nature is more cruel and more dangerous" ... This is the Typical Criminal feared by most law-abiding Americans. His crime, according to former Attorney General John Mitchell (who was by no means a typical criminal), is forcing us "to change the fabric of our society, ... forcing us, a free people, to alter our pattern of life, ... to withdraw from our neighbors, to fear all strangers and to limit our activities to 'safe' areas."

Just as we have images of the typical criminal, we also have mental images of the typical crime. Once again, Reiman (1995:59–60) describes the mental image most people have of a "crime";

> Think of a crime, any crime. Picture the first "crime" that comes into your mind. What do you see? The odds are you are not imagining a mining company executive sitting at his desk calculating the costs of proper safety precautions and deciding not to invest in them. Probably what you see in your mind's eye is one person physically attacking or robbing something from another on the threat of physical attack.

Not only is crime rampant, dangerous, and threatening to explode in America, but it is the worst kind of crime. It is the kind of crime portrayed by George Bush's infamous "Willie Horton" commercials during the 1988 presidential campaign. The Bush campaign took a single case where one convicted violent offender participating in a highly successful prison furlough program in Massachusetts committed a violent crime while on furlough. The ad campaign had a devastating effect on the governor of the state, Michael Dukakis, in his presidential election bid. It also played to the worst fears and prejudices Americans harbor about crime. It portrayed a violent crime, with a weapon, committed by a stranger, who was sent to prey on society by a "soft" criminal justice system. Perhaps even more important was the fact that Willie Horton was an African-American male whose predations were directed at white females.

The Bush campaign exploited our worst images of crime—violent crime, committed by sociopathic strangers, preying upon otherwise sober, cautious, ascetic, industrious and righteous citizens. Is it any wonder that 81 percent of the public favors life imprisonment for anyone convicted of three serious crimes or that 65 percent of the public favors the imposition of a 10 P.M. curfew for citizens under the age of 18? (Lacayo, 1994). Is it any wonder that politicians clamor for more police, more prisons, and more severe sentences to combat an ever-increasing panoply of crimes? The mood of the American public is becoming increasingly ugly toward these violent predators, leading to an attitude of "Line them up and pull, pull, pull."

Before we "line them up," perhaps a moment of sober reflection is necessary—sober reflection isolated from the ritualistic wailing of politicians for more police and prisons; sober reflection detached from the hysterical reports of the tabloid media; sober reflection disconnected from the self-serving warnings of law enforcement executives seeking to enhance their powers, personnel, and budgets. As this [selection] will suggest, a period of sober reflection results in very different conclusions about this wave of crime allegedly gripping America and threatening the innocent. Facts have been curiously missing from the debate about crime in America, and the facts, once uncovered, are startling:

- There is no crime wave in the United States. Criminal victimization has been steadily and drastically declining for the past two decades. The American crime wave is a myth.
- Of those crimes that do occur, the overwhelming majority are the result of minor incidents involving neither serious economic loss nor extensive physical injury. Most crimes are not the serious, violent, dangerous crimes which compose the public stereotype of America as a predatory jungle.
- Of those violent crimes which do threaten our well-being, most are committed by relatives, intimate friends and acquaintances—those we trust the most—not by psychopathic, predatory strangers lurking in urban shadows.
- Most crimes, even violent crimes, do not involve the use of a weapon.
- Most crimes, particularly violent crimes, are intraracial, thereby contradicting the subtle and not so subtle appeals to racism by our crime fighters.

HOW MUCH CRIME IS THERE?

Crime statistics must be treated with great caution and not an inconsiderable amount of skepticism. When numbers are bandied about purporting to reflect the danger of crime in society, two primary questions must be asked before accepting their validity. The first is, are they measuring what they claim to measure? And the second is, where do these numbers come from? Do they emanate from a source which has something to gain from the way crime is presented to the public?

The most commonly recognized measures of crime in America are to be found in the Federal Bureau of Investigation's (FBI) *Uniform Crime Reports (UCR)*. Despite its popularity since its inception in 1930 (Thompson, 1968), the *UCR* has drawn strong criticism (see, Wolfgang, 1963). These reports are issued annually and are compilations of "crimes known to the police." Crimes known to the police is a relatively ambiguous category, for the most part composed of complaints from citizens indicating that a crime has occurred (Chambliss, 1988). This does not mean that a crime has actually occurred. In reporting "crimes known to the police," the FBI does not insist that a suspect be arrested, or, for that matter, that the crime even be investigated and "founded" (Chambliss, 1988:29). The only requirement is that someone, somewhere, for some reason, believed that a crime may have been committed.

In addition, the crime categories and definitions used by the FBI are designed in such a way as to maximize both the severity of the crime and the number of crimes that are reported by local police departments. As Chambliss (1988:29–30) points out:

> The crime categories used in the *UCR* are often ambiguous. For example, burglary requires the use of force for breaking and entering in many states, but the FBI tells local police departments to report the crime as burglary simply if there is unlawful entry. Merging these two types of offenses makes statistics on "burglary" ambiguous. More important is the way police departments are instructed to fill out the forms. In every instance, the instructions are designed to show the highest incidence of crime possible. The *Uniform Crime Reporting Handbook* states: "If a number of persons are involved in a dispute or disturbance and police investigation cannot establish aggressors from the victims, count the number of persons assaulted as the number of offenses."
>
> In reporting homicides, the instructions to the police are equally misleading from the point of view of gathering scientifically valid information. The instructions tell police departments that they should report a death as a homicide regardless of whether other objective evidence indicates otherwise: " . . . the findings of coroner, court, jury or prosecutor do not unfound [change the report of] offenses or attempts which your [police] investigations establish to be legitimate."

In addition, studies of the police reporting of crime by social scientists have demonstrated with regularity that these statistics are subject to political manipulation. For example, Richard Nixon, while president, instituted a crime control experiment in Washington, D.C., to demonstrate the effectiveness of his crime control proposals for the nation. The Nixon administration wanted the crime rate to go down to claim success. The crime rate did indeed go down—not because of any diminution in crime but because of bureaucratic manipulation in the reporting of crime by the police. The District of Columbia police simply began listing the value of stolen property at less than $50, thereby removing a vast number of crimes from the felony category and thus "reducing" the crime rate (Seidman and Couzens, 1974).

Selke and Pepinsky (1984) in a study of crime reporting practices over a thirty-year period in Indianapolis found that local police officials could make the crime rate rise or fall, depending upon political exigencies, virtually at will. Other studies have also demonstrated the ease with which crime rates can be manipulated (Mcleary, Nienstedt and Erven, 1982).

Finally, *UCR* data are presented in ways which are far from scientific. The FBI creates "Crime Clocks" and other highly visual gimmicks designed to exaggerate the incidence of crime and the threat it poses to the public (see also, Tunnell, 1992). For example, the 1993 *UCR* tell us that one criminal offense occurs every two seconds; one violent crime occurs every sixteen seconds; one forcible rape occurs every five minutes; one burglary occurs every eleven seconds. These presentations of *UCR* data are designed to exaggerate the amount of crime in society and to leave the impression that violent victimization is imminent. Chambliss (1988:31) commented on the use of such gimmicks: "This makes good newspaper copy and serves to give the law enforcement agencies considerable political clout, which is translated into ever-increasing budgets, pay raises, and more technologically sophisticated 'crime-fighting' equipment. It does not, however, provide policy makers or social scientists with reliable data."

Further indication of the suspect nature of *UCR* data comes from an article in the *Wall Street Journal* which begins "This is the tale of crime in two cities" and goes on to use the most recent *UCR* data to show New York City's rate of serious crime is 56 percent lower than Tallahassee's. The FBI includes seven crimes—murder, rape, robbery, aggravated assault, burglary, larceny and motor-vehicle theft in its index. In 1993, New York City had 600,346 reported index crimes for a population of 7.3 million. Its crime rate is therefore 82 crimes per 1,000 people. Tallahassee reported 19,426 crimes and has a population of 132,252. Its rate was 147 crimes per 1,000 (Bennett, 1995). According to the FBI, Tallahassee residents were almost 60 percent more likely to be assaulted and almost three times more likely to be raped (Bennett, 1995). Clearly, the "facts" represented by the FBI figures need additional explanation. The first clarification is to note, again, that these figures are based on *reported* crime. If New Yorkers have been conditioned to accept some crimes as inevitable and not worth reporting, that skews the rate. If crimes must be reported in person at the precinct station versus a squad car being dispatched to take a report, that's another significant factor. If residents of both cities do not take the same precautions (locked car doors, valuables hidden, windows secured in houses), the rates will differ. Tallahassee has a large number of college students, which can affect the likelihood of certain crimes. There are a number of essential details that need to be addressed before numbers tell us anything.

Crime rates tell us virtually nothing about crime. "Crimes known to the police" is an ambiguous category, subject to political manipulation, and easily adjusted to the bureaucratic requirements of law enforcement agencies. They may tell us a little about police department practices and policies, but they tell us absolutely nothing useful about crime. Nonetheless, it is on the basis of "crime rates" that both criminal justice officialdom and the media inform us about the ever-increasing threat from crime and criminals. It is, in part, based on these very questionable statistics that FBI Director Freeh warns us about massive increases in violent crime in the past thirty years.

Having said all of this, it may be startling to note that the FBI has reported a 3 percent decline in violent crime and 4 percent decline in crime overall for the first six months of 1993 based on their aggregation of "crimes known to the police" (Lacayo, 1994:51). At the close of 1994, the *UCR* showed that serious crime reported to the police had declined for the third consecutive year (BJS, 1995). The first quarter of 1995 shows a continuation of that decline (Staff, 1995). Even more startling is the fact that any decline in "crimes reported to the police" is remarkable for two reasons having nothing to do with the actual incidence of crime. First, there are many more police on the streets today than in the past. The number of police officers has increased about 20 percent in the last two decades; there are about 800,000 police on the streets today (BJS, 1994). More police, patrolling a greater area with greater frequency, should be reporting a greater amount of crime. If the number of police officers increased by 20 percent, we would expect reported crime to increase about the same amount. Instead we find a significant decline. Second, citizen reporting of crime is up markedly in the past two decades (see table 1). Every single category of crime shows an increase in the percentage of victims reporting crimes to police. This means that the decrease in reported crime rates is even greater than it appears at first glance because people are reporting much more crime.

As we shall see, this reported decline in the crime rate is not a result of greater care in the culling of data or a sudden change in the direction of the political manipulation of crime rate statistics. It is, in fact, a vast understatement of just how much decline in the amount of crime in society there really has been.

Victimization Rates

Another, and a far better, source of crime data is the National Crime Victimization Survey (NCVS). Since 1972, the Department of Justice has conducted an annual survey of 100,000 households across the country, asking respondents if they or any member of their households had been a victim of crime in the past year. The victimization surveys are clearly superior to *UCR* data in that they measure both reported and unreported crime, and they are unaffected by technological changes in police record keeping, levels of reporting by victims to the police, and the other factors that call into question the validity of *UCR* data (Bureau of Justice Statistics, 1993). The NCVS data comes from questionnaires (carefully designed for validity and reliability by social scientists) administered to a very large, demographically representative sample of the U.S. population. While no survey is perfect, the NCVS represents the best available source of data on crime victimization in the United States. While the way the data are reported and presented is subject to political manipulation, the data themselves are scientifically valid.

The NCVS data speaks volumes about crime in America. Most importantly, it tells us that crime has been decreasing in America for the past two decades—and that the decrease has been precipitous. From 1973 to 1991 personal crimes (rape, robbery, assault, and personal larceny) have decreased

TABLE 1

Percentage of Victimizations Reported to the Police in 1973 and 1991

	Percent of Victimizations Reported	
Crime	*1973*	*1991*
Rape	49%	59%
Robbery	52%	55%
Aggravated Assault	52%	58%
Simple Assault	38%	42%
Larceny with Contact	33%	38%
Larceny without Contact	22%	28%
Household Burglary	47%	50%
Household Larceny	25%	28%
Motor Vehicle Theft	68%	74%

Source: Bastian, L. D. (1982). *Criminal Victimization 1991.* Washington, DC: Bureau of Justice Statistics, p. 5.

by 25.3 percent and household crimes (burglary, household larceny and motor vehicle theft) have decreased by 25.2 percent. The victimization rate for rape is down 11.6 percent; for robbery 17.2 percent, for aggravated assault 22.2 percent, and for burglary the victimization rate has declined 42.1 percent (see table 2). Only simple assault, a relatively minor crime which will be discussed later, and motor vehicle theft have shown increases. The simple, indisputable fact is that crime in the United States is down 25 percent. It appears that a massive decrease in the incidence of crime has somehow sparked a massive increase in concern about crime. As Samuel Walker (1994:5) succinctly puts it: "This is one of the longest and most significant declines in the crime rate in American history. Much of the public hysteria about crime is misplaced."

Let us be very clear about this. The only reliable, scientific data we have on crime in America tell us that crime is decreasing, has been decreasing, and continues to decrease. Furthermore, those decreases are not small or marginal, they are consistent decreases which have resulted in a 25 percent diminution in the amount of crime in America. The irony of this prolonged and significant decrease in crime resulting in so much public hysteria should not be lost on us.

The decrease in crime over the past eighteen years is only a part of the story. The victimization survey also tells us that 90.8 percent of the American population was *not* the victim of any kind of personal crime. In addition, the vast bulk of crime that does occur is not the heinous, violent predatory crime that we imagine. By the victims' own accounts, most crime is of relatively little impact and importance.

TABLE 2

Victimization Rates Per 1,000 Households in 1973 and 1991

	Victimization Rates		
Crime	1973	1991	Percent Change
Rape	1.0	0.8	-11.6
Robbery	6.7	5.6	-17.2
Aggravated Assault	10.1	7.8	-22.2
Simple Assault	14.8	17.0	+15.1
Larceny with Contact	3.1	2.3	-23.5
Larceny without Contact	88.0	58.7	-33.3
Household Burglary	91.7	53.1	-42.1
Household Larceny	107.0	88.0	-17.7
Motor Vehicle Theft	19.1	21.8	+14.3

Source: Bastian, L. D. (1992). *Criminal Victimization 1991.* Washington, DC: Bureau of Justice Statistics, p. 4

THE REALITY OF CRIME

For 1991, the NCVS victimization rate for crimes of violence was 31.3 per 1,000 households. Roughly, this victimization rate suggests that about 3 percent of the population aged 12 and older was the victim of a violent crime. As defined by the NCVS, these crimes of violence include rate, robbery, and aggravated and simple assault (see table 3). When the victimization rates for rape, robbery, and aggravated assault are totaled independent of simple assault, we arrive at a figure of 14.2 victimizations per 1,000 households. Thus, the majority of violent crime victimizations are the result of simple assault (17.0 per 1,000 households).

While simple assault is a crime, and no argument is made that it should be ignored or condoned, it is not the kind of violent crime emphasized by the media or law enforcement officials—nor is it the type of violent crime consistent with the public stereotype. What is simple assault and how threatening is it to public safety? As William Chambliss (1984:169) has pointed out in analyzing victimization survey data: "The most likely crime of violence that one will experience is 'simple assault,' an attack without a weapon resulting either in minor injury (e.g., bruises, black eye, cuts, scratches, swelling) or an undetermined injury requiring less than 2 days hospitalization. Also includes attempted assault without a weapon."

Unlike the public image of a typical crime, simple assault involves no weapon and only minor injury. Furthermore, unlike our image of the typical crime, the offender in a simple assault is usually a friend, relative, or acquain-

TABLE 3

Victimization Rates for Personal and Household Crimes, 1991

Crime	Victimizations per 1,000 persons age 12 or older or per 1,000 households
Personal Crimes	92.3
Crimes of Violence	31.2
Rape	0.8
Robbery	5.6
Assault	24.8
Aggravated	7.8
Simple	17.0
Crimes of Theft	61.0
Personal Larceny with Contact	2.3
Personal Larceny without Contact	58.7
Household Crimes	62.9
Household Burglary	53.1
Household Larceny	88.0
Motor Vehicle Theft	21.8

Source: Bastian, L. D. (1992). *Criminal Victimization 1991.* Washington, DC: Bureau of Justice Statistics, p.6.

tance, and the crime takes place in the course of normal social interaction, not in a dark alley:

> Almost half the "simple assaults" were altercations between people who were "not strangers" ... As other research has shown, there is an interaction process characteristic of assaults which always lays open the question of who is the victim and who is the offender. Since only the viewpoint of the victim is being surveyed, these figures on assault ... , while not very high, are nonetheless probably an overstatement of the stereotyped picture of an "assault" in which someone who is "doing nothing" is suddenly and maliciously attacked by a stranger. Further details on the circumstances may reveal that many of the so-called assaults were (a) arguments where one person started swinging ... first or (b) trivial pushing and shoving. This interpretation is also supported by the fact that two-thirds of the assaults were not reported to the police, and the reasons for not reporting most often given were that the incident was unimportant or that "nothing could be done" because of "lack of proof" (Chambliss, 1984:169–70).

So, while simple assault is a crime, it is often a private matter, between friends, relatives, and acquaintances, involving no serious injuries, but comprising a majority of all violent victimizations.

Turning to crimes of theft we find a similar situation. The NCVS data tell us that in 1991 the victimization rate for crimes of theft was 61.0 per 1,000 households, or roughly 6 percent of the population over age twelve. Once again, however, considerable ambiguity exists over these victimizations. Crimes of theft are made up of personal larceny with contact and personal larceny without contact. Ninety-six percent of all crimes of theft victimizations are personal larcenies without contact (see table 3). Again, we must ask, what constitutes a personal larceny without contact?

> We do not know what the actual event was that led people to say that they had had something stolen. But given the fact that these incidents consist of the taking of personal property without personal contact when the property was away from home, it is probable that the vast majority of these "crimes" consists of property being taken after the victim left it in a subway station and which was gone when he or she returned to retrieve it, or having small amounts of money or personal property that had been left in an unlocked desk, locker or office removed. Certainly bicycle theft would account for a large share of these "personal crimes without contact" (Chambliss, 1984:168).

There is no doubt that the stealing of bicycle or the removal of a gym bag from a locker or a briefcase from a subway stop is a crime. But, once again, it is not the kind of serious, life-threatening, dangerous crime perpetrated by a weapon-wielding offender which is so prominent in the public mind. The crimes of simple assault and personal larceny without contact make up 75.7 percent of all personal crime victimizations.

In addition, victims often regard the crimes they report as not being very important. In 1990, those respondents to the NCVS who did not report crimes to the police indicated in 6.2 percent of the cases that the crime was "not important enough." In 20 percent of the cases, they did not report the crime because it was a "private or personal matter." And in 4.4 percent of the cases, they reported that these crimes, classified as violent by the NCVS, were so unimportant that they didn't want to take the time or incur the inconvenience of reporting them (*Sourcebook*, 1992–268–69). Once again, this does not mean that a crime was not committed, nor does it meant that the crime should be ignored, but it does mean that the nature of the crime differs greatly from the popular perception of crime. "Making rough estimates from the data presented, we could conservatively conclude that over half of the victimizations were on the borderline of criminal behavior and consisted of acts that in no way pose a serious threat to the 'life and property' of the nation's people" (Chambliss, 1984:169).

In 1992 the National Crime Victimization Survey was redesigned (Department of Justice, 1994). Categories of crime were changed. For example, rape was aggregated with sexual assault to create a new crime classification; aggravated and simple assault were combined with "attempted assault with weapon" and "attempted assault without weapon," thereby creating a new category of crime. This redesign may have simply been part of the ongoing methodological review of the NCVS which attempts annually to increase the reliability and validity of the data. On the other hand, this redesign may have had more sinister and diabolical implications. As we have seen, the NCVS has demonstrated clearly that contrary to politicians' proclamations and public impressions, serious crime has been declining precipitously in America for the past two decades. Those are hardly data which justify new expenditures on law enforcement and prisons;

expansion of the criminal law; the extension of the death penalty to a plethora of new offenses; and a "crime crisis" mentality in policy making. The reclassification of criminal acts in the redesigned survey makes it inevitable that the victimization rates and frequencies will be higher than in the surveys of the previous twenty years. Perhaps the survey redesign was a bit of methodological legerdemain intended to give the appearance that the incidence of victimizations was increasing. Perhaps the intent was simpler. By changing the survey and the classification of crimes in that survey the Justice Department has made it impossible to continue a longitudinal comparison of data into the future. It is therefore not possible to determine if the clear trends of declining victimization have continued through 1992 and 1993. The Department of Justice has, intentionally or otherwise, made continuing analysis of a trend which negates the official position impossible.

While the data for 1992 and 1993 are no longer comparable with earlier data, they do provide clues which indicate that even a change in survey design cannot obfuscate the continuing drastic decrease in serious crime. Based on the NCVS data for those two years it is clear that serious crime is still declining and still declining markedly. For example, the new category of "Rape/Sexual Assault" showed a decrease of 20.9 percent in the two-year period of the new survey. "Completed Rape" showed a decline of 9.2 percent; "Attempted Rape" declined by 24.5 percent; "Sexual Assault" declined by 26.6 percent (Department of Justice, 1994). In other crime categories victimization declines have also continued and are also steep: "Completed Robbery" declined by 5.2 percent; "Simple Assault Completed With Injury" declined by 6.9 percent; "Theft" declined by 2.2 percent; and all "Property Crimes" declined by 0.9 percent (BJS, 1995; Department of Justice, 1994).

The newly designed survey can no longer be compared directly with previous years, but it still demonstrates the simple fact that criminal victimizations continue to decline year after year. The justification for crime-war hysteria is clearly absent in both old and new victimization studies.

Strangers and Crime

There are other strong indicators that tell us that crime is less of a threat than the popular stereotype would have us believe. For example, at least half of all homicides in the United States take place among people who know each other. One out of five homicides (19.7 percent) where the victim-offender relationship can be determined occur in situations in which the offender and victim are members of the same family, and over half of the homicides (57.4 percent) occur among people who are friends or acquaintances (Prothrow-Stith, 1994). The popular image of a homicide as being related to burglary, youth gangs, drug trafficking, stalkers, and serial killers accounts for less than 25 percent of all homicides.

In other crimes the picture is similar. For example, about half of all rapes of females were perpetrated by someone known to the victim, not by a stranger lurking in an alley or hiding behind bushes (Bureau of Justice Statistics, 1993). If we look at the victimization rate for violent crimes we find that males are

TABLE 4

Violent Crime Rates and Victim/Offender Relationships

Victim/Offender Relationship	Violent crime rate per 1,000	
	Females	Males
Strangers	5.4	12.2
Relatives and Acquaintances	11.9	13.4
Intimates	5.4	0.5
Other Relatives	1.1	0.7
Acquaintance	5.4	12.2

Source: Bureau of Justice Statistics (1993). *Highlights from 20 Years of Surveying Crime Victims.* Washington, DC: U.S. Government Printing Office.

more likely than females to be victimized by a stranger, but that both males and females are more likely to be victimized by someone they know (see table 4). Women, in particular, have considerably more reason to fear those close to them than they have to fear predatory strangers. Overall, we are about 60 percent more likely to be victimized by someone known to us. Clearly, it is not the lurking stranger whom we must fear; those closest to us pose the greatest danger.

Weapons, Injury, and Crime

Our images of crime are also filled with weapons, wielded by violent strangers, causing great physical harm. Once again, however, the data indicate that such crimes are the exception not the rule. Only one out of three violent crimes involve the use of a weapon (Bureau of Justice Statistics, 1993). Of all violent crimes 32 percent involved a weapon; in 9 percent of those cases a handgun was used, in 7 percent a knife, and in 6 percent a blunt object of some type. The typical violent crime does not involve a weapon of any type.

Not only do violent victimizations typically not involve weapons, but they typically do not involve injuries. When they do, the injuries are minor. In all violent victimizations less than 33 percent of the victims are injured, and only 4 percent suffer serious injury. Of those who are injured, 84 percent received bruises, cuts, or scratches; 1 percent received gunshot wounds; 4 percent received knife wounds, and 7 percent either suffered a broken bone or had teeth knocked out (Bureau of Justice Statistics, 1993). In summary, less than about 3 out of every 1,000 violent crime victims are shot, about 12 are wounded by a knife, and about 20 or so have broken bones or teeth knocked out. In addition, only 9 percent of all victims of violent crimes lost any time at all from work, and only 10 percent incurred medical expenses as a result of the crime (Bureau of Justice Statistics, 1993). By 1993 less than 1 in 4 violent crimes resulted in an injury and 70 percent of all violent crimes were attempted but not completed (BJS, 1995). Unlike the picture of crime presented by the media, politicians, and the police, the truth is that even in "violent" crimes very few people are injured—and even fewer are seriously injured.

Race and Crime

Finally, we turn to the issue of race and crime. Both crime reporting by the media and anti-crime railing by politicians and law-enforcement executives have played callously and cynically on a deeply ingrained racism in American culture. George Bush's Willie Horton ad was designed not just to raise the issue of crime but to link it with the offender most feared by white middle-class America. Similarly, tabloid media coverage of shootings of white tourists by young African American men at rest stops, gang attacks on innocent passersby in our cities, or acts of vigilantism by the Bernard Goetzes of the world against minority youth appeal to the same racist fears. The fact is, however, that interracial crime is very rare and interracial crime images can be dismissed as blatant and insidious appeals to the darkest parts of the American soul. Seventy-five percent of white crime victims are victimized by whites, and 85 percent of African-American crime victims are victimized by African Americans. In 80 percent of all violent crimes, the victims and offenders are of the same race (Bureau of Justice Statistics, 1993). Furthermore, in 1993 African Americans were almost twice as likely to become the victims of violent crime; persons living in households with income below $7,500 were over twice as likely to be victimized than those with incomes over $75,000 (BJS, 1995). Once again, lack of knowledge about crime statistics leave the public vulnerable to the most divisive myth. Attempts to link crime and race play to the audience's worst impulses.

CRIME AND PERCEPTION

Since crime, particularly serious crime, is and has been declining significantly, why is the fear of crime—accompanied by feelings of public punitiveness—increasing so dramatically? At least three factors appear to be responsible for the lack of congruence between the facts and public perception: the media and their reporting of crime; alarms raised by the law enforcement establishment; and the politicalization of crime.

The media seriously distort our view of crime and its dangers through their presentation of both news and entertainment programming. Tabloid television shows such as *Hard Copy* and *A Current Affair* present almost daily reports on some type of crime. The crimes they choose to feature are hardly the mundane, relatively unimportant crimes that make up the bulk of actual crime committed. After all, few viewers would stay tuned to watch a special segment on the theft of little Tommy's bicycle or the picking of Mr. Jones' pocket during his lunch break. But viewers will tune in for sensational murders, like those of Nicole Brown Simpson, Ronald Goldman, and the Menendez killings in California; for lurid details on the serial murder of a tourist at a Florida highway rest stop. Despite the fact that patricide among the privileged, serial murder, and rest stop killings of tourists are relatively rare events, they are emphasized and highlighted by these programs.

The exaggeration of the violent and the weird can be seen in both "straight" news programming and entertainment programming. The local 6 P.M. evening news predictably leads with a story about a murder committed in the course of a robbery—or even a robbery without a murder, as long as violence was threatened. The hundreds or thousands of normal, mundane crimes that occur daily in every city are scarcely mentioned. Entertainment shows such as *NYPD Blue, Matlock, Law and Order,* and even the somewhat more refined *Murder She Wrote* feature crimes of violence. Few people want to see Matlock vigorously defend a case of "personal larceny without contact" or Jessica Fletcher solve a troublesome case of misplaced luggage in Cabot Cove. A study by Ericson, Baranek and Chan (1989) discovered that crime takes up 20 percent of all local television news shows, 13 percent of all national news shows, and 25 percent of the column inches in newspapers. Beirne and Messerschmidt (1991) suggest that the media distort our images of crime in three primary ways. First, the intense coverage of crime in the media conveys the incorrect image that we are a society suffering an epidemic of violent crime. As they point out, murder constitutes only 0.2 percent of all crimes reported to the police, yet it occupies 25 percent of newspaper reports about crime. Second, the media create the impression, with the help of law enforcement agencies, that crime rates are continually increasing. Finally, the media downplay the amount of nonviolent crime, creating the false image that crime means acts of predatory violence. Simply put, the media, in an attempt to attract viewers and advertising dollars, play up the most atypical, violent, heinous crimes and downplay the recurrent dull crimes which make up the overwhelming majority of crimes committed in the United States.

The law enforcement establishment also has a pecuniary interest in portraying crime as a serious and growing threat. At the state and local level in the United States, there are about 17,500 police agencies, with 800,000 employees—and annual budgets in excess of $28 billion (Cole, 1995). Add to these the approximately 50 to 60 federal agencies employing almost 69,000 officers (BJS, 1994) with budgets in excess of $12 billion and you will find a large interest group for crime control issues. This interest group is even more impressive in size when the 13,000–15,000 courts in the United States are added and the $37 billion spent in the past two decades on prison construction is considered (Smolowe, 1994).

It is in the interests of police administrators, prison officials, judges and prosecutors to keep crime in the forefront of public debate. Enormous sums of money, millions of jobs, and bureaucratic survival depend on permanent concerns about crime. Year after year official statistics have been presented to increase public fear and downplay any decrease in criminal activity. Policy decisions and jurisdictional issues are also concerns for the criminal justice system in presenting crime as a major threat. For example, the "war on drugs" expanded the jurisdiction and police powers of many federal law enforcement agencies. The FBI, the keeper of crime statistics, was the primary beneficiary. Attempts to remove due process protections and to expand the scope of the legal code also depend on an active public interest in crime matters.

Finally, both the media and the criminal justice system find ready allies among those officeholders and office seekers who must court the public. Crime is a relatively easy issue. No one is for it; therefore being against it is a safe political issue. Exaggerating and distorting the amount and shape of the crime threat is standard fare for politicians. Democrats and conservative Republicans both compete to see who can spend the most money and appear the most punitive in putting together crime control legislation. Imagine justifying costly crime control packages by explaining that crime is less of a threat today than in 1973. It is not scientific proof which persuades, it is appeals to fear about serial killings, stalkers, child abductions, drive-by shootings, car-jackings, and violent predators. Supporting such measures will no doubt curry favor with the voting public; telling the truth could lead to premature retirement.

It appears that we have a warped and distorted view of crime in America. Whether it is the media, politicians, police—or a combination of all three—who are responsible, we have created a popular image of crime that is a myth. The American crime wave does not exist. Crime is decreasing and decreasing substantially. The prominent image fixed in the public mind, the "Typical Criminal," does not exist. Crime is committed primarily in social settings by unarmed people who are relatives, friends and acquaintances of their victims. The prototypical crime is also a myth. Most crime is minor in nature and content, and very little crime results in serious injury. We have either been duped or have duped ourselves.

CHAPTER 3

Criminal Law

3.1 DOROTHY E. ROBERTS

Unshackling Black Motherhood

American history is replete with accounts of instrumental and institutional racist policy and practice directed at the black population, and that same history is no less smattered with sexist policies and practices aimed at women. A historical accounting of American black women will illustrate their particularly egregious treatment at the hands of the white, male-dominated social structure. From the slave period through contemporary times black women in the United States have experienced an enhanced discrimination manifest in the intersection of blackness, femaleness, poverty, and motherhood. No research statistics appear more common or consistent than those to describe the typical urban black family as poor and single female–headed. The Moynihan Report of the 1960s went so far as to allege that the primary problem facing the black population in America is the deterioration of the black family and the emergence of the domineering black mother. Historically there has been a great deal of debate as to the propriety and quality of childrearing in nontraditional family structures. Remarkably, the controversy seems to wane when an alternative to the traditional nuclear structure is introduced or embraced by the white middle classes. Conversely, the controversy intensifies when the alternative structure appears to emanate from the lower and minority classes. In fact, any lifestyle originating within the lower echelons of American society is initially viewed as deviant, or at least held suspect, and rejected as characteristic of lower-class culture. Paradoxically, even those lifestyle alternatives that originate and are embraced within the middle classes are often viewed as less than desirable when adopted by the lower classes. It is apparent then, that lower-class and minority lifestyles are viewed as inherently contrary to the middle and upper classes, regardless of their origination or initial legitimacy. Subsequently, the moral entrepreneurs and other agencies of social control are quickly mobilized to counter such alternatives, particularly as they exist within the American black population.

Rutgers University School of Law professor Dorothy E. Roberts, in the selection that follows from "Unshackling Black Motherhood," *Michigan Law Review* (February 1997), presents a compelling thesis on the dynamics of instrumental and institutional racism directed at black motherhood. Within the context of prenatal drug use, namely crack cocaine, she examines the exceptionally harsh treatment of black mothers by numerous societal institutions, particularly the criminal justice, medical, and welfare communities. Roberts advances the idea that black motherhood, specifically, has been systematically degraded in an effort to ameliorate the prenatal drug use problem. She challenges the contention that the overrepresentation of black mothers, in the response to fetal abuse, is more a function of poverty and lower-class standing than of directed racism. Rather, she demonstrates that black mothers receive substantially more negative treatment by all agencies involved, net of the effects of social class. Drawing from the literature and with anecdotal evidence from a South Carolina experiment, the author illustrates the particularly brutal treatment black mothers received by the medical community and the criminal justice system, arguing that such treatment was more racist than it was classist. Roberts concludes that prior legal defense strategies to refrain from "playing the race card," as well intended as they may have been, were simply inadequate to properly address the demonstrably racist nature of the prenatal drug use issue. Rather, she advocates that the blatantly racist nature of the issue be straightforwardly introduced into future defense strategies.

Key Concept: black women's subordination

When stories about the prosecutions of women for using drugs during pregnancy first appeared in newspapers in 1989, I immediately suspected that most of the defendants were Black women. Charging someone with a crime for giving birth to a baby seemed to fit into the legacy of devaluing Black mothers. I was so sure of this intuition that I embarked on my first major law review article based on the premise that the prosecutions perpetuated Black women's subordination. My hunch turned out to be right: a memorandum prepared by the ACLU [American Civil Liberties Union] Reproductive Freedom Project documented cases brought against pregnant women as of October 1990 and revealed that thirty-two of fifty-two defendants were Black. By the middle of 1992, the number of prosecutions had increased to more than 160 in 24 states. About 75% were brought against women of color.

In *Punishing Drug Addicts Who Have Babies: Women of Color, Equality and the Right of Privacy,* I argued that the prosecutions could be understood and challenged only by looking at them from the standpoint of Black women. Although the prosecutions were part of an alarming trend toward greater state intervention into the lives of pregnant women in general, they also reflected a growing hostility toward poor Black mothers in particular. The debate on fetal rights, which had been waged extensively in law review articles and other scholarship, focused on balancing the state's interest in protecting the fetus from harm against the mother's interest in autonomy. My objective in that article was not to repeat these theoretical arguments, but to inject into the debate a perspective that had largely been overlooked. It seemed to me impossible to grasp the constitutional injury that the prosecutions inflicted without taking into consideration the perspective of the women most affected. Nor could we assess the state's justification for the prosecutions without uncovering their racial motivation.

Dorothy E.
Roberts

Taking race into account transformed the constitutional violation at issue. I argued that the problem with charging these women with fetal abuse was not that it constituted unwarranted governmental intervention into pregnant women's lifestyles—surely a losing argument considering the lifestyles of these defendants. Instead I reframed the issue: the prosecutions punished poor Black women for having babies. Critical to my argument was an examination of the historical devaluation of Black motherhood. Given this conceptualization of the issue and the historical backdrop, the real constitutional harm became clear: charging poor Black women with prenatal crimes violated their rights both to equal protection of the laws and to privacy by imposing an invidious governmental standard for childbearing. Adding the perspective of poor Black women yielded another advantage. It confirmed the importance of expanding the meaning of reproductive liberty beyond opposing state restrictions on abortion to include broader social justice concerns.

Most women charged with prenatal crimes are pressured into accepting plea bargains to avoid jail time. When defendants have appealed their convictions, however, they have been almost uniformly victorious. With only one recent exception, every appellate court to consider the issue, including the highest courts in several states, has invalidated criminal charges for drug use during pregnancy. Yet none of these courts has based its decision on the grounds that I argued were critical. Most decisions centered on the interpretation of the criminal statute in the indictment. These courts have held that the state's laws concerning child abuse, homicide, or drug distribution were not meant to cover a fetus or to punish prenatal drug exposure. The Supreme Court of Florida, for example, overturned Jennifer Johnson's conviction in 1992 on the ground that the state legislature did not intend "to use the word 'delivery' in the context of criminally prosecuting mothers for delivery of a controlled substance to a minor by way of the umbilical cord." Other courts rejected the prosecutions on constitutional grounds, finding that the state had violated the mothers' right to due process or to privacy. The defendants' race, however, has not played a role in the courts' analyses.

Thus, attorneys have successfully challenged the prosecutions of prenatal crimes in appellate courts without relying on arguments about the race of the defendants. But failing to contest society's devaluation of poor Black mothers still has negative consequences. Renegade prosecutors in a few states continue to press charges against poor Black women for exposing their babies to crack. Many crack-addicted mothers have lost custody of their babies following a single positive drug test. The continuing popular support for the notion of punishing crack-addicted mothers leaves open the possibility of a resurgence of prosecutions and the passage of punitive legislation. In this essay, I want to explore the strategies that lawyers have used on behalf of crack-addicted mothers to evaluate the importance of raising issues of race. Some lawyers and feminist scholars have tried to avoid the degrading mythology about Black mothers by focusing attention on issues other than racial discrimination and by emphasizing the violation of white, middle-class women's rights. I argue, however, that we should develop strategies to contest the negative images that undergird policies that penalize Black women's childbearing.

I. THE SOUTH CAROLINA EXPERIMENT

Despite the fact that most prosecutors renounce a punitive approach toward prenatal drug use, South Carolina continues to promote a prosecutorial campaign against pregnant crack addicts. The state bears the dubious distinction of having prosecuted the largest number of women for maternal drug use. Many of these cases arose from the collaboration of Charleston law enforcement officials and the Medical University of South Carolina (MUSC), a state hospital serving an indigent, minority population. In August 1989, Nurse Shirley Brown approached the local solicitor, Charles Condon, about the increase in crack use that she perceived among her pregnant patients. Solicitor Condon immediately held a series of meetings, inviting additional members of the MUSC staff, the police department, child protective services and the Charleston County Substance Abuse Commission, to develop a strategy for addressing the problem. The MUSC clinicians may have intended to help their patients, but larger law enforcement objectives soon overwhelmed the input of the staff. The approach turned toward pressuring pregnant patients who used drugs to get treatment by threatening them with criminal charges. As Condon expressed it: "We all agreed on one principle: We needed a program that used not only a carrot, but a real and very firm stick." Condon also pressed the position that neither the physician-patient privilege nor the Fourth Amendment prevented hospital staff members from reporting positive drug tests to the police.

Within two months MUSC instituted the "Interagency Policy on Cocaine Abuse in Pregnancy" ("Interagency Policy"), a series of internal memos that provided for nonconsensual drug testing of pregnant patients, reporting results to the police, and the use of arrest for drug and child abuse charges as punishment or intimidation. Although the program claimed "to ensure the appropriate management of patients abusing illegal drugs during pregnancy," its origin suggests that it was designed to supply Condon with defendants for his new prosecutorial crusade. The arrests had already begun by the time the hospital's board of directors officially approved the new policy. Hospital bioethicists later criticized the hasty process orchestrated by Condon for neglecting the careful internal deliberation one would expect of a program affecting patient care. Condon personally broadcast the new policy in televised public service announcements that advised pregnant women, "not only will you live with guilt, you could be arrested."

During the first several months, women were immediately arrested if they tested positive for crack at the time they gave birth. Then the Interagency Policy set up what Condon called an "amnesty" program: patients who tested positive for drugs were offered a chance to get treatment; if they refused or failed, they would be arrested. Patients who tested positive were handed two letters, usually by Nurse Shirley Brown: one notified them of their appointment with the substance abuse clinic; the other, from the solicitor, warned that "[i]f you fail to complete substance abuse counselling, fail to cooperate with the Department of Social Services in the placement of your child and services to protect that child, or if you fail to maintain clean urine specimens during your substance abuse rehabilitation, you will be arrested by the police and prosecuted by the Office of the Solicitor."

The policy offered no second chances. Women who tested positive for drugs a second time or who delivered a baby who tested positive were arrested and imprisoned. Depending on the stage of pregnancy, the mother was charged with drug possession, child neglect, or distribution of drugs to a minor. Uncooperative women were arrested based on a single positive test.

The Interagency Policy resulted in the arrests of forty-two patients, all but one of whom were Black. Disregarding the sanctity of the maternity ward, the arrests more closely resembled the conduct of the state in some totalitarian regime. Police arrested some patients within days or even hours of giving birth and hauled them to jail in handcuffs and leg shackles. The handcuffs were attached to a three-inch wide leather belt that was wrapped around their stomachs. Some women were still bleeding from the delivery. One new mother complained, and was told to sit on a towel when she arrived at the jail. Another reported that she was grabbed in a chokehold and shoved into detention.

At least one woman who was pregnant at the time of her arrest sat in a jail cell waiting to give birth. Lori Griffin was transported weekly from the jail to the hospital in handcuffs and leg irons for prenatal care. Three weeks after her arrest, she went into labor and was taken, still in handcuffs and shackles, to MUSC. Once at the hospital, Ms. Griffin was kept handcuffed to her bed during the entire delivery.

I opened *Punishing Drug Addicts Who Have Babies* with the recollection of an ex-slave about the method slave masters used to discipline their pregnant slaves while protecting the fetus from harm:

> A former slave named Lizzie Williams recounted the beating of pregnant slave women on a Mississippi cotton plantation: "I[']s seen nigger women dat was fixin' to be confined do somethin' de white folks didn't like. Dey [the white folks] would dig a hole in de ground just big 'nuff fo' her stomach, make her lie face down an whip her on de back to keep from hurtin' de child."

Thinking about an expectant Black mother chained to a belt around her swollen belly to protect her unborn child, I cannot help but recall this scene from

Black women's bondage. The sight of a pregnant Black woman bound in shackles is a modern-day reincarnation of the horrors of slavemasters' degrading treatment of their female chattel.

II. THE *WHITNER* SETBACK

In a dramatic reversal of the trend to overturn charges for prenatal drug use, the Supreme Court of South Carolina recently affirmed the legality of prosecuting pregnant crack addicts. The case involved twenty-eight-year-old Cornelia Whitner, who was arrested for "endangering the life of her unborn child" by smoking crack while pregnant. On the day of her hearing, Whitner met briefly in the hallway with her court-appointed attorney, Cheryl Aaron, for the first time. Aaron advised Whitner to plead guilty to the child neglect charges, promising to get her into a drug treatment program so that she could be reunited with her children. At the April 20, 1992, hearing before Judge Frank Eppes, Whitner pleaded for help for her drug problem. Aaron explained that her client was in a counseling program and had stayed off drugs since giving birth to her son, who was in good health. She requested that Whitner be placed in a residential treatment facility. Turning a deaf ear, Judge Eppes simply responded, "I think I'll just let her go to jail." He then sentenced Whitner to a startling eight-year prison term.

Whitner had been incarcerated for nineteen months before a lawyer from the local ACLU contacted her about challenging her conviction. Whitner's lawyers filed a petition for postconviction relief that claimed that the trial court lacked jurisdiction to accept a guilty plea for a nonexistent offence. They argued that the relevant criminal statute punished the unlawful neglect of a child, not a fetus. On November 22, 1993, Judge Larry Patterson invalidated the conviction and released Whitner from prison.

On July 15,1996, the South Carolina Supreme Court, in a three to two decision, reinstated Whitner's conviction, holding that a viable fetus is covered by the child abuse statute. The court based its conclusion on prior case law that recognized a viable fetus as a person. South Carolina courts allowed civil actions for the wrongful death of a fetus and had upheld a manslaughter conviction for the killing of a fetus. According to the court, these precedents supported its interpretation of the child abuse statute: "[I]t would be absurd to recognize the viable fetus as a person for purposes of homicide and wrongful death statutes but not for purposes of statutes proscribing child abuse." Moreover, punishing fetal abuse would further the statute's aim of preventing harm to children. The court reasoned that "[t]he consequences of abuse or neglect after birth often pale in comparison to those resulting from abuse suffered by the viable fetus before birth."

The *Whitner* holding opens the door for a new wave of prosecutions in South Carolina, as well as in other states that wish to follow its lead. Condon, who had been elected Attorney General in a landslide victory, declared: "This is a landmark, precedent-setting decision. . . . This decision is a triumph for all those who want to protect the children of South Carolina." As the state's chief law enforcement officer, Condon may have visions of replicating his Charleston experiment in other hospitals across South Carolina.

III. SHACKLING BLACK MOTHERHOOD

Not only did South Carolina law enforcement agents brutally degrade Black mothers and pregnant women at the Charleston hospital with little public outcry, but the state's highest court essentially sanctioned the indignity. How could judges ignore this blatant devaluation of Black motherhood? State officials repeatedly disclaim any racial motivation in the prosecutions, and courts routinely accept their disclaimer. Everyone continues to pretend that race has nothing to do with the punishment of these mothers.

The blatant racial impact of the prosecutions can be overlooked only because it results from an institutionalized system that selects Black women for prosecution and from a deeply embedded mythology about Black mothers. These two factors make the disproportionate prosecution of Black mothers seem fair and natural, and not the result of any invidious motivation. These factors also make it more difficult to challenge the prosecutions on the basis of race. As the Black poet Nikki Giovanni recently observed: "In some ways, the struggle is more difficult now. I'd rather take what we did—if we were killed or beaten, you knew you were fighting the system." Giovanni explained that the battle for racial justice is more complicated today than in the 1960s, because "racism is more sophisticated and insidious than segregated drinking fountains."

Prosecutors like Condon do not announce that they plan to single out poor Black women for prosecution. Rather, they rely on a process already in place that is practically guaranteed to bring these women to their attention. The methods the state uses to identify women who use drugs during pregnancy result in disproportionate reporting of poor Black women. The government's main source of information about prenatal drug use comes from hospital reports of positive infant toxicologies to child welfare authorities. This testing is implemented with greater frequency in hospitals serving poor minority communities. Private physicians who serve more affluent women are more likely to refrain from screening their patients, both because they have a financial stake in retaining their patients' business and securing referrals from them, and because they are socially more similar to their patients.

Hospitals administer drug tests in a manner that further discriminates against poor Black women. One common criterion triggering an infant toxicology screen is the mother's failure to obtain prenatal care, a factor that correlates strongly with race and income. Worse still, many hospitals have no formal screening procedures, and rely solely on the suspicions of health care professionals. This discretion allows doctors and hospital staff to perform tests based on their stereotyped assumptions about the identity of drug addicts. Women who smoke crack report being abused and degraded by hospital staff during the delivery. Their experiences suggest that staff often harbor a deep contempt for these women born at least partly of racial prejudice. A twenty-four-year-old woman from Brooklyn, "K," recounted a similar experience:

> Bad... they treat you bad.... That was like I had my daughter, when the nurse came, and I was having the stomach pain and my stomach was killing me. I kept callin and callin and callin. She just said you smokin that crack, you smoke that crack, you suffer.

Accordingly to court papers, Nurse Brown, the chief enforcer of the Charleston Interagency Policy, frequently expressed racist views about her Black patients to drug counselors and social workers, including her belief that most Black women should have their tubes tied and that birth control should be put in the drinking water in Black communities. It is not surprising that such nurses would turn their Black patients over to the police.

A study published in the prestigious *New England Journal of Medicine* discussed possible racial biases of health care professionals who interact with pregnant women. Researchers studied the results of toxicologic tests of pregnant women who received prenatal care in public health clinics and in private obstetrical offices in Pinellas County, Florida. The study found that little difference existed in the prevalence of substance abuse by pregnant women along either racial or economic lines, and that there was little significant difference between patients at public clinics and private offices. Despite similar rates of substance abuse, however, Black women were ten times more likely than whites to be reported to government authorities. Both public health facilities and private doctors were more inclined to turn in Black women than white women for using drugs while pregnant.

Just as important as this structural bias against Black women is the ideological bias against them. Prosecutors and judges are predisposed to punish Black crack addicts because of a popular image promoted by the media during the late 1980s and early 1990s. News of an astounding increase in maternal drug use broke in 1988 when the National Association for Perinatal Addiction Research and Education (NAPARE) published the results of a study of babies in hospitals across the country. NAPARE found that at least eleven percent of women admitted in labor in hospitals across the country would test positive for illegal drugs. In several hospitals, the proportion of drug-exposed infants was as high as twenty-five percent. Extrapolating these statistics to the population at large, some observers estimated that as many as 375,000 drug-exposed infants are born every year. This figure covered all drug exposure nationwide and did not break down the numbers based on the extent of drug use or its effects on the newborn.

The media parlayed the NAPARE report into a horrific tale of irreparable damage to hundreds of thousands of babies. A review of newspaper accounts of the drug exposure data reveals a stunning instance of journalistic excess. Although NAPARE's figures referred to numbers of infants exposed to, not harmed by, maternal drug use, the *Los Angeles Times* wrote that about 375,000 babies were "tainted by potentially fatal narcotics in the womb each year." The NAPARE figure did not indicate the extent of maternal drug use or its effects on the fetus. In fact, the nature of harm, if any, caused by prenatal drug use depends on a number of factors, including the type and amount of drugs ingested, the pregnant woman's overall health, and the baby's environment after birth. Some articles attributed all 375,000 cases to cocaine, although experts estimate that 50,000 to 100,000 newborns are exposed specifically to cocaine each year. In one editorial the figure ballooned to 550,000 babies who have "their fragile brains bombarded with the drug." *The Los Angeles Times* implied in a front-page story that crack was the only drug used by pregnant women, writing, "Crack was even responsible for the creation of an entirely new, and now leading, category of child abuse: exposure of babies to drugs during pregnancy." Of course, babies had been exposed prenatally to dangerous amounts of alcohol, prescription pills, and illicit drugs long before crack appeared in the 1980s.

The pregnant crack addict was portrayed as an irresponsible and selfish woman who put her love for crack above her love for her children. In news stories she was often represented by a prostitute, who sometimes traded sex for crack, violating every conceivable quality of a good mother. The chemical properties of crack were said to destroy the natural impulse to mother. "The most remarkable and hideous aspect of crack cocaine use seems to be the undermining of the maternal instinct," a nurse was quoted as observing about her patients. The pregnant crack addict, then, was the exact opposite of a mother: she was promiscuous, uncaring, and self-indulgent.

By focusing on maternal crack use, which is more prevalent in inner-city neighborhoods and stereotypically associated with Blacks, the media left the impression that the pregnant addict is typically a Black woman. Even more than a "metaphor for women's alienation from instinctual motherhood," the pregnant crack addict was the latest embodiment of the bad Black mother.

The monstrous crack-smoking mother was added to the iconography of depraved Black maternity, alongside the matriarch and the welfare queen. For centuries, a popular mythology has degraded Black women and portrayed them as less deserving of motherhood. Slave owners forced slave women to perform strenuous labor that contradicted the Victorian female roles prevalent in the dominant white society. One of the most prevalent images of slave women was the character of Jezebel, a woman governed by her sexual desires, which legitimated white men's sexual abuse of Black women. The stereotype of Black women as sexually promiscuous helped to perpetuate their devaluation as mothers.

This devaluation of Black motherhood has been reinforced by stereotypes that blame Black mothers for the problems of the Black family, such as the myth of the Black matriarch—the domineering female head of the Black family. White sociologists have held Black matriarchs responsible for the disintegration of the Black family and the consequent failure of Black people to achieve success in America. Daniel Patrick Moynihan popularized this theory in his 1965 report, *The Negro Family: The Case for National Action,* which claimed, "At the heart of the deterioration of the fabric of Negro society is the deterioration of the Negro family." Moynihan blamed domineering Black mothers for the demise of their families, arguing that "the Negro community has been forced into a matriarchal structure which, because it is so out of line with the rest of the American society, seriously retards the progress of the group as a whole."

The myth of the Black Jezebel has been supplemented by the contemporary image of the lazy welfare mother who breeds children at the expense of taxpayers in order to increase the amount of her welfare check. This view of Black motherhood provides the rationale for society's restrictions on Black female fertility. It is this image of the undeserving Black mother that also ultimately underlies the government's choice to punish crack-addicted women.

The frightening portrait of diabolical pregnant crack addicts and irreparably damaged crack babies was based on data that have drawn criticism within the scientific community. The data on the extent and severity of crack's impact on babies are highly controversial. At the inception of the crisis numerous medical journals reported that babies born to crack-addicted mothers suffered a variety of medical, developmental, and behavioral problems. More recent analyses, however, have isolated the methodological flaws of these earlier studies.

The initial results were made unreliable by the lack of controls and the selection of poor, inner-city subjects at high risk for unhealthy pregnancies. Maternal crack use often contributes to underweight and premature births. This fact alone is reason for concern. But many of the problems seen in crack-exposed babies are just as likely to have been caused by other risk factors associated with their mothers' crack use, such as malnutrition, cigarettes, alcohol, physical abuse, and inadequate health care. Researchers cannot determine authoritatively which of this array of hazards actually caused the terrible outcomes they originally attributed to crack, or the percentage of infants exposed to crack in the womb who actually experience these consequences. In addition, the claim that prenatal crack use causes irreparable neurological damage leading to behavioral problems has not been fully substantiated. An article by a team of research physicians concluded that "available evidence from the newborn period is far too slim and fragmented to allow any clear predictions about the effects of intrauterine exposure to cocaine on the course and outcome of child growth and development."

The medical community's one-sided attention to studies showing detrimental results from cocaine exposure added to the public's misperception of the risks of maternal crack use. For a long time, journals tended to accept for publication only studies that supported the dominant view of fetal harm. Research that reported no adverse effects was published with less frequency, even though it was often more reliable.

The point is not that crack use during pregnancy is safe, but that the media exaggerated the extent and nature of the harm it causes. News reports erroneously suggested, moreover, that the problem of maternal drug use was confined to the Black community. A public health crisis that cuts across racial and economic lines was transformed into an example of Black mother's depravity that warranted harsh punishment. Why hasn't the media focused as much attention on the harmful consequences of alcohol abuse or cigarette smoking during pregnancy, or the widespread devastation that Black infants suffer as a result of poverty? In *Punishing Drug Addicts Who Have Babies,* I suggested an answer:

> [T]he prosecution of crack-addicted mothers diverts public attention from social ills such as poverty, racism, and a misguided national health policy and implies

instead that shamefully high Black infant death rates are caused by the bad acts of individual mothers. Poor Black mothers thus become the scapegoats for the causes of the Black community's ill health. Punishing them assuages any guilt the nation might feel at the plight of an underclass with infant mortality at rates higher than those in some less developed countries. Making criminals of Black mothers apparently helps to relieve the nation of the burden of creating a health care system that ensures healthy babies for all its citizens.

Additional medical studies demonstrate the perversity of a punitive approach. Some researchers have found that the harmful effects of prenatal crack exposure may be temporary and treatable. A Northwestern University study of pregnant cocaine addicts, for example, found that "comprehensive prenatal care may improve [the] outcome in pregnancies complicated by cocaine abuse."

Research has also discovered dramatic differences in the effects of maternal alcohol abuse depending on the mother's socioeconomic status. Heavy drinking during pregnancy can cause fetal alcohol syndrome, characterized by serious physical malformations and mental deficiencies. Although all women in a study drank at the same rate, the children born to low-income women had a 70.9% rate of fetal alcohol syndrome, compared to a 4.5% rate for those of upper-income women. The main reason for this disparity was the nutrition of the pregnant women. While the wealthier women ate a regular, balanced diet, the poorer women had sporadic, unhealthy meals. Admittedly, crack is not good for anyone, and we need effective policies to stem crack use by pregnant women. Yet these studies about fetal alcohol syndrome and prenatal crack exposure suggest that crack's harmful consequences for babies may be minimized, or even prevented, by ensuring proper health care and nutrition for drug-dependent mothers. The best approach for improving the health of crack-exposed infants, then, is to improve the health of their mothers by ensuring their access to health care and drug treatment services. Yet prosecuting crack-addicted mothers does just the opposite: it drives these women away from these services out of fear of being reported to law enforcement authorities. This result reinforces the conclusion that punitive policies are based on resentment toward Black mothers, rather than on a real concern for the health of their children.

The medical profession's new information regarding the risks of prenatal crack exposure has had little impact on the public's perception of the "epidemic." The image of the crack baby—trembling in a tiny hospital bed, permanently brain damaged, and on his way to becoming a parasitic criminal —seems indelibly etched in the American psyche. It will be hard to convince most Americans that the caricature of the crack baby rests on hotly contested data.

IV. STRATEGIES FOR UNSHACKLING BLACK MOTHERHOOD

Given the mountain of structural and ideological hurdles that pregnant crack addicts must surmount, their attorneys have a difficult task in presenting them as sympathetic parties. One strategy in opposing a punitive approach to prenatal drug use is to divert attention away from these women and the devaluing racial images that degrade them.

A. Diverting Attention from Race

Attorneys and scholars have suggested three alternative issues to replace attention to the racial images that make their clients so unpopular—concern for the health of the babies exposed to prenatal drug use, the potential expansion of state interference in pregnant women's conduct, and claims of middle-class white women who have been prosecuted for using drugs during pregnancy.

1. Concern for Babies' Health. One of the greatest assets on the defendants' side is the opinion of major medical and public health organizations about the health risks created by the prosecution of substance-abusing mothers. Most leading medical and public health organizations in the country have come out in opposition to the prosecutions for this very reason. In 1990, the American Medical Association issued a detailed report on legal interventions during pregnancy, stating its concern that "physicians' knowledge of substance abuse . . . could result in a jail sentence rather than proper medical treatment." It concluded that "criminal penalties may exacerbate the harm done to fetal health by deterring pregnant substance abusers from obtaining help or care from either the health or public welfare professions, the very people who are best able to prevent future abuse." According to the American Academy of Pediatrics, "[p]unitive measures taken toward pregnant women, such as criminal prosecution and incarceration, have no proven benefits for infant health." The American College of Obstetricians and Gynecologists, the March of Dimes, the National Council on Alcoholism and Drug Dependence, and other groups have also issued policy statements denouncing the criminalization of maternal drug use.

Attorneys have taken advantage of this support by assembling an impressive array of medical experts at trial and amicus briefs on appeal. In the *Whitner* appeal, for example, major medical, public health, and women's organizations, including the American Medical Association and its South Carolina affiliate, the American Public Health Association, the National Council on Alcoholism and Drug Dependence, and NOW Legal Defense and Education Fund, joined in amicus briefs opposing prosecution of women for prenatal drug use.

Lynn Paltrow, Director of Special Litigation at the Center for Reproductive Law and Policy ("the Center") and the leading advocate for women charged with prenatal crimes, has described the focus on the prosecutions' medical hazards as a way of diverting attention from her unpopular clients. A lengthy article in *The Los Angeles Times Magazine* discussed Paltrow's rationale:

> [Paltrow] knows that, as impressive as the intellectual arguments might be in favor of women's reproductive rights, they pale for many in the face of a sickly newborn twitching from a cocaine rush. She knows she'd lose support, even among those committed to women's rights, if people felt forced to choose between pregnant substance abusers and their babies.

The medical community's policy statements provide Paltrow with a way to avoid this perilous choice. "Even if you care only about the baby, even if you don't give a damn about the mother, you should still oppose Charleston's policy," Paltrow finds herself able to argue.

According to this view, a strategy that seeks to avoid the disparaging images of poor Black mothers is more likely to prevail than one that attempts to discredit them.

2. The Parade of Horribles.   A second avoidance tactic is to steer attention to more sympathetic middle-class white women. A common criticism of the prosecution of drug-addicted mothers is that the imposition of maternal duties will lead to punishment for less egregious conduct. Commentators have predicted government penalties for cigarette smoking, consumption of alcohol, strenuous physical activity, and failure to follow a doctor's orders.

If harm to a viable fetus constitutes child abuse, as the *Whitner* court held, then an endless panoply of activities could make pregnant women guilty of a crime. After the *Whitner* decision, Lynn Paltrow pointed out that:

> There are not enough jail cells in South Carolina to hold the pregnant women who have a drug problem, drink a glass of wine with dinner, smoke cigarettes... or decide to go to work despite their doctor's advice that they should stay in bed. Thousands of women are now child neglecters.

I concur in the objective of demonstrating that the prosecution of pregnant crack addicts should be the concern of all women. It may be a more effective tactic to convince affluent women that such government policies also jeopardize their lifestyles. Although valid, this argument tends to ignore the reality of poor Black women who are currently abused by punitive policies. The reference to a parade of horribles to criticize the fetal rights doctrine often belittles the significance of current government action. It seems to imply that the prosecution of Black crack addicts is not enough to generate concern and that we must postulate the prosecution of white middle-class women in order for the challenge to be meaningful.

In fact, it is very unlikely that South Carolina will pursue thousands of pregnant women on child neglect charges. It is hard to imagine police raiding private hospitals and hauling away middle-class women for fetal abuse. Instead, the state will escalate its crusade against the women it has prosecuted in the past—poor Black women who smoke crack.

3. Relying on White Women to Claims.   Feminist strategists have also suggested that challenging the charges brought against white drug users will benefit Black defendants. In her insightful book, *At Women's Expense: State Power and the Politics of Fetal Rights,* Cynthia Daniels stresses the strategic advantages of connecting the charges brought against Black and white middle-class drug users:

> While the threat of prosecution is not shared equally by women of different races and classes, it is critically important to see that the threat is still shared by all women: no woman is exempt from the threat to self-sovereignty posed by the idea of fetal rights. The successful prosecution of a poor black woman for fetal drug abuse has set legal, political, and social precedents that have been used to prosecute white women of privilege. When a prosecutor in Michigan was confronted with allegations that he was targeting only poor black women addicted to crack, he brought similar charges against Kim Hardy, a white woman lawyer who was addicted to cocaine.
>
> This strategy can have unintended results, however. The cultural, economic, and political power that women of privilege use to resist attempts to prosecute them—or to force them to have surgery, or to keep them out of good-paying jobs —can result in critical precedents for the defense of poor women's rights as well. Kim Hardy, for instance, defended herself successfully in court; the precedent set by her case can now be used to defend women of lesser economic means. . . .
>
> The disproportionate privilege of some women, rather than hopelessly dividing rich from poor or white women from women of color, can be used to defend the rights of all women.

This view, while recognizing the special injury to women of color, also proposes a strategy of challenging governmental intrusion in women's reproductive decisions by demonstrating how they thwart the liberties of middle-class women. Again, the rationale is that calling attention to the harm to privileged women is more likely to generate change than decrying the harm to poor minority women. It is based on the hope that the benefit of establishing a strong theory of reproductive liberty for middle-class white women will trickle down to their poor, less privileged sisters.

But this strategy also has limited potential for liberating Black women. The restraints on Black women's reproductive freedom have trickled up to white women. Protections afforded white middle-class women, on the other hand, are often withheld from Black women. Medical and social experiments are tested on the bodies of Black women first before they are imposed on white women. Norplant, for example, was developed to curtail the fertility of poor Third-World women, and then was marketed to white women in this country. As Daniels recognizes, the prosecution of Black women for smoking crack during pregnancy has set a precedent for regulating the conduct of pregnant women in the middle-class. Welfare "family caps" gained popularity as a means of reducing the numbers of Black children on public assistance, but they will throw thousands of white children into poverty. At the same time, the ideology that devalues Black mothers and perpetuates a racial division among women continues to thwart the universal application of gains achieved by white, professional women. Theories of reproductive freedom must start with the lives of the women at the bottom, not at the top.

*Dorothy E.
Roberts*

After winning a number of state court victories, Lynn Paltrow decided to take the offensive. In October 1993, the Center filed in federal district court a class action lawsuit against the City of Charleston and MUSC on behalf of two Black women who had been jailed under the Interagency Policy. The plaintiffs demanded three million dollars for violations of a number of constitutional guarantees, including the right to privacy in medical information, the right to refuse medical treatment, the right to pro-create, and the right to equal protection of the laws.

The plaintiffs' papers identify no less than five discrete aspects of the policy that have a racially discriminatory impact:

> (1) the choice to apply the Policy only at MUSC where the patient population is disproportionately African American by comparison with the community at large; (2) the choice to apply the policy within MUSC, only to patients of the obstetrics clinic where the patient population is even more disproportionately African American, even by comparison with MUSC as a whole; (3) the choice not to test babies or their mothers treated at MUSC but born at other hospitals in Charleston, where a greater proportion of the patient population was white; (4) the choice to use non-medically indicated criteria for testing, including failure to obtain prenatal care, which arose disproportionately in the African-American community; and (5) the choice to arrest only for the use of cocaine, a drug that defendants concede is used disproportionately by African American women.

The response to the lawsuit demonstrates the strength of derogatory images about Black mothers. Despite the overwhelming evidence that the policy was intended to punish Black women alone, South Carolina officials dismissed the race discrimination claim. Condon tried to explain away the program's blatant racial targeting as the innocent result of demographics. He conceded that "[i]t is true that most of the women treated were black. The hospital serves a primarily indigent population, and most of the patient population is black." Condon did not believe he had to explain why he had singled out MUSC as the lone site for the punitive program. Surely hospitals with a white clientele also had pregnant patients who abused drugs. But the image of the pregnant crack addict justified in many people's minds this disparate treatment. Federal Judge C. Weston Houck refused to halt the program pending trial, explaining that "the public is concerned about children who, through no fault of their own ... are born addicted."

An editorial in Denver's *Rocky Mountain News* applauded Houck's decision and made light of the allegations of racial discrimination. "[T]he hospital serves mostly black clients, so naturally most participants were black. And the center talked as though black junkies were being harmed rather than weaned from a hellish habit. A federal judge dismissed the suit for the hogwash it was." The *CBS Evening News* presented a similar view on a 1994 *Eye on America* segment on the South Carolina policy. Co-anchor Connie Chung set the stage by framing the policy as an answer to the "national tragedy" of cocaine use during pregnancy: "Every day in America thousands of pregnant women take cocaine, endangering the health of their children. Now one state is trying to stop women from doing that by threatening to throw them in jail." Correspondent Jacqueline Adams reported that "nurse Shirley Brown says race has nothing to do with it. She believes cocaine is so powerful, mothers need the threat of jail before they'll change their ways."

Paltrow was also afraid that the discriminatory intent requirement would make it hard to establish an equal protection claim. She nevertheless believed that alleging racial bias would bolster the other claims: "[E]ven if the race discrimination claim is not successful, bringing the racially discriminatory pattern to the court's attention in the main or an amicus brief may sensitize the court and create additional pressure to dismiss the charges on the other grounds presented. I believe that there are additional reasons to focus on the defendants' race rather than avoid it."

1. Telling the Whole Story. The diversionary strategy might be worth the neglect of Black women's particular injuries if it presented the only feasible route to victory. Yet this tactic has other disadvantages that weaken its power to challenge policies that devalue Black childbearing. By diverting attention from race, this strategy fails to connect numerous policies that degrade Black women's procreation. In addition to the prosecutions, for example, lawmakers across the country have been considering schemes to distribute Norplant to poor women, as well as measures that penalize welfare mothers for having additional children. Viewed separately, these developments appear to be isolated policies that can be justified by some neutral government objective. When all are connected by the race of the women most affected, a clear and horrible pattern emerges.

Lynn Paltrow recently stated, " 'for the first time in American history . . . what a pregnant woman does to her own body becomes a matter for the juries and the court.' " Paltrow is correct that the criminal regulation of pregnancy that occurs today is in some ways unprecedented. Yet it continues the legacy of the degradation of Black motherhood. A pregnant slave woman's body was subject to legal fiat centuries ago because the fetus she was carrying already belonged to her master. Over the course of this century, government policies have regulated Black women's reproductive decisionmaking based on the theory that Black childbearing causes social problems. Although the prosecution of women for prenatal crimes is relatively recent, it should be considered in conjunction with the sterilization of Black welfare mothers during the 1970s and the promotion of Norplant as a solution to Black poverty.

2. Telling Details About Black Women's Lives. I recently heard on a radio program portions of the audio-taped diary of a Mexican teenager who had migrated across the Rio Grande River into Texas. One day as he was looking at the river he saw the body of a dead man who looked Mexican floating downstream. The youth, breathing heavily and noticeably shaken by the scene, commented into his tape recorder that he was thinking about the man's family back in Mexico. This dead man, he thought, was probably the father of a poor family that was counting on him for their sustenance. It appeared that he had tried to forge the river in search of work so that he could send money back to them. How would they learn about his awful fate? How would his family survive without him? As the teenager told the story, the man in the river was transformed from the popular image of a "wetback" trying to sneak illegally into the United States into a hero who valiantly had risked his life for the sake of his family. The program impressed upon me how telling a story from a different perspective changes the entire meaning of a set of events.

Although the image of the monstrous crack-addicted mother is difficult to eradicate, it will be hard to abolish the policies that regulate Black women's fertility without exposing the image's fallacies. Describing the details of these women's lives may help. Crystal Ferguson, for example, was arrested for failing to comply with Nurse Brown's order to enter a two-week residential drug-rehabilitation program. Her arrest might appear to be justified without knowing the circumstances that led to her refusal. Ferguson requested an outpatient referral because she had no one to care for her two sons at home and the two-week program provided no childcare. Ferguson explained in an interview that she made every effort to enroll in the program, but was thwarted by circumstances beyond her control:

> I saw the situation my kids were in. There was no one to take care of them. Someone had stolen our food stamps and my unemployment check while I was at the hospital. There was no way I was going to leave my children for two weeks, knowing the environment they were in.

3. Highlighting the Abuse of Black Women's Bodies. The Center also attacked the South Carolina policy by filing a complaint with the National Institutes of Health alleging that the Interagency Policy constituted research on human subjects, which MUSC had been conducting without federally mandated review and approval. It argued that the hospital had embarked on an experiment designed to test the hypothesis that threats of incarceration would stop pregnant women from taking drugs and improve fetal health. Yet MUSC had never taken the required precautions to ensure that patients were adequately protected; indeed, it had surreptitiously collected confidential information about them and given it to the police. The strategy proved effective: the NIH agreed that MUSC had violated the requirements for human experimentation. In October 1994, five years after the policy's inception, MUSC dropped the program as part of a settlement agreement with the Department of Health and Human Services, which had commenced its own investigation of possible civil rights violations. Under threat of losing millions of dollars in federal funding, the hospital halted its joint venture with the solicitor's office and the police.

One advantage of the complaint was that it made the Black mothers claimants rather than defendants. Instead of defending against charges of criminality, they affirmatively demanded an end to the hospital's abusive practices. Instead of fending off a host of negative images, claimants can accuse the government of complicity in a legacy of medical experimentation on the bodies of Black women without their consent.

In past centuries, doctors experimented on slave women before practicing new surgical procedures on white women. Marion Sims, for example, developed gynecological surgery in the nineteenth century by performing countless operations, without anesthesia, on female slaves purchased expressly for his experiments. In the 1970s, doctors coerced hundreds of thousands of Black women into agreeing to sterilization by conditioning medical services on consent to the operation. More recently, a survey published in 1984 found that 13,000 Black women in Maryland were screened for sickle-cell anemia without their consent or the benefit of adequate counseling. Doctors have also been more willing to override Black patients' autonomy by performing forced medical treatment to benefit the fetus. A national survey published in 1987 in the *New England Journal of Medicine* discovered twenty-one cases in which court orders for cesarean sections were sought, and petitions were granted in eighteen of these cases. Eighty-one percent of the women involved were women of color; all were treated in a teaching-hospital clinic or were receiving public assistance.

Given the durability of disparaging images of Black mothers, particularly those who smoke crack, it is understandable that lawyers would search for ways to avoid these images altogether. One strategy, then, is to try to make judges forget that the prosecutions of prenatal crimes are targeted primarily at crack-addicted mothers. But I believe that leaving these images unchallenged will only help to perpetuate Black mothers' degradation. A better approach is to uproot and contest the mythology that propels policies that penalize Black women's childbearing. The medical risks of punitive policies and their potential threat to all women only enhance an argument that these policies perpetuate Black women's subordination. The prosecutions are based in part on a woman's pregnancy and not on her drug use alone. The legal rationale underlying the criminal charges depends on harm to the fetus rather than the illegality of drug use. Prosecutors charge these defendants with crimes such as child abuse and distribution of drugs to a minor that only pregnant drug users could commit. Moreover, pregnant women receive harsher sentences than drug using men or women who are not pregnant. Because a pregnant addict can avoid prosecution by having an abortion, it is her decision to carry her pregnancy to term that is penalized.

3.2 MICHAEL W. LYNCH

Enforcing "Statutory Rape"?

An acute problem facing American families is the high rate of unmarried and teenage parenthood. U.S. society has one of the highest rates of births to unmarried women among industrial nations. In California alone there are 60,000 teenage pregnancies every year, with about 35,000 involving 18- and 19-year-old girls. Nationally, nearly one-third of all births are to out-of-wedlock teenage mothers who are disproportionately poor, black, Latino, and American Indian. Undoubtedly, unmarried and teenage parenthood constitutes a major societal problem confronting American families because of the dreadful outcomes that are directly associated with unmarried and teenage parenthood. For example, nearly two-thirds of all children under the age of six who live in female-headed families in the United States live in poverty. As a result, unmarried and teenage parents are often unable to get proper prenatal and postnatal care for their children.

In the first study to measure age differences in sexual relationships of girls age 18 or younger, the New York–based Alan Guttmacher Institute recently found that age-imbalanced relationships have adverse consequences for young girls. Unmarried girls with older partners are nearly four times more likely to become pregnant than girls with partners who are younger or no more than two years older. Nearly 70 percent of girls sexually involved with partners six or more years older become pregnant, while about 18 percent of girls sexually involved with men younger to two years older become pregnant. But girls sexually involved with men closer to their own age are far more likely to have abortions than girls sexually involved with older partners. About 7 percent of girls under the age of 18 have sexual partners that are 6 or more years older. Historically, state governments have attempted to control teenage pregnancy by enacting and enforcing statutory-rape laws whereby older men who engage in sexual relations with teenage girls face incarceration. But, according to Michael W. Lynch, the Washington editor of *Reason* magazine, in the following selection from "Enforcing 'Statutory Rape'?" *The Public Interest* (Summer 1998), although statutory-rape laws have not been diligently enforced in the past, where state legislators, jurists, and law enforcement choose to draw the line between criminal and noncriminal sexual relations among teenage girls and older men remains an inherently problematic and controversial moral issue.

Key Concept: statutory-rape laws, unmarried parenthood, and teenage pregnancy

When I was growing up, there was a saying, 'Sixteen will get you 20,'" remembers Eloise Anderson, director of California's Department of Social Services. "Sixteen" is a girl's age; "20" is the number of years an adult male would spend in prison if he had sex with her. For years, statutory-rape laws languished in disuse. But recent studies show that a significant proportion of teens are impregnated by adult men, prompting politicians to once again apply such laws, which remain on the books in all 50 states. At the federal level, last year's welfare-reform law called on states and localities to "aggressively enforce statutory-rape laws."

In the Golden State, Governor Pete Wilson created a program to do just that. Since its start in 1995, California's Statutory Rape Vertical Prosecution Program, which provides grants to counties to prosecute statutory rape, has convicted more than 1,454 offenders, with 5,000 more under investigation. The program is netting few teenage lovers. According to Michael Carrington, who ran the program until recently, the typical scenario involves a 13-year-old mother and her 25-year-old male partner. Some counties won't even prosecute statutory-rape cases unless there is a five-year age gap between partners. One such county is San Diego where, after a year and a half of prosecution, the average male offender is 25.7 years old; the average girl, 14.4 years.

Yet, in the Washington policy circles where teen pregnancy is studied, such programs have had a very cool reception. One reason for this is ideological. Liberals instinctively dislike the idea of using criminal law to solve social problems. And conservatives fear that an overreaching state, fueled by exaggerated media reports, will prosecute people for victimless crimes. Meanwhile, so-called children's advocates amass data, reinterpret studies, and challenge the assumptions behind efforts to punish adults who impregnate young girls. They are campaigning to convince policy makers and the public that applying these rape laws won't reduce teen pregnancy. By such efforts, some valid assertions have been made, but also some statistical sleight of hand.

YOUNG FATHERS, YOUNGER MOTHERS

Beginning in the mid 1980s, researchers began uncovering data that undermined the assumption behind teen sexuality programs, that teen pregnancies were the unintended consequences of sex between teenagers. In 1989, Family Planning Perspectives, the peer-reviewed journal of the Alan Guttmacher Institute which specializes in fertility issues, published an article that focused on the partners of teen mothers in Baltimore. While the article, "Fathers of Children Born to Young Urban Mothers," found that most partners of teen mothers were under 20, it did find evidence of an age gap. "On average, the fathers of all infants born to white teenage women were four years older than were the mothers, and those of infants born to black teenage mothers were 2–3 years older," the study reported. Such an age gap isn't shocking, considering that it is customary for women to date and marry slightly older men. But later research revealed that the two- to three-year average underestimated the age differences for the youngest girls.

In 1992 and 1993, U.C.-Irvine graduate student Mike Males published a series of studies in scholarly journals that showed significant age differences between these unwed, underage mothers and the fathers of their children. In 1996, an article in the *American Journal of Public Health*, "The Ages of Fathers in California Adolescent Births, 1993," pretty much shattered the assumption that teens were impregnating teens. Examining California data, Males and his colleague Kenneth Chew reported that "adult post-school men father two thirds of the infants born to school-age mothers and average 4.2 years older than the senior-high mothers and 6.7 years older than the junior-high mothers." More alarmingly, they found that the younger the girl, the wider the age gap. Roughly half of the babies born to 15-year-old mothers were fathered by adult men no longer in school. In addition, a 1995 article in *Family Planning Perspectives*, "How Old are U.S. Fathers?" found an average age gap of four years between mothers aged 15 to 17 and their partners.

Such data effectively refuted the notion that girls 15 and younger were pregnant because their male classmates didn't have easy access to condoms. Earlier studies showed that teenage mothers with much older partners are often victims of sexual assault as children. "The possibility that such early childbearing represents an extension of rape or sexual abuse by male perpetrators averaging one to two decades older remains a serious question," Males and Chew wrote.

PLAYING BOTH SIDES

The New York-based Alan Guttmacher Institute plays prominent roles on both sides of the debate over teen pregnancy. Its 1995 journal article, "How Old are U.S. Fathers?" which first noted the substantial age gap between teenage mothers and their partners, was written by two of its in-house researchers, David Landry and Jacqueline Darroch Forrest. "Half of the fathers of babies born to women aged 15–17 were 20 years of age or older," they wrote. "On average, 15–17 year-old mothers were four years younger than their baby's father." Landry and Forrest concluded that "the mean age difference shows generally that the younger the mother is, the greater the age difference between her and her partner." They warned that "this type of age difference suggests, at the least, very different levels of life experience and power, and brings into question issues of pressure and abuse." They also pointed out that since two-thirds of babies born to mothers aged 15 to 17 are fathered by adult men, "some of the assumptions underlying many of the programs and policies aimed at reducing teenage pregnancy and childbearing are not correct."

Landry and Forrest's study was fact based, containing little of what can be interpreted as political spin. Yet looking back, it is clear that others at the Guttmacher Institute and their allies in the field of teen-pregnancy prevention originally welcomed these data as a justification for expanded government programs—programs that would provide outreach to these disenfranchised and misguided men who were impregnating young girls. What they got out of a Republican-dominated Congress and Republican-dominated statehouses, however, was stepped-up emphasis on putting such men in jail. Delaware, Florida, Georgia, and California recently revived efforts to enforce statutory-rape laws. Lawmakers in other states, including Pennsylvania and Texas, are pushing proposals to do so.

It was the empirical findings on pregnant minors with older partners that reinvigorated statutory-rape-law enforcement. In order to arrest the states' rush to the courts, it became imperative for Landry and Forrest's colleagues at the Guttmacher Institute, and their political allies elsewhere, to discredit these statistics. In the spring of 1997, a group of Urban Institute researchers published an article in the *Guttmacher Institute's Family Planning Perspectives* to recast the data. In "Age Differences Between Minors Who Give Birth and Their Adult Partners," the authors, Laura Duberstein Lindberg, Freya L. Sonenstein, Leighton Ku, and Gladys Martinez, note that there is a big difference between a 19- or even an 18-year-old having a baby with a 20- or 21-year-old man and a 14-year-old having a baby with the same man.

"While a 25-year-old man fathering a child with a 15-year-old would probably meet with social disapproval," Lindberg et al. argue, "the same might not be true for a couple consisting of a 21-year-old and an 18-year-old, particularly if they were married." They then note that women aged 18 to 19 account for nearly two-thirds of teen pregnancies (62 percent), and these pregnancies cannot be the result of statutory rape, even if the father was an adult. As a result, statutory-rape laws can affect only a bit more than one-third of all teenage births. Of the remaining 38 percent, Lindberg et al. report that roughly 21 percent meet the definition for statutory rape, which is typically a minor girl at least five years younger than her partner.

MOTHERHOOD AND THE NEW MATH

Lindberg and company's main empirical conclusion, which has been amplified in another study, is that "overall, among births to 15–19-year-olds in 1988, only 8% involved unmarried women aged 15–17 and men who were at least five years older." From this, the authors derive a major policy conclusion:

New state and federal initiatives that emphasize the vigorous enforcement of statutory-rape laws are unlikely to be the magic bullet to reduce rates of adolescent childbearing, since the number of births that result from acts covered by such laws is small. Policymakers need to pay attention to broader means of reducing teenage childbearing, such as sexuality education, youth development and contraceptive services.

Even if the 8 percent figure is an accurate presentation of the problem, one appropriate question might still be, So what? "Why wouldn't we be concerned about just one child who was involved in this type of relationship?" asks California's Anderson, referring to the girls in the 15- to 17-year-old range. "It doesn't matter to us if there is one or a million. For us, the issue is that the guy is breaking the law, [the mother] is powerless, and the outcome of this relationship is detrimental to society."

But, in fact, the 8 percent finding misses the mark by a factor of nearly three. Lindberg et al. produced this low number by excluding the partners of mothers aged 18 to 19 from their calculations, on the reasonable ground that these men cannot be prosecuted for statutory rape. But then, they include these same 18- to 19-year-old women in the pool when calculating what percentage of babies born to teenage mothers have partners at least five years older. Thus 62 percent of the fathers are removed from the numerator while their partners are included in the denominator. "When it is convenient to put them in the equation to minimize the problem of older males, they put them in the equation," says U.C.-Irvine's Mike Males. "When it is inconvenient, they take them out. They have generated a soundbite figure, the 8 percent, that is the least justified, but they are making it the most prominent."

A more honest approach would focus on the relevant group: mothers aged 17 and under. (Actually, since the age of consent is 16 in many states, girls under 16 would be the relevant pool. But the data, in their present form, are not aggregated in a way that would allow this analysis.) If you pull out all the adults, and even the married minors, Lindberg et al.'s data show that 21 percent of babies born to minor girls—an astonishing one in five—were fathered by men at least five years older than the mothers. Deviating little from the previous studies, Lindberg et al. also found that the "youngest mothers in the sample were the most likely to have a partner five or more years older." Four in 10 babies born to 15-year-old girls were fathered by a man who was at least 20 years old.

In June 1997, these findings made their way into a summary report released by the privately funded National Campaign to Prevent Teen Pregnancy, a Clinton-inspired effort to reduce teen pregnancy by one-third by 2005. The report, "Not Just For Girls: Involving Boys and Men in Teen Pregnancy Prevention," was written by Theodora Ooms, a researcher at the Family Impact Seminar, a Washington-based institute that examines family issues. Ooms's paper is based on a "roundtable meeting of scholars, practitioners, and policy officials" which sought to "get the facts straight about the age between teen girls and their male partners and to explore the lessons being learned from the growing number of efforts to target males in teen pregnancy prevention."

In the first section of her paper, Ooms summarizes the results of the studies outlined above. After detailing the stark findings of the earlier studies, she notes that sensational media reports, led by the *New York Times*, "created considerable public alarm and compelled some states and communities to launch initiatives to enforce statutory-rape laws aggressively." Relying on Lindberg et al.'s findings, Ooms stresses that births to girls with much older partners constituted only 8 percent of all births to teenagers. "Put another way," she writes, lest the point be passed over, "the teen mothers who have so captured the public's attention—those under 18 who are unmarried and have a much older partner—constitute less than one in ten of all teen mothers."

QUESTIONS OF OBJECTIVITY

Ooms's paper attracted little attention, since it merely repackaged old studies and reported on a meeting of unnamed scholars. But it was tied to the release of another study that reported new data. This study, "Partners, Predators, Peers, Protectors: Males and Teen Pregnancy," was also commissioned by the National Campaign to Prevent Teen Pregnancy. The co-authors were from Child Trends Inc., a Washington-based nonprofit that researches issues affecting children. They analyzed newly available data from the Department of Health and Human Services' 1995 National Survey of Family Growth, which collects information on pregnancy and childbearing. The study focused on the first sexual experience of teenage girls: Was it voluntary? How old was her partner? Was contraception used? The Child Trends study found that nearly two-thirds of the first sexual partners of teenage girls were within two years of the girl's age and that nearly three out of four couples were going steady at the time. Sixty-nine percent of girls welcomed their first sexual experience.

Strangely, for a study tied to the Ooms paper, the data paint a picture strikingly similar to the findings of the older studies, even though they deal with first sexual experience as opposed to pregnancy. As in the previous studies, the data diverge by age. The younger the girl, the less likely her partner would be sharing a school, much less a classroom, with her. The study reports that "only 18 percent of girls who were younger than 14 when they first had sex had a partner who was within a year of their age; this was the case for 37 percent of teens who were 14–15 years at first sex, and for more than half of teens who were 16 years or older." The data on which the study was based show that 35 percent of girls 15 or younger first had sex with a partner at least three years older. Nearly one in five 13-year-olds lost her virginity to a man at least five years her senior. In addition, the study found that the wider the age difference, the less likely the couple would use contraception (79 percent for same age and 66 percent for difference of five years).

The data from the Child Trends study confirmed that the youngest girls are most vulnerable to the predatory acts of older men. The larger the age gap, the more likely sex was unwanted by the girl. While 26 percent of girls who first had sex with someone of the same age reported it as unwanted, 37 percent of girls whose partner was five or more years older did. Nearly 40 percent of 13- and 14-year-old girls reported their first sexual experience as unwanted; for those who had sex younger than 13, more than 70 percent reported it as unwanted.

The Child Trends study clearly adds to our understanding of teenage sexual activity, but the decision to tie its release to Ooms's paper, in which the data merely spun previously released studies, raises questions of objectivity. A spokesman for the National Campaign to Prevent Teen Pregnancy which commissioned the paper, John Hutchins, says one of the "key goals" of the expert roundtable and Ooms's paper was to examine the issue of statutory rape. "We didn't see the release of these reports as being corrective of these other studies," he says. "We don't dispute what they say. We just wanted to tease out what they meant." But the data are sure to disappoint those who want to make the case that the problem of statutory rape is of minor significance. All available data consistently show that the younger the girl, the older the man. And since it is the youngest girls whom government has the greatest interest in protecting, attempts to muddy the issue with creative statistics run contrary to the realities of teenage pregnancy and the interests of the youngest teenage mothers.

Even the smallest number that can be produced—Ooms's "less than one in ten"—still begs the question: Why shouldn't we care about one in ten? In 1994, about 393,000 babies were born to unmarried women 19 and under. At 8 percent, more than 31,000 of these babies fall into Ooms's "less than one in ten" category. In that year alone, 12,000 babies were born to unmarried women under 15 years old. The data indicate that 40 percent of these babies are the result of unions with a significant age gap. That's 4,800 babies. What California's Anderson wants to know from those researchers who are questioning statutory-rape laws is, "Would they sanction their daughter, who is 15, being impregnated by a guy who is 27? Or is this something that we sanction for other people's children?"

WILL IT WORK?

Realizing that this battle will never be won by data alone, opponents of statutory-rape enforcement are advancing other arguments. Chief among them is the contention that these unproven programs may generate unintended consequences, making them worse than doing nothing at all. The Guttmacher Institute's Patricia Donovan made this case in the January/February issue of *Family Planning Perspectives*. In "Can Statutory Rape Law Be Effective in Preventing Adolescent Pregnancy?" Donovan draws heavily on interviews with "law enforcement officials, reproductive health care providers, women's rights activists and policy analysts" to put forth what seems to be the prevailing liberal view of teen pregnancy, and of why statutory-rape laws will not work. As Michelle Oberman of the DePaul University Law School explains in Donovan's paper, "Adolescent childbearing is the result of an intricate web of factors, including limited opportunity, entrenched poverty, low self-esteem and many other issues that statutory-rape laws do not address." Circumstances, not individual decisions, generate unfortunate outcomes. In this view, adult men who pursue intimate relationships with minor girls are not responsible for getting them pregnant.

But, while intellectuals argue about root causes, most everyone else should be able to see the value in giving meaning back to the term "jail-bait." Donovan recognizes this, quoting California officials who predict that their program, in time, will deter offenders. But she is unconvinced: "The enforcement strategy is only likely to work if the men it targets—and their young partners—know that these relationships are illegal." Donovan then quotes law-enforcement officials who claim that "predators know they aren't supposed to have sex with someone underage." But for balance, she quotes pregnancy-clinic administrators who claim that "very few know the rules."

It may be true that many 25-year-olds don't know they aren't supposed to have sex with 14-year-olds. But this doesn't mean that they won't get the message after an acquaintance, or even an acquaintance of an acquaintance, winds up in jail. This is what Carla Grabert, deputy district attorney in California's Kern County, is discovering, after a year and a half of prosecuting men for statutory rape. "The first time I talked to teen dads on probation, only a few knew there were laws against sex with minors," recalls Grabert. "Now when I ask the boys, 100 percent raise their hands. The word is getting out."

In any event, Donovan's article tries to play both sides of the issue. One of the arguments she advances against the law-enforcement approach is that it would prevent young girls from seeking pregnancy services. This may well be the case in some circumstances, and it is certainly a concern worth addressing; it is probably the reason that no state has mandatory reporting by health providers. But this can only be the case if the girls know that the sex in which they are engaging is illegal. Thus Donovan's argument holds that 15-year-old girls will know relevant details of the laws to which their twenty-something sexual partners are oblivious.

Yet another argument is that enforcement of these laws will put loving and supportive fathers in jail. The short answer to this objection is discretion by law enforcement. Each case need not be prosecuted, and, in questionable cases, juries might not convict. What's important to keep in mind is this: If we threw away all laws against sex between adult men and minor girls out of a misguided fear of jailing supposedly loving fathers, parents would be unable to protect their teenage daughters from the designs of older men.

Drawing a hard line and prosecuting every individual who crosses it would be no less detrimental. There will always be cases where families are supportive of the couple doing the right thing—getting married and raising the child. Researcher Mike Males—who can hardly be accused of being soft on the issue—estimates that only 10 to 20 percent of prosecutable cases should be prosecuted. It is of course problematic to openly advocate that law-enforcement officials selectively enforce a law. Inconsistent enforcement undermines respect for the rule of law and leads to charges that prejudices based on race, class, or other inappropriate criteria are driving enforcement decisions. To minimize abuses of power, citizens must always monitor law enforcement.

The California program shows how such discretion can be used wisely. Prosecutors, who claim to work closely with social-service providers, say that the threat of prosecution is often used to ensure that the man does not simply abandon the young mother and his child. In fact, sentencing recommendations include "establishing paternity; paying support; [and] attending parenting classes." The program provides prosecutors with wide discretion, and the focus has been on cases with the largest age gaps.

The state's law has three categories of statutory rape. Any sex with a minor (under age 18) is a misdemeanor. If the minor is three years younger than the adult, the case can be handled as either a misdemeanor or a felony. In cases where the adult is at least 21, and the minor no older than 15, prosecutors still have discretion between misdemeanor and felony charges, but the felony charges carry longer sentencing guidelines of up to four years in prison.

For those made nervous when prosecutors are afforded excessive discretion, a highly publicized Wisconsin case offered no reassurance. There, an 18-year-old man who had impregnated his 15-year-old girlfriend—as a result of consensual sex—was tried and convicted as a sex offender even though he was planning to marry the girl. Those welcoming strictly drawn legal lines want to make it more difficult for zealous or ambitious prosecutors—who may, for example, be seeking higher conviction rates—to target men as rapists when they have pregnant girlfriends.

Such problems have yet to arise in California. As noted in Donovan's paper, Orange County social-service workers often recommend marriage as a viable alternative to statutory-rape prosecution. While this is often controversial—as one might expect in the case of a 20-year-old marrying a 13-year-old —such flexibility undermines the argument that enforcement will, on balance, make matters worse for both the girl and her baby.

IN DEFENSE OF PREDATORS

Researchers like Donovan appear bent on proving to skeptics that these men are not social pariahs. They want to rehabilitate the "predatory male" in the public mind, to transform him from a victimizer to a man who is himself a victim of society. Lindberg et al.'s study concludes with a call for policy makers to eschew the stick in favor of the carrot. "The disincentives [to sex with minors], such as expanding the reach and increasing the penalties of statutory-rape laws, have already been advanced," they note. "Improving access to economic opportunities and achievement for disadvantaged men may be an equally important avenue to try to discourage adult sexual involvement and childbearing with minors."

The same people who are willing to absolve men of their responsibility want to heap a larger burden on the pregnant girls. In her penultimate paragraph, Donovan writes that, according to pregnancy-service providers, "it is not uncommon for adolescent women to pursue adult men," noting that adult men are more likely than the girls' schoolmates to "have a job, a car and money to spend." Thus it is the girls who should be the focus of government opportunity programs. Donovan concludes that these girls continue to seek out older men until they "have access to good schools and jobs and develop a sense that their lives can improve." This may well be so. And while a district attorney may not take note of a 17-year-old pursuing a 20-year-old, the purpose of enforcing a statutory-rape law is to ensure that the same 20-year-old resists any attempts for affection by a 14-year-old. The purpose of the law is to make clear that it is the responsibility of the adult to act like one.

Donovan and Lindberg et al. also seek to rehabilitate the "predatory male" by showing that he is often an active participant in the young mother's life. As a proxy for the quality of the relationship, they look at cohabitation patterns. Lindberg et al. note that 35 percent of pregnant minors reported living with their partner during most of their pregnancy. Nearly half were living with their partner at the time they were interviewed for the study, which was as long as 30 months after the birth.

One problem with these data is that they don't distinguish 17-year-olds living with 22-year-olds from 15-year-olds living with 24-year-olds. More to the point, they say nothing about the circumstances under which the couples were living. The data say even less about the troubling issue of consent: Is a 14-year-old girl capable of living with a 22-year-old man in a consensual relationship? Carla Grabert, the district attorney who runs the statutory-rape program in California's Kern County, prosecuted a case that illustrates this problem. A local girl was living with a man 14 years her senior. Physical abuse caused her to lose her first child. At age 16, she was pregnant again. This time, she decided, things would be different. On the condition that she obey household rules, her family took her back in. She had the baby. The father was convicted of statutory rape and sentenced to two years. Happy to have escaped the relationship, she is now in college and speaking to other teenagers about her experience. This case is certainly not typical, either in age breakdown or sanguine outcome, but it illustrates an important point: Living together, in and of itself, does not prove that a minor mother and an adult man are in a mutually beneficial relationship.

PRUDENT, MORAL, AND JUST

In the final analysis, opponents of statutory-rape laws simply distrust using the criminal code as a form of social control, a view with a healthy tradition in America. But some acts, such as theft, fraud, and violent aggression, strike the vast majority of Americans as inherently criminal and therefore worthy of criminal sanctions. Few people would place a consensual relationship between a 17-year-old girl and a 19-year-old boy in this category, and any laws that attempt to do so will surely languish in the same disuse that marked statutory-rape legislation for many years. But nearly everyone would place a relationship between a 13-year-old girl and a 20-year-old man in the criminal category. Thus the debate is over where to draw the line and what to do once the line is drawn, not whether to draw it in the first place.

The other fear harbored by those who oppose enforcing statutory-rape laws is that the new criminal focus will drain resources that could otherwise fund what they consider to be more humane social-outreach programs. But statutory-rape and social programs are not mutually exclusive. Anderson says she would be happy to have a law that no longer needs to be enforced because a social program eradicated the problem. Proponents of expanded social programs for adult males who impregnate young girls should expend their energy making the case for these programs based on their own merits, rather than engaging in a futile effort to attack a public policy that has not yet been demonstrated either a success or a failure.

The critics are, no doubt, correct to point out that enforcing statutory-rape laws will not fix America's problem of teen pregnancy and out-of-wedlock birth. But most Americans will still probably feel that statutory-rape enforcement makes sense. It is simply prudent, moral, and just to build barriers to adult sex with minor girls.

Michael W. Lynch

Beyond Anomalies

From a conflict perspective, social control is the central dynamic in any societal system of intergroup domination and oppression. To many in U.S. society the dominant white population seeks to control the group life of nonwhite minorities through various institutional apparatuses of social control. One such institutional apparatus of social control in the United States is the criminal justice system. To one critical theorist, "It is the coercive force of the state, embodied in law and legal repression, that is the traditional means of maintaining the social and economic interests of the dominant group." Accordingly, the official task of law enforcement officers, prosecutors, judges, juries, and even the state executioner in the U.S. criminal justice system is to protect dominant group interests. The function of the criminal justice system, then, is to maintain the social arrangement of differential power relations between the dominant white population and subordinate nonwhite minority populations. Since the power to define social behavior as criminal resides with the dominant group, any social behavior engaged in by members of subordinate groups that the dominant group perceives as a threat to their interests is criminal. State-imposed violence is fundamental to maintaining this social arrangement because physical violence is integral to the U.S. system of control, domination, and exploitation.

But to Darnell F. Hawkins, a professor in the sociology department at the University of Illinois at Chicago, conflict theory as developed in criminology is far too simplistic an explanation of the relationship between race, crime, and U.S. society. Hawkins asserts in the following selection from "Beyond Anomalies: Rethinking the Conflict Perspective on Race and Criminal Punishment," *Social Forces* (March 1987) that empirically based research reveals inconsistencies in the relationship that are not well explained through conflict theory. Furthermore, in many cases nonwhite minorities are treated far more leniently than members of the white majority. Hawkins contends that such contradictions in the research record can be more appropriately explained by revising conflict theory.

Key Concept: conflict theory, race, and criminal punishment

Abstract   *Research on race and punishment for crime has produced inconsistent findings. Most previous reviews of the literature have been focused primarily on the numerous methodological flaws that may give rise to such inconsistencies. In this paper I suggest that inconsistent or anomalous findings in this area of research may also result from problems of conceptualization and theory. More specifically, it is argued that the conflict perspective must be substantially revised to begin to account for various anomalies observed by empirical researchers. Such a need for revision is the consequence of both problems in the original formulation of the perspective and its oversimplification within the empirical literature.*

Darnell F. Hawkins

One of the most widely debated issues in the criminological literature is whether there is racial bias in the administration of justice. In addition to numerous empirical investigations, there have been efforts in recent years to review previous studies and to determine where the weight of the evidence lies (Green 1971; Hagan 1974; Hagan and Bumiller 1983; Hardy 1983; Kleck 1981; Spohn et al. 1981–82). As in other areas of social research, most studies of racial bias in the administration of justice involve black-white comparisons. Reviews of empirical investigations have shown a large number of these studies to report significantly greater rates and levels of punishment for blacks than for whites.[1] Others report no significant differences between the races. Still others find that in certain instances, whites receive significantly more punishment for crime than do blacks (e.g., Bernstein et al. 1977; Bullock 1961; Gibson 1978; Levin 1972). This latter finding is often described as an anomaly or inconsistency given the theoretical model that has guided research on this topic.

Another anomalous finding that has become a part of the literature on race and criminal punishment derives from post hoc regional comparisons. Beginning with researchers such as Sellin (1928), the finding of less punishment for blacks than whites in the South in some instances has been said to be the product of leniency toward black offenders. Other studies have reported substantial punitiveness toward blacks as compared to whites in areas outside the South. Thus, the notion of anomalies has also been linked to unexpected regional differences in criminal punishment, that is, leniency in the South (at least during the 1920–40s) and harshness in the non-South (Kleck 1981).

Although the recent state-of-the-art reviews cited above often treat both theoretical and empirical studies, there has been little effort to probe fully the theoretical and conceptual limitations of previous research. Rather, most have been purely methodological critiques (e.g., Gibson 1978). In this paper I examine the theoretical underpinnings of previous research on race and punishment for crime and suggest direction for future investigation. I propose that the lack of consensus regarding the impact of race on criminal justice outcomes stems as much from a lack of theoretical clarity as it does from the methodological problems noted in earlier reviews of the literature. The need for an examination of theoretical issues is evident when one considers the conclusions reached in recent reviews.

A major source of criticism of the research on racial bias and a reason cited for the inconsistencies across studies has been the failure of researchers to control for relevant legal variables. This criticism has been targeted particularly at studies done during the 1940s and 1950s (Hagan 1974). Yet Hagan and Bumiller (1983) report that of the pre-1968 studies that controlled for offense and record, two of the most relevant legal variables, 3 studies found discrimination while 8 found no discrimination. On the other hand, of the 20 post-1968 studies that controlled for these variables one-half found discrimination while the other half reported none. These and other reviews suggest that apart from methodological flaws there are major problems of conceptualization and theory that underlie the inconsistencies observed across studies of racial discrimination in the administration of justice.

A number of investigators (Kleck 1981; Liska et al. 1985; Peterson and Hagan 1984) have recently raised significant questions regarding the adequacy of existing theory for explaining black-white punishment differentials. But most of these critiques have been done within the context of primarily empirical analyses and there has been little effort devoted to a systematic rethinking of the theoretical frameworks that have guided research on race and criminal punishment. I attempt such a systematic rethinking through an examination of anomalous findings reported in previous research. The major arguments advanced in this discussion are:

1. Researchers have perhaps used the term "anomalies" too hastily to describe findings which, examined in more detail, are not deserving of the label. Some of these seeming anomalies stem from methodological flaws in the empirical investigations; others result from inappropriate conceptualization and theory.

2. Many of what are perceived to be anomalies or inconsistencies in research on racial bias in the criminal justice system result from oversimplification of the conflict perspective, the principal investigatory model used in past studies.

3. This oversimplification stems from two sources. First, there is a lack of specificity within the conflict perspective itself regarding the relationship between race and criminal punishment. Second, researchers have failed to fully acknowledge the existence of what are now termed anomalies or inconsistencies in the body of research that was relied on to devise the conflict perspective. The work of the major conflict theorists and the studies they rely on report rather systematic departures from those patterns predicted by the oversimplified model. Hence various anomalies and inconsistencies could be said to be an integral part of a fully elaborated conflict perspective.

4. Apart from oversimplification, the reported anomalous findings may point to more substantial flaws in the conflict perspective as it has been used in research on social control. Even in its fully elaborated form the conflict perspective fails to account for a wide range of factors that may be relevant for understanding racial differentials in criminal punishment. Thus, despite the complexity of the theoretical and empirical base from which the conflict perspective was derived, it requires substantial rethinking and revision. Among other things, a revised model must begin to explain and predict those findings now considered to be anomalous.

I propose that the conflict perspective must be revised to address more specifically the question of the role played by various contingencies or mediating factors identified in past studies. Such factors as victim characteristics and region have been linked to various anomalous findings. Recent research has also identified other contingencies. The perspective must also be reduced to readily testable hypotheses that will help researchers avoid the errors of interpretation seen in previous empirical work. Below, I discuss several sets of concerns that must be incorporated into a more comprehensive conflict theory. Although I make an effort to reduce these concerns to testable hypotheses, such efforts are more successful in some instances than in others. I do propose that future researchers must proceed to revise more fully the conflict perspective in light of the findings and issues discussed below.

RACE AND THE CONFLICT PERSPECTIVE: AN OVERSIMPLIFICATION

Most of the empirical investigations and reviews of the literature noted above trace the topic of racial discrimination in the criminal justice system to the work of Chambliss and Seidman (1971), Quinney (1970), Sellin (1928), Turk (1969), and a few other researchers described as conflict theorists.[2] As noted above, the conflict perspective in its original formulation was much more complex than those restatements of it found in most empirical studies and recent reviews. Even more complex were the empirical and theoretical bases from which the conflict perspective was derived. What are the forms this oversimplification has taken and how do we explain its persistence in the literature? There are several potential explanations.

As in other areas of social research, the oversimplification of the conflict model is due partly to the fact that it is a perspective rather than a well formulated theory with testable hypotheses. Neither the work of Quinney nor that of Chambliss and Seidman, the principal architects of the perspective, represents a theory per se. Their propositions (Chambliss and Seidman 1971, pp. 473–75; Quinney 1970, pp. 15–25) are stated in forms similar to testable hypotheses but they have many limitations. In addition, there are other problems with the original formulations of the perspective by these two groups of analysts that bear more directly on the issues raised in this paper. A major area of concern is their limited discussion of race. The various propositions outlined in the two studies generally refer to social class rather than racial differences in the administration of justice.

Social Class and Race

Both Quinney's (1970) and Chambliss and Seidman's (1971) theoretical discussions contain references to the treatment of blacks by the criminal justice system. Yet in both instances the attention paid to black crime and discrimination against blacks is minimal when one considers the disproportionate presence of blacks within the American system of criminal justice for more than a century.[3] This relative inattention to issues of race stems partly from the class-based theoretical framework proposed by both sets of theorists. Within this framework, predicted discrimination against blacks by agencies of criminal justice is said to result from their generally low socioeconomic status [SES] in American society. That is, race effects are said to be less important for determining rates and levels of criminal punishment than the effects of social class (Liska et al. 1985). This model predicts similar treatment for blacks, American Indians, Asian-Americans, Hispanics, lower-class whites, and other low-status groups. Thus, it may be argued that the underpinnings of the conflict perspective derive from classical Marxist conceptions of the significance of social class. Although the work of most conflict theorists, including Quinney or Chambliss and Seidman, does not represent an orthodox Marxist interpretation, the ideas of Marx are evident within the perspective.[4]

Regardless of its precise origins, the result of such an orientation has been a lack of debate among advocates of the conflict perspective over one of the most widely discussed issues in American race relations, that is, to what extent is the treatment of blacks in the United States a function of their racial as opposed to their purely social class status?[5] Another result is that most of the statements of Quinney and of Chambliss and Seidman that have been used as examples of the conflict perspective in tests of racial discrimination do not specifically refer to race bias at all. For example, the following propositions of Chambliss and Seidman, taken from their concluding discussion of poverty and the criminal process, are used in several empirical studies as a statement of the conflict perspective.

> Where laws are so stated that people of all classes are equally likely to violate them, the lower the societal position of an offender, the greater is the likelihood that sanctions will be imposed on him.[6]

> When sanctions are imposed, the most severe sanctions will be imposed on persons in the lowest social class (1971, p. 475).

Examples of racial differentials in the criminal justice system are cast within this social class analytic framework.

Although Quinney (1970) does refer to specific problems of blacks within the criminal justice system, his approach is similar to that of Chambliss and Seidman. In discussing the application of criminal definitions, Quinney says "The probability that criminal definitions will be applied varies according to the extent to which the behaviors of the powerless conflict with the interests of the power segments" (1970, p. 18). He discusses racial differentials in the same context as other power-related differentials, for example, those based on social class or age. Neither Quinney nor Chambliss and Seidman raise the question of whether discrimination against blacks may be greater than that against powerless or subordinate segments of the population who are white. Thus, to the extent that racial differences in criminal punishment result from extra-class-based influences, the conflict model as derived from these researchers may not be adequate for explaining the racial patterns observed in many empirical investigations. For example, Liska et al. (1985) report race to be much more significant than social class for explaining rates of arrest across major American cities during recent years.

Perhaps more importantly, the failure of conflict theorists to discuss race has left subsequent researchers without theoretical referents for their empirical research designs and findings. As a result of these limitations, researchers who propose to empirically evaluate the propositions of Quinney and Chambliss and Seidman often use race as a proxy for social class status and proceed to test what is then labeled the "conflict perspective." This perspective is generally credited with proposing that *blacks or other nonwhites will receive more severe punishment than whites for all crimes, under all conditions, and at similar levels of disproportion over time.* This expectation is sometimes qualified with suggestions that (1) given the legacy of racism in the South, black-white differences may be greater there; and (2) as American race relations improve over time, there may be a gradual change in the black-white punishment differential. Yet since most empirical investigations are not longitudinal or comparative, these caveats generally are not applicable. It is ironic that despite the social class orientation of the original conflict perspective, most empirical tests of the model have involved racial comparisons. This may be largely due to the unavailability of SES data for persons charged with crime.

RACE AND PUNISHMENT: MEDIATING FACTORS AND CONTINGENCIES

How well-grounded are the expectations noted above in the work of the original conflict theorists? While it is true that Chambliss and Seidman and Quinney failed to specify possible extra-social class effects of race on criminal punishment, their work does not support a simplistic expectation of greater punishment for blacks than whites under all circumstances. Their investigations and the various studies they cite note at least two major factors found to be associated with the racial patterning of punishment for crime: victim racial characteristics and region. In most early empirical investigations the former was not controlled for and may have been the source of some seemingly anomalous findings.

Victim Characteristics

In a brief discussion of the racial context of arrest, Quinney (1970) cites the earlier work of Johnson (1941) and Banton (1964) which reported that policemen were much less likely to arrest blacks charged with the murder of other blacks than those accused of the murder of whites.[7] In a discussion of differential sentencing by race Quinney (1970) notes similar race-of-victim effects as reported in investigations by Garfinkel (1949), Johnson (1941), and Sellin (1935). At least in regards to homicide it is accurate to say that researchers in the conflict tradition have long been aware of a hierarchy of seriousness based on the race of the victim and offender (e.g., Hawkins 1983). The existence of such a hierarchy suggests that not all black offenders will receive harsher punishment than all white offenders who are convicted of murder and that the race of the victim must be seen as a factor that mediates the level of punishment. In fact, a rapidly growing body of literature reports that the race of the victim is an important factor affecting criminal punishment for a variety of offenses. Victim effects have been reported for cases of rape (LaFree 1980) and robbery (Thomson and Zingraff 1981). Other studies that have reported the race of the victim to be an important factor include Myers (1979), Wolfgang and Reidel (1973), and Zimring et al. (1976). In considering these studies Kleck observed, "There appears to be a general pattern of less severe punishment of crimes with black victims than those with white victims, especially in connection with imposition of the death penalty. In connection with non-capital sentences, the evidence is too sparse to draw any firm conclusions" (1981, p. 799).

The conclusion regarding the imposition of the death penalty has also been supported by several more recent investigations (Baldus et al. 1983; Bowers and Pierce 1980; Gross and Mauro 1984; Paternoster 1983, 1984; Radelet 1981).[8] In fact, Radelet and Paternoster found that in the absence of consideration of the race of the victim there was not a significant difference between the punishments assigned to black and white murderers in Florida and South Carolina. Such findings suggest that earlier reports of more lenient treatment for black murderers (Bullock 1961) must be reexamined to consider the impact of victims' race on black-white punishment differences. Thomson and Zingraff (1981) argued that the failure to consider victim racial characteristics constitutes a major flaw in previous studies of sentencing disparity. Although race-of-victim effects have recently become a firmly established finding in the empirical literature, such effects have not been incorporated fully into the conflict perspective or any alternative model. That is, researchers have seldom asked why the observed patterns exist. What conditions within the larger society and/or the criminal justice system produce these victim-based punishment differentials? Do such effects suggest that conflict theorists should have targeted victim characteristics rather than offender characteristics as the major determinant of differential punishment across racial and social class groupings?

The earlier studies (Garfinkel 1949; Johnson 1941) explicitly reported that punishment varied on the basis of both victim and offender characteristics. For example, the most punishment was observed for those offenses involving black offenders and white victims. From most to least serious Johnson lists the homicide dyads as "(1) Negro versus White, (2) White versus White, (3) Negro versus Negro, and (4) White versus Negro" (1941, p. 98). Johnson specifically argued against a view that the race of the offender was the only variable of significance. He says:

> Our hypothesis is simply that differentials in the treatment of the Negro offenders in southern courts do exist but are obscured by the fact that conventional crime statistics take into account only the race of the *offender*. If caste values and attitudes mean anything at all, they mean that offenses by or against Negroes will be defined not so much in terms of their intrinsic seriousness as in terms of their importance in the eyes of the dominant group (p. 98).

But apart from generalized conceptions of dominant and subordinate roles within a racial caste system, Johnson fails to explain fully why he expected and observed the patterns of punishment noted. For example, why are black-on-black offenses more serious than white-on-black? What societal values are reinforced by such a system of punishment? Two interrelated explanations were implicit in Johnson's analysis and have been made somewhat explicit in later research. One explanation focuses on the victim-offender dyad; the other on the victim qua victim.

The first explanation proposes that black offender/white victim crimes are the most harshly punished because such acts represent the greatest threat to the white structure of authority. A black who murders a white is said to offend against not only an individual whom the state has an obligation to represent in the criminal process, but also against the system of state authority itself. Thus, this victim-offender dyad is unique in comparison to the other three, none of which represents an attack (symbolic or otherwise) on the system of racially stratified state authority. In this respect black-on-white homicide within the racial caste system of the South is similar to the killing of a policeman or an official of the government. Only whites who kill public officials or law enforcement agents would be expected to receive levels of punishment similar to those generally given to black killers of ordinary white citizens. On the other hand, the lesser punishment for the killing of blacks by whites is in conformity with a value system which often allows whites to aggress against blacks with impunity. Like many aspects of southern life this pattern of punishment had its origin in slavery (Hindus 1980). Johnson proposes that it was still operative in the South of the 1930s. But he notes that patterns in northern states may have differed.

The second explanation was also suggested by Johnson and further developed by Garfinkel (1949). It places the greatest emphasis on the racial characteristics of the homicide victim. This explanation centers around the devalued status of the black victim and black life, in general, in the United States. This has been a recurrent theme in studies of black crime and punishment (Hawkins 1983; Kleck 1981; LaFree 1980; Myrdal 1944; Peterson and Hagan 1984; Thomson and Zingraff 1981; Wolfgang and Riedel 1973). This view holds that the lives and persons of whites are more valued than those of blacks in American society. Offenses against whites are said to be more severely punished than those against blacks regardless of the race of the offender. Empirical support for this position has come from recent studies of indictments and sentences for murder in Florida and South Carolina (Paternoster 1983, 1984; Radelet 1981).

Up to this point there have been too few methodologically sophisticated studies of homicide sentencing that have considered the race of victims to determine whether racial punishment patterns are affected by interacting victim-offender traits or are dependent on the victim's race alone. It is likely that both effects are operative in some cases. The Johnson ranking is also not substantially different from that expected if race of the victim were the pivotal concern. The crucial question is whether there are essentially two dyads instead of four as Johnson suggested, that is, any race offender versus white victim and any race offender versus black victim. There are also too few studies that compare the South and non-South to determine whether either of these effects is observable in the processing and punishment of offenders outside the South. Most studies have been done in southern states. Further, although race-of-victim effects have been noted for a variety of nonhomicide offenses involving interpersonal violence (assault, rape, robbery), these studies are also too few to reach definitive conclusions. Johnson noted that studies of offenses less serious than murder would probably show more clear-cut extremes of leniency toward black in-group offenses. Peterson and Hagan (1984) suggested that even the sentencing of drug offenders may be affected by race-of-victim concerns.

Despite the lack of large numbers of followup studies, it is clear that proponents of the conflict perspective and those who attempt to test it must begin to consider race-of-victim effects. It is also clear that it represents something more than simply another extralegal variable to be added to a multivariate model. The limited body of previous research on this issue raises a number of fundamental questions regarding the conceptual and theoretical bases of the conflict perspective—questions which are considered in more detail toward the end of the paper. I propose that victims' race is a significant factor affecting punishment not only for those crimes against the person considered in previous investigations but also for a variety of property-related offenses. For example, one should expect such effects for offenses such as larceny, burglary, fraud, and various other forms of theft and conversion. Of course, many property crimes have no individual victim in some instances. Nevertheless, some of the institutions that are victims of such crimes may be more likely to be perceived as "white" than others. I am proposing that careful study of racial patterns in sentencing for these crimes will reveal harsher punishment when the victimized individual *or* institution is perceived as white than where the victimized entity is nonwhite. That differential may be the result of another factor—racially defined perceptions of appropriate and inappropriate criminal behavior that are partly derived from victim-offender considerations. This is discussed below.

Crime Type, Race, and Appropriateness

Criminologists have consistently shown the influence of crime type on the official response to criminal activity, but this knowledge has seldom been incorporated into models of racial discrimination. This lack of a substantive consideration of crime or offense type occurs despite the fact that crime type is often statistically "controlled" for in many empirical studies (e.g., Hagan 1974; Kleck 1981). Most researchers who attempt to test the conflict model appear to begin with a presumption that nonwhites will receive harsher punishment than whites regardless of the type of crime (offense category) committed. The perspective, unlike various alternative social-threat-oriented explanations (see the power-threat discussion below), does not propose that the level of social control used against blacks and against whites will differ more for some offenses than for others. On the other hand, previous research and theory suggest that the following proposition-like conclusion is warranted:

> Certain types of crime in multiracial societies are perceived by the public at large and by agencies of social control as race-specific or race-appropriate. A member of a given racial group will receive the harshest punishment for committing those crimes perceived to be racially inappropriate.

In order to move such a statement beyond the level of tautology we must more clearly delineate what is meant by "inappropriate" in this context. First, appropriateness or propriety is not merely a measure of the extent of a given criminal activity among one racial group as compared with another. For example, several researchers have noted that law enforcement and judicial officials may "crack down" on those offenses that are at high levels or are increasing at disproportionate rates. The level or rate of increase for a given crime may also vary by race. Blumstein (1982) argued that to some extent racial differentials in imprisonment may result from an effort by the judicial system to punish more severely those black offenders who commit the types of crimes that have the greatest racial imbalance, for example, robbery. Since blacks are more disproportionately involved in robbery than in many other types of crime, the result is an overall pattern of greater punishment for blacks than whites. In addition to this phenomenon, I propose that there are racial status-related notions of propriety and impropriety that adhere to various types of crimes. These notions may be affected by racial differentials in crime type involvement but are also derived from other sources.[9] Some related research may help illustrate the phenomenon.

Because of the system of racial and socioeconomic stratification in the U.S., white-collar offenses are seen primarily as "white crime" whereas most street crimes against property are seen as "nonwhite crime." Within the street crime category, there may be further divisions along racial lines. Mayas (1977) found that violent street crime was generally associated with blacks. There is also evidence that rape is perceived to be a black offense (Abbott and Calonico 1974). Such race-crime typing has also been observed in other societies. O'Connor (1984) observed that a sample of respondents to a social survey in Australia tended to describe the typical violent criminal as a lower-class white male or an aborigine male. On the other hand, the typical swindler was described as a middle-class, white professional. Such crime typing in both the United States and Australia may reflect certain social realities, that is, differential offending by various racial-social groups. Or it may be essentially a status-related stereotype. Such stereotypes may be grounded in notions of the causes of crime. Regardless of its basis such typing may affect the official response to criminal activity.

For instance, Bernstein et al. (1977) analyzed a sample of all males arraigned in a city in New York State from December 1974 to March 1975. An unexpected finding was that white defendants as well as defendants who had been employed for longer periods of time were most severely sentenced. In attempting to explain this finding they used information obtained from interviews suggesting that some judges and prosecutors assume that nonwhites commit crimes because the nonwhite subculture accepts such behavior. These subcultural differences were said to be considered by the judges and prosecutors, thereby making the offenses of nonwhites seem less pernicious. Expectations were said to be higher for white defendants, hence they received greater punishment. Of course, the effects of race and social class-related notions of "normal crimes" on public defense and prosecutorial decision-making have been documented by Sudnow (1965) and Swigert and Farrell (1977). None of these researchers made comparative studies of the sentencing of white and nonwhite offenders across several crime types. But they do propose that certain types of crimes are perceived as more normal or appropriate for some racial and social class groups than for others.

It may also be the case that what is considered race-inappropriate crime varies over time and across various social contexts (Hagan and Bernstein 1979; Peterson and Hagan 1984). For example, Peterson and Hagan observed that between 1963 and 1976 there was a trend away from harsher punishment and toward more leniency for black drug offenders. They related this change to changes in the social significance of race in the locality studied. But they also provided evidence of the continued operation of race-inappropriate differentials. It was observed that lenient treatment of nonwhite drug offenders peaked between 1969 and 1973. This leniency, however, was restricted to *ordinary* nonwhite drug offenders, not big dealers. Nonwhite *big dealers* were said to have received the harshest punishment of all. Small drug sales had perhaps come to be seen as appropriate for black offenders (indeed, expected behavior) while large drug sales were seen as more appropriate for whites.

In another study, Hagan and Bernstein (1979) studied the sentencing of draft resisters during a 14-year period between 1963 and 1976. They found that during the early period black resisters were more likely than white resisters to be imprisoned. During the latter period white resisters were more likely to be imprisoned. They argued that when political dissent becomes widespread, majority group members can present an even greater threat than minority group members to governing authority. In this instance the level of racial inappropriateness appeared to vary with the level of lawbreaking within each group. But their explanation was largely devised to account for this one unexpected finding and leaves many questions unanswered.

I propose that these assorted studies all point to the existence of a race/crime-specific perception of the appropriateness of criminal behavior that affects racial differentials in criminal sentencing and other criminal justice decision-making. On the basis of the operation of such a perception there is reason to predict that:

1. Blacks will be more severely punished than whites for white-collar offenses.[10]
2. The black-white punishment differential will be greater for white-collar offenses than for street crimes against property.
3. After controlling for relevant legal variables and race of victim, smaller black-white differentials will be observed for homicide than for any other type of crime.[11]

This last proposal is based on the idea that elasticity of the race-inappropriateness concept is less for the most serious of offenses. For example, homicide is generally considered to be among the most inappropriate and abnormal of crimes. Yet even for the most morally reprehensible acts, there will likely be racial differences in punishment based on the idea that racial groups adhere to different moral standards (Bernstein et al. 1977; Swigert and Farrell 1977). Homicide may also be seen as normal (Swigert and Farrell 1977) among blacks and the poor simply because of its disproportionate incidence among those groups.

There is also a likely interaction between victim-offender traits and what is deemed to be racially inappropriate crime. Crimes involving white victims will be seen as more inappropriate for nonwhite offenders than the same criminal acts involving nonwhite victims. Thus, in addition to the factors discussed earlier that may lead to harsher punishment for nonwhite offender-white victim offenses, such offenses may be seen as more inappropriate. Similarly, offenses by nonwhites against "white" institutions will likely be seen as less appropriate than similar offenses against "nonwhite" institutions. Support for the significance of both victim characteristics and crime appropriateness considerations can be found in a statement by Myrdal:

> In criminal cases the discrimination does not always run against a Negro defendant. It is part of the southern tradition to assume that Negroes are disorderly and lack elementary morals, and to show great indulgence toward Negro violence and disorderliness 'when they are among themselves'.... As long as only Negroes are concerned and no whites are disturbed, great leniency will be shown in most cases.... The sentences for even major crimes are ordinarily reduced when the victim is another Negro. Attorneys are heard to plead in the juries: 'Their code of ethics is a different one from ours'.... Leniency toward Negro defendants in cases involving crimes against other Negroes is thus actually a form of discrimination.... For offenses which involve any actual or potential danger to whites, however, Negroes are punished more severely than whites (1944, p. 551).

Race and Region

The significance of region for determining patterns of punishment for crime has also been duly noted by conflict theorists within criminology as well as by some race relations theorists. Chambliss and Seidman say, "Regional differences are rather striking. A higher proportion of blacks are convicted and executed in the South than any other section of the country, and they are convicted there for a greater variety of crimes.... Execution for rape is an almost exclusively southern phenomenon" (1971, p. 466). In the study of American race relations and of criminal justice system outcomes, black-white differences across regions have been largely attributed to cultural factors, for example, northern tolerance versus southern bigotry *or* southern paternalism versus northern racial egalitarianism. Such cultural values are said to explain both the finding of harsher punishment for black than for white offenders in the South and the sometimes-observed leniency granted black criminal offenders in the South as compared with those in the North (see Kleck 1981).

Despite the historically based perception of greater racial bias in the South than outside of it and the observations of early researchers such as Johnson (1941) and Sellin (1935), Welch et al. (1985) note that very few studies make simultaneous regional comparisons when evaluating the impact of race on criminal sentencing. In addition, when regional differences are observed a rather simplistic, culture-based northern-southern dichotomy may be too hastily accepted when other factors may be more significant. For example, researchers may not have controlled for race-of-victim effects, rural-urban differences, crime type, etc. A brief summary of some recent findings on regional variations in the sentencing of blacks and whites illustrates the theoretical and methodological issues involved in such research.

Kleck (1981) reported that the death penalty for murder has not generally been imposed in a fashion discriminatory toward blacks except in the South. In a recent study of punishment of burglary and robbery offenders, Welch et al. (1985) found that southwestern and southeastern jurisdictions were more likely to engage in discrimination. Conversely, studies by Spohn et al. (1981–82) and Levin (1977) have found significant discrimination against blacks in incarceration rates in several northern urban jurisdictions. In fact, recent incarceration statistics show a larger gap between black and white rates of imprisonment outside the South than within it (Christianson 1981; Dunbaugh 1979; Hawkins 1985).[12]

These findings suggest that a revised conflict perspective must predict the direction of regional differences in black-white punishment differences and provide plausible explanations for them. As Kleck (1981) observes, current regional differences in black and white punishment for crime are not easily explained. This is due both to the simplistic northern-southern bias assumptions embodied in past research and to seemingly anomalous findings—evidence of both leniency and harshness in the South and discrimination in nonsouthern areas. Below I discuss the theoretical significance of past studies of regional variation in criminal punishment differences by race by considering a recurring theme in the literature—southern leniency.

Kleck (1981; citing Kuhn 1962) correctly notes that past researchers have failed to recognize the significance of anomalies and have thus not been alert to the need to alter their fundamental assumptions. Yet one must first interpret the significance of such anomalies before they can be effectively used to modify existing assumptions. For example, we must determine to what extent the term "leniency" is the appropriate label for the racial-regional differences in punishment for crime reported in previous investigations. A review of the concept of leniency as it has been used in the literature on race and criminal punishment reveals: (1) it is a concept that was based originally on primarily anecdotal data about southern criminal justice practices;[13] (2) the term has been used indiscriminately to refer to any pattern of punishment for blacks that is lower than that observed for whites. Often statistically insignificant differences are so labeled; (3) the term has also been used to explain seemingly anomalous patterns across regions. It is generally predicted that the overall level of punishment for blacks will be higher in the South than in the non-South. However, it is also said that leniency (the underpunishment of blacks in comparison to whites) occurs mainly in the more paternalistic South; (4) recent investigations, especially, have used the term without regard for the contingent factors that originally underlay the concept. For example, they have not considered type-of-offense differences or victim-offender effects. Much of this pattern of usage of the term can be seen in the recent work of Kleck (1981).

Kleck concludes that one of the most important subsidiary findings of his literature review is the identification of studies which report that black defendants are sometimes treated more leniently than whites. He also reaches this conclusion on the basis of his own empirical analysis of the death penalty. He notes that for the nation as a whole, in the remote and recent past, blacks have been less likely than whites to receive the death sentence for homicide (p. 799). He further concludes that this has been especially true outside the South. Thus, for Kleck the anomaly lies in a reversal of predicted outcomes: a pattern of seemingly more lenient punishment for blacks in the non-South than in the South. In attempting to make sense of this pattern, he refers to earlier studies that reported leniency toward blacks in the South. He concludes that there was a southern pattern of leniency toward blacks in an earlier era and that there is a present-day pattern of leniency toward blacks outside the South.

After listing four studies conducted in various regions between 1961 and 1978 which reported less punishment for blacks than whites, Kleck goes on to discuss a pattern of lenient treatment of black defendants in the South during the 1940s and before. Such treatment is attributed to a southern brand of paternalism that viewed blacks as "child-like creatures who were not as responsible for their actions as whites were, and who therefore could not be held accountable to the law to the extent that whites were" (p. 800). Mention of such a view is attributed to Dollard (1937), Garfinkel (1949), and Myrdal (1944). Apart from a question of the accuracy of this description of southern race relations in general (which I discuss below), Kleck fails to reconcile such a conclusion with: (1) the extremely high rates of imprisonment and execution of blacks in the South during the late nineteenth and early twentieth centuries for homicide, rape, robbery, larceny, and numerous minor offenses (e.g., Adamson 1983, 1984); and (2) Violent punitive sanctions are used excessively against "those whose crimes victimize members, interests, or institutions belonging to the dominant group in society." the extent to which presumed leniency may be due to race-of-victim effects. That is, were white officials lenient only for those offenses involving black victims? Unlike the earlier investigations, the studies conducted between 1961 and 1978 generally do not control for the race of the victim.

I propose that: (1) to the extent that there was statistical "underpunishment" of blacks in comparison with whites in the South, it varied with the race of the victim, crime type, and other concerns discussed in the present paper; (2) to the extent that blacks have been treated more leniently than whites in the non-South during more recent years, these patterns, too, are affected by such contingencies; and (3) since black crime in the aggregate is primarily intraracial, is usually within socially "appropriate" categories, and is seldom directed at white structures of authority (Silberman 1978), an aggregate-level finding of lesser punishment for black offenders is to be expected in many instances. It is the variation within that overall pattern of supposed leniency that Kleck fails to fully acknowledge and, that, a revised conflict perspective must explain.

POWER THREAT VERSUS SUBORDINATION

The existence of regional differences in black-white punishment is related to another significant set of issues that must be confronted by a revised conflict model. To what extent are racial differentials in social control due to individual attributes of the victim and/or offender, and to what extent to the attributes of the group from which these persons come? Is the treatment of blacks by the criminal justice system primarily a response to the threat they pose to white authority structures or is it primarily a response to their subordinate status? Since all subordinate groups represent potential threats, how variable is the ability of such groups (e.g., blacks in the U.S.) to pose a substantial challenge to those in power?

Built into the conflict model is the notion that the treatment of individuals by the criminal justice system is largely a function of their *group status*. However, in attempting to explain differential punishment for crime, conflict theorists place greater emphasis on group subordination and powerlessness than on threat. Lower-class individuals are said to have fewer resources with which to resist the imposition of criminal sanctions. This is one of the basic tenets of the conflict model. This distinguishes it from more recent Marxist interpretations of historical patterns of black punishment. For instance, Adamson (1983, 1984) has argued that immediate post-Civil War social control of blacks by criminal justice systems in the South reflected the fact that black criminals were both potential threats to white control and potential assets (prison labor).

In a similar vein, Blalock (1956, 1957, 1967) has proposed that the level of power resources available to minority groups is more variable than that assumed in the conflict perspective. He also proposes that dominant majority groups often must mobilize to maintain their power advantage over subordinate minority groups. Subordinate groups' advantage is a function of their population size and also the socioeconomic resources available to them. Blalock (1967) notes that only under conditions of slavery would minority resources be zero. For several decades, researchers have utilized this hypothesis to examine the relationship between the relative size of the black population and the extent of various forms of inequality between blacks and whites across regions. They have examined such diverse measures of inequality as political participation (Heer 1959; Key 1949), income (Blalock 1956, 1957; Frisbie and Neidert 1977), occupational status (Glenn 1963, 1964), school desegregation (Pettigrew 1957), and lynchings (Corzine et al. 1983).

Blalock (1967) does not specifically discuss criminal justice outcomes as a measure of discrimination. He does argue that the three major areas of discrimination which have characterized American race relations patterns are directly linked to what he calls the "power-threat factor." The percent nonwhite within a given geographical area is said to have an impact on whites' fear of competition and of the threat posed by nonwhites to white authority. Power threat is generally described as the actual or perceived potential of a minority group to pose a realistic challenge to white political or economic control. He proposes that the three types of discrimination or prejudice in which the power-threat factor should predominate are: (1) restriction of a minority's political rights, (2) symbolic forms of segregation, and (3) a threat-oriented ideological system. Some criminological research suggests that the disproportionate processing of blacks within the criminal justice system likely reflects elements of each of these areas of discrimination.

A series of recent studies has probed the links between the size of the nonwhite population, race relations, and police strength. Jacobs (1979) reports that metropolitan areas with larger numbers of blacks had stronger law enforcement agencies than areas with fewer blacks in 1970 but not in 1960. In a followup

Jackson and Carroll (1981) use the racial composition of the city, the level of black mobilization activity, and the frequency of riots in the 1960s as predictors of police strength in a sampling of 90 nonsouthern cities during 1971. They also derive their hypotheses from the work of Blalock (1967). They conclude that police expenditures are a resource that is mobilized or expanded when a minority group appears threatening to the dominant group.

Liska et al. (1981) look at police department strength in 109 U.S. municipal areas between 1950 and 1972. They report that the effect of racial composition depends on geographical region and year (before or after civil disorders). The greatest effects are noted for the South and after the civil disorders of the 1960s. The dramatic increases noted in police size during the late 1960s and early 1970s cannot be accounted for in terms of reported crime rates alone. Instead they suggest that such increases were influenced by the relative size of racially dissimilar groups associated with street crime and in the South by the extent to which such groups were segregated. The latter conclusion is based on the observation that population composition effects were strongest in the South after the desegregation efforts of the 1960s.

A recent study by Liska et al. (1985) provides additional support for the significance of power-threat factors in the social control of blacks. Using data on arrests for 77 U.S. cities over 100,000 population, they find no support for the traditional conflict perspective which holds that class composition has a greater effect on arrest rates than does racial composition. Although percent nonwhite and percent poor are related, percent poor shows no effect on the certainty of arrests. On the other hand, two race-related variables show significant effects. The percent nonwhite and a measure of segregation significantly increase the number of arrests per 100,000 known crimes. However, they do not find that the certainty of arrest is greater for blacks than for whites. Rather, they suggest that their findings support the hypothesis that a high percentage of nonwhites and a low level of segregation increase the perceived threat of crime. These perceptions increase pressure on police to control crime, which in turn increases the certainty of arrests for both whites and nonwhites. Since their study does not examine the post-arrest processing of persons across these cities, most of the questions regarding the effects of these variables on differential punishment remain unanswered.

These criminal justice related findings suggest that Blalock's theory may be relevant for predicting geographical and temporal patterns of black-white social control. Power-threat considerations may also be useful for explaining black-white punishment differences across crime types. Some crimes may be seen as more threatening to white authority than others. To the extent that race-related societal forces exert an influence on police strength, such social control sentiments may also be expected to influence the entire criminal justice system. This is likely to be a result of the facts that the police initiate the criminal justice process and that the police and nonpolice criminal justice personnel and institutions are affected by the same social conditions. A racial power threat can by hypothesized to influence the behavior of not only the police themselves but also various other government officials. Hence prosecutors, judges, correctional officials and others should be similarly affected and likely to produce similar race-related outcomes. More importantly, these findings suggest that the failure of the conflict perspective to consider power-threat considerations constitutes a major obstacle to effectively using it to explain black-white punishment differences, both within and across geographical areas.

OFFENDERS, VICTIMS, AND THE STATE

In the introduction to this paper I suggested that the debate over anomalous findings may point to more substantial flaws in the conflict perspective than the problem of oversimplification. Some of those flaws can be noted in the preceding discussion of power threat. In this final section I discuss other, somewhat more global flaws and relate them to the discussion of anomalous findings. A growing body of literature has provided significant critiques of the conflict perspective on social control. Numerous critics have raised questions similar to those in the present discussion but few have specifically considered the issue of race and punishment. There are two major areas of criticism that have been directed at the conflict perspective which are relevant for the present discussion. One line of critique involves a symbolic interactionist-like evaluation of the processes within the criminal justice system that produce racially different outcomes. The second centers on the failure of the conflict perspective to fully consider the political economy of racial differentials in punishment.

The conflict perspective in both its original and oversimplified form is flawed both from an interactionist perspective and from the view of the larger structural theory from which it was derived. This has led to a failure of conflict theorists to fully incorporate a concern for victim characteristics into their model despite acknowledging race-of-victim effects. The perspective as used in most empirical research presumes that there are only two significant, racially identifiable actors or entities in the administration of justice—a nonwhite offender and a white system of justice (or other subordinate group offender versus dominant group justice). Thus, the perspective has at its core a model of the modern criminal justice system which according to McDonald (1976a, 1976b) has forgotten the victim. McDonald argues that as a result of developments over the last century and more, the victim has come to play a more limited role in the administration of justice than in colonial America or pre-modern England. He further says that often today the victim is twice victimized, first by the offender and then by the criminal justice system itself.

The increased interest in victims by both scholars and politicians over the last 10–15 years suggests that McDonald may be correct. On the other hand the limiting of the role of the victim in the administration of justice and a neglect of the victim's welfare—e.g., lack of monetary compensation—does not necessarily mean that victims have not continued to be actors in the justice system. Victim characteristics have remained as both legal and extralegal influences on decision-making within the criminal justice system. Consideration of certain victim characteristics—age and sex—is built into the criminal law explicitly and implicitly. It is also well documented that prosecutors, judges, jurors, and other decision-makers take into account a variety of victim characteristics even when these are not specified by law. For example, the person who victimizes an old person is likely to receive a more severe punishment than an offender of similar characteristics who commits the same crime against a younger person. In this respect the victim has never left the criminal justice system, and has remained an actor of sorts within that system. In fact, it may be argued that in the absence of victims as active participants, their characteristics may influence decision-making to a greater extent than in the past. And, of course, in a racially stratified society a victim's race will be a significant concern (e.g., see the mock jury studies of Miller and Hewitt [1978], and Ugwuegbu [1976]).

The conflict perspective's failure to fully consider the influence of victim characteristics thus results from a failure to appreciate fully the complexities of the decision-making processes within the criminal justice system, including its diversity of potential actors. Consequently extralegal variables in the conflict model have been seen only as attributes of the offender or official representative of the state. A fuller model must "bring the victim back in" in much the same way as McDonald (1976a) advocates bringing the victim back into the modern system of criminal justice. But the oversimplified decision-making apparatus portrayed in the conflict model's criminal justice system stems from more than just the absence of the victim. Much of it can be attributed to a related but more global weakness of the conflict model—the portrayal of the state as a hegemonic authority. Like the failure to consider victims, such a view of the criminal justice system leads to a tendency to view racial patterns in punishment as more anomalous than they actually are.

Spitzer notes that while there has been a tendency towards rationalization of social control in modern societies, this has not been accomplished without significant countereffects. Among these countereffects are various conflicts of interest that derive from the creation of "pockets of resistance" to the rationalization process (1983, pp. 327–29). He includes professionals, civil servants, bureaucratic functionaries, unionized workers, and other interest groups among such resistors. These groups themselves are said to have been formed as mechanisms to destroy structures of privilege and to facilitate rationalized people-processing in an earlier age. Ignatieff (1983) also notes that one of the flaws of recent research on social control is the idea that the state has a monopoly over legitimate means of violence, including punishment as social control. The observations of Spitzer and Ignatieff together may suggest that no one entity *within* the system of state authority has a monopoly over criminal punishment. In the U.S. there has been a historical pattern of institutionalization and rationalization of racial dominance. The criminal justice system has been one mechanism for achieving this end. Yet to understand the treatment of black criminal defendants within that system, a more complex decision-making process than that described within the conflict perspective must be considered. A brief discussion of the seemingly anomalous finding of leniency toward some black criminal defendants in the South illustrates both the operation of Spitzer's and Ignatieff's countervailing influences and the complexity of the structural and interactional processes that shape criminal justice decision-making.[14]

As earlier noted, many observers of sentencing patterns in the South during the 1930s and 1940s reported finding leniency in the treatment of black defendants. On the basis of a simplified conflict perspective such departures from rational social control aimed at racial dominance should not have occurred and therefore must, it seemed, be explained by the influence of irrational paternalism or unexamined victim traits. Yet a more detailed examination of the social context and political economy within which the reported leniency occurred suggests other possible factors and raises questions about the validity of labeling such findings anomalous or even as leniency.

The South of the early 1900s was characterized by an elaborate system of sharecropping. This system of quasi-serfdom depended less on the criminal justice system as a means of social control than did the political economies of the North. This system of labor use also provided actors for the criminal justice decision-making process in addition to the professionals assigned to such tasks. Landowners frequently saw no benefit in sending black laborers to prison for crime when their labor was needed for sharecropping. In the South of the 1930s and 1940s a decision to send a landowner's sharecropper to prison merely meant that the sharecropper would be assigned as a chain gang laborer on a state project, or more likely to a work project that would benefit other private business proprietors, including other landowners. What developed was a more or less formal system of brokerage in which various landowners used their political influence to divert accused black offenders out of the criminal justice system.[15]

Johnson's (1941) speculation that the least serious offenses would show the greatest leniency was likely accurate. Such diversion probably worked more effectively for minor offenses and perhaps most effectively of all for minor offenses against blacks. The fact that such leniency was not an "intrinsic" characteristic of the southern criminal justice system is illustrated by the fact that extremely large numbers of blacks continued to be sentenced to chain gangs for minor offenses from the 1920s through the 1950s. Many of these came from the urban areas or towns where no organized system of diversion occurred. Given the financial benefit to be derived from the labor of these urban prisoners who were not part of the sharecropping system, leniency was most likely not widely practiced. In fact, there is sufficient evidence to suggest that blacks most often received harsher sentences than whites (Adamson 1983, 1984; Myrdal 1944; Sellin 1935; Zimmerman 1947).

This suggests that a detailed examination of the social processes and actors involved in generating the supposed pattern of leniency in the South may reveal that the term is inaccurately used. The notion of leniency used in previous research generally is seen as an attribute of a prosecutor or judge who assigns less punishment to black than to white offenders without any rational basis for doing so. That is, the rational response (to perpetuate racial dominance) would be to assign greater punishment. If such leniency did exist in the system described above, one must ask to what extent criminal justice system officials alone made the decisions or to what extent they benefitted from such leniency.[16] Many criminal justice officials in the South during the 1930s

BEYOND ANOMALIES

I have argued that what have been labeled anomalies in past reviews of research on race and criminal punishment instead represent patterns that in some instances have long been recognized by researchers. These patterns are anomalous only if one adopts an oversimplified version of the conflict perspective as it has been developed within criminology. Such an oversimplification stems partly from the lack of specificity in the conflict perspective regarding the relationship between race and criminal punishment and a concomitant lack of testable hypotheses. On the other hand, other reported anomalies may point to major flaws in many of the presumptions inherent in the original conflict perspective.

Further research must incorporate a theoretical perspective that includes at least four major departures from the now-traditional conflict model. First, criminal punishment must be seen as contingent not only on the race of the criminal offender but also on the race of the victim. Second, researchers must begin to recognize the theoretical as opposed to the purely methodological significance of grouping crime into categories and using such groupings to assess levels of racial difference in punishment. The use of such categorizations is important for improving our understanding of the dynamics of assigned punishment for crime across racial groups. Third, power-threat considerations must be considered when assessing temporal or regional variations in black and white punishment. Finally, researchers should follow the lead of Peterson and Hagan (1984) in examining the historical and contextual dimensions of the relationship between race and criminal punishment. That is, variations in levels of punishment by race must be more fully analyzed and explained within the context of the larger structural forces from which they emanate and in their proper temporal perspective. Such a historical-contextual analysis would allow for more attention to the political economy of criminal punishment. Indeed, such modifications as those above would produce a conflict perspective that is closer to the Marxist tradition from which the perspective is largely derived.

While I have argued for a systematic rethinking of the conflict perspective, it must also be recognized that much of the discussion above supports Greenberg's (1981; citing Marx) contention that it may not be possible to construct *universal* laws that are not historically contingent. Many of the economic and social conditions that shaped black-white punishment differentials during the early part of this century have undergone significant change over the last quarter-century. Those societal forces that shape the current levels of disproportionate punishment of blacks in the United States may, therefore, differ from those that were operant in the past. On the other hand, the inability of researchers to develop non-historically contingent propositions must not obscure the fact that black-white criminal punishment differentials have remained at similar levels for more than one hundred years.

NOTES

1. I use the word punishment in a generic sense throughout this paper. It refers to all decisions or outcomes within the system of criminal justice. This includes not only sentencing, but also decisions to prosecute and indict, to release on bail or parole, etc. This term also refers both to the likelihood that a criminal sanction will be imposed and to the severity of the sanction. I am largely excluding studies of police decision-making.

2. Although the term has been widely used, there is still substantial disagreement over exactly what constitutes the conflict perspective and which researchers are its major proponents. I have selected the works of Chambliss and Seidman and of Quinney as representative of the perspective largely because they are most often cited in the empirical literature. They are cited largely because in comparison with Sellin or Turk they provide a wider range of proposition-like statements that have proved useful in empirical tests.

3. For example, the index for the Quinney study shows that only 15 of more than 300 pages specifically treat issues of race, minority status, ethnicity, etc. Chambliss and Seidman limit their discussion of such issues to about 20 of 500 pages.

4. Of course, orthodox Marxists have paid relatively little attention to the study of criminal justice, per se. An exception is Bonger (1943, 1969), who also made a valuable contribution to the study of race and crime. In his later work Quinney approaches crime and crime control from an explicitly Marxian stance.

5. The most recent revival of this debate has centered around Wilson's (1978) notion of the declining significance of race. During the early to middle 1900s the debate involved black intellectuals and civil rights leaders who challenged ideas of American communists and socialists regarding the causes of the race problem. See Liska et al. (1985) for an important recent empirical investigation of the comparative effects of race and social class on crime control.

6. This proposition also illustrates other problems (or lack of clarity) within the conflict perspective. There are very few offenses that people of all social classes and races in the U.S. are *equally* likely to violate. Even if one could perfect some measure of "real" crime, the system of socioeconomic and racial stratification is such that it would be expected to differentially "generate" crime across racial and social class groupings. National arrest statistics have consistently shown that blacks are not arrested at rates equal to their share of the general population for most major offense categories. They are consistently overrepresented. For example, the Uniform Crime Reports over the last few years show blacks to be arrested at rates equal to their share of the population for only two offenses—liquor law violations and driving under the influence. Thus, when speaking of black-white comparisons, the "all things being equal" stipulation places an unrealistic constraint on the empirical researcher. On the other hand, the proposition does highlight the fact that the conflict perspective seeks to explain both the probability that sanctions will be imposed and the severity of sanctions.

7. Banton provides a quote from a southern police detective's captain as illustrative of southern views of black and white homicide. The captain was quoted as saying, "In the town there are three classes of homicide. If a nigger kills a white man, that's murder. If a white kills a nigger, that's justifiable homicide. If a nigger kills a nigger, that's one less nigger" (1964, p. 173). Unfortunately, researchers have not investigated the impact of such racial bias on police decisions to arrest or gather evidence.

8. Most recent work on race-of-victim effects in the administration of punishment for homicide has a decidedly legal slant and shows little concern for the development of theory. Much of it may be described as applied social-legal research whose purpose is to encourage the federal courts to consider *proportionality* questions when adjudging the constitutionality of the death penalty. This is an important objective, but such a goal means that researchers pay little attention to explaining the patterns observed. The focus is also exclusively on race-of-offender effects in homicide cases (as opposed to other crime types).

9. It is possible that crimes that are disproportionately committed by one racial group will come to be associated with that group over time. On the other hand, the linking of some categories of crime to certain racial groups may not be dependent on comparative levels of criminal activity. For example, although for the nation at large and for most local areas the black burglary rate is considerably lower than the black robbery rate, it is likely that both will be seen by the public as "typical" black crimes. Further, on the basis of arrest statistics, embezzlement is nearly as typical for blacks (as compared to whites) as is burglary.

10. There is no agreement as to what is meant by white-collar offenses. I am using the term in its traditional sense to refer to crime committed by persons of high socioeconomic status, usually in the course of their occupation. I am excluding most organizational crime, for example, corporate malfeasance or nonfeasance. I include FBI crime categories such as embezzlement and fraud. I also include the numerous offenses not included in official crime statistics.

11. It is important to control for legally relevant variables when ascertaining the effects of crime type. For example, Jankovic (1978) found that nonwhites convicted of driving under the influence were more likely than whites to receive a prison term. Some evidence suggests that this is largely a result of an interaction among race, social class, and the availability of paid counsel. Affluent whites are more likely to be convicted of this offense than of other offenses. These individuals are also more likely than poorer blacks to afford paid counsel who can help them avoid prison terms. A result is that the white DUI offender will have a greater advantage over black DUI offenders than white burglars will have over black burglars.

12. Rural-urban differences have also been found to be a possible factor affecting racial punishment patterns. For example, Pope (1975) reported that discrimination against blacks was greater in rural than in urban areas of California.

13. The notion of leniency is generally attributed to Myrdal (1944), who bases his conclusion on the work of Johnson (1941) and others. It is anecdotal in the sense that such conclusions are not based on extensive empirical research but instead are based on statements by some observers of southern judicial practices.

14. One of the more promising areas of investigation along these lines involves analyses of prosecutorial discretion. Researchers must determine how prosecutors take victim characteristics into account in indicting or plea bargaining with black and white offenders. For example, Radelet and Pierce (1985) reported that prosecutors for 1,017 homicide defendants in Florida were most likely to "upgrade" police homicide classifications where blacks were accused of killing whites. Concomitantly, these offenses

were least likely to be "downgraded." Such effects were found after controlling for various legally relevant sentencing-related criteria.

15. See Myrdal (1944) for a discussion of southern sentencing practices. Of particular interest also is Myrdal's discussion of the sentencing of black petty offenders (drunkards and vagrants) and the benefits derived from the intercession of whites.

16. Many of the criminal justice officials, such as policemen, prosecutors, and judges, in the rural South during the period likely had vested interests in diverting some black offenders from the formal system of punishment. Many were landowners or operators of businesses that depended on the availability of cheap labor. Others were likely to have been "controlled" by persons with such interests.

CHAPTER 4 Law and Criminality

4.1 DONNA M. BISHOP AND
CHARLES E. FRAZIER

Race Effects in Juvenile Justice Decision-Making

Criminologists and sociologists alike have long theorized about and re-searched the pervasiveness of racial and ethnic discrimination throughout the criminal justice system. It has been manifest in instrumental forms, such as blatant prejudicial and racist behavior on the part of criminal justice officials, and in more subtle institutional forms, such as lawmaking and en-forcement practices that greatly disadvantage minority groups. In any case, the preponderance of the criminological literature reports that nonwhite groups are more likely than their white counterparts to be (1) arrested, (2) formally charged, (3) convicted, and (4) incarcerated. While the theory and research has historically focused on the adult system, it should pose no surprise to find that criminal justice outcomes are quite similar for juveniles. While the juvenile justice system has never lacked the willingness nor the capacity for harshness, since its inception as unique from the adult system, juvenile justice has primarily advanced the philosophy that juveniles are redeemable, forgivable, and more likely to respond to remedial judicial and correctional strategies. In addition, juvenile justice has recognized the preventive potential of intervening in youthful delinquency, even at the precriminal stage. That is, status offenses were created to allow state inter-vention into juvenile misconduct before it became an adult criminal matter.

However, is this "benevolent" philosophy meted out equitably amongst juveniles as a category? The answer is a resounding no! The adjudication of juveniles, whether as young criminals or as unruly children, has been inequitably differentiated across racial and ethnic lines. Nonwhites and other disadvantaged groups are more likely to experience the harsher side of juvenile justice, while their white counterparts are more likely to experience the redemption and remedial options.

The selection that follows is from "Race Effects in Juvenile Justice Decision-Making: Findings of a Statewide Analysis," *The Journal of Criminal Law and Criminology* (vol. 86, no. 2, 1996). In it, Donna M. Bishop, of the Department of Criminal Justice and Legal Studies at the University of Central Florida, and Charles E. Frazier, of the Department of Sociology at the University of Florida, provide a contemporary example of the propensity of juvenile justice to treat young offenders differentially along racial lines. The authors employed a combined quantitative and qualitative research design to investigate the handling of juveniles by the Florida juvenile justice system. In their quantitative analysis, they found that in delinquency cases (criminal offenses), nonwhites were treated more harshly than whites at virtually every decision point in the adjudication process. That is, nonwhites referred for delinquent acts were more likely to proceed to the juvenile court, to be held in juvenile detention, to be formally adjudicated, and ultimately to be incarcerated or otherwise institutionalized. In dependency cases (status offenses) they found that whites were the most likely to be referred for formal processing, but no effects of race were noted at judicial disposition. In their qualitative analysis, the authors found that decisions to facilitate offenders' further penetration into the system were driven by family structure and stability and prior offense history, both of which directly disadvantage nonwhites. Due to an array of sociodemographic disadvantages experienced by nonwhites, they are more likely than whites to come from unstable family structures and to have a prior history with the law. That, coupled with both instrumental and institutional biases in the juvenile justice system, produces the enhanced probability that nonwhites will continue to receive disparate treatment, which, in all likelihood, will set the stage for advancement to the adult system.

Key Concept: race effects in the juvenile justice system

I. INTRODUCTION

Overrepresentation of minorities in the juvenile justice system is well-established. On a national level, minority youths are arrested in numbers greatly disproportionate to their numbers in the general population. While black youths comprise approximately 15% of the ten to seventeen year old population at risk for delinquency,[1] recent figures indicate that they constitute approximately 28% of youths arrested.[2] Further, according to the Office of Juvenile Justice and Delinquency Prevention's (OJJDP) "Children in Custody" census, minority overrepresentation increases dramatically as one moves beyond arrest to later stages in processing. For example, minorities constitute approximately 62% of youths held in short-term detention facilities, and approximately 60% of those committed to "deep end" long-term institutional programs.[3]

Donna M. Bishop and Charles E. Frazier

Quite apart from issues related either to the extent or causes of differential minority involvement in crime, a number of researchers have expressed concern about whether the juvenile justice system operates with a selection bias that differentially disadvantages minority youths. The research reported here is intended to add to the growing body of literature addressing that question.[4] However, this research differs in significant respects from past research because it focuses on differences between the processing of delinquency and status offense (dependency) cases, rather than simply the juvenile justice system in general. Additionally, we supplement our statistical analyses with qualitative data to aid in understanding sources of racial disparity.

Our discussion is divided into two parts. In Part I, we report the findings of quantitative analyses conducted using official records of cases processed through the juvenile justice system in Florida. In Part II, we supplement and provide a basis for a more detailed interpretation of the quantitative findings, drawing upon in-depth interviews with system insiders—juvenile judges, state's attorneys, public defenders, and social service personnel. Based on those interviews, we explore the social and organizational processes underlying the findings reported in Part I.

II. PART I

A. Considerations Guiding the Quantitative Analyses

Because the juvenile justice system consists of multiple decision points, it is essential that researchers track cases from arrest to final disposition through as many stages as possible. This is desirable for at least two reasons. First, decisions made at different points reflect the actions of different decision-makers —such as social service workers at intake, prosecuting attorneys at case filing, judges at court disposition—whose professional philosophies, organizational subcultures, and discretionary authority differ in ways that may render either intentional discrimination or institutional discrimination[5] more or less likely to occur.[6] The identification of more and less problematic decision points may facilitate both an understanding of sources of racial disparity as well as the development of strategies to reduce it.

Second, if a researcher examines only a single decision point, such as judicial disposition, the researcher's analyses may underestimate or altogether miss the effect of race. If disparities occur at early decision points that are not examined, analyses of late-stage outcomes are likely to produce findings of no discrimination.[7]

Another consideration guiding the quantitative portions of the research is the importance of estimating multivariate models that include controls for legally-relevant factors that might explain or justify race differentials in processing outcomes. At a minimum, we wanted to include as precise a measure of offense severity as the data would permit, as well as a measure of offense history that would take into account both the frequency and severity of individuals' prior records.[8]

A final consideration guiding the quantitative analyses is the possibility that the effect of race might be conditioned by other variables. Frequently, those who have explored racial disparities in justice system processing have restricted their estimates of additive or main effects models, which can obscure substantial race differences in treatment. Suppose, for example, that nonwhites and whites charged with serious offenses receive similar dispositions, while nonwhites charged with minor offenses receive harsher dispositions than whites.[9] In this instance, an additive model might show little or no racial impact, while an interactive model would reveal a significant race effect contingent upon offense severity.[10]

B. The Data Set

Data for the quantitative portions of this study were obtained from the Client Information System maintained by Florida's Department of Health and Rehabilitative Services ("DHRS"). The data set includes the total population of youths referred for juvenile intake processing throughout the state between January 1, 1985 and December 31, 1987. Because Florida law requires that all juvenile complaint reports be processed through the intake division, the data set is quite comprehensive and includes records of all police contacts other than those resulting in informal field adjustments, as well as referrals from parents, school officials, and other non-police sources.[11] The case records were organized to permit tracking of decisions made at multiple stages in processing, from initial intake through judicial disposition.

Because the Client Information System tracks referrals rather than individuals, we reorganized the data set around individuals so that multiple referrals of a youth to the juvenile justice system over the three year period could be chronicled and examined. We accomplished this by restricting our analyses to the last delinquency referral in 1987 for each individual, a procedure that allowed us to capture at least two full years of offense and processing history information for each youth. The total number of individuals at the point of initial intake is 161,369. This includes 137,028 youths referred for delinquent acts and 24,341 youths referred for status offenses. Because status offenses are treated as dependency cases in Florida, and because the actors/agencies and processing decisions involved in dependency cases differ from those involved in delinquency referrals, we analyze these cases separately.

In the analyses that follow, the juvenile justice system is viewed as a series of decision points, each of which is simplified to represent a dichotomous contrast. Four stages are involved in delinquency case processing, two in status offense processing.

1. Delinquency Case Processing. 1. *INTAKE SCREENING:* DHRS officials review all referrals originating from police arrests or from complaints by non-police sources. In addition to reviewing the facts presented in each referral, they are expected to interview the juvenile and his/her parents or guardians. They then make nonbinding recommendations to the state's attorney regarding the preferred method of handling each case. Intake officers may recommend that a case be closed without action, that it be diverted from the juvenile justice system for informal handling, or that it be referred to court for formal processing. We classify intake outcomes to differentiate between those cases closed without action or handled informally (coded 0) and those cases recommended for formal processing (coded 1).

2. *DETENTION STATUS:* Decisions regarding detention status are made shortly after delinquency referrals are received. Detention decisions are made jointly by intake staff, law enforcement officials (when referrals are police-initiated), and state's attorneys. Juveniles held in detention for any period between initial referral and the ultimate disposition of their cases are coded 1; those released prior to disposition are coded 0.

3. *PROSECUTORIAL REFERRAL:* State's attorneys decide whether a delinquency case proceeds to court. We coded prosecutorial referral as 1 in cases in which a decision was made to file a formal petition of delinquency or to seek transfer to adult court. Cases in which a decision was made not to seek formal action (e.g., no petition was ever filed or, if filed, a petition was subsequently withdrawn) are coded 0.

4. *JUDICIAL DISPOSITION:* The final stage in the processing of delinquency cases modelled in these analyses is judicial disposition of cases. Although the court has a wide range of options, our analyses compare youths who were returned to the community (e.g., those ordered to do community work service, placed on informal probation, placed on formal probation) (coded 0), with those who were committed to residential facilities (e.g., youth camps, training schools) or transferred to adult criminal court (coded 1).[12]

2. Status Offense Processing. 1. *INTAKE REFERRAL:* Status offenders also enter the juvenile justice system at initial intake. However, because status offenders are legally defined as dependents, their processing differs somewhat from youths charged with offenses that would be crimes if committed by adults. At the time these data were collected, specialized intake caseworkers were responsible for processing dependency actions. Because these are the same officials responsible for handling cases of child abuse and neglect, their orientations may differ from those of delinquency intake personnel. For example, dependency caseworkers may be more oriented toward responding to a youth's family situation, rather than to the actions of the adolescent. Consequently, they may be more likely than delinquency intake officers to choose formal intervention in cases where the family is seen as troubled or dysfunctional. Unlike delinquency intake decisions, dependency intake decisions are unaffected by the anticipated reactions of prosecutors; in status offense cases, caseworkers have sole decision-making authority to file a formal petition. The first stage in status offender processing, then, is intake referral and is coded to distinguish between cases closed without action or handled informally (coded 0) and those petitioned to juvenile court (coded 1).

2. *JUDICIAL DISPOSITION:* Status offenders referred to court face some of the same dispositional options available to delinquent offenders, although they are not eligible to receive the most severe of the dispositions applied to delinquents (e.g., they may not be placed in secure detention, committed to training school or youths camps, or transferred to criminal court). At the most severe end of the continuum, status offenders may be placed in non-secure residential facilities, such as runaway shelters, foster homes, or group homes. Judicial disposition is coded to distinguish between youths who were ordered into some sort of residential placement (coded 1) and those referred for counseling or some other community-based treatment (coded 0).

3. *Independent Variables.* SOCIODEMOGRAPHIC CHARACTERISTICS: The *RACE* categories in the Client Information System include "white," "black," "American Indian," "Asian or Pacific Islander," and "unknown."[13] Because the number of persons classified as "American Indian," "Asian or Pacific Islander," and "unknown" was very small (less than 1% of the cases), we restrict the analysis to blacks, whom we hereafter refer to as nonwhites[14] (coded 0), and whites (coded 1). Other sociodemographic characteristics included in the analysis are *GENDER* (coded male = 1; female = 0) and *AGE* (coded in one year intervals from 7–18).

For the analysis of delinquency cases, we used the most serious offense cited in the arrest or complaint to characterize the *CURRENT OFFENSE.* We coded this variable using the following scoring scheme: felony offense against person = 6; felony property offense = 5; felony offense against public order = 4; misdemeanor offense against person = 3; misdemeanor property offense = 2; misdemeanor offense against public order = 1.[15]

We also included *CONTEMPT STATUS* as a variable to distinguish cases referred for contempt (coded 1) from all other delinquency cases (coded 0). At the time these data were collected, state law permitted judges to place juveniles found in contempt into secure detention facilities for up to five months and twenty-nine days, not in the pre-adjudicatory phase, but as a disposition of their cases. This authority was frequently used as a vehicle to place status offenders otherwise ineligible for secure placement into detention facilities. That is, judges employed their contempt powers to incarcerate status offenders who disobeyed court orders by refusing to attend school or running away from home. These violations of court directives were treated as delinquent acts even though the behavior in which the youth engaged constituted a repeat status offense.[16]

We operationalized *PRIOR RECORD* by measuring the severity of prior referrals to the juvenile justice system. This measurement allowed us to account for both the frequency and severity of prior offending, and we constructed it by adding the severity scores of all offenses in each prior referral (using the same severity values as described above for *CURRENT OFFENSE*),[17] then dividing by the number of prior referrals.

Where appropriate, we also included case processing outcomes as independent variables in the analyses. That is, we explored the effects of decisions made at earlier stages in processing on subsequent stage outcomes (e.g., the effect of being held in secure detention on judicial disposition). This procedure allowed us to identify and assess possible indirect effects of race on case outcomes.

C. Analysis and Findings

Because we defined each of the processing outcomes in terms of a dichotomous contrast, we used logistic regression as the method of estimation. In addition to estimating the main effects of each predictor in additive models, we also estimated models for each processing outcome that included all two-way interactions involving race. These interaction models allowed us to determine whether the influence of race at each decision point is conditioned by values of other variables in the model. We report models containing interaction terms in the tables only where the interaction model produced a significant increment in fit over the additive model.

In Figure One we present a bar chart that depicts the juvenile justice system as a series of dichotomous decision points. The figure shows the relationship between race and each processing outcome, comparing the proportions of white and nonwhite youths receiving the most severe treatment at each stage. Before reviewing the bar chart, it is important to note that nonwhites comprise 21% of the population at risk (ages ten to seventeen) and 29% of the group referred to delinquency intake, but only 19% of the group referred to dependency intake.

Figure One indicates that, among those referred for delinquent acts, a greater proportion of nonwhites than whites received the more severe disposition at each successive stage in processing. Racial disparities are most pronounced at intake screening and judicial disposition. For example, 53% of nonwhite youths referred to intake are recommended for referral to court, compared to 42% of white youths. At judicial disposition, 31% of nonwhite youths are incarcerated or transferred, compared to 18% of white youths. The cumulative effect of these decisions is that the racial composition of the cohort becomes increasingly nonwhite as it moves through the system: while nonwhites make up 21% of the population at risk (ages ten to seventeen) and 29% of the cohort referred to delinquency intake, they make up 44% of the cohort incarcerated or transferred.

For status offenses, on the other hand, the picture is quite different. Figure One's last three comparisons show that there is evidence of racial disparity in processing which suggests a tendency to treat whites more harshly than nonwhites. At intake, decisions are made to refer to court slightly greater proportions of white status offenders than nonwhite status offenders. Although the proportions of whites and nonwhites receiving judicial dispositions of residential placement are approximately the same, there is a fairly marked tendency to incarcerate higher proportions of white repeat status offenders under the court's contempt power (36% of whites, compared to 26% of nonwhites).

Figure One is useful in two respects. First, it provides an indicator of potential discrimination at the bivariate level of analysis. It remains to be seen whether these race-patterned differences in outcomes can be explained by other variables in multivariate models. Second, the figure points to patterns of race differentials in processing that are quite different for delinquency and dependency cases. This is an important issue for further exploration in the analyses and discussion that follow.

FIGURE 1

*Proportions Receiving More Severe Processing
Outcomes Within Racial Categories*

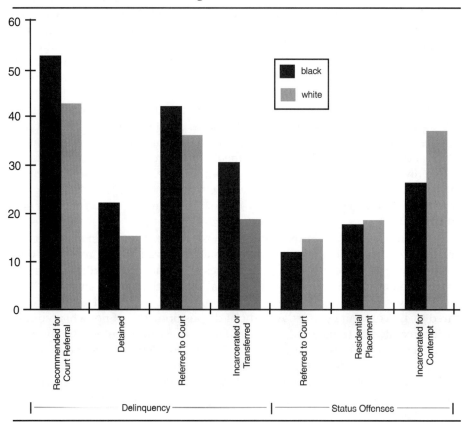

Table One presents results of logistic regression analyses in which we have modelled the processing of delinquency cases. Panel One shows results for intake referral outcomes. Consistent with other studies, the findings indicate that the seriousness of the current offense weighs heavily in intake decision-making, and is the strongest predictor of outcomes at this stage. As might be expected, intake officers also consider youths' prior records of offending and are more likely to recommend formal processing for youths with lengthy and serious prior records. In addition, however, there is evidence that individual characteristics of youths influence intake referral decisions. Nonwhites, older

TABLE 1

Logistic Regression Results for Delinquency Cases

	Intake Screening		Detention Status				Prosecutorial Referral		Judicial Disposition			
	1	SE	2	SE	3	SE	4	SE	5	SE	6	SE
Intercept	-4.818		-7.272		-7.597		-3.202		-8.015		-8.323	
Race	-.311*	.015	-.360*	.017	.143*	.040	-.118*	.014	-.645*	.025	-.219*	.075
Gender	.338*	.155	.243*	.020	.500*	.037	.258*	.015	.455*	.038	.604*	.061
Age	.175*	.003	.256*	.005	.254*	.005	.087*	.003	.340*	.009	.342*	.009
Prior Record	.288*	.003	.085*	.002	.131*	.004	.123*	.002	.090*	.002	.132*	.005
Offense Severity	.507*	.004	.467*	.005	.470*	.005	.254*	.004	.128*	.008	.130*	.007
Contempt Status	1.178*	.142	3.006*	.068	2.988*	.068	1.095*	.070	.913*	.099	-.291*	.184
Detention Status							.973*	.017	1.283*	.025	1.280	.026
Race x Gender					-.402*	.044					.259*	.078
Race x Prior Record					-.063*	.004					-.055*	.006
Race x Contempt											1.692*	.215
Ȳ	.451		.175		.175		.360		.220		.220	
N	137,028		137,028		137,028		137,028		47,747		47,747	
-2 Log Likelihood	140,602		105,438		105,075		155,701		41,126		40,945	
Model x2	41,041,6d.f.		21,533,6d.f.		21,916,8d.f.		23,582,7d.f.		9345,7d.f.		9526,10d.f.	

*Coefficient significant at the .001 level. SE = Standard error

youths, and males are significantly more likely to be recommended for formal processing than are whites, younger adolescents, and females.

Because logistic regression coefficients do not have a clear, intuitive interpretation, it is helpful to discuss the effect of race on the probability that intake will recommend a case for formal processing. To do this, we illustrate with the case of a typical youth referral: we calculate the predicted probability of a recommendation for formal processing for white and nonwhite youths with values of other variables in the model set at their respective means. In these data, the typical youth referred to delinquency intake is a fifteen year old male referred for a misdemeanor against person (e.g., simple battery), with a prior record score consistent with having one prior referral for a misdemeanor against property (e.g., criminal mischief). The probability that a white youth with these characteristics will be recommended for formal processing is 47%. For a similar nonwhite youth, the probability of a recommendation for formal processing is 54%—a substantial difference of seven percentage points.

Panel Two presents logistic regression results for detention outcomes. The results indicate that detention decisions are influenced to a modest degree by race when other important variables are controlled. For the typical case, the probability of being held in secure detention is 12% for a white youth, compared with 16% for a nonwhite youth. The strongest predictors of detention status are the legal variables of current offense and prior record. Gender and age are also significant predictors, although, as is the case with race, their effects are modest.

Panel Three presents an interaction model that provides a significant improvement in fit over the additive model. The panel shows that the effect of race on detention status is conditioned by both gender and prior record. Nonwhite males and females are handled much more similarly than are white males and females: among whites, the probability of being detained for females is significantly lower than is the case for males. Nonwhite females, on the other hand, are detained at a rate that approximates that of nonwhite males. The effect of race is also conditioned by severity of a youth's prior record. When youths have no prior record, or their prior record is not serious, non-whites and whites are rarely detained, and there is little difference in their detention rates. When the prior record is indicative of serious or frequent offending, however, the risk of being detained is much higher for nonwhites than for whites.

Two illustrations may help to clarify the nature of these interaction effects. Consider, for example, a white male with a relatively high prior record score of eight. His probability of detention is 17%. A nonwhite male with the same prior record has a probability of detention of 23%, a difference of six percentage points. A nonwhite female with a similar prior record has a detention probability of 21% (higher than that of the white male), while a similar white female has a probability of detention under these circumstances of 16%. When the prior record score is low, however, these race and gender differences are almost nonexistent.

Panel Four presents model estimates for the prosecutorial referral stage. As was the case with the initial two processing stages, offense seriousness and prior record each have significant effects on prosecutorial decision-making, as do gender and age. The impact of race is very modest: the typical white youth has a 32% chance of being referred to court, compared to a 34% chance for the typical nonwhite youth. After controlling for other variables, being detained has the effect of increasing the likelihood of referral to court. Consequently, some of the influence of race on prosecutorial decision-making is subsumed by the effect of detention status. Nonwhites are more likely than whites to be detained, and those who are detained are more likely to be prosecuted. Thus, racial inequality at the prosecutorial referral stage is more pronounced than the race coefficient in this model would suggest.

Panels Five and Six present results for judicial disposition. The main effects model (Panel Five) indicates that severity of the current offense and prior record each have significant, though fairly modest, effects on dispositional outcomes. Juveniles who are detained are also more likely to receive dispositions of incarceration. Once again, race, operating through detention status, indirectly affects disposition. Those found in contempt also are significantly more likely to receive harsher judicial dispositions. At this final stage in processing, each of the sociodemographic characteristics has a significant effect on case outcomes, the effect of race being relatively strong. The typical white delinquent has a 9% probability of being committed or transferred, compared to a 16% probability for nonwhites.

The results for judicial disposition become considerably more complex when we examine Panel Six, which includes three significant interaction terms in a better fitting model. The effects of race on case outcomes at this stage are conditioned by gender, prior record, and contempt status. To summarize briefly, while nonwhite and white youths with more serious prior records are dealt with similarly, nonwhite offenders with nonserious prior records are more likely to be incarcerated or transferred than white offenders with nonserious prior records. The findings also indicate that the treatment of nonwhite females more closely approximates the treatment accorded nonwhite males than does the treatment of white females approximate the treatment of white males. Finally, being held in contempt increases the likelihood of a more severe outcome selectively among whites, but not among nonwhites. We will return to this finding later in our discussion of status offender processing.

Table Two presents results for status offenders. Panel One provides estimates for intake referral outcomes. The model indicates that those with prior records of offending are more likely to be referred for formal processing. Additionally—and in direct contrast to delinquency cases—whites, females, and younger youths are more likely to be referred to court. There is a small race effect. The typical non-white status offender has a probability of referral to court of 9%, compared to a probability of 11% for the typical white status offender.

Judicial disposition decisions for status offenders are modelled in Panel Two. The variables in the model do a poor job of predicting status offense outcomes. Of the four predictors, only age reaches statistical significance. Younger youths referred to court are more likely than their older counterparts to be ordered into residential placements. Recall, however, that when repeat offenders are referred to delinquency court for contempt, white status offenders are significantly more likely to be incarcerated than are nonwhite status offenders.

TABLE 2

Logistic Regression Models for Status Offense Cases

	Court Referral		Judicial Disposition	
	1	SE	2	SE
Intercept	-1.691*		.070	
Race	.227*	.05	.387	.140
Gender	-.254*	.04	.022	.118
Age	-.023*	.01	-.115*	.031
Prior Record	.061*	.008	.067	.024
$\overline{Y}$	.13		.14	
N	24,341		2,747	
-2 Log Likelihood	18,768		2,181	
Model X^2	105, 4 d.f.		34, 4 d.f.	

*Significant at the .001 level
SE = Standard Error

D. Summary of Findings of the Quantitative Analysis

Our analysis points to clear disadvantages for nonwhites at multiple stages in delinquency case processing. While the magnitude of the race effect varies from stage to stage, there is a consistent pattern of unequal treatment. Nonwhite youths referred for delinquent acts are more likely than comparable white youths to be recommended for petition to court, to be held in pre-adjudicatory detention, to be formally processed in juvenile court, and to receive the most formal or the most restrictive judicial dispositions. For status offense cases, a very different pattern emerges. Whites are slightly more likely to be referred for formal processing than nonwhites. Although there are no significant race differences in status offender outcomes at the judicial disposition stage, when repeat status offenders are referred to delinquency court for contempt, whites are significantly more likely than nonwhites to be incarcerated. This difference in the way race impacts juvenile justice processing for delinquents and status offenders is intriguing. It is an issue we explore in some detail in the following section.

III. PART II

A. Interview Data

To supplement and provide a basis for interpreting our quantitative findings, we conducted telephone interviews ranging in length from one to four hours with a randomly selected sample of thirty-four juvenile justice officials.

The sample includes intake supervisors, assistant state's attorneys assigned to juvenile divisions, public defenders assigned to juvenile divisions, and juvenile court judges from each judicial circuit. A primary reason for conducting the interviews was to examine more deeply and from different perspectives the race differences uncovered in the quantitative portion of our analyses. We wanted to determine what officials working in the system observed and believed with regard to race effects, as well as how they interpreted these effects. Although most of our respondents are seasoned insiders with years of experience in juvenile justice, the explanations they offer must be considered tentative, because the sample is small. We are confident, however, that their observations point to potentially fruitful avenues for further research.

Findings of race differentials in processing, while consistent with the notion of intentional race bias or discrimination, are subject to a number of other interpretations as well. It would be too simplistic to conclude that our findings provide evidence of widespread racial prejudice. As we shall see, the reasons offered by justice officials for the racial disparities that we have observed are multiple and complex.

A majority of the juvenile justice officials whom we interviewed were quick to indicate that our findings of racial disparities in processing were consistent with their experiences and observations. There was, however, variation by functional role. For example, all of the DHRS caseworkers and defense attorneys in the sample perceived race disparities in processing. A smaller proportion of prosecutors and judges perceived race effects. There was also variation in interviewees' perceptions of the kinds of racial bias present in the juvenile justice system. Some respondents, for example, believed the main problem was individuals who held and applied prejudicial attitudes. Many more saw the problem as endemic to the system, the consequence of well-intended policies and practices that impact differentially on whites and nonwhites.

This latter group of respondents suggested that racial disparities in delinquency case processing are in part a result of agency policies and practices that focus on family support and family cooperation as considerations for diversion, for detention, and for final disposition. They noted that, in some instances, these considerations are incorporated into formalized agency decision criteria.

For example, DHRS policy renders youths referred for delinquent acts ineligible for diversion programs if their parents or guardians (a) cannot be contacted, (b) are contacted but are unable to be present for an intake interview, or (c) exhibit attitudes and styles of behavior that are perceived as uncooperative to intake staff. It is important to note that availability of a telephone and access both to transportation to DHRS offices and child care for young children who must remain at home are all taken for granted in this diversion policy.

DHRS intake supervisors reported that minority parents often are single working mothers or single mothers on welfare with other young children at home. If employed, they are often employed in low-paying, low-status occupations; unlike those in managerial and professional positions, these parents often lack the flexibility to take time from work to be interviewed. In addition, many may be embarrassed to make such requests of their employers. Those who are unemployed and on welfare frequently lack access to child care for young children remaining at home. Many must depend on public transportation which may not operate near their homes or DHRS offices. Some do not have telephones and this makes it more difficult for DHRS officials to contact them. Intake officials also indicated that minority parents tend more often than white parents to be distrustful of the juvenile justice system. Intake staff.tend to see these families as less cooperative with DHRS. Similar references to family support and cooperation were cited by prosecutors as key considerations in detention decisions. Generally, these considerations have a negative and differential impact on nonwhite delinquents. Typical is the view illustrated in the following comment by a delinquency intake supervisor:

> Our manual told us to interview the child and the parent prior to making a recommendation to the state's attorney. We are less able to reach poor and minority clients. They are less responsive to attempts to reach them. They don't show. They don't have transportation. Then they are more likely to be recommended for formal processing. Without access to a client's family, the less severe options are closed. Once it gets to court, the case is likely to be adjudicated because it got there. It's a self-fulfilling prophecy.

Thus far, we have noted that respondents identified criteria for diversion and detention that render nonwhite offenders more likely to be recommended for formal processing and held in secure detention. It is interesting to note the interface between these comments and the findings of our quantitative analyses. Note, for example, that race had no direct effect on prosecutorial filing decisions, and that both prosecutorial filing decisions and judicial dispositional decisions to incarcerate were influenced by detention status. The race effect on both the decision to formally prosecute and on the judicial decision to incarcerate appears to emanate in no small part from decisions made at earlier stages in the system—decisions to recommend formal prosecution and secure detention—that are tied to well-intended but inadvertently discriminatory front-end agency policies.

Many of the interviewees were aware that policies of Florida's juvenile justice system locked them into decisions that ultimately disadvantage nonwhites. Respondents from all levels of the system commented on the unfairness of a structure which renders nonwhite youths more vulnerable to formal processing because their families are unable to comply with agency policies.

Many respondents also reported that juvenile justice decisions in delinquency cases are affected by differentials in access to retained counsel and private treatment resources, differentials that impact negatively on low-income —especially minority—clients. Especially in later stages of delinquency processing, respondents observed that the system emphasizes treatments (e.g., psychological counseling, drug treatment) that are often best obtained through private agencies. Youths from affluent families may take advantage of these treatment options and avoid formal processing. Minority youths who are less affluent can only obtain comparable services by being adjudicated delinquent and then committed to residential facilities.[18] As one of the judges in our sample observed:

> Minorities and low income kids get more [juvenile justice system] resources. If parents can afford [an expensive private treatment facility], the child gets probation. If not, he gets committed. Income is significant in that a lot of early interventions are directed to middle income groups. If a child needs constructive activity, a middle class family can afford it. Maybe there is institutional bias.

As might be expected, some respondents were very critical of practices which resulted in minorities receiving harsher treatment by justice officials. Others argued that these practices were quite defensible. In their view, justice officials were merely trying to provide needed services to the disadvantaged that wealthy families could purchase on their own. To become eligible for these services, however, youths had to be formally processed—e.g., referred to court, adjudicated delinquent, and placed on formal probation or committed to residential programs. Only then could these services be provided at state expense. Moreover, this sort of policy negatively impacts on nonwhites anytime they come back to the system on a subsequent charge. A juvenile's prior record and prior disposition history are primary predictors of (and primary justifications for) formal processing and more severe sanctions.[19] What may begin with good intentions at an earlier stage ultimately becomes a self-fulfilling prophecy. The influence of race is obscured as decisions to formally prosecute and detain in the past are used to justify more severe sanctions for youths returning to the system.

In addition, many respondents indicated that juvenile justice officials make decisions influenced in part by perceptions (or misperceptions) of youths' family backgrounds and circumstances. Respondents frequently reported that delinquent youths from single-parent families and those from families incapable of (or perceived to be incapable of) providing good parental supervision are more likely to be referred to court and placed under state control. In other words, when justice officials perceive that there is family strength and support, they are more likely to select less intrusive treatments and sanctions. For the most part, our respondents believed that these distinctions were fair and appropriate. They also indicated that, at least in delinquency cases, black family systems generally tend to be *perceived* in a more negative light, that predisposition reports give disproportionate attention to assessments of family situations, and that judges rely heavily on pre-disposition reports in reaching dispositional decisions.

Several comments made by state's attorneys and judges are instructive:

Judge: "Inadequate family correlates with race and ethnicity. It makes sense to put delinquent kids from these circumstances in residential facilities."
State's Attorney: "Detention decisions are decided on the basis of whether the home can control and supervise a child. So minorities don't go home because, unfortunately, their families are less able to control the kids... I think the way the system sets up programs shows some institutional bias.

If family stability was not a prerequisite to admission to less severe program options, race differences would be less."

State's Attorney: "In black families who the dad is, is unknown, while in white families—even when divorced—dad is married or something else. The choices are limited because the black family is a multi-generational non-fathered family. You can't send the kid off to live with dad."

One of the key findings of our quantitative analyses was that nonwhites are disadvantaged in delinquency case processing while the processing of status offenders in dependency cases appears to disadvantage whites.[20] One of the more experienced judges in our sample, who had served on the bench in both delinquency court and dependency court, shed some potential light on this issue when he observed that there is a "mysterious irony" in the way black and white families are viewed in delinquency courts versus dependency courts. He reported that it is common for judges in delinquency courts to justify harsher sentences for black youths by noting that the black family structure is weak and incapable of dealing effectively with troubled youths. At the same time, he observed that black youths in dependency actions are less likely to be made wards of the court because, in this context, the black extended family network is perceived more positively. In fact, he noted that in the dependency system the black family in particular is seen as strong. Thus, in delinquency proceedings, the black family is stereotyped as generally inept and the white family is seen as generally capable, while in dependency proceedings, these stereotypes are reversed—whites need help and blacks can handle their own problems.

One plausible explanation for these divergent views regarding black and white family systems may be that different organizational cultures have evolved in delinquency and dependency processing agencies. Social workers in dependency cases, for example, are accustomed to seeking out extended family networks (grandparents, aunts, uncles, etc.) to assist in the care of abused and neglected children. In the traditional extended kin networks of black families they find alternative sources of support, so the black family may be viewed in a more positive light. Intake officials in delinquency cases, in contrast, tend to wear two hats: those of social workers and law enforcement officers. Their orientations are geared more toward ensuring public safety, and in their organizational cultures, the broken family is more likely to be seen as a harbinger of future trouble.

Another possible interpretation for these findings is suggested when we consider differences in the ideologies and orientations of delinquency versus dependency proceedings. In delinquency proceedings, the rhetoric of treatment and rehabilitation coexists uneasily with an orientation to punish those who have violated the law. Indeed, in recent years, much has been written about the shift to an increasingly retributive mentality in delinquency courts, a shift that elevates concerns about punishment and public safety over the historical concern for treatment.[21] Dependency proceedings, on the other hand, traditionally have been and remain more often couched in the language of care and protection.[22] Dependent children—who include abused and neglected children as well as status offenders—are more often viewed as victims (i.e., children from troubled families who are without proper care). Viewed from this perspective, court referral and incarceration in delinquency cases are means of providing sanctions for those whose behavior is most strongly condemned (older youths, males, nonwhites). In the dependency system, by contrast, court referral and even incarceration are regarded as treatments more in keeping with the traditional *parens patriae* goals of protective care and rehabilitation. In the dependency system, these responses are means of providing services to those for whom the system has the greatest compassion (younger youths, females, whites).

Following this line of argument, the different responses to nonwhites and whites in delinquency versus dependency proceedings may be understood as official manipulation of cultural stereotypes to fit justice system goals. From this vantage point, minorities are disadvantaged in both delinquency and dependency courts. When the system is oriented toward punishment (delinquency cases), nonwhites receive more of it. When the system is oriented toward beneficent care and protection, nonwhites receive less of it. The view of the family that is invoked may merely be a means by which race-biased organizational responses are rationalized.

B. Conclusions

Our findings show clear indications of race differentials in justice processing. The quantitative analyses demonstrate appreciable effects of race on delinquency case processing that disadvantage minority offenders. These findings are consistent with perceptions of juvenile justice officials at all levels of professional involvement. That minority offenders are disadvantaged is not surprising. A number of previous studies have reported similar findings. What is surprising is our finding that the effect of race on the processing of status offenders differs so markedly from that of delinquents. Here, differentials in processing by race are less pronounced and when they do appear, they indicate that whites, rather than minority youths, are more likely to penetrate further into the system and to receive dispositions involving incarceration.

Had we only the quantitative data, these contrasts would have caused us concern; we would have had no basis for offering an explanation. Interviews with justice officials conducted as a second phase of this research have offered an intriguing glimpse into the dynamics of justice work, into organizational policies, practices, and philosophies, and into the possibility of manipulative use of race realities and perceptions.

Our qualitative findings support several interpretations. Intentional race discrimination does not appear to play a major role in accounting for racial disparities in processing. Although some officials whom we interviewed believed that some justice officials were motivated by prejudicial attitudes, few recounted specific instances of racially motivated actions. Without question, there are some justice officials who hold and act upon racially prejudicial attitudes. As long as race bias exists in the general culture, it would be surprising indeed if it did not operate through individuals in the juvenile justice system as

Donna M. Bishop and Charles E. Frazier

well. However, we are not inclined to conclude that the disparities we observed are largely attributable to intentional race discrimination.

Instead, we see much evidence of institutional racism. This is evident both in criteria for diversion and pre-trial release that focus on family support and cooperation, and in efforts to provide the economically disadvantaged with resources at state expense that the more affluent can purchase on their own. Obtaining these resources exacts a price in terms of adjudications of delinquency and sentences to confinement.

Finally, our qualitative findings support the need to take a closer look at the climate of organizations that do delinquency work versus dependency work. The differing orientations of these two systems, and the differing foci of the professionals who work within them, may support very different views of nonwhite families as facilitators or inhibitors of the achievement of organizational goals for children. Whether the differing orientations of delinquency processing versus dependency processing agencies account for the inverted race disparities we have observed across the two systems—or, alternatively, whether these inverted disparities reflect a manipulation of perceptions of race realities to consistently disadvantage minorities—is an important issue for future research.

In closing, we wish to emphasize the tentative nature of our conclusions. Though randomly selected, our interview sample was small. Moreover, the sample was not stratified to include representative numbers of intake officials and judges from both delinquency and dependency courts. Further research is needed to explore the alternative interpretations offered here for the quantitative findings. Interviews with large samples of individuals drawn from both the dependency and delinquency systems would be helpful. In addition, participant observation and other field studies may provide clearer insights into informal agency policies and practices, and organizational climates that provide the context within which race effects may be most fully understood.

NOTES

1. U.S. BUREAU OF THE CENSUS, U.S. DEP'T OF COMMERCE, U.S. POPULATION ESTIMATES, BY AGE, SEX, RACE, AND HISPANIC ORIGIN: 1980 to 1991, at 2 (1993) (Table 1—Resident Population—Estimates by Age, Sex, Race, and Hispanic Origin).

2. FED. BUREAU OF INVESTIGATION, U.S. DEP'T OF JUST., CRIME IN THE U.S. 1993, at 235 (1994). When national arrest data are examined by offense type, it appears that minority youths are vastly overrepresented among youths arrested for property offenses, drug offenses, and, especially, violent crimes, but only slightly overrepresented among status offenders. *Id.* The latter observation is based on arrests for curfew violations and runaways. The FBI does not report counts of other status offenses, such as truancy and "beyond control."

3. OFFICE OF JUVENILE JUSTICE AND DELINQUENCY PREVENTION, U.S. DEP'T OF JUST., *in* CHILDREN IN CUSTODY 1989, at 6 (1991) (Table 5—Juveniles in Custody by Minority Status and Type of Public Facility: 1989).

4. For comprehensive reviews, see U.S. DEP'T OF JUSTICE, MINORITIES AND THE JUVENILE JUSTICE SYSTEM (1992); Carl E. Pope & William Feyerherm, *Minority Status and Juvenile Justice Processing, Pt I*, 22 CRIM. JUST. ABSTRACTS 327 (1990); Carl E. Pope & William H. Feyerherm, *Minority Status and Juvenile Justice Processing, Pt. II*, 22 CRIM. JUST. ABSTRACTS 327, 527 (1990).

5. Following JOE R. FEAGIN, RACIAL AND ETHNIC RELATIONS (3d ed. 1984), institutional discrimination refers to practices having a negative and differential impact on members of a subordinate race even though organizationally-prescribed norms or regulations guiding those actions have been established and carried out with no intent to harm.

6. For further discussion, see BARRY KRISBERG & JAMES F. AUSTIN, REINVENTING JUVENILE JUSTICE (1993).

7. *See* Donna M. Bishop & Charles E. Frazier, *The Influence of Race in Juvenile Justice Processing*, 25 J. RES. CRIME & DELINQ. 242 (1988); Margaret A. Bortner & Wornie L. Reed, *The Preeminence of Process: An Example of Refocused Justice Research*, 66 SOC. SCI. Q. 413 (1985).

8. One might wish to include controls for social variables as well. For example, recent research suggests that juvenile detention decisions are affected by such factors as socioeconomic status, family structure, and school performance. *See, e.g.,* Madeline Wordes et al., *Locking Up Youth: The Impact of Race on Detention Decisions*, 31 J. RES. CRIME & DELINQ. 149 (1994). Unfortunately, the data used in this research do not permit us to explore the impact of these variables. However, in a very real sense, this does not constitute an important limitation. Insofar as these variables are correlated with race, their inclusion might help specify the considerations that produce institutional discrimination, but they would in no way negate findings of racial disparity. Stated differently, that blacks and whites may be treated differently because blacks are more likely than whites to come from single-parent families would not alter a finding of differential treatment by race. It would merely specify the mechanism by which such differential treatment might arguably be justified.

9. This is not an unlikely scenario, given that justice officials exercise much greater discretion in decision-making with respect to minor offenses. For an extensive review and discussion, *see* MICHAEL R. GOTTFREDSON & DON M. GOTTFREDSON, DECISION MAKING IN CRIMINAL JUSTICE: TOWARD THE RATIONAL EXERCISE OF DISCRETION (2d ed. 1988).

10. *See, e.g.,* Bishop & Frazier, *supra* note 7; Margaret Farnworth & Patrick M. Horan, *Separate Justice: An Analysis of Race Differences in Court Processes*, 9 SOC. SCI. RES. 381 (1980); Terance D. Miethe & Charles A. Moore, *Racial Differences in Criminal Processing: The Consequences of Model Selection on Conclusions about Differential Treatment*, 27 Soc. Q. 217 (1986); Marjorie S. Zatz, *Race, Ethnicity and Determinate Sentencing: A New Dimension to an Old Controversy*, 22 CRIMINOLOGY 147 (1984).

11. An important limitation of the data is that we were unable to examine the effect of race on police decision-making. The question remains whether race impacts police decisions to arrest youths and refer them to intake; there is evidence from much prior research that it does, especially with respect to minor offenses. *See, e.g.,* NATHAN GOLDMAN, THE DIFFERENTIAL SELECTION OF JUVENILE OFFENDERS FOR COURT APPEARANCE (1963); Donald J. Black & Albert J. Reiss, Jr., *Police Control of Juveniles*, 35 AM. SOC. REV. 63 (1970); Darlene J. Conley, *Adding Color to a Black and White Picture: Using Qualitative Data to Explain Racial Disproportionality in the Juvenile Justice System*, 31 J. RES. CRIME & DELINQ. 135 (1994); Dale Dannefer & Russell K Schutt, *Race and Juvenile Justice Processing in Court and Police Agencies*, 87 AM. J. SOC. 1113 (1982); Jeffrey Fagan et al., *Blind Justice? The Impact of Race on the Juvenile Justice Process*, 33 CRIME &

DELINQ. 224 (1987); Richard J. Lundman et al., *Police Control of Juveniles: A Replication*, 15 J. RES. CRIME & DELINQ. 74 (1978); Irving Piliavin & Scott Briar, *Police Encounters with Juveniles*, 70 AM. J. SOC. 20 (1964); James Q. Wilson, *The Police and the Delinquent in Two Cities*, in CONTROLLING DELINQUENTS 9 (Stanton Wheeler ed., 1968). Thus, there is a racial selection bias already built in that we are unable to estimate at the point in processing at which our data begins.

12. Transfer to adult court is the harshest sanction option for adolescent offenders. Once youths in Florida are transferred to criminal court, they may be fined, placed on adult probation, or sentenced to jail or prison. Moreover, their juvenile status is terminated and any subsequent offenses are automatically handled in the criminal courts.

13. Although Florida has fairly large Hispanic, Cuban, and Haitian populations, members of these ethnic groups cannot be identified with the data available to us.

14. The bulk of the persons coded as "black" are African-Americans. However, especially in South Florida, there are substantial numbers of persons of Hispanic origin who are frequently coded as "black" depending on their skin color. We use the term "nonwhite," then, to refer to a group made up predominantly, but not exclusively, of African-Americans.

15. Because many youths had multiple offenses recorded on a single day, we also constructed a measure of *CURRENT OFFENSE* that summed the severity value of each of the allegations contained in the referral. The results using the summated score did not differ significantly from those obtained when we scored only the most serious offense. Consequently, we used the simpler measure.

16. While the Florida legislature subsequently abolished judicial contempt power in such cases, the new juvenile justice reform legislation reinstated the power. For further discussion of the uses and abuses of the law of contempt in juvenile proceedings, see Donna M. Bishop & Charles E. Frazier, *Gender Bias in Juvenile Justice Processing: Implications of the JJDP Act*, 82 J. CRIM. L. & CRIMINOLOGY 1162 (1992); Randall R. Beger, *Illinois Juvenile Justice: An Emerging Dual System*, 40 CRIME & DELINQ. 54 (1994).

17. In cases where a youth's offense history included a status offense, the status offense was assigned a value of 1.

18. Even then, some respondents noted, there are too few spaces available for poor minority youth who need such treatment, and this results in their receiving the harshest dispositions, often for no real benefit.

19. Ronald A. Farrell & Victoria L. Swigert, *Prior Offense Record as a Self-Fulfilling Prophecy*, 12 L. & SOC'Y REV. 437, 450–51 (1978); John C. Henretta et al., *The Effect of Prior Case Outcomes on Juvenile Justice Decision-Making*, 65 SOC. FORCES 554, 559–61 (1986).

20. Recall that in dependency case processing, whites are more likely to be petitioned to court by DHRS Intake and white repeat status offenders referred to delinquency court for contempt are more likely to be sent to secure facilities than their minority counterparts.

21. *See, e.g.,* BARRY KRISBERG & JAMES F. AUSTIN, REINVENTING JUVENILE JUSTICE (1993); Barry C. Feld, *The Juvenile Court Meets the Principle of Offense: Punishment, Treatment and the Difference it Makes*, 68 B. U. L. REV. 821 (1988); Barry C. Feld, *The Punitive Juvenile Court and the Quality of Procedural Justice: Disjunctions Between Rhetoric and Reality*, 36 CRIME & DELINQ. 443 (1990).

22. In many jurisdictions, the dispositions that status offenders may receive have been severely restricted, while in others, status offenses have been removed from juvenile court jurisdiction entirely.

Minority and Female: A Criminal Justice Double Bind

Evidence suggests that the vast majority of minority female criminal offenders are poor, uneducated, and unskilled. Minority women are overburdened with the social conditions of unemployment, poverty, and racism. Minority women, poor women, and economically dependent women experience discrimination in the criminal justice system. The average female offender is a minority between the ages of 25 and 29 who has either never been married or who was a single parent living alone with one to three children before incarceration.

In the following selection from "Minority and Female: A Criminal Justice Double Bind," *Social Justice* (Winter 1989), Coramae Richey Mann, a professor of criminal justice at Indiana University in Bloomington, Indiana, contends that the most cogent conclusion one can draw from an examination of the minority woman offender in the U.S. criminal justice system is that despite awakening interest in female criminality, little attention is devoted to the black, Hispanic, or Native American female offender. All the same, she concludes, as racial minorities and females, nonwhite women are doubly discriminated against at every level of the criminal justice system, from arrest to incarceration. Minority women, especially black women, are disproportionately represented in U.S. prisons and jails when compared with white women. Mann maintains that minority women are more likely to be incarcerated than white women because racial and ethnic bias against minority women by criminal justice professionals increases their likelihood of arrest and conviction.

Key Concept: discrimination against nonwhite minority females in the criminal justice system

*T*his article addresses the status of minority (Black, Hispanic, Native American) women offenders from arrest to incarceration. As such, it examines and synthesizes the scattered information on a group that is doubly discriminated against because of their gender and race/ethnicity status.[1] For many decades the study of women's deviance was rare and the reports available were limited to examinations of prostitution and other sexual deviance thought to be "typical" female offenses. It was gradually recognized that all women offenders did not fit this stereotype and that women were involved in a wide variety of actions that are labeled "criminal." In the 1970s, and more so in the 1980s, criminological inquiry and research turned to women as offenders, but there is still a dearth of studies of the processing of women at each level of the criminal justice system. This neglect is exacerbated in the case of minority or nonwhite women, especially Black women, who comprise the largest proportion of women caught in the criminal justice double bind. The scarcity of documented sources necessarily circumscribes the discussion presented here.

THE CRIMINAL JUSTICE PROCESSING OF MINORITY WOMEN: ARREST, PROSECUTION, AND SENTENCING

The Crimes

The Uniform Crime Reports (UCR) compiled by the Federal Bureau of Investigation are the most frequently utilized sources of arrest information in the United States today.[2] Unfortunately, the UCRs are not crosstabulated by gender and race, which makes it impossible to isolate the offenses for which minority women are arrested. Nonetheless, the parameters of the incidence of female crime can be estimated from aggregated data on race and gender when combined with a number of studies specifically addressing minority female offenders.

The latest available data reveal that in 1987, 31.3% of the total arrests were of minority persons, 29.7% of whom were Black (U.S. Department of Justice, 1988: 183). Blacks also made up 47.3% of persons arrested for Index violent crimes in 1987, yet comprised only 13% of the U.S. population.[3] Women, on the other hand, accounted for 17.7% of total 1987 arrests and 11.1% of Index violent crime arrestees (UCR, 1988: 181). Clearly, women make up a small proportion of arrests, especially for serious offenses, a pattern that has persisted since 1960 when female arrests were first recorded in a separate category (Rans, 1978). Of course, these statistics tell us little about the crimes of minority women, but a number of research efforts suggest that when each subgroup is compared with their white counterparts, the Black woman is as likely to be involved with the law as is the Black man.[4] Homicide and drug offenses are serious crimes of contemporary public concern and, excluding prostitution, are probably the offenses involving women that are most frequently examined.

Early studies of criminal homicides by gender and race reveal that Black females are second to Black males in frequency of arrests (Wolfgang, 1958; Pokorny, 1965) and their conviction rates have been reported as 14 times greater than those of white females (Sutherland and Cressey, 1978: 30). More recent efforts tend to corroborate the previous studies by Wolfgang and Pokorny in showing extremely high proportions of Black females as both victims and offenders. As homicide offenders, Black females have been found to predominate in every major study where women offenders were included (e.g., Suval and Brisson, 1974; Briggers, 1979; Riedel and Lockhart-Riedel, 1984; Weisheit, 1984; Block, 1985; Formby, 1986; Goetting, 1987; Mann, 1987). Black men are their principal victims, since homicide is not only an intraracial, but also an inter-gender event. Homicide has been reported as the leading cause of death among young Black males from 15 to 24 years of age (Mercy, Smith, and Rosenberg, 1983). Since the average age of the Black male homicide victim is older in cases of domestic homicide (about 38 years old) and in instances of nondomestic killing by a Black female assailant (about 29 years old, see Mann, 1988a), it is clear that Black men are at a high risk of death throughout their lifetimes. Thus, it is not surprising that homicide has been designated by the U.S. Public Health Service as the primary public health risk for Black men in the U.S.

In 1970, Williams and Bates reported an overrepresentation of Black females in female admissions to the Public Health Service Hospital in Lexington, Kentucky, for narcotic addiction. Most of these women (63.8%) were urban residents from New York, Chicago, and Washington, D.C., compared to only 22.8% of the white female addicts. More recently, Pettiway (1987: 746) found female heroin and other opiate users to be ethnically split: Blacks were 35%, whites 33.8%, and Hispanics 31.2% (Puerto Rican 16.4% and Cuban 14.8%). Both studies found a strong correlation between women's drug usage and crime. Mann (1988b) compared random samples of female homicide offenders in six major U.S. urban areas on the basis of drug and nondrug use. Few differences were found between the two groups; the majority of whom were Black (77.7%). This led to the conclusion that women who kill are similar to each other on a number of important characteristics, regardless of their substance abuses (alcohol or narcotics). While there were proportionately fewer Blacks in the homicide user group, Mann found there were almost twice the proportion of Hispanic assailants in the abuser group, compared to the nonabuser Hispanic group.

Arrests

Black women are seven times more likely to be arrested for prostitution than women of other ethnic groups (Haft, 1976: 212). Yet, it cannot be empirically established that Black prostitutes are more prevalent than prostitutes in other female racial/ethnic groups. One possible explanation for the disproportionate number of arrests is that Black prostitutes are forced to practice their profession on the streets instead of under the benevolent protection of a hotel manager or in luxury apartments, as predominantly white call girls are able to do. "Street walking" increases the likelihood of police contact and harassment as well as possible law enforcement racial bias:

> As might be expected, the largest proportion of arrests of Black prostitutes takes place in the inner cities where living standards are low, the level of desperation high, and police prejudice endemic (*Ibid.*).

Are harassment and readiness to arrest indicative of police reactions to Black women offenders? A study of incarcerated female offenders reveals that Black women are more likely than white women to perceive police officers as excessively brutal, harassing, and unlikely to give them a break through nonarrest (Kratcoski and Scheuerman, 1974). The researchers conclude that the police discretionary power not to arrest was used more liberally with white women than with Black women.

Moyer and White (1981) hypothesized that police officers would apply more severe sanctions to a Black woman than to a white woman, especially if the Black woman was "loud, boisterous, aggressive, vulgar, and disrespectful" —characteristics seen by some whites as typical of Black people. In the second instance, the researchers reasoned, demeanor could also potentially predict law enforcement bias. While neither hypothesis was supported, type of crime in association with demeanor strongly influenced decisions of police officers where women were concerned, more so than with male offenders.

Pre-Trial, Prosecution, and Sentencing

In minority communities it is generally believed that in addition to the racial prejudice exhibited by the police toward minorities, the white-dominated judicial system also treats them more stringently (Deming, 1977). The few studies of the criminal justice processing of men and women appear to indicate differential treatment of nonwhite women offenders at every stage of the process.

According to earlier studies, at the pre-trial stage minority women are frequently unable to make bail and are held in jail until their court hearing, or they are excessively detained relative to the type of offense committed (see, e.g., Barrus and Slavin, 1971; Nagel and Weitzman, 1971). Many judges deny bail or insist upon higher and higher bail for each prostitution arrest, and since 53% of arrested prostitutes are Black women, the impact upon this minority group is obvious (DeCrow, 1974). An analysis of grand larceny and felonious assault cases sampled from criminal cases in all 50 states isolated a *disadvantaged pattern* of discrimination which resulted in adverse treatment of Black women at virtually all stages of the criminal justice process, including the likelihood of being jailed before and after conviction more so than white women (Nagel and Weitzman, 1971).

Recent research suggests that, in some jurisdictions, the detention status of women offenders may not be related to race/ethnicity. Mann (1984: 168) reports that in the Fulton County (Georgia) criminal courts,

> no overall relationship was found between race and whether a defendant was held in detention before the court hearing, since 66.7% of the Black women and 63.6% of the white women were in jail at the time of their court hearing.

Mann did find that not a single Black female was released on her own recognizance compared to nine percent of non-Blacks and that there was a slight tendency for higher bails set for Black women.

A court study by Daly (1987) compared Seattle and New York City jurisdictions and found that in both jurisdictions the Black and Hispanic female detention rates were lower than those of white women. And apparently being married was found to mitigate more strongly against detention for Black women than Hispanic women in New York City, where 62.6% of the female defendants were Black (a higher proportion than for Black men) and 28.8% were Puerto Rican (*Ibid.*: 161).

The poverty of most minority women offenders may contribute to either a lack of legal counsel or the necessity to rely upon public defenders instead of private attorneys for the defense of their cases. There are as many excellent public defenders as there are inept private attorneys, but it is generally acknowledged that the overwhelming case loads of public defenders permit little attention to individual defendants.[5]

Bias on the part of judges may also affect the appointment of free legal counsel. In one Alabama study, 42% of the white female defendants were afforded court-appointed counsel compared to only 26% of the Black females (Alabama Section, 1975). The reverse should have been indicated, since at that time the median income of Black families in Alabama was one-half that of white families.

A Washington, D.C., study noted the "Black-shift phenomenon," that is, 63% of the adult female population of the District of Columbia was Black. Yet the proportion of first bookings into detention was 73% Black, with Black women comprising 83% of those returned to jail from the initial court hearing, 92% of them receiving 30 days or more. For those given prison sentences, 97% were sentenced for three months or more (McArthur, 1974). For the District's white females, the comparable proportions were in descending order: 37% of adult female population, 27% of first detention bookings, 17% of returns to jail, eight percent 30 days or longer sentence, and only three percent sentenced to three months or longer (Adams, 1975: 185). In a re-analysis of these data, Adams did not find that the type of offense adequately explained the racial differences, but rather that "compared with whites, black women seem underdefended and oversentenced." Further, "they may have been overarrested and overindicted as well" (*Ibid.*: 193).

Foley and Rasche (1979: 104) found that "differential treatment is definitely accorded to female offenders by race." Over a 16-year period, they had studied 1,163 women sentenced to the Missouri State Correctional Center for Women. Their comparison of sentence lengths for all offenses, combined, showed no significant differences between Black and white female sentence lengths, but Black women did receive longer sentences (55.1 months) than white women (52.5 months). An examination of individual crimes revealed that Blacks received significantly longer sentences (32.8 months) than whites (29.9 months) for crimes against property, and served longer periods in prison. Although white women were accorded lengthier sentences for crimes against the person (182.3 months) at almost double the length for Black women (98.5 months), the actual time served was longer for Black women (26.7 months versus 23 months). In fact, the white women imprisoned for murder served one-third less time than did Black women who committed the same offense. The same held true for the analysis of drug offenses between the two groups.

There was no significant difference in mean sentence length between them, yet Black women served significantly more time in prison (20.4 months) when compared with white female drug law violators (13.2 months).

Sentencing outcomes based on the race of the victim and offender are a source of much controversy where men are concerned,[6] but little attention has been devoted to the interracial homicides of women and the sentences received. Two recent studies suggest that the race of the victim influences sentencing of women homicide offenders. In a study of female homicide offenders in six U.S. cities for 1979 and 1983, Mann (1987) found modest (although not statistically significant) support for a devaluation hypothesis.[7] When Black women killed other Blacks, 40% of them received prison sentences, but if the victim was non-Black, 66.7% were imprisoned. Conversely, if both the victim and offender were non-Black, 45.3% of the female offenders were incarcerated, while 50% of non-Black women who killed Blacks went to prison. The other study, conducted by Shields (1987), examined female homicide in Alabama from 1930 to 1986. He found that in the few cases which crossed racial lines, the offenders—who were all Black—received severe sentences. In fact, the majority of convicted Black females received life sentences.

The Punishments

Another method of investigating the relationship between gender, race, and the criminal justice system is through examining the crimes for which women are imprisoned.

According to a national survey by the U.S. General Accounting Office (1979), of the women offenders released from prison in 1979, almost two-thirds (64.3%) were minorities, and more than one-half (50.2%) were Black. As seen in Table 1 ... , each minority group is disproportionately represented in the inmate population according to its proportion in the general female population. On the other hand, as an incarcerated group, white females are substantially less populous.

Data excerpted from a national survey of incarcerated women reported by Glick and Neto (1977), shown in Table 2, reveal that Black women were more likely to be imprisoned for drug offenses (20.2%) and murder (18.6%). Drug offenses and forgery/fraud made up almost one-half (44.8%) of the crimes for which Native American women were in prison. Even more startling was the 40.3% of Hispanic women who were incarcerated for drug offenses—twice as frequently as Blacks.

An examination of the prison statistics from states with large numbers of minority women offers a more detailed picture of the offenses of these women. California, for example, incarcerates more women than any other state in the nation. In 1979, 19% of the women cited and arrested were Black,

TABLE 1

*Proportions of Incarcerated Women in Federal and State
Prisons, 1978, Compared to Proportions in the General
Female Population, by Race/Ethnicity**

	% in Prison	*% in Female Population*
White	35.7	82.0
Black	50.2	11.0
Hispanic	9.1	5.0
Native American	3.2	0.4
All Other	1.8	1.6
TOTALS	100.0	100.0

*Source: U.S. Government Accounting Office, Washington, D.C., 1979, p. 8.

17.3% were Mexican-American, 0.96% were Native American, and 0.44% were Asian-American (Hegner, 1981). Similar to the national results reported above, excluding the UCR catch-all "all other offenses," Table 3 shows that in California, Hispanic women (in this case, Mexican-American) were more frequently arrested for drug offenses (24.2%), with burglary second (21.8%), and theft third (16.5%). Black women's arrests were primarily for theft (19.6%), assault (17.8%), and drugs (17.8%). Assault was the first-ranked offense of Native American women (30.5%), followed by drugs (11.8%) and theft (11.2%).

Kruttschnitt (1981) examined the sentencing outcomes of a sample of 1,034 female defendants processed in a northern California county between 1972 and 1976. She found that:

> ... in three of five offense categories either the defendant's race or her income significantly affects the sentence she receives. Specifically, black women convicted of either disturbing the peace or drug law violations are sentenced more severely than their white counterparts; lower-income women convicted of forgery receive the more severe sentences.... [T]he status of welfare is generally given the greatest weight and appears to have a more consistent impact than either race or income alone on the sentences accorded these women (*Ibid*, 256).

In a separate analysis to determine if the relatively severe sentences were due to race, low-income, or welfare status, Kruttschnitt (*Ibid:* 258) found that most of the effect of race on sentencing was direct and not indirect through welfare, or that "the impact of race on sentencing appears to have little to do with the fact that blacks are more likely to be welfare recipients than whites."

In terms of incarceration in the California prison system, Table 4 compares the three major offenses of each minority group with that of white females and gives the proportions of those receiving prison sentences. Although there may be mitigating circumstances involved in the dispositions of individual cases, Table 4 reveals some curious race/ethnic differences between the women felons in

TABLE 2

*Offense Data on U.S. Incarcerated Women by
Race/Ethnicity, 1979,* in Percentages*

Offense	White	Black	Hispanic	Native American	Total
Murder	12.9	18.6 [2]	8.6	13.4 [3]	15.3 [3]
Other Violent	2.2	2.3	0.9	3.0	2.1
Robbery	9.2	13.8	8.7 [3]	6.6	11.3
Assault	3.2	7.5	1.6	5.8	5.5
Burglary	6.2	4.2	12.7 [2]	6.0	5.7
Forgery/Fraud	22.3 [1]**	11.3	8.2	23.8 [1]	15.6 [2]
Larceny	8.1	14.1 [3]	8.6	7.2	11.2
Drugs	20.4 [2]	20.2 [1]	40.3 [1]	21.0 [2]	22.1 [1]
Prostitution	1.3	3.1	2.4	0.7	2.4
Other Nonviolent	14.1 [3]	5.0	8.0	12.5	8.7
TOTALS***	100.0	100.0	100.0	100.0	100.0

*Compiled from Glick and Neto (1977), Table 4.10.14.
**Numbers indicate rank order.
***Rounded to 100.0.

California. Whereas 50% of the Mexican-American women arrested for homicide end up in prison, only 30.2% of whites, 24.8% of Blacks, and 20% of Native American women convicted of this offense were sentenced to prison, despite comprising higher proportions of those originally arrested for this crime. Similarly, although Black women accounted for 21.2% of women arrested for drug law violations, only 25.8% of those offenders were sent to prison. Mexican-American women were more likely than Black women to receive a prison sentence for drugs (33.3%) compared to their arrest proportion (13.4%). In contrast, white women drug violators, who represent the primary group arrested for this offense (65.1%), were far less likely to be imprisoned (39.4%) than any minority female group. It seems that in terms of homicide and drug violations, minority women, and particularly Mexican-Americans, are treated differentially by the California criminal justice system. As seen in Table 4, the offenses of robbery, assault, and burglary also show disproportionate prison sentences for Mexican-Americans, when compared to white and other minority females.

It has been demonstrated that the Black female offender is more likely to be arrested and imprisoned than any other female minority group, but the California statistics just cited indicate that the number of arrests of Hispanic women are slowly gaining on those of Black women. The similarities of the crimes of California and New York Hispanic women, who are culturally different and from opposite shores of the country, are provocative. The most frequent offense for which a Puerto Rican woman offender in New York State was sentenced in 1976 was also dangerous drugs (53.8%), with robbery second (17.9%) and homi-

TABLE 3

*Arrest Offenses of Woman Felons in California, 1979, by Race/Ethnicity**

Coramae Richey Mann

Arrest Offense	White		Black		Mexican American		Native American	
	N	%	N	%	N	%	N	%
Homicide								
N=228	86	(0.7)	113	(1.5)	24	(0.7)	5	(2.7)
%=100.0	37.7		49.6		10.5		2.2	
Rape								
N=17	9	(0.07)	4	(0.05)	4	(0.01)	0	----
%=100.0	52.9		23.5		23.5		-	
Robbery								
N=919	355	(3.0)	403	(5.5)	143	(4.2)	18	(9.6)
%=100.0	38.6		43.9		15.6		1.9	
Assault								
N=3,082	1,232	(10.3)	1,310	(17.8)[2]	483	(14.2)	57	(30.5)[1]
%=100.0	39.9		42.5		15.7		1.9	
Burglary								
N=3,320[3]	1,649	(13.7)[3]	908	(12.4)	744	(21.8)[2]	19	(10.2)
%=100.0	49.7		27.4		22.3		0.6	
Theft								
N=3,793[2]	1,771	(14.7)[2]	1,437	(19.6)[1]	564	(16.5)[3]	21	(11.2)[3]
%=100.0	46.7		37.9		14.9		0.5	
Auto Theft								
N=845	402	(3.3)	283	(3.9)	147	(4.3)	13	(7.0)
%=100.0	47.6		33.5		17.4		1.5	
Drugs								
N=6,172[1]	4,017	(33.4)[1]	1,309	(17.8)[3]	824	(24.2)[1]	22	(11.8)[2]
%=100.0	65.1		21.2		13.4		.36	
All Other								
N=4,590	2,502	(20.8)	1,577	(21.5)	479	(14.0)	32	(17.1)
%=100.0	54.5		34.4		10.4		0.7	
Totals								
N=22,966	12,023	(100.0)	7,344	(100.0)	3,412	(100.0)	187	(100.0)
%=100.0	52.4		32.0		14.9		0.8	

Notes 1–3: Rankings excluding "all other" offense category.

**Source*: California Bureau of Criminal and Special Services, 1980.

cide third (10.3%) (Wright, 1981). New commitments to the facilities of the New York State Department of Correctional Services in that year reveal that Puerto Rican female commitments comprised 22.1% of all New York State female commitments for drugs compared to 51.5% Black and 25.3% white. Puerto Rican women were also eight percent of the women imprisoned for homicide, while comprising only a portion of the five percent of the national Hispanic female population. Black women were 80% of the women sent to prison for homicide in New York that year; whites were 12%.

One might wonder why it is that in California white women are less likely to be imprisoned for drug law violations than Mexican-American women when this crime is the primary arrest offense for both groups. Are white women referred to drug treatment programs while minority women are sent to prison? Why are white California women more likely to go to prison for robbery than Black women? Could it be because they rob from business establishments and Blacks rob from individual Blacks? Currently there are no hard and fast answers to such questions, but scattered evidence seems to indicate that minority women are not treated equitably by the criminal justice system.

INCARCERATED MINORITY WOMEN

Jails, particularly rural Southern jails are "targets for the sexual abuse" of the women who occupy them, especially Black inmates, according to Sims (1976: 139). Sexual harassment is typical, but cases such as that of Black inmate, Joan Little, who killed the white jailer in Beaufort County, North Carolina, who had sexually molested her, are atypical. Few women in jails kill the jailers and male inmates who sexually humiliate and molest them.

Many jails housing women are dirty and unsanitary. Health care is rare; so are recreational programs. There is no way to separately house women who would participate in work release programs, and, thus, such programs are rare for jailed women. Because of their small numbers in comparison to men, training and education programs for women in jails are generally impossible. Yet a great number of the women in the nation's jails, most of whom are Black, are misdemeanants (43.5%) or unsentenced (46.7%), and have committed victimless crimes (Glick and Neto, 1977: 70). Female offenders of all ages—the sentenced as well as the unsentenced, the mentally ill, the potentially dangerous psychotics, from prostitutes to accused murderers—are confined together in jail because of a lack of housing for female offenders (U.S. General Accounting Office, 1979).

Prisons for women have their own psychologically devastating effects on women, especially for the over 50% minority population occupying them (Goetting and Howsen, 1983). The appalling lack of interest in women's prisons is typically attributed to their small numbers when compared to male felons. Thus, the majority of correctional funds are directed towards men's prisons to

TABLE 4

*Proportions of California Women Felons Arrested and Imprisoned in 1979, by Race/Ethnicity**

Coramae Richey Mann

Race/Ethnicity: Offense	White N	%	Black N	%	Mexican American N	%	Native American N	%	Totals N
Homicide									
Arrest	86	(37.7)	113	(49.6)	24	(10.5)	5	(22)	228
Prison	26	(38.8)	28	(41.8)	12	(17.9)	1	(1.5)	67
% Arrest/Prison	--	30.2	--	24.8	--	50.0	--	20.0	--
Rape									
Arrest	9	(52.9)	4	(23.5)	4	(23.5)	--	--	17
Prison	1	(100.0)	--	--	--	--	--	--	1
% Arrest/Prison	--	11.6	--	--	--	--	--	--	--
Robbery									
Arrest	355	(38.6)	403	(43.9)	143	(15.6)	18	(1.9)	919
Prison	41	(51.2)	23	(28.8)	16	(20.0)	--	--	80
% Arrest/Prison	--	11.6	--	5.7	--	11.2	--	--	--
Assault									
Arrest	1,232	(39.9)	1,310	(45.2)[2]	483	(15.7)	57	(1.9)[1]	3,082
Prison	14	(37.8)	21	(56.8)	2	(5.5)	--	--	37
% Arrest/Prison	--	(1.1)	--	1.6	--	2.3	--	--	--
Burglary									
Arrest	1,649	(49.7)[3]	908	(27.4)	744	(22.3)[2]	19	(0.6)[2]	3,320[3]
Prison	30	(53.9)	12	(36.5)	17	(28.3)	--	--	59
% Arrest/Prison	--	1.8	--	1.3	--	2.3	--	--	--
Theft									
Arrest	1,771	(47.6)[2]	1,437	(37.9)[1]	564	(14.9)[3]	21	(.05)[3]	3,793[2]
Prison	28	(53.9)	19	(36.5)	4	(7.7)	1	(1.9)	52
% Arrest/Prison	--	1.6-	--	1.3	--	0.7	--	4.8	--
Auto Theft									
Arrest	402	(47.6)	283	(33.5)	147	(17.4)	13	(1.5)	845
Prison	4	(57.1)	3	(42.9)	--	--	--	--	7
% Arrest/Prison	--	0.9	--	1.1	--	--	--	--	--
Drugs									
Arrest	4,017	(65.1)[1]	1,309	(21.2)[3]	824	(13.4)[1]	22	(0.36)	6,172[1]
Prison	26	(39.4)	17	(25.8)	22	(33.3)	1	(1.5)	66
% Arrest/Prison	--	0.6	--	1.3	--	2.7	--	4.5	--
All Other									
Arrest	2,502	(54.5)	1,577	(34.4)	479	(10.4)	32	(0.7)	4,590
Prison	74	(55.6)	42	(31.6)	15	(11.3)	2	(1.5)	133
% Arrest/Prison	--	2.9	--	2.7	--	6.7	--	6.3	--
Totals									
Arrest	12,023	(52.4)	7,344	(32.0)	3,412	(14.9)	187	(0.8)	22,966
Prison	244	(48.6)	165	(32.9)	88	(17.5)	5	(1.0)	502
% Arrest/Prison	--	2.0	--	2.3	--	2.6	--	2.7	--

Notes 1–3: rankings excluding "all other" category.

**Source*: California Bureau of Criminal Statistics and Special Services, 1980.

the neglect of female prison facilities. As a result, medical and health services —particularly those peculiar to women's special gynecological and obstetrical needs—are poor or lacking. The federal General Accounting Office found that women in prisons have fewer vocational programs at their disposal compared to men, or an average of three compared to the 10 in men's facilities (U.S. General Accounting Office, 1979). The existing programs follow the sex stereotype of the traditional female role—clerical skills, cosmetology, and food services (Glick and Neto, 1977: 77)—and are geared toward lower-paying jobs. Prison industries in women's facilities rarely provide training beyond that leading to employment as a hotel maid, cook, waitress, laundry worker, or garment factory worker (Simon, 1975).

The frequent location of women's prisons in rural areas introduces special problems for a woman offender. To be physically distant from one's children, family, friends, and legal counsel results in a deprivation of communication that reinforces the female inmate's feeling of isolation and powerlessness (Gibson, 1976). Those women who are mothers (variously estimated at 56% to 70% [Glick and Neto, 1977])—and most minority women in prison are mothers—experience special problems related to custody, support, and other legal matters pertaining to their children (McGowan and Blumenthal, 1976). Because of these distances, an imprisoned woman has greater difficulty obtaining legal counsel or conferring with her attorney.

In an atmosphere that is tense and oppressive, minority women face additional problems related to the rural locations of women's prisons. Most of the staff are whites recruited from the farm and rural areas surrounding the prisons, while the majority of the inmates are nonwhites from urban areas, a mixture that contributes to ever-present friction. A majority of both white and nonwhite (Black and American Indian) female inmates in Kruttschnitt's study (1983) of the Minnesota Correctional Institution for Women felt that race/ethnicity influenced correctional officers' treatment of the female inmates. Over two-thirds of the minority women perceived racial discrimination in the institution and 29.4% felt that job assignments were influenced by race (35.3% had no opinion). Nonwhite women, who comprised 42% of the Minnesota prison population (where 93% of the staff and administration were white) cited "race relations" as the most frequent response for intra-inmate assaults (Kruttschnitt, 1983: 585).

In many institutions for women felons, Hispanic women are not permitted to speak Spanish, to read or write letters in their native language, to subscribe to Spanish-language magazines or newspapers, or to converse with their visitors in Spanish (Burkhart, 1973: 153). Since many Hispanic inmates do not speak English, these customary procedures tend to isolate these women even more than other minorities.

Alejandrina Torres, a Puerto Rican nationalist, who has never been convicted of an act of violence, was arrested in 1983 on charges of possessing weapons and explosives and seditious conspiracy against the government (Reuben and Norman, 1987: 882). Upon conviction in 1985, Ms. Torres received a sentence of 35 years in prison. She and a white self-proclaimed revolutionary, Susan Rosenberg, who has been associated with the Weather Underground group (McMullian, 1988: C1), were put in a new "high security" facility in

Lexington, Kentucky, on October 29, 1986. Below is a graphic description of the
conditions under which they were housed:

177

*Coramae Richey
Mann*

> The two women…are confined to subterranean cells twenty-three hours a day.
> They are permitted one hour of exercise in a yard measuring fifty feet square; upon
> their return they are strip-searched. That daily outing is the only time they see
> sunlight, except when they leave the facility for medical or dental treatment. On
> those occasions they are handcuffed and manacled by chains around their waists.
> In their cells they are kept under constant surveillance by guards or television
> cameras…. They say they are exposed to various forms of sensory deprivation
> designed to alter their personalities. The lights in their cells glare down on them
> continuously, and they are forbidden to cover them in any way (Reuben and Nor-
> man, 1987: 881).

Distance also denies a woman access to her parole board (Arditi et al.,
1973). In the criminal justice system parole is not a right, but a privilege. One
earns parole by demonstrating the ability to function in society in an "acceptable way." The criteria parole boards use to grant parole are vague, and
both institutional and noninstitutional criteria are used in decisions. In addition to the institutional behavior of a woman, industrial time, meritorious
"good time" earned, as well as original and prior offense records may be a part
of the release decision. Women convicted of property crimes, drug offenses,
or alcohol-related offenses are those who experience less successful parole
outcomes (Simon, 1975), yet these are the crimes that usually result in the incarceration of minority women. Parole boards expect higher standards of proper
conduct from women than they do from men. A double sex standard which
holds that "extra-marital sex is normal for men but depraved for women"
might more readily lead to denial or revocation of parole for women (Haft,
1974). Minority women, particularly unwed minority mothers, are frequently
viewed by society as being more carefree sexually and of looser moral fiber.

Whatever thoughts occupy the minds of parole board members concerning minority women inmates, there is some evidence that their release from
prison differs significantly because of race/ethnicity. Foley and Rasche (1979:
103) found that white women in Missouri more frequently received parole than
did Black women (41.3% versus 33.3%), while Black women were more likely
to be released from prison through commutation of their sentences. As a result, Blacks served a highly significant 30% more actual time (19.4 months) than
whites (14.9%).

Excluding the lynchings of untold numbers of Black females in the early
years of this nation, a preliminary inventory of confirmed lawful executions
of female offenders from 1625 to 1984, reported by Strieb (1988), reveals that
for the 346 female offenders for whom race is known, 229, or 66% were Black
women, and 108 were white women (31%). Apparently these proportions have
reversed in recent years. In their compilation of a list of the women executed
since 1900, Gillispie and Lopez (1986) found that of the 37 women killed, 32%
were Black and 68% white. Nonetheless, relative to their numbers in the general
population, Black women are disproportionately represented on the death rows
of this country. As of August 1, 1988, to the time of this writing, seven of the 22

female death-row inmates are Black (31.8%), and one of the two female inmates under the age of 18 awaiting death is Black.

CONCLUSIONS AND RECOMMENDATIONS

The most cogent conclusion one can draw from an examination of the minority woman offender in the United States criminal justice system is that despite awakening interest in female criminality, little attention is devoted to the Black, Hispanic, or Native American female offender. Vernetta Young incisively describes the dilemma that confronts Black women in American society, a depiction which is equally applicable to all minority women:

> Black women in American society have been victimized by their double status as blacks and as women. Discussions of blacks have focused on the black man; whereas discussions of females have focused on the white female. Information about black females has been based on their position relative to black males and white females. Consequently, black women have not been perceived as a group worthy of study. Knowledge about these women is based on images that are distorted and falsified. In turn, these images have influenced the way in which black female victims and offenders have been treated by the criminal justice system (Young, 1986: 322).

The other obvious conclusion is that the few available studies of the minority woman offender tend to document differential treatment due to her racial/ethnic status. Discrimination and a lack of concern for her needs and those of her family are witnessed on every level of the system—arrest, pretrial, judicial, and corrections.

Since the number of incarcerated women is not large, comprising only a little over four percent of the inmate population in the United States, a comprehensive national survey of all female offenders in the District of Columbia, and all 50 states and territories would provide a sound, empirical basis for policy changes that could ameliorate the status and condition of arrested, incarcerated, probationed, and paroled minority female offenders in this nation.

Law enforcement personnel, on the streets and in the station houses, should be sensitized to the special situations faced by the minority mothers whom they arrest. Further, they should be intensively trained in race and community relations as a part of their academy curriculum, as well as in continuing training sessions throughout their careers. Emphasis in such training should be on the cultural nuances of the various racial/ethnic groups in the nation, human relations training, and cross-cultural interactions. Since the majority of police officers are men, special training should be available in the psychology of women and intergender relations.

Efforts should be made to release minority women on their own recognizance, since they are often low income and cannot make bail. If bail is felt to be required, it should be within the realm of possibility for the specific female offender. Since a majority of minority woman offenders are heads of households, any alternatives to outright release of a minority female offender should minimize the disruption of family ties.

Many changes are needed in the laws and the administration of justice by the criminal courts in regard to all women offenders. The following items should be considered:

1. Indeterminate sentencing exclusively applied to women should be eliminated;
2. Prostitution should be decriminalized, particularly since such laws have a discriminatory effect against minority women, while ignoring the male customer who is usually white;
3. Other victimless crimes, such as drug and alcohol abuse, should be viewed as the diseases they are and decriminalized;
4. Educational programs should be initiated to orient both Native Americans and criminal justice personnel to the rights of Native Americans and the discretion and powers of tribal laws and courts; translators should be provided at every level of the criminal justice system for those minorities who are not English speaking; and
5. More women and minority judges and other administrators should be installed at every level of the judicial system.

The corrections system is probably the area most in need of change, yet it is the most entrenched and resistant of all the elements of the criminal justice system, despite its potential for administrative policy change due to its strong state control. In their plea for treatment intervention for female offenders, Iglehart and Stein (1985: 152) note that "historically, the female offender has been forgotten, ignored, or merely footnoted when the treatment and rehabilitation of offenders are discussed." Every effort should be made to maintain and strengthen the fragile family ties of minority woman offenders incarcerated in jails and prisons through widened avenues of communication, more home furloughs, conjugal visits, and family life and childcare educational programs. Pregnant inmates should be permitted to keep their new-born infants while in prison to enhance the bonding process. Legal services, law libraries, and access to courts should be afforded to all women in prison to assist them in preparing defenses and appeals and to properly deal with legal problems concerning their children.

All language restrictions should be eliminated and translators should be available for those minority women not proficient in the English language. Corrections officers should be bilingual in those areas with large numbers of Spanish-speaking inmates. More and better medical, vocational, and educational programs should be provided in women's correctional facilities to maintain sound health and prepare women for nontraditional jobs to gainfully support themselves and their families upon release. Finally, minority women offenders should be released from prison under the same conditions and with the same considerations as nonminority women through timely determination by parole boards and commissions containing minority women in equal proportions to those in the prison system of each state.

For over 15 years I have labored over the etiology of crime and thought that understanding female crime would offer the key to a general theory of crime causation based on the political, economic, and social realities of an inequitable society such as ours. The notion of generating theory diminishes in importance with the realization of the injustices perpetrated against *all* racial/ethnic minorities in the U.S. criminal justice system through institutional racism. Particularly distressing is the double discrimination experienced by minority women offenders simply because they are nonwhite and happen also to be female; they are the most powerless of the powerless.

Perhaps in another 15 years, the real meaning of a criminal justice system dominated by white males will be sufficiently documented that the "grand" theory will fall into place. But somehow I doubt it. According to Sophocles, "knowledge must come through action," to which Disraeli would add, "justice is truth in action." The path is clearly demarcated.

NOTES

1. Two groups of female offenders are excluded from this discussion—Asian American women offenders and adolescent female offenders. In the first instance, the small numbers preclude an examination of this offender group, since Asian American women comprise less than one percent of arrested women. Girls present peculiar problems because of their age and the uniqueness of their processing through the juvenile justice system.

2. Reporting problems from the various jurisdictions introduce multiple potential errors, but more importantly, these statistics are based upon the U.S. Census which consistently undercounts minorities, especially Blacks and Hispanics.

3. Beginning in 1987, the UCR program ceased collection of "ethnic origin" data; however, in 1986 Hispanics were listed separately and were 12.7% of total arrests and 14.7% of arrests for Index violent crimes.

4. As the female minority group most studied and most involved in the U.S. criminal justice system, the focus throughout this article is on Black women. However, it is contended that other minority women share the same type of experiences in the system.

5. Observations of women's criminal court cases indicated that the public defenders observed in the 11 courts were sorely pressed for time. Many had only minutes to talk to their clients, most of whom were assigned at the arraignment. As a result, over 95% of the cases were plea bargained.

6. The most cogent example is capital punishment. According to the NAACP Legal Defense Fund, since the 1976 reinstitution of capital punishment, 30.69% of those executed were minority defendants with white victims, but not a single white defendant with a minority victim had been executed as of August, 1988.

7. The idea here is that the criminal justice system "values" white lives and "devalues" Black and other minority lives in the imposition of harsher sentences if the victim is white rather than Black. This devaluation is particularly appropriate in an interracial crime.

PART THREE

The Criminal Justice Process

On the Internet . . .

Sites appropriate to Part Three

This site was designed as a resource for those who are interested in sentencing and corrections. It contains many links to a variety of criminal justice sources.

    http://www.correctionalpolicy.com

This is the official Web site of the Fully Informed Jury Association (FIJA), a nonprofit educational association whose mission is to inform all Americans about their rights, powers, and responsibilities when serving as trial jurors. FIJA also seeks to restore the political function of the jury as the final check and balance on the American system of government.

    http://www.fija.org

This American Probation and Parole Association (APPA) site offers information and resources related to probation and parole issues, position papers, the APPA code of ethics, and research and training programs and opportunities.

    http://www.appa-net.org

This site contains resources on prisons and on the death penalty debate. Many writings by prisoners and death-row inmates themselves are included.

    http://www.prisonwall.org

CHAPTER 5 Police and Lawlessness

5.1 MICHAEL HUSPEK, ROBERTO MARTINEZ, AND LETICIA JIMENEZ

Violations of Human and Civil Rights on the U.S.-Mexico Border, 1995 to 1997: A Report

One of the most controversial issues confronting policing in the United States is the use of excessive force. A number of high-profile police brutality cases have renewed concerns of misconduct by law enforcement officers. While many social critics contend that police brutality does not occur as often as some people might think, others contend that police brutality is endemic to American policing and not simply comprised of isolated incidents of rogue cops out of control. Many qualitative studies show that nonwhite minorities, drug offenders, and homosexuals are disproportionately victimized through police misconduct. Although the true extent of police use of excessive force is unknown, according to Amnesty International in a 1998 report entitled *Shielded from Justice: Police Brutality and Accountability in the United States,* there were over 3,000 federal criminal civil rights cases referred to the U.S. federal judicial district in 1996 involving police misconduct. Yet there is little accountability for police brutality—less than 100 of the cases were sent to grand juries for prosecution. Federal law enforcement officers are repugnant in their proliferation of brutality and lawlessness toward private citizens, often engaging in deadly force and physical and verbal abuse and intimidation.

One aspect of immigration that has yet to surface in the national debate on immigration to the United States is the extent to which immigrants are victims of police violence. One reason for this may be that much of the violence against immigrants is precipitated by law enforcement agents who continue to escape criminal culpability. In the following selection from "Violations of Human and Civil Rights on the U.S.-Mexico Border, 1995 to 1997: A Report," *Social Justice* (Summer 1998), Professor Michael Huspek of California State University at San Marcos and Roberto Martinez and Leticia Jimenez of the U.S.–Mexico Border Program with American Friends Service Committee in San Diego, California, consider complaints from 267 individuals whose civil rights have been violated by various law enforcement agencies patrolling the United States–Mexico border. Their research reveals that the violations range from illegal searches, to physical and psychological victimization, to child abuse and murder. They suggest that law enforcement officers must receive better training and monitoring, that an external review board must be instituted to deal with public complaints of police lawlessness on the border, and that "the relationship between immigration and law enforcement policies be placed at the top of the agenda for national debate."

Key Concept: police lawlessness, the U.S. Border Patrol, and the United States–Mexico border

*T*his report considers a number of complaints by persons who maintain that law enforcement officials have violated their human and civil rights. The violations include illegal search of persons and their private property, verbal, psychological, and physical abuse of persons, child abuse, deprivation of food, water, and medical attention, torture, theft, use of excessive force, assault and battery, and murder. The complaints are directed at a number of law enforcement agencies located principally in Southern California, including the U.S. Border Patrol, U.S. Customs, U.S. Port Security, the Sheriff's Departments of San Diego, Vista, San Marcos, Fallbrook, and Riverside, the San Diego Police Department, the California Highway Patrol, and the California National Guard. The Immigration and Naturalization Service (INS), including the U.S. Border Patrol, is mentioned most frequently in the majority of complaints. The subjects responsible for voicing the complaints include 267 individuals who are highly diverse with respect to age, social class, gender, life ambition, and legal status. Many are undocumented immigrants, but many others are holders of valid border crossing cards as well as citizens and legal residents of the United States. All of the subjects share an Hispanic ethnicity.

The complaints were collected in two ways. First, during 1996, the San Diego office of the American Friends Service Committee (AFSC) charted a decline in the number of human and civil rights abuses reported on the northern side of the California/Baja California border. In the same year, an increase in the number of reports of abuse on the Mexican side of the border suggested that victims of abuse were being apprehended and deported before they could file reports with human rights workers in the United States. In December 1996, therefore, the AFSC-San Diego met with human rights representatives from Baja California to formulate a strategy for interviewing migrants immediately after they were deported to Mexico by U.S. authorities. As a result of this meeting, students from the Universidad Autónoma de Baja California conducted interviews from January to April, 1997, at the Tijuana, Tecate, and Mexicali ports of entry. The binational study documented 204 cases of abuse.

Second, staff of the AFSC-San Diego office carried out 63 interviews of victims of human and civil rights abuses for the years 1995, 1996, and 1997. During the course of these interviews, respondents were encouraged to provide detailed narratives that identified the nature of the abuses and the contexts within which they occurred. Each narrative is highly individualized, offering a uniquely human story that provides a glimpse of the queries, shouts, interrogations, and threats that were used in the course of the law's applications, as well as the felt humiliation, intimidation, frustration, fear, and other life interruptions such applications imposed upon narrators and their family or friends. The narratives also form a collection; considered in conjunction with the binational study, they validate the following statements:

1. That violations of persons and their most basic rights by law enforcement officials are a routine occurrence;
2. That there is a pattern in the delivery of wrongful law enforcement practices;
3. That an identifiable logic motivates and legitimates such delivery; and
4. That the delivery and logic of law enforcement practices together may amount to a routinized infliction of terror upon persons who are targeted by the practices or who feel themselves likely to be so targeted.

The remainder of this report further develops and provides illustrative support for the above statements. The report begins by focusing on the complaints raised by 204 persons released into Mexico after being apprehended by agents of the U.S. Border Patrol, the INS, U.S. Customs, and other law enforcement agencies. The report emphasizes the nature of the complaints and their statistical frequency, but also draws upon the additional 63 narratives to supply meaningful content to the complaints and to address the substantive practices of law enforcement at the specific points of their application. Insofar as the practices are revealed to be patterned, an attempt is made to describe the logic that motivates and legitimates the practices as well as their consequences.

Second, in an attempt to explain the nature of abusive law enforcement practices and the logic that drives them, the report offers an overview of the general climate of law enforcement in the southwest region of the United States.

Recent developments throughout the region include a steady build-up of military and police personnel, an increased integration of military and police units, heightened deployment of surveillance technology, intensified criminalization of activities related to illegal immigration, and an inflamed rhetoric that both vilifies targeted subjects and legitimates the tactics used by law enforcement agencies against them. The report concludes with a set of recommendations as to what is needed in the way of practical, remedial policies.

I. HUMAN AND CIVIL RIGHTS ABUSES AND THEIR CONTENTS

Human and civil rights violations by law enforcement officials have long been a regular feature in the southwest region of the United States. This is especially true of the United States Border Patrol, whose agents have demonstrated a penchant for cruelty and violence toward those they have been commissioned to hunt down and apprehend. The forms of conduct range from the labeling by Border Patrol agents of the undocumented immigrants they apprehend as "tonks," in reference to the sound of a flashlight striking a human's skull, to unwarranted discharging of firearms (ILEMP, 1992). Concerning the latter, a recent study by Americas Watch (1992: 9) reports that "since 1980, Border Patrol agents have shot dozens of people along the U.S.-Mexico border, killing at least eleven and permanently disabling at least ten." The study goes on to state that further killings resulted from a joint Border Patrol-San Diego Police task force, referred to as the Border Crime Prevention Unit. From 1984 to 1989, members of the task force were involved in 26 shooting incidents in which 19 people were killed and 24 wounded.

Many complaints detailed in this report point specifically to what appears to be a continuation in recent years of violent and abusive conduct on the part of law enforcement officials. This statement finds backing in the binational study's statistical breakdown of statements by 204 persons released into Mexico after being apprehended: 43% reported witnessing excessive use of force either to themselves or to others; 12% reported instances of physical/sexual abuse; 23% reported hearing verbal abuse; 11% reported being made to hear racial insults; 46% reported denial of food or water; 14% reported denial of medical attention; 21% reported being recklessly transported; and 15% reported having been threatened.

A. In No Man's Land: Flight and Punishment; Surrender and Punishment

Reported abuses often refer to the treatment undocumented immigrants receive after being intercepted in remote areas. On the one side are enforcement agents who are assigned to hunt down and capture illegal immigrants, which may entail traversing dangerous terrain, made even more dangerous once the hunters and hunted enter into the heat of a chase. On the other side are undocumented immigrants who may have a great deal to lose upon being apprehended. In addition to financial loss (e.g., coyote fees) and possible imprisonment, there may be strong emotional factors at work. At one moment, they are concealed under cloak of darkness in the isolated wild, only to be struck by utter panic in the next upon being sighted in the search beams of a hovering helicopter or pursuing Ford Bronco. Because the undocumented immigrant may have been the victim of violence in the past, or has heard about violence being directed against others, fear may also come into play. In any event, the undocumented immigrant, having been detected, must make a rapid calculation: Do I attempt to flee, or do I submit?

Running places the targeted subject at great risk, for upon being captured one may receive physical punishment from angry law enforcement officers. So attests Francisco Valdez Lopez who, after being apprehended along the U.S.-Mexico border in July 1995, had a foot placed upon his head as he was forced to the ground and handcuffed. First threatened with death by a Border Patrol agent, he was then beaten with closed fists and batons by a number of agents, causing his nose and mouth to bleed. In February 1995, Juan Carlos Guzman Velasquez also ran after Border Patrol agents spotted him smuggling undocumented immigrants through the San Clemente checkpoint. Wrestled to the ground and handcuffed, he was then punched and had his head slammed into the ground repeatedly. One agent pulled his hair back and punched him in the face. The beating Guzman sustained was so severe that he was transferred to a hospital, though the Border Patrol's formal written account of the incident neglected to mention the injuries.

After hopping the border fence at a railroad crossing near the San Ysidro Port of Entry in July 1996, Jorge Soriano Bautista also ran, until he was hit hard in the back by a Ford Bronco that pursued him, knocking him to the ground and causing him to lose consciousness. Upon regaining consciousness, Bautista heard his arm snap while being handcuffed by a Border Patrol agent, and he again lost consciousness. Bautista was given no medical attention for either his broken arm or the blow to his body caused by the Ford Bronco. Instead, he was returned to the border and stuffed by agents back under the fence onto the Mexican side where he later received medical attention at a Tijuana hospital.

Even if the targeted subject does not run, he or she may nevertheless suffer violence at the hands of arresting officers. In June 1996, Sergio Ponce Rodriguez stopped when he was so ordered after having crossed the border near Tecate, but he was then beaten to the ground by a Border Patrol agent and kicked several times in the head. In February 1996, Carlos Sanchez Zamora stopped upon being commanded to do so, yet he too was kicked repeatedly in the ribs and hit on the arm with a baton. In January 1996, Roman Gonzalez Garcia, after stopping and being handcuffed near the San Ysidro Port of Entry, was pulled up by the handcuffs while at the same time an agent stomped on his ankle with his entire weight, breaking the ankle. Near Campo in August 1995, after Rogelio Hernandez was stopped by Border Patrol agents, his head, hip, and testicles were injured as he was pulled out of his car window by the hair and arm. Agents then threw him to the ground, jumped on his back with their knees, beat him with batons, and held his face in the dirt, almost smothering him. All the while, the agents directed obscenities and racial insults at him, including "stupid Mexican."

Verbal abuse seems to frequently accompany the excessive use of force; the binational study indicates that almost half the time such abuse is punctuated with racial insults. Along the border in September 1995, while Jorge Hernandez Samano was being beaten with closed fists and batons by three Border Patrol agents, a fourth agent approached and asked, "Why do you want to run, . . . wetback?" Yet another agent hit Hernandez on the head with a flashlight, opening a wound. Near the San Ysidro Port of Entry in February 1996, as Carlos Sanchez Zamora was being kicked by a Border Patrol agent, the agent said: "Shut up, . . . Mexican; son of a bitch, I'm tired of Mexicans. Stop or I will be killing one or somebody." In May 1995, in East San Diego County, as Jesus Hector Gaspar Segura attempted to dissuade a Border Patrol agent from hitting a woman companion with a long black club, the agent retorted that "migrants smell" and then stated several times: " . . . you *hediondos* [stinking persons]."

After violence is inflicted upon persons, efforts may be made to conceal the nature of the resultant injuries as well as how they were sustained. Jorge Soriano Bautista was stuffed by Border Patrol agents back under the border fence where he was left on his own to seek medical treatment for his broken arm. Jesus Hector Gaspar Segura was beaten severely enough to warrant professional treatment of his wounds, yet the Border Patrol agent who beat him warned against Gaspar mentioning the beating to anyone. Ramon Gonzalez Garcia, whose ankle was broken by a Border Patrol agent, was turned over to Grupo Beta in an ironic show of cooperation between U.S. and Mexican law enforcement agencies. Juan Carlos Guzman Velasquez was beaten so badly by Border Patrol agents as to require hospitalization, yet his injuries received no mention on the Border Patrol's report (I-213) form. Alberto Muñoz Juarez, whose chest was pinned against the U.S.-Mexico border fence by a Ford Bronco in October 1995, was told he would not be deported if he decided against filing charges.

If serious injury is inflicted upon an undocumented immigrant, life can become very difficult. Consider Juan Carlos Lizalde Yanez, who in October 1995 was marched up a mountainside, placed into a vehicle, and handcuffed without his body being fastened by a seatbelt. During the bumpy ride, Border Patrol agents went at a very high speed, causing Lizalde to be tossed around in the back of the vehicle and to hit his head repeatedly on the roof of the vehicle. Once the Border Patrol agents saw Lizalde vomiting and showing other signs of discomfort, they took him to a hospital where it was determined he had suffered a stroke that paralyzed him. Three days later, and still paralyzed, he was asked by Border Patrol agents to sign voluntary departure forms, which he refused to do. Both the Border Patrol and hospital administrators were apparently anxious to shuffle Lizalde back to Mexico. While at the hospital, Lizalde suffered frequent physical and mental abuse from an attending physician. He was left to lay in his own waste, staff neglected to change his clothes and bed pan, and refused him bathroom or shower privileges. Eventually, Lizalde was put out on the street and today remains paralyzed on the entire left side of his body.

B. The Gaze, Queries, and Commands

Most of the above applications of law enforcement practice occurred in the field, along the border, in no-man's-land, where agents' suspicions are unlikely to be challenged and where witnesses to their actions are likely to be scarce. There are, however, numerous other points of contact between law enforcement officials and the persons they target: at ports of entry and inland checkpoints, along U.S. roads and highways, in fields and campsites, at weddings and funerals, and in homes and workplaces. Such areas admit of greater ambiguity for authoritative intervention. Has the subject done anything to warrant questioning? Is the subject documented? Are the documents genuine or not? Does the subject have a criminal record? Might the subject be in the process of committing a crime? Is the subject telling the truth, or not?

To reduce such ambiguity, law enforcement officials must first interrupt a subject's movements. This is usually followed by a prolonged and studied gaze used to identify the subject's ethnic markings, as well as any physical signs of nervousness, such as fidgeting or sweating.[1] Questions may then be used not only as an invitation for the subject to disclose various types of information, but also to elicit a language marker—Does the subject speak English?— or to detect lies, contradictions, overt gaps, or silences in the subject's accounts. Commands may also come into play, requiring the subject to reveal papers and possessions or to proceed to a secondary inspection site where a body search may be conducted.

For the person who is targeted, a great deal may be at stake. The gaze, query, or command can ultimately result in separation from loved ones, loss of income or possessions, deportation, or incarceration. When inspection occurs at a port of entry, it may also mean that the subject is denied entry into the United States, as well as having papers and other belongings confiscated. This is what happened to Brenda Catalina Ramos, an 18-year-old U.S. citizen who was detained in November 1996 while attempting to pass through the San Ysidro Port of Entry despite showing INS officers her birth certificate, social security card, and California ID. She was taken to a room and surrounded by seven inspectors who, over 5 hours, grilled her, laughed at her replies, and threatened to imprison her and her mother unless she confessed to being an illegal alien. Frightened and crying, Ramos falsely confessed. After being sent to an INS detention center in Las Vegas, she was returned to San Diego and then deported by an immigration judge. INS officers confiscated all of her valid documentation of U.S. citizenship.

A similar experience befell Abel Arroyo in June 1995 at the same port of entry. A 19-year-old U.S. citizen who attended the San Diego Regional Center for the Developmentally Disabled, Arroyo went on a brief shopping trip to Tijuana. Upon returning to San Diego through the San Ysidro Port of Entry, he declared his U.S. citizenship and showed his birth certificate, state ID, and social security card. INS agents taunted Arroyo, hurled racial insults at him, and then punched him in the stomach. For seven hours he pleaded with officers to be allowed entry, but to no avail. Without identification documents, he then wandered the streets of Tijuana for days until he met a man who agreed to smuggle him across the border for a fee. Eleven days after being denied entry into his own country, Arroyo was smuggled across the border and reunited with his family.

Even for the subject who is innocent of any criminal wrongdoing, contact with authority may prove to be more than a casual encounter. Beyond the inconvenience of being stopped, inspected, or queried, there is the possibility that the encounter may escalate into something painfully more threatening. It may be fear of this type of escalation that prompts those who are relatively free of markings of suspicion to render themselves both visible and vocal to the inspecting official by removing sunglasses, saluting, waving, verbally hailing, or giving a robust "thumbs up." However, for subjects who bear markings that draw suspicion—skin color or other physical appearances—fear of an escalated encounter with authority may produce uncertainty with respect to how to respond. For example, the tendency might be to conceal one's more visible markings by shrinking before authority's intrusive gaze. Alternatively, in response to an official's query, one might minimize one's verbal offerings for fear that traces of an accent or an inability to speak English with facility might provoke heightened suspicion from the inspecting official. Either stratagem might be ill-conceived, however: shrinking from the gaze may heighten the official's suspicion and suppressing information may be viewed as indication of guilt.

On the other hand, to possess the markings of suspicion and to return the gaze or to counter the query with a question of one's own may invite harsh recriminations. This was the experience of Raul Nuñez, who in May 1997 asked a Riverside Sheriff's deputy a question as to the nature of the problem that prompted the deputy's attention. After Nuñez was commanded by the deputy to "shut [his] mouth and step inside," he was then sprayed in the face with mace. When Nuñez's son, Victor, asked for the deputy's badge number, the deputy countered with: "Are you trying to be a smart ass, [you] punk? . . ." In August 1997, Jose Gonzales was arrested after he asked a sheriff's deputy his name and to whom he could complain about the treatment he was receiving. In July 1997, as Rigoberto Lopez and his friend, Emigdio, were entering the U.S. at the San Ysidro Port of Entry, the men were directed by U.S. Customs officials to secondary inspection. When they asked for the rationale, orders to spread their legs were accompanied with kicks and shoves. Emigdio was struck in the testicles by a U.S. Customs agent while both men were continually being yelled at to keep quiet and not ask any questions. In September 1997, Noel Alarid asked two INS officers at the San Ysidro Port of Entry why he needed to be queried further in an office and whether he had done anything wrong. The officers simply grabbed his arm, and in response to Alarid's protestations, began slamming him against one wall, then another. In April 1995, after David Garcia Cruz was apprehended by Border Patrol agents at the San Clemente checkpoint, he dared to glance at the badge of one of the agents. The agent retaliated by punching Garcia three times in the chest, causing a visible indentation in the rib area, and then laughing at him.

C. Intensified Tactics

Once the dynamic between officials and the subject under their suspicion is intensified, the scrutinizing gaze may be replaced by a thorough search of the subject's body and possessions; queries may be converted into a fullfledged interrogation. Commands come increasingly into play as subjects are ordered to exit vehicles and submit to an assortment of authoritative probes.

Commands interpellate the subject as a possible criminal who may be dangerous and in need of restraint. This process may be humiliating when performed upon the subject while friends or family members are forced to observe; when performed upon the subject in isolation from friends or loved ones, the process may be frightening. No doubt, such was the case for the Sandoval family and friends who in May 1995 were directed by U.S. Customs officials to secondary inspection where the mother, father, their two teen-aged sons and two young women (aged 14 and 15) were all questioned separately after being made to remove their shoes and socks. Or consider 14-year-old Jessica Patricia Soto and her mother, both U.S. citizens, who were separated from one another as they attempted passage through the Otay Mesa Port of Entry in May 1995. After Jessica became nervous in response to INS officials' questions, she was shoved and pulled into an office while being kneed and called a "bitch." Once in the office, Jessica was grabbed by the neck by a male officer and had her face shoved into a corner. All the while, Jessica's mother could hear her daughter's pleas for help, but could not go to her.

As authority steps up its tactical applications, the subject's previously predictable world is quickly transformed into one of insecurity and fear. Eighteen-year-old U.S. citizen Brenda Catalina Ramos was questioned at the San Ysidro Port of Entry in a rapid-fire manner over a five-hour period by no less than seven different INS agents. During this time she was accused of lying, possessing phony documentation, and being from the Philippines (because of her slanted eyes). In August 1996, Pedro Sanchez was queried by Border Patrol agents at his workplace in San Diego. He showed his green card and social security card, but the agents questioned the authenticity of the latter and asked Sanchez repeatedly, "Where did you buy it?" and "How much did you pay for it?" Juan Carlos Aguirre Zazueta attempted to use a valid passport to pass through the San Ysidro Port of Entry in May 1996. When he attempted to assure a U.S. Customs official of the passport's authenticity, however, the official slapped him on the forehead and insisted that Aguirre tell the truth. Later, the official threw the passport into the trash. Juan Ramon Avalos, a U.S. citizen, had the authenticity of his documents questioned by INS agents during his attempt to pass through the San Ysidro Port of Entry in August 1995; yet when Avalos attempted to respond to an agent's queries, he was told to "shut up." At the same port of entry in July 1997, Berta Alicia Chavez, a U.S. citizen, drew attention to herself on account of not speaking English. INS agents then threatened to imprison her unless she signed papers testifying that her documentation was fraudulent. After signing the papers, Chavez was deported and had to wait several days before her family eventually proved her citizenship. Katarina Galvan Ledezma, also a U.S. citizen, ran into similar difficulty at the same port of entry since she lacked full command of the English language. After threatening Ledezma with jail unless she admitted to lying, U.S. Customs officers took her birth certificate and state ID card and sent her and her family back to Tijuana.

Such interrogating procedures may have the effect of making the targeted subject feel inferior. In fact, this might be their logic: to reduce the subject's confidence so that a range of tactics might be more effectively applied. By the same logic, should the subject object to the rough treatment or the shouts or the threats, officials may interpret such assertions of personhood as a resistance that is to be countered by an application of (increased) force. A torrent of violence may then result. In August 1997, for example, 83-year-old Mrs. Ruiz witnessed San Diego Police officers roughing up her son in response to his insistence that he be told why he was being ordered to "hit the ground." When Mrs. Ruiz begged the officers to stop slamming her son's head into the ground, she was kicked in the stomach twice by an officer and then knocked to the ground. In June 1997, Beatrice Avila, a legal resident of the United States, encountered a similar experience involving the Border Patrol. Objecting to the intimidating behavior of Border Patrol agents, her arm was twisted behind her as she was thrown face down to the ground, injuring her chin and face. While handcuffed and lying prone on the ground, Avila was then kicked by an agent in the back and leg.

In May 1995, when 14-year-old Denise Elizabeth Garcia Velez, a U.S. citizen, attempted to enter the United States at the Otay Mesa Port of Entry, she showed her Los Angeles birth certificate. This apparently upset a U.S. Customs Official who yelled, "Stupid bitch! I don't want to see your stupid trash." Denied entry, Garcia was then pushed out of the inspection office. When she protested, the agent sprayed her eyes with pepper spray and asked her if it hurt. Fifteen-year-old Noel Alarid, also a U.S. citizen, protested when INS officers at the San Ysidro Port of Entry directed him to secondary inspection and grabbed his arm. Three officers responded by slamming him against the wall. Witnesses observed that Alarid struggled with the officers, but would periodically stop struggling, which seemed to provoke even greater use of force from his assailants. Alarid's cousin, Ramon, who was witnessing the violence, was commanded to leave the scene when he told officers to stop hurting Noel. When an officer grabbed for Ramon's hand, Ramon kept his arm firm. Despite being placed in handcuffs, Ramon continued to insist that the officers stop hurting Noel. The officers yelled at him to "shut... up," and they then tightened the handcuffs on his wrists. Both Noel and Ramon were placed in holding cells. Noel was placed alone in a small cell that reeked from toilet paper and garbage that lay scattered on the floor. Ramon was placed in a crowded cell with approximately 15 other men. The toilet in this cell had no seat and there was no toilet paper. The smell inside the cell was so bad that the men were using blankets to cover their noses.[2]

Jesus Payan, a U.S. citizen, made the mistake in December 1994 of getting angry when an INS agent at the San Ysidro Port of Entry denied him entry into the United States and told him to "go back to Mexico." After Payan told the agent to ["go away"], the agent ran after him and grabbed him by the neck until several other agents arrived. With Payan's friends watching, the agents slammed his head twice against the edge of a table. At the same port of entry, U.S. citizen Luisa Torres Garcia was treated as if she were resisting when, falling as a result of her neck being grabbed and her arm being pulled behind her, she reached toward an officer for balance. For this action she was accused of striking the officer.

Asserting one's rights and personhood in the way of asking for explanations or rationale for the treatment they are receiving is often mocked or ignored by officials. At the Tecate Port of Entry in March 1995, an INS officer threatened to seize Eva Gonzalez Mendoza's valid U.S. passport. When she asked for a rationale, the officer stated that he did not need a reason. He then seized the passport and refused to listen while Mendoza begged for her document back so she could take her child, a U.S. citizen, to a U.S. doctor. Mendoza never learned why her passport was cancelled, though the officer's report indicates that she shouted and refused to follow orders, both of which she has subsequently denied. In October 1997, when Juan Manuel Moreno was being beaten by Vista Sheriff's deputies who took turns kicking him, his girlfriend asked for an explanation. One of the deputies responded: "Because we don't like Mexicans." When Noel and Ramon Alarid's friends and relatives were overheard discussing human rights, an INS officer shouted: "What... rights? You don't have any... rights!"

D. Patterned Delivery of Law Enforcement Practices

In all likelihood, the experiences of so many over a three-year period are not exceptional cases, but representative of a general pattern of occurrences. The 204 statements collected as part of the binational study over a relatively brief period of time provide support for the above claim. The narratives also offer substantial evidence that it is not the absence of civil and human rights abuses that explains a "mere" 63 complaints being filed through the San Diego AFSC office, but more likely the fear and intimidation tactics that are directed against targeted subjects.[3] In an atmosphere where physical and verbal abuse are being inflicted upon persons, the threat becomes commonplace. Thus, in June 1996 near Tecate, after Sergio Ponce Rodriguez was kicked by a U.S. Border Patrol agent at least seven or eight times, he was told to run while the agent had his hand placed on his service revolver as if it were a dare. In February of the same year, near San Ysidro, Carlos Sanchez Zamora endured kicks and racial taunts while one of the agents had his service revolver pointed at him. In August 1995 along the border, as Francisco Valdez Lopez was bleeding at the nose and mouth from Border patrol agents' closed fists and batons, he was told they were going to kill him. In October 1997, while her car was being directed to secondary inspection at the San Ysidro Port of Entry, a U.S. Customs inspector warned Angelica Navarro that he would "shoot her" if she did not slow down.

Even to witness the lawless behavior of agents is enough to warrant a threat. Such was the case with Rosario Cardenas and Maggie Bauer who in November 1996 were shaken after viewing the rough treatment a young man was receiving at the hands of several INS agents at the San Ysidro Port of Entry. When the witnesses inquired as to the reasons for such behavior, one agent... gave them the middle finger, while another agent yelled, "get ... out of here" and placed his hand on his service revolver. The effects of such threats should not be underestimated: in August 1995 they caused Jorge Hernandez Samano, after receiving a severe beating from four Border Patrol agents, to state that his numerous injuries were caused when he was climbing into a Border Patrol van after being apprehended along the border.

This recognition of human and civil rights abuses as routine occurrences discloses the workings of a logic of law enforcement as it is constituted by practices aimed against a select group of targeted subjects to interrupt their previously free passage, direct a searching gaze upon them, to query and issue authoritative commands to them, and to detain them or to apply other modes of restraint. Each of these practices can be backed by authoritative legitimation. Nevertheless, it is impossible to judge them without recognition that they are directed selectively only against some subjects to the exclusion of others. Further, inasmuch as the practices tend to exceed just limits—the limits of a person's body or one's right to privacy, or one's right to be secure from authoritatively instituted physical or verbal abuse—so they may have cumulative effects upon those who are most frequently targeted.

The effects themselves are fraught with fear and indecision. When the helicopter's search light beams down on its prey, the subject can hardly know whether to run or submit when it appears that excessive punishment may be inflicted regardless of the decision that is made. Once the authoritative gaze is directed upon the subject, does one shrink from it and thereby attempt to conceal visible markings of one's identity? Or does one return the gaze and, by so doing, offer an invitation to harassment or abuse? As the subject is queried from all sides, asked personal or irrelevant questions, or told that one is lying, does one cower and disclose all that is asked, perhaps even signing false confession papers? Or does one counter with questions of one's own that seek a rationale for having such queries directed at oneself, despite the near certainty that such countering will provoke further assaults upon one's sense of personal dignity? When authoritative commands to submit are questionable, does one acquiesce despite the humiliation this entails? Or does one resist with the knowledge that to do so might provoke a brutal response?

The logic that generates practices that produce these kinds of seemingly no-win life dilemmas transgresses the established limit of law. Perhaps the most important question is why it does this. What is it that prompts and normalizes this transgressing logic?

II. EXPLANATIONS

The general atmosphere of law enforcement in Southern California provides some explanation for the frequency of complaints regarding civil and human rights violations. This atmosphere consists of a steady build-up of military and police personnel, increased integration of military and police units, heightened deployment of surveillance technology, intensified criminalization of activities related to illegal immigration, and inflamed rhetoric that vilifies targeted subjects and legitimates the tactics used by law enforcement agencies. Contributing most to these developments has been Operation Gatekeeper, a federal project launched by the Clinton administration in October 1994 in response to the high numbers of undocumented immigrants entering the United States across what is referred to as the San Diego Sector.[4] Behind a steadily increasing amplification of presidential and congressional support, the presence of the operation has expanded dramatically over a short period of time. This includes sizable increases in law enforcement personnel and a formidable build-up of surveillance and control technology. In the San Diego area, for example, over the past year 1,665 Border Patrol agents have been supplemented by an additional 462 additional hires (Doyle, 1997). Congress has also committed at the national level a minimum of 1,000 additional Border Patrol agents per year over the next five years (GAO, 1997). This new force is being equipped with an increasingly sophisticated arsenal of law enforcement equipment consisting of "improved image enhancement vehicles," portable electronic ground sensors, infrared night scopes, sophisticated surveillance helicopters, low-level light television cameras, and high-power stadium-style lighting used to illuminate sections of a triple wall, developed over 1996 and 1997 at a cost of $8.6 million, that separates the U.S. from its Mexican neighbor *(Ibid.).* A recent Government Accounting Office (GAO) report states that since 1994, "the San Diego sector alone acquired an additional 28 infrared scopes, about 600 underground sensors, about 500 vehicles, about 600 computers, and several advanced computer systems" (1997:23).

At least as notable as the build-up of personnel and technology has been the increased integration of military and police forces. Thus, the Border Patrol, a paramilitary force that has been given expanded law enforcement powers since the late 1980s, routinely receives added support from military, police, and other enforcement agencies (Dunn, 1996; Palafox, 1996). The support is made visible in coordinated maneuvers and joint operations involving the Border Patrol and U.S. Army, Air Force, and Marines. Further, on any given day the National Guard, whose primary task is to build and maintain the wall, may provide the Border Patrol with tactical ground and aviation support. Further plans are also underway for deploying the National Guard in other capacities, which may include manning night-vision scopes, maintaining electronic sensors, assisting with communications and transportation, and conducting aerial surveillance of border activities (U.S. House Hearings, 1995). The Border Patrol also integrates its efforts with some 135 local police and sheriff's deputies who provide escort during nighttime missions. In 1997, U.S. Forest Service personnel were also enlisted to set up and staff inland checkpoint stations for purposes of stopping and interrogating visitors of national parks.

The intensification of law enforcement activity has been fueled by a rhetoric of fear (e.g., Calavita, 1996; Mehan, 1997).[5] This rhetoric, which feeds upon the idea of the dangerousness of the immigrant population, has been made concrete by recent law and a revamped charging policy that effectively increases the criminalization of the immigrant population. Special emphasis has been placed on prosecuting those who have committed "serious felonies," such as for illegally transporting aliens, which can earn sentences of up to five years for a first offence and up to 15 years for a second, as well as for attempting illegal entry with prior felony conviction, which typically earns a two-year sentence, for attempting illegal entry by means of document fraud, which is prosecuted as a felony with a two-year maximum sentence, and for attempting illegal entry after having been previously arrested for a similar act (U.S. Code, Title 8).

Beyond providing a rationale for stepped-up law enforcement, the prevailing rhetoric also has enabled military and police agencies to sidestep otherwise problematic constitutional constraints. Thus, although the National Guard is constitutionally prohibited from enforcing federal immigration laws, it is empowered to provide counterdrug support along the border to federal agencies in the way of "photo reconnaissance," "intelligence analysis," and "aviation support for night thermal imagery" (U.S. House Hearing, 1995:145). Similarly, although U.S. military forces are prohibited by law from pursuing and apprehending suspected criminals within the U.S. interior, they do have jurisdictional authority in marijuana eradication efforts and so are deployed in tandem with the Border Patrol to monitor and surveil suspected criminal activities as well as to assist in the pursuit of criminal suspects (Dunn, 1996; Palafox, 1996). A most telling example of this has been Joint Task Force Six (JTF–6), which was responsible for the fatal shooting of Emanuel Hernandez in Texas as he tended his goats along the U.S.-Mexico border (e.g., Reza, 1997).

The Border Patrol was granted limited authority in 1986 to interdict drugs. The agency may only arrest suspected drug traffickers if they are clearly also suspected of being illegal aliens. To overcome this limitation, local police agencies provide assistance by escorting the Border Patrol on its nightly rounds. The California Highway Patrol is now also regularly called upon for assistance, following a rash of fatal vehicular crashes caused by high-speed chases involving the Border Patrol that led to restrictions on the scope of the agency's authority in this regard.

Spokespersons for various law enforcement agencies claim that the stepped-up campaigns of militarization of the border, criminalization of immigration-related activities, and the integration of military, paramilitary, and police units have been highly successful. The once highly visible flow of undocumented immigrants in and around the San Diego area has been dramatically reduced, with traffic redirected into the mountains, deserts, and vast stretches of no-man's-land to the east. Further, in the past year alone over 110,000 illegal immigrants have been ousted from the United States. California leads the way with the expulsion of over 46,000 people. This represents a 35% jump in deportation of criminals and a 93% jump in deportation of noncriminals (GAO, 1997).

However, critics have pointed to the costs of such proclaimed successes, emphasizing how Operation Gatekeeper has induced changes in behavior among the tens of thousands of undocumented immigrants pulled by the jobs magnet in the U.S. (Huspek, 1998). The rechannelling of immigrant traffic to the perilous eastern terrain has brought with it immense human tragedy. In the nighttime pitch of the mountains, falls resulting in injury are common, as are snakebites. Because the trek across the border now may take up to four days and nights, those setting out without adequate provisions are especially at risk. Climatic conditions in the mountains and desert also tend to be harsh and unpredictable. Thirty-eight immigrants are known to have died in 1996 while attempting to traverse the rugged landscape, with the causes of their deaths being primarily dehydration (in the summer desert heat) and hypothermia (in the cruel mountain snow and cold). In 1997, at least 85 people are known to have died while attempting passage. Countless others have surely disappeared after falling into rocky crevices or wandering disoriented in vast stretches of no-man's-land.

Other shifts in behavior are indicated by a heightened desperation among those who are targeted by U.S. law enforcement agencies. Perhaps most dramatic has been the resort by coyotes to increasingly risky means of avoiding arrest. For example, there has been a marked upswing in vehicular crashes following chases that involve fleeing immigrants and law enforcement agencies. In the San Diego area alone, six violent wrecks that left at least 15 dead and 68 injured have occurred since the inception of Operation Gatekeeper.[6] Despite ongoing construction of the triple wall, coyotes have recently resorted to daring daylight border crossings; after high-speed chases into congested neighborhoods, the fleeing truck or van unloads dozens of clients who then flee on foot.

The state has pointed to the immigrants' increasingly desperate acts to legitimate its own build-up of forces. Specifically, as new behaviors are adopted by those targeted by stepped-up police and military tactics, the state further extends the net of its criminalization categories. This is especially true for coyotes, who have been increasingly spotlighted as a primary source of blame. Thus, the unabated heavy influx of undocumented immigrants is said to be due to the greed and desperate cunning of the coyote. If incidents of drug smuggling have risen along the borderlands and into the interior, this is said to be because coyotes are forcing their clients to carry drugs as partial payment for their passage. If injuries and deaths are on the upswing, this is because smugglers take them into dangerous environs and then leave them to die. Since passage of the 1996 Illegal Immigration Reform and Immigrant Responsibility Act (IIRIRA), the penalty for high-speed vehicular flights or evading immigration checkpoints carries a penalty of up to five years and is grounds for deportation of noncitizens, regardless of status. The U.S. Attorney for the Southwest Region of the United States, Alan Bersin, has repeatedly gone on public record in support of capital punishment for coyotes whose activities result in fatalities.

Stepped-up militarization and policing have contributed to increased law enforcement presence throughout the community: more white Ford Broncos are now positioned along the borderline; more surveillance helicopters are in the sky; more joint operations are being conducted along the border; more inland checkpoints are being installed.[7] With intensified criminalization policies aimed at immigration-related activities, the potential offenses loom larger in the estimates of the targeted subjects as well as those who are commissioned to apprehend and detain them. This may be contributing to even more desperate evasion tactics by the former and more drastic enforcement measures by the latter (Huspek, 1998). In this state of heightened alert, law enforcement officials increasingly encounter their targeted subjects in remote stretches of mountain and desert terrain where, outside any effective monitoring controls, the fear and panic of targeted subjects and the anger and fear of enforcement officials may combine to contribute to an increasingly volatile situation.

It is important to acknowledge how such an atmosphere might be felt by those most frequently targeted by militarization, criminalization, and inflamed rhetoric. Nearly 70% of California's agricultural labor force now consists of undocumented workers. Yet, the state has done virtually nothing to police employers who knowingly hire undocumented workers. In fiscal 1997, there was not a single prosecution of an employer of undocumented workers in San Diego County (Huspek, 1997). Further, as grounds for denying California growers' requests for a guest worker program, top government officials pointed to the adequate labor supply already represented by undocumented workers in the state and projected no discernable decline in the available labor force. As such, undocumented workers seeking to satisfy personal or familial economic need may have some understanding of the ready economic demand for his or her services and the government's own complicity in sustaining existing labor-capital arrangements. Consider, too, that many of these tens of thousands of workers may have labored on U.S. soil for many years.[8] We can only imagine the dissonance that must be felt for undocumented immigrants whose labor is so valued, but who must render themselves invisible, skulking from campsite to workplace and back under cover of darkness.

Finally, consider the legal resident or U.S. citizen who perhaps has struggled over most of a lifetime to attain such a status. One can imagine the sense of righteous indignation in the face of law enforcement officials who show negative dispositions toward persons of Hispanic appearance. This might contribute to the likelihood of escalated tension during points of contact between the subject and law enforcement officials. For their part, officials may be inclined to place the targeted subject of their gaze into one of the many categories that stepped-up criminalization has provided. Short of easy categorization, and faced with a person who may not be showing what in the official's estimate is proper deference to authority, there may be the temptation to provoke some form of conflict that ultimately proves to "confirm" the official's predisposition. In short, if the person does not readily fall into an available criminalization category (beyond ethnic appearance), perhaps some provocation will incite an act of resistance to produce an applicable category where none had existed before.

III. RECOMMENDATIONS

Law delegates to enforcement agencies material and symbolic means of authoritative intervention into people's lives. Frequently, such interventions are violent. This may involve directing an intrusive, inspecting gaze upon subjects, questioning, interrogating, and judging them, searching their personal belongings, including their bodies and private body parts, imposing physical restraints upon them, as well as confiscating personal belongings, money, and documents, inflicting physical harm upon them, incarcerating them, and, in extreme instances, executing them.

With such means of violence and control at their command, law must place proper constraints upon the agents vested with the authority to enforce the law. There are boundaries that simply cannot be transgressed. The law is not to be enforced arbitrarily, or selectively against some while a blind eye is turned toward others. Above all, law enforcement officials cannot abrogate subjects' human and civil rights. To do so constitutes a breaking of the law, a form of lawlessness that instills terror in us all. If the officials entrusted with enforcement routinely violate the law, then we must all live in fear. It is imperative, therefore, that officials are carefully selected, trained, and monitored so as to ensure that they conduct themselves in a highly professional manner. Perhaps most important, they must be made accountable to the public they are commissioned to serve.

The data compiled in this report suggest that law enforcement in the southwest region of the United States may be verging on lawlessness. This statement receives fuller support from announcements emanating from the INS. In December 1997, John Chase, head of the INS Office of Internal Audit (OIA), announced at a press conference that public complaints to the INS had risen 29% from 1996, with the "vast majority" of complaints emanating from the southwest border region. Over 2,300 complaints were filed in 1997 as opposed to the 1,813 complaints filed in 1996. Another 400 reports of "minor misconduct" were placed in a new category. Chase was quick to emphasize, however, that the 243 "serious" allegations of abuse and use of excessive force that could warrant criminal prosecution were down in 1997, as compared with the 328 in 1996. These "serious" cases are considered to be distinct from less serious complaints, such as "verbal abuse, discrimination, extended detention without cause."

On the day Chase spoke to the press, the INS also issued a spate of press releases detailing the Action Plan being implemented in response to recommendations specified in the Final Report of the INS' Citizens' Advisory Panel. According to the INS, much of the Action Plan has already been implemented. The plan consists of increasing the information made available to the public, expanding dialogue between the INS and community groups, enhancing dissemination of INS information, increasing public knowledge about complaint procedures, improving complaint process case management, using a complaint database as the basis for personnel decisions, offering greater consistency in INS disciplinary actions, and incorporating local community-based training of INS staff.

Such changes are to be commended, particularly in an increasingly volatile atmosphere of militarization, criminalization, and anti-immigrant rhetoric. Better training and monitoring are clearly needed since agents are being placed in the field at an unprecedented rate. The steady rise in state funding, coupled with increasing points of contact between agents and the public, makes it essential for the community to have a better understanding of the application, logic, and effects of law enforcement practices. Such measures, moreover, need to be implemented not only for the INS, but also for U.S. Customs and all other law enforcement agencies whose operations are continually being integrated with the INS in response to the war against undocumented immigrants.

This report on human and civil rights violations by law enforcement agencies strongly emphasizes, however, that such proposed changes do not go nearly far enough in the right direction. Most vitally needed is an external review board—with genuine citizen participatory input—that can objectively determine the validity of complaints. This need is patent in light of the track records of the two offices most responsible for dealing with public complaints: the INS' OIA and the Office of the U.S. Attorney of the Southern District.

The experience of the American Friends Service Committee in San Diego is that complaints are routinely buried within the OIA. The U.S. attorney's office fares no better. In response to all 63 AFSC-assisted complaints filed at different times over the 1995 to 1997 period, an identical form letter was received that stated: "After careful review . . . we have concluded that there is insufficient evidence to establish a prosecutable violation of the federal criminal civil rights statutes." This standardized response raises a question: How can an office commissioned to implement and defend law enforcement policies and practices be independent in its investigations? The abysmal record of case review by the U.S. attorney's office suggests that the office is not adequately suited for the task.

Beyond institution of an external review board, further discussion needs to be devoted to the frequency and nature of abuses being committed by law enforcement personnel. Perhaps the most obvious and disturbing inference to be drawn from both data sets is that law enforcement in the southwest region of the United States is being applied discriminatorily against Hispanics. This appears to be true irrespective of the subject's citizenship or other forms of documented identity. This is not to state that all law enforcement practices are racially motivated or to claim that all law enforcement agents who engage in such practices are driven by racist sentiments or beliefs. Yet the number and frequency of complaints, as well as their contents, are sufficient to suggest that law enforcement practices are being applied discriminatorily against some, but not others, and that the practices are driven by a logic that is racially discriminatory. Further, the effects of the practice are understandably felt to be racist by those toward whom the practices are often directed. Indeed, as to the latter, the application and logic of law enforcement practices may amount to a routinized infliction of terror upon the persons it targets and upon those who feel themselves likely to be so targeted.

The current process of distinguishing "serious" abuses, such as rapes or shootings, from "less serious" abuses is inadequate. Verbal abuse, discrimination, and extended detention without cause must be treated as the crimes that they are. What distinguishes the verbal abuses that frequently accompany excessive use of force by law enforcement officials from hate crimes? In an atmosphere where immigrant strawberry pickers have been sighted between the crosshairs of an intensified criminalization strategy, it seems fitting that law enforcement officials' violations of the law also be treated as crimes and not merely as forms of institutional misconduct. Indeed, law enforcement officials need to be fully aware that such violations take on a greater magnitude when they are committed by the personnel whom we entrust with the authority to intervene in so many ways in our lives.

Finally, this report is limited in scope in that it restricts itself to human and civil rights abuses by law enforcement officials in the southwest region of the United States. Nevertheless, the report notes that the number and type of abuses are best understood only when considered within an atmosphere of heightened militarization and policing of our border and interior regions, intensified criminalization of undocumented immigrants, and an increasingly inflamed anti-immigrant rhetoric. As such, this report is intended to stand as a sobering counter to claims from the INS and U.S. attorney's office that we are deporting more illegal aliens and incarcerating more criminals than ever before. We conclude with the recommendation that critical questions involving the relationship between immigration and law enforcement policies be placed at the top of the agenda for national debate. To what lengths are law enforcement agencies resorting in their zeal to apprehend and convict? And how far will the general public permit them to go?

NOTES

1. Based upon an interview conducted January 7, 1998, with Senior Border Patrol Agents Farrens and Villareal at the Temecula checkpoint.

2. Since September 1997, when Noel and Ramon were incarcerated, conditions of the holding cells have not improved. The AFSC-San Diego office continues to hear of 30 to 50 people being kept in a single cell that measures no more than 10 feet wide by 25 feet long. Each cell has only one toilet and no shower or bathing facilities. No beds are provided; people are given a blanket and are required to sleep on the floor. All inhabitants must relieve themselves, and female inhabitants must attend to their feminine hygiene needs, in full view of others. Because trash receptacles are not provided, the floor is frequently covered with litter.

3. Other problems abound. States Nuñez (1992:1577): "alien victims often will not report incidents of confrontation or abuse. Fears of discovery and deportation lead many illegal aliens to believe that the better course is to not report such incidents." He continues: "because the undocumented immigrant's mere presence in this country is viewed as 'illegal,' courts and scholars are faced with the dilemma of whether the 'illegal alien' should be afforded the same constitutional and civil rights as citizens and legal resident aliens" (p. 1578).

4. Along with similar operations—Operation Safeguard in Tucson, Operation Hold the Line in El Paso, and the recently mobilized Operation Rio Grande in Brownsville—Operation Gatekeeper draws from a federally allocated fund of $3.1 billion, nearly twice the $1.6 billion allocated in 1993, and almost four times the $807.8 million allocated in 1988 (Dunn, 1996:35). The San Diego sector is a 66-mile stretch along the U.S.-Mexico border that runs eastward from the Pacific Ocean into desert and mountain areas.

5. State officials have shown a strong penchant for using war terms when discussing border issues. In the context of eliciting support for death penalty sentences for smugglers of aliens whose actions result in death for their clients or others, U.S. Attorney for the Southwest Region, Alan Bersin, announced: "We are declaring war on them" (Gross, 1996). U.S. Attorney General Janet Reno has also repeatedly stressed that the U.S. "will not surrender" the border to aliens (U.S. Senate Hearings, 1994). Perhaps such terms are unavoidable when so much of Operation Gatekeeper involves the use of U.S. military forces for purposes of offering "ground tactical and aviation support," operations that are assessed according to whether they are, in the words of Deputy Commander of the California National Guard, General Edmund Zysk, "militarily sound" (U.S. House Hearings, 1995). States Mehan (1997:267):

   During the Cold War, the state constructed an external enemy, a military enemy, to discipline the citizenry. Now the state and aligned elites are directing our gaze inward, constructing an economic enemy, one who lives among us, but is not part of us.

6. On June 13, 1996, a fleeing van carrying suspected illegal aliens crashed, killing one and injuring 12; on April 26, 1996, a fleeing van carrying suspected illegal aliens crashed, killing two and injuring 19; on April 6, 1996, a fleeing pick-up truck carrying suspected illegal aliens crashed, killing eight and injuring 17; on September 1, 1995, a fleeing car carrying suspected illegal aliens crashed, leaving one dead and several others injured; on April 19, 1995, a fleeing van carrying suspected illegal aliens smashed into a pick-up truck, leaving three dead and 16 injured (Hunt, 1996).

7. According to a GAO report (1997:15), "the number of Border Patrol agents on board along the southwest border increased 76% between October 1993 and July 1997."

8. John Locke's (1960:329) words may be apposite here:

The Labour of his Body, and the Work of his Hands, we may say, are properly his. Whatsoever then he removes out of the State that Nature hath provided, and left it in, he hath mixed his Labour with, and joyned to it something that is his own, and thereby makes it his Property. It being by him removed from the common state Nature placed it in, hath by this Labour something annexed to it, that excludes the common right of other Men. For this Labour being the unquestionable Property of the Labourer, no Man but he can have a right to what that is once joyned to, at least where there is enough, and as good left in common for others.

5.2 DAVID E. BARLOW AND MELISSA HICKMAN BARLOW

Cultural Diversity Training in Criminal Justice

When considering the sociohistorical context within which modern policing emerged, the evolution of community-police relations involves a basic contradiction. On the one hand, both the police and a not-so-small segment of the population have traditionally held that policing is basically the enforcement of law. Toward that end, policing technology, from the recruitment of new officers to the frequent violent encounters between police and the public, has been dedicated primarily to the expediency and efficiency of law enforcement. Such a focus has led to the inevitable bifurcation of relations between the police and community—the we-they split. On the other hand, a certain segment of both the police and the public have viewed policing as a public safety issue as much as a law enforcement function. That is, the role of the police agency is to both "protect and serve." And in contemporary times we can witness some semblance of this focus in the recent moves toward community policing models. These functional arrangements are ostensibly designed to diminish the we-they split, lend credibility and legitimacy to the police role, and to ultimately form a police-community partnership whereby both parties are at least in part responsible for public safety and law enforcement. Currently the traditional view and paramilitary model of policing prevails, and, despite the theoretical soundness of the community policing model, it is not likely that this strategy will be implemented to any significant degree in the foreseeable future. Rather we are more likely to see "token" police programs and policies that provide only slightly more than lip service to what is now considered "politically correct" policing attitudes. In fact, it is quite likely that the concept of community policing will simply serve as a rubric under which "reforms" toward a police-public partnership will actually be "a wolf in sheep's clothing." That is, such reforms may serve more to quiet public concerns and quell the tide of litigation than to embrace a policing model aimed at improving community relations. No substantive or widespread evidence yet exists that would lead us to believe that anything other than the traditional policing model is in store for the future.

The following selection by David E. Barlow and Melissa Hickman Barlow, both of whom are associate professors in the Criminal Justice Program at the University of Wisconsin–Milwaukee, is from "Cultural Diversity Training in Criminal Justice: A Progressive or Conservative Reform?" *Social Justice* (vol. 20, no. 3–4, 1993). It illustrates the dubious and suspect nature of efforts within contemporary policing agencies to improve public-police relations, particularly among minority and other socially subordinated groups. The authors examine the "fashionable" trend in many police agencies to mandate cultural diversity training for its personnel. After observing firsthand the effects of cultural diversity training and the purported rationale for its implementation, they conclude that such training is at best a pawn in the ubiquitous and enduring contradiction inherent to the traditional police role. They argue that, by design, policing is intended to enforce laws that manifest and promote the dominance of one group and the subordination of another.

Key Concept: community-police relations

It is disconcerting to find oneself in the midst of a progressive and critical movement in criminal justice and to face the possibility that efforts aimed at challenging structures of control will serve to strengthen them instead. Perhaps it should come as no surprise that the current movement to develop cultural diversity awareness training for police officers and other criminal justice personnel is already showing signs of supporting rather than transforming the status quo. After all, our own research locates all major criminal justice innovations in the United States (e.g., public police, institutionalization, community-based corrections) within the context of social structures of accumulation and efforts by the capitalist state to control problem populations (Barlow, Barlow, and Chiricos, 1993). Still, dramatic and tragic incidents have drawn public attention to the racist nature of U.S. law enforcement and have created a window of opportunity for efforts to bring multicultural education to police officers. It seems like the right thing to do.

At the same time, participants in the current movement to develop cultural diversity training for police officers will do well to heed the counsel of history and look critically at the impetus for the movement as well as its outcomes. In this article, we describe the cultural diversity training movement as arising out of a growing sense of urgency regarding the tensions in police-minority relations; we discuss our own observations from having been intimately involved in this movement at the local, state, and national levels during the past four years;[1] finally, these observations are located within a broader historical perspective on criminal justice innovations in the United States.

THE MOVEMENT

Cultural diversity, cultural sensitivity, or race relations training are a central component of many recent proposals for reform in the area of police-community relations.[2] Police departments and training bureaus across the nation are developing cultural diversity awareness training programs with

205

*David E.
Barlow and
Melissa
Hickman
Barlow*

conspicuous urgency, often in response to grievous incidents in interactions between police and racial, ethnic, and cultural minorities. The videotaped beating of Rodney King by Los Angeles police officers is certainly among the most dramatic and tragic of such incidents. The Christopher Commission—appointed to investigate police-community relations in Los Angeles County in the aftermath of the Rodney King beating and videotaping, the acquittal of the accused officers, and the 1992 riots in South Central Los Angeles—strongly recommended increasing efforts in cultural sensitivity training for Los Angeles police officers (Christopher Commission, 1992).

Little more than a decade earlier, events remarkably similar to those in Los Angeles in 1992 transpired around the police beating of another African-American man, Arthur McDuffie, in Miami.[3] The Liberty City riot, which ensued following the acquittal of police officers accused of beating Arthur Mc-Duffie to death, was "more violent and destructive than any of the American urban disorders of the 1960s" and, like the recent Los Angeles riots, became the impetus for efforts to improve relations between police and minorities (Skolnick and Fyfe, 1993: 182). A central component of these efforts, according to Deputy Director Eduardo Gonzalez of the Metro-Dade Police Department, has been the development of "Humanity and Community Relations" training in the Miami-Dade County area (Gonzalez, 1992).

In the period between Arthur McDuffie in Miami and Rodney King in Los Angeles, police-minority relations across the nation have been characterized by tensions that typically remain just below the surface until something happens to bring them to the forefront of community and, at times, national concern. The growing movement to develop cultural diversity awareness training for police officers reflects a recognition among law enforcement administrators and experts that the situation is becoming untenable. Ron McCarthy, director of the Deadly Force Training Program for the International Association of Chiefs of Police (IACP) and the retired senior supervisor of the LAPD's SWAT unit, recommends Race and Cultural Awareness Training for police officers to combat unreasonable fear of racial minorities and the excessive use of force (Solomon and McCarthy, 1989). Nancy Taylor's (1991) book, *Bias Crime: The Law Enforcement Response,* contains numerous articles by prominent police executives who recommend training that emphasizes the importance of policing bias crimes. These police executives suggest that bias crime training should focus on understanding the impact on both minority populations of bias crime and on human relations in general.

The Law Enforcement Steering Committee (LESC) is an organization made up of representatives of the Police Executive Research Forum (PERF), the Federal Law Enforcement Officers Association, the Fraternal Order of Police, the International Brotherhood of Police Officers, the Major Cities Chiefs, the National Association of Police Organizations, the National Organization of Black Law Enforcement Executives (NOBLE), the National Troopers Coalition, and the Police Foundation. LESC met in 1992 to discuss public safety and to formulate a series of policy recommendations for improving police-community relations and reducing crime. A central recommendation of this committee was that police departments should initiate "cultural bias training" programs "to enable officers to do their jobs better" (PERF, 1992: 6). NOBLE made cultural awareness training for police officers a primary area of focus in 1993 and developed a series of conferences around the country to showcase "exemplary programs that address the emerging cultural issues facing law enforcement" (NOBLE and PERF, 1993). The cultural diversity training movement is further institutionalized within the newly formed National Law Enforcement Cultural Awareness Association, complete with a quarterly newsletter that goes out to members all across the United States.

Although the ultra-conservative, religious Right opposes acceptance of alternative lifestyles and diversity, traditionally conservative police executives and organizations do support the development of cultural diversity awareness training for police officers because they are acutely aware of the problems in police-minority relations. Conservative police organizations and government executives have vigorously supported training efforts designed to strengthen conflict-resolution and communication skills and to improve police-community relations. The National Organization of Black Law Enforcement Executives (NOBLE) and the Police Executive Research Forum (PERF) support human relations or cultural diversity awareness training because it fits well with their growing support for problem-oriented or community-oriented policing. Their stated concerns include officer safety, liability issues, and increasing the effectiveness of law enforcement (Benson, 1992).[4] Police chiefs have an obvious interest in insulating themselves from citizen complaints of police brutality, misconduct, and abrasiveness, given the lawsuits that accompany such charges. Police organizations are waking up to the fact that enhanced understanding and sharpened communication skills will protect officers from departmental discipline and civil suits. In addition, police agencies are concerned about the current tension in police-community relations and the declining sense of authority among police officers. They often express the hope that such training will be a two-way street, in which the public simultaneously learns about the difficulties and hazards of police work. Law enforcement organizations can see that traditional forms of policing are not successful in reducing crime or making inner-city streets safer. Community- or problem-oriented policing and cultural diversity awareness training are viewed as strategies that might make a difference.

Cultural diversity awareness training has also received significant support from liberal groups such as the American Civil Liberties Union, the National Rainbow Coalition, gay and lesbian organizations, and grass-roots community groups. Like their more conservative counterparts, liberal groups see cultural diversity awareness training as a component of community policing. Yet community activists support such training for reasons differing from those whose primary concerns are legal liability and police effectiveness. Instead, they desire police departments that are more responsive to diverse groups and individuals in their communities. They are concerned about police brutality, misconduct, and abrasiveness, not because of lawsuits, but on behalf of those who are victimized by these acts. The belief is that cultural diversity awareness training will enlighten police officers regarding the concerns of racial and cultural minorities as well as the poor and lead to better treatment of these groups by police officers.

Some programs have developed in response to pressure from grass-roots organizations, while others are proactive initiatives of criminal justice and government executives. In short, efforts to develop cultural diversity awareness training are enjoying widespread support from both liberal and traditionally conservative individuals and organizations. On one level, the current, almost unquestioned acceptance of the need for cultural sensitivity training results from the convergence of liberal and conservative ideologies within this criminal justice policy innovation.[5] Within this context, then, it is reasonable to ask whether cultural diversity training will be progressive or ultimately conservative in its effects. What can be expected from cultural diversity awareness training for police officers? Is it reasonable to expect fundamental changes in police-community relations to occur as a result of these training programs, or will such programs merely treat the symptoms of a deeper contradiction of policing in the United States? Is the problem of police-minority relations simply a matter of police officers not empathizing with minority concerns? Or is the problem much more fundamental to the very structure of society in the United States? Part of the answer must come from looking at the history of this particular criminal justice innovation and of criminal justice innovations in general.

David E. Barlow and Melissa Hickman Barlow

A RECYCLED INNOVATION

The current trend toward developing cultural diversity awareness training for police officers is not truly an innovation; rather, it represents a renewal of interest in this particular approach to making police more sensitive to diverse cultures and lifestyles. Cizon and Smith (1970) state that the Philadelphia Police Department implemented human relations training for police officers in the 1950s. They note, however, that the development of techniques for training police officers in the area of community relations became a high priority beginning with the Law Enforcement Assistance Act (LEAA) of 1965. Cizon and Smith's (1970) paper, *Some Guidelines for Successful Police-Community Relations Training Programs,* is a review of numerous training programs that were implemented during the 1960s and funded by LEAA.

The Kerner Commission Report of 1968 is perhaps the most extensive investigation into police-community relations to date. In this report, the National Advisory Commission on Civil Disorders asserted that to improve police-minority relations, it is essential for officers to receive special training on ghetto problems and conditions (Harris and Wicker, 1988). Similarities between the findings and recommendations of the Kerner Commission and reports of recent commissions are striking.[6] The similarities are even more dramatic in light of a statement made to the Kerner Commission by Kenneth B. Clark:

> I read that report...of the 1919 riot in Chicago, and it is as if I were reading the report of the investigating committee on the Harlem riot of '35, the report of the investigating committee on the Harlem riot of '43, the report of the McCone Commission on the Watts riot.... I must again in candor say to you members of this

commission—it is a kind of Alice in Wonderland—with the same moving picture re-shown over and over again, the same analysis, the same recommendations, and the same inaction (Ibid.: 483).

Longstanding problems in police-minority relations, and repeated efforts to ameliorate them through the development of cultural sensitivity training, give rise to questions concerning the viability of such training in the 1990s. Such questions must be addressed, however, in relation to the history of criminal justice reforms in general.

CONTRADICTION AND CRIMINAL JUSTICE REFORM

The history of criminal justice policy innovations in the United States is fraught with contradiction and the current movement in cultural diversity awareness training for police officers continues this tradition. Throughout the 19th and 20th centuries, seemingly progressive criminal justice innovations have had decidedly conservative impacts, both in terms of preserving the status quo in relations of power and authority and in their effects on immigrants and racial minorities, which have been particularly deleterious (Barlow, Barlow, and Chiricos, 1993). For example, reforms in penal policy—such as institutionalization, indeterminate sentencing, probation, and community corrections—initially appeared to be progressive policies designed to make the criminal justice system more humane. Yet, a closer look at the impetus behind each of these reforms reveals a greater concern for enhancing the effectiveness of penal policy than for making it more humane. As Miller (1980: 79) notes regarding community-based corrections:

> Increased use of community programs is not necessarily synonymous with an anti-incarceration movement. Furthermore, community programs are not necessarily more "humane" or progressive. Institutions exist outside of the walls, and considerable argument may be mounted to posit the notion that…community-based programs are just as coercive, intrusive, and dehumanizing as the methods of walled institutions. They also involve surveillance and control.

The same is true of other criminal justice reforms, such as the transition from private to public policing, police professionalization, the intervention of the federal government into street crime, and the expansion of defendants' and victims' rights (Barlow et at., 1993).

An excellent example is the creation of the Office of the Capital Collateral Representative in the early 1980s in Florida. This agency was created by then-Governor Bob Graham to provide state-funded legal defense for inmates on Florida's death row who file appeals. The creation of this agency might be perceived as a humane effort to provide adequate counsel for these defendants at the expense of the state. However, the governor quickly followed this official act with a dramatic increase in the issuance of death warrants. Indeed, there were numerous indications that Governor Graham's purpose in creating the agency was, in fact, to remove inadequate counsel as a basis for 11th-hour stays of execution by the courts.[7]

A crucial element in all criminal justice reforms is that they are incapable of resolving the fundamental contradictions that exist in a class society. Although efforts may be made to appease certain segments of the population or to make their situation in relation to the criminal justice system more tolerable, the class structure that places them in jeopardy remains intact. No criminal justice reform can change the fundamental class relations that produce the conditions calling for reform. We have previously argued that criminal justice is a part of the overall social structure of accumulation in the capitalist political economy of the United States (Ibid.). Like other aspects of the social structure of accumulation, mechanisms of social control become outdated and ineffective, leading state managers either to improve upon them or to seek new mechanisms of control. The less offensive these mechanisms of control are to democratic sensibilities, the better. Thus, criminal justice innovations have tended to amount to little more than system tinkering and have not produced significant changes in the fundamental nature of criminal justice in a capitalist society.

THE FUNDAMENTAL NATURE OF POLICING

Within this context, current and historical problems in police-community relations may be viewed as manifestations of the inherent contradictions of policing in a class society. Bittner (1980) states that the legitimate use of force is the fundamental distinguishing characteristic or function of police work and describes three central characteristics of policing. First, police work is a "tainted profession," meaning that police forces were granted the legitimate use of violence in an effort to prevent the arbitrary use of violence by the public. In other words, in order to preserve the rights of certain citizens, police officers must choose to restrict the rights of others. Cultural diversity awareness training cannot change the fact that police officers serve the specific social control function of repressing certain activities and restricting freedoms.

The second characteristic of police work that Bittner identifies is that it is necessarily crude. The nature of police work requires police officers to reduce complex human conflicts and profound legal and moral questions to simple decisions. Police work involves a significant amount of crisis intervention, which requires definitive decision-making and quick action. Cultural diversity awareness training may introduce police officers to a whole series of complex social, political, economic, and racial/ethnic issues, but the officers will still be required to function as a crisis unit and to resolve conflicts in an inherently swift and crude manner.

The third characteristic of police work, Bittner notes, is that it is discriminatory: it focuses primarily on the crimes of lower classes. Thus, to the extent that certain minority groups are disproportionately concentrated in the lower classes, they will be disproportionately stopped, investigated, observed, searched, arrested, and killed by police. No amount of cultural diversity awareness training will change the power relations that maintain certain segments of the population within the lower class.

It should be emphasized here that we do not wish to subsume the significance of race in the United States within conceptions of class. As Omi and Winant (1986: 2) point out, the period between the 1960s and 1980s reveals a "complex and contradictory trajectory" in the pattern of race relations that suggests the inadequacy of theories which fail to capture the "centrality of race in American politics and American life."

In the 1960s, race occupied the center stage of American politics in a manner unprecedented since the Civil War era a century earlier. Civil rights struggles and ghetto revolts, as well as controversies over state policies of reform and repression, highlighted a period of intense conflict where the very meaning of race was politically contested. The 1970s, by contrast, were years of racial quiescence when the racial minority movements of the previous period seemed to wane. Racial oppression had hardly vanished, but conflicts over race receded as past reforms were institutionalized (Ibid.).

With regard to the period coinciding with the origins of the current movement in cultural diversity training for criminal justice personnel, Omi and Winant (Ibid.) write that:

> Issues of race have once again been dramatically revived in the 1980s, this time in the form of a "backlash" to the political gains of racial minority movements of the past. Conservative popular movements, academics, and the Reagan administration have joined hands to attack the legacy and logic of earlier movement achievements. They have done this, moreover, in a way that escapes obvious charges of "racism."

The interaction of race and class in the United States creates a web of contradictions that permeates all aspects of U.S. life, including social control through criminal justice. Although the process of implementing cultural diversity awareness training involves efforts to assuage some of the injuries that result from the police role with regard to problem populations, it does nothing to resolve the fundamental contradictions that produce these injuries. The social relations that have contributed to the formation and development of police departments are left completely intact and, therefore, the contradictions of race and class relations continue to manifest themselves in the function of police, police-community relations, and tensions between police and minorities.

Platt et al. (1982) use the concept of the "iron fist and velvet glove" to describe the contradictory nature of policing in a class society. The iron fist, or hard side of policing, is the capacity of the police to use force and developments (such as increasingly sophisticated technologies) that enhance that capacity. The velvet glove, or the softer side of policing, consists of efforts in the area of community pacification and programs that sell the police to the public. These two aspects of policing operate simultaneously, each supporting the other. Both are strategies of repression. Neither the obviously conservative interest in developing more effective strategies of control nor the liberal interest in seeking community input challenge structures of privilege and exploitation in the United States. Indeed, both support that structure "by making the system of repression that serves it more powerful or more palatable or both" (Ibid.: 49).

David E. Barlow and Melissa Hickman Barlow

Manning (1988) posits a similar critique of community-oriented policing, interpreting it as a major dramatic device designed to control public opinion regarding police. He suggests that this criminal justice innovation emerged in response to a crisis of legitimacy, a response to large segments of the U.S. population who had come to believe that they were not receiving their fair share of society's benefits. As the rising populations of minorities in urban areas were systematically denied opportunities and adequate services in the 1960s, the effectiveness of traditional forms of ideological social control, symbols of community integration, and appeals to commitment to the moral order began to deteriorate. As the symbolic authority of the police and other social-control institutions declined, police sought to control what came to be viewed as a dangerous underclass "by a reduction of social distance, a merging of communal and police interests, and a service and crime control isomorphism" (Ibid.: 28). Community policing, in this view, is a strategy for ideological and material social control. The rhetoric of community policing is designed to secure legitimacy for the authority of the police. Klockars (1988) describes community policing as the latest concealment strategy designed to mask the fundamental nature of policing: coercion. Cultural diversity awareness training emerged from the same pressures that produced community policing and, thus, critiques of community policing are applicable to cultural diversity training as well.

OBSERVATIONS FROM WITHIN THE MOVEMENT

In the late 1980s, following a series of racially charged incidents in police-community relations in South Carolina, the South Carolina Chapter of the National Rainbow Coalition requested that we evaluate police training at the South Carolina Criminal Justice Academy (SCCJA) with respect to police use of deadly force, crisis intervention techniques, and race relations. We approached the academy's executive director on behalf of the Rainbow Coalition and simply asked that we be allowed to sit in on a number of their regular training sessions related to each of the above concerns. Our goal was to assess whether inadequate training was a source of problems in police relations with African Americans. The process was informal, in the sense that communication took place within discussions rather than through official reports and press releases. Early on, the executive director of SCCJA expressed responsiveness to the concerns of the Rainbow Coalition by forming a Human Relations Curriculum Development Committee and appointing one of us as a founding member. The committee, which also included community leaders, law enforcement executives, and police trainers, spent most of its time preparing press releases, conducting public forums, and discussing who else should be appointed as members. After two years of work, not one word of the curriculum had been written. Despite the sincere desire of several members to effect real change in law-enforcement practices with regard to African Americans, the process became more important than the goal. Convincing the public that the law-enforcement community was "doing something" became more important than the task of actually educating officers in the area of cultural diversity.

In the summer of 1991, tensions between police and minorities in Milwaukee, Wisconsin, were intensified by the Dahmer-Sinthasomphome case and related allegations that police officers involved in the case were insensitive to the concerns of the gay community and people of color.[8] Faced with a rising tide of disdain for police and what was essentially a crisis of legitimacy for the Milwaukee Police Department, the Mayor appointed a Blue Ribbon Citizen's Commission on Police-Community Relations. As is often the case for politically appointed commissions, members of Milwaukee's Blue Ribbon Commission had well-established connections to power within the Milwaukee community, but were also representative of diverse groups, in terms of race, ethnicity, gender, occupation, and sexual orientation. However, in the aftermath of the Dahmer-Sinthasomphome incident, African Americans and gay rights groups without ties to the Milwaukee power structure announced publicly that they were not fairly represented on the Mayor's Blue Ribbon Commission. These groups formed Black Ribbon and Lavender Ribbon Commissions, respectively, to conduct their own investigations into police-community relations and to make their own recommendations to the mayor. A central component of each group's recommendations was the development of cultural diversity awareness training for police officers. Indeed, the most specific and costly item within the Blue Ribbon Commission's recommendations was for the Milwaukee Police Department to request proposals for the development of cultural diversity awareness training for its officers, supervisors, staff, and executives (Mayor's Citizen Commission on Police-Community Relations, 1992). The Milwaukee Police Department ultimately contracted with the Police Foundation to develop a training program and, at this writing, has begun implementation of that program.

Within this context, other initiatives in the area of cultural diversity training for police officers have emerged in Wisconsin as well. One of us serves on a steering committee for an outreach effort of two University of Wisconsin campuses, the mission of which is to produce cultural diversity awareness training opportunities for local law enforcement and corrections agencies, by selecting both instructors and their programs as well as organizing seminars. The steering committee is made up of outreach staff, university faculty, police administrators, and other criminal justice personnel.

The project was begun with a high degree of enthusiasm and commitment to having a significant impact on officers' knowledge, appreciation, and behavior toward diverse cultures. However, after the first series of training programs, committee members fell into the trap of supporting programs based upon popularity rather than substantive merit. Relying almost exclusively on the participants' program evaluations, the committee reinvited instructors who received high marks and terminated the services of those with lower scores. Some consideration was given to the strong possibility that the "best" programs may be those that the officers don't like, because they confront prejudices and challenge perceptions and attitudes. Yet, ultimately, invitations were extended to instructors with high ratings, despite the uneasy recognition that high ratings may be given to instructors who make participants feel comfortable with their prejudices and the way they are currently doing their jobs.

This connection between participant evaluations and course content is supported by the observations of one of the authors who has conducted cultural diversity awareness training over the past three years. Initially, the lesson plan directly exposed the fundamental contradictions of policing in a class society. It also provided statistical evidence of race and class discrimination within the criminal justice system and used actual examples and cases indicating racism in law enforcement. The evaluations by participants were predominately negative, describing the training and the (ex-cop) instructor as "too liberal," "antagonistic," and a "waste of time." Attendance to the training seminars and calls from police departments to conduct more sessions quickly diminished. Conversely, requests for the instructor's program and attendance at the sessions offered increased in direct proportion to adjustments in the content that rendered the training more empathetic and less confrontational, eliminated material on the fundamental contradictions of policing, and removed the statistical data. Through an interactive process between those providing cultural diversity training and those purchasing it, training programs are altered in ways that give rise to serious questions regarding their worth.

In conversations with a representative of a national criminal justice training institute, the dilemma for those who provide police training is expressed in terms of the potential fallout of a sponsored cultural diversity awareness training program. While the representative was personally committed to the idea of such training, she was concerned that it may be impossible to provide a meaningful and substantive training class without hurting her organization's established reputation as a provider of "good" police training.

Part of the problem is the different expectations held by police practitioners and those who wish to have a substantial impact on police behavior. It is clear from course evaluations and comments that the officers themselves are often looking for guidance on how to manipulate specific groups of people more effectively. Trainers across the country agree that the most effective way to increase the receptivity of police officers to the training is to convince them that it is beneficial in terms of officer safety, liability, and effectiveness.[9]

This basic contradiction within the mission of cultural diversity awareness training is revealed in a question asked by an officer participating in a training session. The officer asked, "How can I stop a Black family in an automobile without being viewed as a racist?" When questioned about the purpose of the traffic stop, the officer replied that he had to stop the family because they were Black and this is cause for suspicion in his suburban township. For this officer, the purpose of cultural diversity training was to provide information that would help him to mask the racism that is a daily part of his job.

CONCLUSION

Each of the circumstances described above, which we have observed as participants in the cultural diversity awareness training movement, we believe arise out of the fundamental contradictions of policing within U.S. society. Police restrict the rights of certain citizens in order to protect the rights of others and this process is certain to reflect existing power relations in society at large. Cultural diversity awareness training cannot change the fact that the basic purpose of policing is to maintain social control by repressing certain activities and restricting freedoms. Police necessarily reduce complex human conflicts and profound legal and moral questions to simple decisions. Cultural diversity awareness training may introduce police officers to a complex set of social, political, and economic issues, but officers must still make quick decisions and resolve conflicts in an inherently crude manner. Law enforcement is inherently discriminatory because of its focus on the crimes of lower classes. Although the disproportionate concentration of racial minorities in lower economic classes doesn't completely explain police discrimination against minorities, it certainly contributes to the rates at which they are stopped, investigated, observed, searched, arrested, and killed by police. Cultural diversity awareness training for police officers does not address existing relations of power and authority, which it is the job of police to defend.

Perhaps even more important, though, are the ways in which the view from within the cultural diversity training movement authenticates theoretical approaches to social phenomena that take seriously the interaction between human agency and social structure.[10] Certainly, we conceive of our own actions and those of individuals with whom we have interacted (including grassroots activists, state-level policymakers, personnel in national foundations, and police trainers and administrators) as relevant to present and future police-minority relations. At the same time, we are keenly aware of the ways in which political and economic structures impede and (for the present, at least) delimit movement toward greater justice in police interaction with racial minorities and other subordinate populations. As long as the very purpose of law enforcement in U.S. society remains focused on the control of problem populations, the very concept of criminal justice is enigmatic. One needs only to listen to the litany of indictments against criminal justice emanating from African-American popular culture (specifically rap music) to conclude that problem populations as human subjects, in a very real sense, know what's going on. As Giddens (1993: 125) suggests:

> It is not implausible to suppose that, in some circumstances, and from some aspects, those in subordinate positions in society might have a greater penetration of the conditions of social reproduction than those who otherwise dominate them.

What, then, can be expected as outcomes of cultural diversity awareness training for police officers? In the short run, such training may play an important role in reducing individual incidents of cultural miscommunication, misunderstanding, and mistreatment. It may have a significant impact on improving the surface relationships between the police and the public for a time.

However, in the long run, police-minority relations are not likely to be fundamentally altered, because the social conditions and relations that produce racism, sexism, ethnocentrism, xenophobia, and bigotry remain fully intact.

Although many of the promoters of cultural diversity training are well-intentioned people who hope to improve the quality of life for all citizens in this country, the historical record suggests that the outcomes of cultural diversity awareness training programs may well include a strengthening of existing social/power relations in the United States. This criminal justice innovation, like so many before it, may help to secure legitimacy for structures of control in a country experiencing a crisis of control. Even if it succeeds in reducing racism and bigotry among police officers, cultural diversity training will not alter the social conditions and power relations that produce social and economic injustice. The application and rhetoric of cultural diversity awareness training tend rather to cloak existing injustice within the language and promise of fundamental fairness and equality before the law.

Our conclusion, however, is not that cultural diversity awareness training should be abolished or that efforts to improve police-minority relations should be discouraged. On the contrary, it is hoped that the movement will proceed with a clear sense of its history, an understanding of its limits within present conditions, and a firm commitment to being part of a larger agenda of social change for a future in which fairness and equality characterize the lived experience of all members of U.S. society in relation to its system of justice.

215

*David E.
Barlow and
Melissa
Hickman
Barlow*

NOTES

1. We have been involved in the planning, curriculum development, and instruction of cultural diversity awareness training for police officers for approximately four years in several states. In addition, we have conducted and participated in seminars, organized a national discussion panel, reviewed numerous lesson plans, and interviewed trainers and police administrators regarding cultural diversity training in the United States, Canada, and Great Britain.

2. The movement in the 1990s toward implementing cultural diversity training programs is not unique to police work. An article in *U.S. News & World Report* states that a "whole diversity industry has sprung up" to teach firms how to function in a culturally diverse marketplace. The products of this industry include annual conferences, training packages, consultants, books, games, videotapes, and newsletters. For example, Pacific Gas & Electric Company in California is sending each of its 27,000 employees through "diversity-awareness sessions" ("Managing Diversity," July 20, 1992: 62).

3. For a detailed description of this case, see Skolnick and Fyfe (1993).

4. These justifications for both community policing and cultural diversity training were clearly expressed at the 1992 conference entitled "Unfinished Business: Racial and Ethnic Issues Facing Law Enforcement II," sponsored by NOBLE, PERF, and the Reno Police Department. Three similar conferences were held in 1993 in Atlanta, Chicago, and Los Angeles.

5. Support for a particular criminal justice innovation from within different ideological camps is not without precedent. The emergence of the Justice Model in corrections in the mid-1970s was supported by both conservatives and liberals, though for different reasons (Paternoster and Bynum, 1982; Paternoster and Hickman, 1982; and Humphries and Greenberg, 1981). Liberal supporters of the Justice Model, such as the American Friends Service Committee, saw its premises as an improvement on the repressiveness of the indeterminate sentence and the intrusiveness of the policy of rehabilitation. Conservatives envisioned the philosophies behind the Justice Model as ideological supporting mandatory sentencing models, a welcome change from what they saw as coddling criminals within the Rehabilitation Model. The Justice Model appeared on the surface to promote more humane and equitable treatment for those who come in contact with the criminal justice system. Yet its consequences in practice have been longer prison sentences, higher rates of incarceration, and the abolition of parole in the federal correctional system (Paternoster and Bynum, 1982).

6. Both the Christopher Commission (1992) and the Mayor's Citizen Commission on Police-Community Relations (1992) in Milwaukee contain recommendations similar to those in the Kerner Commission report.

7. One of the authors worked (as a legal secretary) at the Office of the Capital Collateral Representative (CCR) when it was first created in Florida. Many death penalty abolitionists and lawyers who had previously defended death-row inmates on a voluntary basis went to work in this office because of the massive resources that it would make available for appeals. The inherent contradiction of carrying out this work, funded by the state in which "Bloody Bob" Graham (whose nickname derived from his zealous signing of death warrants) was governor was apparent to everyone who worked at CCR in the early days. Everyone knew that the purpose for creating the office (from the perspective of Governor Graham and Attorney General Jim Smith) was to undermine appeals based on an inadequate defense.

8. "News reports that police officers had (1) been called to a scene involving Dahmer (who is white) and one of his victims (a young Laotian boy) in May 1991, (2) determined that what they were dealing with was a domestic situation between homosexual lovers, (3) returned the naked and incoherent Konerak Sinthasomphome to the custody of Jeffrey Dahmer, who killed him later that evening, and (4) ignored repeated attempts by Glenda Cleveland, her daughter, and her niece (women of color) to convince police that the Asian male was a child, ushered in a period of intense concern in Milwaukee about relations between police and minorities" (Barlow, Barlow, and Stojkovic, forthcoming: 1).

9. The authors have suggested this in a previous paper (Barlow and Barlow, forthcoming) and it was a major theme in a roundtable discussion among trainers, scholars, police administrators, and others at the 1993 meetings of the Academy of Criminal Justice Sciences.

10. See, for example, Maynard and Wilson (1990), Giddens (1983, 1993), and Melossi (1985), as well as Marx' Theses on Feuerbach (1978: 143), in which he wrote that "the chief defect of all hitherto existing materialism . . . is that the thing, reality, sensuousness, is conceived only in the form of the object or of contemplation, but not as human sensuous activity, practice, not subjectively."

CHAPTER 6 Courts and Partiality

6.1 PAUL BUTLER

Racially Based Jury Nullification

In the history of criminology, there is probably nothing more commonly understood and empirically verified than the concept of racial inequality in the dispensing of American justice. From the criminalization of behavior, to the policing and apprehension of suspects, to the finding of guilt and ultimate imprisonment of offenders, the justice system has demonstrated a propensity at all decision points to favor members of the white, male-dominant group over all others, particularly blacks. Black citizens experience arrest, conviction, and imprisonment rates grossly in excess of their representation in the general population. Past efforts to remedy racial inequality within or through due process channels have generally met with dismal failure. Rather, history has shown that it has been the long and arduous application of unorthodox protest, petition, civil disobedience, and often violence that has produced the lion's share of success. The criminal justice system is no stranger to competition and conflict and, in its best interest, can legitimately mobilize violent coercion. However, its weapon of choice is the advantage inherent in the power accrued by law, and that power is notably manifest in the administrative and jurisprudential procedures of the criminal court. While the adversarial nature of criminal proceedings ostensibly offers a semblance of fairness, in reality it reproduces the inequalities endemic throughout the system. Hence, the black defendant must draw upon unconventional methods to accommodate the imbalance in the scales of justice.

In the following selection from "Racially Based Jury Nullification: Black Power in the Criminal Justice System," *Yale Law Journal* (December 1995), former U.S. attorney Paul Butler reviews the doctrine of jury nullification as an effective, although unconventional, means through which African Americans may rectify the injustices they often receive at the hands of the American criminal justice system. After reviewing two notable Washington, D.C., criminal cases, the author advances the premises that (1) counsel for black criminal defendants should continue to introduce courtroom strategies that are racially biased in favor of their clients, and (2) defense counsel are righteous in their attempts to persuade black jurors to acquit black defendants whether or not the evidence supports a finding of guilt. Butler argues that black jurors are legally and morally right to nullify their fact-finding charge in favor of racially driven decision making. That is, blacks who are called upon to participate in the white-dominated criminal justice system should recognize its inherent racism and respond in a manner to neutralize or mitigate those effects. The author concludes that black defendants are better judged by other blacks, who are more likely than whites to understand and appreciate the social, political, economic, historical, and cultural contexts of black criminality.

Key Concept: strategies to combat racism in the criminal justice system

INTRODUCTION

I was a Special Assistant United States Attorney in the District of Columbia in 1990. I prosecuted people accused of misdemeanor crimes, mainly the drug and gun cases that overwhelm the local courts of most American cities. As a federal prosecutor, I represented the United States of America and used that power to put people, mainly African-American men, in prison. I am also an African-American man. While at the U.S. Attorney's office, I made two discoveries that profoundly changed the way I viewed my work as a prosecutor and my responsibilities as a black person.

The first discovery occurred during a training session for new Assistants conducted by experienced prosecutors. We rookies were informed that we would lose many of our cases, despite having persuaded a jury beyond a reasonable doubt that the defendant was guilty. We would lose because some black jurors would refuse to convict black defendants who they knew were guilty.

The second discovery was related to the first, but was even more unsettling. It occurred during the trial of Marion Barry, then the second-term mayor of the District of Columbia. Barry was being prosecuted by my office for drug possession and perjury. I learned, to my surprise, that some of my fellow African-American prosecutors hoped that the mayor would be acquitted, despite the fact that he was obviously guilty of at least one of the charges—he had smoked cocaine on FBI videotape. These black prosecutors wanted their office to lose its case because they believed that the prosecution of Barry was racist.

Federal prosecutors in the nation's capital hear many rumors about prominent officials engaging in illegal conduct, including drug use. Some African-American prosecutors wondered why, of all those people, the government chose to "set up" the most famous black politician in Washington, D.C. They also asked themselves why, if crack is so dangerous, the FBI had allowed the mayor to smoke it. Some members of the predominantly black jury must have had similar concerns: They convicted the mayor of only one count of a fourteen-count indictment, despite the trial judge's assessment that he had " 'never seen a stronger government case.' " Some African-American prosecutors thought that the jury, in rendering its verdict, jabbed its black thumb in the face of a racist prosecution, and that idea made those prosecutors glad.

As such reactions suggest, lawyers and judges increasingly perceive that some African-American jurors vote to acquit black defendants for racial reasons, a decision sometimes expressed as the juror's desire not to send yet another black man to jail. This Essay examines the question of what role race should play in black jurors' decisions to acquit defendants in criminal cases. Specifically, I consider trials that include both African-American defendants and African-American jurors. I argue that the race of a black defendant is sometimes a legally and morally appropriate factor for jurors to consider in reaching a verdict of not guilty or for an individual juror to consider in refusing to vote for conviction.

My thesis is that, for pragmatic and political reasons, the black community is better off when some nonviolent lawbreakers remain in the community rather than go to prison. The decision as to what kind of conduct by African-Americans ought to be punished is better made by African-Americans themselves, based on the costs and benefits to their community, than by the traditional criminal justice process, which is controlled by white lawmakers and white law enforcers. Legally, the doctrine of jury nullification gives the power to make this decision to African-American jurors who sit in judgment of African-American defendants. Considering the costs of law enforcement to the black community and the failure of white lawmakers to devise significant non-incarcerative responses to black antisocial conduct, it is the moral responsibility of black jurors to emancipate some guilty black outlaws.

Part I of this Essay describes two criminal cases in the District of Columbia in which judges feared that defendants or their lawyers were sending race-conscious, "forbidden" messages to black jurors and attempted to regulate those messages. I suggest that the judicial and public responses to those cases signal a dangerous reluctance among many Americans to engage in meaningful discourse about the relationship between race and crime. In Part II, I describe racial critiques of the criminal justice system. I then examine the evolution of the doctrine of jury nullification and suggest, in light of this doctrine, that racial considerations by African-American jurors are legally and morally right. Part II proposes a framework for analysis of the kind of criminal cases involving black defendants in which jury nullification is appropriate, and considers some of the concerns that implementation of the proposal raises.

My goal is the subversion of American criminal justice, at least as it now exists. Through jury nullification, I want to dismantle the master's house with the master's tools. My intent, however, is not purely destructive; this project is also constructive, because I hope that the destruction of the status quo will not lead to anarchy, but rather to the implementation of certain noncriminal ways of addressing antisocial conduct. Criminal conduct among African-Americans is often a predictable reaction to oppression. Sometimes black crime is a symptom of internalized white supremacy; other times it is a reasonable response to the racial and economic subordination every African-American faces every day. Punishing black people for the fruits of racism is wrong if that punishment is premised on the idea that it is the black criminal's "just deserts." Hence, the new paradigm of justice that I suggest in Part III rejects punishment for the sake of retribution and endorses it, with qualifications, for the ends of deterrence and incapacitation.

In a sense, this Essay simply may argue for the return of rehabilitation as the purpose of American criminal justice, but a rehabilitation that begins with the white-supremacist beliefs that poison the minds of us all—you, me, and the black criminal. I wish that black people had the power to end racial oppression right now. African-Americans can prevent the application of one particularly destructive instrument of white supremacy—American criminal justice—to some African-American people, and this they can do immediately. I hope that this Essay makes the case for why and how they should.

I. SECRET MESSAGES EVERYONE HEARS

Americans seem reluctant to have an open conversation about the relationship between race and crime. Lawmakers ignore the issue, judges run from it, and crafty defense lawyers exploit it. It is not surprising, then, that some African-American jurors are forced to sneak through the back door what is not allowed to come in through the front: the idea that "race matters" in criminal justice. In this part, I tell two stories about attempts by defense attorneys to encourage black jurors' sympathy for their clients, and then I examine how these attempts provoked many people to act as though the idea of racial identification with black defendants was ridiculous or insulting to black people. In fact, the defense attorneys may well have been attempting to encourage black jurors' sympathy as part of their trial strategies. The lesson of the stories is that the failure of the law to address openly the relationship between race and crime fosters a willful and unhelpful blindness in many who really ought to see and allows jury nullification to go on without a principled framework. This Essay offers such a framework and encourages nullification for the purpose of black self-help.

A. United States v. Marion Barry

The time is January 1990. The mayor of the District of Columbia is an African-American man named Marion Barry. African-Americans make up approximately sixty-six percent of the population of the City. The mayor is so popular in the black community that one local newspaper columnist has dubbed him "Mayor for Life." Barry is hounded, however, by rumors of his using drugs and "'chasing women.'" Barry denies the rumors and claims that they are racist.

On January 18, 1990, the mayor is contacted by an old friend, Rasheeda Moore, who tells him that she is visiting for a short time, and staying at a local hotel. The mayor stops by later that afternoon and telephones Ms. Moore's room from the lobby of the hotel. He wants her to come downstairs to the lobby for a drink, but she requests that he come up to her room. The mayor assents, joins Ms. Moore in the room, and the two converse. At some point, Ms. Moore produces crack cocaine and a pipe, and invites the mayor to smoke it. He first demurs, then consents, and after he inhales smoke from the pipe, agents of the FBI and the Metropolitan Police Department storm the room. It turns out that Ms. Moore is a government informant, and the police have observed and videotaped the entire proceeding in the hotel room. The mayor is arrested and subsequently charged with one count of conspiracy to possess cocaine, ten counts of possession of cocaine, and three counts of perjury for allegedly lying to the grand jury that had investigated him. The mayor publicly asserts that he is the victim of a racist prosecution.

It is the last week in June 1990. The mayor is on trial in federal court. The judge is white. Of the twelve jurors, ten are African-American. Rasheeda Moore, the government's star witness, is expected to testify. The mayor has four passes to give to guests he would like to attend his trial. On this day, he has given one pass to Minister Louis Farrakhan, the controversial leader of the Nation of Islam. Farrakhan has publicly supported Barry since his arrest, in part by suggesting that the sting operation and the prosecution were racist. When Farrakhan attempts to walk into the courtroom, a U.S. deputy marshal bars his entry. When Barry's attorney protests, the judge states, outside of the jury's hearing, that Farrakhan's "'presence would be potentially disruptive, very likely intimidating, and he is a persona non grata for the [rest] of this case.'" Rasheeda Moore then takes the stand.

The next day, the Reverend George Stallings appears at the trial with one of Barry's guest passes in hand. Stallings is a black Roman Catholic priest who, the previous year, received extensive publicity when he accused the Catholic Church of being hopelessly racist, left it, and founded his own church. When Stallings reaches the courtroom, the deputy marshal, following the instructions of the judge, does not let him enter. The judge explains, again outside of the jury's hearing, that Stallings is "'in my judgment, not an ordinary member of the public and his presence would very likely have the same effect as Mr. Farrakhan's.'" The judge also indicates that there are "'others who fit the same category.'" Barry's attorney asks for a list of those persons. The judge replies, "'I think you will know them when you see them.'"

In the wake of these two episodes, the American Civil Liberties Union, representing Barry, Farrakhan, and Stallings, files an emergency appeal of the trial judge's decision. It argues that the judge's refusal to allow Barry's guests to attend the trial violated Barry's Sixth Amendment right to a fair trial and the First Amendment rights of the guests. In response, the judge's attorneys state that the judge excluded Farrakhan and Stallings because their presence in the courtroom would send an "'impermissible message'" of "'intimidation'" and "'racial animosity'" to jurors and witnesses. The judge's attorneys argue that the excluded persons' views of the prosecution had been highly publicized and that their appearance at the trial was consistent with Barry's " 'publicly avowed strategies of seeking a hung jury and jury nullification.' " The judge's attorneys argue that Farrakhan and Stallings attended the trial " 'not to view the proceedings or to show generalized concern, but instead to send a forbidden message to the jury and witness.' "

The U.S. Court of Appeals for the District of Columbia Circuit rules that Farrakhan and Stallings should have presented their constitutional claims to the trial judge prior to seeking relief in the appellate court. Accordingly, it remands the case back to the trial judge. Because the trial has been halted pending appeal, however, the D.C. Circuit, in light of the "exigent circumstances," lists several "pertinent considerations" for the trial judge on remand. The considerations mainly concern the judge's power to regulate the attendance of those who threaten physically to disrupt a courtroom. The court does note, though, that:

> No individual can be wholly excluded from the courtroom merely because he advocates a particular political, legal or religious point of view—even a point of view that the district court or we may regard as antithetical to the fair administration of justice. Nor can an individual be wholly excluded from the courtroom because his presence is thought to send an undesirable message to the jurors except that of physical intimidation.

The trial judge hears the message of the court of appeals. In lieu of resolving Farrakhan and Stalling's constitutional claims, he instead seeks assurances from their attorneys that their clients know how to conduct themselves in a courtroom. Indeed, the judge provides the attorneys with his own "special rules" of decorum regarding the trial, stating that "any attempt to communicate with a juror may be punished as criminal contempt of Court." Farrakhan and Stallings's attorneys assure the court that their clients will act with decorum in the courtroom. The trial continues. The mayor is eventually convicted of one of the indictment's fourteen counts (for perjury), but not of the count in which he smoked the cocaine on videotape.

B. The Attorney Who Wore Kente Cloth

It is now June 11, 1992. John T. Harvey, III is an African-American criminal defense attorney who practices in the District of Columbia. Harvey represents a black man who is charged with assault with intent to murder. The case is scheduled for arraignment before a white judge. At the arraignment, Harvey wears a business suit and tie, and his jacket is accessorized by a colorful stole made of kente cloth. Kente cloth is a multihued woven fabric originally worn by ancient African royalty, and many African-Americans have adopted it as a fashion statement and a symbol of racial pride.

In pretrial proceedings, the judge had warned Harvey that he would not be permitted to wear kente cloth before a jury. According to Harvey, the judge told him that wearing the fabric during a jury trial " 'was sending a hidden message to jurors.' " The judge had informed Harvey that he had three options: He could refrain from wearing the kente cloth; he could withdraw from the case; or he could agree to try the case before the judge, without a jury. Harvey's client decided to plead guilty. At the June 11 hearing, however, Harvey refuses to enter his client's plea before the judge because he doubts that the judge will be impartial. The judge then removes Harvey from the case, " 'not on the basis of [the] kente cloth, but on the basis that [Harvey] will not enter a plea which [his] client wishes to enter.' "

The same day, another client of Harvey's is scheduled to go to trial, also for assault with intent to kill, before another white judge. During the voir dire, the judge asks if any of the jurors are familiar with Harvey, whose battle with the other judge was well publicized. Four of the potential jurors know of the controversy. " '[T]he concern we think we have here,' " the judge says, is " 'that we won't influence a juror improperly.' " He also informs them of case law in another jurisdiction suggesting that a court may prevent a Catholic priest from wearing a clerical collar in court. When Harvey asks the judge to inform the potential jurors of contrary cases, the judge refuses. The judge subsequently states:

> "For the record, Mr. Harvey is black. Aside from the courtroom clerk, he is the only black person who is participating in this trial.... He is wearing a so-called kente cloth around his neck, and he has recently received wide publicity, which I am sure he loves. I have wondered with my own conscience whether for me to simply wait for the government or someone else to object is the proper approach to avoid a war with Mr. Harvey, which I am not anxious for—either personally or on behalf of the Superior Court....
> I also note that this is costing us all a lot of time ... and I don't appreciate it."

Ultimately, the judge allows Harvey to wear the cloth, but he suggests that when Harvey submits an attorney fee voucher to him for approval, he might not allow Harvey to be paid for the time the kente cloth issue has consumed. Harvey's client is tried before an all-black jury and is acquitted.

C. The Judicial and Popular Response: Willful Blindness

As described above, the trial judge's attempt to exclude Farrakhan and Stallings from Barry's trial met with disapproval from the D.C. Circuit. In the case of John Harvey, no higher court had occasion to review the judge's prohibition against the kente cloth, but, as discussed below, much of the public reaction to the judge's prohibition was critical. These responses scorned the trial judge's fears that black jurors might acquit on the basis of racial identification rather than the "evidence." The D.C. Circuit and many observers, however, failed to acknowledge the significance of the "forbidden" message. I believe that this failure was deliberate. It reflected an intention to avoid serious consideration of the issue of black jurors acquitting black defendants on the basis of racial identification. Simply put, the D.C. Circuit and some of the public did not want to face the reality that race matters, in general and in jury adjudications of guilt and innocence.

1. THE D.C. CIRCUIT: WE HATE FIGHTS   The D.C. Circuit's per curiam opinion discussed the issue before it as though the judge's concern was that

Barry's invitees would cause some type of physical disruption. The court listed a series of five "pertinent considerations," four of which actually were not pertinent because they involved the physical disruption of courtrooms or physical threats to witnesses.

The only relevant consideration was so vague that it was nearly useless: The trial judge must exercise his discretion to exclude people from attending criminal matters "consistently with the First and Fifth Amendment rights of individuals to attend criminal trials." The court's discussion of this consideration is even more ambivalent: No one can be "wholly" excluded from a trial, even if he advocates a point of view that "we may regard as antithetical to the fair administration of justice" or if his presence sends an "undesirable message" to jurors. Because the appellate court did not suggest a procedure for partial exclusion of courtroom spectators, the trial judge's response was to pretend as though he had been concerned all along about physical disruption and subsequently to insist that Farrakhan and Stallings act in accordance with his rules of decorum. In the view of the D.C. Circuit, trial guests should keep their hands and their feet to themselves, but their messages may run amuck. In reality, Farrakhan's and Stallings's manners in the courtroom were an issue created by the appellate court. Ironically, the trial judge's response—the patronizing insistence that Farrakhan and Stallings agree to behave themselves—smacks of racism more than does his initial decision to exclude them from the courtroom.

United States v. Barry suggests that no trial spectator can be barred from a courtroom unless she threatens physically to disrupt the trial. In this respect, the court established a severe restriction on the discretion of judges to control public access to trials. Not all courts have taken this position, however. Two of the few other federal appellate courts that have considered symbolic communication by trial spectators have found it appropriate to regulate this type of communication. In one case, the Ninth Circuit stated that "[w]hen fair trial rights are at significant risk . . . the first amendment rights of trial attendees can and must be curtailed at the courthouse door." In another case, the Eleventh Circuit ordered the retrial of a man convicted of the murder of a prison guard, partly because of the presence, at the first trial, of numerous uniformed prison guards. The court was concerned that the guards' presence posed an unacceptable risk of prejudicing the jurors.

Significantly, the decisions from the Ninth and Eleventh Circuits involved cases in which the presence of the spectators was not thought to implicate race. The D.C. Circuit is the first appellate court to consider a "forbidden" racial message. My intention in noting this distinction is not to criticize the restrictive standard the D.C. Circuit established; indeed, there are potentially troubling implications of standards that allow trial judges more discretion in terms of which "secret" messages to regulate. I suggest, however, that the D.C. Circuit's holding was not mandated by clear constitutional dictates and was not supported by precedent from other federal jurisdictions. Indeed, other appellate courts have considered and regulated the contents of the messages that trial spectators were thought to be sending. Those cases suggest that the D.C. Circuit could have talked about race, and yet it did not.

2. THE SKEPTICS: WHAT'S RACE GOT TO DO WITH IT? The response of a number of commentators to the controversy over John Harvey's kente cloth was disdainful of the trial judge's apprehension about race-based appeals to black jurors. For example, the *Washington Times* characterized one of the judge's concerns as "[s]heer, unadulterated goofiness." The editorial continued:

> [The judge] apparently believes that the [kente] cloth is no innocent fabric but rather possesses hypnotic powers of seduction, powers that will turn the judicial system on its head and hold jurors in its sway....
> ....[W]hile most of us common folk are puzzled by this kind of judicial behavior, lawyers are widely inured to the fact that judges are free to act like fools with impunity—even when it is an abuse of discretion, an abuse of power, a waste of time and an injustice to someone who has come before the court seeking justice.

The *Washington Post* opined:

> There is absolutely no reason in logic or law for Judge Scott to tell Mr. Harvey that he cannot wear a kente cloth before a jury—regardless of the jurors' race. The very suggestion is offensive to black jurors, that they somehow lose their judgment and objectivity at the sight of a kente cloth.

The National Bar Association, an African-American lawyers' group, expressed a similar concern, and one black attorney called the judge's actions "'almost unbelievable'"... and wondered why the judge "'injected race... into the trial proceedings by making an issue of the kente cloth. Even the prosecutors in the kente cloth case "remained conspicuously silent" and refrained from endorsing the judge's concerns about the cloth.'"

D. The Forbidden Message Revealed

I am fascinated by the refusal of these actors to take seriously the possibility and legal implications of black jurors' sympathy with black defendants. The criminal justice system would be better served if there were less reluctance to consider the significance of race in black jurors' adjudications of guilt or innocence. The remainder of this Essay argues that race matters when a black person violates American criminal law and when a black juror decides how she should exercise her power to put another black man in prison.

The idea that race matters in criminal justice is hardly shocking; it surely does not surprise most African-Americans. In the Barry and Harvey stories, I believe that it was known by all of the key players: judges, jurors, attorneys, defendants, and spectators. The trial judges in those cases were correct: Somebody —the controversial black demagogue, the radical black priest, the kente-cloth-wearing lawyer—was trying to send the black jurors a message. The message, in my view, was that the black jurors should consider the evidence presented at trial in light of the idea that the American criminal justice system discriminates against blacks. The message was that the jurors should not send another black man to prison.

There is no way to "prove" what Farrakhan's and Stallings's purposes were in attending Barry's trial—nor can I "prove" the intent of the kente-cloth-wearing lawyer. I believe that my theory that they were encouraging black jurors' sympathy is reasonable, based on the relevant players' statements, the trial judge's observations, and common sense and experience. Even if one is unwilling to ascribe to those players the same racially based motivations that I do, acknowledgement and concern that some black jurors acquit black defendants on the basis of race are increasing, as my experience at the U.S. Attorney's Office showed. For the remainder of this Essay, I focus on the legal and social implications of this conduct by black jurors.

II. "JUSTICE OUTSIDE THE FORMAL RULES OF LAW"

Why would a black juror vote to let a guilty person go free? Assuming that the juror is a rational actor, she must believe that she and her community are, in some way, better off with the defendant out of prison than in prison. But how could any rational person believe that about a criminal? The following section describes racial critiques of the American criminal justice system. I then examine the evolution of the doctrine of jury nullification and argue that its practice by African-Americans is, in many cases, consistent with the Anglo-American tradition and, moreover, is legally and morally right.

A. The Criminal Law and African-Americans: Justice or "Just Us"?

Imagine a country in which more than half of the young male citizens are under the supervision of the criminal justice system, either awaiting trial, in prison, or on probation or parole. Imagine a country in which two-thirds of the men can anticipate being arrested before they reach age thirty. Imagine a country in which there are more young men in prison than in college. Now give the citizens of the country the key to the prison. Should they use it?

Such a country bears some resemblance to a police state. When we criticize a police state, we think that the problem lies not with the citizens of the state, but rather with the form of government or law, or with the powerful elites and petty bureaucrats whose interests the state serves. Similarly, racial critics of American criminal justice locate the problem not so much with the black prisoners as with the state and its actors and beneficiaries. As evidence, they cite their own experiences and other people's stories, African-American history, understanding gained from social science research on the power and pervasiveness of white supremacy, and ugly statistics like those in the preceding paragraph.

For analytical purposes, I will create a false dichotomy among racial critics by dividing them into two camps: liberal critics and radical critics. Those are not names that the critics have given themselves or that they would necessarily accept, and there would undoubtedly be disagreement within each camp and theoretical overlap between the camps. Nonetheless, for the purposes of a brief explication of racial critiques, my oversimplification may be useful.

1. THE LIBERAL CRITIQUE   According to this critique, American criminal justice is racist because it is controlled primarily by white people, who are unable to escape the culture's dominant message of white supremacy, and who are therefore inevitably, even if unintentionally, prejudiced. These white actors include legislators, police, prosecutors, judges, and jurors. They exercise their discretion to make and enforce the criminal law in a discriminatory fashion. Sometimes the discrimination is overt, as in the case of Mark Fuhrman, the police officer in the O.J. Simpson case who, in interviews, used racist language and boasted of his own brutality, and sometimes it is unintentional, as with a hypothetical white juror who invariably credits the testimony of a white witness over that of a black witness.

The problem with the liberal critique is that it does not adequately explain the extent of the difference between the incidence of black and white crime, especially violent crime. For example, in 1991, blacks constituted about fifty-five percent of the 18,096 people arrested for murder and non-negligent manslaughter in the United States (9924 people). One explanation the liberal critique offers for this unfortunate statistic is that the police pursue black murder suspects more aggressively than they do white murder suspects. In other words, but for discrimination, the percentage of blacks arrested for murder would be closer to their percentage of the population, roughly twelve percent. The liberal critique would attribute some portion of the additional forty-three percent of non-negligent homicide arrestees (in 1991, approximately 7781 people) to race prejudice. Ultimately, however, those assumptions strain credulity, not because many police officers are not racist, but because there is no evidence that there is a crisis of that magnitude in criminal justice. In fact, for all the faults of American law enforcement, catching the bad guys seems to be something it does rather well. The liberal critique fails to account convincingly for the incidence of black crime.

2. THE RADICAL CRITIQUE   The radical critique does not discount the role of discrimination in accounting for some of the racial disparity in crime rates, but it also does not, in contrast to the liberal critique, attribute all or even most of the differential to police and prosecutor prejudice. The radical critique offers a more fundamental, structural explanation.

It suggests that criminal law is racist because, like other American law, it is an instrument of white supremacy. Law is made by white elites to protect their interests and, especially, to preserve the economic status quo, which benefits those elites at the expense of blacks, among others. Due to discrimination and segregation, the majority of African-Americans receive few meaningful educational and employment opportunities and, accordingly, are unable to succeed, at least in the terms of the capitalist ideal. Some property crimes committed by blacks may be understood as an inevitable result of the tension between the dominant societal message equating possession of material resources with success and happiness and the power of white supremacy to prevent most African-Americans from acquiring "enough" of those resources in a legal manner. "Black-on-black" violent crime, and even "victimless" crime like drug offenses, can be attributed to internalized racism, which causes some African-Americans to devalue black lives—either those of others or their own. The political process does not allow for the creation or implementation of effective "legal" solutions to this plight, and the criminal law punishes predictable reactions to it.

I am persuaded by the radical critique when I wonder about the roots of the ugly truth that blacks commit many crimes at substantially higher rates than whites. Most white Americans, especially liberals, would publicly offer an environmental, as opposed to genetic, explanation for this fact. They would probably concede that racism, historical and current, plays a major role in creating an environment that breeds criminal conduct. From this premise, the radical critic deduces that but for the (racist) environment, the African-American criminal would not be a criminal. In other words, racism creates and sustains the criminal breeding ground, which produces the black criminal. Thus, when many African-Americans are locked up, it is because of a situation that white supremacy created.

Obviously, most blacks are not criminals, even if every black is exposed to racism. To the radical critics, however, the law-abiding conduct of the majority of African-Americans does not mean that racism does not create black criminals. Not everyone exposed to a virus will become sick, but that does not mean that the virus does not cause the illness of the people who do.

The radical racial critique of criminal justice is premised as much on the criminal law's effect as on its intent. The system is discriminatory, in part, because of the disparate impact law enforcement has on the black community. This unjust effect is measured in terms of the costs to the black community of having so many African-Americans, particularly males, incarcerated or otherwise involved in the criminal justice system. These costs are social and economic, and include the perceived dearth of men "eligible" for marriage, the large percentage of black children who live in female headed households, the lack of male "role models" for black children, especially boys, the absence of wealth in the black community, and the large unemployment rate among black men.

3. EXAMPLES OF RACISM IN CRIMINAL JUSTICE   Examples commonly cited by both liberal and radical critics as evidence of racism in criminal justice include: the Scottsboro case; the history of the criminalization of drug use; past and contemporary administration of the death penalty; the use of imagery linking crime to race in the 1988 presidential campaign and other political campaigns; the beating of Rodney King and the acquittal of his police assailants; disparities between punishments for white-collar crimes and punishments for other crimes; more severe penalties for crack cocaine users than for powder cocaine users; the Charles Murray and Susan Smith cases; police corruption scandals in minority neighborhoods in New York and Philadelphia; the O.J. Simpson case, including the extraordinary public and media fascination with it, the racist police officer who was the prosecution's star witness, and the response of many white people to the jury's verdict of acquittal; and, cited most frequently, the extraordinary rate of incarceration of African-American men.

4. LAW ENFORCEMENT ENTHUSIASTS   Of course, the idea that the criminal justice system is racist and oppressive is not without dissent, and among the dissenters are some African-Americans. Randall Kennedy succinctly poses the counterargument:

> Although the administration of criminal justice has, at times, been used as an instrument of racial oppression, the principal problem facing African-Americans in the context of criminal justice today is not over-enforcement but under-enforcement of the laws. The most lethal danger facing African-Americans in their day-to-day lives is not white, racist officials of the state, but private, violent criminals (typically black) who attack those most vulnerable to them without regard to racial identity.

According to these theorists, whom I will call law enforcement enthusiasts, the criminal law may have a disproportionate impact on the black community, but this is not a moral or racial issue because the disproportionate impact is the law's effect, not its intent. For law enforcement enthusiasts, intent is the most appropriate barometer of governmental racism. Because law enforcement is a public good, it is in the best interest of the black community to have more, rather than less, of it. Allowing criminals to live unfettered in the community would harm, in particular, the black poor, who are disproportionately the victims of violent crime. Indeed, the logical conclusion of the enthusiasts' argument is that African-Americans would be better off with more, not fewer, black criminals behind bars.

To my mind, the enthusiasts embrace law enforcement too uncritically: They are blind to its opportunity costs. I agree that criminal law enforcement constitutes a public good for African-Americans when it serves the social protection goals that Professor Kennedy highlights. In other words, when locking up black men means that "violent criminals ... who attack those most vulnerable" are off the streets, most people—including most law enforcement critics —would endorse the incarceration. But what about when locking up a black man has no or little net effect on public safety, when, for example, the crime with which he was charged is victimless? Putting aside for the moment the legal implications, couldn't an analysis of the costs and benefits to the African-American community present an argument against incarceration? I argue "yes," in light of the substantial costs to the community of law enforcement. I accept that other reasonable people may disagree. But the law enforcement enthusiasts seldom acknowledge that racial critics even weigh the costs and benefits; their assumption seems to be that the racial critics are foolish or blinded by history or motivated by their own ethnocentrism.

5. THE BODY POLITIC AND THE RACIAL CRITIQUES   I suspect that many white people would agree with the racial critics' analysis, even if most whites would not support a solution involving the emancipation of black criminals. I write this Essay, however, out of concern for African-Americans and how they can use the power they have now to create change. The important practicability question is how many African-Americans embrace racial critiques of the criminal justice system and how many are law enforcement enthusiasts?

According to a recent *USA Today/CNN/*Gallup poll, sixty-six percent of blacks believe that the criminal justice system is racist and only thirty-two percent believe it is not racist. Interestingly, other polls suggest that blacks also tend to be more worried about crime than whites; this seems logical when one considers that blacks are more likely to be the victims of crime. This enhanced concern, however, does not appear to translate into endorsement of tougher enforcement of traditional criminal law. For example, substantially fewer blacks than whites support the death penalty, and many more blacks than whites were concerned with the potential racial consequences of the strict provisions of the Crime Bill of 1994. While polls are not, perhaps, the most reliable means of measuring sentiment in the African-American community, the polls, along with significant evidence from popular culture, suggest that a substantial portion of the African-American community sympathizes with racial critiques of the criminal justice system.

African-American jurors who endorse these critiques are in a unique position to act on their beliefs when they sit in judgment of a black defendant. As jurors, they have the power to convict the defendant or to set him free. May the responsible exercise of that power include voting to free a black defendant who the juror believes is guilty? The next section suggests that, based on legal doctrine concerning the role of juries in general, and the role of black jurors in particular, the answer to this question is "yes."

B. Jury Nullification

When a jury disregards evidence presented at trial and acquits an otherwise guilty defendant, because the jury objects to the law that the defendant violated or to the application of the law to that defendant, it has practiced jury nullification. In this section, I describe the evolution of this doctrine and consider its applicability to African-Americans. I then examine Supreme Court cases that discuss the role of black people on juries. In light of judicial rulings in these areas, I argue that it is both lawful and morally right that black jurors consider race in reaching verdicts in criminal cases.

1. WHAT IS JURY NULLIFICATION?   Jury nullification occurs when a jury acquits a defendant who it believes is guilty of the crime with which he is charged. In finding the defendant not guilty, the jury refuses to be bound by the facts of the case or the judge's instructions regarding the law. Instead, the jury votes its conscience.

In the United States, the doctrine of jury nullification originally was based on the common law idea that the function of a jury was, broadly, to decide justice, which included judging the law as well as the facts. If jurors believed that applying a law would lead to an unjust conviction, they were not compelled to convict someone who had broken that law. Although most American courts now disapprove of a jury's deciding anything other than the "facts," the Double Jeopardy Clause of the Fifth Amendment prohibits appellate reversal of a jury's decision to acquit, regardless of the reason for the acquittal. Thus, even when a trial judge thinks that a jury's acquittal directly contradicts the evidence, the jury's verdict must be accepted as final. The jurors, in judging the law, function as an important and necessary check on government power.

2. A BRIEF HISTORY   The prerogative of juries to nullify has been part of English and American law for centuries. In 1670, the landmark decision in Bushell's Case established the right of juries under English common law to nullify on the basis of an objection to the law the defendant had violated. Two members of an unpopular minority group—the Quakers—were prosecuted for unlawful assembly and disturbance of the peace. At trial, the defendants, William Penn and William Mead, admitted that they had assembled a large crowd on the streets of London. Upon that admission, the judge asked the men if they wished to plead guilty. Penn replied that the issue was not " 'whether I am guilty of this Indictment but whether this Indictment be legal,' " and argued that the jurors should go "behind" the law and use their consciences to decide whether he was guilty. The judge disagreed, and he instructed the jurors that the defendants' admissions compelled a guilty verdict. After extended deliberation, however, the jurors found both defendants not guilty. The judge then fined the jurors for rendering a decision contrary to the evidence and to his instructions. When one juror, Bushell, refused to pay his fine, the issue reached the Court of Common Pleas, which held that jurors in criminal cases could not be punished for voting to acquit, even when the trial judge believed that the verdict contradicted the evidence. The reason was stated by the Chief Justice of the Court of Common Pleas:

> A man cannot see by anothers eye, nor hear by anothers ear, no more can a man conclude or inferr the thing to be resolv'd by anothers understanding or reasoning; and though the verdict be right the jury give, yet they being not assur'd it is so from their own understanding, are forsworn, at least in foro conscientiae.

This decision "changed the course of jury history." It is unclear why the jurors acquitted Penn and Mead, but their act has been viewed in near mythological terms. Bushell and his fellow jurors have come to be seen as representing the best ideals of democracy because they "rebuffed the tyranny of the judiciary and vindicated their own true historical and moral purpose."

American colonial law incorporated the common law prerogative of jurors to vote according to their consciences after the British government began prosecuting American revolutionaries for political crimes. The best known of these cases involved John Peter Zenger, who was accused of seditious libel for publishing statements critical of British colonial rule in North America. In seditious libel cases, English law required that the judge determine whether the statements made by the defendant were libelous; the jury was not supposed to question the judge's finding on this issue. At trial, Zenger's attorney told the jury that it should ignore the judge's instructions that Zenger's remarks were libelous because the jury " 'ha[d] the right beyond all dispute to determine both the law and the facts.' " The lawyer then echoed the language of Bushell's Case, arguing that the jurors had " 'to see with their eyes, to hear with their own ears, and to make use of their own consciences and understandings, in judging of the lives, liberties or estates of their fellow subjects.' " Famously, the jury acquitted

Zenger, and another case entered the canon as a shining example of the benefits of the jury system.

After Zenger's trial, the notion that juries should decide "justice," as opposed to simply applying the law to the facts, became relatively settled in American jurisprudence. In addition to pointing to political prosecutions of white American revolutionaries like Zenger, modern courts and legal historians often cite with approval nullification in trials of defendants "guilty" of helping to free black slaves. In these cases, Northern jurors with abolitionist sentiments used their power as jurors to subvert federal law that supported slavery. In *United States v. Morris*, for example, three defendants were accused of aiding and abetting a runaway slave's escape to Canada. The defense attorney told the jury that, because it was hearing a criminal case, it had the right to judge the law, and if it believed that the Fugitive Slave Act was unconstitutional, it was bound to disregard any contrary instructions given by the judge. The defendants were acquitted, and the government dropped the charges against five other people accused of the same crime. Another success story entered the canon.

3. SPARF AND OTHER CRITIQUES   In the mid-nineteenth century, as memories of the tyranny of British rule faded, some American courts began to criticize the idea of jurors deciding justice. A number of the state decisions that allowed this practice were overruled, and in the 1895 case of *Sparf v. United States*, the Supreme Court spoke regarding jury nullification in federal courts.

In *Sparf*, two men on trial for murder requested that the judge instruct the jury that it had the option of convicting them of manslaughter, a lesser-included offense. The trial court refused this request and instead instructed the jurors that if they convicted the defendants of any crime less than murder, or if they acquitted them, the jurors would be in violation of their legal oath and duties. The Supreme Court held that this instruction was not contrary to law and affirmed the defendants' murder convictions. The Court acknowledged that juries have the ... " 'physical power' " to disregard the law, but stated that they have no " 'moral right' " to do so. Indeed, the Court observed, "If the jury were at liberty to settle the law for themselves, the effect would be ... that the law itself would be most uncertain, from the different views, which different juries might take of it." Despite this criticism, *Sparf* conceded that, as a matter of law, a judge could not prevent jury nullification, because in criminal cases " '[a] verdict of acquittal cannot be set aside.' " An anomaly was thus created, and has been a feature of American criminal law ever since: Jurors have the power to nullify, but, in most jurisdictions, they have no right to be informed of this power.

Since *Sparf*, most of the appellate courts that have considered jury nullification have addressed that anomaly and have endorsed it. Some of these courts, however, have not been as critical of the concept of jury nullification as the *Sparf* Court. The D.C. Circuit's opinion in *United States v. Dougherty* is illustrative. In *Dougherty*, the court noted that the ability of juries to nullify was widely recognized and even approved "as a necessary counter to case-hardened judges and arbitrary prosecutors.' " This necessity, however, did not establish "as an imperative" that a jury be informed by the judge of its power to nullify. The D.C.

Circuit was concerned that "[w]hat makes for health as an occasional medicine would be disastrous as a daily diet." Specifically:

> Rules of law or justice involve choice of values and ordering of objectives for which unanimity is unlikely in any society, or group representing the society, especially a society as diverse in cultures and interests as ours. To seek unity out of diversity, under the national motto, there must be a procedure for decision by vote of a majority or prescribed plurality—in accordance with democratic philosophy. To assign the role of mini-legislature to the various petit juries, who must hang if not unanimous, exposes criminal law and administration to paralysis, and to a deadlock that betrays rather than furthers the assumptions of viable democracy.

The idea that jury nullification undermines the rule of law is the most common criticism of the doctrine. The concern is that the meaning of self-government is threatened when twelve individuals on a jury in essence remake the criminal law after it has already been made in accordance with traditional democratic principles. Another critique of African-American jurors engaging in racially based jury nullification is that the practice by black jurors is distinct from the historically approved cases because the black jurors are not so much "judging" the law as preventing its application to members of their own race. The reader should recognize that these are moral, not legal, critiques because, as discussed above, the legal prerogative of any juror to acquit is well established. In the next section, I respond to these moral critiques.

C. The Moral Case for Jury Nullification by African-Americans

Any juror legally may vote for nullification in any case, but, certainly, jurors should not do so without some principled basis. The reason that some historical examples of nullification are viewed approvingly is that most of us now believe that the jurors in those cases did the morally right thing; it would have been unconscionable, for example, to punish those slaves who committed the crime of escaping to the North for their freedom. It is true that nullification later would be used as a means of racial subordination by some Southern jurors, but that does not mean that nullification in the approved cases was wrong. It only means that those Southern jurors erred in their calculus of justice. I distinguish racially based nullification by African-Americans from recent right-wing proposals for jury nullification on the ground that the former is sometimes morally right and the latter is not.

The question of how to assign the power of moral choice is a difficult one. Yet we should not allow that difficulty to obscure the fact that legal resolutions involve moral decisions, judgments of right and wrong. The fullness of time permits us to judge the fugitive slave case differently than the Southern pro-white-violence case. One day we will be able to distinguish between racially based nullification and that proposed by certain right-wing activist groups. We should remember that the morality of the historically approved cases was not so clear when those brave jurors acted. After all, the fugitive slave law was enacted through the democratic process, and those jurors who disregarded it subverted the rule of law. Presumably, they were harshly criticized by those whose interests the slave law protected. Then, as now, it is difficult to see the picture when you are inside the frame.

In this section, I explain why African-Americans have the oral right to practice nullification in particular cases. [I] do so by responding to the traditional moral critiques of jury nullification.

1. AFRICAN-AMERICANS AND THE "BETRAYAL" OF DEMOCRACY   There is no question that jury nullification is subversive of the rule of law. It appears to be the antithesis of the view that courts apply settled, standing laws and do not "dispense justice in some ad hoc, case-by-case basis." To borrow a phrase from the D.C. Circuit, jury nullification "betrays rather than furthers the assumptions of viable democracy." Because the Double Jeopardy Clause makes this power part-and-parcel of the jury system, the issue becomes whether black jurors have any moral right to "betray democracy" in this sense, I believe that they do for two reasons that I borrow from the jurisprudence of legal realism and critical race theory: First, the idea of "the rule of law" is more mythological than real, and second, "democracy," as practiced in the United States, has betrayed African-Americans far more than they could ever betray it. Explication of these theories has consumed legal scholars for years, and is well beyond the scope of this Essay. I describe the theories below not to persuade the reader of their rightness, but rather to make the case that a reasonable juror might hold such beliefs, and thus be morally justified in subverting democracy through nullification.

2. THE RULE OF LAW AS MYTH   The idea that "any result can be derived from the preexisting legal doctrine" either in every case or many cases, is a fundamental principle of legal realism (and, now, critical legal theory). The argument, in brief, is that it is indeterminate and incapable of neutral interpretation. When judges "decide" cases, they "choose" legal principles to determine particular outcomes. Even if a judge wants to be neutral, she cannot, because, ultimately, she is vulnerable to an array of personal and cultural biases and influences; she is only human. In an implicit endorsement of the doctrine of jury nullification, legal realists also suggest that, even if neutrality were possible, it would not be desirable, because no general principle of law can lead to justice in every case.

It is difficult for an African-American knowledgeable of the history of her people in the United States not to profess, at minimum, sympathy for legal realism. Most blacks are aware of countless historical examples in which African-Americans were not afforded the benefit of the rule of law: Think, for example, of the existence of slavery in a republic purportedly dedicated to the proposition that all men are created equal, or the law's support of state-sponsored segregation even after the Fourteenth Amendment guaranteed blacks equal protection. That the rule of law ultimately corrected some of the large holes in the American fabric is evidence more of its malleability than of its virtue; the rule of law had, in the first instance, justified the holes.

The Supreme Court's decisions in the major "race" cases of the last term underscore the continuing failure of the rule of law to protect African-Americans through consistent application. Dissenting in a school desegregation case, four Justices stated that "[t]he Court's process of orderly adjudication has broken down in this case." The dissent noted that the majority opinion effectively... overrule[d] a unanimous constitutional precedent of 20 years standing, which was not even addressed in argument, was mentioned merely in passing by one of the parties, and discussed by another of them only in a misleading way." Similarly, in a voting rights case, Justice Stevens, in dissent, described the majority opinion as a "law-changing decision." And in an affirmative action case, Justice Stevens began his dissent by declaring that, "[i]nstead of deciding this case in accordance with controlling precedent, the Court today delivers a disconcerting lecture about the evils of governmental racial classifications." At the end of his dissent, Stevens argued that "the majority's concept of stare decisis ignores the force of binding precedent."

If the rule of law is a myth, or at least is not applicable to African-Americans, the criticism that jury nullification undermines it loses force. The black juror is simply another actor in the system, using her power to fashion a particular outcome; the juror's act of nullification—like the act of the citizen who dials 911 to report Ricky but not Bob, or the police officer who arrests Lisa but not Mary, or the prosecutor who charges Kwame but not Brad, or the judge who finds that Nancy was illegally entrapped but Verna was not—exposes the indeterminancy of law, but does not create it.

3. THE MORAL OBLIGATION TO DISOBEY UNJUST LAWS   For the reader who is unwilling to concede the mythology of the rule of law, I offer another response to the concern about violating it. Assuming, for the purposes of argument, that the rule of law exists, there still is no moral obligation to follow an unjust law. This principle is familiar to many African-Americans who practiced civil disobedience during the civil rights protests of the 1950s and 1960s. Indeed, Martin Luther King suggested that morality requires that unjust laws not be obeyed. As I state above, the difficulty of determining which laws are unjust should not obscure the need to make that determination.

Radical critics believe that the criminal law is unjust when applied to some antisocial conduct by African-Americans: The law uses punishment to treat social problems that are the result of racism and that should be addressed by other means such as medical care or the redistribution of wealth. Later, I suggest a utilitarian justification for why African-Americans should obey most criminal law: It protects them. I concede, however, that this limitation is not morally required if one accepts the radical critique, which applies to all criminal law.

4. DEMOCRATIC DOMINATION   Related to the "undermining the law" critique is the charge that jury nullification is antidemocratic. The trial judge in the Barry case, for example, in remarks made after the conclusion of the trial, expressed this criticism of the jury's verdict: " 'The jury is not a mini-democracy, or a mini-legislature.... They are not to go back and do right as they see fit. That's anarchy. They are supposed to follow the law.' " A jury that nullifies "betrays rather than furthers the assumptions of viable democracy." In a sense, the argument suggests that the jurors are not playing fair: The citizenry made the rules, so the jurors, as citizens, ought to follow them.

What does "viable democracy" assume about the power of an unpopular minority group to make the laws that affect them? It assumes that the group has the power to influence legislation. The American majority-rule electoral system is premised on the hope that the majority will not tyrannize the minority, but rather represent the minority's interests. Indeed, in creating the Constitution, the Framers attempted to guard against the oppression of the minority by the majority. Unfortunately, these attempts were expressed more in theory than in actual constitutional guarantees, a point made by some legal scholars, particularly critical race theorists. The implication of the failure to protect blacks from the tyrannical majority is that the majority rule of whites over African-Americans is, morally speaking, illegitimate. Lani Guinier suggests that the moral legitimacy of majority rule hinges on two assumptions: 1) that majorities are not fixed; and 2) that minorities will be able to become members of some majorities." Racial prejudice "to such a degree that the majority consistently excludes the minority, or refuses to inform itself about the relative merit of the minority's preferences," defeats both assumptions." Similarly, Owen Fiss has given three reasons for the failure of blacks to prosper through American democracy: They are a numerical minority, they have low economic status, and, " 'as a discrete and insular' minority, they are the object of 'prejudice'—that is, the subject of fear, hatred, and distaste that make it particularly difficult for them to form coalitions with others (such as the white poor)."

According to both theories, blacks are unable to achieve substantial progress through regular electoral politics. Their only "democratic" route to success—coalition building with similarly situated groups—is blocked because other groups resist the stigma of the association. The stigma is powerful enough to prevent alignment with African-Americans even when a group—like low income whites—has similar interests.

In addition to individual white citizens, legislative bodies experience the Negrophobia described above. Professor Guinier defines such legislative racism as

> a pattern of actions [that] persistently disadvantag[es] a ... legislative minority and encompasses conscious exclusion as well as marginalization that results from "a lack of interracial empathy." It means that where a prejudiced majority rules, its representatives are not compelled to identify its interests with those of the African-American minority.

Such racism excludes blacks from the governing legislative coalitions. A permanent, homogeneous majority emerges, which effectively marginalizes minority interests and "transform[s] majority rule into majority tyranny." Derrick Bell calls this condition "democratic domination."

Democratic domination undermines the basis of political stability, which depends on the inducement of "losers to continue to play the political game, to continue to work within the system rather than to try to overthrow it." Resistance by minorities to the operation of majority rule may take several forms, including "overt compliance and secret rejection of the legitimacy of the political order." I suggest that another form of this resistance is racially based jury nullification.

If African-Americans believe that democratic domination exists (and the 1994 congressional elections seem to provide compelling recent support for such a belief, they should not back away from lawful self-help measures, like jury nullification, on the ground that the self-help is antidemocratic. African-Americans are not a numerical majority in any of the fifty states, which are the primary sources of criminal law. In addition, they are not even proportionally represented in the U.S. House of Representatives or in the Senate. As a result, African-Americans wield little influence over criminal law, state or federal. African-Americans should embrace the antidemocratic nature of jury nullification because it provides them with the power to determine justice in a way that majority rule does not.

D. "[J]ustice Must Satisfy, the Appearance of Justice": The Symbolic Function of Black Jurors

A second distinction one might draw between the traditionally approved examples of jury nullification and its practice by contemporary African-Americans is that, in the case of the former, jurors refused to apply a particular law, e.g., a fugitive slave law, on the grounds that it was unfair, while in the case of the latter, jurors are not so much judging discrete statutes as they are refusing to apply those statutes to members of their own race. This application of race consciousness by jurors may appear to be antithetical to the American ideal of equality under the law.

This critique, however, like the "betraying democracy" critique, begs the question of whether the ideal actually applies to African-Americans. As stated above, racial critics answer this question in the negative. They, especially the liberal critics, argue that the criminal law is applied in a discriminatory fashion. Furthermore, on several occasions, the Supreme Court has referred to the usefulness of black jurors to the rule of law in the United States. In essence, black jurors symbolize the fairness and impartiality of the law. Here I examine this rhetoric and suggest that, if the presence of black jurors sends a political message, it is right that these jurors use their power to control or negate the meaning of that message.

As a result of the ugly history of discrimination against African-Americans in the criminal justice system, the Supreme Court has had numerous opportunities to consider the significance of black jurors. In so doing, the Court has suggested that these jurors perform a symbolic function, especially when they sit on cases involving African-American defendants, and the Court has typically made these suggestions in the form of rhetoric about the social harm caused by the exclusion of blacks from jury service. I will refer to this role of black jurors as the "legitimization function."

The legitimization function stems from every jury's political function of providing American citizens with "the security . . . that they, as jurors actual or possible, being part of the judicial system of the country can prevent its arbitrary use or abuse." In addition to, and perhaps more important than, seeking the truth, the purpose of the jury system is "to impress upon the criminal defendant and the community as a whole that a verdict of conviction or acquittal is given in accordance with the law by persons who are fair." This purpose is consistent with the original purpose of the constitutional right to a jury trial, which was "to prevent oppression by the Government." When blacks are excluded from juries, beyond any harm done to the juror who suffers the discrimination or to the defendant, the social injury of the exclusion is that it "undermine[s]... public confidence—as well [it] should." Because the United States is both a democracy and a pluralist society, it is important that diverse groups appear to have a voice in the laws that govern them. Allowing black people to serve on juries strengthens "public respect for our criminal justice system and the rule of law."

The Supreme Court has found that the legitimization function is particularly valuable in cases involving "race-related" crimes. According to the Court, in these cases, "emotions in the affected community [are] inevitably... heated and volatile." The potential presence of black people on the jury in a "race-related" case calms the natives, which is especially important in this type of case because "[p]ublic confidence in the integrity of the criminal justice system is essential for preserving community peace." The very fact that a black person can be on a jury is evidence that the criminal justice system is one in which black people should have confidence, and one that they should respect. But what of the black juror who endorses racial critiques of American criminal justice? Such a person holds no "confidence in the integrity of the criminal justice system." If she is cognizant of the implicit message that the Supreme Court believes her presence sends, she might not want her presence to be the vehicle for that message. Let us assume that there is a black defendant who, the evidence suggests, is guilty of the crime with which he has been charged, and a black juror who thinks that there are too many black men in prison. The black juror has two choices: She can vote for conviction, thus sending another black man to prison and implicitly allowing her presence to support public confidence in the system that puts him there, or she can vote not guilty," thereby acquitting the defendant, or at least causing a mistrial. In choosing the latter, the juror makes a decision not to be a passive symbol of support for a system for which she has no respect. Rather than signaling her displeasure with the system by breaching "community peace," the black juror invokes the political nature of her role in the criminal justice system and votes "no." In a sense, the black juror engages in an act of civil disobedience, except that her choice is better than civil disobedience because it is lawful. Is the black juror's race-conscious act moral? Absolutely. It would be farcical for her to be the sole color-blind actor in the criminal process, especially when it is her blackness that advertises the system's fairness.

At this point, every African-American should ask herself whether the operation of the criminal law in the United States advances the interests of black people. If it does not, the doctrine of jury nullification affords African-American jurors the opportunity to control the authority of the law over some African-American criminal defendants. In essence, black people can "opt out" of American criminal law.

How far should they go? Completely to anarchy? Or is there some place between here and there, safer than both? The next part describes such a place, and how to get there.

To allow African-American jurors to exercise their responsibility in a principled way, I make the following proposal: African-American jurors should approach their work cognizant of its political nature and their prerogative to exercise their power in the best interests of the black community. In every case, the juror should be guided by her view of what is "just." For the reasons stated in the preceding parts of this Essay, I have more faith in the average black juror's idea of justice than I do in the idea that is embodied in the "rule of law."

A. A Framework for Criminal Justice in the Black Community

In cases involving violent malum in se crimes like murder, rape, and assault, jurors should consider the case strictly on the evidence presented, and, if they have no reasonable doubt that the defendant is guilty, they should convict. For nonviolent malum in se crimes such as theft or perjury, nullification is an option that the juror should consider, although there should be no presumption in favor of it. A juror might vote for acquittal, for example, when a poor woman steals from Tiffany's, but not when the same woman steals from her next-door neighbor. Finally, in cases involving nonviolent, malum prohibitum offenses, including "victimless" crimes like narcotics offenses, there should be a presumption in favor of nullification.

This approach seeks to incorporate the most persuasive arguments of both the racial critics and the law enforcement enthusiasts. If my model is faithfully executed, the result would be that fewer black people would go to prison; to that extent, the proposal ameliorates one of the most severe consequences of law enforcement in the African-American community. At the same time, the proposal, by punishing violent offenses and certain others, preserves any protection against harmful conduct that the law may offer potential victims. If the experienced prosecutors at the U.S. Attorney's Office are correct, some violent offenders currently receive the benefit of jury nullification, doubtless from a misguided, if well-intentioned, attempt by racial critics to make a political point. Under my proposal, violent lawbreakers would go to prison.

In the language of criminal law, the proposal adopts utilitarian justifications for punishment: deterrence and isolation. To that extent, it accepts the law enforcement enthusiasts' faith in the possibility that law can prevent crime. The proposal does not, however, judge the lawbreakers as harshly as the enthusiasts would judge them. Rather, the proposal assumes that, regardless of the reasons for their antisocial conduct, people who are violent should be separated from the community, for the sake of the nonviolent. The proposal's justifications for the separation are that the community is protected from the offender for the duration of the sentence and that the threat of punishment may discourage future offenses and offenders. I am confident that balancing the social costs and benefits of incarceration would not lead black jurors to release violent criminals simply because of race. While I confess agnosticism about whether the law

239

can deter antisocial conduct, I am unwilling to experiment by abandoning any punishment premised on deterrence.

Of the remaining traditional justifications for punishment, the proposal eschews the retributive or just deserts" theory for two reasons. First, I am persuaded by racial and other critiques of the unfairness of punishing people for "negative" reactions to racist, oppressive conditions. In fact, I sympathize with people who react "negatively" to the countless manifestations of white supremacy that black people experience daily. While my proposal does not "excuse" all antisocial conduct, it will not punish such conduct on the premise that the intent to engage in it is "evil." The antisocial conduct is no more evil than the conditions that cause it, and, accordingly, the "just deserts" of a black offender are impossible to know. And even if just deserts were susceptible to accurate measure, I would reject the idea of punishment for retribution's sake.

My argument here is that the consequences are too severe: African-Americans cannot afford to lock up other African-Americans simply on account of anger. There is too little bang for the buck. Black people have a community that needs building, and children who need rescuing, and as long as a person will not hurt anyone, the community needs him there to help.

Assuming that he actually will help is a gamble but not a reckless one, for the "just" African-American community will not leave the lawbreaker be: It will, for example, encourage his education and provide his health care (including narcotics dependency treatment) and, if necessary, sue him for child support. In other words, the proposal demands of African-Americans responsible self-help outside of the criminal courtroom as well as inside it. When the community is richer, perhaps then it can afford anger.

The final traditional justification for punishment, rehabilitation, can be dealt with summarily. If rehabilitation were a meaningful option in American criminal justice, I would not endorse nullification in any case. It would be counterproductive, for utilitarian reasons: The community is better off with the antisocial person cured than sick. Unfortunately, however, rehabilitation is no longer an objective of criminal law in the United States, and prison appears to have an antirehabilitative effect. For this reason, unless a juror is provided with a specific, compelling reason to believe that a conviction would result in some useful treatment for an offender, she should not use her vote to achieve this end, because almost certainly it will not occur.

B. Hypothetical Cases

How would a juror decide individual cases under my proposal? For the purposes of the following hypothesis, let us assume criminal prosecutions in state or federal court and technically guilty African-American defendants. Easy cases under my proposal include a defendant who possessed crack cocaine, and a defendant who killed another person. The former should be acquitted, and the latter should go to prison.

The crack cocaine case is simple: Because the crime is victimless, the proposal presumes nullification. According to racial critiques, acquittal is just, due in part to the longer sentences given for crack offenses than for powder cocaine offenses. This case should be particularly compelling to the liberal racial critic, given the extreme disparity between crack and powder in both enforcement of the law and in actual sentencing. According to a recent study, African-Americans make up 13% of the nation's regular drug users, but they account for 35% of narcotics arrests, 55% of drug convictions, and 74% of those receiving prison sentences. Most of the people who are arrested for crack cocaine offences are black; most arrested for powder cocaine are white. Under federal law, if someone possesses fifty grams of crack cocaine, the mandatory-minimum sentence is ten years; in order to receive the same sentence for powder cocaine, the defendant must possess 5000 grams. Given the racial consequences of this disparity, I hope that many racial critics will nullify without hesitation in these cases.

The case of the murderer is "easy" solely for the utilitarian reasons I discussed above. Although I do not believe that prison will serve any rehabilitative function for the murderer, there is a possibility that a guilty verdict will prevent another person from becoming a victim, and the juror should err on the side of that possibility. In effect, I "write off" the black person who takes a life, not for retributive reasons, but because the black community cannot afford the risks of leaving this person in its midst. Accordingly, for the sake of potential victims (given the possibility that the criminal law deters homicide), nullification is not morally justifiable here.

Difficult hypothetical cases include the ghetto drug dealer and the thief who burglarizes the home of a rich family. Under the proposal, nullification is presumed in the first case because drug distribution is a nonviolent, malum prohibitum offense. Is nullification morally justifiable here? It depends. There is no question that encouraging people to engage in self-destructive behavior is evil; the question the juror should ask herself is whether the remedy is less evil. I suspect that the usual answer would be "yes," premised on deterrence and isolation theories of punishment. Accordingly, the drug dealer would be convicted. The answer might change, however, depending on the particular facts of the case: the type of narcotic sold, the ages of the buyers, whether the dealer "marketed" the drugs to customers or whether they sought him out, whether it is a first offense, whether there is reason to believe that the drug dealer would cease this conduct if given another chance, and whether, as in the crack case, there are racial disparities in sentencing for this kind of crime. I recognize that, in this hypothetical, nullification carries some societal risk. The risk, however, is less consequential than with violent crimes. Furthermore, the cost to the community of imprisoning all drug dealers is great. I would allow the juror in this case more discretion.

The juror should also remember that many ghetto "drug" dealers are not African-American and that the state does not punish these dealers—instead, it licenses them. Liquor stores are ubiquitous on the ghetto streets of America. By almost every measure, alcoholism causes great injury to society, and yet the state does not use the criminal law to address this severe social problem. When the government tried to treat the problem of alcohol use with criminal law, during Prohibition, a violent "black" market formed. Even if the juror does not believe that drug dealing is a "victimless" crime, she might question why it is that of all drug dealers, many of the black capitalists are imprisoned, and many of the non-black capitalists are legally enriched. When the juror remembers that the cost to the community of having so many young men in jail means that law enforcement also is not "victimless," the juror's calculus of justice might lead her to vote for acquittal.

As for the burglar who steals from the rich family, the case is troubling, first of all, because the conduct is so clearly "wrong." As a nonviolent malum in se crime, there is no presumption in favor of nullification, through it remains an option. Here, again, the facts of the case are relevant to the juror's decision of what outcome is fair. For example, if the offense was committed to support a drug habit, I think there is a moral case to be made for nullification, at least until drug rehabilitation services are available to all.

If the burglary victim is a rich white person, the hypothetical is troubling for the additional reason that it demonstrates how a black juror's sense of justice might, in some cases, lead her to treat defendants differently based on the class and race of their victims. I expect that this distinction would occur most often in property offenses because, under the proposal, no violent offenders would be excused. In an ideal world, whether the victim is rich or poor or black or white would be irrelevant to adjudication of the defendant's culpability. In the United States, my sense is that some black jurors will believe that these factors are relevant to the calculus of justice. The rationale is implicitly premised on a critique of the legitimacy of property rights in a society marked by gross economic inequities. While I endorse this critique, I would encourage nullification here only in extreme cases (i.e., nonviolent theft from the very wealthy) and mainly for political reasons: If the rich cannot rely on criminal law for the protection of their property and the law prevents more direct self-help measures, perhaps they will focus on correcting the conditions that make others want to steal from them. This view may be naive, but arguably no more so than that of the black people who thought that if they refused to ride the bus, they could end legally enforced segregation in the South.

C. Some Political and Procedural Concerns

1. WHAT IF WHITE PEOPLE START NULLIFYING TOO?   One concern is that whites will nullify in cases of white-on-black crime. The best response to this concern is that often white people do nullify in those cases. The white jurors who acquitted the police officers who beat up Rodney King are a good example. There is no reason why my proposal should cause white jurors to acquit white defendants who are guilty of violence against blacks any more frequently. My model assumes that black violence against whites would be punished by black jurors; I hope that white jurors would do the same in cases involving white defendants.

If white jurors were to begin applying my proposal to cases with white defendants, then they, like the black jurors, would be choosing to opt out of the criminal justice system. For pragmatic political purposes, that would be excellent. Attention would then be focused on alternative methods of correcting antisocial conduct much sooner than it would if only African-Americans raised the issue.

2. HOW DO YOU CONTROL ANARCHY?   Why would a juror who is willing to ignore a law created through the democratic process be inclined to follow my proposal? There is no guarantee that she would. But when we consider that black jurors are already nullifying on the basis of race because they do not want to send another black man to prison, we recognize that these jurors are willing to use their power in a politically conscious manner. Many black people have concerns about their participation in the criminal justice system as jurors and might be willing to engage in some organized political conduct, not unlike the civil disobedience that African-Americans practiced in the South in the 1950s and 1960s. It appears that some black jurors now excuse some conduct—like murder—that they should not excuse. My proposal, however, provides a principled structure for the exercise of the black juror's vote. I am not encouraging anarchy. Instead, I am reminding black jurors of their privilege to serve a higher calling than law: justice. I am suggesting a framework for what justice means in the African-American community.

3. HOW DO YOU IMPLEMENT THE PROPOSAL?   Because *Sparf*, as well as the law of many states, prohibits jurors from being instructed about jury nullification in criminal cases, information about this privilege would have to be communicated to black jurors before they heard such cases. In addition, jurors would need to be familiar with my proposal's framework for analyzing whether nullification is appropriate in a particular case. Disseminating this information should not be difficult. African-American culture—through mediums such as church, music (particularly rap songs), black newspapers and magazines, literature, storytelling, film (including music videos), soapbox speeches, and convention gatherings—facilitates intraracial communication. At African-American cultural events, such as concerts or theatrical productions, the audience could be instructed on the proposal, either verbally or through the dissemination of written material; this type of political expression at a cultural event would hardly be unique—voter registration campaigns are often conducted at such events. The proposal could be the subject of rap songs, which are already popular vehicles for racial critiques, or of ministers' sermons.

One can also imagine more direct approaches. For example, advocates of this proposal might stand outside a courthouse and distribute flyers explaining the proposal to prospective jurors. During deliberations, those jurors could then explain to other jurors their prerogative—their power—to decide justice rather than simply the facts. *Sparf* is one Supreme Court decision whose holding is rather easy to circumvent: If the defense attorneys cannot inform the people of their power, the people can inform themselves. And once informed, the people would have a formula for what justice means in the African-American community, rather than having to decide it on an ad hoc basis.

I hope that all African-American jurors will follow my proposal, and I am encouraged by the success of other grass-roots campaigns, like the famous Montgomery bus boycott, aimed at eliminating racial oppression. I note, however, that even with limited participation by African-Americans, my proposal could have a significant impact. In most American jurisdictions, jury verdicts in criminal cases must be unanimous. One juror could prevent the conviction of a defendant. The prosecution would then have to retry the case, and risk facing another African-American juror with emancipation tendencies. I hope that there are enough of us out there, fed up with prison as the answer to black desperation and white supremacy, to cause retrial after retrial, until, finally, the United States "retries" its idea of justice.

CONCLUSION

This Essay's proposal raises other concerns, such as the problem of providing jurors with information relevant to their decision within the restrictive evidentiary confines of a trial. Some of theses issues can be resolved through creative lawyering. Other policy questions are not as easily answered, including the issue of how long (years, decades, centuries?) black jurors would need to pursue racially based jury nullification. I think this concern is related to the issue of the appropriate time span of other race-conscious remedies, including affirmative action. Perhaps, when policymakers acknowledge that race matters in criminal justice, the criminal law can benefit from the successes and failures of race consciousness in other areas of the law. I fear, however, that this day of acknowledgment will be long in coming. Until then, I expect that many black jurors will perceive the necessity of employing the self-held measures prescribed here.

I concede that the justice my proposal achieves is rough because it is as susceptible to human foibles as the jury system. I am sufficiently optimistic to hope that my proposal will be only an intermediate plan, a stopping point between the status quo and real justice. I hope that this Essay will encourage African-Americans to use responsibly the power they already have. To get criminal justice past the middle point, I hope that the Essay will facilitate a dialogue among all Americans in which the significance of race will not be dismissed or feared, but addressed. The most dangerous "forbidden" message is that it is better to ignore the truth than to face it.

6.2 RONALD STIDHAM AND ROBERT A. CARP

Indian Rights and Law Before the Federal District Courts

The most recent compilation and analysis of new data on the effects and consequences of violent crime among American Indians by the U.S. Department of Justice reveals an extremely disturbing portrait of American Indians as both victims and offenders of violent crime in the United States. The rate of violent victimization of American Indians is more than twice the national average, and roughly 70 percent of the violent victimization suffered by American Indians is by persons of a different race. Also, the incarceration rate of American Indians is about 38 percent higher than the national rate, with some 4 percent of the American Indian population in custody or otherwise under the control of the American criminal justice system. Although American Indians constitute about .08 percent of the U.S. population, nearly 2 percent of all federal cases filed in U.S. district courts in 1997 involved American Indians; roughly half of these cases were for such violent crimes as murder and rape.

Moreover, a study of the impact of crime and criminal justice on American Indians by the National Minority Advisory Council on Criminal Justice found that the displacement of American Indian sovereignty by the encroaching Anglo-European system of laws and values has had pernicious, debilitating effects. The council asserted that "the discriminatory law enforcement experienced by American Indians is perpetuated in the US judicial system, where it assumes the more subtle form of institutionalized discrimination and racism." Preserving American Indian rights has not been a major objective of the American judiciary. In the following selection from "Indian Rights and Law Before the Federal District Courts," *The Social Science Journal* (vol. 32, no. 1, 1995), Ronald Stidham, an associate professor of political science and criminal justice at Appalachian State University, and

Robert A. Carp, a professor of political science and associate dean of social sciences at the University of Houston, provide the first study of the voting behavior of U.S. trial judges on American Indian rights and law. These scholars have found that federal judges appointed by Democratic presidents are significantly more likely to support Indian litigants than federal judges appointed by Republican presidents.

Key Concept: federal judiciary and American Indian rights and law

*T*his study subjects to quantitative analysis the decisional behavior of U.S. trial judges on the subject of Indian rights and law. Following a general discussion of the status of Native Americans in the U.S. legal system we focus more specifically on current case law regarding Indian rights and law. Not unexpectedly, there is a great deal of ambiguity in this legal realm. Since the judicial behavior literature indicates that ambiguous legal areas are fertile realms for judges to manifest their personal/partisan values in their judicial decisionmaking, we test the hypothesis that judges appointed by Democratic presidents respond differently to the pleas of Native American petitioners than do their colleagues selected by Republican chief executives. Our findings reveal that judges placed on the bench by a Democratic president are significantly more likely to support the Indian litigant.

This study is the first attempt to subject to quantitative analysis the voting behavior of U.S. trial judges on the subject of American Indian rights and law. We begin with a general discussion of the status of Native Americans in the U.S. legal system and then focus more specifically on current case law as it applies to the rights of this cultural and legal subgroup. After documenting a great deal of ambiguity in this legal realm, we call to mind the judicial behavior literature which indicates that ambiguous legal areas are fertile realms for judges to manifest their personal/partisan values in their judicial decision making. We then seek to determine empirically whether U.S. jurists appointed by Democratic Presidents respond differently to the pleas of Native American petitioners than do their colleagues selected by G.O.P. Chief Executives.

INDIAN RIGHTS AND LAW IN THE AMERICAN POLITICAL SYSTEM

Observers of the American political system have long recognized that certain individuals and groups have a more difficult time within the system than others. Judicial scholars typically refer to such individuals and/or groups as underdogs or disadvantaged minorities.

Indians would surely have to be included in a listing of underdogs or disadvantaged minorities. In fact, Sigler describes American Indians as "among the most neglected and abused Americans." It has also been noted that "few historical relationships are marked by a starker imbalance of economic and political power than that which developed between the United States and Indian tribes." Such assessments should come as no surprise when one considers that "before the turbulent 1960s, non-Indian America generally viewed Indians as barriers to the growth of the United States and as romantic and/or savage people." During the 1960s, Native American activists aimed to set the record straight and present a more accurate picture of the many injustices endured by Indians. Several demonstrations protesting violations of treaty rights garnered national media attention and aroused public awareness of Indian discontent. New books, some written by Native Americans, appeared on the scene to chronicle the atrocities committed against Indians by the United States. Subsequent decades have seen the publication of several surveys of Indian history, studies of Native American political and legal issues, and casebooks in the field of federal Indian law.

In short, much of the story of the Indian struggle has been well chronicled. Among other things, we know that by the middle of the nineteenth century "Native Americans were portrayed as in most everybody's way, and they had lost much of the force they once had to resist the relentless pressures to give up what land remained theirs." The area east of the Mississippi River, once inhabited by thousands of Indians, had been largely taken away from them. The federal government, by forcing them to move westward to reservations, took their land and disrupted their cultures.

The policy of separation provided by the reservation system had changed by the end of the nineteenth century, however, as Congress changed course and adopted a policy [of] "assimilation and destruction of Indian culture." Concerning this new policy, Kermit L. Hall says that

> White economic self-interest explains part of the change; western farmers, ranchers, and railroad men hungered for reservation lands. There were less materialistic impulses as well. Well-documented abuses on the reservations had an impact on public opinion, and white reformers sought to solve the Indian problem by simply absorbing the native American population.

After nearly two centuries of alternating between two policy extremes, one calling for the physical and political separation of tribes from the rest of the population and another aimed at assimilating Indians into the larger society, the federal government opted for a new approach. Michael Reese says that by the late 1960s "coerced assimilation was out of fashion, and federal attention was riveted on a policy of promoting tribal self-determination."

Although the changing nature of the federal government's policies is disconcerting enough, the picture with regard to Native Americans is further complicated by the fact that

> the complexity of American Indian law is almost inversely related to the size of the Indian population, which constitutes one of the smallest groups of minorities in America today. The law is extensive in its scope, span, and the constitutive sources.

Among those sources are treaties, the U.S. Constitution, federal statutes, executive orders, administrative rules, court decisions, state statutes, and tribal government policies. Furthermore, legal recognition has also been based upon the land status of the tribe. Some are federally designated land trusts, others are treaty-based reservations or executive-order reservations, while still others are congressionally-created reservations.

The individual rights of Indians in the American political system "largely flow from one of two sources—the common rights of U.S. citizenship or the implications of membership in a recognized tribe." Therefore, an Indian may have three separate sets of rights: federal, state, and tribal. Unlike whites, however, Indians were not initially considered citizens simply by virtue of being born in this country. In *Elk v. Wilkins* the U.S. Supreme Court ruled that the Fourteenth Amendment does not confer citizenship on Indians born in the United States. The Court likened Indians to "the children of subjects of any foreign government born within the domain of that government, or the children born within the United States of ambassadors of other public ministers of foreign nations." This situation was altered in 1924 with passage of the Indian Citizenship Act. Since that time, Indians have held citizenship in the United States and their state of residency in addition to having the rights of membership within a tribe.

Membership within a tribe has at times been a mixed blessing, however. For example, consider the events leading to the U.S. Supreme Court's decision in *Ex Parte Crow Dog.* That case began on August 5, 1881 when Spotted Tail, chief of the Brule Sioux, was shot and killed by his fellow tribesman, Crow Dog. A tribal council was quickly called to determine how to restore harmony. Crow Dog was ordered to give Spotted Tail's relatives considerable property and services as compensation for their loss. Despite the immediate, and apparently acceptable, application of Brule Sioux law, Crow Dog was arrested, tried, and sentenced to be hanged by a U.S. territory court in Deadwood, Dakota. Following an unsuccessful appeal, Crow Dog's lawyer filed for a writ of habeas corpus at the U.S. Supreme Court. The Court's decision, based on readings of federal statutes, U.S. treaties with the Sioux, and the idea that tribes maintain their own legal systems as an attribute of sovereignty, held that criminal justice was a prerogative of the tribes alone. Justice Matthews left the door open, however, with his statement that any new criminal jurisdiction policy by the U.S. government would require " a clear expression of the intention of Congress." According to Shattuck and Norgren "these words gave explicit direction to the political activity of the [Bureau of Indian Affairs] bureaucrats, and to the reformers, who saw the Court's acknowledgement of tribal jurisdiction as a setback." Mobilization of a lobbying effort resulted in passage of the Major Crimes Act of 1885 which removed from tribal jurisdiction seven serious crimes: murder, manslaughter, rape, assault with intent to kill, arson, burglary, and larceny. A year later, in *U.S. v. Kagama,* the Supreme Court upheld the legislation.

The issue of whether Indians are entitled to the protections of the Federal Constitution provides another good example. Prior to 1968, Indians had no federally protected rights while living on reservations. Instead, tribal law, as interpreted by tribal courts, determined their fate. In its well-known decision in *Talton v. Mayes* the U.S. Supreme Court held that the Fifth Amendment did not apply to an Indian tribunal. The Court justified its decision on the ground that the powers of local self-government enjoyed by the Cherokee nation preceded adoption of the Constitution. As recently as 1963 a federal district court held in *Glover v. United States* that the due process clause and the right to counsel requirements did not apply to tribal courts.

To be sure, some tribes provided, in their own codes and constitutions, basic protections for fundamental rights. For example, the Blackfoot Constitution guaranteed freedom of worship, speech, press, assembly and association, in addition to providing the accused with such rights as an open and public hearing, due notice, and a jury trial. Other tribes either made no provisions for such protections or did not guarantee them in actual application. Complaints that tribal governments denied fundamental civil liberties were quite common by the early 1960s and prompted at least one senator, Quentin Burdick of North Dakota, to describe tribal judicial proceedings in his state as "kangaroo courts."

Passage of the Indian Civil Rights Act [ICRA] of 1968 was designed to change the situation. However, it was only partially successful in that regard. According to Michael Reese,

> the Act reflected a deliberate attempt to balance the interests in individual justice on the one hand with notions of tribal sovereignty and tradition on the other. In this respect, it is obvious that the ICRA does not mirror the Bill of Rights. There are notable differences, such as the absence of a religious establishment clause and the provision that defendants may have council, but at their own expense. Legislatively then, the ICRA did not completely eliminate the dual standard of justice.

Since major crimes had earlier been removed from tribal jurisdiction, Congress, by 1968, had claimed a great deal of authority over the Indian tribes.

However, tribal courts remained in control of civil suits and minor criminal cases. Indian judges, subject to confirmation by Indians of the reservation and the Bureau of Indian Affairs, handle such matters. Indian customary law may be enforced by tribal courts, but resort to state or federal tribunals may also be available. In short, there is a good deal of jurisdictional confusion.

INDIANS AND THE COURTS

A leading student of Indian law recently said,

> Federal Indian law presents uniquely formidable obstacles to the development of consistent and unitary legal doctrine. There are a number of scattering forces that push Indian law away from any center. Taken together, these splintering influences have the potential of creating a body of law almost without precedent, of reducing each dispute to the particular complex of circumstances at issue—the tribe, its treaty or enabling statute, the races of the parties, the tract-book location of the land where the case arose, the narrow tribal or state power involved, and other factors. Further, the task of rendering coherent judicial decisions in Indian law is profoundly complicated by the passage of time. In most cases a crucial issue—seldom mentioned in the opinions but implicitly a weighty presence to the parties and judges—is how an old treaty, statute, or court decision should be applied in times bearing little resemblance to the era in which the words of law were originally written.

Charles Wilkinson says that the U.S. Supreme Court's 1959 decision in *Williams v. Lee* ushered in the modern era of federal Indian law. The case involved a non-Indian's suit in the Apache County, Arizona Superior Court to enforce a debt entered into by Indians on the Navajo Reservation. Although an action on a contract is normally a transitory cause of action that can be brought to suit in a judicial forum other than the one in which the contract was executed, the Court in *Williams* ruled that the case should be heard exclusively with the tribal system in order to protect and promote tribal self-government. Wilkinson sees the *Williams* decision as a watershed for several reasons. First, he says that for several decades prior to *Williams* the tribes and the federal government instituted few cases to establish or expand tribal powers. Since *Williams* the pace of litigation has accelerated. Secondly, the magnitude of the controversies and affected interests has grown. A third factor cited by Wilkinson is the fact that the *Williams* paradigm of exclusive tribal jurisdiction is a prime example of the special rules the Court has recognized during the modern era to protect tribal government. Finally, he says that *Williams* is especially significant in defining eras in the field because for the first time the Court was presented with Indian issues in a modern context.

In order to fully understand the challenges faced by judges developing Indian law policy we should briefly examine some of the major Supreme Court cases decided prior to the "modern era." Again, Wilkinson's study is especially illuminating. He says that "as the modern era began, the construct of Indian law ultimately rested on two separate braces of opinions." The first line of opinions began with the Marshall trilogy which included *Johnson v. McIntosh, Cherokee Nation v. Georgia,* and especially *Worcester v. Georgia.* In this group of cases Chief Justice Marshall developed a model that called for largely autonomous tribal governments subject to overriding federal authority, but basically free of state control. Later opinions which continued this theme were *Ex Parte Crow Dog* and *Talton v. Mayers.* These cases recognized tribes as independent sovereigns which were free of constitutional restrictions and general federal laws unless Congress had expressly limited tribal powers. This group of opinions is generally referred to as the *Worcester-Crow Dog-Talton* line.

The second group of opinions, handed down in late nineteenth and early twentieth century cases, saw the Court recognize a seemingly unlimited federal power to alter tribal property and jurisdictional prerogatives dealt with by treaties and treaty substitutes. *United States v. Kagama* upheld congressional power to enact the Major Crimes Act which interfered with internal tribal resolution of disputes. In *McBratney v. United States* the Court upheld state court jurisdiction over a murder of a non-Indian within Indian country even though there was no congressional grant of such authority to the states. Finally, the Court's decision in *Lone Wolf v. Hitchcock* upheld the federal sale of tribal land although an 1867 treaty requirement of consent of three-fourths of all adult male Indians to any land sale was not met. This latter line of cases, "implicitly conceptualized tribes as lost societies without power, as minions of the federal government."

Not surprisingly, the lower courts have also offered a variety of opinions in cases involving Indian rights and law. Nonetheless, they too can be divided into two separate, irreconcilable bodies of jurisprudence. One group of opinions, based on the *Kagama-McBratney-Lone Wolf* line of cases, is premised on modern realities. These decisions, reasoning that the Indian tribes are small and powerless, argue that state governments are in a position to exercise police power which serves the needs of state citizens.

Other lower-court judges have relied on the *Worcester-Crow Dog-Talton* line and eschewed the so-called modern realities. They focus on the traditional tribal justice systems which held complete power before contact with European nations. In this view Indian tribes are recognized as "permanent separate sovereigns, a third level of government in this constitutional democracy."

In spite of their mixed record, one scholar says that "in truth the judiciary has been the sole friend of Indian tribes among the branches of the federal government."

THEORETICAL FRAMEWORK

As the above brief review of the literature makes abundantly clear, the field of Indian rights and law is a confusing one. Congress, presidents, state officials, and judges have expressed a wide variety of views on the status of Indians and their collective and individual rights. Furthermore, although there has been a lot of litigation in the field of Indian law there is still a great deal of ambiguity. It is in this setting of confusion and ambiguous precedents that we explore federal district court opinions in cases involving Indian rights and law.

We begin with a basic question. What guides a judge's decisionmaking process when legal precedents are nonexistent, conflicting, or ambiguous? Political scientists exploring this question are likely to argue that judges faced with such a predicament are obliged to look to the democratic subculture, an amalgam of determinants that include their own political inclinations, for guidance in their decision making.

More specifically, many scholars exploring the democratic subculture as an explanation of judges' decisions have found the answer in social background analysis. "Social background analysis moves from the assumption that a judge's decisions are influenced by his or her attitudes, which in turn are shaped by social, political, and legal background factors and experiences." This occurs through a natural process whereby judges develop certain attributes which may be "linked to regularities in decisional behavior through the formation and development of influential attitudes and values." Although social background attributes are not the same as attitudes and values, Robert Bradley, in a recent study on the issuance of structural reform decrees in correctional litigation, says

> I assume that certain attributes either directly reflect or develop into deep-seated attitudes held by federal district judges. Furthermore, these attitudes are assumed

to come to the forefront of a judge's decision in cases where legal precedent is either nonexistent or ambiguous and political aspects are prevalent.

In other words, there are many court cases where the situation is ripe for extra-legal influences on a judge's policy preferences to be substantial. Naturally, it is impractical, if not impossible, to identify and analyze all the possible social background attributes of every federal district judge who served since 1933. For this reason we will follow the lead of Robert Bradley's recent study and treat one social background trait as an independent variable. That one trait, appointing president, has been used frequently in research on federal district judges.

THE APPOINTING PRESIDENT VARIABLE

It is generally assumed that one of the most important factors affecting presidential nominations to the federal bench is the potential judge's beliefs and philosophy. If the potential nominee is in basic agreement with the president, then his or her chances for a judgeship are much better than those of one who does not share such agreement. Furthermore, some presidents have adopted a judicial recruitment strategy which carefully screens potential nominees in order to determine whether they share his ideological and policy preferences. When a president takes such steps he presumably has an interest in exerting some influence over the choices those judges will make once they are on the bench.

Democratic presidents, for instance, have generally been associated with promoting the interests of the disadvantaged and using the power of the government to address social ills. Republican presidents, on the other hand, have traditionally been seen as advocating a less active role for government and favoring a restraintist philosophy for the federal courts. Thus, one might intuitively expect judicial appointees of Democratic presidents to be more supportive of the claims of disadvantaged minorities than judges placed on the bench by a Republican president.

Based upon these assumptions, our basic hypothesis is: In cases involving the issue of Indian rights and law, there is a relationship between the policymaking behavior of federal district judges and the party of their appointing president. The independent variable is the party of the appointing president. This variable consists of federal district judges who were appointed to the bench by either Republican or Democratic presidents. The dependent variable is the policymaking behavior of federal district judges. Policymaking behavior is represented by the liberal or conservative nature of the decisions of federal district judges. The formal hypothesis may be stated as follows:

H1. In cases involving Indian rights and law, a significantly greater proportion of liberal decisions will be provided by federal district judges appointed by a Democratic president than by federal district judges appointed by a Republican president.

Our basic data source is the *Federal Supplement,* which includes all opinions written and submitted by federal district judges. We extracted those cases which pertain to Indian rights and law. Typical examples include suits between Indian tribes and a local government, suits between an Indian tribe and a state, and suits involving an Indian tribe and the national government. Not included are suits between one Indian tribe and another Indian tribe or suits involving an individual suing an Indian tribe.

We are well aware of the fact that only a small percentage of district court decisions are ever formally published. The vast majority are either not justified in written form at all, or merely appear as slip opinions or memoranda which accompany a case on appeal. Although evidence suggests that opinions dealing with important issues are more likely to find their way into print than opinions of a more trivial or routine nature, our data base is somewhat limited by the absence of published opinions for all Indian rights cases. The major reason for not including the unpublished written and oral opinions is, of course, that they are very difficult to obtain. We would note, however, that other researchers have relied on the *Supplement* as their primary data source in a variety of studies that have been well received by public law scholars.

Opinions published between 1933 and 1991 which fit into the Indian rights and law case category and contain a clear underlying liberal-conservative dimension are included in our data set. Each was coded according to whether the decision was liberal or conservative, with a liberal decision being defined as one favoring the Indians. Each opinion also provided us with the identity of the judge/author, which in turn enabled us to determine which president appointed that particular judge. All total, our data set includes over 300 opinions written by the appointees of Presidents Woodrow Wilson through George Bush.

FINDINGS AND DISCUSSION

Our analysis of opinions published during the 1933–1991 period in Indian rights and law cases indicates that 50 percent of the decisions of federal trial court judges in such cases were liberal. Data on other underdog or disadvantaged minority litigants, presented in Table 1, indicate that the mean liberal score in Indian rights cases is exceeded only by that in cases involving rights of the handicapped, which stand at 53 percent.

Table 1 also reveals that women's rights cases yielded the same overall liberal score (50 percent) as cases involving Indian rights and law. Somewhat lower levels of support for the claims of disadvantaged minority or underdog litigants were found in racial minority discrimination cases (46 percent), cases involving the rights of aliens (45 percent), and age discrimination cases (44 percent).

Given the long time period covered by our study and the fact that it extends over three major eras of federal Indian policy, we explore opinions for each era in Table 2. During the era of Indian reorganization (opinions from the 1933–1945 period) a slight majority (52.5 percent) of all decisions in Indian rights cases were liberal. During the period when a policy of termination was dominant (1946–1961), 55.6 percent of the opinions were liberal. As we move to the era of self-determination (1962–1991) we find that the percentage of liberal opinions declined by almost seven points to 48.8 percent. The difference in liberal scores between the latter two periods is not statistically significant, however.

TABLE 1

Percentage of Liberal Opinions by Federal District Judges in Cases Involving Indians and Other Disadvantaged Minorities[a]

Disadvantaged Minority Case Category	Percent Liberal
Age Discrimination	44
Alien Petitions	45
Racial Minority Discrimination	46
Indian Rights and Law	50
Women's Rights	50
Rights of the Handicapped	53

Note: [a] The figures on the other disadvantaged minorities categories are for 1933–1987.

Source: Robert A. Carp and Ronald Stidham, *Judicial Process in America,* 2nd ed. (Washington, DC: Congressional Quarterly Press, 1993), p. 286.

Our data concerning opinions published in Indian rights and law cases by the appointees of Democratic and Republican presidents is presented in Table 3. Of the 162 opinions published by judges named to the bench by a Democratic president, nearly 55 percent were liberal. On the other hand, only about 45 percent of the opinions authored by a Republican appointee were liberal. A difference of proportions test reveals that the difference between the proportion of liberal opinions written by the appointees of Democratic presidents and the proportion of those authored by judges named to the bench by a Republican chief executive is statistically significant beyond the commonly accepted .05 level. Thus, our hypothesis is confirmed.

This finding is compatible with several other studies analyzing the impact of an appointing president on the decisional patterns of his appointees to the federal bench. In one extensive analysis, Carp and Rowland compared the percentage of liberal decisions handed down by the federal district court appointees of Presidents Wilson through Ford and found that, almost without exception, the results were in the expected direction. Other studies have found significant differences between presidential appointment cohorts on the district court in economic cases, criminal justice cases, and cases involving disadvantaged minorities and civil rights and liberties claimants.

Although the findings are compatible, our analysis differs from these other studies in one important respect. Whereas the above-noted studies

TABLE 2

*Percentage of Liberal Opinions by Federal District Judges in Cases
Involving Indian Rights and Law, 1933–1991: By Era*

Reorganization (1933–1945)		Termination (1946–1961)		Self-Determination (1962–1991)	
% Liberal	N	% Liberal	N	% Liberal	N
52.5	61	55.6	36	48.8	215

were able to compare decisions of one specific presidential appointment co-hort with the decisions of another presidential appointment cohort (such as Nixon v. Johnson appointees or Reagan v. Carter appointees), the problem of small numbers of Indian rights cases among the decisions of some presidential appointment cohorts in our study made such comparisons impossible. For example, there were only three opinions written in Indian rights cases by Wilson appointees, five by Harding appointees, and six by Ford appointees. However, by combining the Harding, Coolidge, Hoover, Eisenhower, Nixon, Ford, Reagan, and Bush appointees into one category and comparing their decisions with the appointees of Wilson, Roosevelt, Truman, Kennedy, Johnson, and Carter, we have a sufficient number of decisions for comparison.

We also feel justified in lumping together appointees of Democratic presidents in one group and appointees of Republican presidents in another group since we are focusing on general ideological compatibility between judges and their appointing presidents rather than specific policy positions. On the other hand, to take one notable example, if we were interested in assessing the success of Nixon's pledge to appoint law and order advocates to the federal bench it would be vital to isolate only his appointees for comparison with other presidential appointment cohorts. To our knowledge, none of the presidents covered by our study has ever made judges' views on Indian rights and law a major campaign issue or criticized the Supreme Court for its decisions on Indian policy in the same fashion that Nixon criticized the Warren Court for some of its criminal justice decisions.

It should be noted, however, that in 1968 President Lyndon Johnson delivered a special message to Congress on Indian affairs and two years later, President Richard Nixon issued his "Message From the President of the United States Transmitting Recommendations for Indian Policy." Both messages were critical of past federal government policies, especially termination, and criticized the judicial system as well as the other branches of government.[1]

SUMMARY AND CONCLUSIONS

In recent years, presidents and students of the courts alike have realized that the federal district courts, like other levels of the federal judiciary, play an im-

TABLE 3

Opinions by Federal District Judges in Cases Involving Indian Rights and Law, 1933–1991: By Party of Appointing President

Judges Appointed by Democratic Presidents		Judges Appointed by Republican Presidents	
% Liberal	N	% Liberal	N
54.9	162	44.6	148

$$Z = 1.81$$
$$p < .04$$

portant role in the policymaking process. Students of the judiciary have also realized over the years that when judges are faced with ambiguous or nonexistent cues from the legal subculture they may have to turn to cues from the democratic or political subculture as guidance for reaching a decision. We have argued that policy concerning Indian rights and law presents a good example of an area where the legal subculture is of little help. Judicial precedents abound for regarding Indian tribes as sovereign nations on the one hand or subject to controls by state and federal governments on the other. Clearly, then, the state of the law concerning the rights of Indian tribes, as well as the rights of individual Indians in the American political system, has never been quite settled. Given this lack of clarity from the legal subculture, federal district judges have little choice but to look to their own values, their political party affiliation, or other factors from the democratic subculture, for help in making decisions.

The one aspect of the democratic subculture most amenable to analysis by our data, the appointing president, did prove helpful in explaining differences between judges deciding Indian rights cases. Future studies, with larger data bases might uncover other variables from the democratic subculture which prove helpful in understanding judicial policymaking concerning Indians. Until that time, however, the present study has taken an important first step.

NOTES

1. Despite the fact that Nixon is closely associated with criticism of termination programs and support for self-determination, his judicial appointees show an overall liberal score of only 39.2 percent (N = 51), a full five percentage points below that of the liberal score for judges named to the bench by all Republican presidents com-

bined. It is possible, however, that Nixon appointees serving in districts with large Indian populations were screened more carefully for their views on Indian rights and law by the president and/or the state' senators. Thus, although it is beyond the scope of this study, a state-by-state analysis of judges' opinions in Indian rights cases might reveal such regional patterns.

Ronald Stidham and Robert A. Carp

CHAPTER 7 Sentencing Disparity

7.1 MARVIN D. FREE, JR.

The Impact of Federal Sentencing Reforms on African Americans

The relationship between African Americans and the criminal justice system in the United States can best be illustrated by their *representativeness* within the criminal justice system. Social researchers use representativeness to determine the extent to which a minority (nonwhite) population is *overrepresented* in the criminal justice system compared with its numerical size in the general population. Criminal justice statistics, for example, show that African American males are more likely to enter the criminal justice process than white and Latino males. The incarceration rate for African American males in their 20s is nearly 10 times the incarceration rate for white males and over 3 times the incarceration rate for Latino males. The incarceraton rate for African American males is 8,630 per 100,000 U.S. residents, compared with 868 for white males and 2,703 for Latino males. While blacks compose about 12 percent of the U.S. population, Latinos are about 9 percent, and whites are about 72 percent.

The overrepresentation of a population in the criminal justice system permits researchers to examine the operation of extralegal factors, such as biased attitudes and perceptions, in the population's processing by the criminal justice system. In the following selection from "The Impact of Federal Sentencing Reforms on African Americans," *Journal of Black Studies* (November 1997), Marvin D. Free, Jr., an associate professor of sociology at the University of Wisconsin–Whitewater, brings forth compelling evidence that the racial disproportionality of African Americans in federal prisons results from the differential treatment that African Americans receive from the imposition of U.S. sentencing and mandatory minimum sentencing guidelines related to the differential treatment of crack cocaine versus powder cocaine offenders.

Key Concept: U.S. sentencing guidelines and incarceration rates for African American males in federal prisons

African Americans are disproportionately found in the inmate population of federal penal institutions. Although composing 12.1% of the total United States population (U.S. Bureau of the Census, 1992, p. 17), African Americans constituted 33.8% of all federal inmates in 1993 (Maguire & Pastore, 1994, p. 628). The overrepresentation of African Americans in federal prisons raises an interesting question: What effect have the U.S. sentencing guidelines, which emerged from the Sentencing Reform Act of 1984, and mandatory minimum statutes had on African Americans?[1] Before reviewing the relevant empirical research, however, a succinct overview of recent sentencing reform is in order.

SENTENCING REFORM IN THE UNITED STATES

Recent changes in federal sentencing are the result of two simultaneous and related forces. First, "mandatory minimums" (i.e., statutory requirements that a person convicted of a specific offense shall receive at least the minimum sentence prescribed by that statute), which, until lately, were used sparingly, have today been expanded to include entire classes of offenses (U.S. Sentencing Commission, 1991b). Second, the Sentencing Reform Act of 1984 has altered the processing of federal defendants. This act created the U.S. Sentencing Commission and charged it with the responsibility of developing sentencing guidelines for federal offenses. The guidelines, submitted to Congress in April 1987, became effective on November 1, 1987 (Heaney, 1991).

To place these changes in proper perspective, it is necessary to discuss separately mandatory minimum sentencing provisions and the sentencing guidelines. Because mandatory minimum statutes preceded the sentencing guidelines, mandatory minimums are examined first.

Mandatory Minimums

Federal mandatory minimum sentences were not widely used until 1956 when the Narcotic Control Act required mandatory minimum sentences for most offenses involving the distribution and importation of drugs. By 1970, however, virtually all mandatory penalties for drug violations were abolished when Congress passed the Comprehensive Drug Abuse Prevention and Control Act (U.S. Sentencing Commission, 1991b).

Federal mandatory minimum penalties returned in 1984.[2] The same comprehensive legislation that led to the development of the sentencing guidelines also established mandatory minimum penalty statutes. Within 10 years, more than 60 federal offenses carried mandatory minimum sentences (Vincent & Hofer, 1994, p. 2). Federal legislation emphasized crimes involving drugs and violence, with drug offenders being particularly affected by the mandatory minimum sentences. Between 1984 and 1990, 91% of the federal defendants sentenced to mandatory minimum sentences were convicted of drug-related crimes (Vincent & Hofer, 1994, p. 3). Moreover, the Bureau of Prisons estimates that 70% of the growth in the federal prison population can be attributed to longer sentences given to drug offenders (Vincent & Hofer, 1994, p. 9).

Changes in the processing of drug offenders occurred as a consequence of new legislation reflecting the "get tough" policy of the so-called War on Drugs. The Anti–Drug Abuse Act of 1986 established mandatory minimum penalties for offenses involving drug trafficking based on the quantity of drugs associated with the offense (U.S. Sentencing Commission, 1991b) and differentiated crack cocaine from powder cocaine for sentencing purposes (McDonald & Carlson, 1993). Given that African Americans were disproportionately likely to be charged with possession of crack cocaine, whereas Whites were substantially more likely to be charged with possession of powder cocaine (see *State v. Russell*, 1991), the establishment of stiffer sentences for crack cocaine possession had serious implications for Blacks.[3] Further contributing to racial disparity in sentencing was the *lack* of emphasis on treatment and prevention. Only 14% of the allocated funding was set aside for the treatment and prevention of drug abuse (Johnson, Golub, & Fagan, 1995, p. 288).

Two years later, Congress passed the Omnibus Anti–Drug Abuse Act, which provided for a mandatory minimum of 5 years in prison for possession of 5 grams of crack cocaine, the approximate weight of two pennies (Wallace, 1993, p. 10).[4] As with the earlier act, this legislation stressed law enforcement over treatment and prevention. The effect of this and similar federal legislation was that, by 1993, drug offenses composed the single most common offense in federal trials (Miller, 1995).[5]

Sentencing Guidelines

Although the sentencing guidelines are a form of mandatory sentencing in that they limit judicial discretion and eliminate parole, they are somewhat more flexible than the statutory minimum penalties in that upward and downward departures from the guideline range are permitted under certain circumstances. Additionally, if the minimum of the guideline range does not exceed 6 months, nonimprisonment sentences (e.g., home confinement) can be imposed (Vincent & Hofer, 1994).

The sentencing commission, in developing the guidelines, was given the mandate that its guidelines and policy statements should be "entirely neutral as to race, sex, national origin, creed, and socioeconomic status of offenders" (cited in Heaney, 1991, p. 203). Under the guidelines, judges are prohibited from taking into consideration many personal attributes of the defendant, including (a) the defendant's mental health or alcohol or drug dependence, (b) the defendant's background, (c) prior victimization of the defendant, and (d) the potential impact of the sentence on the defendant or the defendant's family (Tonry, 1995). Depending on the offense, such information as victim injury, drug quantity, amount of dollar loss, and use of a weapon may be relevant to the sentencing process. Moreover, the guidelines stipulate that a judge *must* consider these facts, if present, even if they are not charged and even if the participants in the case have agreed that such facts will not be included (Nagel & Schulhofer, 1992).

A sentencing table is used for ascertaining the appropriate guidelines sentence. The table has two axes—one for the offense level (there are 43 offense levels), the other for the offender's criminal history (Karle & Sager, 1991). To locate the correct guidelines range, one must simply find the intersection of these two axes. A sentencing range between the maximum and minimum sentences of approximately 25% is typically specified by the guidelines (Nagel & Schulhofer, 1992).

Departures from the guidelines are tolerated under certain conditions. Downward departures (i.e., reductions in sentence length) under section 5K1.1, the substantial-assistance provision, are permitted in cases where a defendant has provided assistance in the prosecution of other offenders and the government has moved for a downward departure based on this assistance. Further, a two-level reduction for "acceptance of responsibility" may be awarded. If granted, this can have the effect of reducing the length of the sentence by about 25% (Nagel & Schulhofer, 1992).

Although parole was abolished for individuals engaging in federal crimes after the effective date of the guidelines, sentence reductions were still possible using good time credits earned in prison. Credit for up to 50 days annually can accrue to inmates exhibiting good behavior while incarcerated (Karle & Sager, 1991).

SENTENCING REFORM AND RACIAL DISCRIMINATION

As indicated earlier, sentencing reform in the United States came packaged as either the U.S. Sentencing Commission's sentencing guidelines, which applied to *all* federal crimes committed on or after November 1, 1987, or legislatively mandated minimum sentences, which applied to only specified *classes* of crimes. Thus, to the extent possible, an evaluation of sentencing reform should analyze separately these two alterations in sentencing policy. Some caveats are necessary, however, prior to assessing the impact of sentencing reform on African Americans.

Whether a researcher finds evidence of differential treatment in sentencing is, in part, a function of the type of model the investigator employs. Commonly used in research are additive models that look at the effect of race on sentencing outcome. Alternatively, an interactive model allows the investigator to examine if race, in conjunction with other relevant variables, might result in differential processing. Terance Miethe and Charles Moore (1986) observed that the additive model conceals and suppresses racial differences in criminal processing, whereas the interactive model uncovers differential criminal processing between and within the two racial groups.

At least two additional problems related to statistical procedures can be identified. First, conventional regression techniques can distort one's findings so that the investigator incorrectly accepts the null hypothesis of no racial differences (Myers, 1985). Additionally, overreliance on statistical significance as a gauge of the importance of race in discrimination in the criminal justice system can result in overemphasizing minor relationships because statistical significance is, in part, a function of sample size.

Moreover, the way in which discrimination is operationalized will affect the conclusions of the investigator. Samuel Myers (1993) suggests that many researchers examining discrimination use measures of discrimination that are too narrow. Arguing for the employment of "residual differences" methodology, he posits that discrimination can exist even when systematic decisions are based on legitimate standards if their application differentially affects Blacks and Whites.

Difficulties further arise when investigators attempt to interpret their findings. Although harsher sanctions against African American defendants are typically construed as discriminatory in nature, do less severe penalties necessarily signify an *absence* of discrimination? As Wilbanks (1987) points out, greater leniency accorded African American offenders can, depending on the circumstances, be symptomatic of either nondiscriminatory or discriminatory behavior. For instance, a judge who devalues the lives of African Americans might sentence less severely the killers of Blacks than the killers of Whites. Because much murder is intraracial (i.e., offenders and victims are of the same race), this prejudicial attitude would typically translate into African American defendants receiving lighter sentences than their White counterparts. Racial discrimination might also be operative in cases where Black murderers are given shorter sentences because they are perceived as being prone to irrationality and impulsiveness and consequently less responsible for their actions.

The finding that Whites receive more severe sentences than African Americans may also mask racial discrimination if "selection bias" occurred during the presentencing stage (Blumstein, 1993). Illustrative of this would be a situation where a prosecutor is more likely to institute legal proceedings against African Americans than Whites. Hence, the White defendants coming to trial would, on average, have been involved in more serious crimes than their Black counterparts. Thus, even if a judge handles all cases the same, Whites would be subjected to more severe sentences due to their greater involvement in serious crime, thereby concealing the earlier discrimination.

Moreover, the use of aggregate data may result in a "canceling-out effect" that disguises the presence of racial bias (Wilbanks, 1987). If some judges are more likely to severely sanction African Americans, whereas others are more likely to severely sanction Whites, the overall impact would be a washing out of these differences if aggregate data were employed in the analysis. To effectively determine if individuals within the criminal justice system discriminate against African Americans, studies of individual decision makers are needed; yet, such research is almost nonexistent.

Further complicating the assessment of sentencing reform on African Americans are four problems associated with sentencing guidelines research. One such problem is a weak research design (Tonry, 1993). Evaluations typically compare sentencing patterns before and after the implementation of the guidelines, instead of the ideal (but legally impossible) situation where defendants are randomly assigned to the two sentencing systems.

Another problem stems from changes occurring in the federal criminal justice system since 1987, the year the guidelines took effect (Tonry, 1993). Since the mid-1980s, federal criminal justice policy has become increasingly politicized. The conservative political agenda of the Reagan and Bush presidencies culminated in the appointment of many conservative judges, such that by 1992, a majority of all federal judges were conservative. Given these changes, it is difficult to know if any detected changes are the result of the guidelines or some other factor(s).

Meaningful comparisons of pre- and postguidelines data are also problematic because preguideline data often do not contain information used in sentencing decisions under the guidelines (Tonry, 1993). Quantity of drugs, presence of an unused firearm, and other uncharged crimes are all relevant factors under the guidelines, yet preguideline cases do not regularly contain such information.

Additionally, the shifting of sentencing power from judges to prosecutors since the arrival of sentencing guidelines makes comparisons of pre- and postguidelines cases more onerous (Tonry, 1993). Under the new standards, such items as the specific offense with which one is charged and the quantity of drugs one is alleged to have sold or possessed take on even greater significance. With judges having limited discretion and prosecutors deciding what data will be included in the case, prosecutorial decisions become even more important under the new system. And with data on prosecutors' decisions being largely unavailable, racial bias can go undetected.

These limitations notwithstanding, a critical examination of the extant research is warranted given the racial disparity in federal incarceration rates. Although no single investigation is likely to lead to definitive statements about the impact of sentencing reform on African Americans, drawing on multiple studies makes it possible to derive some general conclusions.

Mandatory Minimums and Racial Bias

Using data for fiscal year 1990, the U.S. Sentencing Commission (1991b) observed that African Americans were more likely than Whites to be convicted under mandatory minimum provisions, even though they constituted a much smaller percentage of all federal defendants than their White counterparts. African Americans, who constituted 28.2% of all federal defendants, accounted for 38.5% of all federal defendants convicted under mandatory minimum provisions. Comparable figures for Whites were 46.9% and 34.8%, respectively.

The study also found that African Americans were more likely than either Whites or Hispanics to be sentenced at or above the indicated mandatory minimum. More than two thirds (67.7%) of all Black federal defendants convicted under the mandatory minimum provisions received sentences that were at or above the indicated mandatory minimum. In contrast, 54% of the White and 57.1% of the Hispanic federal defendants convicted under the mandatory minimum provisions received these sentences (U.S. Sentencing Commission, 1991b, p. 80).

Why are African Americans disproportionately convicted under the mandatory minimum provisions and why are they more likely than Whites and Hispanics to receive severe sentences under the mandatory minimum provisions? Much of the disparity can be attributed to the emphasis on drug offenses. This is readily seen by analyzing data from pre- and postguidelines periods, in that the guidelines reflected the increasingly severe penalties required under the mandatory minimum provisions. In 1986, the last full year prior to the implementation of the guidelines,[6] only 19% of all African Americans convicted in federal court were convicted of drug trafficking. By the first half of 1990, however, this figure had risen to 46%. The comparable White rates were 26% in 1986 and 35% for the first 6 months of 1990 (McDonald & Carlson, 1993, p. 10). Thus, prior to the implementation of mandatory minimum provisions for drug offenses, Whites were more likely than Blacks to be convicted of drug trafficking, whereas the reverse was true after these provisions went into effect.

The dramatic increase in drug convictions for African Americans mirrors the harsher sanctions attached to crack cocaine offenses. With the law equating 1 gram of crack cocaine with 100 grams of powder cocaine, even relatively modest quantities of crack cocaine can lead to rather severe penalties. A serious user of crack cocaine, for instance, could require 5 or more grams of the substance for the weekend. Yet, this amount presently carries a mandatory minimum prison term of 5 years (Vincent & Hofer, 1994, p. 23). Prior to this, federal judges typically placed first-time offenders on probation (Alschuler, 1991).

Not only are crack cocaine offenses more heavily sanctioned, they also somewhat more likely than offenses involving powder cocaine to be sentenced at or above the indicated mandatory minimum. Data analyzed by the U.S. Sentencing Commission (1991b, p. 72) revealed that 67.5% of the offenses involving crack cocaine, compared to 64.9% of the offenses involving powder cocaine, were sentenced at or above the indicated mandatory minimum.

The significance of the harsher sanctions attached to crack cocaine offenses is disclosed in an investigation by Douglas McDonald and Kenneth Carlson (1993). They conclude that the single most important difference that contributed to the longer sentences for Black federal offenders was their overrepresentation in crack cocaine trafficking. Examining the potential impact of sentencing crack and powder cocaine traffickers the same for identical amounts of the drug,

McDonald and Carlson (1993, p. 21) report that instead of African Americans receiving sentences that averaged 30% longer than that of Whites, the average sentence for African American cocaine traffickers would have been 10% *shorter* than that of their White counterparts. In addition, it would have reduced by half the Black/White difference in average prison sentence for all federal crimes.

Evidence of potential racial bias in the charging of Black defendants in federal court with the selling of crack cocaine has been detected by Richard Berk and Alex Campbell (1993).[7] Analyzing data sets from Los Angeles, they observed that although state charges for the sale of crack cocaine were similar to the sheriff's department arrest patterns, African Americans were overrepresented in federal cases when compared to their patterns of arrest by the sheriff's department. Also indicative of possible racial bias was the finding that over a 4-year period in federal court, *no* Whites were charged with the sale of crack cocaine.

Arguments in favor of maintaining a legal distinction between crack and powder cocaine frequently center on the assumption that crack is more dangerous because it is instantly addicting and is related to violence. Contradictory evidence, nonetheless, is beginning to surface. Data from the Careers in Crack Project tend to refute the notion that crack is any more instantly addicting than powder cocaine. Additionally, crack use did not appear to substantially alter the involvement of men in nondrug offending. Moreover, whereas the *use* of crack was unrelated to violent behavior, the *sale* of crack was strongly related to violence, thereby suggesting that the violence associated with inner-city crack culture is probably the result of systemic violence involved in the sale of illicit drugs, rather than the pharmacological properties of the drug itself (Johnson et al., 1995).

The continuation of a legal distinction between the two types of cocaine can also be challenged on other grounds. First, the mood-altering ingredient is the same in both. Second, powder cocaine, if dissolved in water and injected intravenously, has a similar effect to that of smoking crack cocaine. Finally, powder cocaine can be converted into crack cocaine by using baking soda and water to remove the hydrochloride from the powder cocaine (see *State v. Russell,* 1991).

Sentencing Guidelines and Racial Bias

Because the sentencing guidelines are anchored by mandatory minimum sentences, any discussion of the impact of the guidelines on African Americans is somewhat arbitrary. Though numerous studies have attempted to evaluate the effect of the new system on sentencing, few have specifically analyzed racial differences. Accordingly, care must be exercised when assessing the extant research.

Data analyzed by the U.S. Sentencing Commission (1991a) disclosed little sentencing disparity under the guidelines if offenders with similar criminal records are compared. When the commission limited the analysis to four major offenses (bank robbery, powder cocaine distribution, heroin distribution, and bank embezzlement), race was a factor ($p \leq .05$) in sentencing outcome only for heroin distribution. Whereas 92.3% of all Whites convicted of heroin distribution were given sentences at the bottom of the guideline range, the comparable figures for African Americans and Hispanics were 82.6% and 56.7% respectively (U.S. Sentencing Commission, 1991a, p. 310). Nonetheless, the small samples employed in the analyses of different offenses make any generalizations uncertain (for a critique of the study, see Tonry, 1993). The report further revealed that across all offense categories for the last half of fiscal year 1990, African Americans were *more* likely than either Whites or Hispanics to be sentenced at the bottom of the guidelines range.

An investigation by McDonald and Carlson (1993) found that substantial racial disparity in sentencing occurred after the guidelines were implemented. During the period 1986 to 1988, prior to full implementation of the new system,[8] White, African American, and Hispanic defendants received similar sentences in federal district courts. Average maximum prison sentences ranged from 51 months for Whites and Hispanics to 55 months for African Americans (p.3). However, between January 20, 1989, and June 30, 1990, racial disparities in sentencing appeared. African Americans and Hispanics convicted of federal offenses and subject to the provisions of the Sentencing Reform Act of 1984 were more likely than Whites to be sentenced to prison. Further, African Americans received longer average prison sentences (71 months) than either Whites (50 months) or Hispanics (48 months) (p.4). These disparities, the investigators note, were primarily the result of differences in the characteristics of the offenses and offenders that the law recognizes as legitimate for sentencing purposes. McDonald and Carlson (1993) conclude that the sentencing disparities they observed were generally not a consequence of the guidelines themselves with the exceptions of "the mandatory minimum sentencing laws passed for drugs, especially crack cocaine, and the particular way the Sentencing Commission arrayed guideline ranges above the statutory minima" (p. 21).

A study conducted by the U.S. General Accounting Office (1992) revealed that the effect of race on sentencing was not consistent under the guidelines. There were, nevertheless, some situations in which African Americans were at a disadvantage. Bank robbery and larceny, for instance, are offenses in which African Americans and Whites were less likely than Hispanics to have their counts reduced or dismissed and consequently received longer sentences for these crimes. Additionally, the data disclosed that African Americans were less likely than Whites and Hispanics to have their counts reduced or dismissed before going to trial for heroin distribution. And, though the reasons are unclear, African Americans were less likely than Whites to plead guilty, despite the fact that offenders convicted by plea generally received shorter sentences than those convicted at trial.

It additionally appears that the sentencing guidelines have increased the proportion of minority defendants processed in federal court. Methodological criticisms aside (see Schulhofer, 1992; Wilkins, 1992), Gerald Heaney's (1991, 1992) comparison of offenders sentenced under the guidelines to those sentenced under preguidelines law disclosed that African Americans accounted for 22.3% of the preguidelines defendants but composed 26.2% of the guidelines defendants. Hispanics fared even worse, going from 8.5% of the defendants under the preguidelines to 26.3% of the defendants under the guidelines (Heaney, 1991, p. 204; 1992, p. 781). In other words, Black representation increased by almost 4% and Hispanic representation grew by nearly 18% under the guidelines.

The investigator contends that two factors are primarily responsible for these changes (Heaney, 1991). First, he asserts, many law enforcement officials pursued their cases through federal court instead of state court believing that the defendants would be imprisoned longer under the new federal standards. The second factor attributed to the changes involves the filing of marginal cases. According to Heaney, some cases were filed in federal court that would otherwise not have been filed in either state or federal court because the guidelines now made the prosecution worth the effort.

Heaney (1991) also observed that under the guidelines, the average sentence increased most dramatically for African Americans. Although the average sentence for African Americans under preguidelines law in 1989 was 27.8 months, this figure swelled to 68.5 months for cases sentenced the same year under the guidelines. To be sure, the average sentence for Whites and Hispanics expanded as well under the guidelines, but the increases of 19 months for Whites and 13.7 months for Hispanics (p.207) pale in comparison to that experienced by African Americans.

What accounts for the greater Black/White disparity under the new system? Heaney (1991) suggests that the emphasis on curtailing crack cocaine traffic, accompanied with the stiffer penalties attached to crack cocaine, contributed to the expansion of the average sentence for African Americans. Moreover, being more likely than Whites to possess a criminal record, African Americans are at a greater disadvantage in sentencing.

The negative impact of the guidelines on African Americans is apparently not confined to longer sentences: On average, African Americans are less likely than Whites to be given a probation-only disposition in federal court cases prosecuted under the new system (Heaney, 1991, 1992). The probability of receiving straight probation, of course, varies depending on the offense. For instance, Whites are over 3 times more likely than African Americans under the new standards to receive probation-only for offenses involving drugs and violence. On the other hand, African Americans are slightly more likely than Whites to receive a straight probation disposition for property crimes and have a 6% greater chance than Whites to receive this disposition in immigration cases (Heaney, 1991, p. 207; 1992, p. 780).

Most recently, *The Tennessean* newspaper in Nashville conducted a study of all 1992–1993 federal convictions using data furnished by the U.S. Sentencing Commission. The analysis of approximately 80,000 cases controlled for offense severity and prior record. Overall, the investigation revealed that African Americans received sentences that averaged 10% longer than those of comparable Whites (p. 1A). Although Hispanics received sentences similar to those of Whites, in 74 of the 90 federal court districts, African Americans received longer sentences than Whites charged with the same crimes (p. 6A). The amount of disparity, however, varied from one federal district to another, with the largest disparity occurring in the East Missouri district where, on average, African Americans were given sentences that were 40% longer than those of Whites

(p. 1A). Additionally, the disparity was not due to the imposition of mandatory minimum sentences as the disparity remained even after omitting drug
convictions.

DISCUSSION AND CONCLUSION

That mandatory minimum statutes have had an adverse effect on African
Americans is corroborated by the literature. Research shows that African Americans are more likely than Whites to be convicted under mandatory minimum
provisions and more likely than Whites to be sentenced at or above the indicated mandatory minimum. Much of the disparity is apparently a consequence
of the differential treatment accorded crack cocaine offenders.

The disparity between sentences involving crack and powder cocaine has
recently been investigated by the U.S. Sentencing Commission. In a 220-page
report submitted to Congress in February 1995, the Commission revealed its
plans to modify the sentencing guidelines to remedy this disparity (Locy, 1995).
Whether the sentencing standards will undergo alterations is unclear, though,
as the Justice Department has exhorted Congress to reject the commission's proposal to make the penalty for crack cocaine the same as that for powder cocaine
("Justice Agency Urges," 1995).[9]

Sentencing guidelines research suggests that racial disparities have been
enhanced under the new sentencing structure. Investigators have observed that
African Americans are more likely than Whites, under the guidelines, to be sentenced to prison and to receive longer sentences. Overall, African Americans are
less likely than Whites to receive a disposition of probation only. They are also
less likely than other groups to have their counts reduced or dismissed for certain crimes. Furthermore, since the guidelines have become effective, minority
representation in federal court has grown substantially.

Explanations of the inefficacy of sentencing reform to alleviate racial disparity focus on several areas largely concealed from empirical analysis. According to Heaney (1991, 1992) the guidelines have created the possibility of
additional sentencing disparity by giving greater power to prosecutors. With
judges having carefully circumscribed discretion in sentencing decisions under
the new standards, prosecutors now have greater influence on sentencing outcomes. As prosecutors decide who and what to charge, prosecutorial decisions,
in effect, establish the appropriate sentencing guideline range. Moreover, prosecutors control the flow of information about the offense that will be used by
probation officers in their presentence investigation reports. To the extent that
racial bias might enter into prosecutorial decision making, additional disparity
is possible.

Another source of disparity involves the decision regarding the court of
jurisdiction (Heaney, 1991, 1992). The decision to prosecute in state court or
federal court can have important consequences for defendants, particularly in
drug cases, because mandatory minimum statutes have influenced the sentencing guidelines in cases prosecuted under federal law. The possibility of more
severe sentences in federal court can be readily seen by examining background

data from *United States v. Williams* (1990). In this U.S. District Court case, the defendants, who were African American, had been referred to federal court where their crack cocaine distribution carried a sentencing range of 188 to 235 months under the guidelines. In contrast, conviction of the same offense by the state would result in a sentence of under 2 years.

Sentencing guidelines are additionally unlikely to eliminate racial disparity because sentence length is tied to the defendant's criminal history and Black defendants are more likely than their White counterparts to have prior criminal records ("Developments in the Law," 1988; Heaney, 1992). Any previous racial bias in enforcement of the law is, therefore, amplified under the new standards.

The investigative and preprosecution practices of law enforcement officials can further lead to hidden sentencing disparities. This is especially evident in the enforcement of drug laws. Because sentence severity increases as the quantity of drugs bought or sold increases, some drug enforcement agents have encouraged their suspects to purchase or sell larger quantities to impose stiffer penalties when they are apprehended (see *United States v. Rosen*, 1991). Another practice leading to a longer sentence is to postpone the arrest until the cumulative amount purchased results in a statutory minimum sentence (Heaney, 1991). Given that drug law enforcement typically focuses on areas of the city where the poor and minorities are concentrated (Mauer, 1991), African Americans are adversely affected by these practices.

A final feature of the new sentencing system that precludes its being an effective deterrent to racial disparity in sentencing is its failure to address racial disparity during the first phase of the sentencing process. Sentencing typically involves two decisions. The first, the in/out decision, involves a decision as to whether the defendant should be incarcerated. If the defendant is to be incarcerated, then another decision must be made regarding the length of the prison term. The guidelines attempt to reduce racial disparity during the second phase of sentencing only. And yet, a review of numerous sentencing studies by Free (1996) found that empirical support for racial bias in sentencing is stronger for the in/out decision than for the decision on sentence length.

In conclusion, neither mandatory minimum sentences nor the guidelines have been effective in eliminating racial disparity in sentencing in federal court. Much of the disparity can be attributed to drug laws (especially those pertaining to crack cocaine). Although changing the law to make penalties for identical amounts of powder and crack cocaine the same would reduce the disparity, it would not eradicate it because of the greater likelihood of drug enforcement to concentrate on inner-city neighborhoods. Moreover, selective law enforcement at preprosecutorial stages of the criminal justice system has an adverse effect on African Americans by producing criminal records that culminate in longer sentences under the new standards. Therefore, any meaningful attempt to promote equality between African Americans and Whites must address the dual issues of possible preprosecutorial racial bias as well as possible racial bias during sentencing.

NOTES

1. For a more thorough discussion of the Sentencing Reform Act of 1984 and the sentencing guidelines that ensued, see Wilkins, Newton, and Steer (1991).

2. Legislation of mandatory minimums at the state level began in 1973 in New York. By 1983, only one state had not passed some mandatory minimum legislation (U.S. Sentencing Commission, 1991b).

3. The minimum prison sentences established by this act for crack cocaine are identical to the minimum prison sentences for persons convicted of selling 100 times that amount of powder cocaine (McDonald & Carlson, 1993).

4. For second and third offenses, the amount of crack cocaine required to trigger the 5-year mandatory minimum sentence declines to 3 grams and 1 gram, respectively (Wallace, 1993, p. 17).

5. In 1993, 44% of the federal caseload involved drug offenses. The next most common offense was fraud, representing only 13% of the federal cases (Miller, 1995, p. 184).

6. Mandatory minimum sentences for drug offenses did not go into effect until October 27, 1986 (Vincent & Hofer, 1994, p. 26).

7. This study has been heavily criticized by Joseph Finley (1993). He notes that the investigators failed to examine such data as quantity of narcotics and the offender's previous criminal record, which might account for at least some of the reported disparity. Furthermore, a conclusion of selective prosecution in crack cocaine cases at the federal level is considerably weakened by the small number of federal cases involving this drug ($n = 43$).

8. The constitutionality of the sentencing guidelines was questioned by many federal officials until a 1989 Supreme Court decision (*United States v. Mistretta*, 1989) declared the Sentencing Reform Act of 1984 constitutional. Hence, inconsistent application of the sentencing standards was common for several years after the guidelines went into effect.

9. Although rejecting the view that crack cocaine and powder cocaine cases should be identically sentenced, the Justice Department intimated that some adjustment of the structure might be warranted ("Justice Agency Urges," 1995).

7.2 ED A. MUNOZ, DAVID A. LOPEZ, AND ERIC STEWART

Misdemeanor Sentencing Decision: The Cumulative Disadvantage Effect of "Gringo Justice"

"Gringo justice" has become a widely used concept as it applies to the inequitable treatment of Latino populations at the hands of the American criminal justice system. Over the past two decades, people of Latino ancestry, particularly recent immigrants to the southwestern United States from Mexico and Central America, have experienced an increasing amount of discriminatory handling by the police, the courts, and the correctional system. In fact, the representation of Latino populations at all points in the criminal justice system has nearly doubled since the mid-1980s. While Latinos have populated virtually all areas of the United States for at least two centuries, most sociological and criminological studies of this phenomenon have concentrated efforts on the urban centers of the southwest, i.e., Texas, New Mexico, Arizona, and California. And the criminal focus has been on drug trafficking, gangs, and interpersonal violence. Thus, the stereotypical classification of Latinos has been that of a criminogenic, male-dominated, violent culture of *machismo* and territoriality. But what of the nonurban Latino? A significant and important segment of the Latino population in the United States lives, works, and participates in the social life of rural America. These Latinos are, and historically have been, an indispensable part of the agribusiness landscape and, unlike their urban counterparts, are not subject to the same classifications and stereotypes. Rather, they are generally employed to provide cheap manual labor, under very trying conditions, for relatively little reward. But, similar to the urban Latino, rural Latinos also occupy minority and disadvantaged status, and under the rubric of "gringo justice," one would expect to find that the rural criminal justice system's disparate reaction to Latino criminality is similar to that of the urban population. If so, we can safely conclude that Latinos in general, without regard for geography

271

or historical migratory patterns, are subject to inequitable treatment at the hands of the criminal justice system wherever those hands apply.

The selection that follows is from "Misdemeanor Sentencing Decision: The Cumulative Disadvantage Effect of 'Gringo Justice'," *Hispanic Journal of Behavioral Sciences* (vol. 20, no. 3, 1998). In it, Iowa State University's Ed A. Munoz, Creighton University's David A. Lopez, and Iowa State University's Eric Stewart address the issue of rural Latinos and their experiences with the criminal justice system. These researchers conducted a study of misdemeanor arrest rates in three rural counties of Nebraska that hosted large Latino populations. They found that Latinos were arrested and charged with misdemeanor offenses, except minor traffic violations, at a significantly higher rate than their Anglo counterparts. Specifically, Latinos were significantly more likely to be charged and convicted of minor alcohol and drug offenses. Likewise, they were charged with more counts, received higher fines, and were sentenced to more probation time than Anglos. The latter finding begs the premise that Latinos are a valued labor source that would be compromised if incarcerated for any significant period. Conversely, fines and probation are viable methods to control the Latino population economically and socially without jeopardizing their labor power. Additionally, a higher rate of conviction for misdemeanor offenses ensures that Latinos will have a higher rate of prior offenses, which is considered a valid predictor of future convictions. Thus, while misdemeanor convictions alone do not predicate serious criminal activity, in the case of the Latino, it sets the stage for future disparate encounters with the criminal justice system.

Key Concept: "gringo justice" and misdemeanors

*R*acial/ethnic bias in criminal sentencing has been studied extensively (Austin, 1985; Blumstein, Cohen, Martin, & Tonry, 1983; Farrell & Holmes, 1991; Hagan, 1974; Holmes & Daudistel, 1984; Holmes, Hosch, Daudistel, Perez, & Graves, 1993; Hood & Harlan, 1991; Kleck, 1981; LaFree, 1985a, 1985b; Myers & Talarico, 1986; Petersilia, 1985; Pope, 1979; Spohn, 1995; Tinker, Quiring, & Pimental, 1985; Unnever, 1982; Welch, Gruhl, & Spohn, 1984; Zatz, 1985, 1987). Nevertheless, empirical support for racial/ethnic bias in sentencing decisions has been inconsistent due to inadequate theoretical conceptualizations, methodologies, and data (Hagan, 1974; Kleck, 1981; Zatz, 1987). Theoretically, the overwhelming abundance of research on racial/ethnic bias in criminal sentencing has focused on African Americans, precluding explanations on criminal sentencing differentials found among other racial/ethnic groups. Similarly, the limited research on Latinos and criminal sentencing focuses on Hispanic criminal justice experiences primarily in the southwestern United States, which may be different than that of Puerto Ricans in the Northeast, Cubans in Miami, and other Latino ethnic groups throughout the country.

The tendency to categorize Latinos as White according to pre-1970 U.S. Census Bureau procedures is methodologically troublesome. This undoubtedly calls into question not only criminological research but also most sociological research based on the all-too-common Black/White or White/non-White racial dichotomy (Georges-Abeyie 1989, 1992; U.S. Bureau of the Census, 1990). Also of concern when examining the effects of race/ethnicity on sentencing dispositions are specific regional concentrations of racial/ethnic groups. Research suggests that some of the greatest White/Black disparity in imprisonment is in characteristically rural and predominantly White north-central states (Bridges & Crutchfield, 1988; Christianson, 1980a, 1980b). Research also shows non-Whites receiving harsher sentencing in urban as well as rural counties where their presence is relatively large. Hence, employing counties as units of analysis can shed light on criminal sentencing research because large, official aggregate data sets may have the ultimate effect of masking racial/ethnic discrimination in the legal system due to intrastate variations in minority population density (Hawkins & Hardy, 1989).

With this in mind, our study addresses a void in empirical sentencing research. In particular, we examine misdemeanor sentencing decisions in three non-urban Nebraska counties with relatively large, Latino, and primarily Mexican populations for two reasons. We contend that the significant growth of the Latino population in not only Nebraska (Aponte & Siles, 1994; Rochin & Siles, 1996) but also throughout the midwestern region of the country has evoked historical and socially constructed stereotypical images of and beliefs about Mexican criminality. These socially manipulated images and beliefs provide the justification and rationale for the dual standard of enforcement and punishment of misdemeanor criminal codes that favor Anglos over Latinos. We further contend that bias in the enforcement of misdemeanor criminal codes is part of the cumulative disadvantage (Zatz, 1987) that Latinos are susceptible to throughout all stages of the criminal justice system. More specifically, bias in the enforcement and punishment of misdemeanor criminal codes poses negative implications in the enforcement and punishment of felony criminal codes for Latinos. This double standard of justice is what Mirande (1987) has aptly coined "gringo justice."

GRINGO JUSTICE

Early research on Mexicans and criminal sentencing (i.e., Bogardus, 1943; Kluckholm, 1954; Rudoff, 1971; Sanders, 1958) distorted the image of Mexicans by portraying them as innately criminal and prone to thievery and lawlessness (Mirande, 1987; Trujillo, 1974), an image often associated with non-White racial/ethnic groups (Romero & Stelzner, 1985). Assuredly, early researchers of Mexican criminality failed to take into account preconceived notions of Mexicans prevalent among Anglos in U.S. society since initial interactions between the two groups began on the northern Mexican frontier in the early 19th century. The socially constructed criminal nature of Mexicans became solidified with the 1848 Treaty of Guadalupe Hidalgo, which in theory ended wartime hostilities between the United States and Mexico. More specifically, Mexicans remaining in forfeited Mexican territory, now more commonly known as the southwestern United States, were guaranteed not only land ownership rights but also political and cultural rights. However, an unscrupulous process began in which land, property, and status were legally stripped from Mexicans—legal in the sense that unethical and often violent commercial ventures were sanctioned by all levels of the U.S. civil and criminal justice systems. Responding to injustices, many Mexicans went outside of the American legal system to rectify the situation, which repeatedly produced furious, bloodstained confrontations between Mexicans and Anglos. Subsequently, the image of the cutthroat Mexican bandit preying on law-abiding American citizens and territory was easily created. Stripped of any social, economic, and political clout, Mexicans were next to helpless in combating Anglo law enforcement officials and the cultivation and maintenance of this criminal image by journalists, politicians, and intellectuals. At various points in time, these forces have worked to mobilize bias against Mexicans, rationalizing and justifying the differential treatment they encounter in the American criminal justice system (Mirande, 1987; Trujillo, 1974).

A contemporary example is evident in ongoing local and national media debates on the impact of Latino immigrants in emergent rural meatpacking communities throughout the Midwest. Numerous quotes by politicians, police officials, community leaders, and intellectuals alike mention the resultant crime problem apparently associated with Latino immigrant populations. Despite solid evidence to support this claim, the mere presence of Latino immigrants instills fear among longtime residents (Bergstrom, 1995; Carney, 1995; Cooper, 1997; Hedges, Hawkins, & Loeb, 1996; Hendee, 1996; Norman, 1996; Yearwood, 1995). Becker (1963) long ago defined an outsider as one who "may be seen as a special kind of person, one who cannot be trusted to live by the rules agreed on by the group" (p. 1). Thus, cultural differences between Anglos and Mexicans and the history of labeling Mexicans as criminally prone makes this status of an outsider pronounced for Mexicans in the Midwest and suggests that they will be dealt with more harshly for the commission of criminal acts.

Clearly, an increase in the Mexican population increases their visibility, which in turn can increase ethnic conflict by representing an actual and/or a subjective economic threat (Bobo, 1983). For example, even though Mexicans in the Midwest do not represent a real economic threat because they primarily work in lower status, lower paying jobs than do Whites (Rochin & Siles, 1996), they may be perceived as an economic threat due solely to their increased presence. Moreover, Whites have an interest in maintaining the status quo because it functions "as a powerful basis for the development of self-identity and perceptions of individual interests" (Bobo, 1983, p. 1200). Hence, keeping Mexicans socially, economically, and politically subordinated reduces any threat to conceptions of ethnic superiority that may be held by some Whites. One way to keep Mexicans subordinated and to propagate White ethnic superiority is through the system known as gringo justice (Mirande, 1987).

Support for gringo justice arises in sentencing research that focuses primarily on Mexican Americans, which in general suggests that they have higher arrest and incarceration rates than do non-Latino Whites. In fact, the Sentencing Project's (a criminal justice research and advocacy group) recent report based on a review of Department of Justice data found the percentage of Latinos sentenced to prison almost doubling from 7.7% to 14.3% during the years 1980 to 1993 (Nixon, 1996). This trend corresponds to research showing Latino imprisonment doubling in Nebraska from 1987 to 1991 (Munoz, in press). It is also consistent with dissimilar sentencing patterns that favor Whites over Latinos in Florida (Unnever, 1982), Arizona (LaFree, 1985a), Texas, Michigan, California (Holmes & Daudistel, 1984; Holmes et al., 1993; LaFree, 1985a; Petersilia, 1985; Zatz, 1985), and Washington (Hood & Harlan, 1991).

Moreover, sources of disparate sentencing practices for similar types of crimes between Anglos and Latinos arise from juries (Holmes & Daudistel, 1984) as well as judges (Holmes et al., 1993; Petersilia, 1985). Differential criminal processing is another avenue that leads to sentencing differential; Latinos often receive less favorable pretrial release outcomes than do their White counterparts (Holmes & Daudistel, 1984; Petersilia, 1985). Evidence also depicts that plea bargaining may not be as advantageous to Latinos as it is for Whites (Petersilia, 1985; Zatz, 1985). These sources for differentials in felony sentencing research point to the importance of previous criminal justice encounters for convicted felons. Nevertheless, there are findings of no racial/ethnic bias in sentencing between Whites and Latinos (LaFree, 1985b; Tinker et al., 1985).

SETTING FOR THE STUDY

Evidence of gringo justice outside of the American Southwest where Latinos historically have resided can serve as a measure of society's reaction to Mexican criminality in particular and the diffusion of stereotypical beliefs of Mexicans in general. Presently, Nebraska provides an excellent social laboratory to explore these claims. Overall, the U.S. Latino population increased by 53% between 1980 and 1990. Latinos in the Midwest increased 35.2% between 1980 and 1990 (Aponte & Siles, 1994). Although Latinos in the Midwest increased by a lower proportion than Latinos nationwide, their proportional increase in the Midwest is in stark comparison to minimal gains and losses in the non-Latino White population for the region. To illustrate, Nebraska experienced a paltry 0.5% increase in its total population from 1980 to 1990. More telling, however, is that the 1990 Nebraska non-Latino White population decreased by 1.1%, whereas the 1990 Nebraska Latino population increased by 30.8%. Furthermore, four fifths of the 1990 Nebraska Latino population is of Mexican origin, and this population increased by 32.2% between 1980 and 1990 (Rochin & Siles, 1996). Nevertheless, non-Latino Whites still comprise 92.5% of the 1990 Nebraska population of 1,578,385. For comparative purposes, non-Latino Blacks comprise 3.6% of the 1990 Nebraska population; whereas Latinos comprise 2.3%, non-Latino Native Americans comprise 0.7%, non-Latino Asians comprise 0.8%, and non-Latino other comprise 0.1% (U.S. Bureau of the Census, 1992).

To be sure, the Latino presence in Nebraska is both long and overlooked. For instance, Spanish and Mexican exploration into the Nebraska geographic region dates back to the early 18th century when a portion of it was then part of Spanish colonial holdings. But not until the late 19th century did Mexican and Mexican American migration to Nebraska become solidified. Railroad and agricultural economic opportunities provided the major attraction. Notably, the development and entrenchment of the sugar beet industry in the far western rural panhandle of Nebraska led to Scottsbluff County becoming the major enclave of Mexican settlement early in the 20th century (Rochin & Siles, 1996; Valdes, 1991). Continued immigration—but more so natural growth from a settling-out process—has made the 1990 Scottsbluff County Latino population the largest racial/ethnic minority proportional concentration throughout the state at 14.5% (Nelson, 1997; U.S. Bureau of the Census 1992).

Latinos are highly visible in rural Scottsbluff County, which only accounts for 2.3% or 36,025 of the state's total population. Native Americans are the next largest minority group in the county and comprise 1.6% of the county total. Similar to the state trend, the Scottsbluff County non-Latino White population decreased by 9.2% between 1980 and 1990, whereas the Latino population increased by 11.1%. This increase, although relatively smaller than the overall state trend, coupled with the relatively large size of the Latino population in the county is a good indication of the stability of this approximately century-old Latino enclave (U.S. Bureau of the Census, 1992).

In contrast, the urban and eastern county of Douglas bordered by the Missouri River has the largest absolute number of Latinos in Nebraska. Yet, Latinos in Douglas County proportionately account for only 2.7% of the county's 1990 total population of 416,444. Moreover, Latinos merely rival the dominant Black racial/ethnic minority group, which consists of 10.8% of the 1990 population in this urban area (U.S. Bureau of the Census, 1992). Summarily, this racial/ethnic minority population pattern of settlement is characteristic of the state. Blacks predominate in metropolitan counties, with Latinos and Native Americans predominant in rural counties and, oftentimes, with the deciding factors being proximity to Native American reservations and/or developing agribusiness in the rural hinterlands.

Unquestionably, railroad and meatpacking employment provided the early attraction for Latinos to the eastern part of the state. More recently, the reemergence of the meatpacking industry employing nonunion immigrant labor in northeastern rural counties accounts for the increase in Latino populations for Dakota and Madison Counties (Aponte & Siles, 1994; Freed, 1996; Gonzalez, 1994; U.S. Bureau of the Census, 1992). For example, in 1990, IBP, Inc. recruited 770 immigrant and nonimmigrant Mexican workers from Texas to work in plants located in Dakota and Madison counties. Although high employee turnover is characteristic of the new meatpacking industry, it has not precluded the settling-out process for many recruited laborers and their families (Gonzalez, 1994). Indeed, births of Mexican ancestry in 1990 in Dakota County (25.7%) and Madison County (15.6%) are higher than the 1989 national proportion of 8.1% and are a reliable indicator of a settling-out process (Nebraska Department of Health, 1996). These relatively high proportions of Mexican births are major contributors to the 111.2% and 306.4% increases in Dakota and Madison Counties' 1990 Latino populations, respectively. The increased Latino presence in both counties has allowed for an overall net increase in population for both of these nonmetropolitan counties, a trend directly opposite for 83 of the 93 counties in Nebraska (U.S. Bureau of the Census, 1992).

In any case, the increased visibility of Latino workers in the rural hinterlands has strained interethnic relations in all facets of community life (Nelson, 1997). A logical indicator of strained interethnic relations in rural communities described above is disparate treatment in the criminal justice system, particularly because European and non-European immigrants alike historically have been linked with criminal behavior (Mirande, 1987). For the most part, respected legitimate public and private officials are highly adept and successful in mobilizing internalized beliefs of the inherent criminal nature of immigrants. It then follows that action must be taken to secure the well-being of native citizens. Hence, we hypothesize that the proportion of Latinos charged with more serious misdemeanor offenses other than traffic violations will be significantly higher than Whites in Dakota, Madison, and Scottsbluff Counties. We also hypothesize that Latinos on average will be charged with more offenses and receive harsher sentences.

DATA AND METHODS

Corresponding with the tremendous growth of the Latino population in Nebraska was an increase in formal and informal complaints of law enforcement mistreatment of Latinos filed with the Nebraska Mexican American Commission. This state agency acts as the primary liaison between the Latino/Mexican American community and state government. Because of the growing dissatisfaction of Latinos with the state's criminal justice system, the commission employed a private consulting entity to examine the situation further. In the summer of 1993, the lead author, as a graduate student, was employed by consultants to help design and implement the commission's sentencing research project. The original sentencing project called for the collection and analysis of court data from seven Nebraska counties. These included the two urban counties of Douglas and Lancaster as well as the rural county of Scottsbluff, where a definite Latino enclave was well established. Also selected for analysis were Dakota, Madison, Hall, and Dawson counties. These counties were selected because of their rapidly growing Latino populations induced by the recruitment of Latino immigrant labor by meatpacking corporations.

However, administrative oversight on the sheer volume of cases disposed caused an early termination of data collection because of limited funding. Furthermore, the untimely oversight forced project administrators to employ hastily additional data collectors with limited training, which led to a significant amount of missing data, particularly dealing with the race/ethnicity of offenders (approximately 3,000 cases). Nevertheless, information was collected from more than 12,000 misdemeanor and felony criminal cases filed in Dakota, Madison, and Scottsbluff County courts in the calendar year of 1992. Because felony cases were proportionally minimal in all three counties, and because they are forwarded to and later adjudicated in separate district courts, they were excluded from analyses. More important and as we will demonstrate, focusing on misdemeanor cases fills a void in criminal sentencing research: the cumulative disadvantage effect (Zatz, 1987) that racially biased enforcement and punishment of misdemeanor laws has in other aspects of criminal adjudication.

For the sample, Dakota County registered 25.6% of the total cases observed, whereas Madison County registered 32.9%, and Scottsbluff County registered 41.4%. The gender and date of birth of individual defendants were readily available from court files and were recorded. The overwhelming majority of males (72.1%) in the sample and in all three counties accounts for the lack of noteworthy gender effects in the overall sample analyses.... The mean age of male misdemeanants is between 28 and 31 years for the sample and in all three counties. Of the 6,381 male cases in which racial/ethnic identification was recorded, 63.8% were identified as White, 1.3% as Black, 2.6% as Native American, 1.1% as Asian, and 4.6% as other. Latino ethnic ancestry was not indicated in court records, so Spanish surname was employed to identify Latinos, and they accounted for 26.7% of the male sample. For brevity and focus, discussion on the remainder of the analysis will be between White and Latino male misdemeanants.

Population disproportionality is evident when comparing the 1990 combined non-Latino White male population of 89.0% in Dakota, Madison, and Scottsbluff counties to the sample's respective White male population of 63.8%. Corresponding figures further demonstrate population disproportionality, as the combined 1990 Latino male population for the counties is 8.3% percent compared to the sample's 26.7% Latino population. The degree of county Latino disproportionality is also evident as Dakota Latinos account for 6.8% of the total Dakota County population but account for 22.8% of Dakota County Latino male misdemeanants. Latinos make up 2.2% of the total 1990 Madison County male population and 16.5% of Madison County Latino male misdemeanants. Finally, 14.7% of the 1990 male population in Scottsbluff County identifies as Latino, whereas 37.8% of Scottsbluff County male misdemeanants were identified as Latino (U.S. Bureau of the Census, 1992).

Chi-square tables are employed to determine if Latinos are charged with more serious misdemeanor crimes than their White counterparts and, if so, in which counties and for what specific age groups (10–17, 18–24, 25–39, or 40 and older). Although some individuals were charged with more than one specific offense, our focus of analysis is on the first offense listed in a specific case because it is usually the offense of record. Small-cell totals were collapsed to reduce the number of offense type categories for analysis. Personal, domestic, and sexual assaults are combined into one category. We combine resisting arrest and disturbing the peace together but examine them separately from assaults, because they are not always violent in nature. Drug and alcohol offenses are combined to form another category. Trespassing offenses are combined with property offenses. The multitudes of traffic offenses are examined separately. The category of other consists of all other offenses not closely related to the above, such as leash laws, administrative, and so forth. The 66.2% of traffic offenses are the overwhelming majority of misdemeanor charges brought forth in the total male sample and for all three counties ranging from a high of 74.6% in Madison County to 66.2% in Scottsbluff County and a low of 55.6% in Dakota County. Percentages of other offense types vary widely by county.

Analysis of variance is then used to determine if Latinos, on average, receive more total charges than do their White counterparts when controlling for county, type of offense, and age. A higher mean number of charges carries probable negative implications on the severity of a sentence. Consequently, we analyze the effects that Latino ethnicity has on the mean dollar amount of a fine, the mean number of days probation, and the mean number of days jail when controlling for county, offense type, age, and total number of offenses.

FINDINGS AND DISCUSSION

Support for gringo justice emerges from data . . . in which the combined proportions of Latinos charged with misdemeanor offenses other than traffic violations are significantly higher than the combined proportions of their White counterparts for all four age groups observed in the total sample. The combined proportions of White males being charged with something other than traffic violations ranges from a low of 6.5% among the oldest age group (40 and older) to a high of 13.5% among the 18 to 24 age group. The combined proportions of Latino males charged with something other than traffic violations is also lowest among the elderly but practically five times the amount at 35.2%. Similarly, the 49.3% of Latino males age 18 to 24 charged with something other than traffic violations is 3 1/2 times higher than that of Whites.

Interestingly, however, disaggregating the data by county shows that differentials, in most cases, are insignificant in both Dakota County and Madison County, which are experiencing an influx and settlement of Latino (im)migration. Particularly striking are differentials in Scottsbluff County, where the Latino population has been established for approximately four generations. From the data, approximately 98% of Scottsbluff County White male misdemeanants of all ages are charged with traffic violations rather than with any other offense type. On the other hand, the proportions of Latino traffic misdemeanors range from a low of 41.7% among 18- to 24-year-olds to 60.4% among those 40 years of age and older. With the exception of the 10 to 17 age group, the next most common misdemeanor offense for Latinos is alcohol or drug related. These differences are consistently significant ($p \leq .001$) for each age category, and furthermore, Cramer's V statistics indicate that Scottsbluff County associations are stronger than differences found in the sample's two youngest age groups.

In addition to having higher combined proportions of individuals charged with misdemeanor crimes other than traffic violations, Latinos are also, on average, recipients of more than one charge even when controlling for county, offense type, and age. More specifically, increasing age significantly decreases the mean number of charges that one receives. Significant interaction effects are present in addition to independent significant county, racial/ethnic, and offense type effects. However, beta scores suggest that the county of offense is the strongest standardized factor effect in the model. Adjusted mean scores and deviations indicate that Dakota County misdemeanants receive higher average number of charges than Madison County and Scottsbluff County misdemeanants. Nevertheless, Latinos in all three counties receive higher average number of charges than do their White counterparts, and this is reflected in adjusted means and deviations for the sample. Offense type also has a significant effect, particularly when one is charged with the offenses of resisting arrest or disturbing the peace.

In terms of punishment, each additional offense significantly costs misdemeanants approximately $57 in fines.... Increasing age has a significant effect on the mean amount of a fine but only increases a fine by less than $1. Significant effects on the mean dollar amount of a fine are evident for county and offense type. Latino ethnicity has no significant independent effect on the mean dollar amount of a fine. Standardized betas indicate that offense type has the largest significant impact on the mean amount of the fine, followed closely by county of offense. Significant interaction effects are present for all combinations of factors. Adjusted means indicate that Dakota County misdemeanants receive the highest mean fine. And although Latino ethnicity had no significant independent effect, when combined with other factors, Latinos have higher mean fines than do their White counterparts in the overall sample. Last, alcohol and drug misdemeanants receive the highest mean fine in the overall sample, which does not bode well for Latinos who have higher proportions of individuals charged with these types of offenses....

This same general pattern is evident when examining the mean number of days probation received for the conviction of a misdemeanor offense.... Increasing age significantly increases the mean number of days probation by less than a day, whereas each additional charge significantly increases probation by approximately 28 days. Latino ethnicity once again has no independent significant effect, whereas county and offense type do have independent significant effects on the mean number of days probation. Unlike previous findings, standardized beta scores indicate that county effects are stronger than offense type effects, with mean days of probation longest for individuals sentenced in Dakota County. Significant interaction effects among all factors once again produces longer mean days of probation for Latinos over Whites in the sample. And corresponding to previous results, the longest sentences of probation in the sample are for those individuals charged with alcohol- or drug-related offenses.

Curiously, support for gringo justice disappears in sentencing dispositions that involve jail time.... Unlike earlier dispositions, increasing age has a negative insignificant effect on average number of days of jail received for a misdemeanor conviction. Not surprising is the significant extra 19 days of jail time for each additional charge. Although jail sentences are significantly longer for Madison County misdemeanants, what is most surprising is the significant positive effect that White racial identity has on the average number of days jail time received. Whites in the sample receive an adjusted 7.49 mean days of jail time in comparison to the 1.78 mean days of jail time for Latinos in the sample. Much like before, however, and displayed in standardized beta scores is the strong significant effect that offense type has in determining the length of jail time.

CONCLUSION

The extent to which Mexican criminal stereotypes affect enforcement and punishment decisions is unclear from this study. Findings are open to two interpretations due to the limitations of cross-sectional data. On one hand, it could be argued that Latinos commit a wider variety of criminal misdemeanors with more frequency, unlike Whites, who commit a simple traffic violation from time to time. On the other hand and as argued here, Latinos are the victims of biased enforcement and punishment due to key public officials' mobilization of criminal stereotypes associated with immigrants in general and Latinos in particular. To be sure, more social-psychological study is needed to explore the nature and scope of Latino stereotypes and how they affect decision-making processes for all public and private officials.

More important are the criminological research designs that use unconventional data sources and methodologies to examine racial/ethnic bias in the criminal justice system rather than relying solely on those official crime statistics. Official crime statistics allow for after-the-fact examination of a social phenomenon that may be better detected through observation of social action and/or communication. Technological advancements are beginning to provide researchers with data sensitive to an investigation of this sort. Analysis of tape-recorded dispatch logs and the resultant officer action taken can go a long way in determining differential enforcement practices. Research designs with the objective of gaining insight into legal processes from not only legal authorities but also convicted and acquitted misdemeanants and/or felons can better aid our understanding of racial/ethnic bias in sentencing decisions.

At present, analysis of misdemeanor sentencing data demonstrates the existence of gringo justice in the rural heartland of the United States. Evidence of disparate enforcement and punishment of misdemeanor crimes in a combined sample of three rural Nebraska counties that have relatively large, growing Mexican populations casts a gloomy outlook in need of remedy. Overall, Latinos not only were charged with a wider variety of misdemeanor offenses other than simple traffic violations but also were recipients of a higher mean number of charges than were their White counterparts in the sample. This translated into Latinos receiving higher mean fines and mean number of days of probation in misdemeanor sentencing dispositions but not in higher mean number of days of jail time delivered.

Of particular interest in disaggregated county findings is the highly consistent differential pattern of enforcement favoring Whites over Latinos in Scottsbluff County, a county with a historical Hispanic presence dating back to the turn of the 20th century. The data depict a scenario in which apparently few Latinos drive motor vehicles and, therefore, are not susceptible to traffic violations in proportion to their driving age population. In contrast, the near absence of White individuals cited for alcohol and assault-related charges depicts a complacent community abstinent of alcohol and its resultant problems. It is probable that curtailed differentials in Dakota and Madison Counties may worsen if these illusory circumstances take root in developing social relations between longtime White residents and Latino immigrant workers.

Even more problematic is how disparate treatment for minor criminal violations affects future criminal behavior. As it is often said, "What's good for the goose is good for the gander." In other words, if Latinos, particularly adolescents, observe their White peers escaping sanctions for deviant behavior, will they be more willing to risk such activities? Moreover, Latino deviant behavior that is not discounted as an adolescent prank and is punished to the full extent of the law carries negative overtones in future criminal justice encounters. For instance, it is highly likely that racially and ethnically biased enforcement and punishment of misdemeanor criminal codes carry over into the enforcement and punishment of felony criminal codes. This no doubt produces a higher rate of incarceration for longer periods of time for non-White individuals convicted of felony crimes, as published scholarly research claims (Hagan, 1974; Kleck, 1981; Zatz, 1987). Simply stated, gringo justice in misdemeanor courts is but one part of the cumulative disadvantage that individuals of Mexican ancestry face in the overall criminal justice system (Zatz, 1987).

CHAPTER 8 Correctional Inequality

8.1 AMY E. LADERBERG

The "Dirty Little Secret"

The female imprisonment rate is at its highest percentage in U.S. history. The number of female prisoners in the United States has increased by over 400 percent since the early 1980s. With an increase in the female prison population has been an increase in the risk of sexual assault of female inmates by male corrections officers. The pervasiveness of sexual assaults of female inmates results from the American criminal justice system's leaving female prisoners virtually unprotected from abuse by male prison guards, staff, and wardens. Although the abuse of women prisoners occurs nationwide, the extent and frequency of the abuse of female prisoners cannot be accurately determined, because prisons fail to keep records of assaults. Female inmates are subjected to rape, sexual assault, and unlawful invasions of privacy, including prurient viewing during showering and dressing. The sexual abuse of female inmates includes such atrocities as "forced abortions, women prisoners left stripped and bound for weeks, and inmates taken off the grounds to work as prostitutes." The Women's Rights Project recently issued a comprehensive report detailing the sexual abuse of women in prisons in California; Washington, D.C.; Michigan; Georgia; and New York. The report found that male correctional employees have vaginally, anally, and orally raped female prisoners. Another study described prison life for female inmates as tantamount to "a climate of sexual terror that women are subjected to on a daily basis."

The following selection is from "The 'Dirty Little Secret': Why Class Actions Have Emerged as the Only Viable Option for Women Inmates Attempting to Satisfy the Subjective Prong of the Eighth Amendment in Suits for Custodial Sexual Abuse," *William and Mary Law Review* (vol. 40, no. 1, 1998). In it, Amy E. Laderberg, associate editor of the *William and Mary Journal of Women and the Law,* examines the reason why the sexual assault of female inmates who are guarded by men remains pervasive in the U.S. penal system. To correct for the inadequacies of prison officials to sufficiently control the violent behavior of prison employees against female inmates and to take complaints of female prisoners seriously, Laderberg suggests that the class action lawsuit is a viable option for women inmates attempting to satisfy the subjective prong of the Eighth Amendment in suits for custodial sexual abuse because class action lawsuits attract significant publicity and allow courts to characterize the abuses as occurring in a "sexualized environment" within the prison system.

Key Concept: female inmates and sexual abuse

Women [prisoners] complain of male corrections officers refusing to leave their cells so they can dress, caressing their breasts and other parts of their bodies, pulling down their pants in front of them, touching themselves, making lewd and offensive comments, following them around the facility, assigning them to their offices as clerks, watching them use the bathroom and shower, coming on the unit without warning of their presence, and frequently promising them favors and presents for sexual activity.

Despite a growing concern for the vast number of frivolous claims filed on behalf of prisoners, sexual abuse of women inmates by their male guards is a pervasive and legitimate problem in both state and federal prisons of the United States. The media and the legal profession have devoted increased attention to sexual abuse in prisons for several reasons, including the rapid increase in the number of incarcerated women guarded by men, the unique perceptions of women inmates who often have a prior history of sexual abuse, the disturbing lack of prosecutions for custodial sexual misconduct, and the ultimate failure of the lawsuits actually filed by women prisoners.

The power dynamics inherent in the inmate/guard relationship and in the nature of confinement itself contribute to the problem of seeking a remedy for sexual abuse. "An inmate's word alone will not suffice as grounds for disciplining a staff member. . . . " Sexually abused female inmates are often reluctant to come forward to report incidents of abuse because they fear staff reprisal, worry that others will accuse them of lying, or want to avoid being labeled a snitch. As a result, "prison officials, critics and inmates conclude that more sexual misconduct goes on than is reported." The problems in calculating and remedying the frequency of sexual abuse in prisons mirror those in other areas of the law. As with sexual abuse of children and sexual harassment in both the workplace and the military, the physical environment and established power structures foster opportunities for sexual abuse in prisons:

> [M]ost sexual harassment takes place without witnesses between people of unequal power in a highly structured, hierarchical organization. If there are no witnesses, the tendency of most people in that organization, and in our society, will be

to believe the more highly-ranked and credentialed person in any contest between the two as to what happened.

The prison setting greatly magnifies this power disparity, and women prisoners have no ability to escape from the abuse.

Prisoners face yet another problem in attempting to remedy sexual abuse: custodial sexual abuse is a virtually invisible phenomenon. Witnesses rarely observe the incidents, victims are hesitant to make complaints, and the departments of corrections often fail to record complaints or investigate them in an organized and centralized manner. At the state and national level, the prevalent misconduct by male guards is not apparent outside of the prison system itself, and therefore is difficult to eradicate. While suits under the Eighth Amendment against guards in their individual capacities for monetary damages have occasionally prevailed, these types of lawsuits have neither acknowledged the problem of sexual abuse in America's prisons nor offered solutions. Eighth Amendment suits for injunctive relief against members of the prison administration in their official capacities or against the penal institution itself would attract desperately needed visibility to custodial sexual abuse, but these suits rarely have been successful. Instead, class action suits under the Eighth Amendment have emerged as the best option for prisoners wishing to obtain injunctive relief from custodial abuse in American prisons.

Class action suits have many unique features that contribute to the plaintiffs' success in achieving relief from sexual abuse while incarcerated. For example, media coverage of such suits attracts significant publicity. Wide-spread national exposure in turn creates pressure for internal investigations within the prison system and fosters external public awareness of the problem. Under the weight of this intense scrutiny, the departments of correction have allowed the involved officers to resign or "retire" in order to end criticism of the prison and avoid public embarrassment. In fact, female inmates may consider the removal or relocation of the "offending" officers as an additional aspect of "relief." Defining the class bringing the suit as "all women prisoners who are [currently] incarcerated in the... correctional system... and all women prisoners who will hereafter be incarcerated in the... correctional system" enhances the inmate's credibility and reduces the chance that the officer's version will prevail over the inmate's version of events. The vast number of inmates coming forward with comparable stories of sexual abuse makes it more difficult for the officers to claim that the plaintiffs fabricated the allegations or consented to the sexual encounters.

Another beneficial aspect of a class action suit is that the combined consideration of each female prisoner's complaint allows courts to characterize the abuses as occurring in a "sexualized environment" within the prison system instead of simply isolated incidents happening on an individualized basis. "[A] focus on 'the combined acts or omissions' of the state's agents, rather than the search for a particular bad actor whose individual culpability could support liability" also could lead to a greater perception of harm by the courts and the public. This Note suggests that the characterization of the harm as occurring in a "sexualized environment" makes it easier for a class of female prisoner plaintiffs to satisfy the subjective prong of the Eighth Amendment.

The nature of the Eighth Amendment standard is the primary reason for the seemingly insurmountable challenge facing the inmate-plaintiff. The subjective prong of the Supreme Court's Eighth Amendment analysis requires an inquiry into the state of mind of the defendant-prison official, and the requisite state of mind differs depending on the type of challenged act. Plaintiffs' claims of patterns of custodial sexual abuse constitute "conditions of confinement" under the Court's Eighth Amendment analysis. In "conditions of confinement" cases, acting with "deliberate indifference" satisfies the definition of "wanton" and therefore embodies "cruel and unusual punishment in violation of the Eighth Amendment." In a class action, once the plaintiffs establish a pattern of abuse, courts then may determine that the defendants acted with "deliberate indifference" to the women prisoners' endurance of the condition of sexual abuse. As this Note suggests, however, inmate-plaintiffs proceeding individually actually have little opportunity to gain injunctive relief under the Eighth Amendment.

This Note explores the implications of using the subjective prong of the Eighth Amendment to bring claims to remedy custodial sexual abuse. The first section analyzes the Eighth Amendment framework established in *Farmer v. Brennan,* the Supreme Court decision resolving the dispute over the test for "deliberate indifference," and notes the harshness of this standard. The second section describes the pervasiveness of sexual abuse in U.S. prisons and offers first-hand perspectives on its nature and effects. The third section discusses several suits by individual women inmates and offers explanations for the failure of these actions. The fourth section explores *Women Prisoners v. District of Columbia* and suggests why this particular class action suit was successful. The fifth section questions whether the existing Eighth Amendment standard poses an insurmountable obstacle to all inmate-plaintiffs except those involved in class action suits alleging custodial sexual abuse, and also offers possible solutions. This Note concludes that the level of proof required to satisfy the subjective "deliberate indifference" prong of the Eighth Amendment is too demanding for individual prisoners to meet when they are suing for injunctive relief against prison administrators in their official capacities or against the prison itself. This analysis ultimately determines that the present standard has deterred women from coming forward with allegations of abuse, and has created enormous obstacles for those who have pursued their claims on an individual basis.

FARMER V. BRENNAN AND THE EIGHTH AMENDMENT FRAMEWORK

The Eighth Amendment standard established by the Supreme Court in *Farmer v. Brennan* has left inmate-plaintiffs in general, and individual inmate-plaintiffs in particular, with little hope of obtaining relief from custodial sexual abuse. *Farmer* provided minimal support for future inmate-plaintiff cases because it involved the claim of a single inmate and was ambiguous in its exploration of the plaintiff's demand for injunctive relief. *Farmer* did, however, establish the current definition of "deliberate indifference" as applied to "conditions of confinement" cases. While the Supreme Court has upheld the view that "[b]eing violently assaulted in prison is simply not 'part of the penalty that criminal offenders pay for their offenses against society,'" *Farmer* and the preceding line of cases actually demonstrated a shift away from concern for prisoners' safety.

The Supreme Court's decision in *Estelle v. Gamble* marked the first major departure from the "hands-off" approach to prison administration abuse issues arising from practices of incarceration. The Court concluded that "deliberate indifference to serious medical needs of prisoners constitutes the 'unnecessary and wanton infliction of pain.'" Mere negligence was not enough to make a valid claim under the Eighth Amendment, as "only such [deliberate] indifference that can offend 'evolving standards of decency'" was sufficient.

In *Rhodes v. Chapman* the Court solidified the judicial role in prison oversight by unequivocally declaring that "'[c]onfinement in a prison... is a form of punishment subject to [judicial] scrutiny under the Eighth Amendment standards.'" The Court also recognized that the consideration of prison conditions alone or in combination "may deprive inmates of the minimal civilized measure of life's necessities." This realization was a necessary step in favor of prisoners' rights, as the *Rhodes* Court observed that despite the "magnitude" and "complexity" of the problems of prison administration, "[c]ourts certainly have a responsibility to scrutinize claims of cruel and unusual confinement."

In *Wilson v. Seiter*, the Court elaborated on several doctrines established in earlier cases, and then departed from precedent by establishing an intent requirement. The Court refused to accept the inmate's suggestion that it "should draw a distinction between 'short-term' or 'one-time' conditions (in which a state-of-mind requirement would apply) and 'continuing' or 'systemic' conditions (where official state of mind would be irrelevant)." The Supreme Court instead held that all "conditions of confinement" cases require an inquiry into the state of mind of the official in order to determine whether the official acted with "deliberate indifference." In its refusal to recognize the difference between "one-time" and "systemic" conditions, the Court opined that there was no basis for drawing such a distinction and that such a distinction "defie[d] rational implementation."

The Court's elaboration on the consideration of conditions "in combination" was the only aspect of *Wilson* of any consolation to the inmate-plaintiff.

> Some conditions of confinement may establish an Eighth Amendment violation "in combination" when each would not do so alone, but only when they have a mutually enforcing effect that produces the deprivation of a single, identifiable human need.... Nothing so amorphous as "overall conditions" can rise to the level of cruel and unusual punishment when no specific deprivation of a single human need exists.

The opportunity to combine individual complaints is of great value to inmate-plaintiffs, especially in the context of class action suits.

Justice White's concurrence in *Wilson* classified the majority opinion as overreaching in its application of the "deliberate indifference" analysis to cases with systemic violations. He noted that the majority's intent requirement departed from precedent, and made it virtually impossible to apply in certain cases:

> Inhumane prison conditions often are the result of cumulative actions and inactions by numerous officials inside and outside a prison, sometimes over a long period of time. In those circumstances, it is far from clear whose intent should be examined, and the majority offers no real guidance on this issue.

As Justice White asserted, such a muddled inquiry into a subjective intent standard is not very meaningful in practice when a plaintiff challenges an entire prison system or staff.

In *Farmer v. Brennan*, the Supreme Court defined "deliberate indifference" as applied to "conditions of confinement" cases, and left future inmate-plaintiffs with a seemingly insurmountable challenge in satisfying the subjective prong of the Eighth Amendment. The plaintiff in *Farmer* was an inmate diagnosed by the medical personnel of the Federal Bureau of Prisons (BOP) as a transsexual. She was serving a twenty-year federal sentence for credit card fraud. In accordance with the Federal Bureau of Prisons' policy, Farmer was incarcerated in all-male prisons, despite having noticeably feminine attributes after undergoing estrogen therapy, silicone breast implants, and an unsuccessful surgery attempt to have her testicles removed. On April 1, 1989, a prisoner approached Farmer, demanding that she have sexual intercourse with him, and upon her refusal, he forcibly raped her at knife point. "As a result of the rape, Farmer suffered 'mental anguish, psychological damage, humil[i]ation, a swollen face, cuts and bruises to her mouth and lips and a cut on her back, as well as some bleeding.'" Farmer filed a *Bivens* action,* seeking damages and an injunction from future confinement in any penitentiary. Farmer alleged that the prison officials had acted with "deliberate indifference" in violation of the Eighth Amendment by placing her in the general prison population despite knowledge that "the penitentiary had a violent environment and a history of inmate assaults, and... [Farmer] would be particularly vulnerable to sexual attack."

In *Farmer,* the Supreme Court narrowed the relevant issue to a choice between a civil or a criminal recklessness standard. Farmer urged the Court to adopt the more lenient civil law standard that defined recklessness as acting, or failing to act, in response to a high risk of harm that was either known, or so obvious that it should have been known. As a general principle, the harsher criminal law standard only permitted a finding of recklessness if a person disregarded a risk of which he was personally aware. In defining the standard for "deliberate indifference," the Court in *Farmer* rejected the civil law standard of recklessness and adopted the criminal law standard. The Court held that it could not find a prison official liable under the Eighth Amendment for denying a prisoner humane confinement conditions unless the official actually knew of, and then disregarded, an "excessive" risk to the prisoner's health or safety. As

---

* [A *Bivens* claim is a judiciously created constitutional claim to combat blatant constitutional violations by federal agents and authorities.—Eds.]

the Court wrote: "the official must both be aware of facts from which the inference could be drawn that a substantial risk of serious harm exists, and he must also draw the inference."

In essence, the only flexibility that remained for prisoners after *Farmer* was that an official's knowledge of a risk could be inferred from the existence of an "obvious risk to inmate health or safety." As one scholar noted, "by allowing circumstantial evidence of knowledge and not requiring prisoner notification... [m]ore failure-to-protect cases are likely to reach the jury." Inmates who allege that an obvious risk of harm existed within the prison may succeed in at least raising a reasonable inference that the prison official had knowledge of the potential risk of abuse. To prove obviousness, however, prisoners need to produce concrete evidence of the harm. Otherwise, a one-sided inquiry that weighs the prisoner's word against the guard's will govern the determination of obviousness. If an inmate-plaintiff is able to combine her account of abuses with the complaints of her fellow inmates, the obviousness of the harm will be more difficult for a guard to challenge.

Justice Blackmun recognized the burden that the harsh criminal recklessness standard would place on prisoner-plaintiffs. In his concurrence, Blackmun challenged the "deliberate indifference" state of mind requirement in the context of systemic abuses:

> [B]arbaric conditions should not be immune from constitutional scrutiny simply because no prison official acted culpably. *Wilson* failed to recognize that "state-sanctioned punishment consists not so much of specific acts attributable to individual state officials, but more of a cumulative agglomeration of action (and inaction) on an institutional level." The responsibility for subminimal conditions in any prison inevitably is diffuse, and often borne, at least in part, by the legislature.

Farmer did not specifically address the issue of institutional liability, but the Court did recognize "considerable conceptual difficulty" in trying to ascertain the subjective state of mind of an entire government entity, as distinguished from a single government official.

In suits for injunctive relief, however, courts have traditionally held upper-level officials accountable for violations committed by the lower-level staff, and have ultimately treated an "'official capacity suit... in all respects other than name... as a suit against the entity.'" The Court in *Farmer*, however, did not adopt the section 1983 standard for "deliberate indifference" put forth in *City of Canton v. Harris*. Some commentators believe that the Court in *Farmer* recognized that "*Canton*'s definition of deliberate indifference was an interpretation of 42 U.S.C. [sections] 1983, a statute containing no independent state of mind requirement. *Canton* itself had noted that the standard it announced for municipal liability did not turn on the standard governing the underlying constitutional claim." The test also served a different purpose in *Canton* by "identifying the threshold" for municipal liability. The Court in *Farmer* therefore held that *Canton* did not govern the requirements of the subjective prong of the Eighth Amendment. Some may applaud the decision to apply the strictest definition of "deliberate indifference" for "send[ing] a clear message to prison officials that their affirmative duty under the Constitution to provide for the safety of inmates is not to be taken lightly." Prisoner-plaintiffs, however, will be unlikely to share this positive outlook as this new standard simply requires more proof and more tangible evidence, resources that victims of sexual abuse often lack, especially when only one inmate's grievances are heard.

Justice Blackmun further criticized the majority opinion in his concurrence in *Farmer*, recognizing that the holding was "fundamentally misguided; indeed it defies common sense." He also argued that "punishment does not necessarily always imply a culpable state of mind on the part of an identifiable punisher." "[S]evere, rough, or disastrous treatment" may constitute punishment of a prisoner regardless of whether the punisher, such as a prison official, subjectively intended the treatment to be cruel. Blackmun advocated overruling *Wilson v. Seiter*, and argued that a violation of the Constitution "'should turn on the character of the punishment rather than the motivation of the individual who inflicted it.'" In his *Wilson* concurrence, Justice White predicted what would become the aftermath of *Farmer*: "'serious deprivations of basic human needs'... will go unredressed due to an unnecessary and meaningless search for 'deliberate indifference.'" Justice White's prediction has held true in many ways. The next section will focus on these "deprivations" and their effects in greater detail by considering the reality of sexual abuse of women inmates.

SEXUAL ABUSE IN THE PRISON ENVIRONMENT: A VIEW FROM THE INSIDE

> Sex in general, sex in particular, is the primary subject of interest in here [in prison], for the [correctional officers] as well as the inmates. I know a [correctional officer] who impregnated both an inmate and another [correctional officer] in a short space of time, while he was married to yet another. He was found out, suspended for six months, and told he was a naughty boy.

For female inmates, several aspects of incarceration make the problem of custodial sexual abuse a unique threat in desperate need of a remedy. As argued earlier, custodial sexual abuse is "invisible" to outsiders. The view from the other side of the bars, however, provides a very different perspective.

A surprising percentage of women in prison share a history of sexual abuse prior to incarceration. Statistics indicate that anywhere from forty to eighty-eight percent of these women have been the victims of domestic violence and sexual or physical abuse even before their arrival in prison. The American Correctional Association published a profile in 1990 indicating that the typical female prisoner was sexually abused between the ages of five and fourteen, usually by a male in her immediate family. As a result of past abuse, many female prisoners fear their male guards:

> More than half the women in here have been sexually abused at one time in their lives, some as small children by father, uncle, granddad, mother's lover. They fear men, even despise men. There are hookers who hate men. There are some very young girls in here who are afraid to function in prison without a "protector."

As prior victims, incarcerated women become hypersensitized to sexual abuse and often are more vulnerable to attacks in prison. "[S]exual abuse is an important consideration when you look at incarcerated women." A history of sexual abuse has an enormous impact on how these women respond to incarceration. Through their relationships with male guards, women who have experienced sexual abuse often re-live the trauma and suffer flashbacks of prior abuse, particularly when the male guards search them and perform pat-frisks. Incarcerated women respond to abusive male authority in prison in the same manner as they did before their confinement in prison. "The women are so needy and in need of love, they are set up for oppression. The only way they know is to exchange their bodies [to meet this need]." From her observations while incarcerated in a District of Columbia prison, Elizabeth Morgan shares the view that a prior history of abuse affects the behavior and perceptions of female inmates. Arguing that "the [f]ear of male violence and the need to be safe are central to women's experiences," Morgan suggests that the prison environment serves to exacerbate these perspectives. She notes that "[b]eliefs about life and about oneself are profoundly affected by survival of traumatic events." Women inmates share largely negative outlooks. Morgan suggests that these women simply have no experiences that enable them to envision "any positive outcome for themselves in any [type of] situation involving men." Clinical studies have suggested that battered women should be provided with safe experiences in order to take the first step in changing their beliefs about their own lack of power. Not only do prisons fail in their attempt to change these women's beliefs, but the women inmates become entrapped in a different, and seemingly inescapable cycle of abuse. "The jail . . . provide[s] yet more proof that they [a]re powerless to change."

In *Jordan v. Gardner,* the Ninth Circuit finally acknowledged and documented the fact that many women inmates have a history of sexual abuse. The court noted that the psychological impact of clothed body searches by male prison guards of women inmates with a history of sexual abuse amounted to an "infliction of pain." The Court in *Jordan* recognized that women are disproportionately victims of rape and sexual assault, and therefore have a stronger incentive to be concerned with and sensitive to sexual behavior. "Men, who are rarely victims of sexual assault, may view sexual conduct in a vacuum without a full appreciation of the social setting or the underlying threat of violence that a woman may perceive."

When combined with the abusive pasts of women inmates, the retention of powerful positions by male guards fosters an opportunity for continued abuse. Simply put, "[p]olice officers have relatively frequent opportunities for sexual harassment and sexual contact with offenders. Offenders are not only aware of the authority of the officer but are also in a position where their complaints may be disregarded or played down." The fact that the guards literally control the lives of the inmates, including ultimately how long the actual period of confinement will be, adds to the power the guards have over the inmates. The only "bargaining power" women have is their bodies.

Women inmates have come to accept the reality that there is no way to avoid sexual abuse. They also fear that somehow they ultimately will receive punishment for reporting the abuse, instead of the guard receiving punishment for inflicting it. In the words of one inmate:

> "There's not much I can do about it... If I write it up, first thing they are going to do is not believe me, then it's PCU [Protective Custody Unit] and then a transfer. That's how it goes with sexual misconduct.... There are so many females back there that this happens to and they don't tell. They do not want to speak... It's the fear... they're scared... I'm tired of being scared. I'm tired of things not being done."

Women inmates' fears of retribution and endurance of accusations that they are lying when they report abuse only have contributed to the external invisibility of custodial sexual abuse.

The prison administration often has ignored or dismissed individual incidents of sexual abuse, but when viewed in combination with other incidents, these occurrences reveal a "sexualized environment" inside the prison walls. The prison emerges as a psychologically destructive setting in which abuse continually plagues hypersensitized inmates: "Each example of harassment is petty. Piled one on top of another they can become what nervous breakdowns are made of, an obsession, the last miserable straw." The lack of privacy inherent in a prison environment necessarily means that women are exposed and vulnerable on a twenty-four-hour basis. While in prison, women inmates "are in a position where sexual harassment behaviors can take place with relative impunity." Jails are not constructed with the privacy of inmates as a major concern. Male guards may observe prisoners undressed in their cells, showers, toilets, or during searches by jail matrons. "Some officers apparently seek out opportunities to observe females in various degrees of undress." After a while, the constant exposure of women's bodies and the sexual relations between inmates and staff become accepted occurrences. "You get the impression from the [prison] staff... that it was a sexual smorgasbord and they could pick and choose whom they wanted."

After experiencing incarceration in the District of Columbia, Elizabeth Morgan noted some of the effects of the sexualized environment existing in women's prisons. She first characterized the prison administration as functioning as a " 'mind control' sexual abuser." Aside from making the prisoners relive their past histories of sexual abuse, this sexualized environment forces the inmates to acquire defensive tactics to protect themselves: "Entries [in Morgan's diary] described female inmates who refused to shower because it required exposing themselves to men a few feet away who were screaming sexual obscenities, insults, and threats. Women inmates also tried to use poor personal hygiene to diminish the risk of rape. Although women prisoners were able to develop certain defensive tactics, none of these responses successfully directed the administration's attention to the sexual abuse, so patterns of abuse continued unnoticed.

Sexual abuse of women prisoners by their male guards unfortunately has become an accepted reality. Prison administrators "allowed this whole culture of abuse (to develop). Abuse was OK. It didn't matter.... Everybody became sort of inoculated to the abuse that was ongoing." The victims of sexual abuse in prison are silent for several reasons. They fear that no one will believe them, that prison officials will punish them, or they simply blame themselves for somehow provoking the abuse. The few inmates who have recently come forward with individual allegations of abuse have lost in court and have been subject to retaliation by prison staff, thereby deterring other victims of sexual abuse from breaking their silence. An inquiry into the circumstances and the reasons for the failures of recent custodial sexual abuse claims under the Eighth Amendment by individual inmates demonstrates why other victims perceive such a grim chance for relief.

THE UNSUCCESSFUL CASES AND THE DANGERS INHERENT IN BRINGING AN INDIVIDUAL CLAIM

This section focuses on key cases brought in the federal courts since 1995 where the individual inmate-plaintiff unsuccessfully attempted to obtain relief against prison supervisors in their official capacities by instituting claims for sexual abuse under the Eighth Amendment. In each of these cases, the plaintiff was unable to satisfy the subjective prong of her Eighth Amendment claim because of her inability to show that the prison supervisors acted with "deliberate indifference." The myriad of failed cases suggests that the "deliberate indifference" standard is too demanding for an individual plaintiff to overcome in actions against prison officers in their official capacities.

In *Downey v. Denton County,* an employee of the county sheriffs department sexually assaulted an inmate when they were left alone for nearly two hours, unmonitored and unsupervised, in a room with a disconnected voice-activated security device. Downey gave birth to a child as a result of the incident. Downey filed suit against Denton County, the offending officer, and several supervisory officers. With respect to the plaintiff's section 1983 claims, the district court granted the county and supervisory officers' motion for judgment on partial findings, yet denied the offending officer's motion for the same.

On appeal, the Fifth Circuit determined that the trial court did not err in granting the county and supervisory officers' motion for judgment on partial findings. It upheld the trial court's decision that there was no evidence in the record to support a finding of "deliberate indifference" as outlined in *Farmer v. Brennan.* The court further held that the trial judge did not clearly err in his findings of fact to the effect that the plaintiff failed to show sufficient direct evidence that Sheriff Robinson, one of the supervisory officers, actually was aware of a substantial risk of harm to Downey, or that he disregarded this risk. The court concluded that "[a]lthough requisite knowledge of a substantial risk of serious harm can be demonstrated by inference from circumstantial evidence, a survey of the trial record convinces us that there is no evidence of such knowledge on the part of Sheriff Robinson."

In *Carrigan v. Delaware*, plaintiff Dorothy Carrigan filed suit against the State of Delaware, the offending officer, the Delaware Department of Corrections, and several administrative officials in both their individual and official capacities. Carrigan claimed that Peter Davis, the offending officer, entered her room while she was taking a nap, woke her, told her to be quiet, and then raped her. Carrigan reported the incident, and claimed that during the investigation, officers threatened her with additional jail time and prosecution under a law prohibiting sex in prison. She also claimed that the prison transferred her from a minimum security unit to a maximum security unit in retaliation for reporting the incident. Carrigan subsequently attempted suicide as a result of the intense pressure she experienced after reporting the rape. Defendant Davis eventually "admitted to having oral sex with [Carrigan], but claimed that [she] seduced him and the act was consensual." Carrigan remarked that the retaliation against her by other guards continued even after Davis admitted to engaging in oral sex.

In analyzing "deliberate indifference" as defined in *Farmer,* the court concluded that unlike the plaintiff in *Farmer,* the plaintiff in *Carrigan* failed to establish additional facts sufficient for a reasonable jury to conclude that the conditions of her confinement posed a "substantial risk of serious harm" and that the Administrative Defendants acted with "deliberate indifference" to her health and safety. The court in *Carrigan* noted that

> [p]laintiff's brief is replete with rumors and innuendos of sexual impropriety between inmates and prison guards designed to illustrate that the Administrative Defendants were aware of a risk of sexual assault to Plaintiff; however, these allegations are insufficient to establish that the Administrative Defendants were aware of a risk of harm to Plaintiff.

The court further distinguished *Carrigan* from the plaintiff in *Farmer,* by asserting that Carrigan had failed to give the Administrative Defendants advance notice of the risk of harm, and did not present other sufficient evidence to support her claim. The court, however, based its finding on the fact that Carrigan's allegation of rape was the first rape claim brought to the Administrative Defendants' attention. The court erroneously assumed that inmates actually report most rape or sexual abuse incidents, while in reality the exact opposite is true. The court's refusal to rely on a correctional officer's affidavits describing rumors about additional incidents of sexual misconduct also ignored the reality that only a small percentage of women, on both sides of the prison wall, report such occurrences.

In addition, the court pointed to the Department of Corrections Code of Conduct that strictly forbids " '[a]ny sexual contact with offenders,' " as well as the additional training guards receive, to suggest that the prison maintained a practice of "careful attention, rather than deliberate indifference to correctional officer training." The court ultimately granted the Administrative Defendants' motion for summary judgment, concluding that simply because the "[p]laintiff may have suffered [as a result of sexual contact] does not indicate that the Administrative Defendants demonstrated deliberate indifference toward her mental and physical health."

In *Adkins v. Rodriguez*, the plaintiff, Shelly Adkins, brought an Eighth Amendment claim against Deputy Rodriguez, the offending officer, and other county officials in their official capacities. The trial court dismissed her complaint, finding no right under the Eighth Amendment for a prisoner to be free from verbal sexual harassment. Adkins claimed that Rodriguez verbally harassed her and appeared in her cell without authorization. Rodriguez allegedly "made verbal comments to Ms. Adkins about her body, his own sexual prowess, and his sexual conquests," and continued to make such comments even after being warned by prison officials to stop his inappropriate behavior. On one occasion, Rodriguez entered Adkins's cell in the middle of the night, and when she awoke to find him standing beside her bed, he said, " '[b]y the way, you have nice breasts.' " After being threatened with termination, Rodriguez ultimately resigned. Adkins argued that Rodriguez's acts violated her rights "to be free from threats of violence and sexual assault and/or sexual intimidation, to be free from cruel and unusual punishment, [and] to be free from unjustified harassment."

On appeal, the Tenth Circuit affirmed the district court's grant of summary judgment for the defendant. Focusing on the fact that Rodriguez did not actually touch Adkins, the court concluded that, "we cannot infuse defendant's words of sexual harassment with the sort of violence or threats of violence cognizable in the conditions of confinement cases the [Supreme] Court has addressed." The court, however, seemed to suggest that because the plaintiffs complaint only concerned an isolated incident, Adkins could not establish a constitutional violation. The court implied that an individual incident of sexual harassment or sexual abuse, regardless of the nature or severity of the attack, would not constitute deliberate indifference.

A recent, well-documented, and highly-publicized case, *Fisher v. Goord*, popularly known as the "Amy Fisher" case, followed the pattern of inmate-plaintiffs' inability to satisfy the "deliberate indifference" standard in suits against prison supervisors in their official capacities. Fisher alleged that while incarcerated in a New York prison, several corrections officers raped and sexually abused her. She also claimed that prison authorities failed to act on her complaints, and that they retaliated against her as a result of her charges. Fisher named as defendants seven present or former corrections officers at the prison, several high ranking officials in the Department of Correctional Services, and a number of supervisory officers at the prison. Fisher filed a motion for a preliminary injunction, seeking an order requiring her transfer to Danbury prison during the pendency of the action and an order requiring one of the defendant-officers to provide a blood sample. A party seeking a preliminary injunction must show that she will suffer irreparable harm in the absence of an injunction and demonstrate either: "(1) a likelihood of success on the merits or (2) sufficiently serious questions going to the merits to make them a fair ground for litigation and a balance of hardships tipping decidedly in the movant's favor."

On the likelihood of succeeding on the merits, the district court held that Fisher had failed to establish a clear or substantial likelihood of success on her Eighth Amendment sexual abuse claims. After the court considered the testimony during trial and the other evidence in the record, it found that Fisher's claims of rape and sexual abuse were not worthy of belief. "Neither Fisher nor her mother was a credible witness and their testimony was contradicted both by other witnesses... and other evidence in the record." The court attacked Fisher's credibility and suggested that it "appears that [Fisher] and her mother are trying to manipulate the system by capitalizing on this sensitive and important issue." The court further criticized Fisher's case because she failed to present any witnesses to the rapes or sexual abuse. Judge Arcara also remarked that Fisher did not come across in court as the type of individual who had been the victim of multiple rapes.

The fact that New York had not yet established a law mandating that sexual relations of any kind between a corrections officer and an inmate constitutes statutory rape presented a difficult challenge to Fisher's claim. Although New York now has such a law, it was not in effect at the time of the alleged misconduct in *Fisher*. As a result, the court found that Fisher's sexual relationships with the defendants "can only reasonably be interpreted as... consensual in nature." According to the court, even if her testimony was true, Fisher was unable to affirmatively demonstrate a lack of consent.

The court supported the consent defense by applying a recent Eighth Circuit decision to the facts of Fisher's case. In *Freitas v. Ault,* an inmate brought a section 1983 action against a warden and prison employee, alleging sexual harassment in violation of the Eighth Amendment. The Eighth Circuit in *Freitas* affirmed the district court's determination that the relationship between the inmate and the prison employee was consensual, and noted that "[t]he record contained no evidence, other than [the inmate's] unsubstantiated assertions, supporting his claim that he succumbed to [the employee's] advances because she was his boss and he feared the possible negative consequences of reporting her actions." *Fisher* argued, in response to *Freitas,* that there was a "power discrepancy" between guard and inmate, "making it impossible for an inmate to ever truly consent to having sexual relations with a correction officer," but the court did not find this argument persuasive.

Even though the court in *Fisher* did not accept that the "power discrepancy" demonstrated a lack of consent, it still labeled these types of sexual relations as inappropriate:

> Sexual interactions between correction officers and inmates, no matter how voluntary, are totally incompatible with the order and discipline required in a prison setting. Further, the court is disturbed by the notion that an inmate might feel compelled to perform sexual favors for correction officers in order to be on the officer's "good side." Such quid pro quo behavior is inappropriate, despicable and serves no legitimate penological purpose.

Judge Arcara seemed to recognize that sexual relations between inmates and guards constitutes bad prison policy, but failed to consider the inmate's perspective on such relationships. Within the walls of a prison, the inmate becomes comparable to a victim of child sexual abuse. In both situations, two key factors of sexual abuse are present: "a bigger and more powerful person used his/her strength or authority over a smaller, weaker and more vulnerable individual," and the victim was unable "to resist, and therefore... there was no real or true choice in the matter."

Recognizing the implications of his ruling that a prisoner may consent to sex with a guard, Judge Arcara concluded with a disclaimer: "The Court['s] ... decision here should not be viewed as a ringing endorsement of the situation at Albion. Despite the Court's determination that Fisher's claims of rape and sexual abuse are not credible, there are indications that all is not right at Albion." Amy Fisher did not necessarily lose her case because of her reputation or her lack of credibility; rather, her failure likely is attributable to the reality that as an individual plaintiff, she could not offer enough proof of sexual abuse in Albion to prevail.

Fisher's tabloid notoriety created a great deal of media attention and several commentators noted the implications of the decision. Fisher's lawyer, Glenn Murray, reacted to Judge Arcara's ruling by stating, " 'I'm afraid that with this decision ... the (Department of Correctional Services) won't take rape accusations more seriously, but rather, less seriously, if such a thing is imaginable.' " Supporters of Judge Arcara's verdict accused Fisher of tarnishing the name of Albion by questioning the integrity of its officers. Others viewed the whole suit as entirely fabricated by Fisher in order to obtain a transfer to Bedford Hills prison. A union official representing Albion's guards claimed "[s]he dragged down a whole lot of people who worked at Albion who had absolutely nothing to do with this.... The only reason for this lawsuit ... is a book or a movie deal that will come out afterward."

Regardless of their interpretation of Judge Arcara's ruling, commentators agreed that the decision would impact the prison system. As Roger Gangi, executive director of the Correctional Association of New York observed: "It's definitely no joke ... I'm not making any judgments about [Fisher's] accusations, but things like this do happen in the state prisons." Despite her notoriety, however, even Fisher was unable to generate enough media scrutiny to actually remedy the problems of sexual abuse in New York prisons.

WOMEN PRISONERS AND THE SUCCESS OF CLASS ACTION SUITS

The ruling in *Women Prisoners v. District of Columbia* had two major effects on Eighth Amendment litigation for claims of custodial sexual abuse. First, it attracted necessary recognition of the pervasiveness of the problem. Second, the plaintiffs' success suggested at least one possible method through which inmate-plaintiffs might satisfy the subjective prong of the Eighth Amendment. In *Women Prisoners*, women inmates in the District of Columbia (D.C.) prisons brought a class action suit against the District of Columbia, its Department of Corrections (DCDC), the District of Columbia General Hospital Commission, and numerous District officials, all in their official capacities. Among their claims for declaratory and injunctive relief, the plaintiffs alleged that women prisoners in the D.C. prisons were subjected to sexual harassment in violation of the Eighth Amendment.

One noticeable benefit of using a class action suit was the plaintiffs' ability to mount a more "exhaustively-prepared case." The trial itself lasted three weeks and included the submission of close to nine hundred exhibits and hundreds of pages of transcript and deposition testimony. Prisoner testimony revealed allegations of sexual assault, sexual harassment, the inadequacy of the corrections officers' responses, and retaliation by the guards after complaints were filed. Women took the stand and told of rapes, forced sodomy, sexual touching, and fondling. In addition to this physical abuse, the women inmates complained of a lack of privacy stemming from the ability of male guards and fellow inmates to view the women in various states of undress. The women inmates also described how they were subjected to sexually explicit comments and verbal sexual harassment.

As a class, the inmate-plaintiffs benefited from being able to present expert testimony on the effects of sexual abuse on women inmates, especially those with prior histories of sexual abuse. Dr. Susan Fiester testified that among the population of women in prison, "between 70 to 80 percent have been sexually abused at some point in their lives." In addition to the harmful physical and psychological effects of sexual abuse and sexual harassment on women prisoners, Dr. Fiester explained that those with backgrounds of abuse suffered even further. For these women, the recent episodes of sexual abuse or sexual harassment brought flashbacks of prior abuse, which could lead to severe depression, reinforcement of a 'victim' self-image and a belief that, as in childhood, they have no control over their lives."

Witnesses for the plaintiffs also addressed the flaws in the Inmate Grievance Procedure, the lack of specific staff training, the absence of confidentiality of complaints, the inadequacy of the investigations, and the prisons' repeated failures to take remedial action. Officers regarded inmates' complaints as a "joke" or "gossip." One of the plaintiffs' expert witnesses testified that "in approximately 90 percent of all sexual harassment cases [that] she has confronted, the Defendants often fail to reach any conclusions in their investigations." One inmate concluded that the grievance system "was like a game to everybody there. They didn't care about anybody's feelings." Despite these allegations, the DCDC maintained that it did "everything an institution can do to prevent sexual misconduct."

In light of the extent of the accounts of sexual abuse and sexual harassment, Judge Green could not dismiss the plaintiffs' claims as isolated or fabricated. In her findings of fact, she noted:

> Within the [DCDC] there is a general acceptance of sexual relationships between staff and inmates which creates a "sexualized environment" where "boundaries and expectations of behavior are not clear." ... [One former correctional administrator has noted] "[Y]ou just get this sense that [sexual misconduct] has always happened and it is always going to happen." ... The most disturbing evidence of sexual harassment involves sexual assaults on women prisoners and the inadequacy of the Defendants' response to these attacks.

Unlike Judge Arcara in *Fisher,* Judge Green adopted the inmate's perspective and recognized the harmful and pervasive effects of this "sexualized environment." She viewed sexual abuse of prisoners not merely as an administrative problem, but also as a physical and mental threat to the women inmates.

Judge Green ruled in favor of the inmate-plaintiffs because, as a class, they were able to satisfy the subjective prong of the Eighth Amendment claim. She found that the defendants had acted with "deliberate indifference" to the women prisoners' endurance of the condition of sexual harassment. The evidence demonstrated that the defendants both knew of and disregarded an excessive risk of sexual assaults and sexual harassment of the women prisoners. Judge Green inferred the presence of deliberate indifference from the obviousness of the sexual harassment. "Indeed, assaults are widely known by DCDC staff, vulgar comments are made openly and women are fondled publicly." She concluded that the plaintiffs had proven violations of the Eighth Amendment "by demonstrating a level of sexual harassment that is objectively cruel and to which the Defendants are deliberately indifferent."

This "victory" for the plaintiffs was the result of several factors that can be attributed to the fact that the case was a class action suit. The inmates had the ability to combine the individual incidents of sexual harassment to create the "sexualized environment" recognized by Judge Green:

> In combination, vulgar sexual remarks of prison officers, the lack of privacy within CTF [Correctional Treatment Facility] cells and the refusal of some male guards to announce their presence in the living areas of women prisoners constitute a violation of the Eighth Amendment since they mutually heighten the psychological injury of women prisoners.

Judge Green focused on the effect of these abuses in combination, and noted that the prison setting heightens psychological impact of abuse further because "the women are tightly confined, making their escape from harassment as unlikely as escape from the jail itself." Unlike an isolated occurrence, this "sexualized environment" surrounds and literally consumes the inmates. The combination of sexual abuse, harassment, and the continual unannounced presence of male guards in the women's cells provided a constant "reminder to women prisoners that their exposure to abuse is almost endless."

The publicity generated by *Women Prisoners* was useful in drawing attention to the problem of sexual abuse within the D.C. prison system, breaking the tradition of invisibility and giving the inmates hope that they could obtain a remedy. Brenda Smith of the National Women's Law Center told Human Rights Watch that in working on the case since 1990, she had received numerous reports of sexual assaults within the prisons and assisted women on an individual basis. She noted, however, that the sheer magnitude and pattern of sexual abuse was exposed only after the class action suit was filed. She told Human Rights Watch that "[i]t is really like this dirty little secret that everyone in corrections knows about and doesn't want to talk about. It is a huge problem."

The *Washington Post* coverage of the case also informed the public of the existence of sexual abuse in prison and appealed to the public's sentiments. The exposure of the problem contributed to its remedy, and responses to sexual misconduct have improved since the decision in *Women Prisoners*. In August 1995, for example, prison officials in the District of Columbia suspended seven corrections officers following allegations that they attended a party held within the prison at which two female inmates were asked to perform a striptease.

The most telling example of the acknowledgement of the problem of custodial sexual abuse occurred shortly after Judge Green rendered her decision in *Women Prisoners*. In December 1994, the D.C. City Council modified its rape law as it applied to individuals in police or correctional custody. Now, any type of sexual intercourse or sexual contact involving an incarcerated individual is a felony. Legislators, at least, are finally beginning to recognize the uniquely vulnerable position of women prisoners and the greatly magnified power disparity between inmate and guard that increases the risk of custodial sexual abuse in prison.

RECOGNITION OF THE PROBLEM AND POSSIBLE SOLUTIONS

As Justice Blackmun noted, concurring in *Farmer v. Brennan*, "regardless of what state actor or institution caused the harm and with what intent, the experience of the inmate is the same. A punishment is simply no less cruel or unusual because its harm is unintended." Unfortunately, since *Farmer*, the focus on the intent of the guard or supervisor has become the deciding factor, notably in cases involving claims seeking injunctive relief for custodial sexual abuse against officers in their official capacities.

After *Farmer*, plaintiffs face a dilemma in determining how to go about establishing that the prison had knowledge of harm. In *Farmer*, the Court's reference to the requirement that the inmate prove the prison officials' state of mind "in the usual ways" indicated that "statistics, institutional and municipal reporting of assaults, and the existence of systemic predictive factors, among other indicia of 'institutional knowledge' of prison violence," are acceptable forms of "circumstantial evidence that plaintiffs may introduce to establish knowledge of the risk of harm." If the plaintiff proves that this risk is

> longstanding, pervasive, well-documented, or expressly noted by prison officials in the past, and the circumstances suggest that the defendant-official being sued had been exposed to information concerning the risk and thus 'must have known' about it, then such evidence could be sufficient to permit a trier of fact to find that the defendant-official had actual knowledge of the risk.

The documentary proof required by this circumstantial evidence standard places a great deal of confidence in the internal investigative systems of prisons, which, in cases of sexual abuse, are frequently less effective than usual.

Victims of sexual abuse and harassment often are very cautious in their reliance on any sort of internal grievance system. Inmates share this lack of faith in the formal complaint resolution mechanisms. They feel that "the grievance procedure is 'just for show,' unanimously agreeing that only those inmates with particularly egregious complaints can prevail in the [grievance] process." The *Farmer* Court placed special emphasis on these prison grievances, noting that, "even when [grievance procedures] do not bring constitutionally required changes, the inmate's task in court will obviously be much easier." The necessity of these prisoner grievances is problematic:

> Violence in prison is often substantially underreported, as a result either of prisoner intimidation or of staff indifference or discouragement, and some prison records—especially those dealing with staff use of force—have been found to be too self-serving to meet the reliability requirements of the public records and reports rule.

Cases of sexual abuse magnify the problem of underreporting. In her findings of fact in *Women Prisoners*, Judge Green recognized some of the problems of established internal grievance procedures and investigations in addressing sexual harassment. Judge Green found that not only did prison officials often fail to reach any conclusions in their investigations of prison sexual harassment claims, but the prison administration's typical response to an inmate's internal grievance was to conclude that the allegations "could not be validated." In some instances, the offending officers often were not even reassigned after an incident was reported, making the inmate hesitant to reveal incidents of abuse for fear of retaliation. In examining prisons in the District of Columbia, Judge Green concluded that the failures of the DCDC Internal Grievance Policy itself constituted "deliberate indifference." She recognized that within the D.C. prisons, "there is no clear understanding of what constitutes sexual harassment and how it should be reported." In addition, the noticeable lack of confidentiality caused women prisoners to suffer the trauma of having the small prison community know the details of a personally degrading assault.

Women prisoners also are the targets of retaliation. Prison officials often leak confidential information, coercing women prisoners and the staff into silence while simultaneously insulating their own actions from scrutiny. "The invariable result is that cases 'cannot be resolved' and officers who commit the assaults are often reassigned to another facility or allowed to remain in the same facility." The very procedures that the Court in *Farmer* found to be virtually indispensable in bringing a successful claim against prison officials were recognized by the court in *Women Prisoners* as being a source of "deliberate indifference" itself.

The plaintiffs in *Women Prisoners* took on the responsibility of exposing to the court the inherent flaws in the process through which inmates obtain proof of the officers' knowledge of harm. The class action form of the suit gave the plaintiffs access to resources and strategies that an individual plaintiff would lack:

> In class action litigation, where counsel and expert witnesses are involved on an ongoing basis, additional opportunities exist for proving knowledge. For example, testimony or a declaration from an expert that a risk was obvious may suffice to prove that prison officials had knowledge of it. A letter from plaintiffs' counsel apprising prison officials or their counsel of a risk of harm should serve the same function.
>
> Individual plaintiffs do not have these resources, and they face intimidation from the same internal grievance procedures that must filter requisite proof of knowledge on the part of the officials. Courts should not require plaintiffs to

become a class in order to succeed in bringing Eighth Amendment claims for custodial sexual abuse.

CONCLUSION

[B]eing a woman prisoner in U.S. state prisons can be a terrifying experience. If you are sexually abused, you cannot escape from your abuser. Grievance or investigatory procedures, where they exist, are often ineffectual, and correctional employees continue to engage in abuse because they believe they will rarely be held accountable, administratively or criminally. Few people outside the prison walls know what is going on or care if they do know. Fewer still do anything to address the problem.

The "deliberate indifference" standard outlined by the Supreme Court in *Farmer v. Brennan* has left inmates who are victims of sexual harassment with few alternatives. To succeed in a systemic violations case against prison officers in their official capacities, inmates need the resources that only a class action can afford. Proceeding on an individual basis forces a plaintiff to rely on ineffective, intimidating, and retaliatory internal grievance procedures to obtain proof of the prison officer's knowledge of harm.

Experts have recommended class actions as an "appropriate vehicle" for sexual harassment suits in the employment setting, and the rationale for this preference extends to women inmates' suits for custodial sexual abuse. "Inherent disincentives for bringing an individual ... claim, such as embarrassment and fear of retaliation, could be overcome through the use of class actions." Class actions allow plaintiffs to rely on multiple incidents and accounts of sexual assault in order to demonstrate the obviousness of the abuse, allowing for an inference of "deliberate indifference." In light of the "deliberate indifference" standard articulated in *Farmer,* a class action lawsuit remains not merely a good option for inmate-plaintiffs, but the only option.

In the future, as Justice White suggested in *Wilson v. Seiter,* courts must make a distinction between cases involving an individual claim against the offending officer and claims for systemic violations against officers in their official capacities. For the latter category of cases, the "deliberate indifference" standard should not apply. As the numerous unsuccessful cases brought by female inmates have shown, if courts do not make this distinction, custodial sexual abuse will remain a "dirty little secret" within the prisons, kept quiet by self-serving internal grievance procedures.

Justice for All?

The United States in general and the state of California in particular, have a long history of social inequality. The unfair treatment of disadvantaged groups in virtually all public arenas (e.g., housing, education, policing, public assistance, and employment) has clearly demonstrated the abject failure of policies and programs ostensibly designed to promote "equality and justice for all." Sociological conflict theory holds that most forms of social inequality are nested in the tenets of capitalism and can be best understood in the context of the perpetual social struggle for power and resources. In that context, the competition for scarce and purportedly finite resources provokes competitors to employ whatever means available to maximize their chances of success, even at the expense of others. It follows, then, that the socially powerless, or otherwise disadvantaged, lack a competitive edge and are subsequently subordinated to the more advantaged and powerful. And it does not matter whether the powerless and disadvantaged are so because of their own devices and shortcomings or whether they are so due to circumstances beyond their control. They are nevertheless subject to the same victimization and subordination by the same dynamics of struggle.

The foregoing principles are highly evident in the workings of the criminal justice system. It is well understood that "justice" is a function of power and privilege, not "blindness," and it has been clearly shown that disadvantaged groups are the most likely to be surveilled, arrested, convicted, and incarcerated. Those arrested are less likely to effect pretrial release; thus, they are more likely to be convicted. Those convicted are more likely to receive longer and more incapacitating sentences (e.g., incarceration versus community-based corrections). Those incarcerated are less likely to be exposed to rehabilitative or remedial options and more likely to experience the full harshness of imprisonment. And the prison experience is more likely to produce recidivists than properly reintegrated citizens.

It cannot be said that local, state, and federal government agencies have not recognized the need for criminal justice reform. Nor can it be said that actual attempts at such reform have not been made. What can be said is that despite the recognition and the attempts at reform, the problem persists and, in fact, seems to be getting worse. More and more states and local jurisdictions are effectively using executive order, legislative mandate, and the democratic process to enact more and more policies and practices aimed at controlling, subjugating, and alienating disadvantaged and powerless groups.

Joan Petersilia is a professor of criminology, law, and society in the School of Social Ecology at the University of California, Irvine. In the following selection from "Justice for All? Offenders With Mental Retardation and the California Corrections System," *The Prison Journal* (December 1997), she traces the inequitable treatment of mentally retarded offenders in California from arrest through imprisonment and beyond. Despite a history of legislation and public policy to ameliorate the problems of inequality, the California corrections system persists in its less-than-even-handed treatment of this special class of inmates. Initially, the selection compares the lot of the mentally retarded prisoner with that of any other disadvantaged group, but it ultimately suggests that those with mental retardation are subjugated even further within the general prison population. The special characteristics of the mentally retarded prisoner are such that he does not do time well and is consequently treated not as needing special attention but rather as needing longer, more severe, and more restrictive imprisonment. This selection presents several examples of more effective prison programming elsewhere in the United States and offers a number of remedial strategies to recognize and properly handle this special class of offender, all of which are designed to protect rather than persecute.

Key Concept: victimization of disadvantaged groups in the U.S. corrections system.

DIMENSIONS OF THE PROBLEM

Duane Silva, a 23-year-old from Tulare County, California, sits today in a California prison cell serving 25 years to life, having been convicted of stealing a VCR and jewelry in a 1994 residential burglary. Silva is mentally retarded (MR; also stands for mental retardation), with an IQ of 70, the mental age equivalent to that of a 10- or 11-year-old.[1] Silva was one of the first offenders to be sentenced under California's Three Strikes Law, having had two previous strikes for arson, one involving a fire he started in a trash can and another involving a fire that began in a parked truck where it appears he was playing with matches.

Silva and the other estimated 6,400 MR California adult and juvenile inmates represent a complex, troubling, and increasingly costly issue for the corrections system. On one hand, we do not wish to excuse the criminal behavior of criminals who are MR, but many offenders with MR are not so much lawbreakers as they are low-functioning citizens who lack training on how to function responsibly in a complex society.

MR and developmentally disabled (DD) persons are usually defined as those with less than a 70 IQ, but practically speaking, such persons can be described with fair accuracy as having a childlike quality of thinking, coupled with slowness in learning new material.[2] MR persons have little long-term perspective and little ability to think in a causal way to understand the consequences of their actions. They are usually followers, easily manipulated, and often used by others with more intelligence and/or experience.

Studies have shown that although their rates of crime are similar to those of nondisabled persons, and consist mostly of less serious felonies and property crimes, the offender with MR is disproportionately represented in correctional agencies.[3] The prevalence of MR is about 1% to 2% in the population at large, but in the criminal justice system, it is estimated to be about 4% to 10% (although prevalence rates in the literature range from 1% to 30%).[4] A number of cumulative factors explain this.

POLICE AND PROSECUTION DECISION MAKING

Offenders with MR come disproportionately from low-income minority groups, where police presence and the probability of arrest is high. MR persons cannot think quickly, often make no attempt to disguise what they have done, nor do they run from the scene. As a result, they are generally easily arrested and convicted. As one police officer put it, "They are the last to leave the scene, the first to get arrested, and the first to confess." Studies show that many MR persons cannot understand their rights when arrested (e.g., the term waiver), especially in the form read by the police (Edwards & Reynolds, 1997). People with MR often exhibit low self-esteem and have a heightened desire to please authority figures. As such, they often will acquiesce to the wishes of other individuals who are perceived to be more influential (delinquent peers as well as police officers).

For most offenders with MR, official justice system processing (from arrest through sentencing) will proceed without officials becoming aware of the offender's intellectual disability.[5] Most justice personnel are not trained to identify the MR (indeed, they often confuse mentally ill with MR), and there are seldom any formal procedures for identifying such persons.[6] Moreover, MR offenders, anxious to fit in, are rather clever at masking their limitations and rendering the magnitude of their disability invisible to the criminal justice system (CJS) personnel. Only when impairments become visible enough, such as when the offender acts in a bizarre or disruptive manner, are formal evaluations completed.

Even if the offender with MR is identified, special handling or programming is extremely rare. Psychological evaluations are seldom performed prior to trial or sentencing, the result being that their condition is sometimes not discovered until incarceration, when it is too late to employ special procedures to ensure a fair trial. Defendants are often simply viewed as slow and uncooperative, especially in cases involving minority defendants (McGee & Menolascino, 1992).

INCARCERATION BEFORE TRIAL

Offenders with MR are unlikely to meet the criteria for personal recognizance or bail, because the individual is probably unemployed and living with less stable surroundings, two of the major criteria used in bail decision making. The MR defendant is usually held in the local jail prior to the case disposition, and research has shown that other factors being equal, defendants held for trial in lieu of bail are convicted more often. In addition, when convicted, they go to prison more often and receive longer sentences that those who post bail (Goldkamp, 1979; Toberg, 1992). Although it is difficult to isolate the detention factors from other variables such as the severity of the crime, research has consistently found a relationship between being held in jail pretrial and the severity of court disposition. Persons who remain in the community while their case is being adjudicated have the opportunity to assist in their defense, secure employment or training, and, generally speaking, show the court that they can "make it" in the community. The hardship of detention before trial also puts pressure on defendants to waive their rights and to plead guilty.

PLEA BARGAINING, COURT PROCESSING, AND SENTENCING

Persons with MR confess more readily, provide more incriminating evidence to authorities, and are less successful in plea bargaining. As a result, they are more likely to be convicted and receive longer sentences. The offender with MR is subjected to the same judicial procedures—confrontational, legalistic, and impersonal—as are persons having greater intellectual capacities. The result is that offenders with MR do poorly in plea negotiations. Studies show that the vast majority of MR defendants are represented by public defenders, confess to the crime, plead guilty to the original (not reduced) charge, and waive their right to a jury trial (Moschella, 1982; Santamour, 1986). When MR persons do go to trial, their ability to remember details, locate witnesses, and testify credibly is limited. Defense attorneys know they make less-than-ideal defendants and are easily manipulated by prosecutors pretending to be on their side.[7]

At sentencing, MR offenders do not often look like a good prospect for probation, which is more commonly granted to individuals with higher intelligence and greater educational and work achievement. Again, studies show that even when presentence investigations are prepared for the court to use in sentencing, the MR condition is not usually noted and the offender is evaluated similarly to the nondisabled person (Laski, 1992). Probation is less frequently granted for offenders with MR (Haskins & Friel, 1973; Santamour & West, 1979). When intermediate sanctions (e.g., boot camps) or diversion programs (e.g., work release) are available to the court, eligibility requirements often explicitly exclude those who are physically or mentally handicapped.

Recent studies show that MR offenders are most often convicted of property crimes (often arson and theft)—although a minority are convicted of violent and sex-related offenses (often assault, indecent exposure, and pedophilia).[8] Legislative changes in sentencing laws in the 1980s made it routine to send such offenders to prison for long terms. California increased its prison population by 400% between 1980 and 1993 (to 125,605 inmates), yet only 27% of the additional prison space confined people convicted of violent offenses; the remaining 73% were convicted of nonviolent crimes (Zimring & Hawkins, 1997). Recidivism rates for MR offenders are fairly high; therefore, MR offenders are increasingly coming under mandatory sentencing laws, such as California's Three Strikes Law, which requires imprisonment for all but the first conviction.[9]

INCARCERATION, PAROLE, AND RECIDIVISM

While in prison or jail, it is estimated that less than 10% of all inmates with MR receive any specialized services, even if the system officially identifies them (Hall, 1992). California, for example, identifies some inmates as K class offenders, but they receive no special services and are mainstreamed with the general prison population. Housed with the general prison population, the offenders with MR are often cruelly abused or victimized (Sobsey, 1994). Their personal property may be stolen, they may be forced to participate in homosexual acts (increasing exposure to AIDS), or they may be used by more intelligent inmates to violate institutional rules.

The responses of MR inmates to such threatening situations are more likely to be physical than verbal or intellectual. The result is that MR inmates are more prone to getting into fights and becoming correctional management problems, both because of their outbursts and their high profile for victimization by others. The offender with MR takes up an inordinate amount of staff time, and many are eventually reclassified to a higher (and more expensive) security level and moved to maximum-security cells. Their poor institutional behavior and "over-classification" also means that they fail to earn good-time or work-time credits, are unable to participate in institutional or early release programs, and in states with parole, fail to become eligible for parole because they have not finished the programs or procedures required for parole consideration.

When inmates with MR are considered for parole release, they will likely have a poor prison record with little program participation, many infractions and violations, and a very weak postdischarge plan. Also, inmates with MR generally do not do well in interviews with the parole board, because those types of intense verbal interactions are particularly difficult for them. The result is that MR offenders end up serving a greater portion of their court-imposed sentence than non-MR offenders.[10]

When released, there is usually no distinction made between MR and non-MR parolees, and the likelihood is that people with MR will be no more successful at navigating the parole supervision situation than they were at being a successful inmate within the correctional institution. Placed on regular supervision caseloads and told to abide by strict rules and procedures (e.g., report to parole officer, get a job, submit to drug testing, and pay victim restitution), they often experience technical and other rule violations. Moreover, with few rehabilitation programs suited to their special needs, they have little opportunity to participate in substance abuse, education, and/or work training programs. Now possessing a criminal record, the MR offender will have almost no possibility of getting a job. Even for nondisabled persons, studies have shown that any involvement with the criminal justice system (even an unsubstantiated arrest) significantly lowers employment prospects (Hagan, 1993). For offenders with MR, such stigmatization is likely to be devastating.

Resulting rearrest rates are correspondingly high, and the cycle described above repeats itself (New York State Office of Mental Retardation and Developmental Disabilities, 1987).

In sum, it appears that offenders with MR do more time, do harder time, get less out of their time, and are more likely to be returned to prison after release than persons who are not mentally handicapped. Clearly, this situation is intolerable. It not only raises questions of fundamental equality under the law but also offends our sense of common decency when our weakest and most vulnerable citizens are further subjected to an unduly harsh and victimizing legal system. It is not that we wish to excuse the crimes of the MR, but rather, we wish to create a fairer system—one that provides appropriate treatment, protection from victimization, and equal opportunity for rehabilitation.

THE PROBLEM IS LIKELY TO WORSEN

Although the details above may be new to some, this troubling situation is well known to corrections professionals. Interviews conducted in recent months with officials throughout the nation reveal a heightened awareness and concern for the handling (and more accurately, the mishandling) of MR persons in correctional facilities.[11] Officials realize that this group requires greater patience, assistance, and specialized programming, and yet, due to prison crowding, staff are increasingly unable to provide it. As Rowan (1976) noted more than 20 years ago, "The care and treatment of MR offenders is one of the most consistently frustrating problems that confront administrators of both correctional institutions and facilities for the retarded. Both types of facilities are geared to treat their predominant groups, and offenders with mental retardation are misfits in both settings" (p. 4).

Experts predict the problem will worsen considerably over the next several years, as the factors known to be associated with MR and DD prevalence increase. Factors related to epidemiological rates of MR and related developmental disabilities are prenatal care, low birth weight, adolescent pregnancy, and substance abuse during pregnancy (Fryers, 1993; President's Commission on Mental Retardation, 1988). Fetal Alcohol Syndrome and prenatal substance abuse are major causes of MR.

Moreover, a greater number of young people of all intellectual abilities are now under correctional control, and the rates are increasing fastest for Black minority youth living in the inner city. Mauer (1990) estimated that in 1990, 1 in 4 young Black men (ages 20 to 29) was under correctional control—meaning either in jail, in prison, on probation, or on parole. By 1995, he found a worsening situation, with 1 in 3 young Black men under correctional control (Mauer & Huling, 1995). More young persons are choosing to commit crime, and the MR are easy prey for their delinquent peers, both as victims and accomplices. As one Los Angeles police officer noted, "With the growth of gangs in urban areas of California, we are finding greater incidence of exploitation of the mentally retarded offender in criminal activities."

It is also now well established that abuse as a child increases the chances of perpetrating crime later in life by the victims themselves. One recent national study showed that being the victim of abuse and neglect as a child increases the chances of later juvenile delinquency and adult criminality by 40% (Widom, 1995). And importantly, recent studies also show that children with disabilities suffer significantly higher rates of criminal abuse than children without disabilities. Considerable research demonstrates that both children and adults with disabilities experience greater risks of criminal physical abuse and sexual assault; minimally, it is estimated that they are at least twice as likely to suffer sexual assault (Sobsey, 1994). Moreover, research shows that abuse against disabled persons is reported at a much lower rate, and results in fewer prosecutions and convictions, than crimes against nondisabled persons (Sobsey, 1994). As a result, the criminal justice system seldom intervenes, and the disabled victim often suffers repeated victimization. Sobsey and Doe (1991) found that of the 86% of women with developmental disabilities in their study who had been sexually assaulted, half of them had been sexually assaulted 10 or more times. This situation has led one author to observe that disabled persons are "invisible victims"—unnoticed and unprotected by the justice system (Sorensen, 1997).

These facts, coupled with an overall trend toward deinstitutionalizing large numbers of MR persons, have led to a rise in the number of such persons who live on the streets or in shelters. Lakin and Prouty (1996) report that in 1994, national MR institution populations were barely one third of their 1967 populations, decreasing from 194,650 to 65,735 over the time period. Ironically, of the 99 state institutions closed or planned for closing between 1970 and 2000, the majority have become state and federal correctional facilities; and the staff, laid off from the state MR institutions, are being hired to staff the new jails and prisons (Braddock, Hemp, Bacheldner, & Fajiura, 1995). For many MR offenders, the well-intentioned deinstituionalization movement has produced disastrous effects. Many get released from state mental hospitals to community settings with few services and little support. Without services, many flounder and eventually come to the attention of the police and the courts. The result is they end up trading one institutional address for another, and the number of MR persons in correctional institutions continues to grow.

It is troubling that the size of the MR (and other low-income) populations living in the community under poor conditions and the American prison population both increased dramatically in the 1980s. The U.S. prison population quadrupled during the last decade, whereas the average rate of poverty increased 17% overall and for African American children increased an astonishing 44% (U.S. Department of Commerce, 1994). Worse, the growth of each seemed to feed off the growth of the other. This is because funding for prison expansion came largely at the expense of funding for programs designed to alleviate poor community conditions.

For example, the California state budget for 1997–1998 proposes the largest spending increase (11%) for corrections-related programs. In contrast, proposed 1997–1998 spending for social services programs declines by 7% (Legislative Analysts Office, 1997–1998). In California, this upward spending trend for corrections, coupled with a downward trend in social services spending, began in the late 1980s. Between 1988 and 1998, the state adopted a series of reductions in both grants to low-income persons in families with children under the Aid to Families With Dependent Children (AFDC), and grants to elderly, blind or disabled persons under Supplementary Security Income (SSI) (Legislative Analysts Office, 1997–1998). Programs to support employment, training, welfare, and health-related programs for the low-income and disabled persons were cut. We spend billions of dollars to lock up hundreds of thousands of people while cutting billions of dollars for programs that might provide them opportunities to avoid committing crime in the first place. In this context, an increase in the prevalence of MR and other low-income persons within the California justice system is expected.

ESTIMATING THE SCOPE OF THE CURRENT CALIFORNIA PROBLEM

No one knows the exact number of MR housed in jail or prison, or on probation or parole. Such statistics are not maintained for any of these populations, and only for the prison population have national estimates been attempted. In fact, all available data on the prevalence rates or characteristics of persons with MR or DD within the criminal justice system must be viewed with extreme caution. Despite universal agreement that individuals with MR are not handled appropriately in the justice system, little official attention has been paid to the problem, and basic statistics in every aspect of the problem are lacking.

The most recent estimate of the prevalence of MR and other disabilities in the prison population comes from a survey of all federal and state prisons by Veneziano and Veneziano (1996). Researchers asked each facility for information on inmates with the following five types of disability: visual deficits, mobility or orthopedic deficit, hearing deficit, speech deficit, and psychological disability. Administrators reported the results shown in Table 1, estimating that 4.2% of all prison inmates are MR and 10.7% are learning disabled. These authors had conducted a similar survey in 1987, and at that time, found that 1.8% of the prison population was MR (Veneziano, Veneziano, & Tribolet, 1987). These data suggest that the national prevalence rate of MR in prisons has more than doubled—in fact, increased by 133%—in less than a decade.[12]

If the prevalence of persons with MR in California prisons is similar to the national estimate of 4.2% (and there are reasons to believe it might be higher), then at a minimum, we estimate that the California Youth Authority (CYA) now houses about 360 MR youths and the California Department of Corrections (CDC) now houses about 6,000 MR adults. There are no national estimates of the prevalence of offenders with MR on probation, so as a conservative estimate for that population, we use half the institutional rate, or 2.1% (see Table 2). If we included those who are borderline retarded (defined as having an IQ of between 70 and 85) or the broader category of the developmentally disabled, the figures would be significantly higher.

TABLE 1

Percentages of Total U.S. Prison Populations With Disabilities

Type of Disability	Percentage Prevalence
Physical disabilities	
Visual deficit	0.2
Mobility or orthopedic deficit	0.3
Other major health problems	14.2
Cancer	0.2
Cardiovascular disease	3.4
Diabetes	3.1
Epilepsy	0.9
Hypertension	6.6
Human immunodeficiency virus (HIV)	2.4
Communicative disabilities	
Hearing deficit	0.2
Speech deficit	0.06
Psychological disabilities	
Learning disabilities	10.7
Mental retardation	4.2
Psychotic disorders	7.2
Other psychological disorders	12.0

Note: All figures, except for the HIV rate, are from Veneziano and Veneziano (1996). The HIV estimate is from the Bureau of Justice Statistics (1995). Neither study reports multiple conditions.

Some may argue that relative to the total of 700,788 persons under correctional control in California, 21,479 persons with MR are not a high-priority problem. As Brown and Courtless noted in 1971, when the problem was much less pronounced, "the problem of the mentally retarded offender is small in absolute numbers and large in significance" (p. 77). The problem is now both large and significant.

FINDING WORKABLE SOLUTIONS

Recognizing the problem is far easier than identifying a solution. Philosophically, the issue of how to handle the MR in criminal justice matters quickly becomes mired in debates concerning normalization. Nirje (1969) defined normalization as "making available to the mentally retarded patterns and conditions of everyday life which are as close as possible to the norms and patterns of the mainstream of society" (p. 369). If full normalization is the goal (and to many MR advocates, it is), then, logically, it follows that people with MR are fully responsible for complying with normal laws and expectations, and violations should result in the same kinds of punishments given to those without such disabilities. Yet, MR professionals profusely debate how the normalization concept should be applied to corrections. The emerging consensus within the profession seems to be that there are highly unique aspects to the correctional environment and that the normalization goals for the MR should not fully apply in this setting (Association of Retarded Citizens, 1992).

TABLE 2

Mentally Retarded Offenders in California Corrections (estimated)

	1996 Offender Population	Percentage Mentally Retarded (MR)
Adults		
Probation	300,000	6,300
Jail	66,358	2,654
Parole	98,013	4,116
Prison	141,017	5,923
Adult total	605,388	18,993
Juveniles		
Probation	70,000	1,470
Halls	6,400	256
Ranches and camps	4,000	160
California Youth Authority	9,000	360
Parole	6,000	240
Juvenile total	95,400	2,486
Combined total	700,788	21,479

Note: The population figures are from the California Department of Corrections; the California Youth Authority; the California Probation, Parole, and Corrections Association; Legislative Analysts Office; and the U.S. Bureau of Justice Statistics.

Beyond these philosophical debates, there are also serious practical problems. Is it really beneficial to identify MR offenders? As Petrella (1992) observed, many defendants with MR are identified and then unidentified because it better serves their legal interests. The common assumption that if only individuals with MR were identified, they would be appropriately served, may not be valid. Sometimes, the MR label creates more difficulties and limits the available options more significantly than any lack of identification.

If identification is deemed desirable, how and at what point in the process should MR persons be identified? What types of additional training would criminal justice personnel need to more accurately identify and appropriately handle the MR offender? If programs were developed, which MR offenders could be successfully diverted to them: That is, what types of programs seem to work, for which offenders, and at what cost? Which agencies should be responsible for operating such programs, and what collaboration is necessary? If incarceration is warranted, what are the implications of different housing arrangements? Should the MR be segregated from the rest of the population, housed with the total inmate population, or something in between? Do specialized probation and parole caseloads make a difference to offender success and recidivism rates? What expectations are reasonable for supervising the MR offender on probation or parole? And the important unanswered questions go on and on.

It is not that these questions cannot be answered but, rather, we have not devoted the public policy attention necessary to answering them. The MR offender has never attracted the attention that other specialized populations have or that their numbers alone should warrant. For example, we spend inordinate amounts of time and energy debating programs and policies for elderly inmates, child molesters, spouse assaulters, and offenders with AIDS. Yet, often, their prevalence is less than that for offenders with MR or DD. As shown in Table 1, for example, about 2% of federal and state prison inmates are known to be infected with the HIV virus that causes AIDS, and yet there are hundreds of articles, federal data-collection activities, and special study groups and conferences on the topic. It is not that the AIDS issue is unimportant, but rather that one wonders why there is no similar scholarly or policy attention paid to the MR offender. As Talent and Keldgord (1975) wrote, "Less effort has been expended in the US to the MR offender than any other group of offenders" (p. 23). Their statement is still true more than 20 years later.

Some believe that the lack of attention reflects a long history of callous disregard for the lives of individuals with MR and a constant devaluing of their worth. Others suggest it results from the fact that MR offenders lack a committed, well-organized and fiscally sound advocacy group. Whatever the reason, it is certainly true that the topic has garnered little scholarly, public, or policy interest.

It is not that the issue has received no attention. President Kennedy, whose sister was MR, created the President's Committee on Mental Retardation in 1962. Over the ensuing years, it tackled a number of issues related to MR and in 1989, sponsored a presidential forum on the special issues that arise when people with MR commit crimes or become crime victims. Subsequently, the papers presented at the forum were published in *The Criminal Justice System and Mental Retardation* (Conley, Luckasson, & Bouthilet, 1992), which remains the major piece of scholarly work in this field.[13] Dick Thornberg, then the attorney general of the United States, in writing the foreword to the book, called on the justice system to develop special procedures for the appropriate handling of persons with mental disabilities. Thornberg wrote the following:

> Disabled offenders must at times be treated differently from others to ensure protection of their rights and to ensure an equal opportunity to benefit from services. People with mental retardation cannot be "processed" exactly like others who come into contact with the criminal justice system because, for them, it may be a system they do not understand or a system that does not understand them. Thus, we must take care to ensure that our criminal justice system does not compound the challenges that individuals with disabilities face in other aspects of their lives. (p. xvi)

The President's Committee on Mental Retardation encouraged a major program of national reform, incorporating legal, program, and policy changes. They outlined the necessary training and agency collaboration that was needed; described exemplary program models; and encouraged a serious program of national data collection, research, and program demonstration.

Despite their good intentions and the high quality of the undertaking, the committee's report never got the attention it deserved, and most of the recommendations were never implemented. Prison crowding and budget shortfalls reached catastrophic proportions in the early 1990s, and corrections officials became singularly preoccupied with providing enough secure cells to house an increasing number of inmates. Dollars had to be allocated, and prisons and jails had to be sited and built. Concerns for individualized justice gave way to the doctrine "do the crime, do the time." The U.S. prison population exploded, increasing from 319,598 in 1980 to 1,182,169 in 1996, a 370% increase (Bureau of Justice Statistics, 1997). Probation, parole, and jail populations grew similarly, but their budgets did not increase commensurately, and in many counties, dollars to support local probation and jail services actually declined, whereas populations more than doubled (Petersilia, 1997b). Within this context, then, focusing on any one special offender population—regardless of their recognized differences—simply became impossible. And, offenders with MR do not seem to be anyone's primary responsibility. Correctional programs cannot handle the health and behavioral problems, and mental health programs cannot handle the criminal or disruptive behavior. In our interviews, we continually heard that this was a group that concerned professionals, but that it "wasn't really their problem." However, a few jurisdictions have implemented special corrections programs for the MR offender, and their success rate appears high. Although few formal program evaluations exist, persons who operate and fund the programs believe they protect the public, teach the offender with MR to obey the law, and save tax dollars. For example,

- The Boston MassCAPP (Community Assistance Parole Program) is operated by the Massachusetts Parole Board to provide MR parolees with extra assistance on prison release. Although parolees who are MR have the same parole conditions on release as other inmates, they are given additional help in following them. MassCAPP uses volunteer community assistants to assist the parole offender by providing advocacy, positive role modeling, and guidance in use of leisure time, and academic training or tutoring. MassCAPP also provides a weekly counseling group and resource meeting led by a forensic psychologist and a social work intern. The program, funded by the state, has been operating for 15 years and is judged highly successful.

- Texas has a wide variety of programs within and outside institutions. In Fort Worth, Volunteers of America works with the Adult Probation Department in specialized programs for MR probationers. The goal of the 24-hour residential program includes eliminating drug and alcohol problems, obtaining employment, and developing basic hygiene and survival skills. All inmates entering the Texas Department of Corrections (DOC) are given group intelligence tests. Inmates identified as MR are transferred to a specified unit where they receive habilation, social support, and help in pre- and post-release planning.

- Cuyahoga County: Cleveland, Ohio; Tucson, Arizona; and Lancaster County, Pennsylvania, all operate exemplary programs for probationers with MR. Each of these programs incorporates a wide variety of activities designed to assist the probationer in the community with social support and vocational education, but most also involve an educational component. The educational component attempts to familiarize the person with MR with the workings of the justice system and the law.

- New York has a number of small residential halfway houses specifically for the MR offender. These programs, which accept both full-time residents and day-reporting offenders, accept referrals from corrections facilities throughout the state, and can be used as a probation alternative, a prison or jail diversion, or as a means of transitioning from prison. Individuals receive training on basic skills, as well as training on building socialization skills.

- The Association of Retarded Citizens (Arc), a voluntary national organization with chapters in every state, operates the Developmentally Disabled Offenders Program (DDOP) in New Jersey. The DDOP is one of the few programs nationwide that specifically provides alternatives to incarceration for defendants with DD and MR. The program, directed by an attorney with a background in criminal law, acts as a liaison between the criminal justice and human services systems. DDOP, through the use of a personalized justice plan (PJP), offers the court alternatives to incarceration by identifying community supports and programs to appropriately treat and sanction disabled offenders. If the PJP is accepted by the judge, the offender is diverted to DDOP and then appropriately monitored by probation staff and Arc volunteers until the sentence is completed. The DDOP also provides training and technical assistance to professionals on matters relating to identifying and processing disabled defendants, as well as developing materials for disabled persons on what to do if they are arrested. The Arc of New

Mexico operates a similar program called the Justice Advocacy Project (Reynolds & Berkobien, 1997).

The goal of all these programs is to help offenders attain the skills and discipline needed so that they can live independent, productive, and crime-free lives. Program operators say that such programs help break the cycle of crime and recidivism, and as such, end up saving taxpayers money.

THE GROWING SIGNIFICANCE OF THE MENTALLY HANDICAPPED OFFENDER TO CORRECTIONS POLICY

The MR in corrections are attracting renewed policy interest for two reasons. First, as states continue to struggle to fund the growth in prison populations, the positive experiences of specialized MR programs are attracting attention as a means of diverting low-risk inmates to community-based programs, thereby saving the state the cost of providing an expensive prison or jail cell. Second, public interest law firms have begun to file class action civil rights lawsuits against correctional facilities for their failure to apply the Americans with Disabilities Act (ADA) to the MR population within corrections facilities. The California DOC, housing the largest prison population in the nation, is currently the subject of such a lawsuit: *Clark and Woods v. California.*

DEVELOPING INTERMEDIATE SANCTIONS FOR OFFENDERS WITH MR

In the past decade, every state in the nation has experimented with intermediate sanction programs (ISPs). ISPs are community-based programs that are tougher than traditional probation, but less stringent and expensive than prison. The most popular intermediate sanctions are intensive probation supervision, house arrest, electronic monitoring, substance abuse treatment, and boot camps. All these programs are considerably cheaper to operate than prison because they do not require the state to provide secure structures, guards, food, or the other round-the-clock expenses of prison. Hundreds of programs have been implemented, primarily in the hopes of saving money, and the evaluation evidence is in: they have not saved the dollars that program proponents had hoped for (Tonry and Lynch, 1996).

The problem is basically one of "target group." ISPs will only save prison funds if those who would have otherwise served a significant time in prison are diverted to them. But, those sentenced to longer than average prison terms are likely to have been convicted of serious property or person offenses or have lengthy criminal records (hence, the longer sentence), and that is exactly the group that the public wants to remain in prison. As such, intermediate sanction programs have ended up serving as a prison diversion program only for very low-risk prisoners, usually those returned to prison for a technical violation of their probation or parole conditions, rather than the commission of a new offense. But because such persons serve only a few months' prison time, diverting them to the community may serve justice goals, but the prison cost savings are negligible. Recent California analysis by Petersilia (1997a) reveals that technical violators and other lower risk inmates serve, on average, about 4 months in prison, at a state (operational) cost of about $7,300 per inmate. (The average time served in CDC is now 21 months.) Diverting these persons to community-based ISP programs, which often last for 1 year, may actually end up costing the state more, especially if the programs employ more intensive surveillance that detects a higher rate of violations and thus results in increased recommitments to prison.

The system is caught in a catch-22: To realize true cost savings through intermediate sanctions, one must identify segments of the prison population who are both nonserious (so that the public and judiciary will support their diversion, and public safety is not compromised) and who now spend a significant time in prison (so that true cost savings are realized).

The offender with MR represents an ideal target group for ISPs. As discussed above, the MR offender is usually convicted of less serious offenses but spends a longer than average term in prison due to institutional behavior and an inability to participate in early release programs or to put together an acceptable prerelease plan. Because of poor prison behavior, this inmate requires greater attention and therefore larger staffing. Eventually, the MR inmate may be reclassified to a higher security status, and as a medium or maximum inmate, he or she is occupying a more expensive prison cell. California estimates that the construction costs alone for a maximum-security cell average $113,000 each, whereas a minimum-security cell costs $60,000 each. The 2:1 cost differential between maximum- and minimum-security inmates also applies to operational costs that now average about $21,000 per year per inmate (Lasley, Hooper, & Dery, 1997). These cells could be more appropriately reserved for violent, repeat offenders.[14]

Finally, there is emerging evidence that the offenders with MR can be safely supervised in intermediate sanctions given the right support, and importantly, that recidivism can be reduced—meaning that the costs of subsequent incarcerations are also avoided. The Lancaster County, Pennsylvania, intensive probation or parole program for MR offenders reports maintaining a 5% recidivism rate, compared to the often-cited national rate of 60% (White & Wood, 1986).

Importantly, there is also likely to be widespread public support for handling the MR offender outside of an institution. Officials interviewed during the past several months continually voiced their concern over the mishandling of this population and often noted that sending these persons to prison or jail was not out of malevolence but rather because of a lack of options. As one person observed, "Nine out of the ten times, it is the lack of alternatives, not the nastiness of the court, that sends the mentally retarded to miserable incarceration."

OFFENDERS WITH MR, CORRECTIONS, AND THE AMERICANS WITH DISABILITIES ACT (ADA)

The ADA, signed into law July 26, 1990, bans discrimination based on disability and guarantees equal opportunity for individuals with disabilities in employment, transportation, state and local government services, and public accommodations. It is generally conceded that the ADA is probably the most sweeping civil rights legislation passed since the enactment of the Civil Rights Act of 1964. Of importance, the ADA has provided the foundation for court intervention on the operations of correctional agencies on behalf of MR inmates. Significant litigation has already began and will likely accelerate in the near future. There is no doubt that such litigation will profoundly affect the manner in which corrections identifies and treats MR inmates. The ADA significantly expands the requirements previously defined in *Ruiz v. Estelle* (1980), which, until the ADA was passed, represented the most comprehensive attempt by the federal judiciary to intervene in the operation of a correctional agency. It profoundly affected how Texas handles MR offenders, establishing the first statewide correctional screening process for their identification and programming specifically targeted toward their specialized needs.

Two recent Department of Justice reports have been written to assist states in interpreting the implications of the ADA for corrections. The reports by Rubin and McCampbell (1994, 1995) make clear that states are no longer able to mainstream MR offenders, with little or no recognition of how their disability affects their corrections experience. ADA requires that all corrections agencies (including probation, parole, jail, and prisons) establish screening and rehabilitation programs specifically for offenders with MR. The ADA further requires that each correctional facility and program evaluate each program, service, and activity in such a way so that, when viewed in its entirety, the program service or activity is readily accessible to and usable by eligible inmates with disabilities. Legally, corrections must now examine all programs— including work release, parole heatings, education, recreation, substance and alcohol abuse, boot camps, halfway houses, community service, and visitation —and facilities to assure that procedures do not eliminate eligible inmates from programs and services on the basis of a mental disability. In short, the ADA (1990) requires that all corrections programs be "readily accessible and usable" by inmates with MR.

As the ADA mandates have become clearer, so too has the fact that most corrections systems are not in compliance. In April of 1996, the Prison Law Office (PLO) and two private law firms filed a class action civil rights suit on behalf of all MR inmates in California against Governor Pete Wilson, the director of the CDC, and various state officials. Believed to be the first statewide, class action civil rights suit filed on behalf of MR prison inmates since the passage of the ADA, the case was filed in the U.S. District Court in San Francisco under the ADA and for violations of the Sixth, Eighth and Fourteenth Amendments of the U.S. Constitution.

The suit, *Clark and Woods v. California*, alleges that Derrick Clark and Ambrose Woods, two CDC inmates with mental retardation, and others similarly situated cannot "obtain necessary and adequate accommodations, protection, and services necessitated by their disabilities as required by the US Constitution and federal law." Furthermore, because they cannot adapt to prison without such accommodations, protection and services, they are more likely to be "beaten or raped than non-disabled prisoners, to be manipulated by other prisoners, are less able to comprehend and to comply with prison rules and procedures than non-developmentally disabled prisoners, and do not have access to the full range of services and privileges available to non-developmentally disabled prisoners" (p. 2). The suit asserts that Clark has been continually abused by other inmates and has not been separated from the general prison population, despite staff recommendations that he be removed. Woods has been denied access to prison work and education programs as a result of his disability, and was rejected from a reading class because he was "too stupid."

Clark and Woods v. California is now proceeding through the U.S. District Court, Northern District of California, but, a resolution is not expected quickly. There is no doubt that the case—and those that will undoubtedly follow in other states—will mandate that the DOC implement revised procedures for the special handling of the MR within corrections. Debate will likely center on the desirability of one of three policy positions: segregation and the use of special facilities; normalization and mainstreaming within the general prison populations; or the use of alternatives to incarceration. But, without empirical data on characteristics of MR inmates, the kinds of crimes they commit, and what programs and procedures work best, in what settings, and for whom, changes are likely to be ill informed and misguided.

ANSWERING THE IMPORTANT QUESTIONS

There is a serious need for more and better information on offenders with MR. At a minimum, we need to know the following:

- What is the prevalence of MR offenders coming into contact with various correctional agencies—probation, parole, jail, and prison—in different states? How does their mental handicap affect their interactions with justice agencies?
- What training is now provided correctional personnel regarding the characteristics, behavior, and handling of MR offenders? Do corrections agencies make any distinctions made between mentally ill, MR, and DD offenders?
- What systems are used, in different states, to identify the MR offender at different points in the correctional system? If identified or more information on the offender's disability is known—or known at different stages in the process—what difference does it make in decision making?
- What have been the demonstrated and perceived effects of alternative approaches to correctional handling of MR inmates—on costs, system management, and offender performance?

There are no simplistic solutions to the problem of the mentally handicapped offender in corrections. For one thing, there are a multitude of local jails, probation, parole, and prisons throughout the nation, each of which operates rather independently when it comes to these issues, and most are already overburdened in dealing with their "dominant" populations. The author does believe, however, that more knowledge and analysis could significantly influence the priority the nation places on this topic and the program and policy changes that are considered. In short, the issue of the MR offender needs to be brought to the forefront of corrections policy attention.

There will probably always be some persons who, like Silva, continue to sit in prison and jail cells bewildered and unable to comprehend and negotiate correctional rules and conditions. But, hopefully the numbers will decrease, and it should not be because we have "swept these persons" under the rug or failed to devote sufficient energy and analysis to considering alternative options. If a culture is measured by how it treats its weakest members, then the handling of the mentally handicapped in corrections reveals an American justice system at its basest. As Sobsey (1994) put it, "We must strive to make right what is currently so very wrong" (p. 370). Our respect for the human rights of all persons and our system of justice demands no less.

NOTES

1. The most widely accepted definition of mental retardation (MR; also stands for mentally retarded) is that developed by the American Association on Mental Deficiency (AAMD). This definition states that MR is based on "significant subaverage general intellectual functioning existing concurrently with deficits in adaptive behavior" (AAMD, 1983, p. 1). An IQ level below 70 is the criteria for measuring the deficit in intellectual function for retardation.

2. A developmental disability (DD) may be defined as a severe chronic disability attributable to a mental or physical impairment that manifests before age 22 and is likely to continue indefinitely. DDs may consist of epilepsy, MR, and/or severe learning disabilities. The California Department of Developmental Services estimates that 86% of those served by the state system for those labeled DD, are MR.

3. Despite the common perception that the MR population commits many violent crimes, studies show that the majority of offenses committed by MR persons are less serious offenses (although data on the subject is rare and affected by selection biases). See Illinois Retarded and Mentally Ill Offender Task Force (1988) and White and Wood (1986).

4. The earliest reported estimate of the MR of offenders appears to have been made by Zeleny (1933), who examined the intelligence tests of more than 60,000 inmates and reported that the number of retarded offenders was close to 30% of the inmate population. A more comprehensive effort was conducted by Brown and Courtless (1971) who reported that 9.5% of the inmate population was MR (IQ below 70). Texas reported a rate of 10% for adult offenders and 12% to 16% for juvenile offenders, Georgia estimated its figure to be 27% for prison inmates, and the South Carolina Department of Corrections reported a figure of 8% (Santamour & Watson, 1982).

The varying estimates result from different testing instruments and methods, and underlying differences in the prevalence rates across the nation.

5. See McAfee and Gural (1988) who found that 75% of MR offenders were not identified at arrest, and more than 10% were not identified until they were in prison.

6. MR and mental illness (MI) are quite distinct conditions. MR refers to subaverage intellectual functioning; MI has nothing to do with IQ. A person with MI may be a genius or subaverage. MR refers to impairment in social adaptation; a person with MI may be very competent socially but have a character disorder. MR is usually present at birth; MI may strike at any time. The intellectual impairment of MR is permanent; MI is often temporary and in many cases reversible. An MR person can be expected to behave rationally at his or her operational level; a person with MI may vacillate between normal and irrational behavior. MR persons are unlikely to be violent except in those situations that cause violence in non-MR persons; a person with MI may be erratic and violent (see Montgomery, 1982). There is no accurate count of the number of the mentally ill in correctional institutions, but it has been estimated that 5% to 10% of incarcerated inmates reveal serious psychopathology, and more than half could be diagnosed as having some type of psychiatric problem, most commonly a personality disorder. See McShane (1996) for a complete discussion.

7. The President's Committee on Mental Retardation (1991) noted that MR persons are in a uniquely damned position before the courts. If their disability remains undetected, the chances of receiving special court handling are impossible. But if the impairment is recognized, he may receive a long, institutional commitment without a trial for the alleged offense, because very often laws make no distinction between MI—where a lengthy civil commitment is possible without a criminal conviction—and MR.

8. It is important to point out that selection biases seriously affect our ability to know the distribution of crime types committed by MR or DD offenders or their personal characteristics. Criminal justice agencies do not routinely test or record the MR or DD condition unless some unusual behavior on the part of the offender brings it to their attention. This selection bias means that those who are IQ tested do not represent the MR or DD population at large but rather a biased subpopulation (e.g., those who are "acting out"). Much of the literature inappropriately uses such data to describe the general characteristics of MR or DD offenders. For example, it is asserted that a high proportion of MR offenders are dual diagnosed as MI (Rockowitz [1986] estimates the figure to be as high as 40%). Clearly, this high prevalence rate is due to selection biases in the population studied. Offenders often do not get IQ tested unless they are exhibiting unusual behavior, which is more characteristic of persons with MI. Therefore, those who get IQ tested have a higher probability of having both the MR and MI conditions, whereas the prevalence rate of dual diagnosis in the overall MR or DD population would be much lower if all (not just a select group) of MR persons were IQ tested. Such selection biases influence much of the data we have on MR and DD offenders, making them appear more handicapped and seriously criminal than they are.

9. Frank Zimring's 1997 analysis of the increase in California's prison population showed that "the greatest impact of the growth in the California prison population since 1980 has been on convictions for burglary and thefts, two nonviolent offenses that have experienced 366% and 635% increases" (p. 23). In 1996, about 59% of inmates incarcerated in California prisons were convicted of nonviolent offenses (Legislative Analysts Office, 1997–1998). The same is true with the growth in the U.S. prison population—fully 84% of the increase in state and federal prison admissions

since 1980 was accounted for by nonviolent offenders (Bureau of Justice Statistics, 1996). These crimes are exactly the ones MR offenders are usually convicted of.

10. Lampert (1987) observed that in a sample of Texas prisoners, inmates with MR served a significantly longer portion of their sentence when contrasted to inmates with normal intelligence.

11. As part of this RAND research project, informal telephone and personal interviews were conducted by the author with about two dozen persons interested in the issue of the developmentally disabled offender. These persons represented criminal justice and mental health agencies, citizen advocacy groups, and national associations for the MR. All interviews were conducted in the spring and summer of 1997.

12. It is also important to note that estimates of MR incarcerated youth are much higher than those for adults and have been estimated to be as high as 40% (Wolford, Nelson, & Rutherford, 1997). The higher rate is probably because legal mandates require correctional agencies to test for the MR condition so that required special education services can be provided according to the Education of the Handicapped Act (PL 94-142) and its amendments (PL 101-476, the Individuals With Disabilities Education Act of 1990).

13. The other major treatise of the topic is published in Santamour and Watson (1982).

14. There is also evidence that adopting special procedures for the MR while in jail or prison reduces the number and severity of disciplinary infractions and reduces staff time necessary to supervise such inmates (Hall, 1992).

CHAPTER 9 The Death Penalty

9.1 JON SORENSEN AND DONALD H. WALLACE

Prosecutorial Discretion in Seeking Death

Many criminal justice investigators believe that the imposition of the death penalty in the United States has developed into a systematic pattern of differential treatment of nonwhite minorities. Indeed, about 42 percent of all death row inmates are black—more than three times their representation in the U.S. population. Nearly half of all prisoners executed in the United States since 1976 have been nonwhite minorities, and in 83 percent of these cases the race of the victim has been white. One of the most troubling statistics concerning the imposition of capital punishment in the United States is that a black man is 20 times more likely to be executed for killing a white man than is a white man for killing a black man. Jurists, legal scholars, and social scientists have looked to the U.S. Supreme Court to redress the effects of racism in the application of the death penalty. Yet the major capital punishment cases handed down by the Court concerning the application of the death penalty in the United States indicate that the Court has moved from a position of formally recognizing that imposition of the death penalty is imbued with racial prejudice, as noted in *Furman v. Georgia* (1972); to imposing what many believe are meaningless procedural safeguards established in *Gregg v. Georgia* (1976); to acceptance of the risk of racial prejudice in imposing the death penalty in *McCleskey v. Kemp* (1987). The U.S. Supreme Court held in *McCleskey* that empirically based statistical evidence showing that blacks who kill whites are more likely to be executed than white defendants who kill blacks does not "prove that race enters into any capital sentencing decisions or that race was a factor in petitioners' cases."

The following selection is from "Prosecutorial Discretion in Seeking Death: An Analysis of Racial Disparity in the Pretrial Stages of Case Processing in a Midwestern County," *Justice Quarterly* (September 1999). In it, Jon Sorensen, an associate professor of criminal justice at the University of Texas, Pan American, and Donald H. Wallace, a professor of criminal justice at Central Missouri State University, examine prosecutorial discretion in post-*McCleskey* capital trials. They find that black defendants with white victims are more likely to be charged with aggravated murder and tried as capital offenders than other defendant-victim racial combinations. To these researchers, prosecutorial discretion amounts to intentional discrimination against black defendants with white victims.

Key Concept: the race factor in death penalty cases and prosecutorial discretion in capital cases

*I*n *the 1987 case of* McCleskey v. Kemp, *the U.S. Supreme Court appeared to foreclose the possibility of challenging racial bias in capital sentencing by using statistically based claims of discrimination.* McCleskey, *however, does not prevent a challenge to decisions made by particular individuals during the capital punishment process. In this study we examined pretrial decisions made by, or under the direction of, one prosecutor to determine whether those decisions had been influenced by race. We found that homicide cases involving black defendants and white victims fared worse than other racial combinations in all of the pretrial decisions made: They were more likely to result in first-degree murder charges, to be served notice of aggravating circumstances, and to proceed to capital trial.*

In the 1987 case of *McCleskey v. Kemp*, the U.S. Supreme Court appeared to foreclose the possibility of challenging racial bias in capital sentencing by using statistically based claims of discrimination. In that case, the appellant presented evidence from the most extensive empirical study ever conducted on racial bias in the administration of capital punishment (see Baldus, Woodworth, and Pulaski 1990). Although the study showed that race influenced the sentencing decision even after controlling for 230 nonracial variables, the Court held that the correlation between race and sentence did not rise to the level of constitutionally unacceptable risk in violation of the Eighth Amendment. Nor did the appellant meet his burden of proof under the equal protection clause of the Fourteenth Amendment which, according to the majority, required a showing of "purposeful discrimination" against the appellant.

The debate surrounding systemic racial bias in the administration of capital punishment did not end with the *McCleskey* decision. Prompted by Justice Powell's admonition that such questions are more appropriately addressed by legislatures, Congress ordered the Government Accounting Office (GAO) to conduct a study of racial bias in the administration of capital punishment in conjunction with the Anti Drug Abuse Act of 1988. More commonly known as the "drug kingpin" statute, that act included a provision for the death penalty as punishment for murders related to drug trafficking. According to the GAO report, victim's race influenced decision making in capital sentencing in 82 percent of the 28 empirical studies reviewed; this confirming the statistical findings presented to the Court in *McCleskey.*

Since that time, various members of Congress have proposed legislation that includes provisions for challenging capital convictions on the basis of racial bias in the court system using evidence similar to that employed in *McCleskey.* Various versions of a Racial Justice Act were introduced between 1988 and 1994 (Bedau 1997; also see Baldus et al. 1994). The proposed legislation would have empowered the federal courts to review capital cases for possible racial bias and to place the burden on the government to overcome a prima facie showing of racial bias (Bedau 1997). Although the resulting Omnibus Crime Control Bill passed the House in 1994, the House-Senate Conference Committee dropped that provision from the final version (Bedau 1997).

A report prepared for Congress in 1994 showed that 89 percent of the defendants selected by federal prosecutors for capital punishment under the drug kingpin statute were African American or Mexican American, whereas the majority of those charged under the general statute had been white (Subcommittee 1994). Despite overwhelming evidence of racial bias, the Violent Crime Control Act of 1994 added numerous offenses to the list of capital crimes, bringing to nearly 60 the number of federal crimes eligible for capital punishment. Although the proposed racial justice provisions were not included in the final enactment, Attorney General Reno instituted a protocol whereby a hearing was required before U.S. attorneys would be authorized to seek the death penalty. The protocol allows defense attorneys to challenge a prosecution on the grounds of racial bias. This appears, however, to be an empty formality; almost immediately after its implementation, it was bypassed in the Oklahoma City bombing prosecution (Christianson 1996).

In view of the refusal of Congress and the U.S. Supreme Court to remedy obvious instances of racial discrimination in implementing capital punishment, the question of statistical analyses of racial bias might appear at first to be purely academic. After all, federal and state courts have interpreted *McCleskey* broadly, routinely refusing to grant hearings on claims of racial discrimination in applying the death penalty (Baldus et al. 1994).[1] States initiating their own Racial Justice Acts have also enjoyed little success.[2] Further, in response to *McCleskey,* the State of California abandoned a probe into the issue of racial bias and the death penalty (Cox 1987).

Some states, however, offer more protection and potential remedies for racial discrimination in imposing capital punishment than does the federal government. The New Jersey Supreme Court has held that the level of disparity found in *McCleskey* would be considered significant under the Equal Protection Clause of the New Jersey Constitution (*State v. Marshall* 1992). It also appears that states with a comparative proportionality review process, such as New Jersey and Florida, are more likely than states without such a process, if it is taken seriously, to discover unexplained differences among cases involving particular racial categories and to treat those differences as constitutionally suspect (see *Foster v. State* 1992; *State v. Bey* 1994).

Despite *McCleskey* and the response of lower federal courts, there is still hope of remedy in federal court. The most immediate and most influential critics of the *McCleskey* decision were members of the U.S. Supreme Court. The 5–4 decision was fraught with internal inconsistencies. Justice Brennan, joined by the other dissenting justices, argued that the Baldus study showed that race probably entered into the decision in cases involving defendants convicted of killing white victims; such a capricious pattern of sentencing would show an equal protection violation if not for the majority's "crippling burden of proof" (*McCleskey* 1987:337). Ironically, Justice Lewis Powell, a prisoner in reconciling the demands of consistent sentencing and individual fairness, head of a commission charged with finding ways to accelerate the federal postconviction process in death penalty cases, and author of the majority opinion in *McCleskey*, admitted that the inability to conduct executions expeditiously and in a nonarbitrary and noncapricious manner had since led him to reject the post-*Furman* jurisprudence with which he had been so intimately involved. Referring to the Supreme Court's post-*Furman* jurisprudence as "a failed experiment," Powell said he regretted his decision in *McCleskey* (Jeffries 1994:451–54).

It is shortsighted to perceive that all race-based challenges to capital punishment in the Supreme Court are foreclosed by *McCleskey*. In its ruling the Court realized that it had to distinguish some cases in which it had accepted statistics as proof of intent to discriminate so as to establish a prima facie case. In *Arlington Heights v. Metropolitan Housing Dev. Corp.* (1977:266) the Court accepted statistical disparities as proof of an equal protection violation in the selection of the jury venire.[3] To prove employment discrimination under Title VII of the Civil Rights Act of 1964, the Court accepted similar statistics (*Bazemore v. Friday* 1986). The convincing point for the Court was the nature of the decision maker in these contexts, in contrast to the compositions of the numerous individual juries that had decided on the sentences in the Baldus et al. research.

> The decisions of a jury commission or of an employer over time are fairly attributable to the commission or the employer. Therefore, an unexplained statistical discrepancy can be said to indicate a consistent policy of the decision maker. The Baldus study seeks to deduce a state "policy" by studying the combined effects of the decisions of hundreds of juries that are unique in their composition. (*McCleskey v. Kemp* 1987:295, n.15).

An additional point convincing the Court was that the decision maker has an opportunity to explain the statistical disparity in the contexts of venire selection and Title VII. In McCleskey's challenge, in light of the number, diversity, and temporal nature of the decision makers addressed by the Baldus study, the state has no practical opportunity to rebut its findings.

Although it imposes limitations, the *McCleskey* decision does not preclude a court from adopting the statistical examination of the results by a single decision maker. Thus the U.S. Supreme Court has yet to address the impact of a study of the decisions made by one prosecutor over a period of time. Individual juries decide on individual sentences; in contrast, a single prosecutor, over a span of time, decides, with a number of homicide cases, whether to file capital charges, to serve notice of aggravating circumstances, and to proceed to capital trial. A statistical examination of these decisions should not raise the concerns expressed in *McCleskey*. Such evidence should demonstrate a prima facie case of an equal protection violation, as it would in venire selection or Title VII cases. After reviewing the relevant literature, we examine the various decisions made by a single prosecutor in homicide cases to examine the extent, if any, of racial disparity in outcomes.

PRIOR RESEARCH

Studies of racial bias in implementing capital punishment typically are reviewed in chronological order, by jurisdiction studied, or by the stage of case processing analyzed. What follows here, however, is not meant to be an exhaustive review of the literature but a guide for constructing a sound empirical study. In developing this guide, we examine previous studies in terms of their strengths and weaknesses. In the report issued by the Government Accounting Office, the research designs and analyses of 28 previous studies were scrutinized. Three major limitations among the studies were identified: "(1) the threat of sample selection bias, (2) the problem of omitted variables, and (3) small sample sizes" (GAO 1990:3–4).

Sample selection bias occurs when cases chosen for analysis do not represent the universe of cases from which they are drawn, but have certain characteristics in common which make them dissimilar to the cases excluded from the analysis. Sample selection bias is most likely to result when the pool of cases is limited to those in which a decision was made overtly during the later stages of case processing, such as the sentencing decision in a pool of convicted first-degree murderers who have advanced to the penalty stage of a capital trial. When samples are limited in this manner, the effects of racial discrimination occurring at earlier decision points are not taken into consideration. Cases involving particular racial combinations of offenders and/or victims may be systematically included or excluded from the pool of convicted capital murder cases because of bias in the pretrial stages of case processing. At the same time, the sentencing decision may be found to lack racial bias, thus giving the appearance that the system of capital punishment in the jurisdiction studied is not influenced by race (Heilburn, Foster, and Golden 1989; Klein and Rolph 1991).

If murders involving particular racial combinations (e.g., blacks who kill whites) are regularly selected for prosecution as capital murder even in the least aggravated cases, then during the sentencing phase, when legally relevant case criteria are taken into consideration, one should expect a lower death-sentencing rate among those cases than among cases involving other offender/victim racial combinations. A finding of no difference in the rates of death sentencing among racial combinations actually could indicate racial bias, masked by researchers' failure to consider decisions made earlier in the process.

Studies that include a broader pool of cases and earlier decision-making stages are not immune from sample selection bias if the decisions are analyzed consecutively. Most studies that have analyzed both pretrial and trial decisions have not found evidence of racial bias in sentencing (Nakell and Hardy 1987; Paternoster and Kazyaka 1988; Radelet and Pierce 1985; Sorensen and Marquart 1991; Vito and Keil 1988). To determine whether sentencing decisions are influenced indirectly by earlier decisions, one must factor into subsequent models the effects of race on pretrial decision making (Berk 1983; Keil and Vito 1990).

Another limitation of previous empirical studies identified by the GAO is that important variables are often omitted from consideration. Many variables related to the egregiousness of the offense and to the defendant's culpability may legitimately influence decision making in capital cases. Unless these factors are controlled in statistical models along with race, one cannot determine whether apparent racial disparities are warranted by legally relevant case characteristics. Only the residual racial disparity remaining after controlling for these characteristics may be presumed to result from racial bias.

Many post-*Furman* studies have compared the racial makeup of death row inmates with the racial proportions of those arrested for homicide, using information available in the *Supplemental Homicide Reports* (SHR) (Bowers and Pierce 1980; Ekland-Olson 1988; Gross and Mauro 1984; Kleck 1981; Radelet and Pierce 1985; Smith 1987; Zeisel 1981). These studies often find large discrepancies based on the victim's race or on the offender/victim racial combinations. The main problem with studies using the SHR is that they omit important variables, including most of those which determine death eligibility under various state statutes.[4]

The last major limitation identified in the GAO report concerned small sample size. Studies that examine one jurisdiction during a limited period typically suffer from this limitation (Arkin 1980; Murphy 1984). The advantage of studying one jurisdiction is that data collection is easier and more comprehensive within one locale; thus it is easier to analyze pretrial decision making. Furthermore, with comprehensive data on one jurisdiction, legal challenges can target individual decision makers more readily. The main disadvantage is that the studies of one jurisdiction may begin with a reasonable number of homicide cases in the pool, but only a handful typically result in a death sentence. When such small numbers of cases result in death sentences, it is also difficult to determine whether any differences found to exist are statistically significant or the result of chance. Further, when the dependent variable of interest is divided in this manner, it is difficult to control simultaneously for the many necessary control variables in order to perform a rigorous statistical comparison.

In addition to limitations, the GAO set criteria for determining the quality of the studies reviewed. In the GAO report, a study was considered to be of high quality if it "was characterized by a sound design that analyzed homicide cases throughout the sentencing process; included legally relevant variables (aggravating and mitigating circumstances); and used statistical techniques to control for variables that corresponded with race and/or capital sentencing" (GAO 1990:3). According to these criteria, the study completed by Baldus and colleagues and offered as evidence in the *McCleskey* case is the highest-quality study ever conducted: It uses sophisticated statistical techniques to control for

230 nonracial variables in a broad pool of homicide cases in examining the effects of racial bias during various decision-making stages.

In agreement with the findings of the Baldus study, the GAO's synthesis revealed that the victim's race influenced the processing of capital cases. Whether the defendant's race influenced outcomes was uncertain, but many of the studies included in the GAO synthesis found that the racial combination involving black defendants and white victims was most likely to receive the death penalty. Among the studies included in the GAO report, statistical disparities based on the victim's race or the offender/victim racial combination were strongest in the presentencing stages of case processing.

THE CURRENT STUDY

In the current study we take into account the strengths and weaknesses identified in previous studies in order to conduct a methodologically defensible analysis. To meet the criteria for a high-quality study and to avoid the shortcomings identified by the GAO, we analyze a pool of homicide cases from inception through the early pretrial stages. We include indicators of the statutory aggravating and mitigating circumstances in addition to other legally relevant variables found in previous studies, to be most consistently related to decision making, and we employ appropriate multivariate statistical techniques to control for variables that correlate with race and decision making. Taking cues from court decisions, particularly the dicta in *McCleskey*, we limit the sample to decisions made by, or under the direction of, a single individual in a particular jurisdiction.[5]

Pool of Cases

To determine the extent of racial disparity, if any, resulting during the current tenure of a prosecutor in one jurisdiction here called "Midwest County," we examine all potential capital cases acted upon in the pretrial stages of processing after the prosecutor assumed official duties on January 1, 1991. This universe of cases, compiled from lists provided by the State Supreme Court and the Department of Corrections, includes Midwest County cases disposed of from 1991 through 1996.[6]

The pool of cases to be used in the analysis, however, was limited to those in which the prosecutor could exercise complete discretion, at least theoretically, in seeking the death penalty.[7] Some observers may suggest that the pool of cases should be limited to those resulting in first-degree murder convictions. Information contained in police reports and files kept by the Parole Board, however, suggested that nearly all of the cases eventually resulting in second-degree murder convictions, and even those resulting in convictions for voluntary manslaughter, could be considered death-eligible. In fact, the majority of defendants convicted of those lesser degrees of homicide were charged initially with first-degree murder. Further, it was impossible to conclude that any of the cases did not include some circumstances that could be construed as aggravating under the broad statutory criteria used in death sentencing (see Suni 1986:553). To exclude any of the cases, an arbitrary decision would have to be made. Because indicators of the statutory criteria are included in the code sheet, the analyses performed can control for the inevitability that at least some of the cases are less death-eligible than others. The final pool of cases examined in the following analyses includes 133 cases in which defendants were convicted of first-degree murder, second-degree murder, or voluntary manslaughter.[8]

Data Collection

We collected data from official records of state agencies. The State Department of Corrections files kept by the Parole Board served as the primary source of information. These files typically included police reports, presentence investigations, intake summaries, and clinical reports. Together these documents contained a wealth of official information from which data could be collected. Trial judge reports maintained by the State Supreme Court were a strong secondary source of information, although somewhat more limited and less complete than the inmate files. Midwest County Court records were accessed to code the pretrial decisions made in each case. In some instances, Midwest County Coroner's records were consulted to fill in missing information concerning the victim. Through comparison of the sources the strengths of each data source were utilized, while verification held in check the weaknesses of each individual data source.

Measurement

Prosecutorial decision making. In one approach to measuring prosecutorial discretion, the dependent variable, the researcher examines each stage at which the prosecutor makes an identifiable decision to chart or continue a case on a death penalty course. The prosecutor makes three identifiable decisions during the pretrial stages of capital case processing: (1) the decision to charge first-degree murder, (2) the decision to file aggravating factors as notice to seek the death penalty, and (3) the decision to proceed to capital trial before a death-qualified jury.[9] The initial decision to charge the defendant with first-degree murder rather than a lesser degree of murder is a result of the prosecutor's unhampered discretion, as is the decision to file aggravating circumstances in the case.[10] Filing notice of aggravating circumstance, in essence, is the means of communicating to the court and the defense that the prosecutor intends to seek the death penalty. The final pretrial decision made by the prosecutor is whether to proceed to a capital trial—a first-degree murder trial with a death qualified jury and notice of aggravating factors filed.

Each stage of prosecutorial decision making can be treated as a binary dependent variable. In addition, the number of stages of prosecutorial decision making through which a case passes, when charted on a death-penalty course, serves as a summary measure of prosecutorial discretion. In this summary measure, a case that is not charged as first-degree murder is coded 0; other cases are coded 1 through 3, corresponding to the stages of decision making described above. This measure translates into the number of unfavorable pretrial decisions made by the prosecutor in a particular case; "unfavorable" means decisions that would lead to imposing the death penalty.

Most of the previous studies examined each of the binary responses separately. By using a summary measure, however, we can examine simultaneously the incremental steps made during the pretrial stage of case processing so as to take full advantage of the ordered nature of the dependent variable. By doing so we ameliorate some of the problems associated with small samples and sequential analyses, such as a loss of explanatory power, the inability to control for numerous legally relevant variables, and the threat of sample selection bias.

Racial disparity. Racial disparity, the independent variable, is often defined broadly as significant differences in the treatment of blacks and whites. Racial disparity usually refers to the offender's race, but also may refer to disparity based on the victim's race or on the combination of offender's race. As we stated earlier, the review of post-*Furman* empirical studies by the GAO found a pattern of racial disparity in capital punishment, resulting mainly from decisions made by prosecutors during the pretrial stages of case processing. The racial combination found most likely to result in a capital murder charge and to proceed to capital trial was that of blacks who kill whites (BkW).

Another dimension of racial disparity is that cases involving blacks who kill blacks (BkB) may be marginalized. Because blacks are less likely than other racial groups to marshal the resources of the justice system, BkB cases may be less likely to result in capital murder charges and proceed to capital trials.

The coextensive laxity in processing black-on-black homicide and harshness in processing black-on-white homicides, if not taken into consideration, could mask racial differences in the treatment of black and white offenders, as may have occurred in previous studies. In this analysis, in line with previous research findings, we consider the race of offenders and victims simultaneously to determine their influence on prosecutorial decision making.

Unadjusted racial disparity. [Unadjusted racial disparity] is defined as the difference in the proportions of particular offender/victim racial categories that advance through various stages of pretrial case processing charted on a death-penalty course. To determine the unadjusted level of racial disparity, one can compare these proportions as they advance through each of the pretrial stages. Because we are concerned mainly with the possibility of disparate treatment of black offenders based on their victims' race, we compare the proportion of BkW and BkB cases advancing through each stage of case processing with the proportion of all other cases advancing through each stage. We calculate a ratio of proportions indicating how much more or less likely it is that a case involving BkW or BkB will advance through each stage, in comparison with all other cases.

Unwarranted racial disparity. [Unwarranted racial disparity] refers to the difference in treatment of particular racial groups that is not justified by the nature of the offenses committed by members of those groups. Legally relevant factors concerning the egregiousness of the offense and the offender's culpability can rightly be expected to influence prosecutorial discretion. Racial disparities are warranted insofar as racial groups differ in the seriousness of the crime and the defendants' culpability. Only the effects of race beyond legally relevant considerations may be considered unwarranted and hence discriminatory.

Case seriousness measures. To determine the extent of unwarranted racial disparity, if any, the analyses must include measures of case seriousness as control variables. The code sheet used to collect data includes indicators of all the statutory aggravating and mitigating circumstances (see appendix). Because some of the statutory circumstances are broad and subjective, we used objective indicators to measure multiple dimensions of the statutory criteria. The indicators encompass most of the measures of case seriousness and offender culpability used in previous studies of pretrial racial disparity (e.g., number of victims, defendant's criminal record); we also coded additional variables found to be significant predictors in prior studies (e.g., victim's age, relationship between offender and victim). We use these control variables to measure the level of seriousness of a case; thus we consider them legitimate predictors of pretrial decision making.[11]

From these variables we created two types of measures. The first, an aggregate measure, simply sums the numbers of aggravating and mitigating factors present in each case. The second, a fact-specific measure, includes only the specific variables which are statistically significant predictors of prosecutorial decision making. In two separate equations using both of these measures, the influence of the legally relevant factors on prosecutorial decision making is considered simultaneously with the influence of race. Any warranted racial disparities in case processing are indicated by the coefficients of the legally relevant factors in these equations. Any disparities not attributable to legally relevant factors are indicated by the coefficients for BkW.[12]

In other words, if blacks who kill whites pass through more stages of prosecutorial decision making charted on a death-penalty course because of the level of seriousness or the specific aggravating factors present in their cases, the coefficient for BkW will be 0. Yet, should these legally relevant considerations not account entirely for the harsher treatment, in the pretrial stages of case processing, of blacks who kill whites, the coefficient for BkW will differ significantly from 0. Any effect of race beyond that explained by the legally relevant variables is to be considered unwarranted and hence discriminatory.

ANALYSIS AND FINDINGS

Unadjusted Racial Disparity

The first stage of this analysis involves bivariate comparisons of racial groups by pretrial decisions. Table 1 displays the probabilities that cases advance through successive stages of prosecutorial decision making, by race of defendants and victims. These probabilities show that disparities are based on the race of offenders in conjunction with the race of victims. For cases involving black offenders, the likelihood of advancing through the stages of a death-penalty course depends on the victim's race. Cases involving a black defendant and a white victim are the most likely to pass through each of the three stages.

TABLE 1

*Probability That Cases Will Progress Through Prosecutorial
Decision-Making Stages, by Race of Defendant and Victim*

Prosecutorial Decision-Making Stages	Defendant's Race/ Victim's Race			Rate of Probabilities Between Selected Racial Categories Versus Other	
	Black/ Black/	Black/ White	White/ White	Black/ Black	Black/ White
All Cases	(77)	(31)	(25)	(133)	(133)
First-Degree Murder Charge	.597 (46)	.871 (27)	.640 (16)	.78:1*	1.43:1**
Notice of Aggravating Factors	.143 (11)	.290 (9)	.160 (4)	.62:1	1.97:1*
Capital Trial	.078 (6)	.194 (6)	.120 (3)	.12:1	2.20:1*

*p < .05; **p < .01

The ratio of probabilities presented in the fourth column of Table 1 can be used to examine the likelihood that cases involving BkB will advance through pretrial decision-making stages, in comparison with all cases involving other racial combinations (BkW and WkW). The probabilities listed in the last column can be used to compare BkW with the other cases (BkB and WkW).[13]

Figures in the first row indicate that blacks who kills blacks are charged with first-degree murder at a ratio of .78:1. That is, BkB cases are only about three-quarters as likely to result in first-degree murder charges as are cases involving all other racial combinations. Figures for BkW indicate that blacks who kill whites are 143 percent, or nearly 1½ times, more likely to be charged with first-degree murder than offenders in the other racial categories. The ratios in the remaining rows suggest that this initial disparity increases throughout the stages of processing. BkB are only about two-thirds as likely as other combinations to have notice of aggravating factors filed in their case, and only about one-tenth as likely to proceed to a capital trial. The ratios in these rows indicate that blacks who kill whites are more than twice as likely as all other cases both to be served with notice of aggravating factors and to proceed to capital trial. Although not presented in the table, cases involving BkW were over $4\frac{1}{2}$ times more likely to result in death sentences than cases involving other racial combinations.[14]

Unwarranted Racial Disparity

The probabilities presented in Table 1 are unadjusted race effects that do not include the influence of legally relevant case measures; hence the racial disparity presented is not purged of disparity warranted by the egregiousness of the offense and by the offender's culpability. As mentioned earlier, only disparities remaining after controlling for legally relevant factors may be considered unwarranted and consequently racially discriminatory.

Because the response variable is ordinal, ordered logit is an appropriate statistical technique for estimating models (Kennedy 1992:245). In predicting order categories, ordered logit has an advantage over linear models such as OLS [Ordinary Least Squares] because it is curvilinear. In contrast to the single, linear estimate produced by OLS, ordered logit uses cutpoints along the curve in estimating the model; this approach allows for a closer fit to an ordered polychotomous dependent variable. Specifically, these models isolate the extent of racial discrimination by examining whether, and how extensively, race (BkW) predicts the stage of pretrial processing that a case reaches while charted on a death-penalty course when the effect of legally relevant variables is controlled.

Aggregate measure. The aggregate measure is presented in Table 2. In this model, the sums of aggravating and mitigating factors (see Table 4) were included with the indicator variable BkW. The coefficients presented in Table 2 show that the number of aggravating and mitigating factors is influential in pretrial decision making. As expected, the logit coefficients indicate that the number of aggravating factors present in a case increases the likelihood that the case will advance through the pretrial decisions charted on a death-penalty course. Also as expected, the more mitigating factors present in a case, the less likely that a case will advance through these pretrial stages.

The logit coefficient for the racial indicator variable suggests that when the number of aggravating and mitigating factors is held constant, BkW increases the number of unfavorable decisions made by prosecutors. At the prosecutor's discretion, if two cases are equal in the number of aggravating and mitigating factors, one is significantly more likely than the other to be tracked on a death-penalty course during the pretrial stages of case processing if the offender is black and the victim is white. Other indicators of race could not be included in this model because of collinearity; in models estimated separately, however, the logit coefficients for BkB, victim's race and offender's race were not significant.

Fact-specific measure. In the second logit model, we included along with BkW specific aggravating and mitigating factors found to be statistically significant predictors of prosecutorial decision making. We created the model in Table 3 by reducing the inventory of predictor variables to those which were significant predictors of prosecutorial decision making. We excluded from consideration all variables with a small number of cases in one of their categories and those

TABLE 2

Ordered Logit Model Predicting Prosecutorial Decision Making for Cases Involving Black Defendants and White Victims Compared With All Other Cases, Controlling for the Number of Aggravating and Mitigating Factors

Variable	Logit Coefficient	Standard Error	Z-Value
Black Kill White (BkW)	.685	.405	1.69 *
Aggravating Factors	.445	.119	3.75 ***
Mitigating Factors	-.519	.147	-3.54 ***
Log-Likelihood = -132.45			
Model Chi-Square = 39.45***			
Pseudo-R^2 = .130			

*p < .05; ***p < .001

which were highly correlated with other variables. Otherwise all significant predictors from the inventory of variables were included in the model.

The overall statistics for the model, including the log-likelihood measure and chi-square, reveal a goodness of fit with the data. The pseudo-R^2 also indicates that the model successfully explains a portion of the variance in prosecutorial decision making. A number of aggravating factors increase the likelihood of unfavorable pretrial decisions, while many specific mitigating factors decrease the likelihood that a case will advance through the stages of pretrial decision making when charted on a death-penalty course.

When we controlled for the level of case seriousness and offender culpability by considering the influence of these specific legally relevant case features, unexplained racial disparities still were present. Although several other legally relevant factors helped to explain pretrial decision making, they did not eliminate the significance of race. When the logistic regression coefficient for BkW is transformed and all other statistically significant predictors are held constant, the predicted probability that the prosecutor will advance a case to capital trial is $2\frac{1}{2}$ times greater when a black kills a white than in all other racial combinations.[15]

We estimated separate models with the same predictor variables, but included different racial indicators. In these models, the logit coefficients for the victim's race and for BkB were significant, but not for the offender's race. In the model estimated with the indicator BkB, the predicted probability that the prosecutor will advance a case to capital trial declines to about half as great when a black kills a black as in all other racial combinations.[16] These analyses show that the influence of race on prosecutorial decision making may be masked unless the offender's and the victim's race are considered simultaneously. Blacks who killed whites were treated more harshly; blacks who killed blacks were treated more leniently.

TABLE 3

Ordered Logit Model Predicting Prosecutorial Decision Making for Cases Involving Black Defendants and White Victims Compared With All Other Cases, Controlling for Significant Predictor Variables

Variable	Logit Coefficient	Standard Error	Z-Value
Black Kill White (BkW)	.866	.432	2.00 *
Prior Assaultive Convictions	1.417	.440	3.22 ***
Multiple Victims	1.576	.794	1.98 *
Death by Gunshot	2.033	.519	3.92 ***
Death by Asphyxiation	1.635	.654	2.50 **
Involved Torture/Mutilation	2.706	.677	4.00 ***
Defendant Only an Accomplice	-1.242	.603	-2.06 *
Defendant Intoxicated	-1.085	.407	-2.67 **
Defendant Youthful (< 18)	-1.067	.516	-2.07 *
Defendant Female	-1.895	.880	-2.16 *

Log-Likelihood   -117.98
Model Chi-Square =   68.41***
Pseudo-R^2 =   .225

$^*p < .05; ^{**}p < .01; ^{***}p < .001$

CONCLUSION

Given the findings presented here, we conclude that racial disparity exists in the pretrial stages of decision making for potential capital murder cases processed in Midwest County from 1991 through 1996. Further, the fact that this disparity still was statistically significant after controlling for legally relevant considerations suggests that the disparity is unwarranted and hence discriminatory. Homicide cases involving blacks who kill whites are more likely to result in first-degree murder charges, to be served with notice of aggravating circumstances, and to proceed to capital trials than are similar cases involving other offender-victim racial combinations. This pattern of racial discrimination, occurring during the pretrial stages of case processing in Midwest County, can be attributed to decisions made during the tenure of the current prosecuting attorney.

In the current study we have been able to isolate the discriminatory pattern in the pretrial decisions made by a particular actor in the criminal justice system. *McCleskey* is inapplicable because this study examined the decisions of only a single prosecutor. Such evidence of discriminatory decision making by individual actors in the criminal justice system cannot receive superficial treat-

TABLE 4

Frequency Distribution of Control Variables (N = 133)

*Jon Sorensen
and Donald H.
Wallace*

Indicators of Aggravating Circumstances	Percentage (Frequency)
a. Previous assaultive convictions	32.3 (43)
Previous murder conviction	2.3 (3)
b. Multiple victims	6.8 (9)
c. Additional victims assaulted/shot	7.5 (10)
Great risk to many (drive-by/explosives)	11.3 (15)
g. Gun (not included in index)	67.7 (90)
Multiple shots fired	36.1 (48)
Shotgun, close range	3.0 (4)
Execution style	6.0 (8)
Knife (not included in index)	18.0 (24)
Multiple stabs	11.3 (15)
Arson	2.3 (3)
Bludgeoning objects/fists/feet	17.3 (23)
Strangulation/asphyxiation/drowning	10.5 (14)
Torture involved/mutilation of corpse	15.0 (20)
h. Victim was police officer	1.5 (2)
j. Resisted arrest	6.0 (8)
k. Kidnapping/held hostage	10.5 (14)
Burglary	8.3 (11)
Robbery	26.3 (35)
Carjacking	5.3 (7)
Sexual assault	8.3 (11)
l. Obstruction/retaliation	2.3 (3)
o. Drug deal	25.6 (34)
q. Gang-related	7.5 (10)
Indicators of Mitigating Circumstances	
a. Defendant no prior arrests/warrants	28.6 (38)
Defendant no previous prison incarcerations	70.7 (94)
c. Victim was a participant in defendant's conduct (gang, drugs, provoke)	45.1 (60)
d. Defendant only an accomplice/did not kill	12.8 (17)
f. Defendant lacked capacity/mental illness	4.5 (6)
Defendant mentally retarded/borderline IQ	11.3 (15)
Defendant under influence of drugs/alcohol	39.8 (53)
g. Youthful defendant (under 18)	17.3 (23)
Other Control Variables	
Codefendants	46.6 (62)
Female defendant	6.8 (9)
Female victim	31.6 (42)
Stranger	24.1 (32)
Child victim (under 6)	6.0 (8)
Youthful victim (6 through 17)	12.8 (17)
Elderly victim (over 54)	9.0 (12)

ment as easily as in previous studies, which showed the aggregate disparities of many decision makers.

Although the effects of these results should not be governed by *Mc-Cleskey*'s demands of proof of discriminatory intent in making systemic challenges, they may lead to a further challenge to the statewide policy of capital punishment, of which this prosecutor is a part. Similar findings for other prosecutors in this state may suggest systemic defects. Such a piecemeal approach to a statewide challenge also may reveal equal protection violations in other counties. Yet other, less populous counties may reveal no statistically significant results because of an insufficiently large number of homicides for such a study. If these results are replicated in other populous jurisdictions in the state, however, such replication should meet the demands of *McCleskey* for a systematic challenge to prosecutorial decision making.

Though these findings may not challenge the state's death penalty policy, a statistically based claim of discrimination is well founded. Clearly, a prima facie case of intentional discrimination in this jurisdiction has been made. At the very least, the prosecutor should take up the burden of persuasion in an attempt to justify the apparent discrepancies.

NOTES

1. Baldus et al. (1994) found only one federal district court case that allowed a hearing on the issue, but dismissed the claim for failing to meet *McCleskey's* crippling burden of proof (*Dobbs v. Zant* 1989).
2. Racial justice acts have failed in both Maryland (Senate Bill No. 440, introduced 2/21/1994) and Kentucky (Senate Bill No. 132, introduced 1/17/1996).
3. One year earlier the Court relied on statistical evidence less convincing than that presented in *McCleskey* in reversing a capital conviction, on the grounds that racial bias may have influenced the selection of the jurors (*Batson v. Kentucky* 1986).
4. See Maxfield (1989) for a discussion of numerous other problems with the SHR data.
5. In the *McCleskey* decision, the majority argued that the type of data presented did not lend itself to evaluating decisions made by particular individuals. They also asserted that such evidence would be necessary to meet the burden of proof required in a particular case when racial bias is claimed (*McCleskey* 1987:295, n.15).
6. The list from the State Supreme Court included all first-degree murder cases for which trial judge reports were forwarded to the court by December 1996. The list from the State Department of Corrections included all inmates convicted of first-degree murder, second-degree murder, and voluntary manslaughter received at the institution before October 9, 1996. Therefore these lists included all disposed-of cases for which information was available at the time of this investigation.
7. We excluded cases involving defendants under age 16 at the time of the offense because such cases were not death-eligible. Also excluded were death-penalty cases that had been reversed and remanded to Midwest County. The rationale for excluding these cases is that the original pretrial decisions had been made previously. Further, the decision to seek death for a second time is quite different in that it depends

on the appellate decision and the staleness of the case; these considerations do not influence initial pretrial decisions. For 26 cases pending in the pretrial stages of processing (charged but not tried) on January 1, 1991, the disposition during the current prosecutor's tenure is recorded here.

8. The final pool of cases is limited to homicides resulting in convictions. As suggested by one reviewer, the most inclusive pool would include all homicide arrestees. Under state law, however, records pertaining to cases resulting in dismissals or acquittals are not publicly available, even to researchers. Although it might have been possible to obtain arrest records from a police department if our study had focused on a large urban jurisdiction, that approach is not feasible because the jurisdiction studied here encompassed several suburban police departments.

   The final pool also excludes five cases involving unusual offender/victim racial characteristics, which made their classification problematic. Because our main goal was to determine the effects of race on prosecutorial decision making, these small categories of cases could not be analyzed separately. Simply categorizing them along with "other cases" would have made it difficult to interpret differences between particular racial categories and the referent category. To keep these comparisons as clear as possible, we omitted from the final pool three cases involving whites who killed blacks, and two cases involving offenders and victims of foreign ancestry. Because none of these cases advanced past the stage of first-degree murder indictment, dropping them from the referent category results in a more conservative estimate of racial bias in prosecutorial decision making.

9. By the time of a capital trial, prosecutorial discretion is nearly purged from the process. Typically, if the defendant receives less than a death sentence after a trial begins, it is due to the discretion of other authorities in the adjudication and penalty phase.

10. Although murder charges are brought through grand jury indictment in Midwest County, the decision as to which degree murder to charge is solely the prosecutor's province. As found elsewhere, it appeared that grand juries rarely, if ever, changed the charge issued by the prosecutor (see Jacoby 1980:144–45). Only cases that resulted in indictments are included in this pool.

11. Although the possibility of omitting explanatory variables is omnipresent in attempts to empirically model decision making, the inventory of variables used here is quite extensive; we gave special consideration to variables that had been found significant in previous studies.

12. As we discuss further in the analysis section, BkW is the only racial variable included in the multivariate models because of collinearity. Models using the other racial combinations, however, were estimated separately.

13. As mentioned in note 8, five cases involving other racial combinations were dropped from the analysis.

14. The following figures correspond to the columns in Table 1 for cases resulting in death: black/black, .013 (1); black/white, .129 (4); white/white, .080 (2); ratio of probabilities, black/black to all other cases, .12.:1 ($p < .01$); black/white to all other cases, 4.45:1$p < .05$).

15. Because ordered logit is an extension of logistic regression with a dichotomous dependent variable, a similar formula is used to derive predicted probabilities for coefficients. The main difference is the point on the logistic curve at which the effect of the predictor variable is calculated. In logistic regression with a dichotomous dependent variable, the influence of predictor variables is generally evaluated at the mean of the dependent variable (see Petersen 1985). Because ordered logit involves a polychotomous dependent variable, the influence of a predictor variable can be calculated

at any of k-1 cutpoints that model the categorization of the dependent variable (see Kennedy 1992). In this instance, we evaluated the effect of the predictor variable at the third cutpoint above which a case was predicted to result in a capital trial. Using the formula for expected values ($S_j = B*BkW_j + u_j$) and the third cutpoint (4.773) as provided by STATA, one may compare the predicted probabilities of scoring in the fourth category of the dependent variable with and without the influence of this particular coefficient. In the case of the indicator variable BkW, the expected value for BkW cases is .866; for all other racial combinations, 0. Thus the predicted logistic probability of non-BkW cases moving to a capital trial is $u_j > 4.773$; for BkW cases, $.866+u_j > 3.907$. Familiarity with the logistic curve allows us to transform these into predicted probabilities for non-BkW cases, $1/(1+e^{4.773}) = .008$, and BkW cases, $1/(1+e^{3.907}) = .020$.

16. The model estimated with the indicator BkB yielded an R^2 of .221, a logit coefficient of −.655 for BkB, and a third cutpoint of 4.202. With the formula described in note 15, the predicted probabilities were .015 for non-BkB cases and .008 for BkB cases.

REFERENCES

Arkin, S. D. 1980. "Discrimination and Arbitrariness in Capital Punishment: An Analysis of Post-*Furman* Murder Cases in Dade County, Florida, 1973–1976." *Stanford Law Review* 33:75–101.

Baldus, D. C., G. Woodworth, and C. Pulaski. 1990. *Equal Justice and the Death Penalty.* Boston: Northeastern University Press.

———. 1994. "Reflections on the 'Inevitability' of Racial Discrimination in Capital Sentencing and the 'Impossibility' of Its Prevention, Detection, and Correction." *Washington and Lee Law Review* 51:359–430.

Bedau, H. A. 1997. *The Death Penalty in America: Current Controversies.* New York: Oxford University Press.

Berk, R. A. 1983. "An Introduction to Sample Selection Bias in Sociological Data." *American Sociological Review* 48:386–98.

Bowers, W. J. and G. L. Pierce. 1980. "Arbitrariness and Discrimination under Post-*Furman* Capital Statutes." *Crime and Delinquency* 26:563–635.

Christianson, S. 1996. "Corrections Law: Federal Death Penalty Protocol—Safeguard or Window Dressing?" *Criminal Law Bulletin* 32:374–79.

Cox, G. D. 1987. "Calif. Death Penalty Probe Aborted." *National Law Journal,* November 16, p. 3.

Ekland-Olson, S. 1988. "Structured Discretion, Racial Bias, and the Death Penalty: The First Decade after *Furman* in Texas." *Social Science Quarterly* 69:853–73.

Government Accounting Office (GAO). 1990. *Death Penalty Sentencing: Research Indicates Pattern of Racial Disparities.* Washington, DC: USGAO.

Gross, S. R., and R. Mauro. 1984. "Patterns of Death: An Analysis of Racial Disparities in Capital Sentencing and Homicide Victimization." *Stanford Law Review* 37:27–153.

Heilbrun, A. B., Jr., A. Foster, and J. Golden. 1989. "The Death Sentence in Georgia, 1974–1987: Criminal Justice or Racial Injustice?" *Criminal Justice and Behavior* 16:139–54.

Jacoby, J. E. 1980. *The American Prosecutor: A Search for Identity.* Lexington, MA: Heath.

Jeffries, J. C. 1994. *Justice Lewis F. Powell, Jr.* New York: Scribner's.

Keil, T. J. and G. F. Vito. 1990. "Race and the Imposition of Death Penalty in Kentucky Murder Trials: An Analysis of Post-*Gregg* Outcomes." *Justice Quarterly* 7:189–207.

Kennedy, P. 1992. *A Guide to Econometrics.* 3d ed. Cambridge, MA: MIT Press.

Kleck, G. 1981. "Racial Dicrimination in Criminal Sentencing: A Critical Evaluation of the Evidence with Additional Evidence on the Death Penalty." *American Sociological Review* 46:783–805.

Klein, S. P. and J. E. Rolph. 1991. "Relationship of Offender and Victim Race to Death Penalty Sentences in California." *Jurimetrics* 32:33–48.

Maxfield, M. G. 1989. "Circumstances in Supplementary Homicide Reports: Variety and Validity." *Criminology* 27:671–95.

Murphy, E. 1984. "The Application of the Death Penalty in Cook County." *Illinois Bar Journal* 93:90–95.

Nakell, B. and K. A. Hardy. 1987. *The Arbitrariness of the Death Penalty.* Philadelphia: Temple University Press.

Paternoster, R. and A. M. Kazyaka. 1988. "Racial Considerations in Capital Punishment: The Failure of Evenhanded Justice." Pp. 113–48 in *Challenging Capital Punishment: Legal and Social Science Approaches,* edited by K. C. Haas and J. A. Inciardi. Beverly Hills: Sage.

Petersen, T. 1985. "A Comment on Presenting the Results from Logit and Probit Models." *American Sociological Review* 50:130–31.

Radelet, M. L. and G. L. Pierce. 1985. "Race and Prosecutorial Discretion in Homicide Cases." *Law and Society Review* 19:587–621.

Smith, M. D. 1987. "Patterns of Discrimination in Assessment of the Death Penalty: The Case of Louisiana." *Journal of Criminal Justice* 15:279–86.

Sorensen, J. R. and J. W. Marquart. 1991. "Prosecutorial and Jury Decision Making in Post-*Furman* Texas Capital Cases." *New York University Review of Law and Social Change* 18:743–76.

Subcommittee on Civil and Constitutional Rights. 1994. *Racial Disparity in Federal Death Penalty Prosecutions 1988–1994.* Washington, DC: Death Penalty Information Center.

Suni, E. Y. 1986. "Recent Developments in Missouri: The Death Penalty." *University of Missouri—Kansas City Law Review* 58:523–80.

Vito, G. F. and T. J. Keil. 1988. "Capital Sentencing in Kentucky: An Analysis of the Factors Influencing Decision Making in the Post-*Gregg* Period." *Journal of Criminal Law and Criminology* 79:483–503.

Zeisel, H. 1981. "Race Bias in the Administration of the Death Penalty: The Florida Experience." *Harvard Law Review* 95:456–68.

"An Apology Does Not Assist the Accused"

In 1969 the U.S. Senate ratified the Vienna Convention on Consular Relations (VCCR). This treaty regulates consulates in more than 140 nations. Under Article 36 of the treaty, local arresting authorities are required to notify detained foreign nationals of their right to communicate with their consular representatives. This provision is meant to ensure that foreign nationals confronted by an unfamiliar legal system are not tried and condemned to death without the benefit of support from the authorities of their native countries. As a result, local law enforcement authorities are required under the treaty to notify the consulate of the foreign national's arrest and to permit consular access to the detained national. Unfortunately, while the U.S. government requires that American citizens arrested in foreign countries be promptly advised of their rights to contact consular representatives, American authorities have failed to comply with the terms of the international agreement in the vast majority of cases involving foreign nationals who are arrested domestically. Some 83 foreign nationals are presently being held under a sentence of death. Since 1976 death penalty jurisdictions have executed 14 foreign nationals, and none of them were notified by authorities of their right to communicate with their consular representatives. In response to Virginia's 1998 execution of Angel Francisco Breard, a Paraguayan national, the International Court of Justice (ICJ) has demanded that the U.S. government honor its commitment to the treaty.

The following selection is adapted from " 'An Apology Does Not Assist the Accused': Foreign Nationals and the Death Penalty in the United States," *The Justice Professional* (1999). In it, Margaret Vandiver, an associate professor in the Department of Criminology and Criminal Justice at the University of Memphis, reviews the issues raised by American violations of the Vienna Convention and addresses several cases involving condemned foreign nationals and the rulings of American courts and of the ICJ, particularly as these rulings pertain to the case of Breard. To ensure compliance with the provisions of the Vienna Convention, Vandiver suggests that *Miranda* warnings could be amended to include the right to contact consulates for assistance if the criminal suspect is a foreign national. Or defendants could be advised of their rights to seek consulate assistance at their initial arraignment. Yet, asserts Vandiver, U.S. criminal justice practitioners and the nation's political leadership have met these simple provisions mostly with ignorance of and contempt for international law.

Key Concept: foreign nationals' rights under sentence of death

Margaret Vandiver

INTRODUCTION

Over 80 citizens of at least 29 foreign nations are currently on death row in the United States.[1] Thirteen foreign nationals have been executed in the U.S. under current statutes, five of them in the first half of 1999 (see Table 1)[2]. Executions of foreign nationals raise a number of legal issues, including refusal of abolitionist countries to extradite suspects to the United States without guarantees that the death penalty will not be sought (Kobayashi, 1996; Roecks, 1994; Quigley and Shank, 1989), challenges to the conditions of confinement on American death rows (*Soering v. United Kingdom*, 1989; Lillich, 1991), and claims that foreign nationals have been denied their right to consular assistance.

The focus of this paper is on the legally well established but generally unenforced right of foreign nationals facing the death penalty in the United States to receive consular assistance. This right, grounded in the practices of nations and customary international law, was formalized some 35 years ago by a multilateral treaty, the Vienna Convention on Consular Relations [VCCR]. The United States has consistently required that Americans arrested abroad be promptly advised of their right to consular assistance; American states, however, have violated the Vienna Convention in the vast majority of death penalty cases involving foreign nationals.

Although foreign nationals comprise only a small percent of the total number of condemned persons in the United States (approximately 80 out of over 3,500), the issue of their Vienna Convention rights has considerable legal and practical importance. Legally, executions in violation of the Vienna Convention raise complex questions of the relationship between state, federal, and international law. American failure to honor the right of consular assistance has serious implications for foreign nationals facing capital charges in the United States, as well as for American nationals arrested in other countries. More broadly, the issue has the potential to damage America's reputation and relations with foreign countries, as well as the still fragile structure of international law.

THE VIENNA CONVENTION ON CONSULAR RELATIONS

The Vienna Convention on Consular Relations was drawn up in April 1963, and was ratified without reservation by the United States Senate in 1969. The Convention requires that local authorities of the signatory nations inform arrested foreigners that they have the right to consular assistance. If the detained person

TABLE 1

Executions of Foreign Nationals in the United States, 1976–1998

Name	Date	State	Nationality	Consular Rights Observed or Violated
Carlos Santana	3/23/93	TX	Dominican Rep.	Violated
Ramon Montoya	3/25/93	TX	Mexico	Violated
Pedro Medina	3/25/97	FL	Cuba	Violated
Irineo Montoya	6/18/97	TX	Mexico	Violated
Mario Murphy	9/18/97	VA	Mexico	Violated
Angel Breard	4/14/98	VA	Paraguay	Violated
Jose Villafuerte	4/22/98	AZ	Honduras	Violated
Tuan Nguyen	12/10/98	OK	Vietnam	Violated
Jaturun Siripongs	2/9/99	CA	Thailand	Violated
Karl LaGrand	2/24/99	AR	Germany	Violated
Walter LaGrand	3/3/99	AR	Germany	Violated
Alvaro Calambro	4/5/99	NV	Philippines	Violated
Joseph Stanley Faulder	6/17/99	TX	Canada	Violated

so requests, authorities must notify the consulate of the arrest and permit consular access to the detained person. The relevant paragraphs of Article 36 read:

> (b) If he so requests, the competent authorities of the receiving State shall, without delay, inform the consular post of the sending State if, within its consular district, a national of that State is arrested or committed to prison or custody pending trial or is detained in any other manner. Any communication addressed to the consular post by the person arrested, in prison, custody or detention shall also be forwarded by the said authorities without delay. The said authorities shall inform the person concerned without delay of his rights under this subparagraph;
>
> (c) consular officers shall have the right to visit a national of the sending State who is in prison, custody or detention in their district in pursuance of a judgment. Nevertheless, consular officers shall refrain from taking action on behalf of a national who is in prison, custody or detention if he expressly opposes such action. (Vienna Convention on Consular Relations, Article 36, 21 U.S.T. 77, p. 101)

As a signed and ratified treaty, the Vienna Convention is the supreme law in the United States, comparable to an act of Congress. The Supremacy Clause (Article VI, clause 2 of the U.S. Constitution) states: "This Constitution, and the Laws of the United States which shall be made in Pursuance thereof; and all Treaties made, or which shall be made, under the Authority of the United States, shall be the supreme Law of the Land." Thus, the Vienna Convention is binding upon the federal government and upon the states.[3] Although the federal government has not made any sustained and systematic attempt to bring state law enforcement practices into compliance with the Vienna Convention, regulations of the Department of Justice and the Immigration and Naturalization Service do require compliance (Gisvold, 1994, p. 787, footnote 66).

Under the American system of federalism, states do not make foreign policy; the federal government alone has the power to make policy concerning international relations. The ratification of the Vienna Convention by Congress and the enforcement policies of the executive branch "completely preempt the states from contrary action" (Gisvold, 1994, p. 795). If a state does violate international law, however, it is the federal government that is ultimately responsible for the state's actions. It is an established rule of international law that "central governments are held accountable for the conduct of constituent authorities" (Spiro, 1997, p. 567). Despite this responsibility, the American federal government has been reluctant to assert its authority; indeed, the United Nations Special Rapporteur, in his recent report on the death penalty in the United States, wrote that "domestic laws appear de facto to prevail over international law" (United Nations, 1998). State, rather than federal, authorities have committed the vast majority of violations of the Vienna Convention, but neither they nor the federal authorities have provided a remedy.

The United States has insisted that foreign governments inform arrested American citizens of their right to consular assistance. The U.S. demanded this right for American nationals as a matter of customary international law even before the existence of the Vienna Convention (Shank and Quigley, 1995, p. 734; for examples, see Lee, 1961, pp. 120–124) and more recently the U.S. has relied on the treaty to assert the right of consular assistance, as well as insisting on the enforcement of other provisions of the treaty. When Syria failed to notify the U.S. of the detention of two Americans in 1975, for instance, American officials telegramed Syrian authorities, citing the Vienna Convention "as a solemn treaty obligation and evidence of a norm of customary international law, asserting that 'The Government of the Syrian Arab Republic can be confident that if its nationals were detained in the United States the appropriate Syrian officials would be promptly notified and allowed prompt access to those nationals'" (Doherty 1996, p. 1318, footnote 165). When Americans were held hostage in the Embassy in Iran, the United States invoked the Vienna Convention in its arguments before the International Court of Justice [ICJ] that Iran's actions were illegal (Sands, 1998). In 1975, the Administrator of the Bureau of Security and Consular Affairs told Congress that American consular officers in Mexico were expected to do the following for Americans arrested in Mexico:

> These officers are expected to make every effort to insure that they learn of each new arrest of an American citizen in their district... the consular officer after learning of an arrest seeks access to the accused to establish his identity and citizenship, to ensure he is aware of his rights, to advise him of the availability of legal counsel, to give him a list of local attorneys, to help him get in touch with his family and friends, to alert him to the legal and penal procedures of the host country and to observe if he has been or is in danger of being mistreated... (quoted in Ruiz-Bravo, 1995, p. 396)

American insistence that other countries observe the Vienna Convention with respect to American citizens was recently reiterated by Secretary of State

Madeleine Albright, who said that consular access must be provided to foreigners in the U.S., because it "is something that we will insist on and do insist on when one of our citizens is in trouble abroad" (MacSwan, 1998).

Despite American insistence that other countries promptly meet their obligations under the Vienna Convention, the U.S. has a very poor record of compliance, even in capital cases. The vast majority of foreign nationals on death row in the United States were never informed of their right to receive consular assistance. The most complete effort to track condemned foreign nationals has documented compliance in only three cases, two of which were federal (M. Warren, personal communication, June 14, 1998). Thus, the failure of state law enforcement officials to comply is nearly complete. Reasons for this lack of compliance and possible remedies are discussed in the final sections of the paper.

IMPORTANCE OF CONSULAR ASSISTANCE

The right to consular assistance is anything but academic to a person arrested in a foreign country. A host of problems place him at substantial disadvantage at every point in the criminal justice process. The first and most obvious problem for many foreign nationals is language. Without the ability to communicate fluently, the accused may not even understand the charges against him, much less how to defend himself against them. Even where language is not a problem, understanding a foreign legal system is extremely difficult: "a foreign national is inherently prejudiced when detained or in custody in a foreign criminal justice system. A consul's assistance can place him on par with a non-foreigner" (Kadish, 1997, p. 606, footnotes omitted).

The right to consular assistance is especially important to persons facing capital charges. Somewhat more than half of all countries do not use the death penalty (Bedau, 1997, pp. 78–83); their citizens thus face the possibility of receiving harsher punishment in the U.S. than they could receive for any offense committed in their home country. Foreigners are likely to have little understanding of how to prepare for trial, sentencing, and appeal. American death penalty practice is a highly specialized area of law, obscure even to many attorneys. Although there are outstanding exceptions, the quality of defense lawyers in many death penalty cases is extremely poor (Coyle, Strasser, and Lavelle, 1990; Bright, 1994), making it inadvisable for a foreign national to trust entirely to his lawyer.

The choices a person makes when confronted with criminal charges in a foreign country may be influenced by the type of government in his home country. If he fears beatings or torture from the police, he may confess in order to avoid such treatment. Failure to understand plea bargaining and to take advantage of any offers of a reduced penalty may deprive a foreign national of his best chance to avoid the death sentence. The defendant's home country may not use juries, and he may not understand the role of the jury in the American criminal justice system, especially its central role in capital cases. A consul can explain all these aspects of the American system, and can provide guidance in regard to the various courses of action open to the defendant.

The sentencing hearing in capital cases requires extensive investigation into the defendant's background (Haney, 1995). The defense in a capital case must present to the jury "a painstakingly researched, thoughtfully assembled, and carefully and comprehensively presented chronicle" of the defendant's life (Haney, 1998, p. 376). It is at this point that consular assistance is perhaps most critically important. The consul will have the language skills, contacts, and resources to find records and witnesses in the defendant's home country, an exceptionally difficult task for an American defense team, even one with the inclination to do a thorough and zealous job of presenting mitigating evidence.

Throughout the entire process from arrest to the sentencing hearing, the consul can translate, explain the legal system, and facilitate communication with defense counsel and witnesses. The consul can advise and support the defendant, and can assist contact between the defendant and his family and friends in the home country. And, as Shank and Quigley point out, "the mere involvement of a consul may encourage local government to follow procedural norms and minimize discrimination against a foreigner" (1995, p. 721). In sum, the consul's involvement can make the difference between life and death in capital cases. The right to consular assistance, therefore, is critically important for foreign nationals facing capital charges in this country.

The consulates of a number of countries have clearly indicated their willingness to provide all these services for their nationals facing capital charges in the U.S. In the wake of executions of their nationals, the Mexican government "is prepared to commit resources to hire attorneys, private investigators, expert witnesses and translators ... [to] locate witnesses and family ... and arrange for them to testify in US courts" (Villafranca, 1997). Mexico has provided extensive assistance to several American lawyers representing Mexicans detained on capital charges. An Idaho attorney was delighted to receive a call from Mexican officials offering help: "They've already hired an investigator.... And they're flying me to Mexico, where I'll have a room, meals, car, interpreter and driver and meet with people who know [his client's] background" (Sahagun and Darling, 1994). (See Kadish, 1997, pp. 607–608, footnote 260, for a detailed description of the assistance offered by the Argentine consul to a national charged with a capital offense in Texas and Gisvold, 1994, p. 773, footnote 6, for a listing of the duties of a Canadian consul in assisting an arrested Canadian citizen.)

The following brief case descriptions and the discussion of the *Breard* case below provide examples of foreign citizens who, in the absence of consular assistance, fared poorly in their encounters with the U.S. death penalty system. In each case, timely assistance by the consul might well have made a difference in the choices made by the defendants and in the resources available to their attorneys. Prompt notification of consul might have been especially helpful to those foreign nationals who confessed to police and whose confessions formed a major part of the case against them.

Irineo Tristan Montoya was 18 years old at the time of his arrest, and had about a fifth grade education (Uribe, 1997, p. 414, footnote 235). Montoya's conviction was largely based upon "a signed confession obtained after several hours of police interrogation following his arrest, prior to his initial appearance before any court, and before counsel had been appointed to defend him. Montoya was intoxicated at the time of arrest. Montoya's confession was in English, a language he was unable to read, speak or write" (*ibid.*, pp. 413–414, footnotes omitted). The State Department asked Texas to look into the circumstances of the Vienna Convention violation in Montoya's case, and received a refusal to investigate, based "on the grounds that Texas was not a signatory to the Vienna Convention" (Amnesty International, 1998a). Montoya was executed in June of 1997, despite strong protests by the Mexican government, which made use of all possible legal avenues to avoid the execution (Protestara gobierno[4], 1997). Two weeks after Montoya was executed, the Department of State issued the following apology to Mexico: "The Department of State extends, on behalf of the United States, its most profound apology for the apparent failure of the competent authorities to inform Mr. Tristan Montoya that he could have a Mexican consular officer notified of his detention" (quoted in United Nations, 1998).

Cesar Fierro's conviction was also based on his confession, which was made under extraordinary circumstances. El Paso police arrested Fierro based on a tip they received from "a sixteen-year-old with a history of mental problems" (Shank and Quigley, 1995, p. 725). The murder weapon was never found and the police "had no other physical evidence to connect Fierro to the crime" (p. 725). While Fierro was in custody of the El Paso police, he learned his mother and stepfather had been arrested by the police in Ciudad Juarez. He was allowed to speak with the police officer holding his relatives, and was convinced that they would not be released and that they might be tortured unless he confessed (pp. 725–726), which he promptly did. The prosecutor who won the conviction against Fierro has since filed an affidavit stating that "evidence of possible coercion [in obtaining the confession] was suppressed," and has stated that had he known the circumstances of the confession, he "might not have prosecuted the case" (Rodriguez and Gonzalez, 1994). Fierro remains on death row in Texas.

Another foreign national who could have benefited greatly from consular assistance was Joseph Stanley Faulder, a Canadian citizen. Faulder had organic brain damage and was alcoholic (Gisvold, 1994, pp. 771–774). He was twice tried and convicted of capital murder and sentenced to die without consular assistance or being informed of his right to that assistance. No physical evidence linked him to the crime; his first conviction was supported by a confession and the second by the testimony of a codefendant (*Faulder v. Johnson*, 1996, p. 517). Faulder raised the issue of the violation of his Vienna Convention rights in a federal habeas petition. The Fifth Circuit Court of Appeals noted that Texas admitted violating the Vienna Convention in Faulder's case (p. 520), but the court held that this violation of Faulder's rights was harmless error and therefore was not grounds for a reversal.

In late 1998, Faulder was scheduled for execution. Secretary of State Madeleine Albright contacted Governor George W. Bush of Texas, requesting a 30 day reprieve for Faulder, so that there would be sufficient time to consider the issue of the treaty violation in his case. Bush did not comply with her request, stating, "In general, I will uphold the laws of the state of Texas, regardless of the nationality of the person involved. People can't just come into our state and coldbloodedly murder somebody" (Weinstein, 1998). Faulder came within half an hour of execution before being granted a stay of execution by the United

States Supreme Court (*Faulder v. Johnson*, 1998). The Court determined not to give the case a hearing, however, and lifted the stay January 25, 1999 (*Faulder v. Texas*, 1999). Despite Canada's vigorous protests, Faulder was executed in June 1999.

Mario Murphy, a Mexican citizen, pled guilty in Virginia to a crime committed when he was 19. He had five codefendants. "Murphy fully cooperated with the police and was clearly not the most culpable individual. He was also the only defendant not offered a plea bargain by the prosecution and the only one sentenced to death—and the only foreign national" (Amnesty International, 1998a). Murphy first raised his Vienna Convention claim in a federal habeas petition; the Federal District Court found the claim to be procedurally defaulted, but nevertheless discussed the issue, and concluded "that the violation at issue caused no prejudice to the defendant" (Kadish, 1997, pp. 580–581). The Circuit Court of Appeals dismissed Murphy's appeal on grounds of procedural default (*Murphy v. Netherland*, 1997), and found that any rights created by the Vienna Convention were not constitutional rights, and thus the Federal District Court's ruling against Murphy was not appealable (pp. 99–100). Despite vigorous efforts of the Mexican government to prevent his execution, Murphy was put to death in September of 1997. The day after the execution, the State Department made a formal apology to Mexico for failing to comply with the Vienna Convention in Murphy's case (Amnesty International, 1998a).

Finally, there is the case of Ricardo Aldape Guerra, a Mexican national condemned to death in Texas in 1982 for the murder of James Harris, a Houston police officer. Federal District Judge Kenneth Hoyt ruled that Aldape Guerra's conviction could not stand because of police and prosecutorial behavior he characterized as "outrageous" "intentional" and "done in bad faith" (quoted in Dieter, 1997). Judge Hoyt held that the evidence indicated the killer of Officer Harris was a companion of Aldape Guerra, who was shot and killed in a subsequent manhunt (Mexican long held, 1997). Judge Hoyt's ruling was affirmed by the Federal Court of Appeals (*Guerra v. Johnson*, 1996). Prosecutors did not retry Aldape Guerra, and he was released after 15 years on death row. He received a "hero's welcome" upon his return to Mexico. Hundreds of supporters welcomed him at the Mexican border; hundreds more were at the airport from which he flew to his hometown; and hundreds more stood along the route to his neighborhood, where a crowd of over 1,000 people cheered him (Zuniga and Dyer, 1997). Aldape Guerra became a star in a very popular Mexican soap opera after his release, but he was killed in a car accident only a few months later. He was widely mourned in Mexico (Villafranca, 1997).

THE CASE OF ANGEL FRANCISCO BREARD

The issues raised by American noncompliance with the Vienna Convention have been most fully litigated in the case of Angel Francisco Breard, executed by Virginia in April of 1998. Mr. Breard was a dual citizen of Argentina and Paraguay. He was born in Argentina in 1966 to an Argentine father and a Paraguayan mother (Breard fue ejecutado, 1998). After a traumatic childhood, including a sexual assault by a soldier, Breard moved to Paraguay with his family at 13, and a couple of years later began drinking (*ibid*). The year before he moved to the U.S., Breard was in a car accident which resulted in serious injury to his head. "Family members later reported a distinct change in Breard's personality following the head injury, particularly a tendency to behave impulsively and to lose his temper" (Amnesty International, 1998b). In the U.S., Breard's problems with alcohol worsened, and his marriage to an American woman ended in divorce (Breard fue ejecutado, 1998).

Breard was arrested in Virginia in 1992 for the murder of Ruth Dickie. The evidence against him was very strong, and he admitted having committed the crime (*Breard v. Netherland*, 1996, p. 1259). Breard was offered a chance to plead guilty in exchange for a life sentence, but he rejected his lawyers' advice and refused the plea bargain, apparently believing that a confession to the jury would result in mercy or even in exoneration. On the stand, Breard admitted the crime and told the jury he committed it under a satanic curse, placed upon him by his former father-in-law. The jury found him guilty, and sentenced him to death (Amnesty International, 1998b; Stout, 1998).

Three years after his trial, Breard learned of his right to consular assistance, and raised the issue for the first time in his 1996 appeal in Federal District Court. That court held the claim was procedurally defaulted because Breard had not raised it in state court, and therefore the issue was barred from federal review.[5] The court acknowledged being troubled by "Virginia's persistent refusal to abide by the Vienna Convention" (*Breard v. Netherland*, 1996, p. 1263). The Circuit Court of Appeals affirmed the Federal District Court decision (*Breard v. Pruett*, 1998). Judge Butzner concurred in denying Breard relief, but wrote a separate opinion "to emphasize the importance of the Vienna Convention" (p. 621). He noted:

> United States citizens are scattered about the world.... Their freedom and safety are seriously endangered if state officials fail to honor the Vienna Convention and other nations follow their example.... The importance of the Vienna Convention cannot be overstated. It should be honored by all nations that have signed the treaty and all states of this nation. (p. 622)

At the same time that Breard's appeal was working its way through the courts, Paraguay sued Virginia in Federal District Court, requesting that Breard's conviction be voided. The Paraguayan Consul claimed that his rights under the Vienna Convention had been violated, as well as Breard's. This novel approach failed in the Federal District Court (*Republic of Paraguay v. Allen*, 1996) which ruled it lacked subject-matter jurisdiction under the 11th Amendment grant of immunity to state officials. The Fourth Circuit Court of Appeals upheld this ruling (*Republic of Paraguay v. Allen*, 1998). The Federal District Court wrote that it was "disenchanted by Virginia's failure to embrace and abide by the principles embodied in the Vienna Convention" (p. 1273), and the Court of Appeals noted that it shared this "disenchantment" (p. 629).

Breard's execution was scheduled for April 14, 1998. On April 3rd, Paraguay took its case to the International Court of Justice in The Hague. The International Court of Justice properly had jurisdiction of the matter under

Article I of the Optional Protocol to the Vienna Convention (signed by both Paraguay and the United States), which states: "Disputes arising out of the interpretation or application of the Convention shall lie within the compulsory jurisdiction of the International Court of Justice" (Vienna Convention, Optional Protocol, 21 U.S.T. 77, p. 326). The Court issued a ruling on the 9th of April, unanimously holding that Breard's execution should be stayed until the court could consider the case fully and issue a ruling on the merits: "The United States should take all measures at its disposal to ensure that Angel Francisco Breard is not executed pending the final decision in these proceedings, and should inform the Court of all the measures which it has taken in implementation of this Order" (*Case Concerning the Vienna Convention*, 1998). The President of the ICJ, American Stephen M. Schwebel, voted for the order, although "with disquiet," noting that the United States had apologized to Paraguay for its breach of the treaty. Schwebel wrote, however, that "an apology... does not assist the accused," and based his vote on consideration of the great importance of the Vienna Convention "in the intermixed global community of today and tomorrow" (*ibid*).

The ICJ ruling resulted in an unprecedented situation. The world's highest court was requesting a stay of execution in a domestic criminal case, in order to determine what if any remedy should occur in response to an admitted treaty violation. The state involved was adamant that it had the right to enforce the penalties of its own laws. The federal government, ultimately responsible for the state's actions under international law, split in its reaction to the case. The Department of Justice argued in a brief to the U.S. Supreme Court that the violation of the Vienna Convention should not be grounds for overturning an otherwise legally imposed criminal sentence (EU ejecuta a un paraguayo, 1998). But the State Department requested that Virginia abide by the International Court of Justice ruling. Secretary of State Madeleine Albright wrote to the governor of Virginia asking that he grant a temporary stay of execution pending the final decision of the International Court of Justice (*ibid*).

Under these extraordinary circumstances, the case moved into the U.S. Supreme Court, with Breard's and Paraguay's appeals consolidated. As frequently happens in death cases, the U.S. Supreme Court's ruling came on the very night the execution was scheduled to occur. In a six to three decision, the Supreme Court affirmed the rulings of the lower federal courts, holding that Breard had forfeited any right he might ever have had to consular assistance: "By not asserting his Vienna Convention claim in state court, Breard failed to exercise his rights under the Vienna Convention in conformity with the laws of the United States and the Commonwealth of Virginia. Having failed to do so, he cannot raise a claim of violation of those rights now on federal habeas review" (*Breard v. Greene*, 1998). The Supreme Court briefly acknowledged the International Court of Justice's ruling and the Secretary of State's request for a stay. "If the Governor [of Virginia] wishes to wait for the decision of the ICJ, that is his prerogative. But nothing in our existing case law allows us to make that choice for him" (p. 1356).

Justices Stevens, Breyer, and Ginsburg dissented from the denial of a stay of execution on grounds that the case deserved more consideration than could be given before the scheduled execution. Justice Stevens noted that under the

Supreme Court's own rules, Breard had another month before his certiorari petition was even due in the Court (pp. 1356–1357). Stevens noted the "international aspects of this case" and dissented from "the decision to act hastily rather than with the deliberation that is appropriate in a case of this character" (p. 1357). Despite the three Justices' request for further time to deliberate, the Court gave less time to this capital case raising complex and novel issues of state, federal, and international law than it routinely would give to a non-capital case.

Only Governor Gilmore stood between Breard and execution after the Supreme Court's ruling.[6] The Governor could have complied with the State Department's request and with the ruling of the International Court of Justice by issuing a temporary stay of execution. The U.S. Supreme Court had specifically noted that this option was open to him. Governor Gilmore issued a statement giving his reasons for not granting a stay:

> I am concerned that to delay Mr. Breard's execution so that the International Court of Justice may review this matter would have the practical effect of transferring responsibility from the courts of the Commonwealth and the United States to the International Court.... The U.S. Department of Justice, together with Virginia's Attorney General, make a compelling case that the International Court of Justice has no authority to interfere with our criminal justice system. Indeed, the safety of those residing in the Commonwealth of Virginia is not the responsibility of the International Court of Justice. It is my responsibility and the responsibility of law enforcement and judicial officials throughout the Commonwealth. I cannot cede such responsibility to the International Court of Justice.
>
> Mr. Breard having committed a heinous and depraved murder, his guilt being unquestioned, and the legal issues being resolved against him, and the U.S. Supreme Court having denied the petitions of Breard and Paraguay, I find no reason to interfere with his sentence. Accordingly, I decline to do so. (Governor Gilmore, quoted in Charney and Reisman, 1998, p. 674–675)

Angel Breard received a lethal injection late the night of April 14, 1998. Subsequently, Paraguay dropped its case against the United States (International Court of Justice, 1998). (For legal commentaries exploring various aspects of the Court's decision, see Agora: *Breard*, 1998).

An especially troubling aspect of the *Breard* case is the U.S. Supreme Court's ruling that state and national procedural rules can override international law. The federal district and appellate courts ruled that Breard had forfeited his right to appeal the issue of the Vienna Convention violation by not raising it earlier, and the U.S. Supreme Court agreed. The reasoning of the courts has a Kafkaesque quality, since it was precisely the failure to inform him of his Vienna Convention rights that Breard was appealing; how he could be expected to appeal the failure to inform him of a right that he would only know about if he had been informed of it is never made clear. Breard was not alone in not knowing of his Vienna Convention rights: during a hearing on this issue in Mario Murphy's case, Virginia's Assistant Attorney General and two of the federal judges on the panel admitted they had never heard of the Vienna Convention before the case (Amnesty International, 1998a).

But the issue raised is much broader than the fairness or unfairness of any particular case, or even of all death sentences against foreign nationals. The issue goes to the heart of the enforcement of international law, because if treaty law does not prevail over domestic procedural law, then all any nation has to do to avoid its binding international responsibilities is to find that the assertion of treaty based rights fails to meet some procedural requirement under national law; a government could even pass domestic legislation precisely in order to avoid treaty obligations. This opens the door to the possibility of wide ranging abuses, as it undermines the basis of international law. Amnesty International notes that the Vienna Convention on the Law of International Treaties expressly holds that a country "may not invoke the provisions of its internal law as justification for its failure to perform a treaty" (quoted, 1998c). Yet this is precisely what the federal courts of the United States did in the *Breard* case.

INTERNATIONAL REPERCUSSIONS

Foreign countries are increasingly concerned and angry about U.S. failure to honor the Vienna Convention. This failure goes further than other death penalty related issues in its potential to damage the reputation of the U.S. abroad. America's insistence on using the death penalty, especially against juveniles, has created substantial foreign disgust, but in response, the U.S. can argue that nations have the right to establish their own criminal penalties, and that other countries are not affected. But the violation of the treaty obligation of consular assistance is more difficult to dismiss. The United States is openly and admittedly and frequently violating a law while insisting that other countries promptly and scrupulously observe the same law. This puts the United States in the very odd position of being "both a leading champion and violator of the right to consular protection" (Gisvold, 1994, p. 803). The rest of the world has not been slow to point out the hypocrisy of this position, both through formal government protests and through displays of popular resentment.

Popular resentment toward U.S. policy has been strongly evident in Latin America. The Mexican reaction to the execution of Irineo Tristan Montoya was typical. During the execution, crowds blocked the bridge forming the border crossing at Brownsville/Matamoros in protest. When Montoya's body was brought back into Mexico, he was received almost as a hero and martyr: "hundreds of people mobbed the bridge over the Rio Grande to salute his sacrifice and curse the country that killed him. Mariachis in full costume played 'Beautiful and Beloved Mexico.' The crowd cheered when the car crossed the bridge, and children ran after the convoy" (Price, 1997). Montoya's body was driven back to his childhood village, and "people came out along the 500-mile stretch... to view the procession" (Villafranca 1997). The reports of two Mexican newspapers convey a sense of the sorrow and anger felt by many. *El Manana* reported the execution under a banner headline that read "The nightmare is over for Irineo," with color photographs of weeping protesters and Montoya's family. The paper reported on Montoya's funeral: "this morning approximately 800 people said goodbye to him amidst sobs and shouts [and] threats against Americans, primarily against the Texas authorities" (Ya esta Irineo, 1997). *El Nacional* reported that the town

> wept and went into mourning at the arrival today of the coffin with the mortal remains of Irineo Tristan Montoya. The tiny and humble house of his family was too small to receive the majority of the 4,000 residents who wanted to pay their last respects.... The chants and cries of the name of Irineo merged with shouts of "Murderers, murderers..." by the spectators, who displayed banners with slogans against the justice system of the United States. (Pueblo Viejo se vistio de luto, 1997)

The fact that the condemned prisoners have been convicted of terrible crimes does not lessen the resentment felt by the public in their home countries. Many people doubt that their compatriots received anything like justice in the U.S., and many deeply oppose the death penalty under any circumstances; they are genuinely horrified to see it imposed upon one of their citizens. The execution of the prisoner can assume huge symbolic importance, and become a rallying point for anger and nationalistic feelings. Oscar Gonzalez, president of the Mexican Academy of Human Rights, said of Montoya's execution that it touched "popular sentiments. It has left a deep mark" (Price, 1997). A *New York Times* article reported that Montoya's execution "fanned a national wave of sorrow and solidarity" (Dillon, 1997).

Americans abroad may pay the heaviest immediate price for U.S. failure to observe the Vienna Convention. Honduran authorities had to reinforce security at the American Embassy after the execution of Jose Roberto Villafuerte in Arizona (Reforzada la vigilancia, 1998). The roughly 3,000 Americans arrested abroad each year (Stout, 1998) may find that countries whose citizens' rights were violated by the U.S. feel little inclination to protect those same rights for Americans. This possibility clearly concerned Secretary of State Madeleine Albright when she requested a stay of execution for Angel Breard. Americans already in detention in foreign countries are an especially vulnerable target for rage over the executions of compatriots. After Villafuerte's execution, the Honduran paper *La Tribunal* reported that a number of Americans detained in prison were on the point of being lynched in retaliation for the execution, and that prisoners were threatening to kill a "gringo" for every Honduran executed in the United States (Reos intentan vengarse, 1998).

But the most serious consequence of U.S. failure to observe the Vienna Convention is the inevitable weakening of international law. At the heart of international law is the concept of reciprocity. Reciprocity is a "structural principle of international law, whereby... any state claiming a *right* under that law has to accord all other states the same right" (Byers, 1995, p. 162, footnote omitted, emphasis in original). Because there are no reliably functioning mechanisms for punishing violations of international law, especially those committed by powerful countries, the basis of such law must be "mutual forbearance from deviation from the precepts of international law" (Gisvold 1994, p. 792). This "golden rule" is threatened whenever a nation refuses to honor its obligations.

The U.S. failure to observe its treaty obligations greatly weakens its ability to insist on other countries honoring theirs, and the example of defiance set by the United States is almost sure to be followed by other nations on many international issues, not only the Vienna Convention. Amnesty International, in a scathing report on the *Breard* case, concluded:

> The implications of the Breard execution go far beyond the undermining of U.S. credibility in the international community or the potential danger to U.S. citizens arrested abroad. Even more significantly, the United States has eroded the foundations of international justice and accountability, on which all protection of universal human rights ultimately rests. (Amnesty International, 1998c)

Hardly three months after Breard's execution, the United States invoked the Vienna Convention in a dispute with Belarus over the inviolability of diplomatic residences. The State Department declared that the rights granted by the Vienna Convention are not "privileges to be doled out by a host government, but rather basic legal rights that must be protected in a world based on international law" (U.S. Department of State, 1998a). These words ring hollow when pronounced by the same government that routinely violates the Convention.

REMEDIES

What relief is available for condemned foreign nationals who were not informed of their right to consular assistance? Their options currently are severely limited. Lawyers will probably continue to bring cases before the International Court of Justice and the Inter-American Court of Human Rights, but the United States is unlikely to comply with any rulings of these courts that require granting relief to convicted prisoners. The formal protests of foreign governments have elicited apologies from the U.S., but have not prevented execution of the prisoners. Paraguay's attempt to bring action against the United States failed in federal court under the 11th Amendment. Sims and Carter (1998) note, however, that no foreign government has yet attempted to obtain declaratory or injunctive relief from a pattern of Vienna Convention violations, rather than for a violation in an individual defendant's case. They believe such an approach might avoid problems with the 11th Amendment and with showing that an individual's case was harmed by the failure to notify him of his consular rights.

Attempts to gain relief in federal appellate courts for violations of the Vienna Convention have been unsuccessful, largely because federal courts have held the issue to be procedurally defaulted.[7] This points to the importance of attorneys preserving the issue for appeal by raising it as early as possible, preferably pre-trial. For cases in which the violation is not discovered till after trial, state habeas procedures may serve as a means for litigating treaty violations, and for preserving the issue for appeal in federal court (Sims and Carter, 1998).

While no solution seems to be forthcoming for most convicted foreign nationals, there are measures that can be taken to increase U.S. compliance with the Vienna Convention in future cases. Much of the failure to comply is simply due to ignorance on the part of law enforcement officials in the United States. The federal government up to the present has made only sporadic efforts to inform state law enforcement officers of their duty to inform foreign nationals of the right to consular assistance; given this lack of effort and the highly decentralized nature of American law enforcement, it is not surprising that many police departments have few or no officers who are familiar with the Vienna Convention. While no systematic study of police officers' knowledge of the Vienna Convention has been done, there are indications that such knowledge is rare. Shank and Quigley reported that their telephone calls to "a number of major-city police departments indicated little awareness of the Vienna Convention and an absence of any procedure to inform foreign nationals of their right to consular access" (1995, p. 748). Amnesty International quoted the Executive Director of the National Association of Retired Police Chiefs as saying, "In my 47 years in law enforcement, I have never seen anything from the State Department or FBI about this" (1998a). *The Washington Post* found that the Vienna Convention "is routinely ignored by many Washington [D.C.] area police departments" (Masters, 1998). The low level of knowledge of American officials in general about the international obligations of the U.S. has been noted by the International Commission of Jurists (1997) and the Special Rapporteur of the United Nations (1998).

To the extent that failure to comply with the Vienna Convention results from ignorance rather than resistance, it should not be too difficult to improve compliance. The United Nations Special Rapporteur called for the federal government to "develop an intensive programme aimed at informing state authorities about international obligations undertaken by the United States and at bringing national laws into conformity with these standards" (United Nations, 1998). The State Department is attempting to do just this. A manual on the obligations entailed by the Vienna Convention has been sent to the governor of every state, over 10,000 cards with a summary of the Convention have been given to law enforcement officers, and 29 states have coordinators assigned to increase observance of the Convention at the state level (McClelland, 1998). The State Department manual makes a clear and forceful statement of the obligation of officials to inform foreign nationals of their rights to consular assistance: "When foreign nationals are arrested or detained, they must be advised of the right to have their consular officials notified," and:

> Consular notification is in our view a universally accepted, basic obligation that should be extended even to foreign nationals who do not benefit from the VCCR [whose countries are not signatories] or from any other applicable bilateral agreement. Thus, in all cases, the minimum requirements are to notify a foreign national who is arrested or detained that the national's consular officials may be notified upon request; to so notify consular officials if requested; and to permit consular officials to provide consular assistance if they wish to do so. (U.S. Department of State, 1998b)

The simplest way of insuring broad compliance with the Vienna Convention is to routinely add a brief sentence to the *Miranda* warnings. All persons arrested would be told that if they are foreign nationals, they have the right to contact their consulates for assistance. This procedure would ensure that foreign nationals are informed, while avoiding the need for police officers to determine the nationality of everyone they arrest. Since this procedure would not be helpful to those who don't understand English, police could prominently post the same sentence in various languages in the detention facility. In addition, defendants could be advised of Vienna Convention rights during their first appearance in court; again, it would probably be more efficient to give this information to all defendants rather than to try to determine the nationality of every individual defendant.

Several jurisdictions in the United States have implemented or are considering procedures to ensure compliance. Cook County, Illinois apparently in response to protests by the Polish government of failure to notify one of their nationals, has adopted procedures to ensure that all arrested foreign nationals will be informed of their Vienna Convention rights not later than during their first appearance before a judge (Babcock and Warren, 1998). A California state senator has filed a bill requiring law enforcement officers to notify foreign nationals of their right to consular assistance (Warren, 1999a). Such a statute already exists in Florida, although it seems to be almost unknown to law enforcement. Chapter 901.26 of the Florida Statutes, passed in 1965, holds that when an official arrests or detains a national of any country to which the United States extends diplomatic recognition, the official "shall immediately notify the nearest consul or other officer of the nation concerned or, if unknown, the Embassy in Washington, D.C...." (Warren, 1998).

Statements by a number of American officials indicate a more troubling aspect of American noncompliance than simple lack of knowledge of their obligations under the Vienna Convention. Whether their statements reflect ignorance of or contempt for international law and the Supremacy Clause of the U.S. Constitution is not entirely clear, but the distinctly unhelpful and even inflammatory quality of the remarks is evident. The Attorney General of South Carolina, for instance, seemed to be unaware of the Supremacy Clause when he recently wrote: "The dogmatic application of international law to matters currently covered under the statutes of the states would eventually render the U.S. Constitution moot and signal the end of our federal form of government" (Capital controversy, 1998, p. 36). The prosecutor in the case of a Mexican national executed in Virginia appeared to entirely misunderstand the Vienna Convention when he said, "I mean, what is the remedy? I suppose Mexico could declare war on us. The burden is on [defendants] to say, 'Hey, excuse me, I'm a Mexican citizen. Tell my Embassy'" (LaFay, 1997). A spokesman for Senator Jesse Helms, Chair of the U.S. Senate Foreign Relations committee, said of the ICJ ruling in Angel Breard's case, "It's an appalling intrusion by the United Nations into the affairs of the State of Virginia. There's only one court that matters here. That's the Supreme Court. There's only one law that applies. That's the United States Constitution," apparently forgetting it is that very Constitution which gives treaties the status of the supreme law of the land (quoted in Amnesty International, 1998c). Worst of all, officials in Texas justified their refusal to investigate the violation of the Vienna Convention in Irineo Tristan Montoya's case by asserting that Texas had not signed the Vienna Convention (Amnesty International, 1998a). Unless Texas has seceded from the union and become an independent nation, it is bound by treaties signed and ratified by the federal government. Such comments and the attitudes they reveal must be deeply disturbing to foreign governments hoping for U.S. compliance and seeking redress in cases in which the U.S. has violated the Vienna Convention.

CONCLUSION

As more foreign nationals travel, work, and live in the United States, the need to ensure compliance with the Vienna Convention will only grow more urgent. The State Department is taking steps to encourage, if not to enforce, compliance by state law enforcement officials, and this is a positive move. For those persons already convicted, however, no remedy seems to be available, except perhaps for those few whose exceptionally alert lawyers have preserved the issue for appeal. For the majority of foreign nationals on death row, neither appellate nor diplomatic channels have provided relief. The execution of these persons will increase the resentment and ill will already felt by their home countries for the United States and may place Americans abroad at risk. Most seriously, at a time when the United States frequently calls on other nations to honor international law, continuing to violate our treaty obligations and to deny any remedy to those persons affected undermines international law and invites violations by other countries.

NOTES

1. Citizens of the following countries are on death row in the United States: Argentina, Bangladesh, Cambodia, Canada, Cuba, El Salvador, Estonia, France, Germany, Guyana, Honduras, Hong Kong, Iran, Iraq, Jamaica, Jordan, Laos, Lebanon, Mexico, Pakistan, Peru, The Philippines, Poland, Spain, Thailand, Trinidad, United Kingdom, Vietnam, Yugoslavia (Warren, 1999). Forty-two of the condemned foreign nationals are Mexican citizens; there are far more Mexicans on America's death row than any other foreign nationality. Texas has 24 foreign nationals on death row; California has 23 (Warren, 1999b). All foreign nationals on death row in the U.S. are male (M. Warren, personal communication, June 14, 1998).

2. Information in this table is from Warren, 1999b and M. Warren, personal communication, June 14, 1998. I have omitted from the table one dual national, Nicholas Ingram, executed in Georgia on April 17, 1995. Ingram was a dual citizen of the United States and the United Kingdom.

3. The Vienna Convention has been held to be a self-executing treaty, thus requiring no implementing legislation. For detailed discussion of self-executing versus non self-executing treaties, and whether treaties grant enforceable individual rights, see Gisvold, 1994, pp. 785–789 and Kadish, 1997, pp. 585–602.

4. All articles referenced and quoted from Honduran, Mexican, and Paraguayan newspapers are in Spanish. The translations are mine.

5. The doctrine of procedural default is one of the most complex issues affecting current habeas corpus law. Basically, procedural default means that a defendant forfeits his right to appeal issues if he has not raised those issues in the proper courts at the proper time. For recent articles on procedural default and related issues of habeas corpus, see Jones, 1992, Tabak, 1996, and Tushnet and Yackle, 1997.

6. At least one legal commentator has argued, however, that President Clinton had the authority to issue an executive order postponing Breard's execution under his authority to execute treaties and to conduct foreign policy (Vazquez, 1998, p. 689).

7. A recent non-capital case is apparently the first in which a federal court has ruled that a violation of the Vienna Convention can be grounds for the reversal of a criminal conviction (*United States of America v. Lombera-Camorlinga*, 1999). The government is currently appealing the unanimous decision of a three judge panel of the Ninth Circuit Court of Appeals.

The Wrong Man

Imposition of the death penalty has increased dramatically over the past few decades. Since 1973 death penalty jurisdictions have sentenced over 6,000 capital offenders to death. With 98 executions conducted in 1999, death penalty jurisdictions performed more executions in that year than in any other year since 1951, when 105 condemned prisoners were put to death. To some scholars, an escalating rate of executions in the United States increases the possibility that innocent defendants will be executed. The possibility of executing an innocent defendant has increased so significantly that the American Bar Association (ABA) has called upon capital punishment jurisdictions not to carry out the death penalty until jurisdictions can ensure that they have significantly reduced the risk of executing the innocent. This plea is not without merit. Capital punishment researchers have identified some 350 cases where defendants have been wrongfully convicted of murder in the United States since 1900. Of these cases, states sentenced 159 defendants to death, 23 prisoners were actually executed, and another 22 condemned prisoners came within 72 hours of being executed before their innocence was established and they won release. The Death Penalty Information Center in Washington, D.C., reports that 84 condemned prisoners have been released from death rows across the country through evidence of their innocence since 1973. The majority of innocent defendants released from death row have been nonwhite minorities, and over one-third of these defendants had been wrongfully convicted in Florida and Illinois. Innocent defendants spent an average of 7.5 years on death row before being released, and in eight of the cases identified by researchers with the Death Penalty Information Center, DNA evidence was a significant contributing factor in establishing defendants' innocence.

In the following selection from "The Wrong Man," *The Atlantic Monthly* (November 1999), social critic Alan Berlow identifies several facets of the process under which the U.S. criminal justice system imposes the death penalty that have increased the prospect that wrongfully convicted prisoners will be executed. Death-qualified juries, a "take-no-prisoners" mentality of jurists and politicians, the lack of resources required to fund public-defender organizations, an ever-increasing public condemnation of heinous criminality, an indifference of jurists to the possibility of wrongful convictions, the incompetence of defense counsel, the lawlessness of police officers and prosecutors in suppressing exculpating evidence, and an increasing complexity of the appeals process all indicate that the U.S. criminal justice system's mechanism of imposing death as punishment is faulty, impractical, and ineffectual. To Berlow, the only hope for remedying the problem of executing innocent persons is to declare a moratorium on the death penalty.

Key Concept: wrongful capital convictions and politics and capital punishment

It is better to risk saving a guilty person than to condemn an innocent one.
—Voltaire

On the afternoon of February 25, 1983, a sunny, dimple-cheeked little girl named Jeanine Nicarico reportedly heard a knock on the front door of the comfortable split-level house where she, her two older sisters, and their parents lived in Naperville, a Chicago suburb. The ten-year-old, home from school with the flu, listened through the door as a man said his car had broken down and he needed help. Jeanine, dressed in a nightgown picturing one of Snow White's dwarfs, with the words "I'm Sleepy," told him she was all alone and couldn't let him in. The man kicked in the front door, carried Jeanine to an upstairs bedroom, wrapped her in a sheet, and taped a towel around her eyes. Her body was discovered forty-eight hours later, less than two miles from the house. An autopsy revealed that she had been sodomized and that her skull had been crushed by a blunt instrument.

The Nicarico murder is every parent's worst nightmare, one that Thomas and Patricia Nicarico have lived with for the past sixteen years. It's the kind of case that leads 75 percent of Americans to support the death penalty. For nearly as many years Rolando Cruz has lived with another kind of nightmare. On February 22, 1985, Cruz was convicted of murder, rape, deviant sexual assault, kidnapping, and burglary in the Jeanine Nicarico murder trial. Despite the fact that the police found no physical evidence linking him to the victim, a judge sentenced Cruz to die by lethal injection. Because of a prosecutorial error, the Illinois Supreme Court ordered a second trial for Cruz, and in February of 1990 he was again found guilty and sentenced to death. That verdict was overturned in 1994. Then, on November 3, 1995, as a third trial got under way, one of the police officers who had provided critical evidence against Cruz acknowledged that he had lied under oath. The judge ordered a directed verdict of not guilty, and Rolando Cruz, having spent nearly twelve years in jail, was a free man.

The policeman's revelation alone didn't prove that Cruz was not guilty, but by then the state's case was a shambles. DNA evidence had all but eliminated Cruz as a suspect in the rape, and implicated another man, Brian Dugan, who, astonishingly, had claimed ten years earlier that he raped and killed Jeanine Nicarico. Dugan had also confessed to five other vicious crimes, including the rape and murder of a seven-year-old girl. Those confessions were credible enough for prosecutors in nearby Kane and LaSalle Counties, who used them to win Dugan's conviction and two consecutive life terms without parole. But the state attorney for DuPage County, James Ryan, now the Illinois attorney general, was convinced that Dugan was lying, and Illinois prosecutors fought for another decade to keep Dugan's testimony out of court while they tried Cruz twice more. They continued with their case despite the resignation of one of their own detectives, who was so certain of the state's error that he had offered to testify for the defense in Cruz's first trial. And they pressed on even after an assistant attorney general, too, resigned, protesting that the state was attempting to execute an innocent man. To date the Nicarico murder remains officially unsolved.

"THE WORST KIND OF MISTAKE"

Why prosecutors were so zealous in their pursuit of Cruz has been a matter of considerable speculation. Clearly, there was enormous public and political pressure on the state attorney's office to solve the highly publicized Nicarico case; it is quite possible that the police and prosecutors became convinced of Cruz's guilt before they had accumulated the facts to prove it, and then stuck with their hunch even as the holes in their case multiplied. Short of unimpeachable exculpatory evidence, prosecutors are loath to back away from an indictment, much less a conviction. No doubt Cruz shares responsibility for his lengthy ordeal, because he foolishly sought to sell the police a fabricated story about the murder in exchange for a $10,000 reward, thereby injecting himself into a situation he might otherwise have avoided. If law-enforcement officials had any doubt about Cruz's guilt, it presumably evaporated with the jury's guilty verdict in the defendant's first trial. When that verdict was set aside, prosecutors probably satisfied themselves that the court's decision turned on nothing more than a technicality. By the time Cruz's third trial rolled around, even the exculpatory DNA evidence was insufficient to shake the prosecution's belief in the rightness of its cause. Even today the leading prosecutors and police officers in the Cruz case insist that he was involved in the crime.

If Rolando Cruz were the only person ever mistakenly condemned to death in the United States, one could find any number of ways to explain his case away. But since the Supreme Court reinstated the death penalty, in 1976, more than eighty death-row inmates have been freed from prison, their convictions overturned by evidence of innocence. That may not sound like many, given the huge U.S. prison population, but it is more than one percent of the 6,000 men and women who were sentenced to death in that same period, and equal to almost 15 percent of those actually executed—not good odds for the defendants, given the stakes. The reasons for these miscarriages of justice range from simple police and prosecutorial error to the most outrageous misconduct, such as the framing of innocent people, and everything in between: perjured testimony, erroneous eyewitness testimony, false confessions (including the confessions of innocent defendants), racial bias, incompetent defense counsel, and overzealous police officers and prosecutors who may or may not genuinely believe they have the perpetrator of a heinous crime. Taken together, these miscarriages are not only shocking but also a powerful indictment of the way our criminal-justice system operates, particularly with regard to those at the margins of American society. Although we have no way of knowing how many innocent people remain on death row, or how many are serving life or other lengthy prison sentences for crimes they didn't commit, surely the number of innocent people discovered and freed from prison is only a small fraction of those still incarcerated. The other unanswered question is, of course, how many, if any, innocent people have actually been put to death.

Opponents of the death penalty believe that the execution of an innocent person would have a profound impact on public support for capital punishment. In England several wrongful executions played a crucial role in the decision, in 1964, to abolish the death penalty for murder. The execution of an innocent man in Michigan led to abolition in that state in 1846. Death-penalty supporters in this country have invested considerable energy in reassuring the public that the execution of an innocent person is virtually impossible. William G. Otis, formerly a special counsel to President George Bush and now an adjunct professor of law at George Mason University, in Virginia, says, "The administration of the death penalty ought to be, and in my view in fact is, surrounded with the most elaborate and exacting sort of safeguards of any decision that the government makes, and properly so." Paul G. Cassell, a professor of law at the University of Utah and a leading advocate of capital punishment, is even more categorical. "There is no documented case," he says, "of a factually innocent person who has been executed for at least the last fifty years." Ironically, it is the safeguards Otis refers to—the often time-consuming constitutional and legal challenges to convictions and death sentences—that death-penalty supporters have successfully undermined during the past decade, thereby increasing the likelihood of executing an innocent person.

Proving that an innocent person has been executed is difficult. Once a convicted murderer is dead, few people have any incentive to pursue claims of innocence. Witnesses and evidence disappear, memories fade, and defense resources that may have been marshaled to save a life evaporate. Nevertheless, a handful of cases over the past decade have raised troubling questions as to whether the person executed was guilty "beyond a reasonable doubt."

Last December, Florida Supreme Court Justice Gerald Kogan said he had "grave doubts" that at least two people executed during his twelve years on the bench were guilty. In one of the most controversial capital cases to reach the Supreme Court, the late Justice Harry A. Blackmun pointed out that the condemned man had an affidavit from a former state judge swearing that his own client, and not the defendant, was the actual killer. "The execution of a person who can show that he is innocent comes perilously close to simple murder," Blackmun wrote in 1993 in a dissenting opinion.

The 1992 execution of Roger Coleman remains controversial even today. Only hours before Coleman was scheduled to die in Virginia's electric chair, Governor Douglas Wilder allowed the condemned man to take a polygraph test. Coleman flunked and was executed later the same day. "If he had passed it," Wilder said at the time, "it obviously could have—could have—influenced my decision [about clemency]." Aside from the fact that some polygraph experts claim that administration of a test under such extreme stress would make it virtually worthless, Wilder's action suggested to many people that he had at least some doubt about Coleman's guilt—raising the question of why he allowed the execution to proceed. Today Wilder says he is absolutely certain that Coleman was guilty.

Doubts about the guilt of capital offenders have also been raised by jurors who learned after an execution of evidence they hadn't heard during the trial, and by others intimately involved with the fate of capital defendants. Don Cabana, a former warden of the Mississippi state prison, who presided over the 1987 execution of Edward Earl Johnson, says he believes that Johnson was probably innocent. Howard Marsellus, a former chairman of the Louisiana pardon board, admits that he was responding to political pressure when he voted, in 1984, to execute Timothy Baldwin, a man he believed was innocent of the bludgeoning death of an eighty-five-year-old woman. "I'm guilty as sin," Marsellus says. "I did something morally wrong. I gave in to the prestige and power, the things that went with my job. I knew what the governor, the man who appointed me, wanted: no recommendation for clemency in any death case." Marsellus says he is haunted by Baldwin's execution.

"The man walked in [to the execution chamber], grabbed the microphone, and looked dead in my face and said, 'Y'all are about to execute an innocent man and someday you'll have to answer for this.' Man, I will carry this to my grave."

Indisputable evidence that an innocent person has been executed in recent years has yet to be produced. But the close calls, as much as any actual execution, expose a myriad of potentially lethal fault lines in the administration of death sentences.

In 1972, in the case of *Furman v. Georgia*, the Supreme Court ruled 5–4 that the death penalty as then administered violated the Eighth Amendment's proscription against cruel and unusual punishment and the Fourteenth Amendment's equal-protection clause. Individual justices in the majority found much they didn't like about the death penalty. They said that it was disproportionately applied to the "poor and despised," that it was frequently imposed on the "constitutionally impermissible basis of race," and that it was applied in an "arbitrary and capricious" fashion. Although one can make a compelling case that all these criticisms remain valid today, the Supreme Court has since rejected them. The Court has said, however, that it is concerned about the *risk* of imposing an arbitrary sentence as well as about the proven fact of one. Even Justice Sandra Day O'Connor, a vigorous death-penalty proponent, stated in a 1985 decision that a sentence would have to be struck down if it created "an unacceptable risk that 'the death penalty [had been] meted out arbitrarily or capriciously' or through 'whim . . . or mistake.'" If nothing else, the wrongful sentencing to death of more than eighty innocent people would seem to suggest that there remains something both arbitrary and capricious about the way the death penalty has been administered since *Furman*. "If you have this many mistakes, you can't say we're only executing guilty people," argues Richard Dieter, the director of the Death Penalty Information Center, in Washington, D.C., a nonprofit research organization. "These cases illustrate the possibility of making the worst kind of mistake."

John Justice, the former president of the National District Attorneys Association, and like-minded supporters of capital punishment don't dispute that innocent people have been sentenced to death. But they insist that wrongful death sentences are aberrations. "The system is not perfect," says Justice, a South Carolina district attorney, arguing that "the reversals prove that the system works."

Governor George Ryan, of Illinois, advanced the same argument—"The system does work and . . . the checks and balances are there"—last February, when his state released Anthony Porter from death row after a group of Northwestern University journalism students working with a private investigator proved that Porter was innocent and obtained a videotaped confession from the actual murderer. But as details of Porter's wrongful sixteen-year incarceration emerged, the governor apparently began having second thoughts about Illinois justice. Police officers involved in Porter's case allegedly ignored suspects identified by a relative of one victim and pressured witnesses and other suspects to testify against Porter. Porter's lawyer acknowledged that he had barely conducted any investigation, because his client's family had come up with only part of his fee. Porter, who has an IQ of 51, came within forty-eight hours of execution by lethal injection in September of last year. He was granted a reprieve so that the state could determine whether he was mentally competent to be executed. Had his IQ been 50 points higher, he would almost certainly be dead.

Governor Ryan recently told reporters that he's "not sure the system worked" in the Porter case. "I think everybody understands what's at stake here," Ryan said. "An innocent man was about to die, and thank God he didn't. And now we want to make sure that scenario doesn't . . . come back and haunt us in the future." But Ryan knows as well as anyone that this scenario has reappeared repeatedly in Illinois. Since 1994 ten innocent people have been discovered on the state's death row. Porter's was actually the second Illinois case to be demolished by Northwestern students taking an investigative-reporting class. In 1996 students helped to establish the innocence of four Chicago black men convicted in a 1978 rape and murder involving a young white couple. Dennis Williams, Verneal Jimerson, Kenneth Adams, and Willie Raines spent a combined sixty-five years in prison. Williams and Jimerson spent fifteen and eleven years respectively on death row. In an effort to prevent erroneous death sentences in the future, the Illinois legislature recently passed, and Governor Ryan signed into law, legislation to increase funding for capital defenders and to require that they meet basic standards of competency.

Not surprisingly, Williams, Anthony Porter, and many of the other inmates released from death row over the past two decades are unforgiving of the system's imperfections. Williams says the State of Illinois "attempted to murder me." Immediately after his release Porter told reporters that he'd been "railroaded" by the Chicago police.

That law-enforcement authorities would plot to have a man executed for a crime he didn't commit is probably the most Kafkaesque scenario imaginable for the U.S. justice system—a scenario that gives paranoids and conspiracy theorists a good name. But even if former death-row inmates truly believe they were framed by police officers and prosecutors, such claims are nearly impossible to prove. In the Rolando Cruz case a special prosecutor, William Kunkle, actually indicted four policemen and three former prosecutors for falsely accusing Cruz, charging them with perjury and obstruction of justice. But this is believed to be the only death-penalty case in U.S. history that has led to such high-level indictments, and earlier this year all the defendants were acquitted.

True, courts have frequently ordered murder convictions overturned as a result of official misconduct. But a *Chicago Tribune* investigation published earlier this year found that since 1963 at least 381 homicide convictions nationwide have been overturned because prosecutors concealed evidence of innocence or presented evidence they knew to be false. Not one of those prosecutors has been convicted of a crime or barred from practicing law. Although law-enforcement officials invariably insist that miscreants in their ranks should be punished, in practice prosecutors rarely find any reason to investigate, let alone indict, their colleagues. Under existing law, law-enforcement officials are virtually immune from civil and criminal liability. "If a prosecutor withholds evidence, it's not a crime," says Bennett L. Gershman, a professor at Pace Law School, in White Plains, New York, and the author of *Trial Error and Misconduct*. "The fact is that criminal prosecutions of prosecutors for matters relating to their professional responsibilities in American law are virtually unknown, inconceivable, unthinkable." Gershman believes that there are hundreds of cases of prosecutorial abuse each year, but says that the Justice Department acts on only one or two, "as if to show that they're really being vigorous and diligent in their oversight." And he insists that the same lax oversight prevails among the states. As for the bar associations, which are supposed to discipline their members, Gershman says they are far too timid to take on prosecutors.

The Justice Department contends that instances of prosecutorial misconduct represent a minute percentage of the tens of thousands of criminal cases brought each year. And there is no question that the public generally sees prosecutors as "white hats" who are working to rid our streets of certifiable bad guys like the Unabomber and Timothy McVeigh, who in a single act of terror murdered 168 people in Oklahoma City. Undoubtedly, the country's prisons contain many dangerous predators who are actually guilty of the crimes of which they were convicted, and most of those sentenced to death committed unspeakable acts.

But whether or not one believes that the system works fairly most of the time, there is no denying that innocent people have been found on death row, and that many owe their freedom to factors having little to do with a properly functioning system of justice. The innocence of James Richardson, who was sentenced to death in Florida for the murder of his seven children, was established only after someone broke into a prosecutor's office and stole a file on the case which showed that the state had suppressed evidence of Richardson's innocence and that key witnesses, including a local sheriff, had lied under oath. Richardson spent twenty-one years in prison for a crime he didn't commit. No law-enforcement official was ever held accountable.

Rolando Cruz owes his life to Brian Dugan, who told the police about his own involvement in the Nicarico murder only to escape the death penalty. Joseph Burrows spent five years on death row for murdering an elderly man in 1988. He was freed after the key witness against him, Gayle Potter, was persuaded by a conservative Republican pro-death-penalty lawyer to tell the truth: that *she* had committed the murder. Most murderers never confess to their crimes, and it's fair to assume that most don't care if innocent people are executed in their place.

Walter McMillian, a black Alabaman who spent six years on death row for murdering an eighteen-year-old white woman, probably owes his freedom to a judge who was determined to have him executed. McMillian, who was dating a white woman at the time of his arrest, was sent to death row before even being tried. Although he had no prior felony record and twelve alibi witnesses placed him at a church fundraiser at the time of the murder, a jury convicted him of murder after a trial lasting a day and a half and sentenced him to life in prison without parole. But that wasn't good enough for Judge Robert E. Lee Key Jr., who overruled the jury. Citing the "vicious and brutal killing of a young lady in the first full flower of adulthood," Key condemned McMillian to die in Alabama's electric chair.

Today Judge Key says he doesn't want to talk about the McMillian case, and volunteers that McMillian "had one of the finest criminal attorneys in the state of Alabama representing him—a black attorney, by the way." Key says, "I'll go to my grave believing [McMillian] was guilty as hell." What Key doesn't say is that he had the trial moved from a county that was 40 percent black to one that was 13 percent black; that prosecutors withheld exculpatory evidence; that the state's principal witness avoided a capital murder charge by testifying against McMillian; that other witnesses were paid thousands of dollars for their false testimony; that the state's three primary witnesses all later recanted; and that the State of Alabama eventually admitted it had made a terrible mistake. Had Key not demanded the death penalty, however, Walter McMillian would probably be wasting away in prison along with the scores of other convicted murderers who, precisely because they are not facing execution, generate neither public interest nor the attention of the country's top capital defenders, who employ an emergency-room triage system that focuses on those in greatest need.

Just how often the police actually get the wrong man is nothing short of astounding. A 1996 Justice Department report, *Convicted by Juries, Exonerated by Science: Case Studies in the Use of DNA Evidence to Establish Innocence After Trial,* found that in 8,048 rape and rape-and-murder cases referred to the FBI crime lab from 1988 to mid-1995, a staggering 2,012 of the primary suspects were exonerated owing to DNA evidence alone. Had DNA analysis not been available (as it was not a decade earlier), several hundred of the 2,012 would probably have been tried, convicted, and sentenced for crimes they didn't commit.

DNA testing has without question revolutionized forensic science. Particularly in rape cases, its use is already preventing injustices of the kind that resulted from mistaken eyewitness identifications in the past. The attorney Barry C. Scheck says that his Innocence Project, at the Benjamin N. Cardozo School of Law, at Yeshiva University, has successfully employed DNA evidence to exonerate thirty-six convicted felons, and that nationwide DNA testing has been used to secure the release of sixty-two men sentenced for crimes they didn't commit, including eight on death row. Two death-penalty states, New York and Illinois, have found recent DNA-assisted cases so compelling that they have enacted laws allowing any inmate who feels he has a legitimate claim of innocence to demand post-conviction DNA testing.

The bad news is that there is no logical reason to think that police-error rates in criminal investigations lacking DNA evidence are any better than the 25 percent error rate in those where it is present. In 1984 a Maryland jury concluded that Kirk Bloodsworth, a former Marine with no arrest record, was guilty of raping and murdering a nine-year-old girl, after hearing several eyewitnesses testify that they'd seen him with the girl on the day of the crime. In June of 1993, after Bloodsworth had spent nearly nine years in prison, a new DNA test, unavailable at the time of his trial, demonstrated that semen found on the victim's clothing could not have been his. Had the actual assailant in this case simply murdered the victim and not raped her, DNA testing would have been irrelevant, and Bloodsworth, whose sentence had been commuted to life, would probably still be rotting away in a Maryland prison.

"I was separated from my family and branded the worst thing a man can be called—a child killer and rapist," Bloodsworth says today. "I don't know why all these things happened to me. Maybe God had a reason. Maybe He was trying to say these things happen to ordinary people."

One can, of course, argue that Kirk Bloodsworth is that rare exception to the proper functioning of the judicial system. But one can make the same case for Walter McMillian, and Joseph Burrows, and Anthony Porter. At some point the accumulating aberrations begin to suggest a more pervasive problem. At some point they raise the troubling suspicion that we as a nation may be tolerating the execution of innocent people.

DEATH-QUALIFIED JURIES

Although there is a common perception that the average murderer has endless forums in which to make his case, the reality is that once a defendant is found guilty by a jury, doors to an appeal begin slamming shut, and the burden of proof becomes far greater: where the defendant once had to convince a jury that he was not guilty "beyond a reasonable doubt," he now goes before the court under a presumption of guilt and must attempt to prove his innocence. Therefore a defendant's first trial may be his only real opportunity to present a complete case. In gruesome, high-profile cases like the Nicarico murder, a defendant may go to trial with a theoretical presumption of innocence but he or she will have a difficult time proving that innocence. Jurors are naturally reluctant to acquit someone who may have murdered a child, and the more violent and vicious the crime, the more likely a jury is to convict. So-called death-qualification procedures, in which potential jurors are questioned, often for days on end, about their ability to impose the death penalty (they must be willing to call for the death penalty in order to be seated), tend to create an atmosphere in which jurors go into a courtroom assuming that the defendant is guilty and that their only job is to decide on the appropriate sentence. Numerous studies have demonstrated that death-qualified jurors are more likely to convict.

Mike Callahan, who sat on the death-qualified jury in the first Rolando Cruz trial (in which Cruz was tried with a codefendant), believes that "half of the jurors had their minds made up before the trial even started." Callahan says that on the very first day of the trial, after the judge had ordered jurors not to discuss the proceedings among themselves, the jury foreman said, "Well, they're here, they must have done something." When the jurors finally began their deliberations, Callahan recalls, the first thing the foreman told them was "This'll be a mere formality, so we might as well get on with it." Callahan says he had grave reservations about the defendants' guilt and was stunned when the judge imposed the death sentence. "It wasn't an open-and-shut case, it absolutely wasn't, and to give the death penalty—I was absolutely appalled." Nevertheless, Callahan had voted to convict, because "I was more than willing to say, 'All right, we'll put you in the slammer for a while, and sooner or later the truth is going to come out.'" That's not exactly how the system is supposed to work.

Callahan and his fellow jurors might be forgiven their erroneous verdict, since they were not presented with all the evidence of innocence. If prosecutors present inaccurate, incomplete, or fabricated evidence, even the most unprejudiced and fair-minded juror may vote to convict an innocent man. And although most prosecutors and police officers presumably do not "cook" the facts, it is difficult to ignore the all-too-common exceptions. The Justice Department's DNA study found that eight of twenty-eight rape and rape-and-murder cases in which juries had convicted innocent men involved allegations of perjured trial testimony, fabricated lab evidence or expert testimony, or the withholding of exculpatory evidence by the police and prosecutors. Manufacturing evidence against an accused murderer may not be easy to get away with, but if the defendant has a criminal record, jurors are likely to give prosecutors the benefit of the doubt.

One troublesome and increasingly frequent source of perjured testimony is the "jailhouse snitch"—the convicted felon who will testify to just about anything for the prosecution in exchange for a reduced sentence. Walter F. Rowe, a professor of forensic science at George Washington University, says, "The dirty little secret in this country, and it's not such a secret, is that if you perjure yourself for the prosecution, no one's going to prosecute you." One Los Angeles County Jail inmate, Leslie White, acknowledged that he had fabricated a dozen "confessions" by fellow inmates, which he reported to authorities in exchange for more-lenient treatment.

But perjured evidence may come from sources far more insidious than convicted felons. In West Virginia, Frederick Zain, a police chemist and a popular expert witness for the prosecution, was accused of repeatedly falsifying laboratory results and presenting perjured testimony at trial. No fewer than 170 rape and murder convictions in West Virginia and Texas, all based in part on testimony by Zain, were called into question, and six men who served a total of forty years in prison have had their convictions overturned. In Texas, the nation's execution capital, where more than seventy-nine people have been executed in the past three years, prosecutors relied for years on the expert testimony of Ralph Erdmann, a forensic pathologist, who repeatedly falsified autopsy reports to support prosecution arguments in death-penalty cases. A special prosecutor's investigation of Erdmann concluded, "If the prosecution theory was that death was caused by a Martian death ray, then that was what Dr. Erdmann reported." Texas prosecutors also repeatedly relied on James Grigson, a psychiatrist who became known as "Dr. Death" because his expert opinion in 124 capital cases contributed to 115 death sentences. One of those sentenced was Randall Dale Adams, whose wrongful conviction was the subject of the movie *The Thin Blue Line*. Grigson testified at Adams's 1977 trial that the defendant had a "sociopathic personality disorder" and that "there is no question in my mind that Adams is guilty." Asked if Adams was likely to kill in the future, given the opportunity, Grigson replied, "He will kill again." In fact Adams was innocent, and had never killed anyone. He came within seventy-two hours of execution.

WINNING AT ANY COST

In Canada, which has no death penalty and only a handful of known wrongful murder convictions, the Ontario government conducted a year-long investigation into a case strikingly similar to that of Rolando Cruz. Guy Paul Morin was convicted of raping and murdering a nine-year-old girl and was freed in 1995 after a DNA test helped to establish his innocence. His family was awarded $1.25 million and an official apology from the attorney general's office. When Fred Kaufman, a retired judge, released a 1,400-page report on the case, in April of last year, he said, "This case in not unique. This case is not an aberration. The causes of Mr. Morin's conviction are rooted in systemic problems as well as the failings of individuals." The report made 119 recommendations for reforming the Canadian criminal-justice system.

In contrast, law-enforcement officials in the United States are just beginning to wake up to the fact that the growing numbers of innocent prisoners who are being discovered on death row raise profound constitutional issues. Although the Justice Department and a handful of state legislatures have examined pieces of the wrongful-conviction puzzle, no government agency, federal or state, has conducted a comprehensive analysis of why such miscarriages occur—not even in Florida, where at least eighteen innocent men have been discovered on death row since 1977.

In 1935 Supreme Court Justice George Sutherland wrote that a prosecutor is

> the servant of the law, the twofold aim of which is that guilt shall not escape or innocence suffer.... It is as much his duty to refrain from improper methods calculated to produce a wrongful conviction as it is to use every legitimate means to bring about a just one.

Since 1977 more than 570 people have been executed in the United States. Executions have become so routine that they are rarely given anything but perfunctory notice by the media. Rational debate over the benefits versus the costs of all these executions has been replaced by the rhetoric of "the paladins and pillars of justice and equity," as William Faulkner described them in *Old Man*—men who have become "blind apostles not of mere justice but of all human decency, blind instruments not of equity but of all human outrage and vengeance." In many prosecutorial offices Sutherland's conception of American justice has been replaced by an ethos of winning at any cost.

Examples of the take-no-prisoners approach to justice are legion. In 1995 Newt Gingrich, then the speaker of the House, suggested that Communist Chinese-style executions of "twenty-seven or thirty or thirty-five people at one time" might deter would-be drug smugglers. When flames burst from the head of Pedro Medina during his execution, in March of 1997, Florida's highest law-enforcement official, State Attorney General Bob Butterworth, saw a silver lining. He commented that the incident would send a message to potential lawbreakers: "People who wish to commit murder, they better not do it in the state of Florida, because we may have a problem with our electric chair." Television advertising in recent election campaigns has often featured candidates trying to persuade voters that they're "tougher" with respect to the death penalty than their opponents. Kirk Fordice promised in his campaign for governor that he would make Mississippi the "capital of capital punishment." Texas Governor Ann Richards, who presided over fifty executions during her four years in office, lost to George W. Bush in 1994 after a campaign in which he attacked her for not executing more people more quickly. During his first term Bush presided over seventy-seven executions. To date no fewer than 100 people have been executed on Bush's watch. Elected governors have also taken to boasting about the number of death warrants they have signed, as if this provided some objective yardstick of their fitness to serve. Kentucky Governor Paul Patton signed five execution warrants on his second day in office, though all five cases were still pending in court. Bob Martinez has bragged that he signed some ninety death warrants during his four years as governor of Florida. And Governor Bill Clinton flew to Arkansas during the 1992 New Hampshire presidential primary for the execution of a brain-damaged man who had killed a policeman. Flouting Supreme Court rulings against executing the mentally incompetent, Clinton seized control of the crime issue for the Democratic Party.

Many of these same death-penalty champions dismiss concerns about mistaken convictions and the execution of innocents, assuring voters that gubernatorial clemency provides what Chief Justice William Rehnquist referred to in 1993 as "the fail-safe in our criminal justice system." In several prominent cases where innocent men had exhausted all avenues of redress, clemency proved their only salvation. In Maryland, for example, the wrongfully condemned Kirk Bloodsworth might still be in jail had the pardon power not been available.

Clemency, however, presupposes a degree of integrity and political courage that is not readily apparent among the governors of most death-penalty states. Governors often eschew clemency, citing the sanctity of the jury process and their obligation to carry out the will of the people or to uphold the laws of the state. In cases where evidence of innocence is anything short of overwhelming, a governor facing a tough reelection in a strong pro-death-penalty state might decide against clemency for largely political reasons. The "fail-safe" case that Rehnquist wrote about involved a man convicted of killing two police officers in Texas. No governor would be inclined to grant clemency in that kind of situation.

Since 1973 there have been more than 6,000 death sentences and only forty cases of clemency nationwide. Clemency is most often granted when a governor is leaving office and needn't worry about voter reaction. In Texas, where it's difficult to keep up with reported miscarriages of justice, the Board of Pardons and Paroles almost never consents to defense requests for clemency. The only recent defense request granted was in 1998, when Governor Bush stopped the execution of Henry Lucas, who, although he was an established serial killer, had falsely confessed to dozens of other murders, including the one for which he was about to be executed. Bush wisely decided that it would be unseemly to execute him for a crime he didn't commit.

Unfortunate though political motives may be in the gubernatorial court of last resort, they are far more perfidious in the courthouse. Yet the idea of an independent judiciary—of judges willing to stand above politics—has come under relentless assault. Senate Republicans made it clear at the outset of the Clinton presidency that they would challenge any judicial nominee who lacked strong capital-punishment credentials, although the precise standard of political correctness has sometimes been difficult to discern. When Rosemary Barkett, the chief justice of Florida's Supreme Court, was nominated to the U.S. Court of Appeals, Senator Orrin Hatch said he wanted to see if she was "serious enough about the death penalty," even though Barkett had upheld more than 200 death sentences.

In 1996 Supreme Court Justice John Paul Stevens told the American Bar Association that "a campaign promise to be 'tough on crime,' or to 'enforce the death penalty,' is evidence of bias that should disqualify a candidate from sitting in criminal cases." Such a view probably seems tiresomely old-fashioned to a great many lawmakers today. Nowadays politicians are too busy seeking recalls, resignations, and impeachments of judges whose opinions are politically unpopular to be concerned with judicial independence or the separation of powers. In Tennessee, Republican Governor Don Sundquist proclaimed before a 1996 judicial election that he would appoint only death-penalty supporters to be criminal-court judges. Some judges and judicial candidates who must run for office have clearly imbibed a similar message, campaigning for office with promises to impose the death sentence at every opportunity. In thirty-two of the thirty-eight death-penalty states judges may be subjected to voter approval. In most it is highly implausible that a candidate who refused to take a strong position in favor of the death penalty could be elected. Judges are also elected in eight out of the nine states where it is a judicial prerogative to impose a death sentence or to override a jury's sentence of life. Can such judges fairly examine the facts in a gruesome murder case when the public is demanding execution?

373

Alan Berlow

"HOW MUCH JUSTICE CAN YOU AFFORD?"

No doubt most judges, police officers, and prosecutors are committed to the principle that a defendant is innocent until proven guilty. The single greatest threat to an innocent defendant, however, may be his or her own attorney. In Illinois, Gary Gauger was sentenced to die in 1994 for murdering his parents, after his well-paid attorneys failed to conduct a serious investigation into the prosecution's paper-thin case. Eventually Gauger was released and members of a Wisconsin motorcycle gang were indicted for the crime.

Perhaps Gauger was just unlucky. After all, anyone can hire a bad lawyer. The average capital defendant doesn't have the money to hire O. J. Simpson's "dream team." More likely than not, he has no money at all. At the very least, three fourths of state-prison inmates and half of federal-prison inmates have taxpayer-financed court-appointed counsel. The quality of this representation is questionable.

In its historic 1963 decision in *Gideon v. Wainright* the Supreme Court stated, "In our adversary system of criminal justice, any person haled into court, who is too poor to hire a lawyer, cannot be assured a fair trial unless counsel is provided to him." Since then the Court has ruled that in all criminal proceedings that carry prison sentences adequate counsel also means access to expert witnesses and investigative services. But how those rights are implemented has been left entirely to the states, and often such rights in fact belong only to those who can afford them.

Eighteen death-penalty states lack statewide public-defender organizations, and many of those that have them underfund them so seriously that lawyers end up handling huge caseloads that would be considered unconscionable, to say nothing of impractical, in the private sector. Most public defenders are so poorly paid that many talented lawyers tend to shy away from this sort of practice. Some jurisdictions award capital cases to the attorney making the lowest bid. In one Georgia county the low-bid public-contract attorney tried fourteen cases, entered a grand total of seven motions, and entered 262 guilty pleas for his court-assigned clients from 1993 to 1998. Other states randomly assign lawyers from a general list, a system that almost ensures that lawyers lacking appropriate qualifications will frequently be found. Aden Harrison Jr., a black man indicted for murder in Georgia, was assigned an eighty-three-year-old attorney who had been an imperial wizard of the Ku Klux Klan. Dennis Williams, one of the four men exonerated in 1996 with the help of Northwestern University students, was defended on a murder charge in Illinois by a lawyer who was simultaneously defending himself in disbarment proceedings. Federico Martinez-Macias was represented in Texas by a court-appointed attorney who failed to present witnesses, including an alibi witness who could have disputed the prosecutor's case. Martinez-Macias spent nine years on death row and came within two days of execution before a pro bono attorney in Washington, D.C., having thoroughly investigated his case, managed to demolish the state's evidence. In ruling that Martinez-Macias had been denied his constitutional right to counsel, the court noted that the defendant's trial attorney had been paid $11.84 an hour by the state and that "unfortunately, the justice system got only what it paid for."

In March of last year, on the thirty-fifth anniversary of the *Gideon* decision, Attorney General Janet Reno wrote in *USA Today,* "No prosecutor wants to prosecute someone whose defense counsel lacks the necessary skills and experience to put up a defense, and face the likelihood of having the conviction reversed on appeal." In the real world, however, one doesn't hear the National Association of Attorneys General making the case for better-funded defense lawyers, or complaining that indigents have been defended by law students, clerks, and lawyers with no courtroom or capital-defense experience. In Texas, where a state bar committee has estimated that defending a post-conviction capital client requires 400 to 900 hours of work, the Court of Criminal Appeals limits state-funded attorney compensation to 150 hours. When judges routinely reject defense requests for investigators or expert witnesses, prosecutors don't jump to their feet to object that this will make the proceeding unfair, even though they face no similar constraints on resources. Nor does one hear prosecutors carping about the lack of a level playing field in Mississippi, where attorneys are paid no more than $1,000, plus a small allowance for overhead, to try a capital case. (A private attorney defending a capital case would typically earn $100 to $500 an hour.) If these lawyers actually put in the hours needed to defend complex death-penalty cases, they would earn less than the minimum wage. Many don't put in the necessary time, and their clients pay the price.

Asked if they would favor a judicial system in which only the prosecution could present its case, most Americans would presumably be aghast. But in many courtrooms such *ex parte* proceedings are, for all intents and purposes, what happens. The adversary system simply doesn't exist. *Convicted by Juries, Exonerated by Science* found that a major cause of wrongful convictions was incompetent attorneys who neglected to examine the prosecution's forensic evidence or failed to have it tested. Nancy Gist, the director of the Bureau of Justice Assistance, which dispenses $1.7 billion a year to state and local criminal-justice systems, has described the quality of counsel in capital cases as "mostly abysmal." One innocent man spent eleven years on Georgia's death row because his lawyer failed to have a vital piece of evidence analyzed by a laboratory. In Kentucky an investigation by the Department of Public Advocacy found that 25 percent of death-row inmates had been represented at trial by attorneys who had since been disbarred or had resigned to avoid disbarment. A 1990 study found that 13 percent of the defendants executed in Louisiana had been represented by lawyers who had been disciplined, a rate sixty-eight times as great as that for the state bar as a whole. The pervasive inadequacy of defense counsel in capital cases was a major reason that the American Bar Association's House of Delegates overwhelmingly approved a 1997 resolution calling for a moratorium on executions. "In case after case," a report accompanying the resolution stated, "decisions about who will die and who will live turn not on the nature of the offense the defendant is charged with committing, but rather on the nature of the legal representation the defendant receives."

Death-penalty advocates are right to insist that the public should not be required to provide every capital defendant with a team of $400-an-hour lawyers. Nevertheless, no one seriously doubts that a defendant's prospects—whether he is guilty or innocent—will be improved by a skilled attorney. A study commissioned by the Texas Judicial Council in the mid-1980s showed that a defendant's chances of being convicted in a capital case were 28 percent higher if he was represented by court-appointed counsel than if he retained counsel. The study also showed that 55 percent of those who retained counsel but 79 percent of those with appointed counsel were sentenced to death. Walter Rowe, of George Washington University, says that for a defendant in state court the "unfortunate fact of life is, if you ain't got bucks, you're going to take it in the shorts." Rowe says he asks defendants who solicit his services as an expert witness, "How much justice can you afford?" "Numerous innocent people are presently incarcerated because of the inadequacy of their attorneys," he says.

"ONE HALF JUSTICE"

Almost thirty-seven years after *Gideon v. Wainright* it is difficult to escape the unpleasant conclusion that the failure of state and local jurisdictions to provide adequate legal representation in criminal cases is anything other than a deliberate policy—one that probably arises from a pervasive belief that most criminal defendants are guilty and therefore unworthy of competent counsel. This inattention—by now a matter of tacit national policy—to what should be a fundamental constitutional right is bolstered by a self-justifying logic that becomes almost irresistible when one considers the tangible "benefits." By failing to fund counsel for indigents adequately a state or locality not only saves an enormous amount of money but also makes meaningful defenses difficult if not impossible, thus easing the government's burden in winning convictions and imposing death sentences, and diminishing the likelihood that heinous errors will ever be discovered. In providing counsel to the poor "we set our sights on the embarrassing target of mediocrity" and "halfway justice," Harold Clarke, the chief justice of Georgia, said in 1993. "To my way of thinking, one half justice must mean one half injustice, and one half injustice is no justice at all."

Public officials see themselves, of course, not as skimping on justice or constitutional rights but as conscientious guardians of the budget who are tough on crime and determined to provide law-enforcement authorities with the very best tools possible to get criminals off the streets. Death-penalty advocates avoid questions about the condemning of innocent people by focusing on the number of murderers never prosecuted or mistakenly freed and by asking "How many innocent people will die if we do not execute vicious murderers?" Most prosecutors I have interviewed seemed to accept as an article of faith that adequate legal resources are provided to capital defendants, even when those prosecutors hadn't a clue what the actual resources were in their respective states.

If a hospital assigned a cosmetic surgeon to perform a heart-bypass operation, the hospital would be held accountable when the patient died. But when states make a practice of appointing cosmetic attorneys to defend indigents, they declare that justice has been served, regardless of the outcome. Astonishingly, the Supreme Court has endorsed that position, ruling that jurisdictions appointing incompetent attorneys bear virtually no responsibility for the miscarriages that occur. "The government is not responsible for, and hence not able to prevent, attorney errors," the Supreme Court ruled in 1984 in *Strickland v. Washington*. Who, then, is responsible? According to the Supreme Court, apparently, the defendant is responsible. Under its landmark ruling state courts have typically found no violation of the Sixth Amendment, which guarantees the assistance of counsel in all criminal prosecutions, even when lawyers have been addicted to heroin or cocaine during a trial, have come to court drunk, have conducted no investigation of their clients' claims, or have been unable to cite a single relevant capital case. In one death-penalty case a lawyer presented no evidence during the penalty phase of a trial and made the following closing argument (quoted in its entirety): "You are an extremely intelligent jury. You've got that man's life in your hands. You can take it or not. That's all I have to say." The defendant was executed. In a Texas case in which the defense lawyer slept through most of his client's trial, the judge found no denial of due process. "The right to be heard," the Supreme Court ruled in 1932, in the famous Scottsboro Boys case, "would be, in many cases, of little avail if it did not comprehend the right to be heard by counsel." But the Texas court didn't think it essential that defense counsel hear the case, or even be conscious: "The Constitution doesn't say the lawyer has to be awake," the judge ruled.

How does the highest court in the land justify what to a layman appears to be a brazen denial of due process? By referring the hapless defendant to the healing succor of his national or local bar association. "The Sixth Amendment refers simply to 'counsel,' not specifying particular requirements of effective assistance," the *Strickland* court ruled. "It relies instead on the legal profession's maintenance of standards sufficient to justify the law's presumption that counsel will fulfill the role in the adversary process that the Amendment envisions."

It's an extraordinary presumption. The legal profession has, after all, produced reams of ethical and professional standards to guide lawyers, but they are widely ignored and largely unenforced or unenforceable, and the justices of the Supreme Court know this better than anyone. In 1989 the American Bar Association approved "Guidelines for the Appointment and Performance of Counsel in Death Penalty Cases," which set rigorous standards. Invaluable though these guidelines may be in establishing goals for state and local governments, they remain purely hortatory and are rarely put into practice. The ABA's "Rules of Professional Conduct" require attorneys to communicate adequately and promptly with their clients, and forbid conflicts of interest. The ABA's "Model Rules" include a pie-in-the-sky provision that stipulates, "Every lawyer, regardless of professional prominence or professional workload, has a responsibility to provide legal services to those unable to pay." Yet in a country with a million lawyers more than 200 condemned prisoners await execution without counsel, and thousands of indigents accused of crimes are processed through the courts each year with only the barest semblance of counsel. Naturally, the ABA also has standards regarding ability ("A lawyer shall not handle a legal matter which he knows or should know that he is not competent to handle"), but lawyers routinely handle matters they know little or nothing about with the full complicity of the courts—often with grave consequences to their clients and not a whimper from the state or local bar. The world would truly be a better place if all good people heeded the wisdom of the bar's sage oracles, but they don't. Justice Thurgood Marshall knew they wouldn't when he wrote in his dissent to *Strickland*, "To tell lawyers and the lower courts that counsel for a criminal defendant must behave... like 'a reasonably competent attorney,' is to tell them almost nothing."

The predicament of an innocent defendant represented by an incompetent lawyer has been further complicated by Supreme Court rulings on what is known as "procedural default," which effectively punishes the client for his lawyer's incompetence or stupidity. In practice, procedural default sets up a classic Catch-22 situation. An indigent defendant is assigned a lawyer who fails to investigate the case properly, puts on a perfunctory defense, ignores exculpatory evidence, and collects his fee, while his client goes to prison. When the defendant, now a convicted felon, tries to have the exculpatory evidence raised on appeal, it is barred by the court, which announces that it should have been presented by counsel at the initial trial. Meanwhile, any claim against the lawyer is conveniently executed, thanks to *Strickland*.

In one of its most controversial procedural-default rulings the Supreme Court allowed Roger Coleman to be executed in Virginia after finding that he had no right to present in court what he claimed was evidence of innocence, because his attorney had missed a filing deadline by three days. In a ruling that seemed to give process precedence over life and liberty, the Court concluded that Coleman "must bear the risk of attorney error that results in a procedural default." Justice O'Connor wrote one of the more astounding death-penalty decisions in recent memory: "This is a case about federalism. It concerns the respect that federal courts owe the States and the States' procedural rules when reviewing the claims of state prisoners in federal hebaes corpus" claims —habeas being the procedure that allows prisoners to petition state and federal courts to determine whether a sentence violates the laws or the Constitution of the United States. A 6–3 majority of the Court appeared to be saying that state procedures were more important than Coleman's claim of innocence, and the defendant was executed. Justice Blackmun called the execution "an affront to principles of fundamental fairness," adding, "The more the Court constrains the federal courts' power to reach the constitutional claims of those sentenced to death, the more the Court undermines the very legitimacy of capital punishment itself."

Not only has the Supreme Court given its seal of approval to incompetent counsel; in some capital cases it has even sanctioned a lack of any counsel whatsoever. Coleman's execution was justified by the Court in part on the basis of another precedent-setting Virginia case, *Murray v. Giarratano*, in which the Court ruled that a capital defendant is not entitled to a court-appointed lawyer in a post-conviction proceeding. Citing *Giarratano*, the Court ruled that because Coleman had no right to counsel, he had no basis on which to make a claim of ineffective counsel. But why would the Supreme Court under any circumstances conclude that a person facing the ultimate sanction did not need an attorney—particularly since federal law does recognize a right to counsel in post-conviction proceedings? Because, the Court reasoned, a state "may quite sensibly decide to concentrate the resources it devotes to providing attorneys for capital defendants at the trial and appellate stages of a capital proceeding." This sounds reasonable enough. But the Court's abstract rationale bears no relation to reality. Had the justices bothered to examine what resources Virginia was actually devoting to trials and appeals, they would have found that the state has one of the worst records on indigent defense anywhere in the nation, and routinely ignores the needs of the poor at both the trial and appellate stages.

Then again, perhaps the justices believe that a post-conviction appeal, one of the most complex areas of death-penalty law, is best handled by an illiterate high school dropout facing a lethal injection or the electric chair. If so, they might want to examine the abysmal success rate of capital defendants who try to play lawyer. Stephen Bright, the director of the Southern Center for Human Rights and one of the nation's pre-eminent capital-defense attorneys, says the chance that a person of normal intelligence could successfully represent himself without counsel on a murder charge is "equivalent to our going to the airport, and the pilot isn't there, and we say, 'Well, we'll just fly the Concorde to Paris ourselves.'" Bright recalls the 1996 case of Exzavious Gibson, a man with an IQ below 85, who was condemned to die by the State of Georgia and was forced to represent himself in a state post-conviction proceeding. "It was a farce, of course. The state had an expert lawyer and the defendant had no idea what he was doing."

SPEEDING UP EXECUTIONS

Many of the more than eighty prisoners who have been freed from death row over the past two decades are alive today only because their executions were stayed long enough for the truth about their cases to emerge. Some had to wait fifteen or twenty years. Nevertheless, the drumbeat for speedier executions continues. The Supreme Court, Congress, and many states have moved during the past decade to expedite executions by making it more difficult for defendants to have their appeals heard. States have, for example, placed stringent time limits on appeals. In Virginia a person convicted of murder is given twenty-one days after conviction to present new evidence of innocence. Suffice it to say that new evidence rarely, if ever, materializes in a capital case during the first three weeks following conviction.

In 1995 Congress weighed in on the need for speedier executions when it eliminated the $20 million annual budget for Post-Conviction Defender Organizations, which had provided some of the most sophisticated and effective counsel for death-row inmates in twenty death-penalty states. The following year Congress passed the Antiterrorism and Effective Death Penalty Act, slapping a one-year statute of limitations on the filing of habeas corpus petitions in capital cases. Until then Americans had lived quite comfortably with the notion that there should be no time limit on habeas appeals—that the right to be free from illegal restraint never expired.

The radical revision of habeas law was sold to the House of Representatives by Henry Hyde, the chairman of the Judiciary Committee, as the "Holy Grail" of criminal-justice reform, a long-sought change that would address what he called "the absurdity, the obscenity" of "endless appeals" in death-penalty cases. The average time between sentencing and execution is a little over eight years. "Eight years is ridiculous, fifteen and seventeen years even more so," Hyde proclaimed during House debate on the act, insisting that such delays "make a mockery of the law." Orrin Hatch, the chairman of the Senate Judiciary Committee, declared that "support for an end to frivolous death-penalty appeals is the most authentic evidence of an elected official's support for the death penalty." Hyde and Hatch directed their spleen at the pariahs on death row, but 99 percent of habeas petitions relate to noncapital cases. Still, this fundamental right has now been circumscribed for everyone. As for the one percent of habeas petitions filed by death-row inmates, neither state nor federal courts have found them entirely "frivolous." On the contrary: in nearly two thirds of the cases courts have found violations so serious as to warrant overturning the convictions.

Will the new one-year statute of limitations increase the likelihood that innocent people are executed? Congressman Bill McCollum, of Florida, a leading advocate of capital punishment and one of the authors of the anti-terrorism bill, thinks not. "It simply speeds up the process of execution where someone's truly guilty," McCollum says, adding that there is no time limit on filing a claim of innocence. He would like to see the time between sentencing and execution reduced from the current national average of eight years to four to six years. But in the past, evidence of innocence has taken seven, twelve, fifteen, or more years to surface. McCollum insists that speeding up the process will actually benefit death-row inmates, because the expert resources brought to bear just before an execution will now come into play in the fourth year rather than the fourteenth. That may be wishful thinking. And it clearly doesn't apply to the cases whose outcomes have nothing to do with the typical legal actions brought on behalf of the condemned—the cases that turn on pure serendipity, that need time for the real murderer to step forward and confess, or time for police officers or witnesses who perjured themselves to feel safe in talking. Time may heal all wounds, but it won't do much for a lethal injection.

Robert E. Morin, who got Kirck Bloodsworth released from prison, told a conference at American University in 1995 that speeding up executions will result in the execution of innocent people. "It's not a question of increasing the probability; it's going to happen," Morin says. "It's just a matter of when, and when we discover their innocence." Morin, now a superior-court judge in the District of Columbia, said that "anybody who wants to compress the time" should "sit down and have a conversation with Mr. Bloodsworth and his family about why you wanted to shorten the period of time he had to work on his case."

For its part, the Supreme Court has sought in recent years to give maximum discretion to state-court constitutional determinations. It has, for example, expanded the so-called harmless-error doctrine, making it easier for states to uphold convictions regardless of whether errors or prosecutorial misconduct contributed to an unfair trial. And under Chief Justice William Rehnquist it has seized on every available opportunity to limit federal-court review of state habeas rulings. A provision of the new anti-terrorism law limiting federal habeas review to cases in which a state-court decision "involved an unreasonable application of clearly established federal law" has already been narrowly interpreted by several of the most conservative circuit courts. And if the Supreme Court follows their lead, says John Blume, a habeas expert and the director of the Cornell Death Penalty Project, "it would be impossible for a person to get federal habeas relief."

Where the Court is headed on claims of innocence is not at all clear. In January of 1993, in *Herrera v. Collins,* Rehnquist bemoaned "the very disruptive effect that entertaining claims of actual innocence would have on the need for finality in death penalty cases" and dismissed the argument that "claims of actual innocence based on newly discovered evidence" provide a rationale for habeas relief. At the same time, the court's majority ruled that it would be unconstitutional to execute a defendant with "a truly persuasive demonstration of actual innocence made after trial." What a "truly persuasive" case would be, however, remains unclear, because the court has yet to identify one. Leonel Herrera's case was evidently not what the justices had in mind. He was executed three and a half months after the Supreme Court issued its ruling. His final words were "I am innocent, innocent, innocent. . . . Something very wrong is taking place tonight."

THE PUBLIC-OPINION FACTOR

As executions become increasingly common, the media seem to find them less and less newsworthy, and the public grows decidedly more blasé about them. (The five-hundredth execution since capital punishment was reinstated, in 1976, received a 141–word notice in the *New York Times* "National News Briefs" column.) Dozens of stories about innocent people wrongly condemned to death have provided entertaining fodder for TV newsmagazines, yet they've provoked little public outcry and few demands for compensation of victims or calls for action against police officers, prosecutors, and judges who perpetrate these miscarriages. Only a handful of states have addressed the need for preventive measures, such as better-funded defense services.

Unquestionably, support for the death penalty remains high—the proportion in favor of it has ranged from 70 to 76 percent over the period 1982–1996, as against 38 percent in 1965 and 47 percent in 1970. It is these numbers that drive the debate on capital punishment. Nevertheless, when questioners suggest that the death penalty "has a built-in racism" or that "many people have been sentenced to death who have later been found innocent," support for capital punishment declines abruptly. In one survey 48 percent of respondents had "some doubts" or "serious doubts" when the race factor was introduced, and 58 percent expressed doubts when the possibility of innocence was introduced. Even in the states most strongly in favor of the death penalty support drops dramatically—to anywhere from 50 to 61 percent, depending on the poll—when the alternative of life imprisonment with absolutely no possibility of parole is mentioned to respondents.

Studies of capital juries buttress the idea that Americans are far less gung-ho about the death penalty than the polls suggest. Because capital juries are "death-qualified," one might expect the typical jury to be much more inclined to impose death than the public at large, of which approximately 25 percent opposes the death penalty under any circumstances. But a 1993 Justice Department study indicated that where death was an option, juries imposed it in only one out of eight cases. One reason for this is that almost all death-penalty states now offer life without parole as an option for jurors. Studies also show that in some cases jurors have been concerned about executing an innocent person; they have "lingering doubts" about the defendant's guilt, and although those doubts may not be strong enough to warrant letting the defendant go free, they forestall a vote for death.

Finally, unlike normal citizens responding to the latest sensational murder case on television, jurors are required to consider mitigating evidence in sentencing. Although the idea of a murderer is an abstraction to most of us, jurors must confront flesh-and-blood human beings. And the evidence suggests that when they get to know a defendant, when they learn the details of an individual case, many jurors find it difficult to take a person's life.

BUILDING IN SAFEGUARDS

England's experience might lead one to expect that public support for the death penalty would decline dramatically if it could be proved that an innocent person had been executed. Yet some death-penalty advocates believe, like Congressman Bill McCollum, that what they see as the remote possibility of executing an innocent person is no reason to abolish capital punishment. Others have argued that the occasional accidental execution of an innocent person is the price the country must pay to combat violent crime. William Kunkle, the Chicago prosecutor who both secured the death penalty for the serial killer John Wayne Gacy and brought the unsuccessful case against police officers and prosecutors for allegedly framing Rolando Cruz, argues that the execution of innocent people is inevitable. "Sooner or later it's going to happen," he says. "It comes with the territory. It is not humanly possible to design a system that is perfect. And if people are not prepared for the eventuality that human institutions are going to make mistakes, then they shouldn't support the death penalty, and they shouldn't elect legislators who support it."

Although it is undoubtedly impossible to design a perfect system, that hardly argues for tolerating the status quo. Nevertheless, the idea that this system is the best that human beings can design remains an article of faith among many prosecutors, death-penalty supporters, and citizens in general. William Otis, the former aide to President Bush, argues, "It goes back to first principles. It depends on what a person really believes about the nature, honesty, and legitimacy of government in this country. And a person who basically has faith in those things is more likely to believe that the death penalty is a permissible remedy than the person who doesn't."

But the first principles with which many of us grew up were designed to protect innocent and powerless individuals from an abusive and overweening government, whether federal or state. From that perspective there can be no greater offense by a state, and nothing more damaging to its legitimacy, than the execution of an innocent person. The fact that we are not able to guarantee that no innocent person will be executed remains the most powerful argument against the death penalty. If the government and we citizens want to continue executing men and women, we might at least take some steps to reduce the risk that the ultimate sanction will be imposed on innocent people. That won't be easy. In an environment in which defendants are typically presumed to be guilty, any legislator who tries to provide safeguards for the accused is certain to be attacked as "soft on crime." The problem is one not only of reclaiming some fundamental notions of fairness but also of building in new safeguards at virtually every stage of the criminal-justice process.

First, reforming the system might begin at the investigative level, where the police should be required to record, on either videotape or audiotape, both interrogations and confessions.

Second, serious efforts must be made to eliminate criminal abuses of law-enforcement power. Attorney General Janet Reno knows firsthand the kind of outrageous behavior that goes on in high-profile murder cases. In 1989, as a Florida district attorney, Reno was personally responsible for the release of James Richardson, the man who was sentenced to death for the murder of his seven children, when evidence emerged that police officers and prosecutors had framed him. As the nation's top judicial officer, Reno knows, particularly since Waco, how unwilling law-enforcement officers are to police their own. She should therefore appreciate the need to establish independent special prosecutors or inspectors general in every state to investigate and prosecute police, prosecutorial, and judicial misconduct.

Third, routine DNA testing must be made available to inmates who believe that it will demonstrate their innocence. And better procedures are needed to ensure both that DNA and other evidence is preserved as long as a person is incarcerated and that the defense is given full access to it.

Fourth, the use of jailhouse snitches, many of whom are known pathological liars, must be dramatically curtailed. Such informant testimony should be inadmissible unless it is backed by corroborating evidence.

Fifth, better methods of judicial selection are needed to ensure an independent judiciary. Ultimately this means eliminating the election of judges and thus removing the blight of judges who not only take campaign contributions from the attorneys who try cases before them but also routinely place their own political and financial interests above the Bill of Rights.

Sixth, the American Bar Association should press for adoption by the states of a provision in the American Law Institute's "Model Penal Code" which is designed to minimize the risk of convicting and executing innocent people. The provision would prohibit a death sentence if the evidence, albeit sufficient to sustain a guilty verdict, "does not foreclose all doubt respecting the defendant's guilt." To date no state has adopted this "residual doubt" provision.

Seventh, whether an official's corruption, simple witness error, or the racism of an arresting officer led to wrongful imprisonment, the victims of such miscarriages should be compensated. Unfortunately, those who have been wrongfully sentenced find it nearly impossible to rid themselves of the taint of criminality, and tough-on-crime legislators don't seem terribly distressed about these victims of the system. Only fourteen states have statutory compensation for people who have been wrongfully incarcerated. Federal law provides a miserly $5,000, regardless of time served.

Eighth, and most important, the right to counsel and to due process must be given substance through the creation of adequately funded nationwide public-defender services. Both the existing systems of court-appointed counsel, which are rife with conflicts of interest, and the unconscionable contract systems that rely on low-bid attorneys have to go. In addition, states need to adopt and enforce reasonable standards for the appointment and performance of defense attorneys in capital cases, such as those proposed by the American Bar Association a decade ago. The *Strickland* decision's grant of immunity to incompetent lawyers should be overturned, and the Justice Department should facilitate this by joining the next viable Sixth Amendment challenge to go before the Supreme Court. The history of the Sixth Amendment since *Gideon* demonstrates that it is not enough to assert that everyone has a right to an attorney. Criminal defendants, and capital defendants especially, need attorneys who are well trained, experienced, and adequately paid.

Some outspoken death-penalty supporters who favored defunding the Post-Conviction Defender Organizations now say they favor funding post-conviction representation in capital cases. Others say they want to see competent counsel provided at the trial stage, in order to avoid unnecessary appeals and overturned convictions. But there's a catch: conservatives invariably want to consign the issue of spending to the states, which is where the Sixth Amendment has been moldering, a sort of discretionary constitutional right, since its adoption, in 1791.

How much should the states be spending to ensure equal protection for every U.S. citizen? Nobody really knows. Robert Spangenberg, the country's leading authority on indigent-defense programs, says the country spent about $1 billion on indigent defense in 1986, or about $200 per case—a "totally inadequate" figure, he says. The quality of indigent defense varies state to state, from quite good to reprehensible. Spangenberg says that it would cost the State of Florida, to cite one example, about $25 million a year to properly handle its backlog of capital appeals alone. The state legislature has currently budgeted $6 million. Where the states will get the money to defend the rights of a constituency with no political power remains the big question. What is clearly needed is some sort of permanent funding mechanism that is not subject to annual budget skirmishes and political fashions. One idea is to make indigent defense a fixed percentage of some other annual budget, such as the prosecutor's budget—which, in particular, would lock in the notion that fair representation is a sine qua non for both sides if justice is to be genuine. As a result of lawsuits that successfully challenged the constitutionality of programs that often provided defendants with unqualified or horribly overworked lawyers, several states and counties have been forced to increase indigent-defense spending and to adopt basic standards of competency for their public defenders. Most recently the State of Connecticut agreed to hire approximately eighty new attorneys and support-staff members for its public-defender system in response to a lawsuit brought by the American Civil Liberties Union. More challenges along these lines by, among others, the organized bar should be encouraged.

For its part, the organized bar shares responsibility for the fact that there are currently scores of people on death row without lawyers, and for the state of indigent defense in general. In 1982 the American Bar Association issued a report on what it called "the crisis in indigent defense funding," in which it advised, "We must be willing to put our money where our mouth is; we must be willing to make the constitutional mandate a reality." Seventeen years later there is little for which to thank the ABA. It does provide expert resources to law firms handling capital cases, and it funds its own Death Penalty Representation Project, which over the past eighteen months has enlisted forty-five law firms to defend death-row inmates without charge. But the project's director calls it little more than a "small Band-Aid on a gaping wound." The ABA has done a good job of documenting serious problems with the administration of the death penalty and the crisis in indigent defense. But the ABA, the largest voluntary professional association in the country, also represents one of the wealthiest and most privileged segments of American society. With a few notable exceptions, these generally well-informed professionals from one year to the next do little more than approve high-minded resolutions condemning the status quo that has been so good to them. If state and local bar associations were really serious about addressing these problems (and there's little evidence that they are), they might underwrite a model indigent-defense program or two, or a capital-representation office. If nothing else, they should be standing up for equal justice by lobbying their state legislators to find the money to finance public defenders at levels that don't make a mockery of the Sixth Amendment.

Finally, the Justice Department or a presidential commission should follow the example of Canada, and examine why our courts continue to sentence innocent people to death, and whether we have in fact executed innocent people. The steady accumulation of wrongful convictions and death sentences in the United States constitutes a prima facie case that we are dealing with widespread, systemic flaws in the administration of justice. Until those flaws are corrected, we should declare a moratorium on executions.

ACKNOWLEDGMENTS

1.1 From Herbert L. Packer, *The Limits of the Criminal Sanction* (Stanford University Press, 1968), pp. 149–173. Copyright © 1968 by Herbert L. Packer. Reprinted by permission of Stanford University Press. Some notes omitted.

1.2 From David E. Barlow, Melissa Hickman Barlow, and Theodore G. Chiricos, "Long Economic Cycles and the Criminal Justice System in the U.S.," *Crime, Law and Social Change,* vol. 19 (1993), pp. 143–163. Copyright © 1993 by Kluwer Academic Publishers. Reprinted by permission of Kluwer Academic Publishers and David E. Barlow. Notes and references omitted.

1.3 From Richard Delgado, "Words That Wound: A Tort Action for Racial Insults, Epithets, and Name-Calling," *Harvard Civil Rights–Civil Liberties Law Review,* vol. 17 (1982), pp. 159–165. Copyright © 1982 by The President and Fellows of Harvard College and the *Harvard Civil Rights–Civil Liberties Law Review.* Reprinted by permission. Notes omitted.

2.1 From Donald E. Green, "The Contextual Nature of American Indian Criminality," *American Indian Culture and Research Journal,* vol. 17, no. 2 (1993), pp. 99–119. Copyright © 1993 by The Regents of the University of California. Reprinted by permission of The American Indian Studies Center, UCLA, and the author. Some notes omitted.

2.2 From Robert Staples, "White Racism, Black Crime, and American Justice: An Application of the Colonial Model to Explain Crime and Race," *Phylon,* vol. 36 (1972), pp. 14–22. Copyright © 1972 by *Phylon.* Reprinted by permission.

2.3 From Victor E. Kappeler, Mark Blumberg, and Gary W. Potter, *The Mythology of Crime and Criminal Justice,* 2d ed. (Waveland Press, 1996), pp. 31–49. Copyright © 1996 by Victor E. Kappeler, Mark Blumberg, and Gary W. Potter. Reprinted by permission of Waveland Press, Inc. References omitted.

3.1 From Dorothy E. Roberts, "Unshackling Black Motherhood," *Michigan Law Review,* vol. 95, no. 4 (February 1997), pp. 938–964. Copyright © 1997 by The Michigan Law Review Association. Reprinted by permission of *Michigan Law Review* and the author. Notes omitted.

3.2 From Michael W. Lynch, "Enforcing 'Statutory Rape'?" *The Public Interest,* no. 132 (Summer 1998), pp. 3–17. Copyright © 1998 by National Affairs, Inc. Reprinted by permission of the author.

3.3 From Darnell F. Hawkins, "Beyond Anomalies: Rethinking the Conflict Perspective on Race and Criminal Punishment," *Social Forces,* vol. 65, no. 3 (March 1987), pp. 719–743. Copyright © 1987 by University of North Carolina Press. Reprinted by permission of *Social Forces* and the author. References omitted.

4.1 From Donna M. Bishop and Charles E. Frazier, "Race Effects in Juvenile Justice Decision-Making: Findings of a Statewide Analysis," *The Journal of Criminal Law and Criminology,* vol. 86, no. 2 (1996), pp. 392–414. Copyright © 1996 by Northwestern University, School of Law. Reprinted by permission.

4.2 From Coramae Richey Mann, "Minority and Female: A Criminal Justice Double Bind," *Social Justice,* vol. 16, no. 4 (Winter 1989), pp. 95–111. Copyright © 1989 by *Social Justice.* Reprinted by permission. References omitted.

5.1 From Michael Huspek, Roberto Martinez, and Leticia Jimenez, "Violations of Human and Civil Rights on the U.S.-Mexico Border, 1995 to 1997: A Report," *Social*

386

Justice, vol. 25, no. 2 (Summer 1998), pp. 110–129. Copyright © 1998 by *Social Justice.* Reprinted by permission. References omitted.

Acknowledgments   5.2   From David E. Barlow and Melissa Hickman Barlow, "Cultural Diversity Training in Criminal Justice: A Progressive or Conservative Reform?" *Social Justice,* vol. 20, no. 3–4 (1993), pp. 69–83. Copyright © 1993 by *Social Justice.* Reprinted by permission. References omitted.

6.1   From Paul Butler, "Racially Based Jury Nullification: Black Power in the Criminal Justice System," *Yale Law Journal,* vol. 105, no. 3 (December 1995), pp. 677–725. Copyright © 1995 by The Yale Law Journal Company and Fred B. Rothman & Company. Reprinted by permission. Notes omitted.

6.2   From Ronald Stidham and Robert A. Carp, "Indian Rights and Law Before the Federal District Courts," *The Social Science Journal,* vol. 32, no. 1 (1995), pp. 87–97. Copyright © 1995 by JAI Press. Reprinted by permission of Elsevier Science. Some notes omitted.

7.1   From Marvin D. Free, Jr., "The Impact of Federal Sentencing Reforms on African Americans," *Journal of Black Studies,* vol. 28, no. 2 (November 1997), pp. 268–285. Copyright © 1997 by Sage Publications, Inc. Reprinted by permission. References omitted.

7.2   From Ed A. Munoz, David A. Lopez, and Eric Stewart, "Misdemeanor Sentencing Decision: The Cumulative Disadvantage Effect of 'Gringo Justice'," *Hispanic Journal of Behavioral Sciences,* vol. 20, no. 3 (1998), pp. 298–320. Copyright © 1998 by Sage Publications, Inc. Reprinted by permission. References omitted.

8.1   From Amy E. Laderberg, "The 'Dirty Little Secret': Why Class Actions Have Emerged as the Only Viable Option for Women Inmates Attempting to Satisfy the Subjective Prong of the Eighth Amendment in Suits for Custodial Sexual Abuse," *William and Mary Law Review,* vol. 40, no. 1 (October 1998), pp. 323–363. Copyright © 1998 by *William and Mary Law Review.* Reprinted by permission. Notes omitted.

8.2   From Joan Petersilia, "Justice for All? Offenders With Mental Retardation and the California Corrections System," *The Prison Journal,* vol. 77, no. 4 (1997), pp. 358–381. Copyright © 1997 by Sage Publications, Inc. Reprinted by permission.

9.1   From Jon Sorensen and Donald H. Wallace, "Prosecutorial Discretion in Seeking Death: An Analysis of Racial Disparity in the Pretrial Stages of Case Processing in a Midwestern County," *Justice Quarterly,* vol. 16, no. 3 (1999), pp. 559–578. Copyright © 1999 by The Academy of Criminal Justice Sciences. Reprinted by permission. Case citations omitted.

9.2   Updated and adapted from Margaret Vandiver, "'An Apology Does Not Assist the Accused': Foreign Nationals and the Death Penalty in the United States," *The Justice Professional,* vol. 12 (1999). Copyright © 1999 by Overseas Publishers Association. Reprinted by permission of the author and Gordon and Breach Publishers. References omitted.

9.3   From Alan Berlow, "The Wrong Man," *The Atlantic Monthly* (November 1999), pp. 66–91. Copyright © 1999 by Alan Berlow. Reprinted by permission of *The Atlantic Monthly* and the author.

Index

388

*Notable
Selections in
Crime,
Criminology,
and Criminal
Justice*

389

*Notable
Selections in
Crime,
Criminology,
and Criminal
Justice*

390

*Notable
Selections in
Crime,
Criminology,
and Criminal
Justice*

392

*Notable
Selections in
Crime,
Criminology,
and Criminal
Justice*

*Notable
Selections in
Crime,
Criminology,
and Criminal
Justice*